Price Theory
and Applications

Steven E. Landsburg

University of Rochester

The Dryden Press
Chicago   New York   San Francisco
Philadelphia   Montreal   Toronto
London   Sydney   Tokyo

TO LAUREN AND CAYLEY

Acquisitions Editor: Elizabeth Widdicombe
Developmental Editor: Rebecca Ryan
Project Editor: Karen Steib
Design Director: Alan Wendt
Production Manager: Barb Bahnsen
Permissions Editor: Doris Milligan
Director of Editing, Design, and Production: Jane Perkins

Text and Cover Designer: C. J. Petlick, Hunter Graphics
Copy Editor: Mary Englehart
Indexer: Leoni McVey
Compositor: Dayton Typographic Service
Text Type: 10/12 Palatino

Library of Congress Cataloging-in-Publication Data

Landsburg, Steven E., 1954–
    Price theory and applications.

    Includes bibliographical references and index.
    1. Microeconomics.   I. Title.
HB172.L34 1989   338.5   88-18071
ISBN 0-03-020589-1

Printed in the United States of America
90-016-98765432

Address orders:
The Dryden Press
Orlando, Florida 32887

Address editorial correspondence:
The Dryden Press
908 N. Elm St.
Hinsdale, IL 60521

The Dryden Press
Holt, Rinehart and Winston
Saunders College Publishing

Cover Source: © 1988 Amcal: *Timberline Jack's* from an original painting by Charles Wysocki.

The Dryden Press Series in Economics

Preface

Price theory is both a challenging subject and a rewarding one. The student who masters it acquires a powerful tool for understanding a remarkable range of social phenomena. It illuminates questions about which students are naturally curious. How does a sales tax affect the price of coffee? Why do people trade? What happens to ticket prices when a baseball player gets a raise? How does free agency affect the allocation of players to teams? Why might the revenue of orange growers increase when there is an unexpected frost—and what may we infer about the existence of monopoly power if it does?

Price theory teaches the student how to solve such puzzles. Better yet, it poses new ones. Students learn to be intrigued by phenomena they might previously have considered unremarkable. When rock concerts predictably sell out in advance, why don't the promoters raise prices? Why are bank buildings fancier than supermarkets? What accounts for the price difference between leaded and unleaded gasoline? Why do ski resorts sell lift tickets on a per-day basis rather than a per-ride basis?

Throughout this book I highlight such questions and use them to motivate a careful and rigorous development of microeconomic theory. New concepts are immediately illustrated with entertaining and informative examples, both verbal and numerical. Ideas and techniques are allowed to arise naturally in the discussion, and they are given names (like "marginal rate of substitution") only after the student has discovered their usefulness. Students are everywhere encouraged to develop a strong "seat of the pants" economic intuition and then to test their intuition by submitting it to rigorous graphical and verbal analysis.

I think that students will find this book inviting. There are no mathematical demands or prerequisites and no lists of axioms to memorize. At the same time, the level of economic rigor and sophistication is quite high. In many cases I have carried the analysis beyond what is found in most other books at this level. There are digressions, examples, and especially problems that will challenge even the most ambitious and talented students.

One reviewer characterized the book as "deceptively friendly," in that the applications and the emphasis on verbal reasoning disguise the complexity of the material until after the student has begun to master it. I like that description very much.

To the Instructor

In addition to what has been said above, you will want to know something about the content of this book. All of the standard topics of intermediate price theory are covered. There are also a number of innovations, of which the following are the most important:

The Use of Social Welfare (via Triangles of consumers' and producers' surplus) as a Unifying Concept

Consumers' and producers' surplus are introduced in Chapter 8, immediately following the theory of the competitive industry. There they are used to analyze the effects of various forms of market interference. Thereafter each new concept is immediately related to social welfare and analyzed in this light.

The Economics of Information

Chapter 9 (Knowledge in Society) surveys the key role of prices in disseminating information and relates this to their role in equilibrating markets.

Treatment of the Theory of the Firm

It is often difficult for students to understand the importance of production functions, average cost curves, and the like until after they have been asked to study them for several weeks. To remedy this, Chapter 5 (The Behavior of Firms) provides an overview of how firms make decisions, introducing the general principle of equimarginality and relating it back to the consumer theory that the students have already learned. Having seen the importance of cost curves, students may be more motivated to study their derivation in Chapter 6 (Production and Costs).

The material on firms is presented in a manner that gives a lot of flexibility to the instructor. Those who prefer the more traditional approach of starting immediately with production can easily skip Chapter 5, or postpone it until after Chapter 6. Although Chapter 6 begins with isoquants, Section 6.2 (on production and costs in the short run) is largely independent of isoquants. The instructor who prefers to defer the more difficult topic of long-run production can skip Section 6.1 and begin immediately with Section 6.2, skipping also the few paragraphs in Section 6.2 that relate the short-run production function to the isoquant diagram.

An Extended Analysis of Market Failures, Property Rights, and Rules of Law

This is the material of Chapter 12, which I have found to be very popular with students. The theory of externalities is developed in great detail, using a series of extended examples and illustrated with actual court cases. Section 12.4 (The Law and Economics) analyzes various legal theories and doctrines from the point of view of economic efficiency.

Relations to Macroeconomics

The topic coverage provides a solid preparation for a rigorous course in macroeconomics. In addition, several purely "micro" topics are illustrated with "macro" applications. (None of these applications is central to the book, and all can easily be skipped by instructors who wish to do so.) There are sections on information, intertemporal decision making, economy-wide labor markets, money, and rational expectations. In the chapter on interest rates, there is a purely microeconomic analysis of the effects of federal deficits, including Ricardian Equivalence, the hypotheses necessary for it to hold, and the consequences of relaxing these hypotheses. In the chapter on labor markets, there is a careful presentation of several different labor supply curves (each holding different variables fixed) and the uses of each. There is a discussion of labor markets in general equilibrium (taking account of the fact that all capital is ultimately owned by the suppliers of labor) and of the intertemporal aspects of labor supply, with applications to the theory of business cycles. The section on rational expectations is presented in the context of a purely micro problem, involving agricultural prices, but it includes a discussion of "why economists make bad predictions," with a moral that applies to macroeconomics.

The chapter on money, while nontraditional, is a particularly useful unifying tool. It illustrates a number of purely microeconomic ideas, including social welfare, externalities, the value of an annuity, and optimal taxation. The analysis of inflation is an exercise in pure microeconomics, but students enjoy its macro flavor and the way it ties in with their other courses.

Other Nontraditional Topics

There are extensive sections devoted to topics excluded from many standard intermediate textbooks. Among these topics are: alternative normative criteria (including the concept of an envy-free allocation), efficient asset markets, imperfect information in labor markets, contestable markets, antitrust law, the principal agent problem, mechanisms for eliciting private information about the demand for public goods, job market signaling, job market discrimination, human capital (including the external effects of human capital accumulation), moral hazard, adverse selection and the market for lemons, executive compensation, the Capital Asset Pricing Model, and the pricing of stock options. The book concludes with a chapter on the methods and scope of economic analysis, with examples drawn from biology, sociology, and history.

Pedagogy

The book is distinguished by a large number of exercises and problems. The exercises are scattered throughout the text and (with a few "starred" exceptions) are routine. They are intended primarily to slow down the student and make sure that he understands one paragraph before going on to the next. A student who cannot complete an exercise quickly and accurately has missed an important point. Many exercises simply ask for a fuller explanation of an assertion made in the text.

The problems, by contrast, are often challenging and open-ended, allowing room for deep thought and creativity. I have found it effective to have students solve these problems collectively, either in small groups or as a class.

Another pedagogical innovation is the incorporation of "dangerous curve" signals, which warn the student about the most common misunderstandings. These are marked with the special symbol

Most of the exhibits have extensive explanatory captions that summarize key points from the discussion in the text. Other features, such as the marginal glossary, review questions, and chapter summaries are described in the Introduction, under the heading "Using This Book."

Acknowledgments

I first learned economics at the University of Chicago in the 1970s, which means that I learned most of it, directly or indirectly, from Don McCloskey. Generations of Chicago graduate students were infected by his enthusiasm for economics as a tool for understanding the world, and the members of one generation communicated their exuberance to me. They, and consequently I, learned from Don that the world is full of puzzles—not the abstract or technical puzzles of formal economic theory, but puzzles like: Could the advent of free public education cause there to be less education consumed? We learned to see such puzzles everywhere and to delight in their solutions.

Later, I had the privilege to know Don as a friend, as a colleague, and as the greatest of my teachers. Without him this book could not have been conceived.

The exuberance that Don personifies is endemic at Chicago, and I had the great good fortune to encounter it every day. I absorbed ideas and garnered examples in cafeterias, in the library's coffee area, and especially in all-night seminars at Jimmy's Woodlawn Tap. Many of these ideas and examples appear in this book, their exact sources forgotten. To all who contributed, thank you.

Among the many Chicago students who deserve to be thanked explicitly are Craig Hakkio, Eric Hirschhorn, and Maury Wolff, who were there from the beginning. John Martin and Russell Roberts taught me much and contributed many valuable suggestions specifically for this book. Ken Judd gave me a theory of executive compensation. Dan Gressell taught me the two ways to get a chicken to lay more eggs.

I received much education, and much encouragement, from members of the Chicago faculty. I thank Gary Becker, who enticed me to think more seriously about economics; Sherwin Rosen, who had planted the seeds of all this years before; and José Scheinkman, who listened to my ideas even when they were foolish. Above all, Bob Lucas can have no idea of how grateful I have been for his many gracious kindnesses. I remember them all, and value his generosity as I value the inspiration of his intellectual depth and honesty and rigor.

Since leaving Chicago, my good fortune in colleagues has remained with me. It was with me at Iowa and at Cornell and especially at Rochester, where this book was written. There is no faculty member in economics at

Rochester who did not contribute to this book in some way or another. Some suggested examples and problems; others helped me learn material that I had believed I understood until I tried to write about it; and many did both. I should name them all, but have space for only a few. William Thomson taught me about mechanisms for revealing the demand for public goods and about envy-free allocations and suggested that these were appropriate topics for a book at this level. Walter Oi contributed more entertaining ideas and illustrations than I can remember and told me how Chinese bargemen were paid. Alan Stockman and Ken McLaughlin come in for special mention. Alan has been teaching me both economics and the joys of economics for a dozen years; Ken has crammed a dozen years of teaching into two.

I must also mention the contributions of the daily lunch group at the Hillside Restaurant, where no subject is off limits and no opinion too outrageous for consideration. In the past year the daily discussions about how society is or should be structured have been punctuated by tangential discussions about how to present various ideas in an intermediate textbook. I thank especially the 1986–1987 group, consisting of Stockman, McLaughlin, Mark Bils, John Boyd, Jim Kahn, Marvin Goodfriend (the first inductee into the Hillside Hall of Fame), and various part-timers. Newcomers Eric Bond and Mike Dotsey are thanked heartily as well.

Lauren Feinstone should have been mentioned in nearly all of the above categories, as a Chicago student, a Rochester faculty member, and a sometime Hillsider. She taught me how to think about Ricardian Equivalence and told me the best way to present it to students. For that, I thank her here. For so much more, no words can be enough.

At The Dryden Press, I have had good editors in Liz Widdicombe and Becky Ryan. Besides supplying their outstanding talents in the usual editorial tasks, they have performed remarkably in managing to talk me out of any number of bad ideas. I am grateful for their persuasiveness, and for their patience, and for their skill.

Mary Englehart's copyediting was the very opposite of the nightmare that I had been warned that copyediting must always be. Linda Tesar and Mike Cadwallader proofread the galleys diligently and made numerous good suggestions for improving the exposition. The impressive look of the book is the result of Alan Wendt's superb design, and the miraculous fact that there is a book at all is testimony to Karen Steib's tenacity through an onslaught of disasters, and to her grace under pressure from a temperamental author. As this is written, I do not know the outcome of Mike Roche's marketing direction. But if you bought this book, chances are he had something to do with it.

Steven Landsburg
November 1988

We gratefully acknowledge the contributions of the following reviewers. Their comments and suggestions have helped this project grow from an idea to a textbook, and have improved it every step of the way.

John Antel, University of Houston
Jay Bloom, SUNY–New Paltz
John Conant, Indiana State University
John Conley, University of Rochester
Arthur Diamond, University of Nebraska–Omaha
Richard Eastin, University of Southern California
Dean Hiebert, Illinois State University
Roberto Ifill, Williams College
Paul Jonas, University of New Mexico
Kenneth Judd, University of Chicago
Chris Brown Mahoney, University of Minnesota
Devinder Malhotra, University of Akron
John Martin, Baruch College
Scott Masten, University of Michigan
Sharon Megdal, Northern Arizona University
John Miller, Clarkson University
David Mills, University of Virginia
John Mullen, Clarkson University
Margaret Oppenheimer, DePaul University
Michael Peddle, Holy Cross
James Pinto, Northern Arizona University
Libby Rittenberg, Lafayette College
Russell Roberts, University of California–Los Angeles
Peter Rupert, West Virginia University
Annette Steinacker, University of Rochester
Vasant Sukhatme, Macalester College
Paul Thistle, University of Alabama
Mark Walbert, Illinois State University
Paula Worthington, Northwestern University

Thank you all for the extra efforts that have made this book what it is.

Comprehensive Teaching and Learning Package

We are pleased to offer the most complete set of support materials available for the intermediate microeconomics course.

Landsburg's Exercises and Calculus Supplement, packaged *free* with the text, contains answers to all in-text exercises. It also features a unique calculus supplement for those students who want to apply calculus to intermediate microeconomics.

Study Guide with GraphPac, by William Weber, Eastern Illinois University, makes studying more profitable and enjoyable for your students. It includes for each chapter a section-by-section summary, additional review questions, numerical exercises and problems, and a special annotated "working through the graphs" section that builds the most important graphs from the chapter step by step. Included in the Study Guide at no additional cost, GraphPac features reproductions of 150 key graphs from the text designed to be used as a class note-taking device.

The *Instructor's Manual* includes detailed general overviews for each chapter, teaching notes, many extra problems, and tear-out solution sheets for problems in the text.

A *Test Bank* by William Hallagan, Washington State University, is included in the Instructor's Manual. It contains over 500 multiple-choice test questions, many graph-related. Questions are identified by level of difficulty.

A *Computerized Test Bank* is available for both the IBM and Apple personal computers, allowing you to select and edit the questions found in the printed test bank and add your own questions. Each can be used on floppy and hard disk drive systems.

Transparency Masters help you illustrate important topics through reproductions of 150 key graphs from the text.

Computer-Assisted Instruction Software by Tod Porter and Teresa Reilly at Youngstown State University contains more than 100 problems and inter-active questions on the core intermediate microeconomics topics. This unique tutorial's built-in error-catching routine helps prompt students to improve their weak areas, while its graph-drawing capability enables students to get hands-on practice with working graphs. It is free upon adoption of *Price Theory and Applications.*

About the Author

Steven Landsburg (Ph.D. University of Chicago) is Assistant Professor of Economics at the University of Rochester. He has also taught at Cornell University, the University of Iowa, and the University of Chicago. Professor Landsburg's articles have been published in the *Journal of Economic Theory*, the *Journal of Political Economy* and various other research journals.

Contents

Chapter 18

Transactions and the Role of Money   571

Chapter 19

The Nature and Scope of Economic Analysis   591

Introduction

Many books begin by telling you, at some length, what price theory is. This book begins by showing you. When you finish the first chapter, you will know how to analyze the effects of sales and excise taxes, and you will have discovered the surprising result that it makes no difference to buyers or to sellers which one of them is taxed. When you finish the second chapter, you will know the conditions under which people benefit from trade, and how two people can both gain when they exchange tasks, even if one is apparently more skillful than the other at every task. In each succeeding chapter you will be exposed to new ideas in economics and to their surprising consequences for the world around you.

To learn what price theory is, dig in and begin reading. To encourage you in that direction, this introduction will be brief. The next few paragraphs can give you only a hint of what it's all about.

Price theory, or *microeconomics*, is the study of the ways in which individuals and firms make choices, and the ways in which these choices interact with each other. We assume that each individual has certain well-defined preferences and certain well-defined limits to his behavior. For example, you might enjoy eating both cake and ice cream, but the size of your stomach limits your ability to pursue these pleasures; moreover, the amount of cake that you eat affects the amount of ice cream you can eat and vice versa.

In predicting behavior, we assume that individuals behave *rationally*, which is to say that they make themselves as well off as possible, as measured by their own preferences and within the limitations imposed on them. While this assumption (like any assumption in any science) is only an approximation to reality, it is an extraordinarily powerful one, and it leads to many profound and surprising conclusions.

The entire subject is made richer by the fact that each individual's choices can affect the opportunities available to others. If you decide to eat all of the cake, your roommate cannot decide to eat some too. An *equilibrium* is an outcome in which each person's behavior is compatible with the restrictions imposed by everybody else's behavior. In many situations (you will begin to encounter them in Chapter 1) it is possible to say both that there is only one possible equilibrium and that there are good reasons to expect that equilibrium to actually come about. This enables the economist to make predictions about the world.

Price theory is concerned with two sorts of questions: those that are **positive** and those that are **normative**. A positive question is a question about what *is* or *will be*, whereas a normative question is a question about what *ought* to be. Positive questions have definite, correct answers (which may or may not be known), whereas the answers to normative questions depend on values. For example, suppose that a law is proposed that would prohibit any bank from foreclosing on a farmer's mortgage. Some positive questions are: How will this law affect the incomes of bankers? How will it affect the incomes of farmers? What effect will it have on the number of people who decide to become farmers and on the number of people who decide to start banks? Will it indirectly affect the average size of farms or of banks? Will it therefore indirectly affect the price of land? How will it affect the price of food and the well-being of people who are neither farmers nor bankers? And so forth. A normative question is: Is this law, on balance, a good thing?

Economics can, at least in principle, provide answers to the positive questions. Economics by itself can never answer a normative question; in this case your answer to the normative question must depend on how you feel about the relative merits of helping farmers and helping bankers.

Therefore we will be concerned in this book primarily with positive questions. However, price theory is relevant in the consideration of normative questions as well. This is so in two ways. First, even if you are quite sure of your own values, it is often impossible to decide whether you consider some course of action desirable unless you know its consequences. Your decision about whether to support the antiforeclosure law will depend not only on your feelings about farmers and bankers, but also on what you believe the effects of the law will be. Thus it can be important

Positive question
A question about what is or will be the case; a question with a definite correct answer.

Normative question
A question about what ought to be the case; a question whose answer depends on values.

to consider positive questions even when the questions of ultimate interest are normative ones.

The second way in which price theory can assist us in thinking about normative issues is by showing us the consequences of consistently applying a given normative criterion. For example, if your criterion is "I am always for anything that will benefit farmers, provided that it does not drive any bankers out of business," the price theorist will be able to respond "In that case you must be in favor of such and such a law, because I can use economic reasoning to show that it will benefit farmers without driving any bankers out of business." If such and such a law does not sound like such a good idea to you, you might want to rethink your criterion.

In the first seven chapters of this book, you will receive a thorough grounding in many of the positive aspects of price theory. You will learn how consumers make decisions, how firms make decisions, and how these decisions interact in the competitive market place. In Chapter 8 you will examine some of these outcomes from the viewpoint of various normative criteria. Chapter 9 rounds out the discussion of the competitive price system by examining the role of prices as conveyors of information.

In Chapters 10 through 13 you will learn about various situations in which the competitive model does not fully apply. These include conditions of monopoly and oligopoly and circumstances in which the activities of one person or firm affect others involuntarily (for example, factories create pollution that displeases their neighbors).

The first 13 chapters complete the discussion of the market for goods, which are supplied by firms and purchased by individuals. In Chapters 14 through 16 you will learn about the other side of the economy: the market for inputs to the production process (such as labor) that are supplied by individuals and purchased by firms. In Chapter 16, where you will study the market for the productive input called *capital*, you will also examine the way individuals allocate goods across time, consuming less on one day so that they can have more on another.

Chapters 17 and 18 concern special topics: the role of risk and the role of money.

Chapter 19 provides an overview of what price theory is all about. Most of the discussion in that chapter could have been included here in the introduction. However, we believe that the discussion will be much more meaningful to you *after* you have seen some examples of price theory in action, rather than before. Therefore we make the following suggestion: Dip into Chapter 19. Not all of it will make sense at this point, but much of it will. After you have been through a few chapters of the book, dip into Chapter 19 again. Even the parts that you understood to begin with will be more meaningful now. Later on—say, after you have finished Chapter 7—try it yet again. You will get the most from this final chapter if you read it thoroughly at the end of the course.

Using This Book

This book provides many tools to help you learn. A few hints on how to use them are given below.

Exercises

Exercises are sprinkled throughout the text, and, with a few exceptions (marked with asterisks) they are routine. If you cannot do an exercise quickly and accurately, you have missed an important point. In that case it is probably wise to reread the preceding few paragraphs.

Dangerous Curves

 The dangerous curve symbol appears periodically to warn you against the most common misunderstandings. Passages marked with this symbol describe mistakes that students often make, and explain how to avoid them.

Marginal Glossary

Each new term is defined both in the text and in the margin, where you can easily find it. All of the definitions in the marginal glossary are gathered in alphabetical order in the glossary at the back of the book.

Chapter Summaries

The summaries at the end of each chapter provide concise descriptions of the main ideas. You will find them useful in organizing your studying.

Review Questions

The review questions at the end of each chapter test to see whether you have learned and can repeat the main ideas of the chapter.

Numerical Exercises

About half the chapters have numerical exercises at the end. By working these, you will see concrete examples of how economic theory can be applied to given data to make precise predictions. For example, in the numerical exercises at the end of Chapter 7, you are given some information about the costs of producing kites and the demand for kites. Using this and the theory you have learned, you will be able to deduce the price of kites, the number of kites that are sold by each firm, and even the number of firms in the industry.

Problem Sets

The extensive problem sets at the end of each chapter are often challenging and open-ended, and are intended to give you an opportunity to think deeply and creatively. There is a wide range of difficulty in the problems. A few of the most difficult are marked with asterisks.

Often, problems require additional assumptions that are not explicitly stated. Learning to make such additional assumptions is a large part of learning to do economics. In some cases there will be more than one correct answer, depending on what assumptions you have made. Thus in answering problems you should always spell out your reasoning very carefully. This is particularly so of "true or false" problems, where the quality of your explanations will often matter far more than your conclusion.

If your instructor allows it, you will learn a lot by working on problems together with your classmates. You will often find that you and they have found different answers to a problem, and that both you and they are equally sure of your answers. In attempting to convince each other, and in trying to find the point at which your thinking diverged, you will be forced to clarify your ideas and will discover which concepts you need to study further.

Now we begin.

Chapter One

Supply, Demand, and Equilibrium

You have undoubtedly heard at some time in your life that economics is all about "supply" and "demand," and that statement is true. So our first task is to understand these two crucial concepts. In this chapter we will discuss the meanings and the applications of supply and demand. Using these tools, we will see how prices and quantities are determined in the marketplace. We will then be able to see how these prices and quantities change in response to changes in other economic variables. As an example, we will be able to analyze the effects of various kinds of taxes, and will discover that these effects can be very different from what you might at first expect.

1.1 Demand

Law of demand
The observation that when the price of a good goes up, people will buy less of that good.

When the price of a good goes up, people generally choose to purchase less (or at least not more) of it. This statement is known as the **law of demand** and can be summarized as: "When the price goes up, the quantity demanded goes down." Economists believe that the law of demand is always (or very nearly always) true, and believe so primarily on the basis of observation. In Chapter 3, we will see that this law is also a logical consequence of certain fundamental assumptions about human behavior. Here we shall examine some of its consequences.

Demand versus Quantity Demanded

As an example, suppose that the good in question is coffee. The number of cups of coffee that you choose to purchase on a typical day might be given by a table like this:

Price	Quantity
20¢/cup	5 cups/day
30¢	4
40¢	2
50¢	1

Quantity demanded
The amount of a good that a given individual or group of individuals will choose to consume at a given price.

We say that when the price is 20¢ per cup, your **quantity demanded** is 5 cups per day. When the price is 30¢ per cup, your quantity demanded is 4 cups per day, and so on. Notice that the price is measured *per cup* and the quantity is measured in *cups per day*. If we had selected different units of measurement, we would have had different entries in the table. For example, if we measured quantity in cups per week, the numbers in the right-hand column would be 35, 28, 14, and 7. In order to speak meaningfully about demand, we must specify our units and we must use them consistently.

Demand
A family of numbers that lists the quantity demanded corresponding to each possible price.

The information in the table is collectively referred to as your **demand** for coffee. Notice the difference between *demand* and *quantity demanded*. Quantity demanded is a number, and it changes when the price does. Demand is a whole family of numbers, listing the quantities you would demand in a variety of hypothetical situations. The demand table asserts that if the price of coffee were 50¢ per cup, then you would buy 1 cup per day. It does not assert that the price of coffee actually is, or ever has been or will be, 50¢ per cup.

If the price of coffee rises from 30¢ to 40¢ per cup, then your quantity demanded falls from 4 cups to 2 cups. However, your demand for coffee is unchanged, because the same table is still in effect. It remains true that if the price of coffee were 20¢ per cup, you would be demanding 5 cups per day, if the price of coffee were 30¢ per cup you would be demanding 4 cups per day, and so on. The sequence of "if" statements is what describes your demand for coffee.

A change in price leads to a change in quantity demanded. A change in price does *not* lead to a change in demand.

Demand Curves

Unfortunately, when we represent demand by a table, we do not provide a complete picture. Our table does not tell us, for example, how much coffee you will purchase when the price is 22¢ per cup, or 33½¢. Therefore we

Exhibit 1–1 **The Demand Curve**

Price	Quantity
20¢/cup	5 cups/day
30¢	4
40¢	2
50¢	1

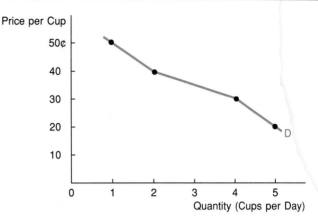

The demand table shows how many cups of coffee you would buy per day at each of several prices. The black points in the graph correspond precisely to the information in the table. The curve connecting the points is your demand curve for coffee. It conveys more information than the table because it shows how many cups of coffee you would buy at intermediate prices like 22¢ or 33½¢ per cup. If the table were enlarged to include enough intermediate prices, then the table and the graph would convey exactly the same information.

Demand curve
A graph illustrating demand, with prices on the vertical axis and quantities demanded on the horizontal axis.

usually represent demand by a graph. We plot price on the vertical axis and quantity on the horizontal, always specifying our units.

Exhibit 1–1 provides an example. There the information in your demand table for coffee has been translated into the black points in the graph. The curve through the points is called your **demand curve** for coffee. It fills in the additional information corresponding to prices that do not appear in the table. If we were to fill in enough rows of the table (and only space prevents us from doing so), then the demand table and the demand curve in Exhibit 1–1 would convey exactly the same information. The demand curve is a picture of your demand for coffee.

Because the demand curve is a picture of demand, every statement that we can make about demand can be "seen" in the curve. For example, consider the law of demand: "When the price goes up, the quantity demanded goes down." This fact is reflected in the downward slope of the demand curve. It is important to remember both of these statements:

When the price goes up, the quantity demanded goes down.

and

Demand curves slope downward.

But it is even more important to recognize that these two statements are just two different ways of saying the same thing, and to understand *why* they are just two different ways of saying the same thing.

Changes in Demand

If a change in price does not lead to a change in demand, does this mean that demand can never change? Absolutely not. Suppose, for example, that your doctor has advised you to cut back on coffee for medical reasons. You might then choose to buy coffee according to a different table such as this:

Price	Quantity
20¢/cup	3 cups/day
30¢	2
40¢	1
50¢	0

Now your rule for deciding how many cups of coffee to purchase at different prices has changed—and this rule is just what we have called *demand.*

We can also use demand curves to illustrate the difference between a change in quantity demanded and a change in demand. A change in quantity demanded is represented by a movement along the demand curve from one point to another. A change in demand is represented by a shift of the curve itself to a new position.

The curve labeled D in Exhibit 1–2 is the same as the demand curve in Exhibit 1–1. The curve labeled D′ illustrates your demand after medical advice to reduce your caffeine intake. Because you now want fewer cups of coffee at any given price, the new demand curve lies to the left of (and consequently below) the old demand curve. We describe this situation as a **fall in demand.**

The opposite situation, a **rise in demand,** results in a rightward shift of the demand curve. If you enrolled in a class that required a lot of late-night studying, you might experience a rise in your demand for coffee.

There are many other possible reasons for a shift in demand. If the price of tea were to fall, you might very well decide to drink more tea and less coffee. The amount of coffee you would choose to buy at any given price would go down. This is an example of a fall in demand. On the other hand, if your aunt gives you a snazzy new coffee maker for your birthday, your demand for coffee might rise.

A change in something *other* than price can lead to a change in demand.

▷ *Exercise 1.1* If the price of donuts were to fall, what do you think would happen to your demand for coffee? Does a fall in the price of a related good always affect your demand in the same way, or does it depend on what related good we are talking about?

▷ *Exercise 1.2* How would a rise in your income affect your demand for coffee?

Fall in demand
A decision by demanders to buy a smaller quantity at each given price.

Rise in demand
A decision by demanders to buy a larger quantity at each given price.

Exhibit 1–2 **Shifting the Demand Curve**

Table A. Your Original
Demand for Coffee

Price	Quantity
20¢/cup	5 cups/day
30¢	4
40¢	2
50¢	1

Table B. Your New
Demand for Coffee after
Medical Advice to Cut
Back

Price	Quantity
20¢/cup	3 cups/day
30¢	2
40¢	1
50¢	0

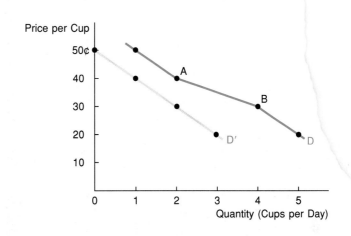

Your original demand curve for coffee is the curve labeled D. A change in price, say from 30¢ per cup to 40¢ per cup, would cause a movement along the curve from point A to point B. A change in something other than price, such as a doctor's suggestion that caffeine is bad for your health, can lead to a change in demand, represented by a shift to an entirely new demand curve. In this case the doctor's advice leads to a fall in demand, which is represented by a leftward shift of the curve.

Example: A Sales Tax

Sales tax
In this book, a tax that is paid directly by consumers to the government. Other texts use this phrase in different ways.

One thing that could change your demand for coffee is the imposition of a **sales tax.**[1] Suppose that from now on you will be required to pay a tax of 10¢ per cup of coffee that you buy. This will make you want to buy less coffee at each given price than you did before.[2] Your demand curve will shift to the left and downward. In fact, we can even figure out how far it will shift.

Let us suppose that your demand for coffee in a world without taxes is given by the table in Exhibit 1–1. Let us figure out your demand in a world where coffee is taxed at 10¢ per cup. If the (pre-tax) price of coffee is 10¢, what will it actually cost you to acquire a cup of coffee? It will cost you 10¢ plus 10¢ tax—a total of 20¢. How many cups of coffee do you choose to buy when they cost you 20¢ apiece? According to the table in Exhibit 1–1, you will buy 5.

---

[1]In this book we will use the phrase *sales tax* to refer to a tax that is paid to the government by consumers. Some other texts use this phrase in a different way.

[2]The word *price* here refers to the pre-tax price. If coffee sells for 50¢ per cup plus 10¢ tax, we will say that the price of coffee is 50¢ per cup.

Using this information, we can begin to tabulate your demand for coffee in a world with taxes. We know that, with taxes, if the price of coffee is 10¢ per cup, you will choose to buy 5 cups per day. This is the first row of your new demand table:

Price	Quantity
10¢/cup	5 cups/day

We can continue in this way. When the price of coffee is 20¢, the actual cost to you will be 30¢. We know from Exhibit 1–1 that you will then choose to buy 4 cups. Thus we can fill in another row of our table:

Price	Quantity
10¢/cup	5 cups/day
20¢	4

If we complete the argument at other prices, we finally arrive at your new demand for coffee, which is shown in Exhibit 1–3. Compare the entries in the two demand tables of that exhibit. Notice that the same quantities appear in each but the corresponding prices are all 10¢ lower in the new demand schedule (Table B). What can we conclude about the demand curves that illustrate these tables? For every point on the original demand curve (D), a corresponding point on the new demand curve (D′) represents the same quantity but a price that is lower by 10¢. This corresponding point lies a vertical distance exactly 10¢ below the original point.

We can summarize by saying that the sales tax causes each point of the demand curve to shift downward by the vertical distance 10¢. Because each point shifts downward the same distance, we can say that the demand curve shifts downward parallel to itself by the vertical distance 10¢. This gives us a precise prediction of how a sales tax will affect demand.

A sales tax causes the demand curve to shift downward parallel to itself by the amount of the tax.

▷ *Exercise 1.3* How would demand be affected by a sales tax of 5¢ per item? How would it be affected by a subsidy under which the government pays 10¢ toward each cup of coffee purchased?

▷ *Exercise 1.4* How would demand be affected by a *percentage* sales tax— say a tax equal to 10 percent of the price paid?

Market Demand

Until now we have been discussing *your* demand for coffee or the demand by some *individual*. We can just as well discuss the demand for coffee by some *group* of individuals. We can speak of the demand by your family, or by your city, or by your country, or by the entire world. The quantity associated with a given price would then be the total number of cups per day that members of the group in question would demand.

Exhibit 1–3 **The Effect of a Sales Tax on Demand**

Table A. Demand for
Coffee without Tax

Price	Quantity
20¢/cup	5 cups/day
30¢	4
40¢	2
50¢	1

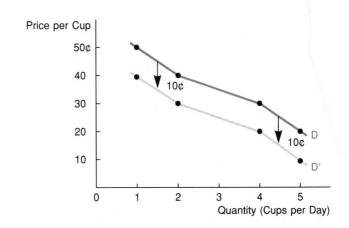

Table B. Demand for
Coffee with Sales Tax of
10¢ per Cup

Price	Quantity
10¢/cup	5 cups/day
20¢	4
30¢	2
40¢	1

If the price of coffee is 10¢ per cup and there is a sales tax of 10¢, then it will actually cost you 20¢ to acquire a cup of coffee. Table A shows that under these circumstances you would purchase 5 cups per day. This is recorded in the first row of Table B. The other rows in that table are generated in a similar manner.

The rows of Table B contain the same quantities as the rows of Table A, but the corresponding prices are all 10¢ lower. Another way to say this is that each point on the new demand curve lies exactly 10¢ below a corresponding point on the original demand curve. Therefore the new demand curve lies exactly 10¢ below the original demand curve in vertical distance. The sales tax causes the demand curve to shift downward parallel to itself by the amount of the tax.

Of course, since we can speak of a group's *demand* for coffee, we can speak of that group's *demand curve* as well. And, of course, this demand curve will slope downward.

The Shape of the Demand Curve

We have discussed the meaning of the demand curve's downward slope, but have not yet discussed how steeply the demand curve slopes downward. Your community's demand curve for shoes might look like either panel of Exhibit 1–4. Both of these demand curves slope downward, but one slopes downward far more steeply than the other. If the demand curve looks like panel A, a small change in the price of shoes will lead to a small change in the quantity of shoes demanded. If the demand curve looks like panel B, a small change in the price of shoes will lead to a much larger change in the quantity of shoes demanded.

There are many circumstances in which it is desirable to have information about the steepness of a particular demand curve. For example, if you owned a shoe store, you would be very interested in knowing whether a

Exhibit 1–4   **The Shape of the Demand Curve**

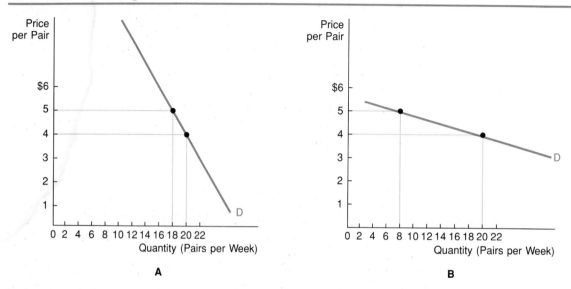

A   **B**

The two panels depict two possible demand curves for shoes. In panel A a given change in price (say from $4 per pair to $5 per pair) leads to a small change in quantity demanded (from 20 pairs of shoes per week to 18 pairs per week). In panel B the same change in price leads to a large change in quantity demanded (from 20 pairs per week to 8 pairs per week).

small price rise would drive away only a few customers or a great many. This is the same thing as asking whether the demand curve for your shoes is very steep or very shallow.

Econometrics
A family of statistical techniques used by economists.

To help resolve such questions, economists have invented a variety of statistical techniques known collectively as **econometrics.** These techniques allow us (among other things) to estimate the slopes of various demand curves on the basis of direct observations in the marketplace. In this book we will not study any econometrics, but it is important for you to know that the techniques exist and work tolerably well. In many circumstances economists can estimate the slopes of demand curves with considerable accuracy.

Example: The Demand for Murder

Many economists have applied the successful techniques of econometrics to the study of demand curves for a variety of interesting "goods" that were previously viewed as outside the realm of economic analysis. Consider, for example, the demand curve for murder.

Murder is an activity that some people choose to engage in for a variety of reasons. We can view murder as a "good" for these people, and the commission of murder as the act of consuming that good. The price of consuming the good is paid in many forms. One of these forms is the risk of capital punishment.

This means that we can draw a demand curve for murder, plotting the probability of capital punishment on the vertical axis and the quantity of murders committed on the horizontal axis. We can ask how steep this demand curve is, which is the same thing as asking whether a small increase in the probability of capital punishment will lead to a small or a large decrease in the number of murders committed. In other words, measuring the slope of this demand curve is the same thing as measuring the deterrent effect of capital punishment.

Now, on the one hand, the deterrent effect of capital punishment is something about which there is much discussion and much interest. On the other hand, the slope of a demand curve is something that economists know how to measure. In the early 1970s Isaac Ehrlich set out to measure the slope of the demand curve for murder, using the same sort of techniques that economists had used for many years to measure things like the slope of the demand curve for shoes.

His results were striking.[3] He found that the demand curve for murder was remarkably shallow. A small increase in the price of murder could be expected to lead to a large decrease in the quantity of murders committed. In fact, he estimated that over the period 1935–1969, one additional execution per year in the United States would have prevented, on average, about eight murders per year.[4]

This is a remarkable example of an application of economics to a positive question: "What is the deterrent effect of capital punishment?" It is emphatically *not* an answer to the related normative question: "Is capital punishment a good thing?" It is entirely possible to believe Ehrlich's results and still oppose capital punishment on a variety of ethical grounds. However, knowing the answer to the positive question is unquestionably helpful in thinking about the normative one. The size of the deterrent effect of the death penalty will certainly affect our assessment of its desirability, even though our assessment depends on many other things as well.

Example: The Demand for Reckless Driving

Reckless driving is another good that people choose to "consume." For this consumption they pay a price, partly by risking death in an accident. When

---

[3]I. Ehrlich, "The Deterrent Effect of Capital Punishment: A Question of Life and Death," *American Economic Review* 65 (1975): 397–417.

[4]Other researchers have questioned this result. See B. Forst, "The Deterrent Effect of Capital Punishment: A Cross State Analysis of the 1960's," *Minnesota Law Review* 61 (1977): 743–767; A. Blumstein, J. Cohen, and D. Nagin, *Deterrence and Incapacitation: Estimating the Effects of Criminal Sanctions on Crime Rates* (National Academy of Sciences, 1968); and P. Passell, "The Deterrent Effect of the Death Penalty: A Statistical Test," *Stanford Law Review* 28 (1975): 61–80.

The disagreements expressed in these articles do not involve attitudes toward capital punishment or attitudes toward econometrics; they are primarily concerned with highly technical matters of statistical theory and implementation. In principle, such issues can be settled on strictly technical grounds.

However, for a warning about how a researcher's prior expectations can affect his results, see E. Leamer, "Let's Take the 'Con' Out of Econometrics," *American Economic Review* 73 (1983): 31–43.

that price is reduced—say by the installation of safety equipment in cars—we should expect the quantity of reckless driving to increase.

This implies that safety equipment (such as seat belts, energy-absorbing steering columns, penetration-resistant windshields, dual braking systems, and padded instrument panels) could lead to either an increase or a decrease in the number of driver deaths. Each individual accident would have a lower probability of being fatal. But the reduction in price (that is, risk of death per accident) would lead to more reckless driving and therefore to more accidents. Whether the number of driver deaths decreased, increased, or stayed the same as a result of the safety equipment would depend on whether the rise in the quantity of reckless driving was small or large compared to the reduction in the probability of fatality. It would depend on whether the demand curve for reckless driving was steep or shallow.

When Sam Peltzman investigated this question, he found that the advent of automobile safety regulation in the 1960s (mandating the installation of safety equipment in all new cars) led to no change in the quantity of driver deaths.[5] Unless the demand curve was moving for some reason, we may conclude that it was remarkably shallow. People chose to engage in enough additional reckless driving as to completely offset the advantages of the new safety equipment. On this interpretation, one would expect to see increases in the number of pedestrian deaths and the amount of property damage. Peltzman found evidence of these results as well.

The Expanding Realm of Economics

Measurements of the demand curves for murder and for reckless driving are examples of the application of economic reasoning to social phenomena once considered to be outside the realm of economics. One of the pioneers in this activity was Gary Becker. In his book *The Economics of Discrimination* (University of Chicago Press, 1957), Becker investigated the effects of racial discrimination on things like wage rates and employment. By applying fundamental economic reasoning, he was able to reach many surprising conclusions about who gained and who lost from the effects of discrimination. Many of the tools that he used will be developed in this book. Since that time, Becker has developed economic theories of love, marriage, and fertility, and his students have written about topics ranging from the economics of religious belief to the economics of cannibalism. The broad applicability of economic reasoning will be a recurrent theme in this book.

The Elasticity of Demand

In the two panels of Exhibit 1–4, we compare a steep and a shallow demand curve. The comparison makes sense because the units are the same in each graph. However, when two curves are plotted using different units, a

---

[5] S. Peltzman, "The Effects of Automobile Safety Regulation," *Journal of Political Economy* 83 (1975), 677–725.

Exhibit 1–5   Slopes versus Elasticities

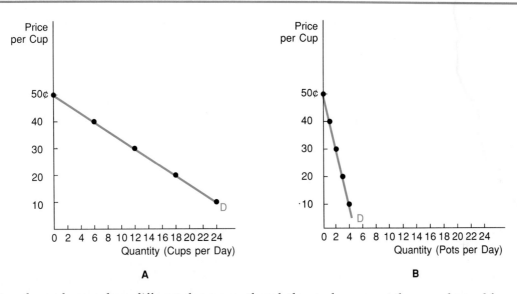

The two demand curves have different slopes even though they each represent the same demand for coffee. The different slopes result from the different choices of units on the quantity axis. However, both curves have the same elasticity. Elasticity is unaffected by the choice of units.

---

comparison of their slopes is always misleading. The two demand curves in Exhibit 1–5 each represent exactly the same demand for coffee, but one is much steeper than the other because it is measured in pots per day rather than cups per day. Indeed, any demand curve can be made to have any slope by an appropriate choice of units.

Because the slope can be so misleading, economists usually measure the relationship between price and quantity demanded in another way. The measure they prefer is called the **elasticity of demand.** To understand the meaning of elasticity and to understand how it differs from slope, consider the following two questions:

Elasticity of demand
The percentage rise in quantity demanded resulting from a 1 percent fall in price.

- If the price of coffee rose by 1¢, how many fewer units of coffee would you buy?

- If the price of coffee rose by 1%, by what percentage would you decrease your consumption of coffee?

The answer to the first question is the slope of your demand curve. It is a number that depends on what units you use. An increase of 1 cup is the same as an increase of 1/6 of a pot. Therefore you will give different answers depending on how you measure coffee. (There is an additional ambiguity resulting from the arbitrary units on the price axis: Instead of measuring money in cents, we could measure it in dollars.)

The answer to the second question is the number that economists refer to as the elasticity of your demand curve. It does not depend on the units of measurement. The percentage increase in your coffee consumption will be the same whether it is measured in cups or in pots.

When the price changes by a small amount ΔP, the percentage change in price is given by $100 \times \Delta P/P$. (If the price has fallen, ΔP will be a negative number.) If this leads to a change in quantity ΔQ, the percentage change in quantity is $100 \times \Delta Q/Q$. Therefore:

$$\text{Elasticity} = \frac{\text{Percentage change in quantity}}{\text{Percentage change in price}}$$

$$= \frac{100 \cdot \Delta Q/Q}{100 \cdot \Delta P/P}$$

$$= \frac{P \cdot \Delta Q}{Q \cdot \Delta P}.$$

The elasticity of a demand curve is negative, because the curve is downward sloping. For example, in the demand curves of Exhibit 1–5 an increase in price from 20¢ to 30¢ leads to a fall in quantity from 18 cups to 12 cups (or from 3 pots to 2 pots). That is, a 50% price rise leads to a 33% fall in quantity, so the elasticity of the curves in this region is $(-33\%)/50\% = -0.67$.

▷ **Exercise 1.5** Calculate the elasticity of the demand curves in Exhibit 1–5 in the region where price varies from 40¢ to 50¢ per cup.

We say that the demand curve is highly *elastic* when the elasticity is very large in absolute value (like $-10,000$) and highly *inelastic* when the elasticity is very small in absolute value (like $-.0001$).

▷ **Exercise 1.6** Calculate the elasticity of a straight-line demand curve at the point where it hits the price axis and at the point where it hits the quantity axis.

When the demand for a good is highly elastic, people are willing to reduce their consumption significantly in response to a given price rise. This is most likely to be the case when a good has many close substitutes. A reasonable expectation is that the demand for Hostess Twinkies is more elastic than the demand curve for packaged cakes; the demand for packaged cakes is more elastic than the demand curve for snack foods; and the demand for snack foods is more elastic than the demand for food generally.

1.2 Supply

The law of demand states that "when the price goes up, the quantity demanded goes down." The **law of supply** states that "when the price goes up, the quantity supplied goes up." By **quantity supplied** we mean the

Law of supply
The observation that when the price of a good goes up, the quantity supplied goes up.

Quantity supplied
The amount of a good that suppliers will provide at a given price.

quantity of some good that a specified individual or group of individuals wants to supply to others per specified unit of time.

The law of supply is not as ironclad as the law of demand. Imagine a manufacturer of bicycles who works 12 hours a day to produce one bicycle that he can sell for $40. If the price of bicycles were to go up to $500, he might choose to work harder and produce more bicycles—but he might choose instead to cut back on production, make one bicycle per week, and spend more time at the beach.[6]

Nevertheless, economists have found that in most circumstances an increase in price leads to an increase in quantity supplied. Throughout this chapter, therefore, we shall assume the validity of the law of supply.

Supply versus Quantity Supplied

Consider the supply of coffee in your city. It might be given by Table A of Exhibit 1–6. According to the table, if the price is 20¢ per cup, then the individuals who supply coffee to your city will wish to supply a total of 100 cups per day. If the price is 30¢ per cup, then they will wish to supply a total of 300 cups, and so forth. All of these hypothetical statements taken together constitute the **supply** of coffee to your city.

Supply
A family of numbers giving the quantities supplied at each possible price.

As with demand, a change in price leads to a change in the quantity supplied (which is a single number). Such changes are represented by movements along the supply curve. A change in something other than price can lead to a change in supply, that is, to a change in the entries in the supply schedule. Such changes are represented by shifts in the supply curve itself.

For example, imagine an innovation in agricultural techniques that allows growers to produce coffee less expensively. This innovation might take the form of a new hybrid coffee plant that produces more beans, or a new idea for organizing harvesting chores so that more beans can be picked in a given amount of time. Such an innovation would make supplying coffee more desirable, and suppliers would supply more at each price than they did before. Table B of Exhibit 1–6 shows what the new supply schedule might look like. The new supply curve is the curve labeled S' in Exhibit 1–6.

Rise in supply
An increase in the quantities that suppliers will provide at each given price.

Fall in supply
A decrease in the quantities that suppliers will provide at each given price.

The shift in supply due to improved agricultural techniques is an example of a **rise in supply.** It is represented by a rightward shift of the supply curve. The opposite situation is a **fall in supply.** If the wages of coffee bean pickers went up, growers would want to provide less coffee at any given price, which is another way of saying that supply would fall. A fall in supply is represented by a leftward shift of the supply curve.

 In Exhibit 1–6 the new supply curve S', with its higher quantities, lies to the right of the old supply curve S. This is because quantity is measured in the horizontal direction, so "higher" translates

---

[6]However, we will see in Chapter 5 that when the supplier is a profit-maximizing firm, the law of supply must hold.

Exhibit 1–6   The Supply of Coffee

Table A. Supply of Coffee
to Your City

Price	Quantity
20¢/cup	100 cups/day
30¢	300
40¢	400
50¢	500

Table B. Supply of Coffee to
Your City Following the
Development of Better
Farming Methods

Price	Quantity
20¢/cup	200 cups/day
30¢	400
40¢	600
50¢	700

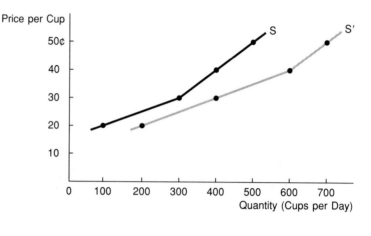

Table A shows, for each price, how much coffee would be supplied to your city. The same information is illustrated by the points in the graph. The curve labeled S is the corresponding supply curve. It conveys more information than the table by displaying the quantities supplied at intermediate prices. The law of supply is illustrated by the upward slope of the supply curve.

The invention of a cheaper way to produce coffee increases the willingness of suppliers to provide coffee at any given price. The new supply is shown in Table B and is illustrated by the curve S'. Although a change in price leads to a movement along the supply curve, a change in something other than price causes the entire curve to shift.

The curve S' lies to the right of S, indicating that the supply has increased.

---

geometrically into "rightward." In the vertical direction, S' lies below S, even though it represents a rise in supply. This is the opposite of what you might at first expect, and you should be on your guard against possible confusion.

▷ *Exercise 1.7* How would the supply of shoes be affected by an increase in the price of leather? How would it be affected by an increase in the price of leather belts?

Example: An Excise Tax

One thing that could lead to a change in supply is the imposition of an **excise tax**—that is, a tax on suppliers of goods.[7] Suppose that a new tax is instituted requiring suppliers to pay 10¢ per cup of coffee sold. Suppose also that in the absence of this tax the supply of coffee in your city is given

Excise tax
In this book, a tax that
is paid directly by sup-
pliers to the govern-
ment.

---

[7]We shall use the phrase *excise tax* to refer to a tax that is paid to the government by producers. As with the phrase *sales tax*, this phrase is not used the same way in all textbooks.

Exhibit 1–7   Effect of an Excise Tax

Table A. Supply of Coffee without Tax

Price	Quantity
20¢/cup	100 cups/day
30¢	300
40¢	400
50¢	500

Table B. Supply of Coffee with Excise Tax of 10¢ Per Cup

Price	Quantity
30¢/cup	100 cups/day
40¢	300
50¢	400
60¢	500

If the price of coffee is 30¢ per cup and there is an excise tax of 10¢, then a seller of coffee will actually get to keep 20¢ per cup sold. The original supply schedule (Table A) shows that under these circumstances suppliers would provide 100 cups per day. This is recorded in the first row of Table B. The other rows in that table are generated in a similar manner.

The rows of Table B contain the same quantities as the rows of Table A, but the corresponding prices are all 10¢ higher. Thus each point on the new supply curve S′ lies exactly 10¢ above a corresponding point on the old supply curve S. Therefore S′ lies exactly 10¢ above S in vertical distance. The excise tax causes the supply curve to shift upward parallel to itself a distance 10¢.

by Table A of Exhibit 1–7 (which is identical to Table A of Exhibit 1–6). Let us compute the supply of coffee in your city after the tax takes effect.

Suppose first that the price of a cup of coffee is 30¢. Then a supplier gets to keep 20¢ for every cup of coffee that he sells (he collects 30¢ and gives a dime to the tax collector). We want to know what quantity will be supplied under these circumstances. The answer is in Table A of Exhibit 1–7: When suppliers receive 20¢ per cup of coffee sold, they provide 100 cups per day.

Therefore, in a world with an excise tax, a price of 30¢ leads to a quantity supplied of 100 cups per day. This gives us the first row of our supply table for a world with an excise tax:

Price	Quantity
30¢/cup	100 cups/day

The entire new supply schedule is displayed in Table B of Exhibit 1–7.

▷ *Exercise 1.8* Explain how we got the entries in the last three rows of Table B in Exhibit 1–7.

Notice that both of the tables in Exhibit 1–7 list the same quantities but that the associated prices are 10¢ higher in Table B. This means that the supply curve associated with Table B will lie a vertical distance 10¢ above the supply curve associated with Table A. The graph in Exhibit 1–7 illustrates this relationship.

Notice that the supply curve with the tax (curve S' in the exhibit) is geometrically above and to the left of the old supply curve S. This is what we have called a lower supply curve (it is lower because, for example, a price of 30¢ calls forth a quantity supplied of only 100, instead of 300).

We can summarize as follows:

An excise tax causes the supply curve to shift upward parallel to itself (to a new, *lower* supply curve) by the amount of the tax.

Elasticity of Supply

Elasticity of supply
The percentage rise in quantity supplied resulting from a 1 percent rise in price.

We can compute the **elasticity of supply** using the same formula that we use to compute the elasticity of demand:

$$\text{Elasticity} = \frac{\text{Percentage change in quantity}}{\text{Percentage change in price}}$$

$$= \frac{100 \cdot \Delta Q/Q}{100 \cdot \Delta P/P}$$

$$= \frac{P \cdot \Delta Q}{Q \cdot \Delta P}$$

The elasticity of supply is positive because an increase in price leads to an increase in quantity supplied. For example, in Table A of Exhibit 1–7 an increase in price from 20¢ to 30¢ (a 50% increase) leads to an increase in quantity supplied from 100 to 300 cups per day (a 200% increase). Therefore the elasticity of supply in this range is $(200\%)/(50\%) = 4$.

1.3 Equilibrium

The language of demand and supply curves enables us to express how buyers and sellers would like to behave in response to various hypothetical prices. We have said nothing about what prices these buyers and sellers will actually face, or whether they will be able to trade their desired quantities at those prices. Demanders cannot purchase more coffee than suppliers are willing to sell them, and suppliers cannot sell more coffee than demanders are willing to buy. In this section we will examine the interaction between suppliers and demanders and the way in which this interaction determines both the prices and the quantities of goods traded in the marketplace.

Exhibit 1–8   **Equilibrium in the Market for Floppy Disks**

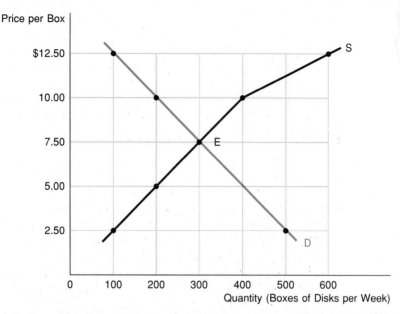

The graph shows the supply and demand curves for floppy computer disks. The equilibrium point, E, is located at the intersection of the two curves. The equilibrium price, $7.50 per box, is the only price at which quantity supplied and quantity demanded are equal.

The Point of Equilibrium

Exhibit 1-8 shows the demand and supply curves for floppy computer disks in your city. We want to find the point on the graph that describes the price of disks and the number of disks that are sold at that price.

 The first thing to notice is that there is only one price at which the quantity supplied and the quantity demanded are equal. That price is $7.50 per box, where the quantities supplied and demanded are each equal to 300 boxes per week. The corresponding point on the graph is called the **equilibrium point.** The equilibrium point is the point at which the supply and demand curves cross.

 To understand the significance of the equilibrium point, we will first imagine what would happen if the market were not at the equilibrium—that is, if the price were something other than $7.50.

 Suppose, for example, that the price is $12.50. We see from the demand curve that all demanders taken together will want a total of 100 disks each week, while suppliers will want to provide 600 disks. The demanders will purchase the 100 disks that they want and will refuse to buy any more. At least some of the suppliers will not be able to sell all of the disks that they want to. Those suppliers will be unhappy.

Equilibrium point
The point where the supply and demand curves intersect.

Satisfied
Able to behave as one
wants to, taking mar-
ket prices as given.

Of course, some demanders may be unhappy too. They may be unhappy because the price of computer disks is so high. They would prefer a price of $7.50 per box, and they would prefer even more a price of $0 per box. But the demanders are perfectly happy in one limited sense: Given the current price of floppy disks, they are buying precisely the quantity that they want to buy. We choose to describe this situation by saying that the demanders are **satisfied.**

In general, a satisfied individual is one who is able to behave as he wants to, taking the prices he faces as given. This is so regardless of how he feels about the prices themselves. We take this as a definition. It is the only definition that really makes sense in this context. Nobody is ever completely happy about the prices themselves: Buyers always wish they were lower and sellers always wish they were higher.

So, when the price is $12.50 per box, the demanders buy 100 boxes a week and are satisfied. The suppliers, who want to sell 600 boxes per week, sell only 100 boxes per week and are unsatisfied. When some suppliers discover that they cannot sell as many disks as they would like at the going price, they lower their prices to attract more demanders.

Suppose that they lower their prices to $10.00 per box. Referring again to Exhibit 1–8, we see that demanders will want to buy 200 boxes of disks per week and suppliers will want to sell 400 boxes. After 200 boxes are sold, the demanders will go home satisfied, and some suppliers will still be left unsatisfied. They will lower their prices further.

We may expect this process to continue as long as the quantity supplied exceeds the quantity demanded. That is, we expect it to continue until the market reaches the equilibrium price of $7.50 per box.

If the price of floppy disks starts out below $7.50, we can expect the same process to work in reverse. For example, when the price is $2.50, demanders want to buy 500 boxes of disks per week, but suppliers want to provide only 100 boxes. The suppliers, having provided 100 boxes, will go home, leaving some demanders unsatisfied. In order to lure the suppliers back to the marketplace, demanders will offer a higher price for the disks. This process will continue until the quantity demanded no longer exceeds the quantity supplied. It will continue until the market reaches the equilibrium price of $7.50 per box.

The story we have just told gives a reason to expect the market to be in equilibrium. The reason is that if the market were not in equilibrium, buyers and sellers would change their behavior in ways that would cause the market to move toward equilibrium. We still have to ask how realistic our story is. Later in this book we will see that there are some markets for which it is substantially accurate, and other markets for which it may not be accurate at all. For the time being, we will focus on the first type of market. That is, for the remainder of this chapter we will assume that the markets we are studying are always in equilibrium. For a wide range of economic problems, this is a safe and useful assumption to make.

Exhibit 1–9   **The Effects of Supply and Demand Shifts**

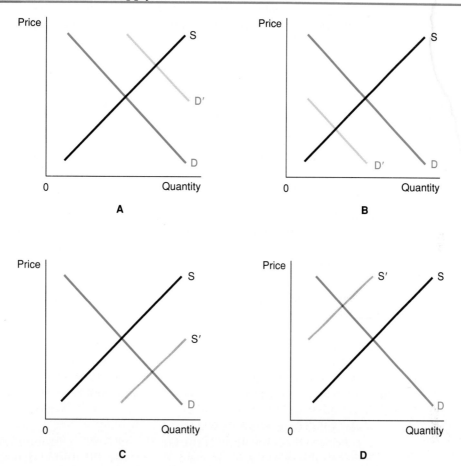

The graphs show the effects of various shifts in demand and supply. For example, in panel A we see that a rise in demand leads to a rise in price and a rise in quantity.

Changes in the Equilibrium Point

Because the equilibrium price and quantity are determined by the supply and demand curves, anything that affects the curves will affect the equilibrium price and quantity. In Exhibit 1–9 we see some of the ways in which changes in demand or supply can affect the point of equilibrium. Using these diagrams, we can predict how various phenomena will affect the price and quantity of computer disks. For example, if the price of computers should fall, there will be an upward shift in the demand curve for computer disks, as shown in panel A of the exhibit. This will lead to an increase in both the price of computer disks and the quantity of computer disks being traded.

▷ *Exercise 1.9* Which panel in Exhibit 1–9 illustrates the effect of a rise in the price of plastic? (Computer disks are made from plastic.) How will a rise in the price of plastic affect the price and the quantity of computer disks?

In general, to see how an event will affect the equilibrium price and quantity, you should first ask how it will affect the demand and supply curves (these are two separate questions) and then ask how the movements in demand and supply affect the equilibrium. *The only way that anything can affect the equilibrium price and quantity is by causing a shift in either the supply curve or the demand curve (or both).* That is why any analysis of a change in equilibrium must begin with the question of how the curves have shifted.

It is important to distinguish causes from effects. For an individual demander or supplier, the price is taken as given and determines the quantity demanded or supplied. For the market as a whole, the demand and supply curves determine both price and quantity simultaneously.

Effect of a Sales Tax

One thing that we know will influence the demand curve for coffee is the imposition of a sales tax paid by demanders. Let's see how such a tax would affect the equilibrium.

Exhibit 1–10 shows the market for lettuce before and after the imposition of a sales tax of 5¢ per head. The curve labeled D is the original demand curve, and the one labeled D' is the demand curve after the tax is imposed. Recall from our discussion of sales taxes in Section 1.1 that D' lies a vertical distance 5¢ below D.

Prior to the imposition of the tax, the market is in equilibrium at point E. When the sales tax is imposed, the downward shift in demand moves the equilibrium to point F. How does point F compare with point E? The first thing to notice is that it is to the left of point E. It corresponds to a smaller quantity than point E does. This gives our first conclusion:

Imposing a sales tax reduces the equilibrium quantity.

What about the equilibrium price? We can see immediately from the diagram that point F is lower than point E. In other words, imposing a sales tax causes the equilibrium price to fall. We can even say something about how far the equilibrium price will fall. You should be able to see from the graph in Exhibit 1–10 that the vertical drop from point E to point F is smaller than the vertical distance between the old and the new demand curves. In other words, it is a drop of less than 5¢. (The vertical distance from point G to point F is 5¢ and the vertical distance from point E to point F is clearly less than this.) In other words:

A sales tax of 5¢ per item will cause the equilibrium price to fall by some amount less than 5¢ per item.

Exhibit 1–10 The Effect of a Sales Tax in the Lettuce Market

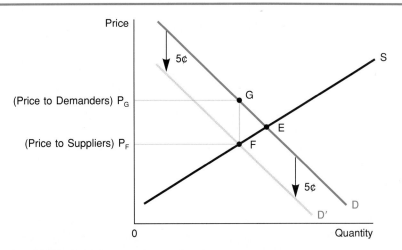

The graph shows the market for lettuce before and after the imposition of a sales tax of 5¢ per head. The original demand curve (D) intersects the supply curve at E, which is the point of equilibrium before the tax. When the tax is instituted, the demand curve moves down vertically a distance 5¢, to D'. The new equilibrium point is F, and the new equilibrium price for lettuce is P_F. However, demanders must pay more than P_F for a head of lettuce—they must pay P_F plus 5¢ tax. Thus the price to demanders is 5¢ higher than P_F. To find the corresponding point, begin at F and move up a distance 5¢ to G. Since F is on the curve D', G must be on the curve D. The price to demanders is P_G.

The exact amount of the fall in price depends on the exact shapes of the supply and demand curves, but it is always somewhere between 0¢ and 5¢.

▷ *Exercise 1.10* Draw some diagrams in which either the demand or the supply curve is either unusually steep or unusually shallow. In which cases will a 5¢ sales tax cause the price to drop very little? In which cases will the tax cause the price to drop by nearly 5¢?

The price P_F shown in Exhibit 1–10 is the new price of lettuce. However, a consumer wishing to acquire a head of lettuce must pay more than P_F: He must pay P_F plus 5¢ tax. To find this price, we must look for a point 5¢ higher than point F. Because point F is on the new demand curve D', a point 5¢ higher than F will be on the old demand curve D. (This is because the vertical distance between the demand curves is exactly 5¢.) That point has been labeled G in the exhibit. The price that the consumer must pay to get a head of lettuce is the corresponding price P_G.

Let us summarize: By shifting the equilibrium from point E to point F, a sales tax of 5¢ per head lowers the quantity sold. It lowers the price that sellers collect from the original equilibrium price P_E to P_F. It raises the price that demanders pay from P_E to P_G.

Effect of an Excise Tax

Now that we have analyzed the effect of a sales tax, let us turn to a different problem: The effect of a 5¢ excise tax. This effect is illustrated in panel B of Exhibit 1–11. The sales tax has disappeared now, so the demand curve has returned to its original position. However, as we discovered in Section 1.2, the 5¢ excise tax will shift the supply curve by a vertical distance 5¢. The new supply curve is labeled S′ in panel B. With the excise tax, the new market equilibrium is at point H. The quantity traded has fallen, and the price has risen by an amount less than 5¢.

▷ *Exercise 1.11* How do we know that the price rise is less than 5¢?

In everyday language, this situation is often described by saying that the suppliers have "passed on" part of the sales tax to consumers through the rise in the market price of lettuce. This is analogous to the situation brought on by the sales tax: In that case demanders "passed on" a portion of the tax to producers through the fall in the market price of coffee.

Referring again to panel B of Exhibit 1–11, the market price has risen to P_H, and that is the price that demanders pay for a head of lettuce. But a supplier who sells a head of lettuce does not get to keep P_H—he can keep only P_H minus the 5¢ that goes to the tax collector. In order to find the amount that the supplier gets to keep, we must drop a vertical distance 5¢ below point H. Because point H is on the curve S′, this vertical drop will land us on the curve S at the point marked J. This gives a price to suppliers of P_J, below the original equilibrium price that was given by point E.

Comparing Two Taxes

Now let's ask an important question: Would you rather live in a world with a 5¢ sales tax or a world with a 5¢ excise tax? Let's deal with this question first from the point of view of a demander. To a demander the net effect of a sales tax is to raise the after-tax price of lettuce to P_G. The net effect of an excise tax is to raise the price of lettuce to P_H. (Refer to Exhibit 1–11 for the relevant graphs.) Because demanders like low prices, the question is really: Which is lower, P_G or P_H?

Before answering this question, let's formulate the corresponding question from the point of view of the supplier. To him, the sales tax lowers the price of lettuce to P_F; the excise tax lowers the price to him (after taxes) to P_J. Suppliers like high prices, so the question from their point of view is: Which is higher, P_F or P_J?

The answer turns out to be that point G is exactly the same as point H and point F is exactly the same as point J! It is easy to see why this is true. We only need three observations:

1.   Point G is on the original demand curve D, point F is on the original supply curve S, and the vertical distance between them is 5¢.

2.   Point H is on the original demand curve D, point J is on the original supply curve S, and the vertical distance between them is 5¢.

Exhibit 1–11   **A Sales Tax versus an Excise Tax**

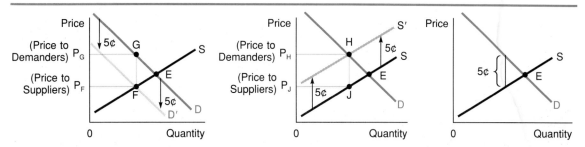

| **A. Effect of a Sales Tax** | **B. Effect of an Excise Tax** | **C. Equilibrium without Any Tax** |

Panel A is a reproduction of the graph from Exhibit 1–10, illustrating the effect of a 5¢ sales tax. Panel B illustrates the effect of a 5¢ excise tax: The supply curve shifts upward a vertical distance 5¢, leading to a new market equilibrium at point H. The corresponding price, P_H, is what demanders must pay for a head of lettuce. But suppliers keep less than P_H when a head of lettuce is sold—they keep P_H minus 5¢ tax. Thus the price to suppliers is 5¢ below P_H. To find the corresponding point, begin at H and move down a distance 5¢ to J. Since H is on the curve S′, J must be on the curve S. The price to suppliers is P_J.

To compare the effects of the two taxes, we must compare the points G and F in panel A with the points H and J in panel B. In each case there is one point on the curve D and one point on the curve S, and in each case the two points are a distance 5¢ apart. There is only one possible location for such points, as shown in panel C. It follows that points G and F are identical to points H and J. In other words, the sales tax and the excise tax have exactly the same effects on both suppliers and demanders.

3.   There is only one place to the left of E at which the vertical distance between the curves D and S is exactly 5¢.

Points 1 and 2 are illustrated in panels A and B of Exhibit 1–11. Point 3 is illustrated in panel C, where only the original demand and supply curves are shown.

From these observations we can conclude that points G and F are identical with points H and J. In other words, the 5¢ sales tax affects suppliers and demanders in exactly the same way that the 5¢ excise tax does. Neither suppliers nor demanders have any reason to prefer either tax over the other.

Economists often summarize this startling conclusion with the slogan:

The economic incidence of a tax is independent of its legal incidence.

Economic incidence
The division of a tax burden according to who actually pays the tax.

In this statement, the **economic incidence** of a tax refers to the distribution of the actual tax burden. The **legal incidence** of the tax is the distribution of the tax burden in legal theory. The sales tax places the legal incidence entirely on demanders, because it is they who are required by law to pay the tax. The excise tax places the legal incidence entirely on suppliers. However, the economic incidence of the sales tax and the economic incidence of the excise tax are the same, because the actual prices paid by suppliers and demanders are the same in both cases.

Legal incidence
The division of a tax burden according to who is required under the law to pay the tax.

Students sometimes misunderstand the conclusion we have drawn by thinking that the sales tax (or the excise tax) imposes equal burdens on demanders and suppliers. This is not correct. The division of the tax burden depends on the shapes of the supply and demand curves. In Exhibit 1–11 point F might be 4¢ below the original equilibrium (E) and point G 1¢ above the original equilibrium; in this case ⅘ of the tax is being passed on to suppliers and ⅕ is being paid by demanders. With differently shaped curves, the suppliers might be paying ⅕ and the demanders ⅘.

What we have argued is that the division of the tax burden will be the same under an excise tax as it is under a sales tax. If suppliers pay ⅘ of the sales tax, they will also pay ⅘ of the excise tax; if they pay ⅕ of the sales tax, they will also pay ⅕ of the excise tax.

▷ *Exercise 1.12* Suppose that an excise tax of 2¢ per head of lettuce and a sales tax of 3¢ per head of lettuce were simultaneously imposed. Show that the combined economic incidence of these taxes will be the same as the economic incidence of either the pure 5¢ sales tax or the pure 5¢ excise tax.

An interesting application is to Social Security taxes. We can view Social Security as a tax on hours worked. "Hours worked" are demanded by firms and supplied by their employees. A Social Security tax that is paid directly by the employees is an excise tax. One that is paid by firms is a sales tax. Whenever Social Security taxes are raised, there is a furor in the legislature about how to divide the legal incidence of the two taxes: Should they be paid entirely by employees, entirely by firms, divided equally, or divided in some other way? The analysis of this section shows that the resolution of this conflict ultimately makes not one bit of difference to anybody.

Summary

The law of demand says that when the price of a good goes up, the quantity demanded goes down. For any individual or any group of individuals, and for any particular good, such as coffee, we can draw a demand curve. The demand curve shows, for each possible price, how much of the good those individuals or groups will purchase in a specified period of time. Another way to state the law of demand is: Demand curves slope downward.

A change in price leads to a change in quantity demanded, which is the same as a movement along the demand curve. A change in something other than price can lead to a change in demand, which is a shift of the demand curve itself.

One example of a change in something other than price is the imposition of a sales tax, paid directly by consumers to the government. (For purposes of drawing the demand curve, we do *not* view the tax as a form of price increase. When coffee sells for 50¢ plus 10¢ tax per cup, we say that the price is 50¢, not 60¢.) Consider the effect of a sales tax on coffee. The sales tax makes coffee less desirable at any given (pre-tax) price and so causes the demand curve to shift downward. In fact, we can calculate that the demand curve will shift downward by a vertical distance equal to the amount of the tax.

The law of supply says that when the price of a good goes up, the quantity supplied goes up. For any individual or any group of individuals, and for any particular good, we can draw a supply curve. The supply curve shows, for each possible price, how much of the good those individuals will provide in a specified period of time. Another way to state the law of supply is: Supply curves slope upward.

A change in price leads to a change in quantity supplied, which is the same as a movement along the supply curve. A change in something other than price can lead to a change in supply, which is a shift of the supply curve itself.

One example of a change in something other than price is the imposition of an excise tax, paid directly by suppliers to the government. Consider the effect of an excise tax on coffee. The excise tax makes providing coffee less desirable at any given price and so causes the supply curve to shift leftward. (The resulting curve is called a lower supply curve, because it has shifted leftward. Geometrically, it lies above and to the left of the original supply curve.) In fact, we can calculate that the supply curve will shift upward by a vertical distance equal to the amount of the tax.

The equilibrium point is the point at which the supply and demand curves intersect. The corresponding equilibrium price is the only price at which the quantity supplied is equal to the quantity demanded. Therefore it is reasonable to expect that this will be the price prevailing in the market. We make the assumption that this is indeed the case. Later in the book we will discover that there are many circumstances in which this assumption is well warranted.

Because the point of equilibrium is determined by the supply and demand curves, it can change only if either the supply or the demand curve changes. To see how a change in circumstances affects market prices and quantities, we first decide how it affects the supply and demand curves and then see where the equilibrium point has moved.

As an example, we can examine the effects of a sales tax on coffee. The sales tax causes the demand curve to shift down by the amount of the tax. This leads to a reduction in quantity and a reduction in the market price. The market price is reduced by less than the amount of the tax. To acquire a cup of coffee, a demander must now pay the new market price plus tax; this adds up to a new post-tax "price to demanders" that is higher than the old equilibrium price.

Another example is the effect of an excise tax on coffee. This shifts the supply curve to the left (vertically, it shifts it up by the amount of the tax), leading to a smaller quantity and an increase in the market price. The market price goes up by less than the amount of the tax. When a supplier sells a cup of coffee, he earns the market price minus the amount of the tax; this leaves him with a new post-tax "price to suppliers" that is less than the old equilibrium price.

The sales and excise taxes both reduce quantity, reduce the post-tax price to suppliers, and raise the post-tax price to demanders. A simple geometric argument shows that the magnitudes of these effects are all the same regardless of whether the tax is legally imposed on demanders or on suppliers. We summarize this by saying that the economic incidence of a tax is independent of its legal incidence. For example, an increase in the Social Security tax will affect both employers and employees in exactly the same way regardless of whether the employers or the employees are required to pay the tax.

Review Questions

R1. What can cause a movement along the demand curve? What can cause the demand curve itself to shift? Which of these is a change in demand and which is a change in quantity demanded?

R2. Explain why a sales tax of $100 per automobile would cause the demand curve for automobiles to shift down a vertical distance $100. Explain why an excise tax of $100 per automobile would cause the supply curve to shift up a vertical distance $100.

R3. What is the elasticity of a horizontal demand curve? Of a vertical demand curve?

R4. Compute the elasticities of the demand and supply curves shown in Exhibit 1–8 at a variety of places along the curves.

R5. How are the equilibrium price and quantity of record albums affected by a rise in demand? A fall in demand? A rise in supply? A fall in supply? Give examples of possible causes for rises and falls in the supply and demand for record albums.

R6. Explain what is meant by the statement "The economic incidence of a tax is independent of its legal incidence." Explain the geometric argument that leads to this conclusion.

Numerical Exercises

N1. Suppose that the demand curve for oranges is given by the equation

$$Q = 200 \cdot P + 1,000,$$

with quantity (Q) measured in oranges per day and price (P) measured in dollars per orange. The supply curve is given by

$$Q = 800 \cdot P.$$

Compute the equilibrium price and quantity of oranges.

N2. Suppose that an excise tax of 50¢ apiece is imposed on oranges. If the original supply and demand curves are as in Problem N1, what are the equations for the new supply and demand curves? What is the new equilibrium price and quantity of oranges? What is the new post-tax price from the supplier's point of view? Illustrate your answer by drawing supply and demand curves.

N3. Repeat Problem N2 for a 50¢ sales tax instead of a 50¢ excise tax.

Problem Set

1. *True or false:* A sharp rise in the price of eggs would be unlikely to last very long; after all, the rise in price would lead to a fall in demand, and this fall in demand would then cause the price to fall.

2. The following item appeared in a major daily newspaper:

Though sales are down, prices continue to rise in apparent violation of the law of supply and demand

Does this observation in fact violate the laws of supply and demand?

3. *True or false:* The discovery of a new method of birth control that is safer, cheaper, more effective, and easier to use than any other method would reduce the number of unwanted pregnancies.

4. Can you think of some other "goods," such as murder and reckless driving, that are not traded in the traditional economic marketplace but for which people nevertheless have demand curves? For each of these goods, what would it mean for the demand curve to be unusually steep? Unusually shallow?

5. In each of the following circumstances, what would happen to the price and the quantity consumed of corn?
   a. The price of wheat goes up.
   b. The price of fertilizer goes up.
   c. An epidemic wipes out half the population.
   d. The wages of industrial workers go up.

6. a. Suppose that the only way to reach a certain restaurant is by train, and the train fare is $2. One day a law is passed requiring the restaurant owner to provide free transportation to his restaurant, which he does by making an arrangement with the railroad whereby his customers ride free and he pays the $2 fare per customer directly to the railroad.
      (i) What does this do to the supply curve for restaurant meals?
      (ii) What does this do to the demand curve for restaurant meals? (*Hint:* it does *not* stay fixed.)
      (iii) What does this do to the price and quantity served of restaurant meals?

   (iv) Of the following, who benefits and who loses as a result of this law? The restaurant owner, the restaurant customers, the railroad?

b. Suppose that no law had been passed but that the restaurant owner had decided on his own to start offering free transportation. What parts of your answer would be different?

c. Nelson Brothers furniture store advertises that "we would never think of charging you for delivery." Do you believe them? Why or why not?

Refer to Answers to Problem Sets for solutions to problems 5a and 5c.

Chapter Two

Prices, Costs, and the
Gains from Trade

The supply and demand curves of Chapter 1 arose from the desires of individuals to trade with one another. Suppliers offered goods to demanders in exchange for money, which they themselves presumably exchanged for other goods. We studied various aspects of those exchanges: the quantities that were traded, the prices at which those trades took place, and the ways in which these were affected by external influences such as various forms of taxation.

Our main goal in this chapter is to understand some of the reasons why people want to trade with each other in the first place. We will begin in Section 2.1 with a more precise discussion of what is meant by the term *price*. Then in Section 2.2 we will relate prices to the more general notion of costs. We will see how differences in costs create opportunities for people to gain from trade. Another source of such opportunities—differences in tastes—will be discussed in Chapter 3.

2.1 Prices

In Chapter 1 we had much to say about prices, on the assumption that everybody knows what prices are. Now it is time for a more precise discussion. In this section we will study alternative interpretations of the word *price*, and will specify exactly what is meant by the concept of price in microeconomics.

Absolute versus Relative Prices

Imagine a world without money. In such a world, people would still trade, and it would make perfectly good sense to talk about prices. For example, if you gave your neighbor two loaves of bread in exchange for one bottle of wine, we would say that the price you paid for the wine was 2 loaves of bread per bottle. At the same time, we would say that your neighbor had purchased 2 loaves of bread at the price of ½ bottle of wine per loaf.

In the real world we use money to make purchases. Consequently, we usually measure the price of wine in terms of dollars rather than in terms of loaves of bread. However, it is still possible to measure the price of wine in terms of bread. If bread sells for $1 per loaf and wine sells for $2 per bottle, it follows that you can exchange 2 loaves of bread for 1 bottle of wine.[1] We can still say that the price of wine is 2 loaves of bread per bottle or that the price of bread is ½ bottle of wine per loaf.

We now have two different meanings for the word *price*, and we must distinguish between them. The number of dollars necessary to purchase a bottle of wine is called the **absolute price** of the bottle, whereas the number of loaves of bread necessary to purchase a bottle of wine is called the **relative price** of wine in terms of bread. In general, the absolute price of a good is measured in dollars and the relative price of a good is measured in units of some other good.

Absolute price
The number of dollars that can be exchanged for a specified quantity of a given good.

Relative price
The quantity of some other good that can be exchanged for a specified quantity of a given good.

Of course, there are many different relative prices of wine. We could measure the relative price of wine in terms of chickens, the relative price of wine in terms of steel, or the relative price of wine in terms of hours of labor.

To illustrate the difference between relative and absolute prices, suppose that the absolute prices of bread and wine in two different years are given by the following table:

	1985	1990
Bread	$1/loaf	$3/loaf
Wine	$2/bottle	$6/bottle

In this example the absolute price of wine has tripled over a 5-year period. However, the relative price of wine in terms of bread has remained fixed at ½ bottle of wine per loaf. This illustrates the important point that changes in absolute prices are not the same thing as changes in relative prices.

---

[1]In order to do this, you might first have to sell the bread for $2 cash and then use the cash to buy the wine. But the end result is the same as if you had exchanged the bread for the wine directly.

Exhibit 2–1   **Absolute and Relative Price Changes**
              in a World with Two Goods

	1989	1990(a)	1990(b)	1990(c)	1990(d)
Bread	$1/loaf	$1/loaf	50¢/loaf	$5/loaf	25¢/loaf
Wine	$2/bottle	$4/bottle	$2/bottle	$20/bottle	$1/bottle

The table shows the absolute prices of bread and wine in 1989 and four possibilities for the absolute prices in 1990. In each of the four cases the relative price of a bottle of wine has risen from 2 loaves of bread to 4 loaves of bread. In each case we can correctly assert that "the price of wine has doubled," because in microeconomics *the price* always means *the relative price.*

In microeconomics the prices that we study are relative prices. This means that the price of wine should always be measured in terms of other goods, such as bread. However, we can still use dollars to measure the relative price of wine *provided* we assume that the dollar price of bread does not change. We simply must remember that the "dollars" in which we express the price of wine are really just stand-ins for loaves of bread.

In microeconomics the single word *price* always refers to a relative price.

Relative Prices When There Are More than Two Goods

If we imagine a world with only two goods, such as bread and wine, the *price of wine* refers to something unambiguous, namely a certain number of loaves of bread. In the real world there are many different relative prices for wine: one in terms of bread, one in terms of chickens, and so on. We can also consider the price of wine relative to a basket containing representative quantities of all goods in the economy. Sometimes we will speak of *the* price of wine, in which case we will be referring to the price relative to that representative basket. Often we will measure this relative price in dollars, keeping in mind that the word *dollar* is being used to refer not to a piece of green paper but to a basket of goods.

Changing Prices

Suppose that in 1989 the absolute price of bread is $1 per loaf, that the absolute price of wine is $2 per bottle, and that these are the only two items you consume. Now suppose that because bad weather has damaged the vineyards, we are led to expect that the price of wine will double in 1990. Because we are studying relative prices, this means that in 1990 one bottle of wine will trade for 4 loaves of bread, rather than for the 1989 price of 2 loaves. The table in Exhibit 2–1 shows only a few of the many different absolute prices at which this could happen.

If in 1990 any of the last four columns of the table describes the prices correctly, then we will be able to say that the price of wine has doubled, just as we predicted it would. All four of these columns fit our prediction equally well. Because microeconomics is concerned only with relative prices, from our point of view there is no real difference between those columns. If you woke up tomorrow morning to discover that all absolute prices (including wages) had doubled (or halved), the world would not really be different in any significant way.

Relative Price Changes and Inflation

Because relative prices and absolute prices are determined independently of each other, it is always misleading to attribute an absolute price change to a relative price change. It is quite common to hear that there has been inflation (a rise in the level of absolute prices) because of a rise in the price of a particular commodity such as oil, housing, or wine. But we can see from Exhibit 2–1 that a rise in the relative price of wine is equally consistent with either a rise or a fall in the absolute price level.

In fact, when the relative price of wine increases from 2 to 4 loaves of bread per bottle, what happens to the relative price of bread? It decreases, from ½ to ¼ bottle of wine per loaf. Any increase in the relative price of wine must be accompanied by a decrease in the relative price of bread.

▷ *Exercise 2.1* Explain why the preceding statement is true.

When you hear the commentator on the nightly news program attribute the latest burst of inflation to a rise in the price of gasoline, reflect on what he means. He means that gasoline is now more expensive relative to, say, shoes than it was before. Another way to say the same thing is to state that shoes are now cheaper relative to gasoline than they were before. If the rise in the relative price of gasoline causes inflation, why doesn't the fall in the relative price of shoes cause deflation? In fact, relative price changes do not cause absolute price changes—and you now know more than the commentator on the nightly news.

2.2 Costs, Efficiency, and the Gains from Trade

In the preceding section we discussed the concept of *price*. In this section we will discuss the related concept of *cost*. Once we understand what costs are, we will be able to see how everyone can benefit when activities are carried out at the lowest possible cost. This will provide us with a powerful example of the gains from trade.

Costs and Efficiency

When you decide to spend an evening at the opera, you must forgo a number of other things. First, you pay a price, say $50, for the ticket. Of course, the money itself is valuable only insofar as you could have used it to buy something else. That "something else"—perhaps 10 movie tickets or 5 pizzas—represents some of the cost of going to the opera.

The ticket price is only part of the cost, because your evening at the opera entails many other sacrifices as well. There is the gasoline that you use to get you to the opera. There is also the time spent actually attending the performance. That time could have been spent doing something else, and the value of that something else is also part of the cost of going to the opera.

Cost
A forgone opportunity.

In summary, a **cost** is a forgone opportunity. The cost of engaging in an activity is the totality of all the opportunities that the activity requires you to forgo.

You may have heard the term *opportunity cost* used to describe such costs as the time sacrificed in attending the opera. This term is quite misleading because it implies that an "opportunity cost" is one of several types of cost. In reality, *every cost is an opportunity cost.* The dollars that you pay for the opera ticket are valuable only insofar as they represent forgone opportunities to purchase other goods. They are of exactly the same nature as the costs represented by your time and your gasoline—forgone opportunities all.

In calculating costs it is important not to double-count. The time spent at the opera could have been used to go to the movies or to study for exams, but not both. Therefore it would not be correct to count both the forgone movie and the forgone studying as costs. The only activities that should be counted as costs are those you would have actually engaged in if you had not gone to the opera.

Example: The Electrician and the Carpenter

Imagine an electrician and a carpenter, each of whom wants his house rewired and his den paneled. As shown in Table A of Exhibit 2–2, the electrician requires 10 hours to rewire his house and 15 hours to panel his den. The carpenter knows how to do his own rewiring, but because he is less skilled at it than the electrician, it takes him 20 hours instead of 10. And what about paneling? The electrician can panel his den in 15 hours, so you might expect a professional carpenter to be able to do it in a shorter time. But we forgot to tell you that this particular carpenter is a tad on the doltish side, and has some paralysis in his left arm to boot. As a result, paneling his den takes him 18 hours to complete. All of these numbers are summarized in Table A of Exhibit 2–2.

Because the electrician can both rewire and panel faster than the carpenter can, you might think that it is correct to say that he can perform both tasks at a lower cost than the carpenter can. But this is definitely not true. To see why not, we have to remember that costs are defined in terms of forgone opportunities. The electrician needs 10 hours to rewire his house. Alternatively, he could use that same 10 hours to complete ⅔ of a 15-hour paneling job. That ⅔ of a paneling job is the cost of his rewiring. Similarly, a paneling job costs him 3/2 rewirings.

Exhibit 2–2   The Electrician and the Carpenter

	Table A			Table B	
	Electrician	**Carpenter**		**Electrician**	**Carpenter**
Rewiring	10 hours	20 hours	**Rewiring**	2/3 paneling	10/9 panelings
Paneling	15 hours	18 hours	**Paneling**	3/2 rewirings	9/10 rewiring

Table A shows the amount of time needed for the electrician and the carpenter to rewire and to panel. Notice that the electrician can complete either job in less time than the carpenter can. We express this by saying that the electrician has an absolute advantage at each task.

Table B shows the costs of rewiring and paneling jobs performed by each individual. The costs are measured in terms of forgone opportunities; thus the cost of a rewiring job must be measured in terms of paneling jobs and vice versa. All of the information in Table B can be derived from the information in Table A.

Notice that the electrician can rewire at a lower cost than the carpenter, but that the carpenter can panel at a lower cost than the electrician. We express this by saying that the electrician has a comparative advantage at rewiring, whereas the carpenter has a comparative advantage at paneling.

Suppose that each individual wants his house rewired and his den paneled. Table C below shows the total amount of time that each will have to work in order to accomplish both jobs. In the first column we assume that each does all of the work on his own house. For example, the electrician spends 10 hours rewiring and 15 hours paneling, for a total of 25 hours. In the second column, we assume that each specializes in the area of his comparative advantage: The electrician rewires both houses and the carpenter panels both dens.

Table C

	Without Trade	**With Trade**
Electrician	25 hours	20 hours
Carpenter	38 hours	36 hours

It is apparent from Table C that trade makes both parties better off. In particular, the electrician can gain from trade with the carpenter, despite his absolute advantages in both areas. This illustrates the general fact that everyone can be made better off whenever each concentrates in his area of comparative advantage and then trades for the goods he wants to have.

We can do the same kind of calculations for the carpenter. The results are displayed in Table B of Exhibit 2–2.

▷ *Exercise 2.2* Explain how we got the entries in the second column of Table B.

The electrician can produce a rewiring job more cheaply than the carpenter can because he rewires a house at a cost of ⅔ of a paneling job, whereas the carpenter rewires at a cost of 10/9 paneling jobs. We express this by saying that the electrician has a **comparative advantage** at rewiring. This simply means that he can do the job at a lower cost than the carpenter

Comparative advantage
The ability to perform a given task at a lower cost.

More efficient
Able to perform a
given task at lower
cost; having a com-
parative advantage.

can. Another way to say the same thing is that the electrician is **more efficient** at rewiring than the carpenter is.

It is a bit more surprising, but equally true, that the carpenter is more efficient than the electrician at paneling. This statement may surprise you, since the carpenter takes 18 hours to do a paneling job that the electrician can do in 15 hours. Nevertheless, it is true. The cost to the carpenter of performing a paneling job is only 9/10 of a rewiring job, whereas the cost to the electrician of performing a paneling job is 3/2 rewiring jobs. This follows from our definition of cost as a forgone opportunity. The cost of paneling is not the number of hours devoted to the job, but the use to which those hours could have been put. The carpenter is therefore a more efficient paneler than the electrician. He has a comparative advantage at paneling.

Students often make statements like "The electrician is more efficient at rewiring than he is at paneling" or "The electrician has a comparative advantage at rewiring over paneling." Such statements are not only wrong; they are without meaning. The correct statements are "The electrician is more efficient at rewiring than the carpenter is, and less efficient at paneling than the carpenter is" and "The electrician has a comparative advantage over the carpenter at rewiring, whereas the carpenter has a comparative advantage over the electrician at paneling." The *comparative* in *comparative advantage* refers to a comparison of two individuals performing the same task, and never to a comparison of different tasks performed by the same individual.

Specialization and the Gains from Trade

We have chosen to define *efficiency* in such a way that the most efficient producer of a good is the one who produces it at the lowest cost, where costs are defined in terms of forgone opportunities. According to this definition, the carpenter is more efficient at paneling than the electrician is. Perhaps this definition strikes you as strange. Why have we chosen it? The answer is that it is the only definition of efficiency that makes the following statement true:

> **Everyone in society can be made better off if each specializes in the area where he is most efficient, and then trades for the goods he wants to have.**

We can illustrate this with the example of the electrician and the carpenter. Suppose that each of these individuals elects to make his own home improvements. Then the electrician spends 10 hours rewiring and 15 hours paneling, for a total of 25 hours. At the same time, the carpenter spends 20 hours and 18 hours for a total of 38 hours.

Suppose, on the other hand, that each specializes in his area of comparative advantage, and that they trade services. The electrician specializes in rewiring, and does both his own house and the carpenter's.

These two 10-hour jobs take him 20 hours. In exchange for this, the carpenter panels both dens. These two 18-hour jobs take him 36 hours. All of this is summarized in Table C of Exhibit 2–2.

As you can see, everybody in this society is better off when each exploits his comparative advantage by specializing in the area in which he is the more efficient producer.

When you first looked at Table A in Exhibit 2–2, you might have thought that the electrician could not possibly have anything to gain by trading with the carpenter. You might have thought that this was so because the electrician appeared to be better than the carpenter at everything. Now you know that the carpenter is actually "better" than the electrician at paneling, in the sense that he panels at a lower cost than the electrician does, giving him a comparative advantage. This is the reason that trade can be a profitable activity for both.

An individual's preferences are not sufficient (or even necessarily relevant) for determining what he should produce. The electrician wants both rewiring and paneling, but he is better off when he produces two rewirings than when he produces exactly what he wants. The same is true of groups of individuals. The people of Finland might collectively love grapefruit, but it would not be intelligent for Finland to specialize in domestic grapefruit production. The Finns can have more grapefruit by specializing in the areas of their comparative advantage (in this case, timber and timber products) and then trading for grapefruit and the other commodities they wish to consume.

The benefits of specialization and trade account for most of the material wealth that you see in the world. Wherever you go in the United States, you will find small towns of 500 or 2,000 or 3,000 people. The residents of these towns consume fresh fruit and power tools and air-conditioning and comic books and Hollywood movies and catcher's mitts and artwork. None of the towns produces such a wide variety of goods on its own. Typically, the residents of the town specialize in a few areas of comparative advantage and acquire the goods they want to have by trading with people in other towns who have specialized in other areas. If a town of 2,000 people attempted to produce its own fresh fruit and power tools and Hollywood movies, very little of anything would be accomplished. The difference between the standard of living in that imaginary isolated town and the standards of living actually observed in America is due entirely to the principle of comparative advantage. The enormous magnitude of that difference is almost impossible to contemplate.

Example: The Middleman

One important task in society is the transfer of goods from producers to consumers. The complexity of this task is often overlooked or underestimated: Somebody has to figure out who wants which products, where these products are to be found, which producers can be relied upon to provide a certain level of quality, what is the most efficient means of transporting those goods, and the solutions to many other problems of this sort. According to the principles we have just established, everybody can benefit when this task is accomplished by specialists with an appropriate comparative advantage. Those specialists are often called *middlemen*.

The middleman is much maligned in popular mythology for his alleged tendency to increase the costs of the products in which he deals. In fact, he does the opposite. Suppose that a bicycle manufacturer is able to make three bicycles per day, from which he earns a net income of $30. One day a week, he delivers the bicycles, using $10 worth of gasoline. The total cost to him of making deliveries is $40: $10 in gasoline plus $30 worth of forgone opportunities to earn income. If he can hire a middleman to make deliveries for him, and if that middleman can produce that service at a cost of less than $40, then the cost of a delivered bicycle will go down, not up.

The middleman might be an employee, or he might be an independent contractor who buys the bicycles and then resells them. The analysis is the same in either case.

Notice that even if the middleman has a poor sense of direction and requires $15 worth of gasoline to make the deliveries instead of $10, he can still be more efficient at delivering bicycles than the manufacturer is. He is more efficient, and is reducing costs, as long as he has a comparative advantage at bicycle delivery.

The fact that the manufacturer chooses to use the middleman's services is already good evidence that those services reduce costs. If this weren't the case, the middleman would soon be eliminated.

We have said that the middleman performs many tasks that would otherwise be performed by the producer. It is also true that he performs many tasks that would otherwise be performed (more expensively) by the consumer. When you go to the sporting-goods store to buy a canoe, the store is acting as a middleman between you and the canoe maker. The three or four brands that are available at the store have been chosen from among the dozens that are manufactured. The store owner has performed an extensive search to find the brands with characteristics that are most likely to appeal to his customers. For this you pay a premium when you buy the canoe. The alternative would be to conduct the search yourself, a process almost surely more expensive than paying the premium. Indeed, it would be fair for an observer to conclude that this is the case, since he sees you choosing to shop at the store. By exercising his comparative advantage as a middleman, the store owner is able to make everybody—the producer, the consumer, and himself—a beneficiary.

Why People Trade

People trade for two reasons, either one of which would be sufficient for trade to take place. They trade because they have different tastes and because they have different abilities.

Imagine a world with only two goods: apples and gasoline. Suppose that the only way in which these goods are produced is that once a week each individual receives five apples and five gallons of gasoline as a gift from heaven. In that world everyone has equal abilities in production—we each "produce" five apples and five gallons of gasoline per week and can do nothing to increase or decrease that production—but we might still trade with one another because of differences in tastes. If you preferred to stay home every night eating apples while your friend preferred to spend his evenings driving through the countryside, you would have an excellent opportunity for a mutually beneficial exchange.

At the other extreme, imagine a world in which everyone has the same preferences regarding apples and gasoline, but some people only know how to grow apples while others only know how to manufacture gasoline. The apple growers will grow apples, the gasoline manufacturers will make gasoline, and then they will trade so that each has a mix of apples and gasoline that is preferable to what the individual could produce for himself.

In each of these imaginary worlds, trade takes place for a different reason. People with identical abilities might trade because of differing tastes, and people with identical tastes might trade because of differing abilities. In a world in which both tastes and abilities differ, people will trade for both reasons.

In this chapter we have explored the meaning of *differing abilities* and have made the term more precise through the concept of comparative advantage. We have seen quite explicitly how individuals with different comparative advantages can gain from trade. Our next task is to make a thorough study of tastes and to incorporate them into our study of market behavior. That will be the subject of Chapter 3.

Summary

In microeconomics the word *price* is always used to refer to the *relative price* of a good. Thus the price of a potato is the quantity of some other good or collection of goods that can be exchanged for a potato. The relative price must be distinguished from the *absolute price,* which measures the number of dollars that can be exchanged for a potato. Nevertheless, we often measure relative prices in "dollars." In doing so, we must remember that these dollars are not pieces of green paper but simply a convenient shorthand for referring to collections of other goods in the economy.

The price of a good or of an activity is typically only one component of the cost of acquiring that good or participating in that activity. The full cost of participation is the totality of all alternative opportunities that must be forgone. In calculating this cost, we must be careful to count only those alternatives that we would have actually pursued.

An individual is said to perform a task more efficiently than another if he performs it at a lower cost. An individual is said to have a comparative advantage at a task if he performs it more efficiently than anyone else. In determining who is the most efficient producer of a good, we must keep in mind that all costs are forgone opportunities. Thus we do not count, for example, time and raw materials, but instead the alternative uses of that time and those raw materials.

Everyone benefits when each person specializes in his area of comparative advantage and then engages in trade. Therefore an individual's preferences need not enter into his decisions about what to produce.

Differences in ability (in other words, differences in comparative advantage) are one reason for trade. Another reason is differences in taste, which will be examined in Chapter 3.

Review Questions

R1. Explain the difference between absolute and relative prices. Which one are we referring to when we use the single word *price?*

R2. Suppose that the absolute prices of bread and wine are $2 per loaf and $6 per bottle in 1990, and that they change to $4 per loaf and $8 per bottle in 1991. Assuming that bread and wine are the only two goods in the world, would you say that the price of wine has gone up or down? Why?

R3. List some of the costs of going to college.

R4. How is efficiency defined in economics? Why do economists choose this definition?

R5. Why might a person who loves potatoes and hates squash nevertheless choose to grow squash in his garden?

R6. What are the reasons that people trade?

Numerical Exercise

N1. Suppose that the amount of time required for the electrician or the carpenter to complete a job of rewiring or paneling is given by the following table:

	Rewiring	Paneling
Electrician	10 hours	20 hours
Carpenter	20 hours	25 hours

a. Compute the costs of performing each of these tasks for each individual.
b. Who has the comparative advantage at rewiring? At paneling?
c. Suppose that the more efficient rewirer does all of the rewiring and the more efficient paneler does all of the paneling. Does this trade benefit the electrician? Does it benefit the carpenter?
d. Suppose that a different trade is worked out whereby the electrician rewires the carpenter's entire house in exchange for the carpenter's doing 3/5 of the electrician's paneling job. Now how much time does each spend working? Do they each benefit?
Note: This problem illustrates the fact that when different parties have different comparative advantages, there is always some trade that will benefit both. However, not *any* trade will benefit both; the trade must take place at an appropriate relative price.

Problem Set

1. The price of personal computers has fallen dramatically in recent years. *True or false:* If it were not for this fact, inflation in the United States would have been higher than it has been.

2. *True or false:* A farmer with a lot of children will find it less costly to harvest his crops than a farmer with no children, since he can put his children to work without pay.

3. *True or false:* If George types 50 words per minute and Mary types 120, then it certainly makes more sense for Mary to be employed as a secretary than for George to be.

4. *True or false:* It is unfortunate for society when the best-qualified candidate for a judicial position refuses to accept that position.

5. *True or false:* A small country with widespread starvation would be well advised to concentrate its resources in the production of food rather than in the production of decorative jewelry.

6. *True or false:* A country that is poor in natural resources and has an unskilled population may be unable to trade profitably because it has no comparative advantage at anything.

7. Sears typewriters are made by Smith-Corona. *True or false:* If Sears made its own typewriters, they would be cheaper for consumers to buy.

8. Explain exactly where the following argument goes wrong: The Anderson-Little clothing store buys clothes directly from the manufacturers, whereas Brand X clothing stores buy from middlemen. In each case there are the same costs of producing, shipping, and marketing the clothes, but with Brand X's system there is also the additional cost of supporting the middlemen. Therefore clothes will be cheaper at Anderson-Little.

9. *True or false:* If everyone had the same income, substandard housing would disappear.

Refer to Answers to Problem Sets for solutions to problems 2, 3, and 8.

Chapter Three

The Behavior of Consumers

A consumer's demand curve for a product displays the quantities that he will choose to purchase at various possible prices. Our next goal is to dig a little deeper and ask where the demand curve comes from. How, for example, does a consumer decide to buy 5 cups of coffee per day when the price is 50¢ per cup but only 3 cups per day when the price is 60¢?

The answer to this question lies in the interplay between *tastes* and *opportunities*. The consumer's choices are limited by factors that are largely beyond his control, such as his income and the market prices of goods. From the available choices (his opportunities), he makes selections on the basis of his tastes.

In Section 3.1 we will discuss the tastes (or *preferences*) of the consumer. In Section 3.2 we will examine the opportunities available to the consumer and how the interaction between tastes and opportunities leads to the consumer's choice. In Section 3.3 we will practice applying these tools. Then in Chapter 4 we will be in a position to use what we have learned to analyze consumer behavior in the marketplace.

3.1 Tastes

The Latin proverb "De gustibus non disputandum" can be translated as "There's no accounting for tastes." Some people like antique wooden furniture, whereas others prefer brass. You are likely to get a variety of answers if you ask different friends whether they would prefer to live in a world without Bach or in a world without clean sheets.

Economists accept the wisdom of the proverb and make no attempt to account for tastes. Why people prefer the things that they do is an interesting topic, but it is not one that we will explore. We take people's tastes as given and see what it is possible to say about them.

Indifference Curves

Imagine a consumer named Beth who lives in a world with only two goods: food and clothing. You might imagine asking Beth which of these two goods she likes better. But although this question sounds sensible at first, it really isn't. There are many reasons why not. First, the answer is likely to depend on what quantities of food and clothing are being compared. Second, the answer is likely to depend on how much of each Beth happens to own already. The question is open to several interpretations: Are we asking which good Beth would least like to do without altogether, or are we asking which she would rather receive for her birthday?

Here is a better question. We can ask Beth: "Which would you rather own: three units of food and five of clothing, or six units of food and two of clothing?" This question can elicit an unambiguous answer, provided that we have carefully specified what our "units" are. In theory, we could discover that answer by starting Beth out with no possessions and then offering her a choice of 2 baskets—one containing 3 units of food and 5 of clothing, and the other containing 6 units of food and 2 units of clothing. A question makes sense when some (possibly imaginary) experiment is capable of revealing the answer.

Of course, there are many possible baskets other than the ones we've described. We can display all of them simultaneously on a graph, as shown in Exhibit 3–1. Each point on that graph represents a basket containing a certain quantity of food and a certain quantity of clothing. For example, point A represents a basket with 3 units of food and 5 of clothing—the first of the two baskets we offered to Beth.

▷ *Exercise 3.1* Describe the baskets represented by points B, C, and D. Which represents the second basket of our imaginary experiment?

What can we say about Beth's preferences among these baskets? Compare basket A to basket B, for example. Which would she prefer to own? Basket B contains more food than basket A (4 units instead of 3) and also more clothing (7 units instead of 5). If we assume that food and clothing are both **goods**—items that Beth would prefer to have more of whenever she can—then the choice is unambiguous. Basket B is better than basket A.

Goods
Items of which the consumer would prefer to have more rather than less.

Exhibit 3–1   **Baskets of Goods**

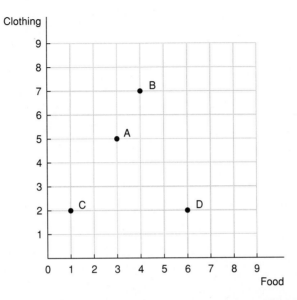

Each point on the graph represents a basket containing a certain quantity of food and a certain quantity of clothing. For example, point A corresponds to 3 units of food and 5 units of clothing.

▷ *Exercise 3.2* Which is preferable—basket A or basket C? How do you know?

When it comes to comparing basket A with basket D, the choice is less clear. Basket D has more food (6 units versus 3) but less clothing (2 units versus 5). Which will Beth prefer? At this point we cannot possibly say. She might like A better than D, or D better than A. It is also possible (though not necessary or even likely) that she would happen to like them both equally.

Now consider this question: Where should we look to find the baskets that Beth likes exactly as much as A? They can't be to the "northeast" of A (like B) because the baskets there are all preferred to A. They can't be to the "southwest" of A (like C) because A is preferred to all of those baskets. They must all be to either the "northwest" or the "southeast" of A (like D). This doesn't mean that D is necessarily one of them—just that they lie in the same general direction from A that D does.

If we draw in a few of the baskets that Beth likes just as well as she likes A, they might look like the points shown in panel A of Exhibit 3–2. Because each of these baskets is "exactly as good" as A, they must all be "exactly as good" as each other. This means that each one must lie either to the northwest or to the southeast of each other one, which accounts for the downward slope that is apparent in the picture.

The baskets shown in panel A of Exhibit 3–2 are only a few of those that

Exhibit 3–2   **Comparing Baskets**

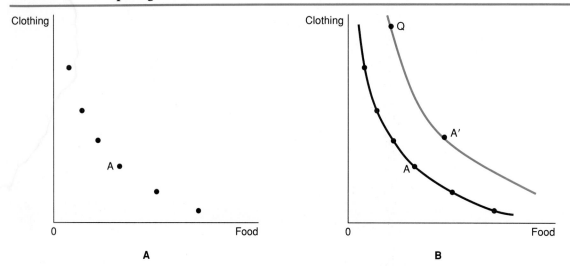

| A | B |

Panel A shows several baskets that Beth considers to be equally desirable. None of these can lie to the northeast or southwest of any other one, because if it did, one would be clearly preferable to the other. As a result, they all lie to the northwest and southeast of each other, accounting for the downward slope.

   The black indifference curve in panel B includes the points from panel A, as well as all of the other baskets that Beth considers equally as desirable as these. The colored indifference curve shows a different set of baskets, all of which are equally as desirable as each other. Knowledge of Beth's indifference curves allows us to make inferences about her preferences that would otherwise be impossible. For example, we know that Beth likes Q and A' equally because they are on the same indifference curve, and that A' is preferred to A because it contains more of everything. We may infer that Beth prefers Q to A.

Indifference curve
A collection of baskets all of which the consumer considers equally desirable.

Beth likes just as well as A. There are many other such baskets as well. The collection of all such baskets forms a curve, shown in black in panel B of the exhibit. From our discussion in the preceding paragraph, we know that the curve will be downward sloping. Because Beth is indifferent between any two points on this curve, it is called an **indifference curve.**

   There is nothing special about basket A. We could as easily have begun with a different basket, such as A' in panel B of Exhibit 3–2. That panel depicts both the indifference curve through A (in black) and the indifference curve through A' (in color).

   The indifference curves do not have to have the same shape, but they do both have to slope downward.

   If we know a consumer's indifference curves, we can make inferences that would not be possible otherwise. Try comparing basket A to basket Q in panel B of Exhibit 3–2. Basket A has more food than basket Q, but basket Q has more clothing than basket A. Without more information, we cannot say which one Beth will prefer. But the indifference curves provide that additional information. We know that Beth likes Q and A' equally, because

Exhibit 3–3   **Indifference Curves Never Cross**

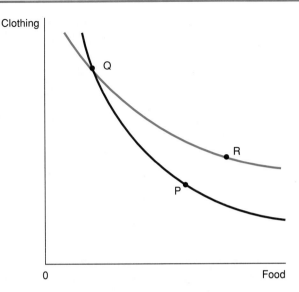

Crossing indifference curves, such as those shown in the graph, cannot occur. The consumer likes P and Q equally well because they are both on the same (black) indifference curve. He also likes R and Q equally well because they are both on the same (colored) indifference curve. We may infer that he likes P and R equally well, which we know to be false (in fact R is preferred to P). Thus the graph cannot be correct.

they are on the same indifference curve. We know that she likes A' better than she likes A, because it is to the northeast of A and therefore contains more of everything than A does. We may infer that she likes Q better than she likes A.

In general, a basket is preferable to another precisely when it is on a higher indifference curve, where *higher* means "above and to the right."

Relationships among Indifference Curves

Of course, Beth has more than two indifference curves. Indeed, we can draw an indifference curve through any point that we choose to start with. Because of this, *the indifference curves fill the entire plane.* (More precisely, they fill the entire quadrant of the plane in which both coordinates are positive.)

An important feature of indifference curves is that *indifference curves never cross.* To understand why this must be true, imagine a consumer with two indifference curves that cross as in Exhibit 3–3.

From the fact that baskets P and Q are on the same (black) indifference curve, we know that the consumer likes these baskets equally well. From the fact that baskets R and Q are on the same (colored) indifference curve, we know that he also likes these equally well. Putting these facts together, we conclude that he likes P and R equally well. But this is impossible, since

Exhibit 3–4 **The Marginal Rate of Substitution**

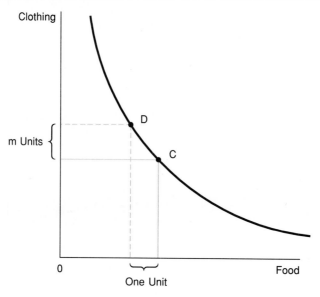

Consider a consumer who owns basket C. Take from the consumer one unit of food, and give him enough clothing to keep him equally happy. Keeping him equally happy means keeping him on the same indifference curve, so the necessary quantity of clothing is the vertical distance from C to D, labeled m in the figure. This vertical distance is called the *marginal rate of substitution*. It is a measure of the value of the consumer's last unit of food in terms of clothing. It is the smallest quantity of clothing for which the consumer would be willing to trade one unit of food.

R is to the northeast of P and therefore contains more of both goods. In other words, if indifference curves cross, impossible things will happen. We conclude that indifference curves *don't* cross.

The Marginal Rate of Substitution

We have said that indifference curves slope downward, but we haven't yet said anything about how steeply. Our next task is to interpret the slope of an indifference curve.

Imagine a consumer who owns basket C in Exhibit 3–4. Imagine the experiment of taking one unit of food away from this consumer and simultaneously giving him just enough units of clothing so that he is exactly as happy as he was when he started out. What basket will he end up with?

Because we are removing one unit of food from basket C, we must end up somewhere on the dashed vertical line. Because we are adjusting things to keep the consumer at a fixed level of happiness, he must end up on the same indifference curve. In other words, he must end up at point D.

How much clothing do we have to give the consumer to compensate for taking away one unit of food? Enough to get us to basket D. In other

Exhibit 3–5 Differing Marginal Rates of Substitution

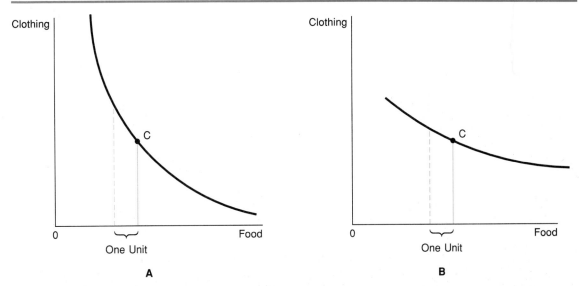

The panels show the indifference curves of two different consumers. The first consumer, in panel A, requires more additional clothing to compensate him for the loss of a unit of food than does the second consumer, in panel B. Another way to say this is that he has a higher marginal rate of substitution between food and clothing. As a result, the first consumer's indifference curve is steeper than the second consumer's at the point C.

Marginal rate of substitution, or MRS, between X and Y
The value of a consumer's last unit of X, measured by the number of additional units of Y that would just compensate him for its loss.

words, an amount equal to the vertical distance from C to D, labeled m in the exhibit. The number m is called the **marginal rate of substitution** between food and clothing. The marginal rate of substitution is often abbreviated MRS.

We can think of the marginal rate of substitution in terms of willingness to trade. The consumer is willing to trade one unit of food for m units of clothing and comes away feeling that he is neither better nor worse off as a result of the trade. He would not be willing to trade a unit of food for anything less than m units of clothing.

If the consumer values additional units of food very highly, how much clothing must we give him to compensate for the loss of a unit of food? Presumably a lot. This means that m will be large, which in turn implies that the indifference curve is very steep. In other words, it is like the indifference curve in panel A of Exhibit 3–5, rather than like the one in panel B.

What we have just argued bears summarizing:

If a consumer with basket C values additional units of food highly relative to additional units of clothing (that is, if his marginal rate of substitution between food and clothing is large), then his indifference curve will be very steep near point C.

▷ *Exercise 3.3* Suppose that a consumer with basket C places very little value on additional units of food relative to additional units of clothing. Explain why his indifference curve through C will be very shallow near C.

▷ *Exercise 3.4* Imagine the experiment of taking one unit of clothing away from a consumer and compensating him with just enough food to keep him equally happy. If the consumer values additional clothing highly relative to additional food, will you have to give him a lot of food or a little? Does this mean that his indifference curve is steep or shallow?

The Marginal Rate of Substitution as a Slope

We have argued that when the MRS is large, the indifference curve is steep, and that when the marginal rate of substitution is small, the indifference curve is shallow. We can make this more precise with a geometric construction.

Consider a consumer starting with basket C in Exhibit 3–6. Take from the consumer one unit of food, and give him just enough clothing to leave him equally happy. The necessary quantity of food is equal to the distance m. Now draw a straight line through the points C and D. The absolute value of the slope of that line is:

$$\frac{\text{Vertical distance from C to D}}{\text{Horizontal distance from C to D}} = \frac{m}{1} = m.$$

In other words, the slope of the line is equal to the marginal rate of substitution.

Economists like to choose their units very small; Coca-Cola can be measured in drops instead of quarts and meat can be measured in milligrams rather than pounds. With this convention, the points C and D are so close together as to be nearly indistinguishable. Then the line drawn through C and D is essentially the tangent line to the indifference curve at point C. Thus our calculation shows that when units are small:

The absolute value of the slope of the tangent line to the indifference curve at point C	=	The consumer's marginal rate of substitution between food and clothing at point C.

When this common number is large, the indifference curve is very steep and the last unit of food is valued very highly. When the number is small, the indifference curve is shallow and food is valued less highly.

The Shape of Indifference Curves

A starving man with a full wardrobe is likely to value food more highly relative to clothing than is a poorly clothed man with a full refrigerator. In other words, we expect indifference curves to be steep near baskets con-

Exhibit 3–6   The Marginal Rate of Substitution as the Slope of the Tangent Line

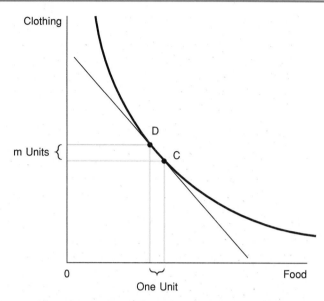

For a consumer starting with basket C, the marginal rate of substitution between food and clothing is given by the vertical distance m. This distance is also equal to the slope of the line through points C and D. When units are chosen very small, D is very close to C and the line through these points is essentially tangent to the curve. Therefore the marginal rate of substitution is equal to the slope of the tangent line to the indifference curve at C.

taining little food and much clothing, and to be shallow near baskets containing little clothing and much food.

Consider the two sets of indifference curves shown in Exhibit 3–7. Both sets slope downward. The first set slopes steeply in the area where baskets contain little food and much clothing (that is in the "northwest" part of the figure) and shallowly in the area where baskets contain little clothing and much food. These are the indifference curves of a consumer who values additional food more highly when he has less food and more clothing. This consumer conforms to the general rule of the preceding paragraph.

Another consumer might have the indifference curves shown in panel B of Exhibit 3–7. This consumer values additional food very little when he is starving and values it very much when he already has a lot of food. Such tastes are possible, but they seem unlikely.

For this reason we will always assume that indifference curves are shaped like those in panel A rather than like those in panel B. That is, we assume that indifference curves bow inward toward the origin. This property is expressed by saying that indifference curves are **convex**. At the end of Section 3.2 we will give another, independent justification for assuming convexity.

Convex
Bowed in toward the origin, like the curves in panel A of Exhibit 3–7.

Exhibit 3–7   **The Curvature of Indifference Curves**

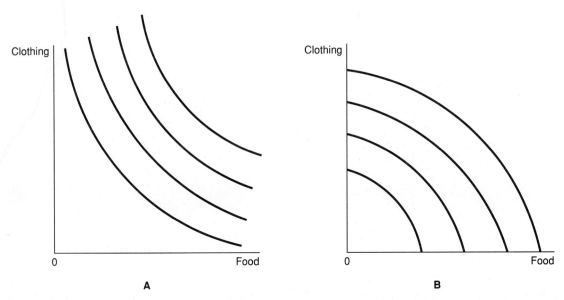

| A | B |

The indifference curves in panel A are convex (bowed in toward the origin), indicating that when the consumer is starving and well-dressed (in the "northwest" part of the diagram), his marginal rate of substitution between food and clothing is high—he would require many units of clothing to compensate him for the loss of one unit of food. We assume that indifference curves have this shape, rather than the alternative shape illustrated in panel B.

▷ *Exercise 3.5* Under what circumstances do you expect the consumer to value additional clothing highly relative to additional food? Combine this answer with your answer to Exercise 3.4 to draw a conclusion about where the indifference curves should be steep and where they should be shallow. Does your conclusion give further support to our assumption that indifference curves are convex, or does it suggest a reason to doubt that assumption?

More on Indifference Curves

Properties of Indifference Curves: A Summary

Here are the fundamental facts about a given consumer's indifference curves:

> **Indifference curves slope downward, they fill the plane, they never cross, and they are convex.**

A consumer's indifference curves between two goods encode everything that there is to say about his tastes regarding those goods. A different consumer is likely to have a different family of indifference curves (also satisfying the fundamental facts). This is just another way of saying that tastes may differ across individuals.

The Composite-Good Convention

In order to draw indifference curve diagrams, we must assume that there are only two goods in the world. This might appear to be a severe limitation. Yet in fact it is not. In many applications we will want to concentrate our attention on a single good—say, food. In that case we divide the world into two classes of goods, namely "food" and "things that are not food," otherwise known as "All Other Goods." This allows us to draw indifference curves between food (on the horizontal axis) and all other goods (on the vertical).

There remains the problem of units. What is a single unit of "all other goods"? The simplest solution to this problem is to measure all other goods in terms of their dollar value.

When we lump together everything that is not food and measure it in a single unit like dollars, we say that we are using the **composite-good convention.**

In the presence of the composite-good convention, the slope of an indifference curve is the MRS between food and other goods, with the other goods measured in dollars. Thus it is the number of dollars for which the consumer would be willing to trade a unit of food. Put another way, the MRS is the minimal price (in dollars) at which the consumer would sell one unit of food; it is the dollar value that he places on that one unit. In this case the MRS is also called the **marginal value** of food to the consumer.

Composite-Good Convention
The lumping together of all goods but one into a single portmanteau good.

Marginal value
The marginal rate of substitution of X for All Other Goods, often measured in dollars.

3.2 The Budget Line and the Consumer's Choice

In order to predict a consumer's behavior, we need to know two things. First, we need to know his tastes, which is the same thing as saying that we need to know his indifference curves. Second, we need to know what options the consumer has available to him. In other words, we need to know his budget.

The Budget Line

Continue to assume a world with two goods. Instead of calling them food and clothing, we're going to start calling them X and Y. You may continue to think of them as food and clothing if you wish. In order to determine which baskets our consumer can afford, we need to know three things: the price of X, the price of Y, and the consumer's income.

Rather than make up specific numbers, let's make up names for the three things we need to know:

$$P_X = \text{the price of X in dollars,}$$

$$P_Y = \text{the price of Y in dollars,}$$

$$I \;\; = \text{the consumer's income in dollars.}$$

Now let's suppose that the consumer is considering the purchase of a particular basket. Suppose that the basket contains x units of X and y units of Y. (Keep in mind that the capital letters X and Y are the *names* of the goods and the small letters x and y are the *quantities*.) How much will it cost him to acquire this basket? The x units of X at a price of P_X dollars apiece will cost him $P_X \cdot x$ dollars. The y units of Y at a price of P_Y dollars apiece will cost him $P_Y \cdot y$ dollars. The total price of the basket is:

$$P_X \cdot x + P_Y \cdot y \text{ dollars.}$$

Under what circumstances can the consumer afford to acquire this particular basket? Clearly he can acquire it only if the price of the basket does not exceed his income. In other words, he can afford the basket precisely if:

$$P_X \cdot x + P_Y \cdot y \leq I.$$

In fact, we can say a little more. Let's take seriously our assumption that X and Y are the only goods in the world. (In view of the composite-good convention, this assumption is not as outrageous as it seems.) Then the consumer will have to spend his entire income on X and Y.[1] He must choose a basket that costs *exactly* I dollars. He can have the basket in question precisely if:

$$P_X \cdot x + P_Y \cdot y = I.$$

It is important to distinguish the meanings of the various symbols in this equation. P_X, P_Y, and I are particular, fixed numbers that the consumer faces. The letters x and y are variables that can represent the contents of any basket. As the consumer considers purchasing various baskets, the values of x and y change. For each basket he plugs the relevant values of x and y into the equation, and he asks if the equation is true. Asking "Does this basket make the equation true?" is exactly the same as asking "Can I afford to purchase this basket?"

The line described by the equation $P_X \cdot x + P_Y \cdot y = I$ is a picture of all the baskets that the consumer can afford. It is called the consumer's **budget line.**

Another way to write the equation of the budget line (using some simple algebraic manipulations) is:

$$y = -\frac{P_X}{P_Y} \cdot x + \frac{I}{P_Y}.$$

Budget line
The set of all baskets that the consumer can afford, given prices and his income.

---

[1] It is possible that the consumer would want to save some of his income, but in that case we would want to consider savings as another good. If we are using the composite-good convention, we can include savings along with "all other goods."

Exhibit 3–8   **The Budget Line**

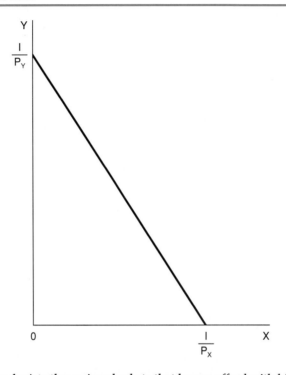

The consumer's budget line depicts the various baskets that he can afford with his income.

If you remember that P_X, P_Y, and I are constants and that x and y are variables, you may recognize this as the equation of a line with slope $- P_X/P_Y$ and y-intercept I/P_Y. The points on that line are those that satisfy the equation, and are therefore those that represent baskets that the consumer can buy. The budget line is shown in Exhibit 3–8.

Here is an easy way to remember how to draw the budget line. If you were the consumer and you bought no X's at all, how many Y's could you afford? Since your income is I and Y's sell at a price of P_Y apiece, the answer is I/P_Y. This means that the point $(0, I/P_Y)$ must be on the budget line. If you bought no Y's at all, how many X's could you afford? The answer is I/P_X. This means that the point $(I/P_X, 0)$ must be on the budget line. The budget line must be the line connecting the points $(0, I/P_Y)$ and $(I/P_X, 0)$.

What if P_X, P_Y, and I were all to double simultaneously? This would have no effect on the ratios I/P_Y and I/P_X. It follows that a simultaneous doubling of all prices and income would have no effect on the budget line. This accords with our expectation that only relative prices matter.

The geometry of the budget line reflects everything there is to know about the opportunities facing the consumer. For example, the slope of the budget line is $- P_X/P_Y$, and the ratio P_X/P_Y is the relative price of X in terms of Y. Therefore the budget line will be steep when X is expensive relative to Y, and it will be shallow when X is inexpensive relative to Y.

The Consumer's Choice

The Geometry of the Consumer's Choice

The budget line conveys an entirely different kind of information than the indifference curves do. The indifference curves reflect the consumer's preferences without regard to what he can actually afford to buy. The budget line shows which baskets he can afford to buy (that is, it shows his opportunities) without regard to his preferences. To determine how the consumer will actually behave, we must combine these two kinds of information. To this end, we draw the indifference curves and the budget line on the same graph, as in Exhibit 3–9.

We now have enough information to determine which basket this consumer will choose. Look at the baskets pictured. Of these, F is on the highest indifference curve and the one that the consumer would most like to own. (There are also many baskets not pictured that the consumer would like even more than F.) Unfortunately, he can't afford basket F—it's outside his budget line. By contrast, point E is inside his budget line and would fail to exhaust his income; therefore E is ruled out as well. The baskets that the consumer can acquire are the ones on his budget line. In Exhibit 3–9 these include A, B, O, C, and D.

Of these, he will choose the one on the highest possible indifference curve. It is clear from the picture that his choice is O. In fact, O is not just the best choice among the five baskets we have considered, but the best choice of any basket on the budget line.

From the picture the following is clear:

> **The basket the consumer chooses will always be located where his budget line is tangent to one of his indifference curves.**

Optimum
The most preferred of the baskets on the budget line.

This basket is called the consumer's **optimum.** Because there is only one such point, the budget line and the indifference curves give sufficient information for us to predict which basket the consumer will choose.

The Economics of the Consumer's Choice

We can analyze the consumer's problem from a different perspective and still reach the same conclusion about the location of his optimum.

Referring to Exhibit 3–9, suppose that the consumer owns basket A. How much Y would this consumer be willing to trade for an additional unit of X? The answer is given by his marginal rate of substitution, which is measured by the absolute value of the slope of his indifference curve at A.

How much Y would this consumer actually have to sacrifice in order to acquire an additional unit of X? The answer is given by the relative price of

Exhibit 3–9   **The Consumer's Optimum**

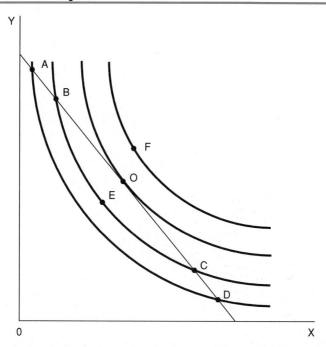

The consumer must choose one of the baskets that is on his budget line, such as A, B, O, C, or D. Of these, he will choose the one that is on the highest indifference curve, namely O. Thus the consumer is led to choose the basket at the point where his budget line is tangent to an indifference curve. This point is called the consumer's optimum.

At the consumer's optimum, the relative price of X in terms of Y (given by the slope of the budget line) and the marginal rate of substitution between X and Y (given by the slope of the tangent line to the indifference curve) are equal. The geometric reason for this is that the budget line is the tangent line to the indifference curve. The economic reason for it is that whenever the relative price is different from the MRS, the consumer will continue to make exchanges until the two become equal.

X in terms of Y, which is the ratio P_X/P_Y, the absolute value of the slope of his budget line.

Of these two, which is greater, the MRS or the relative price? At point A the indifference curve is steeper than the budget line. Consequently, the amount of Y that the consumer is *willing* to pay for a unit of X exceeds the amount of Y that he actually *has to* pay for a unit of X. In such a situation, buying a unit of X is an attractive proposition. The consumer will exchange Y's for X's at the going relative price, ending up with more X and less Y than he started with. This will bring him to a point like B.

Now the same reasoning applies again. At B it is still the case that the MRS exceeds the relative price. The consumer will want to buy another unit of X, which will move him further down the budget line.

This process will continue until the consumer reaches point O. At that point the price that he is willing to pay for X and the price at which he is able to purchase X have become equal. There is no longer anything to be gained from additional trades.

A similar process occurs if the consumer starts out with basket D. Here the MRS is less than the relative price of X; the consumer values his last unit of X at less than the number of Y's he can exchange it for in the marketplace. In this case he will happily trade away his last unit of X, ending up with more Y's and fewer X's, at a point like C.

As long as the MRS is less than the relative price, the consumer will trade X's for Y's. This process stops when the MRS and the relative price become equal, at point O.

Whenever the MRS exceeds the relative price, the consumer will want to buy X's, moving down the budget line. Whenever the MRS is less than the relative price, the consumer will want to sell X's, moving up the budget line. The only point at which he can settle is O, where the MRS and the relative price are exactly equal. Thus the economic reasoning leads to the same conclusion as the geometric reasoning: Of the points available to the consumer, the optimum occurs where his budget line is tangent to one of his indifference curves.

Corner Solutions

There is an exception to the rule that the consumer's optimum always occurs at a tangency. This exception is illustrated in Exhibit 3–10. In this case there is no tangency for the consumer to choose.

To predict the consumer's choice in this situation, we can use simple geometry. We know that the consumer must choose a basket on his budget line. Of all of these baskets, we can see from the picture that the one lying on the highest indifference curve is P. Therefore this is the basket that the consumer will choose.

Here is an alternative path to the same conclusion: Suppose that the consumer begins with basket S. At this point his indifference curve is less steep than the budget line. His MRS between X and Y is less than the relative price of X in terms of Y. His last unit of X is worth less to him than it will bring in the marketplace. Therefore he trades X for Y, bringing him to a point like R. Now the same reasoning applies again, leading him to move first to Q and then to P. The same reasoning would apply no matter what basket the consumer started with.

Corner solution
An optimum occurring on one of the axes when there is no tangency between the budget line and an indifference curve.

The situation depicted in Exhibit 3–10 is called a **corner solution** because the consumer's optimum occurs in a corner of the diagram. As you can see from the picture, he consumes no X's whatsoever and spends all of his income on Y.

More on the Shape of Indifference Curves

In Section 3.1 we justified the assumption that indifference curves are convex with an appeal to the marginal rate of substitution. Now we can give an additional reason for making this assumption.

Exhibit 3–10   **A Corner Solution**

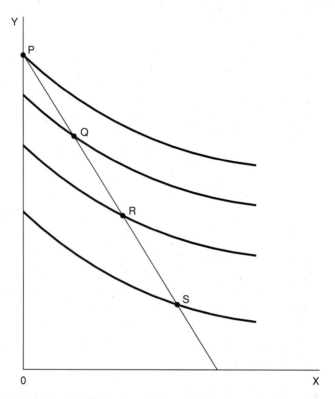

If the consumer's indifference curves look like those pictured, there is no tangency between his budget line and any of his indifference curves. Of all the points on his budget line, he will choose the most desirable, namely P. At any other point on the budget line, his marginal rate of substitution between X and Y is less than the relative price, so the consumer can sell X's for more than they are worth to him. He will continue to do so until he has sold all of his X's, ending up in the corner at P.

Suppose that a consumer has the indifference curves illustrated in Exhibit 3–11. Will this consumer choose to purchase the basket at point O? No! He can do better. Points C and D are both available to him (they are on his budget line) and they are on a higher indifference curve than O. And can he do better than C and D? Yes. Every movement "outward" along the budget line, away from O and toward one of the axes, improves the consumer's welfare. For this reason he will always want to choose a basket on one of the axes—a corner solution. In this case he will choose basket A.

▷ *Exercise 3.6* Why does the consumer choose basket A rather than basket E? How would the budget line have to look for him to choose a point on the X-axis rather than the Y-axis?

Exhibit 3–11   The Consumer's Choice with Nonconvex Indifference Curves

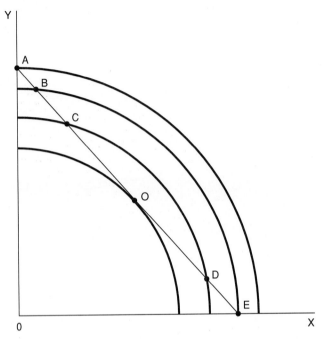

Nonconvex indifference curves always lead to a corner solution. The consumer pictured here will choose point A, which is on the highest possible indifference curve.

Because this consumer always selects a corner solution, he consumes either zero units of X or zero units of Y. But goods that consumers choose to purchase none of are not very interesting from the viewpoint of economics. So now we have our additional reason for assuming that indifference curves are convex. They might not be—but in this case one of the goods in question would not be consumed at all, and we would prefer to turn our attention to goods that *are* consumed. Therefore we usually confine our attention to convex indifference curves.

3.3 Applications of Indifference Curves

Indifference curve analysis is a powerful tool for understanding consumer behavior. The two ways to become proficient with a tool are to observe it in use and to use it. In this section we present three solved problems that illustrate some of the applications of indifference curves. You might want to attempt the problems yourself before reading the solutions. By working through them, you can acquire the ability to work similar problems quickly and accurately. After you have practiced on these, you will find many problems at the end of the chapter that you can use to test out your new skills.

A. Price Indices

A Problem

Suppose that the only goods you consume are X and Y. Suppose further that the price of X is $3 (per unit), that the price of Y is $4, and that at these prices you choose to purchase 4 units of X and 2 units of Y, exhausting your total income of $20. One day the price of X goes up to $4, the price of Y falls to $2, and your income stays fixed at $20. Are you better off or worse off than before?

The Solution

We begin by graphing your original budget line. We are told that (originally) your income is $20, the price of X is $3, and the price of Y is $4. This means that if you buy no X's at all, you can afford exactly 5 Y's, and if you buy no Y's at all, you can afford exactly 6⅔ X's. Your original budget line is the one labeled *original* in Exhibit 3–12. The basket (4,2) is on this line. Because this is the basket you choose with the *original* budget line, it must be where the *original* line is tangent to an indifference curve (that is, it must be your original optimum). The basket (4,2) is labeled O in the exhibit. The graph shows the indifference curve that is tangent there.

Now let's figure out your *new* budget line. The price of X is now $4, the price of Y is $2, and your income is still $20. If you buy no Y's, you get 5 X's, and if you buy no X's, you get 10 Y's. The *new* budget line goes through (5,0) and (0,10).

If we are drawing the *new* budget line freehand and want to draw it accurately, we have to figure out whether point O is above, below, or on the *new* budget line. That is, we must determine whether basket O would cost more than your income, less than your income, or exactly the same as your income at the new prices. At the new prices of $4 for X and $2 for Y, basket O will cost ($4 × 4) + ($2 × 2) = $20, so that you can exactly afford it. This means that the *new* budget line goes right through O, and it is drawn that way in Exhibit 3–12.

Now let's figure out where your *new* budget line is tangent to an indifference curve, that is, the location of your new optimum. First, we can rule out point O. The indifference curve through O is already tangent to the *original* line, so it can't be tangent to the *new* line. (This is because *a smooth curve cannot be tangent to two different lines at the same point*—an important fact about geometry that it will be useful to keep in mind.)

Where, then, is your new optimum? It cannot be anywhere between point A and the Y-axis. If it were tangent in that region, it would be forced by geometry to cross the indifference curve that passes through O—and

Exhibit 3–12   Your Original and New Budget Lines

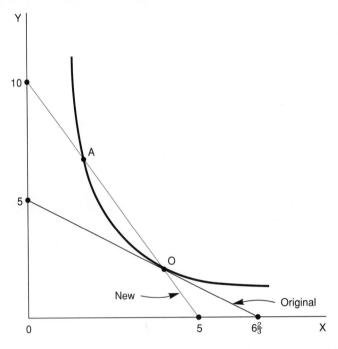

The graph shows the *original* and *new* budget lines that are specified in the problem. We know that an indifference curve is tangent to the *original* line at the point O. We can calculate that the *new* budget line passes through the point O.

this is not allowed. For the same reason there cannot be a tangency anywhere between point O and the X-axis. In panel A of Exhibit 3–13 we reproduce the graph from Exhibit 3–12 with two dashed indifference curves in the forbidden regions. The pictures are dashed precisely because there cannot *really* be any indifference curves tangent there. They are illustrated only to show you what they would look like if they were there— and to show you that they would be forced to cross the curve passing through O.

The only possible locations for the new optimum are the points between A and O, such as at P in panel B of Exhibit 3–13. If you look at that panel, you will see that P must be on a higher indifference curve than O is. In other words, your new basket is preferable to your old basket.

This solves the problem that began this section. The price change unquestionably makes you better off. It allows you to move to a higher indifference curve. Your old basket O is still as expensive as it ever was, but you can now afford better baskets (like P) that were previously outside your budget constraint.

Exhibit 3–13   **Finding the New Optimum**

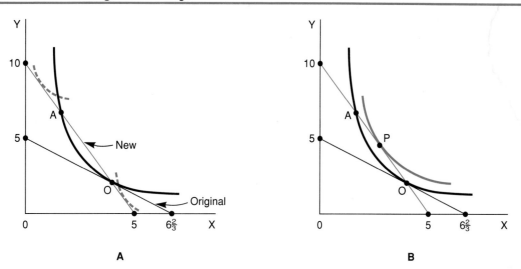

A   **B**

The dashed indifference curves in panel A cannot be correct, since they cross the indifference curve through O. The only correct way to draw an indifference curve tangent to the *new* budget line is with the tangency between A and O, at a point like P as in panel B. The new indifference curve is then necessarily higher than the old one, so you are better off at the new optimum.

Measuring the Cost of Living

Now let's ask another interesting question. What has happened to the "cost of living" (or the "price level") in this problem? When the price of X goes from $3 to $4 and the price of Y goes from $4 to $2, will the newspapers report "inflation" or "deflation"?

The answer is not obvious. The prices of different baskets have changed in different ways. A basket consisting entirely of X will have risen in price and a basket consisting entirely of Y will have fallen in price. In order to report the change in the "cost of living," we must choose a basket and report the change in the cost of that basket. The answer that we get will depend on what basket we choose. This choice is known as selecting a **price index.**

In practice the most commonly quoted price index is the **consumer price index (CPI)** compiled by the Bureau of Labor Statistics of the U.S. Department of Labor. Roughly, the CPI chooses the basket consumed by a typical consumer in the earlier period and reports changes in the price of that basket.

In the situation of Exhibit 3–13, the CPI would report the change in the price of basket O, because that is the basket consumed in the *original* period. Recall that O = (4,2) costs exactly $20 at both the *original* and the *new* prices. Therefore the CPI will report no change in the price level. This

Price index
A measure of the cost of living, based on changes in the cost of some basket of goods.

Consumer price index (CPI)
The price index officially reported by the U.S. Department of Labor.

is so despite the fact that an income of $20 will now buy you more "happiness" than it did before.

Here is another example. Suppose that the only two items you consume are bread and potatoes. You consider buying 4 possible baskets, which we call A, B, C, and D. These baskets are described in Exhibit 3–14. For example, A contains 2 steaks and 2 potatoes. Suppose also that the baskets are listed in your order of preference (A being the best and D the worst). Finally, suppose that in 1990 steaks cost $2 apiece and potatoes cost $1 apiece, whereas in 1995 these prices are reversed. The last two columns in Exhibit 3–14 show the prices of the baskets in each of the two years.

▷ *Exercise 3.7* Verify the last two columns of Exhibit 3–14.

Now assume that your income is $4 per year and that in each year you buy the most desirable basket you can afford. In 1990 you will buy basket C and in 1995 you will buy basket B. In which year are you happier? Clearly 1995.

What has happened to the officially reported "cost of living" in the five-year period from 1990 to 1995? The Consumer Price Index focuses on the basket purchased in the earlier year—in this case basket C. The price of C has gone up 25% from $4 to $5. The CPI will report that the price level has risen 25%, implying that you are worse off than before. Indeed, a naive observer might think that you *are* worse off, because you can no longer afford basket C in 1995. In fact, you are better off, because you can now afford basket B, which you like better.

Laspeyres price index
A price index based on the basket consumed in the earlier period.

A price index that focuses on the basket purchased in the earlier year is called a **Laspeyres[2] price index.** Whenever there is a change in relative prices, a Laspeyres index will make the price changes seem worse for consumers than they really are. Does this mean that the Bureau of Labor Statistics is foolish for choosing such an index? No, it only reflects the fact that there is no such thing as a perfect measure of the cost of living. For example, a **Paasche[3] price index** is one that focuses on the basket purchased in the later period. In Exhibit 3–14 a Paasche price index will focus on basket B and report a 20% drop in the cost of living. A Paasche price index will always make price changes seem better for consumers than they really are. Every price index contains some information, but it must be interpreted with care.

Paasche price index
A price index based on the basket consumed in the later period.

▷ *Exercise 3.8** The examples of Exhibits 3–13 and 3–14 are not perfectly analogous. In Exhibit 3–13 there is no change in the Laspeyres price index, whereas in Exhibit 3–14 the Laspeyres price index rises by 25%.

The goal of this exercise is to construct a graphical representation of the tabular example in 3–14 and a tabular representation of the graphical example in 3–13.

Draw a figure like the ones in Exhibit 3–13 that reflects the situa-

---

[2]Pronounced "La-spears."

[3]Pronounced "Posh."

Exhibit 3–14   **Changing Prices and the Consumer Price Index**

Basket	No. of Steaks	No. of Potatoes	1990 Basket Price (Steak = $2, Potato = $1)	1995 Basket Price (Steak = $1, Potato = $2)
A	2	2	$6	$6
B	2	1	5	4
C	1	2	4	5
D	1	1	3	3

We assume that the 4 baskets in the exhibit are listed in the order of your preference. With a $4 income, you will choose basket C in 1990 and basket B in 1995, making you better off in 1995. However, a Laspeyres price index such as the CPI will report a 25% rise in the cost of living from 1990 to 1995, because basket C costs 25 % more in the later year.

tion described in Exhibit 3–14. Be sure to draw indifference curves that reflect the order of preference given in Exhibit 3–14. Show the *original* and *new* budget lines, and the points where they are tangent to indifference curves.

Now construct a table like the one in Exhibit 3–14 that reflects the situation described in Exhibit 3–13. Be sure to include rows for baskets O and P. (You will have to make up some plausible coordinates for the point P.)

Nobody blames the Department of Labor for the fact that there is no such thing as a perfect price index. However, the CPI has been criticized for a number of reasons unrelated to its being a Laspeyres index. An entertaining catalog of reasons for being skeptical of the CPI can be found in an article by William Kruskal and Lester Telser.[4] A number of these problems have been corrected since the article appeared.

B. Differences in Tastes

A Problem

A Befuddled Former Peanut Farmer (BFPF) living in a rural part of Georgia finds that he can buy grits for $2 per helping and jelly beans for $1 per bag. His total income is $10, with which he buys 4 helpings of grits and 2 bags of jelly beans.

Meanwhile, an Aging Retired Movie Actor (ARMA) living in California must buy jelly beans for $4 per bag, but he can still get grits for $2 per helping. He earns $30 per year, with which he buys 7 bags of jelly beans and 1 helping of grits.

---

[4]W. Kruskal and L. Telser, "Food Prices and the Bureau of Labor Statistics," *Journal of Business* 33 (1960): 258–279.

One night, Dan Rather and Tom Brokaw both host special reports on the buying habits of the BFPF and the ARMA. Dan Rather reports that while both individuals have identical tastes regarding grits and jelly beans, the BFPF is buying more grits than the ARMA because he is poorer and cannot afford the luxury of jelly beans. Tom Brokaw reports that, on the contrary, their tastes are *not* the same and their buying habits reflect their differing tastes.

Who is right?

The Solution

The first panel of Exhibit 3–15 shows the budget lines of the ARMA and the BFPF.

▷ *Exercise 3.9* Make sure that the budget lines are drawn correctly.

The next step is to draw in the optima of the BFPF and the ARMA. The BFPF's optimum is at (4,2) on his budget line. To make the drawing accurate, it is necessary to know whether (4,2) is to the left or to the right of point X. In other words, we must determine whether (4,2) is outside or inside the ARMA's budget line. This is the same as asking whether the ARMA can afford that basket. In California the basket would cost $(4 \times \$4) + (2 \times \$2) = \$20$, which is less than the ARMA's income of $30, so he can afford the basket; it must therefore lie inside the ARMA's budget line. The part of the BFPF's budget line that is inside the ARMA's budget line is the part to the right of point X, so that is where the BFPF's optimum is located. It is the point labeled B in panel B of Exhibit 3–15.

In exactly the same way, we can calculate that the ARMA's optimum of (1,7) is located inside the BFPF's budget line, and so must lie to the left of point X. It is the point labeled A in Exhibit 3–15.

▷ *Exercise 3.10* Justify the assertions of the preceding paragraph.

Clearly the two indifference curves in Exhibit 3–15 will eventually cross. This means that they cannot be part of the same family of indifference curves. The ARMA's family of indifference curves will differ from the BFPF's family. This is another way of saying that the ARMA and the BFPF have different tastes. Dan Rather is wrong and Tom Brokaw is right.

Students sometimes misunderstand this analysis and think that the crucial point is that the two indifference curves in Exhibit 3–15 are not identical. Those students have missed an important point. The key fact is not that the curves are different; it is that they are incapable of belonging to the same family of indifference curves. The observation leading to this key fact is that the two curves must cross.

Do Tastes Change over Time?

The method that we have used to discover taste changes across individuals can also be used to discover changes in taste over time. In Exhibit 3–15 replace the BFPF and the ARMA with "Mr. Jones in 1980" and "Mr. Jones in

Exhibit 3–15   The Befuddled Former Peanut Farmer and the Aging Retired Movie Actor

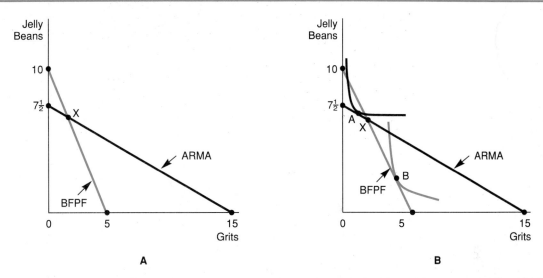

Panel A shows the budget lines of the BFPF and the ARMA. Panel B also shows their optima. The ARMA's optimum is at A and the BFPF's optimum is at B. The ARMA's black indifference curve and the BFPF's colored indifference curve must therefore cross and thus cannot be part of the same family of indifference curves. It follows that the ARMA and the BFPF have different tastes.

1981." Suppose that Mr. Jones in 1980 had the black budget line and chose point A, and Mr. Jones in 1981 had the colored budget line and chose point B. We would then be entitled to conclude that Mr. Jones in 1981 had different tastes from Mr. Jones in 1980. In other words, we could conclude that Mr. Jones's tastes changed.

Whenever possible, economists prefer to assume that people's tastes are relatively constant over time, and that changes in their behavior are due primarily to changes in prices and changes in income (that is, changes in the budget constraint). The reason for this is that tastes are unobservable, and that theories that allow for significant changes in unobservable variables are very hard to test. In fact, the economists Gary Becker and George Stigler have gone so far as to argue for the assumption that all individuals have the same tastes in all things at all times and they never change![5] It is important to know whether such assumptions are consistent with the observable facts about the world. One way to find out is to plot a single consumer's budget lines in different years, draw his optimal points, and see if the picture ever looks like panel B of Exhibit 3–15. If it does, the assumption of constant tastes is in trouble.

[5]G. Becker and G. Stigler, "De Gustibus Non Est Disputandum," *American Economic Review* 67 (1977): 76–90.

This test has been performed via an examination of the behavior of the "typical" British consumer in the years 1900–1955.[6] Using 127 goods in every possible pairing, and plotting budget lines for each pair of successive years, there were hundreds of cases in which the budget lines crossed. Each of these was potentially a source of evidence for taste change. If in any of these cases, the optima had been located like those in Exhibit 3–15, a taste change would have been revealed. In fact, there were no such cases.

Looking for a taste change and not finding it does not *prove* that no taste changes exist. But looking very extensively for a thing and not finding it entitles one to *doubt* its existence. The tests described here are only a fraction of those that were performed and reported on in the paper. Many of these tests had the potential to reveal a taste change, but none of them did so.

C. Head Taxes versus Income Taxes

Which would you rather pay: a percentage income tax (under which the government takes a certain percentage of your earnings) or a head tax (under which the government takes a certain number of dollars per day, regardless of your earnings)? Obviously, the answer depends at least partly on the size of the taxes. A 1% income tax is probably better than a $10,000 daily head tax, whereas a 2¢ daily head tax is probably better than a 90% income tax.

So let's make the comparison fair by assuming that the taxes are set at such levels that your tax bill will be the same under either tax. Now which would you rather pay? The following problem is designed to lead you through an analysis of this question.

A Problem

a) Suppose that you can work up to 24 hours per day at a wage of $1 per hour, with the remainder of your time available for leisure. Draw your budget constraint between "dollars" and "leisure hours."

b) Now suppose that the government institutes a 50% income tax. Draw your new budget constraint. Depict your new optimum. Call it P.

c) Show the number of dollars that you get to keep. Show the number of dollars that you earn before you pay your taxes. Show the size of your tax bill. Call it $T.

d) Now suppose that the income tax is abolished and replaced by a head tax of $T per day. Draw your new budget line. Does it pass over, under, or through point P? How do you know?

e) Which would you rather pay: the income tax or the head tax? Why?

[6]S. Landsburg, "Taste Change in the United Kingdom," *Journal of Political Economy* 89 (1981): 92–104.

Exhibit 3–16   **An Income Tax versus a Head Tax**

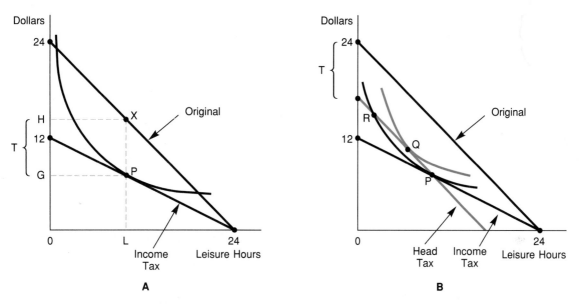

A   B

Panel A shows your *original* (untaxed) budget line and your *income tax* budget line. The optimum on the *income tax* line is at P. Your after-tax income is $G. Your before-tax income is equal to what you would earn if you were on your *original* budget line and working L hours, that is, $H. Your tax bill is the difference, or $T.

Panel B shows the *head tax* budget line, which lies a vertical distance $T below the *original* budget line and consequently passes through point P. The optimum on the *head tax* line must be at a point like Q between P and R, and it is consequently on a higher indifference curve. The head tax is thus preferable to the income tax.

The Solution

a)   If you consume no leisure, you will be able to earn $24 per day, whereas if you earn no income, you will be able to consume 24 hours of leisure per day. Therefore your budget line is the line labeled *original* in each of the two panels of Exhibit 3–16.

b)   Now if you consume no leisure, you will be able to earn only $12 per day. Therefore your new budget line is the one labeled *income tax* in each of the two panels of Exhibit 3–16. Your new optimum occurs where this line is tangent to an indifference curve. Such a tangency is depicted in the exhibit and labeled P.

c)   The number of dollars you get to keep is the number of dollars in basket P. That number of dollars is labeled G in panel A of Exhibit 3–16. With basket P you consume L leisure hours and receive $G in after-tax income.

   To compute your pre-tax income, you must ask yourself this question: If the income tax were abolished, and if I kept working the same number of hours I am working now, how many dollars would I get to keep? (Notice that this question is entirely hypothetical. If the income tax were abolished, you would probably choose to work some different number of hours.)

If the income tax were abolished, you would be back on the *original* budget line. If you continued to work the same number of hours, you would continue to have the same number of leisure hours, namely L. Putting these two facts together, you would be consuming basket X in panel A of Exhibit 3–16, and you would earn $H. $H is your pre-tax income.

Since you earn $H before taxes and keep $G after taxes, the difference must be the size of your tax bill. This difference is represented by the vertical distance from G to H, labeled T in the exhibit.

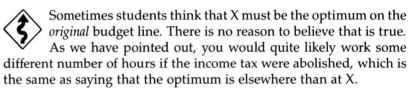 Sometimes students think that X must be the optimum on the *original* budget line. There is no reason to believe that is true. As we have pointed out, you would quite likely work some different number of hours if the income tax were abolished, which is the same as saying that the optimum is elsewhere than at X.

d) First the abolition of the income tax returns you to your *original* budget line. Then the institution of the head tax reduces your income by $T regardless of how many hours you work. Therefore we can get your *head tax* budget line by removing $T from each basket on the *original* budget line; this causes a parallel downward shift by the amount $T. The *head tax* budget line is shown in panel B of Exhibit 3–16.

Since point P lies a distance $T below the *original* budget line, and since the *head tax* budget line lies a distance $T below the *original* budget line, the *head tax* line must pass through point P.

e) The optimum along the *head tax* line must be between P and R (at a point like Q). If this were not true, the indifference curves would cross. It is clear from the exhibit that Q must be on a higher indifference curve than P. The best basket that you can acquire under a head tax (Q) is superior to the best basket that you can acquire under an income tax (P). The head tax is preferable to the income tax.

Discussion

Since your head tax bill is the same size as your income tax bill, you might be tempted to think that either tax is equally unpleasant. To see why this is false, consider your position at point P under the income tax. Here your marginal rate of substitution is such that your last hour of leisure is worth 50¢. If you forgo that last hour of leisure by working another hour, you will take home 50¢ in wages, gaining nothing. However, when the income tax is abolished and replaced by the head tax, you have the opportunity to forgo an hour of leisure in exchange for an additional $1 in wages. This new opportunity is an attractive one. By accepting it, you move up and to the left along the *head tax* budget line, improving your situation. You continue to move in that direction until you reach point Q, where your marginal rate of substitution between leisure and income is exactly $1 per hour.

*Exercise 3.11** A 50% tax on income is an example of a flat-rate income tax—the percentage does not vary with income. A progressive income tax is one that takes a larger percentage of your income when your income is greater.

A progressive income tax would lead to a budget "line" that was not a straight line at all, as in this figure:

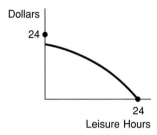

Try to understand why this is so. Now compare a flat-rate income tax to a progressive income tax, assuming that you pay the same number of dollars under either tax. Show that you would prefer living in a world with a flat-rate income tax to living in a world with a progressive income tax.

Summary

A consumer's behavior depends on his tastes and his opportunities. His tastes are encoded in his indifference curves and his opportunities are encoded in his budget line. By combining this information in a single graph, we can predict the consumer's behavior.

Each consumer has a family of indifference curves. Each curve in the family consists of baskets between which he is indifferent. His indifference curves slope downward, fill the plane, never cross, and are convex. A different consumer will have a different family of indifference curves, also satisfying these properties.

The slope of an indifference curve is equal (in absolute value) to the marginal rate of substitution of X for Y. That is, it is the number of units of Y for which the consumer is just willing to trade one unit of X. The marginal rate of substitution can be thought of as the value that the consumer places on his last unit of X, measured in terms of Y.

As the consumer moves along an indifference curve in the direction of more X and less Y, we expect that his MRS will decrease. This accounts for the convexity of indifference curves.

The consumer's budget line depends on his income and the prices of the goods that he buys. Its equation is:

$$P_X \cdot x + P_Y \cdot y = I,$$

where P_X and P_Y are the prices of X and Y and I is the consumer's income. The slope of the budget line is equal (in absolute value) to the relative price of X in terms of Y.

The consumer's optimum occurs where his budget line is tangent to one of his indifference curves. This is the point at which he attains the highest indifference curve that is available to him. At this point the MRS between X and Y is equal to the relative price of X in terms of Y. At any other point either the MRS would exceed the relative price, in which case the consumer would trade Y for X, or the relative price would exceed the MRS, in which case the consumer would trade X for Y. Only at his optimum point is he satisfied not to trade any further.

Review Questions

R1. Explain why indifference curves slope downward.

R2. Explain why two of a consumer's indifference curves can never cross. Can two indifference curves belonging to different consumers ever cross?

R3. What is the meaning of the marginal rate of substitution of X for Y? How is it reflected geometrically?

R4. What is the equation for the consumer's budget line? What is the economic interpretation of the slope of the budget line?

R5. Where does the consumer's optimum occur? What two important quantities are equal at the optimum point?

R6. Suppose that the consumer's marginal rate of substitution between X and Y is greater than the relative price of X in terms of Y. Is the consumer's basket to the left or to the right of his optimum point? Will the consumer want to buy or sell X? Explain how you know. In which direction will this cause the consumer to move along the budget line?

Numerical Exercise

N1. Every day Fred buys wax lips and candy cigarettes. After deciding how many of each to buy, he multiplies the number of sets of wax lips times the number of packs of candy cigarettes. The higher this number comes out to be, the happier he is. For example, 3 sets of wax lips and 5 packs of candy cigarettes will make him happier than 2 sets of wax lips and 7 packs of candy cigarettes, because 3×5 is greater than 2×7. Wax lips sell for $2 a pair and candy cigarettes for $1 a pack. Fred has $20 to spend each day.
   a. Make a table that looks like this:

Pairs of Wax Lips	Packs of Candy Cigarettes
0	
1	
2	
:	
:	
:	
10	

where each row of the chart corresponds to a basket on Fred's budget line. Fill in the second column.
b. Draw a graph showing Fred's budget line and marking the baskets described by your table. Draw Fred's indifference curves through these baskets. If he must select among these baskets, which one will Fred choose?
c. Add to your table a third column labeled MRS for the marginal rate of substitution between wax lips and candy cigarettes. Fill in the MRS for each basket. (*Hint:* For each basket construct another basket that has one less pair of wax lips but enough more packs of candy cigarettes to be equally desirable. How many packs of candy cigarettes have been added to the basket?) Which basket has an MRS closest to the relative price of wax lips? Is this consistent with your answer to part b?

Problem Set

1. Herman buys 10 turnips each year. *True or false:* If the price of turnips goes up by 10¢ apiece, and if Herman's tastes and income remain unchanged, then he will have $1 a year less to spend on other things.

2. *True or false:* If crime prevention is a costly activity, then it is possible for New York City to have too *little* crime.

3. Suppose that you hate typing and you hate filing. Your boss tells you that you may divide your 8-hour day any way you wish between these two activities, but the number of hours you spend typing and the number of hours you spend filing must add up to 8.

   You end up deciding to type for 3 hours and file for 5 hours.

   On an indifference curve diagram between hours of typing and hours of filing, draw your constraint and a plausible set of indifference curves that might have led to your decision.

4. Suppose that you like to own both left and right shoes, but that a right shoe is of no use to you unless you own a matching left one, and vice versa. Draw your indifference curves between left and right shoes.

5. Draw your indifference curves between nickels and dimes, assuming that you are always willing to trade 2 nickels for a dime or vice versa. What is your marginal rate of substitution between nickels and dimes?

6. Basket A contains 1 X and 5 Y's. Basket B contains 5 X's and 1 Y. Basket C contains 3 X's and 3 Y's. On Monday you are offered a choice between basket A and basket C, and you choose A. On Tuesday you are offered a choice between basket B and basket C, and you choose B. *True or false:* We may infer that your tastes changed overnight.

7. **a.** Draw Mr. Jones's budget line between education and All Other Goods, assuming that he can purchase varying quantities of education from private schools at a going price.

   b. One day there opens in Mr. Jones's neighborhood a public school that he may attend for free if he wants to. However, if he attends the public school, he must accept the amount of education that it offers. He can no longer take any private school classes because the public and private schools are in session at the same time of day. Draw Mr. Jones's new budget constraint. (*Hint:* It is no longer a line, but a line plus a point.)

   c. Draw a set of indifference curves that implies that Mr. Jones will increase his consumption of education as a result of the opening of the public school. Draw a set that implies that Mr. Jones will not change his level of education. Draw a set that implies that Mr. Jones will now buy less education than before. Call these the indifference curves of Mr. A. Jones, Mr. B. Jones, and Mr. C. Jones, respectively. Can you rank Mr. A., Mr. B., and Mr. C. in terms of how much they seem to like education?

   d. *True or false:* If most people are reasonably fond of education but not fanatically so, then an offer of free public education could reduce the quantity of education consumed.

8. **a.** Draw a typical set of indifference curves between "Smoking" and "Lung Cancer" for a person who likes to smoke. Draw the relevant "budget line."

   b. Now suppose that a new cigarette is invented that is identical to currently available cigarettes in every way except that it is less likely to cause cancer. Show the new budget line and the new optimum. Could this invention lead to an increase in the number of people who get cancer from smoking?

9. Suppose that the only two goods you consume are bread and circus tickets. When bread sells for $1 a loaf and circus tickets sell for $1 apiece, you buy 7 loaves of bread and 3 circus tickets to exhaust your income of $10. One day the price of bread falls to 50¢ a loaf while the price of circus tickets rises to $2 apiece and your income remains unchanged. You now buy 12 loaves of bread and 2 circus tickets.

   Is it possible to say with certainty whether you are better off? Why or why not?

10. **a.** Suppose that you have an income of $10 per month and can buy meat for $1 per pound. Draw your budget constraint between meat and dollars.

    b. Now suppose that the government subsidizes your meat purchases by agreeing always to pay one-half of your meat bill. Show your new budget constraint and how it compares with the old one. Show your new optimum point. Call it P.

    c. Depict geometrically the amount of money the government is spending on this subsidy. (*Hint:* How much money do you have left after you make your subsidized meat purchase? How much would you have left if you had bought the same amount of meat but were not subsidized? Where is the difference coming from? Call this amount $S.

    d. Suppose that the subsidy is abolished and the government chooses to give you a subsidy of $S per month instead. Is point P above, below, or on your new budget line? How do you know?

    e. Which would you rather have: the subsidy or the gift? Why?

11. Suppose that you have 24 hours per day to allocate between leisure and working at a wage of $1 per hour. Draw your budget line between leisure and dollars. One day the government simultaneously institutes two new programs: a 50% income tax and a plan whereby everybody in the country receives a gift from the government of $6 each year.

    a. Draw your new budget line.

    b. Suppose that the government chose the level of $6 for the gift because it precisely exhausts the income from the tax. Explain why this means that the average taxpayer must be paying exactly $6 in tax.

    c. Assume that you are the average taxpayer and draw your new optimum. Is it on, above, or below your original budget line?

    d. As the average taxpayer, are you working harder or less hard than before the programs went into effect? Are you happier or less happy? How do you know?

12. Suppose that you get rid of your old gas-guzzler and buy a new fuel-efficient car. Driving is now cheaper, but on the other hand you have to make monthly car payments. You find that, on balance, you are exactly as happy as you were before. Illustrate this situation using indifference curves between "Car Rides" and "All Other Goods." Are you driving more or less than you were before?

13. Kramden's Grocery advertises, "We randomly chose 10 of our customers and calculated the costs of their market baskets at Norton's Supermarket. At Norton's, they were an average of 6% higher." Does this convince you that wise shoppers will shop at Kramden's? Why or why not?

Refer to Answers to Problem Sets for solutions to problems 4 and 5.

Cardinal Utility

The theory of cardinal utility is an alternative approach to consumer behavior. It has the advantage of sometimes being easier to work with and the disadvantage that it introduces a new quantity—called *utility*—that can never actually be measured. However, it turns out to be the case that *the cardinal utility approach has exactly the same implications as the indifference curve approach.* Thus the choice between the two is largely a matter of convenience and of taste.

The Utility Function

Utility
A measure of pleasure or satisfaction.

In the cardinal utility approach, we assume that the consumer can associate to each basket a number, called the **utility** derived from that basket, that measures how much pleasure or satisfaction he would get from owning that basket. For the basket containing x units of X and y units of Y, the utility is often denoted U(x,y). Thus, for example, if we write

$$U(5,7) = 6,$$

what we mean is that a basket containing 5 X's and 7 Y's gives the consumer 6 units of utility. The rule for going from baskets to utilities is called the consumer's *utility function*. An example of a utility function is

$$U(x,y) = \sqrt{xy + 1},$$

which would yield the value U(5,7) = 6, as above.

We assume that, given a choice between two baskets, the consumer always chooses the one that yields higher utility. Thus if the consumer with the above utility function were given a choice between basket A, with 5 units of X and 7 units of Y, and basket B, with 6 units of X and 4 units of Y, then he would choose basket A, since U(5,7) = 6 but U(6,4) = 5.

The assumption that consumers seek to maximize utility enables us to pass from utility functions to indifference curves. The consumer with the above utility function is indifferent between the baskets (6,4), (8,3), (12,2), and (4,6) since they all yield utilities of 5. Thus all of these baskets must lie on the same indifference curve. More generally, all of the baskets (x,y) that satisfy

$$U(x,y) = 5$$

lie on a single indifference curve, so that the equation of that indifference curve is given by U(x,y) = 5. Similarly, there is another indifference curve whose equation is given by U(x,y) = 6.

If a consumer has the utility function U(x,y), then his indifference curves are the curves with equations U(x,y) = c, where c is any constant.

Marginal Utility

Marginal utility of X
The amount of
additional utility
derived from an
additional unit of X,
when the quantity of Y
is held constant.

The consumer's **marginal utility of X (MU$_X$)** is defined to be the amount of additional utility he acquires when the amount of X is increased by one unit and the amount of Y is held constant. For example, consider a consumer whose utility function is as above and who consumes 5 units of X and 7 units of Y. His utility is U(5,7) = 6. If we increase his consumption of X by one unit, his utility will be U(6,7) ≈ 6.557. Thus the marginal utility of X for this consumer is about .557.

We define the marginal utility of Y (MU$_Y$) in a similar way. For this consumer, increasing Y by one unit would yield utility U(5,8) ≈ 6.403. The marginal utility of Y for this consumer is about .403.

We assume that the marginal utility of X is always positive (more is preferred to less) but that each additional unit of X yields less marginal utility than the previous unit (always holding fixed the consumption of Y). This is known as the principle of *diminishing marginal utility*. For example, we have seen that a consumer who starts with basket (5,7) has MU$_X$ ≈ .557. After acquiring a unit of X and moving to basket (6,7), his marginal utility of X is reduced to MU$_X$ ≈ .514, as you can verify with your calculator.

Marginal Utility and the Marginal Rate of Substitution

We can relate the concept of marginal utility to the concept of the marginal rate of substitution. Suppose that we reduce your consumption of X by one unit. This reduces your utility by the amount MU$_X$. Now suppose that we increase your consumption of Y by ΔY units. This increases your utility by

$MU_Y \cdot \Delta Y$. Finally, suppose that ΔY is chosen to leave you just as happy as you were before the changes in your consumption. Then ΔY is your marginal rate of substitution between X and Y. Since you are equally happy before and after the changes, the loss of utility from consuming less X must equal the gain in utility from consuming more Y; in other words,

$$MU_X = MU_Y \cdot \Delta Y.$$

Rearranging terms, we get

$$\frac{MU_X}{MU_Y} = \Delta Y = MRS_{XY},$$

where MRS_{XY} denotes the marginal rate of substitution between X and Y.

The Marginal Utility of Income

Suppose that a consumer facing prices P_X and P_Y finds that his income goes up by a dollar. How much additional utility can he achieve?

First, suppose that he spends the additional dollar entirely on X. Then he can purchase $1/P_X$ units of X, each of which yields an additional MU_X units of utility. By spending an additional dollar on X, the consumer increases his utility by the amount $MU_X \cdot (1/P_X) = MU_X/P_X$. Similarly, by spending an additional dollar on Y, the consumer increases his utility by the amount MU_Y/P_Y. We can think of MU_X/P_X and MU_Y/P_Y as the marginal utility of a dollar spent on X and of a dollar spent on Y.

The Consumer's Optimum

The consumer allocates his income across X and Y so as to achieve the highest possible level of utility. We will determine the conditions that describe this optimum.

Consider the marginal utility of a dollar spent on X, MU_X/P_X, and the marginal utility of a dollar spent on Y, MU_Y/P_Y. We will argue that at the consumer's optimum these two quantities must be equal.

To see why, suppose first that MU_X/P_X is greater than MU_Y/P_Y. Then there is a way for the consumer to increase his utility. He can spend one dollar less on Y and use that dollar to buy more of X. In doing so, he will sacrifice MU_Y/P_Y units of utility and gain the greater quantity MU_X/P_X; thus he becomes better off. Having increased his consumption of X, the consumer finds, due to decreasing marginal utility, that MU_X is reduced; and having decreased his consumption of Y, he finds that MU_Y is increased. This brings the quantities MU_X/P_X and MU_Y/P_Y closer together. If MU_X/P_X still exceeds MU_Y/P_Y, the consumer will again cut his expenditures on Y and use the freed-up income to buy more of X. This continues until MU_X/P_X and MU_Y/P_Y become equal.

The same sort of thing happens if MU_Y/P_Y starts out greater than

MU_X/P_X. In this case the consumer can increase his utility by spending less on X and more on Y, which brings MU_X/P_X and MU_Y/P_Y closer together. Again, the process continues until the two are equal.

Thus at the consumer's optimum we must have

$$MU_X/P_X = MU_Y/P_Y.$$

Rearranging terms, we get

$$MU_X/MU_Y = P_X/P_Y.$$

We have encountered the term on the left before in this appendix; we determined that it is equal to the marginal rate of substitution. The term on the right is the relative price of X in terms of Y. So our cardinal utility analysis leads us to conclude that the consumer's optimum occurs at that point on his budget line where the marginal rate of substitution is equated to the relative price of X—exactly the same conclusion that we reached from the indifference curve analysis in Chapter 3!

Chapter Four

Consumers in the Marketplace

A consumer's budget line is determined by his income and the prices that he faces. A change in either of these things (and *only* changes in these things) can cause the budget line to shift, leading to a change in the consumer's behavior. In Section 3.3 we saw some examples of such shifts. In this chapter we will make a systematic examination of shifts in the budget line and the consumer's responses. One reward for our efforts (in Section 4.3) will be a deeper understanding of why demand curves slope down.

Throughout this chapter we want to focus on a consumer's behavior with respect to a particular good, which we will call X. Therefore we will use the composite-good convention, lumping all other goods in the economy into a single category called, appropriately enough, *all other goods*. This will enable us to maintain our assumption that there are only two goods in the economy: There is X, and there is "all other goods," which we will label Y. The fact that there are really many different kinds of "all other goods" need not concern us, provided we confine our attention to situations in which these distinctions are not relevant.

Exhibit 4–1   **How a Change in Income Affects the Budget Line**

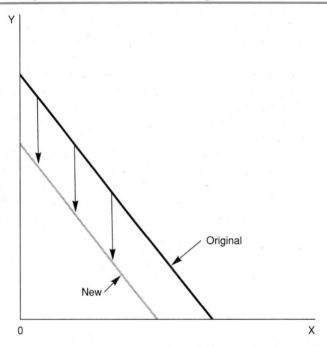

The graph illustrates the effect of a $5 fall in income. For any given quantity of X, the height of the *original* budget line shows how much Y the consumer can afford with his original income, and the height of the *new* budget line shows how much Y he can afford after his income is reduced by $5. Therefore, for any given quantity of X, the difference in height between the two budget lines is equal to $5 worth of Y. This distance, represented by the vertical arrows in the figure, is the same everywhere along the budget line; consequently, the budget line shifts downward parallel to itself.

4.1 Changes in Income

In this section we consider the effects of a change in income.

Changes in Income and Changes in the Budget Line

If your income falls by $5 and your consumption of X remains unchanged, how much less Y can you afford to buy? Obviously, $5 worth. This is so regardless of how much X you are consuming, provided only that your consumption of X does not change.

This is illustrated in Exhibit 4–1. The *new* budget line is the result of a $5 drop in income. For each fixed quantity of X, the *original* line shows how much Y you could afford before the income change, and the *new* line shows how much you could afford after. The difference between these quantities is always "$5 worth." In other words, the vertical arrows in the exhibit all have the same length. That length corresponds to $5 worth of Y. If the price of Y is $1 per unit, the arrows all have length 5. If the price of Y is $2 per unit, the arrows all have length 2½. If the price of Y is 1¢ per unit, the arrows all have length 500. Since the arrows all have the same length, the *new* budget line is parallel to the *original* budget line.

▷ *Exercise 4.1* Draw the new budget line that would result from a $5 increase in income.

The general rule is:

A change in income causes a parallel shift in the budget line.

There is also another way to see why this is so. Recall from Section 3.2 that the equation of the budget line can be written:

$$y = \frac{-P_X}{P_Y} \cdot x + \frac{I}{P_Y}$$

so that income (I) is unrelated to the slope ($-P_X/P_Y$). A change in income affects only the Y-intercept of the budget line, which is another way of saying that it causes a parallel shift.

The Engel Curve

Let's try a numerical example. Suppose that the price of Y is $1 per unit and the price of X is 50¢ per unit. (In order to focus on the effects of income changes, we will assume that the prices of X and Y are fixed.) Panel A in Exhibit 4–2 shows the budget lines that you would have with incomes of $4, $8, and $12.

▷ *Exercise 4.2* Check that the budget lines are drawn and labeled correctly.

By drawing in a few indifference curves, as we have done in Exhibit 4–2, we can see which basket you would consume at each level of income. In this particular example, we see that when your income is $4, you consume 3 X's, when your income is $8, you consume 6 X's, and when your income is $12, you consume 12 X's. We can plot this information on a graph, as in panel B of Exhibit 4–2.

Engel curve
A curve showing, for fixed prices, the quantity of X consumed (on the vertical axis) at each level of income (on the horizontal axis).

The graph in the second panel is called your **Engel curve** for X. The Engel curve shows (for given, fixed prices) how much X you would buy at each possible level of income.

If we know your indifference curves, we can generate as many points on your Engel curve as we want to. Suppose we want to know what point on your Engel curve corresponds to an income of $6. We return to panel A of Exhibit 4–2 and draw in the budget line corresponding to that income. (It would be located between the $4 and the $8 budget lines that are already shown.) Then we draw in the indifference curve that is tangent to that budget line, and we read off the X-coordinate of the tangency. This tells us

Exhibit 4–2   **Income Changes and the Engel Curve**

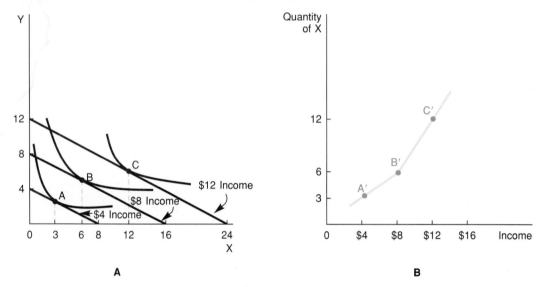

Points A, B, and C in panel A show the consumer's optima with a variety of incomes. (The prices of X and Y are held fixed at 50¢ per unit and $1 per unit throughout the discussion.) Points A, B, and C correspond to points A', B', and C' in panel B, showing how much X is consumed for each level of income. The curve through the points in panel B is the Engel curve.

how many X's you consume when your income is $6, and it gives us a new point on the Engel curve in panel B.

It is important to recognize that the Engel curve contains no information beyond that which is already encoded in the indifference curve diagram. Once we know the indifference curves, we can generate the Engel curve by a purely mechanical process.

Inferior Goods

The Engel curve in Exhibit 4–2 slopes upward. Most Engel curves do. This means that when your income increases, you tend to buy more of most things. However, this is far from a universal rule. Your Engel curve for Hamburger Helper undoubtedly has a downward-sloping portion. When your income goes up, you are likely to consume less Hamburger Helper, not more.

This is illustrated in Exhibit 4–3. Panel A shows your indifference curve diagram between Hamburger Helper and "all other goods." The second panel shows the Engel curve derived from this.

The two budget lines in panel A of the exhibit correspond to incomes of $1 and $2 per year. With an income of $1 per year, you choose basket A with a quantity of Q_A units of Hamburger Helper. When your income is $2 per

Exhibit 4–3   **Income Changes and the Engel Curve: The Case of an Inferior Good**

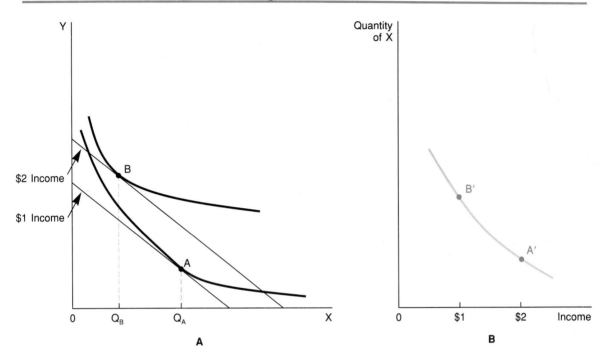

Points A and B in panel A show the optima with incomes of $1 and $2. Points A and B give rise to points A' and B' on the Engel curve in panel B. Because Q_B is less than Q_A, we can say that a rise in income leads to a fall in consumption of Hamburger Helper, or, in other words, that the Engel curve slopes downward. The downward slope is a result of the consumer's particular configuration of indifference curves. Any good for which the Engel curve slopes downward is referred to as an inferior good.

year, you choose basket B with a quantity of Q_B units of Hamburger Helper. For many goods we would expect Q_B to be greater than Q_A. In other words, we would expect point B to be to the right of point A, in which case the Engel curve would slope upward as in Exhibit 4–2.

In the case of Hamburger Helper, however, we find that Q_B is less than Q_A. In other words, point B is to the left of point A. In still other words, the Engel curve slopes downward. These are all different ways of saying the same thing, which we summarize by stating that Hamburger Helper is an **inferior good.**

Inferior good
A good that the consumer chooses to consume less of when his income goes up.

Normal good
A good that the consumer chooses to consume more of when his income goes up.

An inferior good is a good for which the Engel curve slopes downward. The use of the adjective *inferior* is not intended to reflect on the quality of the good itself.

A good that is not inferior is called a **normal good.** A normal good is one for which the Engel curve slopes upward.

Income Elasticity of Demand

Your Engel curve presents a picture of how sensitively your consumption of X reacts to changes in your income. We would like to have a numerical measure of this sensitivity.

One possible measure is the slope of the curve. We imagine that your income increases by $1 and ask by how many units your consumption of X will increase. That number is the slope of your Engel curve.

Unfortunately, this slope is arbitrary. It depends on the units in which X is measured (different units would yield different slopes) and it depends on the units in which your income is measured. (If we asked what happens when your income goes up by one British pound instead of by one American dollar, we would get a different answer.) This is the same problem we ran into when we considered the slope of a demand curve in Section 1.1 (see the subsection on elasticity of demand).

Therefore we adopt a measure that does not depend on arbitrary choices of units. We ask: If your income were to increase by 1%, by what percentage would your consumption of X increase? The answer to this question is a number, and that number is called your **income elasticity of demand** for X. Sometimes it is also called the elasticity of the Engel curve.

Income elasticity of demand
The percentage change in consumption that results from a 1% increase in income.

If a change in income by the amount ΔI leads to a change in consumption of X by the amount ΔQ, then the income elasticity of demand for X is given by:

$$\frac{\Delta Q/Q}{\Delta I/I},$$

which is the same thing as:

$$\frac{I \cdot \Delta Q}{Q \cdot \Delta I}.$$

▷ *Exercise 4.3* What would it mean for your income elasticity of demand for X to be negative?

4.2 Changes in Price

We now shift our attention from changes in income to changes in the price of X.

Changes in Price and Changes in the Budget Line

In order to focus attention on the effects of a change in the price of X, we assume that the price of Y and your income remain unchanged. For example, suppose that the price of Y remains fixed at $3 per unit and your income remains fixed at $24. Exhibit 4–4 shows the budget lines that result when the price of X is $2, $3, and $6.

Exhibit 4–4   **How Changes in Price Affect the Budget Line**

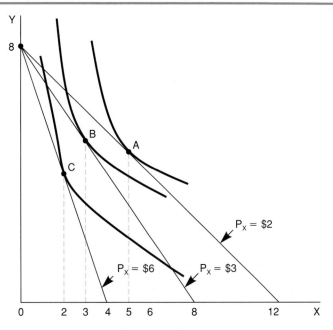

The graph shows budget lines corresponding to various prices of X. (We assume that the price of Y is held fixed at $3 per unit and income is held fixed at $24.) If you buy no X, you can afford 8 Y's, and this is so regardless of the price of X. Therefore the Y-intercept (0,8) is on all of the budget lines; that is, a change in the price of X causes the budget line to swing around its Y-intercept.

▷ *Exercise 4.4* Verify that the budget lines are drawn and labeled correctly.

There are two important facts to notice in Exhibit 4–4. First, a change in the price of X has no effect on the number of Y's you can buy when you buy no X's. In other words, it has no effect on the Y-intercept of the budget line. We summarize this by saying:

A change in the price of X causes the budget line to swing around its Y-intercept.

The second important fact concerns the direction in which the budget line swings. If you buy no Y's, you can afford a lot of X's when the price is low, but you can afford only very few X's when the price is high. In other words, low prices correspond to budget lines that have swung out very far to the right, and vice versa. When the price of X is very low (like $2), we get a budget line that extends out to a high quantity of X (in this case 12 units). The opposite is true when the price is very high (like $6).

We summarize the second important fact by saying:

A fall in the price of X causes the budget line to swing outward, and a rise in the price of X causes the budget line to swing inward.

The Demand Curve

In Section 4.1 we constructed your Engel curve, which keeps track of how much X you will buy at each possible level of income. In this section we will construct a curve that keeps track of how much X you will buy at each possible price of X. Indeed, we've already met such a curve, back in Chapter 1. It is called your *demand curve for X!* We can construct your demand curve in a way entirely analogous to the way in which we constructed your Engel curve.

In drawing the Engel curve, we plot income on the horizontal axis and quantity of X on the vertical. In drawing the demand curve, we reverse the axes, plotting price on the vertical axis and quantity of X on the horizontal axis. There is no strong reason for this, other than tradition.

In panel A of Exhibit 4–5, we have reproduced the graph from Exhibit 4–4. Reading from this figure, we see that when the price of X is $2 per unit, you choose basket A containing 5 units of X. At $3 per unit, you choose basket B containing 3 units of X, and at $6 per unit you buy basket C containing 2 units of X. Points A', B', and C' in panel B reflect this information. Points A', B', and C' lie on your demand curve for X.

Additional points on the demand curve can be generated in the same way. To find a point that corresponds to a price of $4, proceed as follows: Return to panel A of Exhibit 4–5 and draw the budget line corresponding to a price of $4. (It has an X-intercept of 6.) Find the optimum basket along that budget line and see what quantity of X it contains. That is the quantity that corresponds to a price of $4 on the demand curve in panel B.

Every point on the demand curve can be generated in this way. The demand curve contains no information beyond what is already encoded in the indifference curve diagram of Exhibit 4–5.

Students sometimes attempt to draw the demand curve and the indifference curves in the same diagram. This cannot be done correctly, because the two diagrams require different axes (quantities of X and Y for the indifference curves; quantity and price of X for the demand curve).

Other students sometimes think that the labeled points in panel A of Exhibit 4–5 illustrate the shape of the demand curve. This is also incorrect. It *is* true that each point on the demand curve arises from a point in the indifference curve diagram, but translating points from one diagram to the other is not a simple geometric process. The only way to go from one diagram to the other is by the process summarized in the preceding few paragraphs.

Exhibit 4–5 **Price Changes and the Demand Curve**

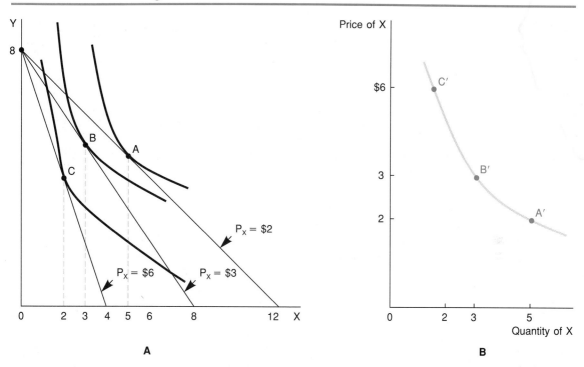

A   **B**

When the price of X is $2 per unit, you choose basket A containing 5 units of X. This information is recorded by point A′ in panel B. Points B′ and C′ are generated similarly. The curve through these points is your demand curve for X.

Price Elasticity of Demand

Price elasticity of demand
The percentage change in consumption that results from a 1% increase in price.

Your consumption of X changes in response to changing market conditions. The income elasticity of demand measures the sensitivity of your consumption to changes in income. The **price elasticity of demand** measures the sensitivity of your consumption to changes in price. The price elasticity of demand is the percentage change in the quantity of X that results from a 1% change in price. This is exactly the same measure that we called the *elasticity of the demand curve* in Section 1.1.

As we saw in Section 1.1, the formula for price elasticity of demand is:

$$\frac{P \cdot \Delta Q}{Q \cdot \Delta P}$$

when the price change is ΔP and the quantity change is ΔQ.

Elasticities with large absolute values indicate that your consumption of X is very sensitive to the price of X. When two demand curves pass through the same point, the shallower one is the one with higher elasticity.

Exhibit 4–6 **A Rise in the Price of X**

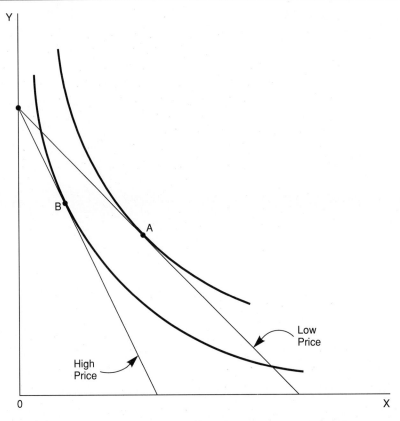

When the price of X goes up from *low* to *high*, your budget line swings inward and you move from point A to point B. This is drawn as a leftward movement, indicating that when the price of X goes up, the quantity demanded goes down.

For a given income and consumption of X, high income elasticity is reflected in a *steep* Engel curve. For a given price and consumption of X, high price elasticity is reflected in a *shallow* demand curve. The apparent paradox is due to the fact that the quantity of X is plotted on the vertical axis for an Engel curve and on the horizontal axis for a demand curve.

4.3 Income and Substitution Effects

We are now prepared to discuss the question of why demand curves slope downward. Exhibit 4–6 shows two budget lines, one corresponding to a *low price* of X and one corresponding to a *high price* of X. It also shows the

Exhibit 4–7   **Income and Substitution Effects**

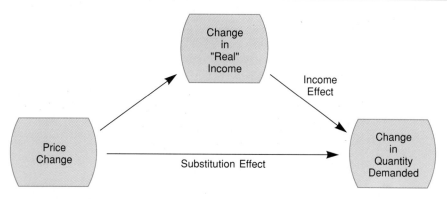

A rise in the price of X affects quantity demanded in two ways. It affects it directly through the substitution effect and indirectly by first making you feel poorer, whereupon (if X is a normal good) you buy fewer X's because of the income effect.

corresponding optima. When the price of X goes up from *low* to *high*, the optimal basket moves from point A to point B. As drawn in the exhibit, point B is to the left of point A. That is, when the price goes up, the quantity demanded goes down. Drawing point B to the left of point A is the same as asserting that demand curves slope downward. In this section we will examine the reasons why we usually expect this to be the case.

Two Effects of a Rise in Price

There are actually two reasons why a price rise leads to a fall in the quantity demanded. The first is the direct effect of the price rise itself: You buy fewer X's than before because each unit of X requires you to sacrifice more units of Y than previously. The terms of trade are less desirable than they were before. You stop buying X's when the marginal rate of substitution becomes equal to the relative price; following a price increase, this happens at a smaller quantity of X.

The second reason is slightly more subtle. Notice that point B is on a lower indifference curve than point A. When the price of X goes up, you are less happy than you were before. Your "real" income (meaning your level of happiness) is lower than it was before. You feel poorer than you were before, and in fact you *are* poorer, in the sense that your income will no longer buy as much as it used to. If X is a normal (as opposed to an inferior) good, you will buy less of it just because your real income is less than it was.

We refer to the first effect as the **substitution effect** (sometimes called the *pure price effect*) and the second as the **income effect.** The directions of causation are indicated schematically in Exhibit 4–7.

Substitution effect
When the price of a good changes, that part of the effect on quantity demanded that results from the change in the terms of trade between goods.

Exhibit 4–8   The Income and Substitution Effects of a Price Increase

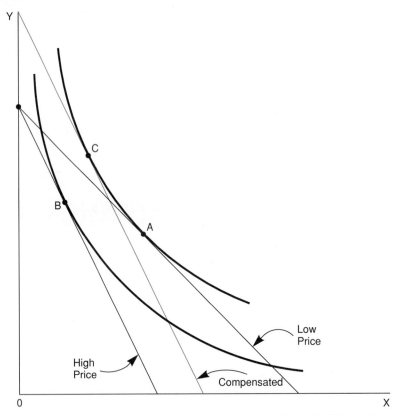

The graph shows the effect of a price increase from a *low price* to a *high price*. When the price goes up, the consumer moves from point A to point B and feels poorer. We imagine that he is compensated for this rise in price by an increase in income just sufficient to enable him to reach his original indifference curve. This causes the *high price* budget line to shift outward parallel to itself until it is just tangent to the original curve at point C. Point C is the consumer's optimum in the (imaginary) situation where the income effect is eliminated by the compensation scheme. Therefore the movement from A to C illustrates the pure substitution effect. Now we imagine the compensation being removed, so that the consumer returns from the *compensated* budget line to the *high price* budget line. This parallel shift, causing the consumer to move from C to B, represents a pure income effect.

▷ *Exercise 4.5* Trace through the meanings of the arrows in Exhibit 4–7 when the price of X *falls.*

Income effect
When the price of a good changes, that part of the effect on quantity demanded that results from the change in real income.

It will be enlightening to separate the substitution effect from the income effect and study them separately. We will accomplish this by describing an imaginary experiment that allows us to observe each effect in isolation. The experiment is illustrated in Exhibit 4–8, which reproduces the graph from Exhibit 4–6 together with some additional information that we will now explain.

An Imaginary Experiment

Exhibit 4–8 shows the result of an imaginary experiment. Suppose that the price of X rises from the *low* price to the *high* price. Initially, this makes you feel poorer. (You move from point A to point B, on a lower indifference curve.) The first step in the experiment is to give you just enough additional income to compensate you for the price rise, in the sense of making you just as happy as you were before the changes took place.

The additional income causes a parallel outward shift in your new *high price* budget line. Since we give you just enough income to restore your original level of happiness, the budget line shifts precisely far enough to become tangent to your old indifference curve. The new *compensated* budget line is also shown in Exhibit 4–8. It is tangent to the original indifference curve at point C. The outcome of the experiment would be your purchase of basket C.

The move from A to C captures precisely the substitution effect of the price change. We have maintained the new prices, but we have eliminated the income effect through our compensation scheme.

The second step in the experiment is to take away the additional income that we gave you in the first step. This causes a parallel shift from the *compensated* budget line to the *high price* budget line. This shift leads to a movement from C to B, entirely as a consequence of the reduction in your income. That movement is the income effect.

The real world is not like this imaginary experiment. In the real world a rise in the price of X is unlikely to be accompanied by an offsetting increase in your income. Therefore what really happens is simply that you move from point A to point B. However, we shall *imagine* that this move takes place in two steps: first, you are income-compensated for the price rise (causing a movement from A to C) and then the compensation is removed (causing a movement from C to B).

Why imagine such a thing? Because the movement from A to C is precisely the substitution effect, and the movement from C to B is precisely the income effect.

Here is a story that parallels the imaginary experiment. Suppose that every day you buy 4 candy bars from a vending machine at 40¢ apiece. One day you arrive at the machine to find that the price has gone up to 50¢, which makes you unhappy. However, almost at the same instant you find a $5 bill lying on the ground, which makes you happy. Indeed, you discover that by coincidence the money you've found exactly offsets the rise in price, leaving you just as happy as before you arrived at the machine. At that moment you decide to buy 2 candy bars instead of 4 because of the price rise. However, before you can make your purchase, you discover that the $5 bill you thought you had found was actually play money. Now you feel poorer and decide to buy only 1 candy bar.

All an observer would ever see is your reduction from 4 candy bars a day to 1. But this reduction was actually accomplished in two steps: the substitution effect leading you to switch from 4 a day to 2 a day, and the income effect leading you to switch from 2 a day to 1 a day.

If you had never spotted the phony $5 bill, you would have simply reduced your consumption from 4 to 1. However, it still makes sense to decompose this into two effects by imagining what you would have done if you had first found and then immediately lost the $5.

▷ *Exercise 4.6* Suppose that the price of X were to fall from the *low price* in Exhibit 4–8 to a *lower price*. Draw the *lower price* budget line, and draw the budget line that would result if you were compensated for the *lower price* by losing income until you were just as happy as when you started out. Show the basket to which you would move if there were only a substitution effect, and show the consequence of the income effect.

The Compensated Demand Curve

Compensated demand curve
A curve showing how much of a good would be consumed at each possible price if the consumer were income-compensated for all price changes.

Your **compensated demand curve** for X is a curve that shows how much X you would consume at each price if all income effects were eliminated. To get a point on the compensated demand curve, we begin by postulating a price, say $10. Then we ask: "If the price of X were to change to $10, and if at the same time you were income-compensated for the price change, then how much X would you buy?" The answer to this question is the quantity that corresponds to a price of $10 on the compensated demand curve.

Exhibit 4–9 illustrates the construction of points on the compensated demand curve, and contrasts this with the construction of points on the ordinary (uncompensated) demand curve.

▷ *Exercise 4.7* Use the graphs you drew for Exercise 4.6 to generate one additional point for each of the demand curves in Exhibit 4–9.

Most consumers of apples do not experience any change in their money income when the price of apples goes up. If you want to know how many apples such a consumer will buy at a given price, you must look on his *un*compensated demand curve in order to take account of both price and income effects. It is the uncompensated demand curve that actually describes behavior in individual markets. *Whenever we use the unqualified phrase* demand curve, *we always mean the ordinary (uncompensated) demand curve.*

Why Demand Curves Slope Downward

In Exhibit 4–9 we have drawn both the compensated and the uncompensated demand curves sloping downward. Let us examine why.

The Compensated Demand Curve

We begin with the compensated demand curve. To say that the compensated demand curve slopes downward is precisely to say that Q_C is less than Q_A; that is, point C is to the left of point A in panel A. Indeed, this must be true as a matter of geometry. The *low price* and *compensated* budget

Exhibit 4–9 **The Compensated and Uncompensated Demand Curves**

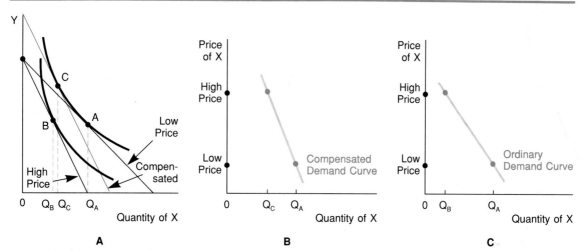

A

B

C

Suppose that X originally sells for a *low price*. The consumer chooses basket A, containing Q_A units of X. Therefore the quantity corresponding to *low price* is Q_A on both the compensated and the uncompensated demand curves.

Now suppose that the price of X rises to *high price*. At this price the consumer chooses basket B, containing Q_B units of X. Therefore the quantity corresponding to *high price* on the ordinary demand curve is Q_B.

We imagine the experiment in which the consumer is income-compensated for the price rise. In that case he would choose basket C, containing Q_C units of X. Therefore the quantity corresponding to *high price* on the compensated demand curve is Q_C.

Points on the compensated demand curve show how much X the consumer would buy at each given price, provided that he was always income-compensated for every price change. Points on the ordinary demand curve show how much X the consumer buys at each given price under the more realistic assumption that he is not income-compensated for price changes.

lines are both tangent to the same indifference curve, and the *compensated* line is the steeper of the two. Because indifference curves become steeper to the left and shallower to the right, this can happen only if the *compensated* tangency (point C) is to the left of the *low price* tangency (point A). In other words:

> **The compensated demand curve must slope downward. It is forced to slope downward by the convexity of indifference curves.**

The Income Effect

Before we turn to the uncompensated demand curve, we must study the relationship between points C and B. The movement from C to B is a pure income effect; it results from a parallel downward shift of the budget line. It reflects the drop in real income resulting from the price rise. Now, a fall in income will lead to a fall in consumption of X when X is a normal good, and to a rise in consumption of X when X is an inferior good. In other words, B is to the left of C if X is normal, and B is to the right of C if X is inferior.

This leads us to consider normal goods and inferior goods as two separate cases.

The Demand Curve for a Normal Good

First, suppose that X is a normal good. In that case point B is to the left of point C. We also know that C is always to the left of A. Using our IQ test skills, we can conclude that B is to the left of A. Thus because Q_B is less than Q_A, the uncompensated demand curve in panel C of Exhibit 4–9 must slope downward.

> **The (uncompensated) demand curve for a normal good must slope downward.**

Although we have phrased the argument in terms of geometry, we can also phrase it in terms of economics. When the price of X goes up, the substitution effect always causes us to reduce our consumption of X. If X is a normal good, the income effect causes us to reduce our consumption of X. Putting the two effects together, our consumption of X is certainly reduced.

The Demand Curve for an Inferior Good

Now we turn to the case of an inferior good. The pure substitution effect (from point A to point C) is still a movement to the left. The income effect (from C to B) will now be a movement to the right (a fall in income causes an increase in the consumption of an inferior good). B will be to the left of A if the substitution effect outweighs the income effect, and B will be to the right of A if the income effect outweighs the substitution effect. Thus Q_B can be either less or greater than Q_A, depending on which effect is bigger. Consequently:

> **The (uncompensated) demand curve for an inferior good slopes downward if the substitution effect outweighs the income effect. It slopes upward if the income effect outweighs the substitution effect.**

Both cases are illustrated in Exhibit 4–10.

Giffen good
A good for which the demand curve slopes upward.

A good for which the demand curve slopes upward is called a **Giffen good.** We have just argued that a Giffen good must be an inferior good for which the income effect is large.

When would there be a large income effect from a change in the price of X? It would have to be the case that a rise in the price of X made you feel very much poorer. It is a reasonable presumption that this could happen only if you spend a large fraction of your income on X. Therefore we conclude that a Giffen good must be an inferior good that consumes a large portion of your income.

For example, suppose that you eat hamburger 6 days a week and steak on Sunday. A rise in the price of hamburger might make you feel so much

Exhibit 4–10   **Income and Substitution Effects: The Case of an Inferior Good**

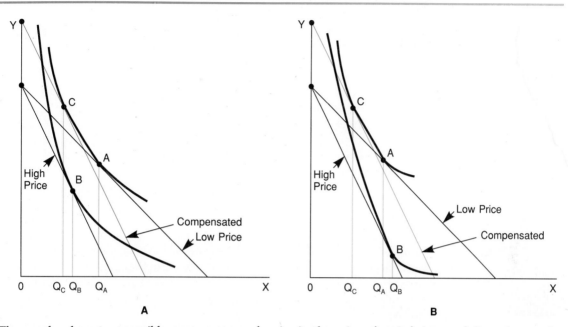

The graphs show two possible consequences of a rise in the price of an inferior good. In each case the substitution effect leads to a fall in quantity demanded (from Q_A to Q_C), and the income effect leads to a rise in quantity demanded (from Q_C to Q_B). In panel A the substitution effect is greater, so that the quantity demanded goes down and the demand curve for X slopes downward. In panel B the income effect is greater, so that the quantity demanded goes up and the demand curve for X slopes upward. In the latter case X is called a *Giffen good*.

poorer that you felt obliged to give up steaks and eat hamburger 7 days a week. The rise in the price of hamburger effectively makes you much poorer, and when you are poor you eat more hamburger.

In the real world it is hard to find examples of Giffen goods. Many economists believe that none has ever been found.

Summary

Changes in the consumer's opportunities lead to changes in his optimal consumption basket. Changes in opportunities arise from changes in income and from changes in prices.

A change in income causes a parallel shift in the consumer's budget line. If we fix the prices of X and Y, we can draw the budget lines corresponding to various levels of income. Then if we know the consumer's indifference curves, we can find the optimal basket corresponding to each level of income and see how much X he would purchase with that income. We can plot this information on a graph, with income on the horizontal axis and quantity of X on the vertical axis. The resulting curve is known as an Engel curve.

If an increase in income leads to increased consumption of X, then the Engel curve slopes upward and we say that X is a normal good. If an increase in income leads to decreased consumption of X, then the Engel curve slopes downward and we say that X is an inferior good.

The Engel curve shows how sensitively the consumption of X responds to changes in income. This sensitivity is measured numerically by the income elasticity of demand, defined to be the percentage change in consumption resulting from a 1% increase in income.

A change in the price of X causes the budget line to swing through its Y-intercept, outward for a fall in price and inward for a rise in price. If we fix the consumer's income and the price of Y, we can draw the budget lines corresponding to various prices for X. Then if we know the consumer's indifference curves, we can find the optimal basket corresponding to each price and see how much X he would purchase at that price. We can plot this information on a graph, with price on the vertical axis and quantity of X on the horizontal axis. The resulting curve is the consumer's demand curve for X.

The demand curve illustrates how sensitively the consumption of X responds to changes in price. It is measured numerically by the price elasticity of demand, also known as the elasticity of the demand curve.

When the price of X goes up, the consumer changes his consumption of X for two reasons. First, there is the substitution effect, resulting from the fact that it is now necessary to sacrifice more Y for each unit of X acquired. Second, there is the income effect, resulting from the fact that the consumer feels poorer as a result of the price rise. The substitution effect of a price rise always leads to less consumption of X. The income effect of a price rise will lead to less consumption of X if X is normal, but it will lead to greater consumption of X if X is inferior.

The compensated demand curve shows, for each price, the quantity of X that the consumer would choose if we performed the experiment of always income-compensating him for any price rise. Therefore the compensated demand curve shows only the substitution effect and consequently must slope downward.

The ordinary uncompensated demand curve, which describes actual behavior in individual markets, includes both substitution and income effects. Consequently it must slope downward for a normal good, where both effects work in the same direction. For an inferior good, the two effects work in opposite directions, so the demand curve will slope downward if the substitution effect dominates the income effect and upward if the reverse is true. In the latter case the good is known as a Giffen good. Giffen goods are rare in nature.

Review Questions

R1. How does a change in income affect the budget line? How does a change in price affect the budget line?

R2. Show how to use an indifference curve diagram to construct points on the Engel curve. Show how to use an indifference curve diagram to construct points on both the compensated and uncompensated demand curves.

R3. Give the formulas for (a) income elasticity of demand and (b) price elasticity of demand.

R4. State under what circumstances each of the following curves slopes upward and under what circumstances it slopes downward: (a) the Engel curve, (b) the demand curve, (c) the compensated demand curve.

R5. Define the income and substitution effects of a price change.

R6. Describe the imaginary experiment that would enable us to measure the substitution effect of a price change. Explain how the geometry of this experiment reveals the direction of the substitution effect.

R7. What is the definition of a Giffen good? Are all Giffen goods inferior goods? Are all inferior goods Giffen goods?

Problem Set

1. *True or false:* It is unlikely that a consumer would view all goods as inferior goods.

2. A *luxury* is defined to be a good with income elasticity greater than 1. Explain, without the technical jargon, what this means. Is it possible for all of the goods you consume to be luxuries? Why or why not?

3. Suppose that the federal government issues $100 worth of food stamps to everybody in your city. These food stamps are coupons that can be exchanged for $100 worth of food at the grocery store, but they can be used only by the person to whom they are issued. Draw your budget constraint between "food" and "all other goods" both before and after the food stamps are issued. *True or false:* If food is a normal (noninferior) good, then the food stamps will lead to more food being eaten in your city.

4. Suppose that the only goods you consume are wine and roses. On Tuesday the price of wine goes up, and at the same time your income increases by just enough so that you are equally as happy as you were on Monday.
   a. What happens to the quantity of wine that you consume? Illustrate your answer with indifference curves.
   b. On Tuesday would you still be able to afford the same basket that you were buying on Monday? How do you know?

On Wednesday there are no new price changes (so the Tuesday prices are still in effect), but your income changes to the point where you can just exactly afford Monday's basket.

   c. Are you happier on Wednesday or on Monday?
   d. Is it possible to say with certainty whether you buy more wine on Wednesday than on Monday? If not, what would your answer depend on?

e. Is it possible to say with certainty whether you buy more wine on Wednesday than on Tuesday? If not, what would your answer depend on?

5. Suppose that your indifference curves between X and "all other goods" are shaped, somewhat unusually, as in panel B of Exhibit 3–7. Draw your Engel curve, your compensated demand curve, and your uncompensated demand curve for X. Compute their elasticities.

6. *True or false:* For a normal good the compensated demand curve is steeper than the uncompensated demand curve, but for an inferior good the reverse is true.

7. Suppose that the only two goods you consume are cakes and ale. You have chosen an optimal basket containing 5 cakes and 7 pints of ale. Now suppose that you are unable to change the amount of ale but that someone starts giving you additional cakes. You find that each additional cake is worth less to you in terms of ale than the previous one. *True or false:* Ale could not possibly be an inferior good.

8. *True or false:* Henry's compensated and uncompensated demand curves for bubble gum are likely to be almost identical, but his compensated and uncompensated demand curves for housing might very well not be.

9. Suppose that the only two goods you consume are X and Y. *True or false:* If the price of Y goes up and X is an inferior good, then you will buy more X. Illustrate your answer with indifference curves. (*Hint:* Draw in an income-compensated budget line.) Explain your answer in terms of income and substitution effects.

10. Suppose that the only two goods you buy are X and Y. One day the price of Y and your income both increase by 10%.
    a. Show your old and new budget lines. (*Hint:* What effect do the changes have on the amount of X you can buy if you buy no Y? On the amount of Y you can buy if you buy no X?)
    b. What will happen to your consumption of X if X is a normal good? If X is an inferior good? If X is a Giffen good? Explain your answers in terms of income and substitution effects.

Refer to Answers to Problem Sets for solutions to problems 2 and 3.

Chapter Five

The Behavior of Firms

In this chapter we will turn our attention from the behavior of individuals to the behavior of firms. Firms are the institutions that produce and supply the goods that individuals demand. Just as our study of individual consumers' behavior led us to a deeper understanding of demand, our study of firms' behavior will lead us to a deeper understanding of supply.

All firms are created and owned by individuals. Some, like many corner grocery stores, have one owner, whereas others, like the General Motors Corporation, have many thousands of owners (in this case the General Motors stockholders). In some firms the owner or owners exert considerable day-to-day control over operations, whereas in others salaried managers serve these functions. With such diversity in the size, nature, and organization of firms, you might wonder how it could be possible to make any statements at all about the behavior of firms in general.

There is, however, one grand generalization about firms that economists have found extraordinarily powerful: We assume that firms act to maximize profits. There are reasons to question this assumption. Why should individuals, who are interested in many things other than profits, choose to organize firms that pursue profits single-mindedly? Even if the owners view profit maximization as desirable, does it follow that the managers will behave accordingly? Economists have given much thought to these and related questions.[1] However, most economists also believe that the assumption of profit maximization, while only an approximation to the truth, leads to deep insights into the ways in which goods are supplied.

Firm
An entity that produces and sells goods, with the goal of maximizing its profits.

Therefore we will use the word **firm** to refer to an entity that produces and supplies goods and that seeks to do so in such a way as to maximize the profits that it earns in any given time period. The goal of profit maximization will enter into every decision that the firm makes. In Section 5.1 we will study a simple problem in which a firm must weigh costs against benefits. This will lead us to the equimarginal principle, which is one of the most fundamental concepts in economics and the key to profit maximization. In Section 5.2 we will see how firms use this principle in deciding how much to produce.

5.1 Weighing Costs and Benefits

In this section we will examine how firms make decisions by imagining a simple problem that a farmer might face: How many acres of his land should he spray with insecticide? The solution to this problem will reveal one of the key concepts in economics, known as the equimarginal principle. Once this principle has been made explicit, we will see that it applies both to the behavior of firms and to the behavior of individuals.

A Farmer's Problem

To begin to understand how firms make decisions, let us imagine a problem Farmer Ryan faces in operating his farm as a firm (that is, as a profit-maximizing enterprise). Farmer Ryan owns 6 acres of land planted with wheat. His problem is to decide how many acres to spray with insecticide.

Suppose that spraying one acre will save $7 worth of crops. What then will be the value of the crops saved when 2 acres are sprayed? Your first guess might be $14, but a more reasonable guess would be something less. Why? Because the 6 acres of land on the farm are not identical. Some acres are more fertile than others, and some acres are more susceptible to insect damage than others. When Farmer Ryan sprays only one acre, he chooses that acre where spraying will yield the greatest benefit. When he sprays 2 acres, he chooses both the one where spraying will yield the greatest benefit and the one where spraying will yield the second greatest benefit.

---

[1]One of the earliest and most enlightening contributions to this literature is R. H. Coase, "On the Nature of the Firm," *Economica* 4 (1937), 386–405.

We can expect that this will generate less than twice the gain from spraying the first acre.

So a reasonable assumption would be that if spraying one acre will save $7 worth of crops, then spraying 2 acres will save $13 worth of crops. We record these numbers in the second column of the following table, along with the total benefit when 3, 4, 5, or 6 acres are sprayed.

No. of Acres Sprayed	Total Benefit	Marginal Benefit
0	$ 0	
1	7	$7/acre
2	13	6
3	18	5
4	22	4
5	25	3
6	27	2

Marginal benefit
The additional benefit gained from the last unit of an activity.

The third column of the table, labeled **marginal benefit,** refers to the value of crops saved on the last acre sprayed. For example, since spraying 2 acres saves $13 worth of crops, of which $7 worth are saved on the first acre, it follows that $6 worth are saved on the second acre. So when two acres are sprayed, we say that the marginal benefit from spraying the second acre is $6 worth of crops saved per acre. If Farmer Ryan sprays 3 acres, he will save $18 worth of crops. Because we know that spraying has saved $13 on the first two acres, we can calculate a marginal benefit of $5 per acre for the third acre sprayed.

▷ *Exercise 5.1* Verify the other numbers in the third column of the table. Explain why it is reasonable for these numbers to be decreasing. Explain why the sum of the first 3 (or 4 or 5) entries in the "marginal" column is equal to the third (or fourth or fifth) entry in the "total" column.

In order to solve the farmer's problem of how many acres to spray, we also need to know something about the costs of spraying. Let us suppose that the farmer can hire a crop duster for a fee of $5 per acre. The second column of the following table shows the total cost of spraying various numbers of acres.

No. of Acres Sprayed	Total Cost	Marginal Cost
0	$ 0	
1	5	$5/acre
2	10	5
3	15	5
4	20	5
5	25	5
6	30	5

Marginal cost
The additional cost
associated with the last
unit of an activity.

The third column of the table shows the **marginal cost** associated with each acre sprayed; that is, it shows the additional cost incurred as a result of spraying each acre. If Farmer Ryan sprays 4 acres, the spraying bill will be $20, of which $15 pays for the first 3 acres sprayed. Therefore the marginal cost of spraying the fourth acre is $5 per acre.

▷ *Exercise 5.2* Explain why the marginal cost of spraying is $5 per acre regardless of how many acres are sprayed.

In Exhibit 5–1 all of our information is gathered together and displayed on graphs. The only new column in the table, labeled "Net Gain," is the total value of crops saved through spraying minus the total cost of spraying.

The graphs in the exhibit display the information from the table. The values in the "net gain" column are illustrated by the lengths of the vertical lines in the first graph, indicating the distance between total cost and total benefit.

The net gain from spraying will add to the farmer's profits, so he wants this net gain to be as large as possible. Looking at the last column of the table, we see that this occurs when the number of acres sprayed is either 2 or 3. To remove the ambiguity, let us arbitrarily suppose that whenever the farmer is indifferent between two options, he chooses the larger one. In that case the number of acres sprayed will be 3.[2]

Farmer Ryan has an easy way of deciding how many acres to spray: Scan the "net gain" column, find the largest possible net gain, and spray the corresponding number of acres. We will call this process *Method 1*. There is an alternative, equally valid process available to Farmer Ryan, which we will call *Method 2*.

To use Method 2, focus on the row of the table corresponding to 1 acre sprayed and look only at the "marginal" columns. Now ask yourself which is greater—the marginal benefit of spraying the first acre or the marginal cost? Since $7 is greater than $5, the marginal benefit is greater, and so spraying that first acre is a good deal. On this basis we decide to spray the first acre.

Next, inspect the row of the table corresponding to 2 acres sprayed, again using only the "marginal" columns. Does the marginal gain from spraying a second acre exceed the marginal cost of doing so? Since $6 is greater than $5, the answer is yes, and so it is a good idea to spray the second acre as well.

When we get to the next row of the table, we find that the marginal gain from spraying a third acre is equal to the marginal cost of spraying that

---

[2]In real life the farmer would have many more than six choices. In addition to the possibilities displayed in Exhibit 5–1, he could choose to spray exactly 3½ acres, or 1.7894 acres, or any other number of acres between 0 and 6. If we had been able to display all of these possibilities, we would have found that the net gain was maximized by only one of them, rather than two. The optimal number of acres to spray might have been somewhere between two and three. You might have been disturbed by our arbitrary rule that the farmer always chooses the larger of the two options that maximize net gain. If so, you should be relieved by the observation that this was necessitated only by the simplicity of our example, and that if we displayed more options, no such arbitrary choice would be required.

Exhibit 5–1   **Maximizing Net Gain**

No. of Acres Sprayed	Total Benefit	Marginal Benefit	Total Cost	Marginal Cost	Net Gain
0	$ 0		$ 0		$ 0
1	7	$7/acre	5	$5/acre	2
2	13	6	10	5	3
3	18	5	15	5	3
4	22	4	20	5	2
5	25	3	25	5	0
6	27	2	30	5	−3

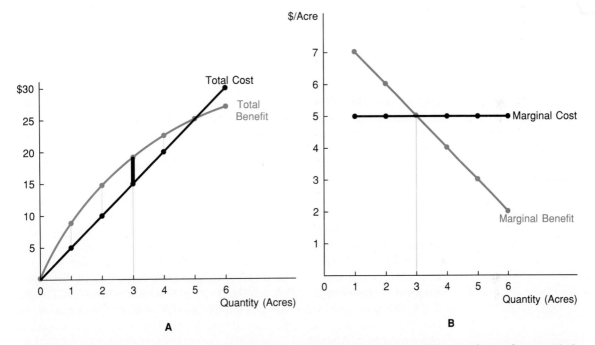

A

B

The graphs display the information in the table. Because Net gain = Total benefit − Total cost, the net gain is equal to the distance between the total cost and total benefit curves in panel A. For example, the heavy vertical line has length $3, representing the net gain of $3 when 3 acres are sprayed. Because the heavy line is the longest of the vertical lines, the farmer will maximize his net gain by spraying 3 acres. An alternative way to reach the same conclusion is to continue spraying as long as marginal benefit exceeds marginal cost and to stop when they become equal, at 3 acres.

acre. Having already decided to spray the first 2 acres, the farmer is indifferent about spraying the third. As before, we arbitrarily eliminate the ambiguity by assuming the farmer always moves forward when he is indifferent, and so he sprays a third acre as well.

When we consider spraying a fourth acre, we find that the marginal value of the crops saved is only $4. This is less than the marginal cost of saving them. Farmer Ryan would be $1 poorer after spraying this fourth acre. Spraying the fourth acre is *not* a good idea, and so Farmer Ryan stops after spraying 3 acres.

Method 2 can be summarized as follows: Continue spraying as long as the marginal benefit from spraying is greater than or equal to the marginal cost; stop spraying when the marginal value and the marginal cost become equal. Here is an even briefer summary of Method 2: Scan the "marginal" columns until you find the row in which the marginal benefit is equal to the marginal cost; then spray the corresponding number of acres. In terms of the graph, Method 2 says to choose the quantity at which the marginal benefit curve and the marginal cost curve cross.

Notice that Method 1 and Method 2 both yield the same answer: Spray 3 acres. They *must* yield the same answer, since each is a perfectly valid way of determining the optimal behavior. In view of this, you may wonder why we went to the trouble of developing Method 2 when Method 1 works perfectly well. The reason for studying Method 2 is that it demonstrates the importance of the "marginal" columns. It shows that the "marginal" information alone is enough to determine the optimal decision. We can say the same thing in a slightly different way: A change in circumstances will not affect Farmer Ryan's behavior unless it causes a change in a "marginal" column.

An example will illustrate this last point. Suppose that the crop duster changes his pricing policy. He now charges a $1 flat fee for coming out to the farm, plus $5 for each acre sprayed. (One dollar is the fee for spraying *zero* acres!) Exhibit 5–2 illustrates the new situation.

The marginal costs and marginal benefits in Exhibit 5–2 are the same as those in Exhibit 5–1. Therefore Method 2 still gives the same result as before: Marginal cost equals marginal benefit when 3 acres are sprayed, and so 3 acres is the optimal number to spray. We can confirm this using Method 1. Net gain is still maximized when 3 acres are sprayed. Graphically, the total cost curve has shifted up parallel to itself a distance $1, so that the maximal distance between it and the total benefit curve still occurs at a quantity of 3 acres.

Now here is the key observation: We really could have predicted this result without ever building the table in Exhibit 5–2. All we had to observe was that the change in the crop duster's pricing policy does not change either of the "marginal" columns in the table, and that only these columns are necessary for predicting the farmer's behavior. Therefore the farmer's behavior will not change under the new pricing policy.

It is true that the crop duster's new pricing policy makes the farmer worse off than before: He used to realize a net gain of $3 when he sprayed 3 acres, and now he realizes a net gain of only $2. What remains unchanged is the number of acres that the farmer will choose to spray: 3 in either case.

▷ *Exercise 5.3* Suppose that the crop duster changes his policy again, so that he now charges $2 to come out to the farm, plus $5 per acre sprayed. How many acres will the farmer spray now? Figure out the

Exhibit 5–2   Maximizing Net Gain

No. of Acres Sprayed	Total Benefit	Marginal Benefit	Total Cost	Marginal Cost	Net Gain
1	$ 7	$7/acre	6	$5/acre	$ 1
2	13	6	11	5	2
3	18	5	16	5	2
4	22	4	21	5	1
5	25	3	26	5	−1
6	27	2	31	5	−4

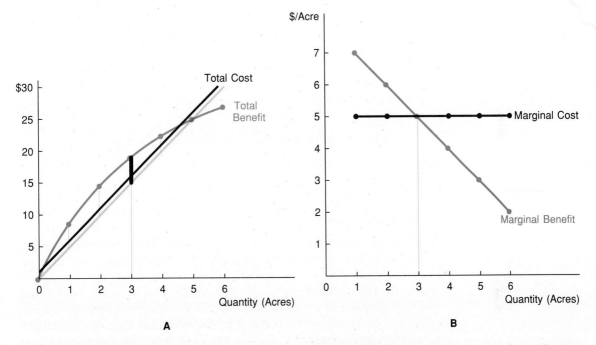

The table describes the situation after the crop duster institutes a $1 flat fee for coming out to the farm. The data from the table are displayed in the graphs. The light-colored curve in panel A is the old Total Cost curve from Exhibit 5–1 and is reproduced here for comparison. The marginal curves are the same as those in Exhibit 5–1. Therefore the optimal number of acres to spray, which is determined by the intersection of the marginal cost and the marginal benefit curves, is unchanged.

answer *without* building a table, and explain how you know that your answer is correct. Now build a table and check that your answer really *is* correct.

▷ *Exercise 5.4* Suppose now that the crop duster lowers his price to $4 per acre sprayed. Does this affect anything "marginal"? Does it change the farmer's decision about how many acres to spray?

There is one exception to the rule we have just learned. The rule is: If nothing marginal changes, then Farmer Ryan's behavior won't change. The exception is: If the only possible net gains from spraying become negative, Farmer Ryan will quit spraying altogether. For example, suppose that the crop duster changes his pricing scheme to: $100 to come out to the farm plus $5 per acre sprayed. If you construct a table like those in Exhibits 5–1 and 5–2, you will see that the "marginal" columns remain unchanged but that the farmer loses money by spraying no matter how many acres he sprays. In this case he will spray not 3 acres but zero acres. So a better way to state the rule is this: If nothing marginal changes and if Farmer Ryan continues to spray at all, then his behavior won't change.

The Equimarginal Principle

Equimarginal principle The principle that an activity should be pursued to the point where marginal cost equals marginal benefit.

Farmer Ryan has discovered the **equimarginal principle,** which is the essence of his Method 2 for deciding how many acres to spray:

> **If an activity is worth pursuing at all, then it should be pursued up to the point where marginal cost equals marginal benefit.**

He has also discovered an important consequence of the principle:

> **If circumstances change in a way that does not affect anything marginal and if an activity remains worth pursuing at all, then the optimal amount of that activity is unchanged.**

The equimarginal principle has broad applicability. It applies not only to firms but also to individuals. Indeed, we have already met the equimarginal principle in Chapter 3, where we studied the consumer's optimum. The consumer moves along his budget line, trading Y for X until the relative price of a unit of X (which is the marginal cost of that unit measured in terms of Y) is equal to the marginal rate of substitution between X and Y (which is the marginal value of that unit measured in terms of Y). Since the benefit to a consumer from owning a unit of X is the same thing as the value to him of that unit, equating marginal cost to marginal value is the same as equating marginal cost to marginal benefit.

Applying the Principle

Occasionally you will read a newspaper editorial that makes an argument along the following lines: "Our town spends only $100,000 per year to run its police department, and the benefits we get from the police are worth far more than that. Police services are a good deal in our town. We should be expanding the police department, not cutting back on it as Mayor McDonald has proposed." This argument is wrong. The editorial writer has observed (we assume correctly) that the total benefit derived from the police department exceeds the total cost of acquiring those benefits. But this is not relevant to the decision between expanding the department or contracting it. For this only marginal quantities matter.

Reconsider Exhibit 5–1. When Farmer Ryan sprays 3 acres, he is getting a "good deal": His gains from spraying exceed his costs by $3. Does it follow that he should expand his spraying program and spray a fourth acre? No, because the *marginal* cost of spraying that fourth acre exceeds the *marginal* gain from doing so. It is true that Farmer Ryan's gains exceeded his costs on each of the first 3 acres he decided to spray. However, if he sprayed a fourth acre, the marginal cost of doing so would exceed the marginal gain by $2, reducing his total net gain from $3 to $1. Spraying the fourth acre is a bad idea.

Imagine Farmer Widdicombe, faced with the same opportunities as Farmer Ryan, who has foolishly decided to spray 4 acres. He is considering cutting back his spraying program. The logic of the editorial would have us say: "Your spraying program is costing you only $20 and the value of the crops it saves is far more than that ($2 more, to be exact). Your spraying program is a good deal. If anything, you should be expanding it, not cutting back." It is true that Farmer Widdicombe's spraying program is a good deal overall, but it is also true that spraying the fourth acre is a bad deal (a $5 marginal cost exceeds a $4 marginal benefit). His spraying program will be an even better deal if that fourth acre is eliminated. Although his total gains exceed his total costs, this is beside the point, because for a decision like this only marginal quantities matter.

5.2 Firms in the Marketplace

We are now prepared to study the market behavior of firms, armed with our key observation that "only marginal quantities matter." The Tailor Dress Company produces dresses and sells them in the marketplace. This firm (like all firms in this book) is interested only in maximizing its profits. The firm's profit for any given period is equal to its revenues in that period minus its costs of production in that period. So to understand profits, we first have to understand revenues and costs. We begin with costs.

Costs

The production of dresses requires many inputs: fabric, thread, labor, the use of various types of machinery, and so on. The cost of producing a dress is the sum total of the costs of all these inputs.

Suppose that Tailor can produce 1 dress for a cost of $4. How much will it cost to produce 2 dresses? Your first guess might be $8, but this need not actually be the case. When the firm produces its first dress, it does so at the lowest possible cost. This means that of all the resources available to it, it uses precisely those that can produce a dress most efficiently. It will choose the fabric that is most appropriate for the pattern, hire the best possible dressmakers, and put them to work on the firm's most efficient sewing machines.

When Tailor decides to produce a second dress, the most efficient inputs will have been used up and the firm will have to resort to its second most efficient production process. Perhaps all of the large pieces of fabric have been used up and it will now be necessary to work with odd-shaped pieces. Perhaps it will be necessary to hire additional, less skillful dressmakers. Perhaps the firm will find that its best sewing machines cannot be run all day without damage, and so make the dress on its second most efficient machines. Alternatively, the firm might go ahead and use the first machines again, but it would incur more repair bills in the process, adding to costs.

The same sort of phenomenon might occur in any industry. The farmer producing 1 acre of wheat plants his most fertile acre of land, resorting to his second most fertile acre when he decides to increase his production to 2 acres. A writer producing 1 short story will work at the time of day when he is most productive and will use his best ideas. When he produces his second story, he will have to work harder.

For such reasons it is plausible to conclude that the cost of producing 2 dresses could well be *more* than $8. Suppose that the cost is $9. Then the marginal cost of producing the second dress is $5, because this is how much it costs to produce the second dress given that the first one has already been produced.

If 3 dresses can be produced for a total cost of $15, then the marginal cost of producing the third is $6. This is the additional cost incurred when the third dress is produced, given that the first 2 dresses have already been produced at a total cost of $9. We have assumed that the marginal cost of the third dress is higher than that of the second, just as the marginal cost of the second is higher than that of the first.

Increasing marginal cost
The condition where each additional unit of an activity is more expensive than the last.

We say that the Tailor Dress Company faces the condition of **increasing marginal cost**. In the preceding few paragraphs we have argued for the plausibility of this assumption. There are also arguments to be made against it; perhaps you can construct some. In Chapter 6 we will make a careful study of how marginal costs arise from the production processes available to the firm. There we will have much to say about the circumstances in which marginal costs can be expected to increase. In the present chapter we will simply make the assumption of increasing marginal cost so that we can study the behavior of firms in the context of a simple example.

Exhibit 5–3 illustrates Tailor's total cost and marginal cost curves. Notice the units used; when total cost is measured in dollars, marginal cost is measured in dollars *per item produced*. There must also be a unit of time agreed upon in advance. The table shows the company's costs per week, for each possible quantity of output per week.

▷ *Exercise 5.5* In Exhibit 5–3 explain how you could derive the numbers in the marginal cost column from those in the total cost column. Explain how you could derive the numbers in the total cost column from those in the marginal cost column.

Exhibit 5–3 Total and Marginal Costs at the Tailor Dress Company

Quantity of Dresses	Total Cost	Marginal Cost
1	$ 4	$ 4/dress
2	9	5
3	15	6
4	22	7
5	30	8
6	39	9
7	49	10
8	60	11

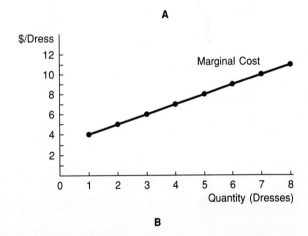

A

B

When 4 dresses are produced, the marginal cost is $7 per dress, which is the total cost of producing 4 dresses minus the total cost of producing 3 dresses. That difference is also the slope of the line that connects the 2 points on the total cost curve at quantities of 3 and 4. When the unit of quantity is small, such a line is nearly tangent to the total cost curve. Thus we say that marginal cost is the slope of total cost.

In Exhibit 5–3 we have plotted total cost on one graph and marginal cost on another. It is necessary to do so because they require different vertical axes: dollars for total cost and dollars per dress for marginal cost. For this reason it is never correct to plot total cost and marginal cost on the same graph.

As the exhibit demonstrates, marginal cost is the slope of total cost. For example, when 4 dresses are produced, the marginal cost is $7 per dress. That is the same as the slope of the line shown in panel A, connecting the points on the total cost curve that correspond to quantities of 3 and 4. When the standard unit of quantity is small, such points are close together, and the line approximates the tangent line to the total cost curve.

Fixed Costs

Fixed cost
A cost that does not vary with the level of output.

Some of the costs of operating a firm may not appear in the marginal cost column at all. These are the costs that are necessary to maintain the existence of the firm; they are costs that have to be met even if the firm produces nothing. These costs are called the **fixed costs** of the firm. They are called *fixed* because they do not depend on the quantity produced. For example, the Tailor Dress Company may find itself in a position where it has to pay $2 per week rent for the factory that it uses. Alternatively, if the firm owns the factory, it forgoes the opportunity to rent that factory to someone else for $2 per week. In either case it has $2 per week of fixed costs, which must be added to the total costs of the firm even though they are not part of the marginal cost of producing any item. Exhibit 5–4 displays such a situation. The marginal cost curve of Exhibit 5–4 is identical to that of Exhibit 5–3, but the total cost curve is shifted upward a distance of $2 due to the new assumption of $2 in fixed costs.

Revenue

Revenue
The proceeds collected by a firm when it sells its products.

Firms are motivated by profit, and profit is the excess of revenue over costs. Therefore to understand firm behavior, we need to understand both costs and revenue. We have completed our initial discussion of costs; we turn now to revenue.

The **revenue** that a firm earns in a given time period can be computed by the simple formula:

$$\text{Revenue} = \text{Price} \times \text{Quantity}.$$

In this formula *Price* refers to the price per unit at which the firm sells its product. *Quantity* refers to the number of units that the firm sells in the time period under consideration. The firm can choose either the price it wants to charge or the quantity it wants to sell, but it cannot choose both simultaneously. The Tailor Dress Company can decide to sell exactly 9 dresses this week, or it can decide to sell dresses at a price of $200 apiece. But it can't decide to sell 9 dresses at $200 apiece, because it may not find demanders willing to purchase 9 dresses at $200. Tailor's options are limited by the quantity of Tailor dresses that demanders are willing to purchase at any given price. That is, its options are limited by the demand curve for Tailor dresses.

Exhibit 5–4   **Total and Marginal Costs at the Tailor Dress Company**

Quantity of Dresses	Total Cost	Marginal Cost
1	$ 6	$ 4/dress
2	11	5
3	17	6
4	24	7
5	32	8
6	41	9
7	51	10
8	62	11

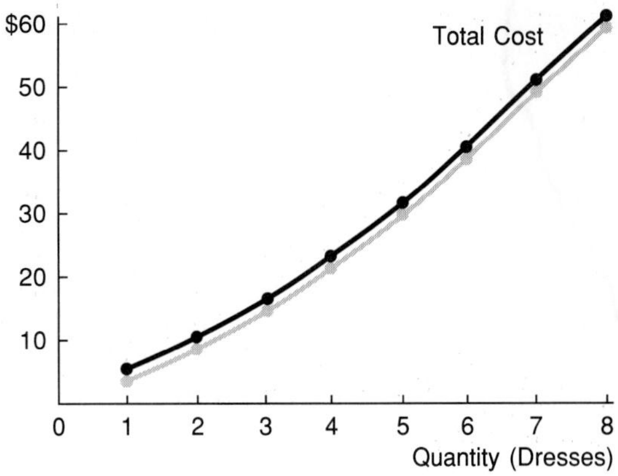

A

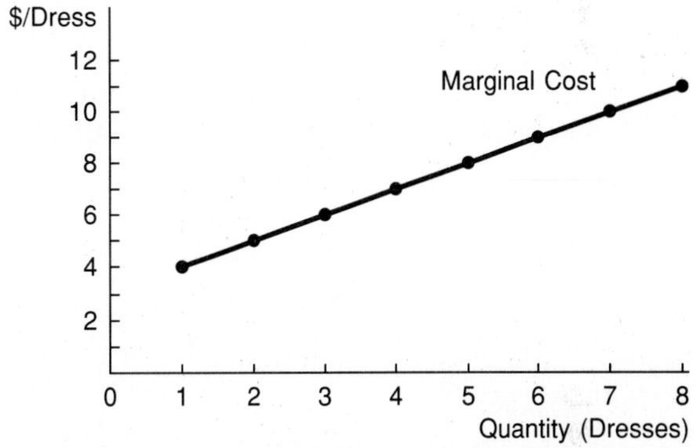

B

The table and the graphs assume fixed costs of $2 at the Tailor Dress Company. This assumption has no effect on marginal costs, so the marginal cost curve is identical to that of Exhibit 5–3. The new $2 fixed cost does cause the total cost curve to shift upward a distance $2. Since the vertical shift is the same everywhere, the shape of the total cost curve remains unchanged. Another way to see that the slope remains unchanged is to recall that marginal cost is the slope of total cost, and this slope has not changed.

Suppose that the demand curve is given by the following table:

Price	Quantity		Price	Quantity
$1	10		5	6
2	9		6	5
3	8		7	4
4	7		8	3

(Remember that this table is not the demand curve for dresses. It is the demand curve for *Tailor* dresses.) If Tailor wants to sell 9 dresses, it cannot charge a price of more than $2. In fact, if it wants to sell 9 dresses, it should charge a price of *exactly* $2. This is the highest price it can charge and still sell 9 dresses.

▷ **Exercise 5.6** If Tailor wants to sell exactly 5 dresses, what price should it charge? Why?

For any given quantity of dresses, Tailor selects the highest price at which it can sell them by reading the demand curve backward. That is, Tailor finds the point on the demand curve with the desired quantity and reads off the corresponding price. Its total revenue from the sales of these dresses is then given by this formula:

$$\text{Revenue} = \text{Price} \times \text{Quantity}.$$

Maximizing Profits

Exhibit 5–5 displays the options available to the Tailor Dress Company. For each quantity the "price" column shows the maximum price at which that quantity can be sold. The "total revenue" column shows how much revenue the company will earn if it sells that quantity. The "marginal revenue" column indicates the amount of additional revenue attributable to the last item sold. (Notice that this can be negative!) The two "cost" columns are taken from Exhibit 5–4, where we assumed fixed costs of $2 per week; we continue with this assumption. The final column shows Tailor's **profit,** defined as:

Profit
The amount by which revenue exceeds costs.

$$\text{Profit} = \text{Revenue} - \text{Cost}.$$

▷ **Exercise 5.7** Verify all of the entries in Exhibit 5–5.

To choose the quantity that will maximize profits, Tailor can use either Method 1 or Method 2. Method 1 is the direct method: Scan the profit column and choose the maximum possible profit. Graphically, this is equivalent to finding the point where the distance between total cost and total revenue is greatest. This occurs at a quantity of either 2 or 3, where the profit is $7. As in Section 5.1, we assume that when firms are indifferent between two choices they take the larger of the two. Therefore, Tailor produces 3 dresses and sells them at $8 apiece, the highest price at which demanders are willing to buy 3 dresses.

Method 2 is the method of scanning only the marginal columns. Taking them row by row, the Tailor Dress Company first asks: Is the first dress worth making? The answer is yes, because the marginal revenue earned from selling that dress exceeds the marginal cost of producing it ($10 is greater than $4). Next the company asks if the second dress is worth making. Here again, comparing a marginal revenue of $8 with a marginal cost of $5, we find that the answer is yes. What about a third dress? Now the marginal revenue is equal to the marginal cost, so it is a matter of

Exhibit 5–5   **Maximizing Profits at the Tailor Dress Company**

Quantity of Dresses	Price	Total Revenue	Marginal Revenue	Total Cost	Marginal Cost	Profit
1	$10/dress	$10	$10/dress	$ 6	$ 4/dress	$ 4
2	9	18	8	11	5	7
3	8	24	6	17	6	7
4	7	28	4	24	7	4
5	6	30	2	32	8	-2
6	5	30	0	41	9	-11
7	4	28	-2	51	10	-23
8	3	24	-4	62	11	-38

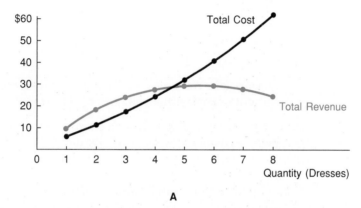

A

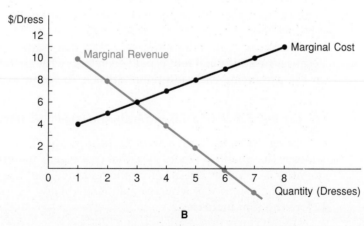

B

There are two ways for the Tailor Dress Company to choose a profit-maximizing quantity, each of which leads to the same outcome. Using Method 1, Tailor scans the profit column looking for the largest entry. This is the same as looking for the point of maximum distance between the total cost and total revenue curves. Using Method 2, Tailor scans the marginal columns and chooses the quantity at which marginal cost and marginal revenue are equal. This is the same as looking for the point where the marginal cost and marginal revenue curves cross. Using either method, Tailor will be led to produce 3 dresses and will earn a profit of $7.

indifference whether to provide the third dress. In accordance with our conventions, we assume that Tailor goes ahead and produces the third dress. Now when we come to the fourth row in the column, Tailor finds that marginal cost exceeds marginal revenue. Making the fourth dress is a bad idea, so Tailor stops after three.

Graphically, Method 2 consists of looking for the point where the marginal cost and marginal revenue curves cross.

The validity of Method 2 is an application of the equimarginal principle. It reveals that:

Any firm produces that quantity at which marginal cost equals marginal revenue.

Changes in Cost Schedules

From the validity of Method 2, it follows that:

Any change in circumstances that does not affect anything marginal will not affect the behavior of the firm.

(There is one exception: A change in circumstances that causes the firm to shut down or go out of business will certainly affect its behavior, in that it will produce a quantity of zero. This will happen precisely when the firm can earn only negative profits.)

To illustrate this point, suppose that the landlord who owns the building where the Tailor Dress Company is located announces a rent increase from $2 to $5 per week. How will this affect the firm's costs? It will raise its total cost by $3 per week regardless of how many dresses it manufactures and sells. However, marginal costs will be unaffected because the additional rent is paid even before the first dress is sewn. The cost of producing each additional dress is the same as it was before this rent increase. Exhibit 5–6 illustrates the new situation.

▷ *Exercise 5.8* Verify the entries in the table in Exhibit 5–6.

Using Method 2 to maximize profits, the Tailor Dress Company chooses the quantity where marginal cost equals marginal revenue. That quantity is 3, just as it was before the rent increase. The price it charges is $8, the highest price at which demanders will buy 3 dresses, just as it was before the rent increase.

We can verify this result by using Method 1: Scan the profit column and look for the largest possible profit. We find that this occurs at a quantity of 3, with a profit of $4 (per week).

The most important point of this example is that we could have predicted in advance that the rent increase would not affect price or quantity, simply on the basis of the observation that the rent increase did not affect anything marginal and the fact that only marginal quantities

Exhibit 5–6   **The Effect of a Rent Increase**

Quantity of Dresses	Price	Total Revenue	Marginal Revenue	Total Cost	Marginal Cost	Profit
1	$10/dress	$10	$10/dress	$ 9	$ 4/dress	$ 1
2	9	18	8	14	5	4
3	8	24	6	20	6	4
4	7	28	4	27	7	1
5	6	30	2	35	8	−5
6	5	30	0	44	9	−14
7	4	28	−2	54	10	−26
8	3	24	−4	65	11	−41

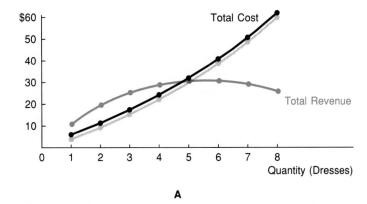

A

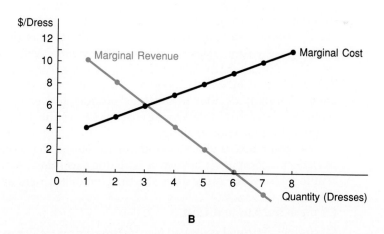

B

The table is derived from the table in Exhibit 5–5 by incorporating a $3 increase in rent. This increases total cost by $3 everywhere, but does not affect marginal cost. Therefore the point of maximum profit is unaffected. The light-colored curve in panel A is the old total cost curve, from Exhibit 5–5. Although the distance between total cost and total revenue has decreased, the point of maximum distance is still at a quantity of 3.

matter. Therefore we know that the same result will hold for any change in costs that does not affect marginal costs.

▷ *Exercise 5.9* Predict what will happen if the rent increases by $4 per week rather than by $3 per week. Make a table to verify your prediction.

Sunk Costs Are Sunk

Prior to the rent increase, Tailor earned a profit of $7. The rent increase leaves Mr. Tailor, the owner, poorer by the amount of $3 per week. You might wonder why Tailor does not attempt to compensate for this loss by changing his price. The answer to this question can be found in Exhibit 5–6: There *is* no price that brings Tailor a profit of more than $4 per week. No change in pricing policy can benefit Mr. Tailor; he can only make himself worse off if he tries.

If this seems counterintuitive, ask yourself the following question: If Tailor could make greater profits by producing some quantity other than 3, or by charging some price other than $8, then why wasn't he already doing so before the rent was increased? If he has been profit-maximizing all along, why would a rent increase cause him to alter his strategy?

If you still aren't convinced, ask yourself these questions: If Tailor had accidentally lost a dollar bill down a sewer, would he change his business practices as a result? If he *did* change his business practices because of this bad luck, wouldn't you wonder whether those practices had been especially well thought out in the first place? Now, is the rent increase any different from losing a dollar bill in a sewer?[3]

Economists sum up the moral of this fable in this slogan:

Sunk costs are sunk.

Sunk cost
A cost that can no longer be avoided.

The dollar rent increase is a **sunk cost** from the moment that the Tailor Dress Company decides to continue producing dresses at all; from that moment it is irretrievable. Once a cost has been sunk, it becomes irrelevant to any future decision making.

However, before you learn too well the lesson that a rent increase does not affect a company's behavior, note one exception: A sufficiently large rent increase will simply drive the firm out of business altogether.

Changes in Marginal Cost

Of course, marginal costs can also change. Suppose, for example, that the price of fabric goes up. In this case the cost of making a dress will certainly rise. The Tailor Dress Company's *total* costs will go up, and its *marginal* costs will go up as well. This example is very different from the example of the

---

[3]There is one way in which the lost dollar is different from the rent increase. Mr. Tailor might be able to avoid the rent increase by going out of business entirely, but there is no way for him to recover his dollar. However, once Tailor decides to remain in business, either dollar is lost irretrievably.

Exhibit 5–7   **An Increase in the Price of Fabric**

Quantity of Dresses	Price	Total Revenue	Marginal Revenue	Total Cost	Marginal Cost	Profit
1	$10/dress	$10	$10/dress	$ 9	$ 7/dress	$ 1
2	9	18	8	17	8	1
3	8	24	6	26	9	−2
4	7	28	4	36	10	−8
5	6	30	2	47	11	−17
6	5	30	0	59	12	−29
7	4	28	−2	72	13	−44
8	3	24	−4	86	14	−62

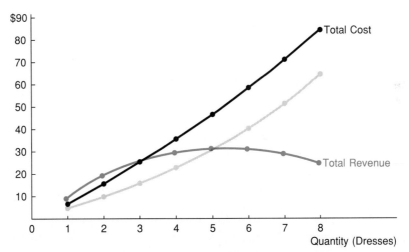

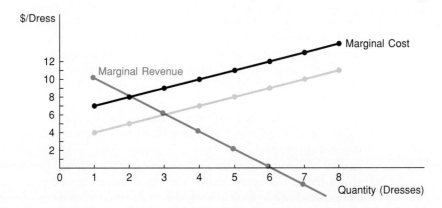

When the price of fabric increases by $3 per square yard, marginal costs increase at the Tailor Dress Company. The new cost curves can be compared with the original (light-colored) curves reproduced from Exhibit 5–5. The shift in total cost is no longer parallel, so the point of maximum distance between it and total revenue is able to shift. The new point of maximum profit occurs at a quantity of 2 and a price of $9.

rent increase, where only fixed costs changed. Returning to Exhibit 5–5 (where the rent is still $2 per week), assume that the price of fabric goes up by $3 per square yard, and each dress requires exactly one square yard of cloth. Now the total cost of making one dress will be $3 higher than before, the total cost of making 2 dresses will be $6 higher, and so on. The marginal cost of making any given dress will be $3 higher than before. The new situation is illustrated in Exhibit 5–7.

In this circumstance the marginal cost curve shifts from its original position in Exhibit 5–5, so that it now crosses the marginal revenue curve at a quantity of 2. This is the new point of maximum profit. Since marginal cost is the slope of total cost, the change in marginal cost is equivalent to a nonparallel shift in total cost. This nonparallel shift allows a change in the point of maximum distance between total cost and total revenue. The new maximum is now at 2, where marginal cost crosses marginal revenue.

Tailor will now sell two dresses at a price of $9 apiece. The change in marginal costs will affect the firm's behavior, even though the earlier change in fixed costs could not.

Changes in the Revenue Schedule

We now understand a great deal about how and when changes in a firm's schedule of costs will affect its economic behavior. However, it is important to realize that this is not the whole story: Changes in the firm's marginal revenue schedule can affect its behavior as well. This is because both marginal revenue and marginal cost are used in the Method 2 calculations for maximizing profits. Therefore it is important to understand the circumstances under which a firm's marginal revenue schedule might change.

Referring to Exhibit 5–5, you will see that when we computed marginal revenue, it was determined completely by the demand curve for Tailor dresses. We used the demand curve to determine the right price to charge for any given quantity, then calculated total revenue by multiplying price times quantity, then calculated marginal revenue from that. What can affect marginal revenue? The answer is: Anything that affects the demand curve.

Our question then becomes: What can affect the demand curve for the Tailor Dress Company? First, anything that affects the demand curve for dresses in general—changes in income, changes in the prices of related goods, and so on. But there are other factors as well. Suppose the Seamstress Dress Company down the street closes up shop for good and its customers have to look elsewhere for dresses. In that case the demand for Tailor's product will probably rise, and so will its marginal revenue curve. It is likely to end up producing a different number of dresses at a different price.

We can continue this line of inquiry one step further back and ask what might have driven the Seamstress Dress Company out of business. One possibility is a very large increase in rent at the Seamstress building. So we have the remarkable conclusion that although a rise in the Tailor Dress Company's rent will not lead to a change in Tailor's prices, a rise in someone *else's* rent very well *could* have that effect—provided that the "someone else" is a competitor who is driven out of business by the rent increase.

Summary

We assume that firms act to maximize profits. This implies that they will act in accordance with the equimarginal principle; that is, they will engage in any activity up to the point where marginal cost equals marginal benefit.

When the firm sells goods in the marketplace, it chooses the profit-maximizing quantity. In accordance with the equimarginal principle, this is the quantity at which marginal cost equals marginal revenue. The firm sells this quantity at a price determined by the demand curve for its product.

The total revenue derived from selling a given quantity is given by the formula Revenue = Price × Quantity, where the price is read off the demand curve. Thus the total revenue curve, and consequently the marginal revenue curve, are determined by the demand curve for the firm's product.

A change in the firm's fixed costs, because it affects nothing marginal, will not affect the quantity or price of the firm's output. There is one exception: A sufficiently large increase in fixed costs will cause the firm to shut down or leave the industry entirely.

A change in marginal costs can lead to a change in the firm's behavior. So can a change in marginal revenue. Any change in the demand curve facing the firm can lead to a change in marginal revenue. For example, a change in the availability of competing products can affect demand, and consequently marginal revenue, and consequently the behavior of the firm.

Review Questions

R1. State and explain the equimarginal principle.

R2. What formula defines a firm's profits? What formula defines its revenue?

R3. How might each of the following affect the behavior of a firm? (a) A change in marginal costs, (b) a change in fixed costs, (c) a change in the demand for the firm's product, (d) a competitor leaving the industry.

Numerical Exercises

In the following exercises suppose that x liters of orange juice can be produced for a total cost of x^2.

N1. Write down a formula for the marginal cost of production when x liters of orange juice are produced. Simplify your formula algebraically.

N2. Suppose now that orange juice is measured in centiliters (there are 100 centiliters in a liter). Write a formula for the total cost of producing y centiliters of orange juice. (*Hint:* When you produce y centiliters, how many liters are you producing? What is the associated cost?)

N3. Write a formula for the marginal cost of production when y centiliters are produced. Your formula gives the marginal cost in dollars per centiliter. Express the same formula in terms of dollars per liter.

N4. On the basis of your answer to Exercise N3, would you be willing to say that the marginal cost when x liters are produced is about $2x per liter? Why or why not?

N5. Now measure orange juice in milliliters (there are 1,000 milliliters in a liter). Write formulas for total cost and marginal cost when orange juice is measured in milliliters. Convert your marginal cost formula from dollars per milliliter to dollars per liter. Are you now more confident of your answer to Exercise N4? What do you think will happen if you measure orange juice in even smaller units?

Problem Set

1. The U.S. government has invested over a billion dollars deploying a weapons system that can now be made operational for less than 1% of the outlays to date. *True or false:* Since 99% of the cost of this weapons system has already been spent, it would be foolish to consider junking the project now.

2. *True or false:* If you bought gold last year for $1,000 an ounce, and if gold is now selling for only $300 an ounce, it would be a mistake to sell now because you'd lose a lot of money.

3. The following problem recently appeared on an examination at a major university:

   Suppose that the current population of the town where you sell soap is 20,000. Suppose that you know from marketing research that 10% of the population will buy your product in a given week. Here is a table of your total revenue (TR) minus total cost (TC) for various sales volumes:

Q	TR – TC
1,000	$4,000
2,000	5,000
3,000	6,000
4,000	7,000

   Suppose that you wish to have profits of $4,000. How much can you spend on advertising?

   List the objectionable assumptions underlying this problem. How would you rewrite the problem to make it a reasonable one?

4. Comment on the following headline from a major daily newspaper: "Rental Vacancies on the Rise: Apartment Owners May Have to Raise Rents to Compensate."

5. Which of the following might affect the price of a hamburger at Waldo's
    Lunch Counter and why?
    a. The price of meat goes up.
    b. A new restaurant tax of 50¢ per hamburger is imposed.
    c. Waldo's is discovered to be in violation of a safety code, and the
        violation is one that would be prohibitively expensive to correct.
        As a result, Waldo is certain to incur a fine of $500 per year from
        now on.
    d. A new restaurant tax of $500 per year is imposed.
    e. Waldo recalculates and realizes that the redecoration he did last
        month cost him 15% more than he thought it had.
    f. Word gets around that a lot of Waldo's customers have been having
        stomach problems lately.

6. a. Suppose that a famous Chicago Cubs baseball player threatens to
        quit unless his salary is doubled, and the management accedes to
        his demand. *True or false:* The fans will have to pay for this through
        higher ticket prices.
    b. Now suppose that the Cubs hire a famous and popular player away
        from the Philadelphia Phillies. Explain what will happen to ticket
        prices now.

7. A firm faces the following demand and total cost schedules.

Demand		Total Cost	
P	Q	Q	TC
$10	1	1	$ 2
8	2	2	7
6	3	3	13
4	4	4	20
2	5	5	29

How much does it produce and at what price? How do you know?

Refer to Answers to Problem Sets for solutions to problems 2 and 7.

Chapter Six

Production and Costs

In Chapter 5 we saw the important role that cost curves play in determining a firm's behavior. In this chapter we will back up a step and ask how the cost curves themselves are determined. The brief answer is that they arise from the technology available for the firm to use in producing goods. Therefore we will begin, in Section 6.1, by developing a graphic representation of the many production processes that a firm might consider using.

In the remainder of the chapter, we will see how the firm's cost curves arise from the available technology. In Chapter 7 we will be able to use these cost curves to develop a deeper understanding of the supply curves of many firms and industries.

6.1 Technology

Consumption goods (or outputs)
Goods that individuals want to consume.

The goods in an economy can be roughly classified into two sorts: **consumption goods** (or **outputs**), which contribute directly to individuals' utility, and **productive inputs**, also called **factors of production**, which are

129

Productive inputs (or **factors of production**)
Goods that are used to produce outputs.

combined to create consumption goods. The job of the firm is to convert factors of production into outputs.

Factors of production are traditionally classified into the three broad categories of land, labor, and capital. Of these, land and labor need no further explanation, but capital does. Students are often confused by the use of the word *capital* in their economics courses, because economists use the word in a way that differs from ordinary usage. As a first approximation, **capital** in economics refers to physical assets, such as machines and factories, that enter directly into the production process.[1] The term does *not* include financial assets, such as stocks and bonds, which are sometimes called *capital* by noneconomists.

Capital
Physical assets used as factors of production.

We will consider a good, X, that is produced with two inputs. For concreteness, we will refer to the inputs as *labor* and *capital*, but the same analysis could apply to any two inputs. We could also study goods produced with three or more inputs. When one of these inputs (say labor) is the immediate focus of discussion, it is often productive to treat labor as one input and "all other inputs" as another.

Isoquants

Typically, there are many ways to produce a unit of X. What can be done by 3 workers with 5 machines can perhaps also be done by 6 workers with only 1 machine. Exhibit 6–1 shows the set of all combinations that suffice to produce one unit of X in a given period of time. The vertical axis, labeled K, represents capital, and the horizontal axis, labeled L, represents labor. (K is traditionally used instead of C for capital in order to avoid any possible confusion with consumption.) The period of time is implicitly fixed; for example, we might be speaking of producing one unit of X per day. Appropriate units for labor and capital are, for example, "man-hours per day" and "machine-hours per day."

Technologically inefficient
A production process that uses more inputs than necessary to produce a given output.

In Exhibit 6–1 every basket of inputs in the shaded part of the graph will suffice to produce a unit of X. However, points that are off the boundary (like B) are **technologically inefficient** in the sense that there are other baskets of inputs, containing both less capital and less labor, that will also suffice to produce a unit of X. (For example, basket A contains smaller quantities of both inputs than basket B does.) No firm would want to produce a unit of X using a technologically inefficient basket of inputs. Thus we will ignore these baskets and concentrate on the technologically efficient ones. In Exhibit 6–1 the technologically efficient baskets for producing a unit of X are represented by the heavy curve that bounds the shaded region. That curve is called the **unit isoquant.**

Unit isoquant
The set of all technically efficient ways to produce one unit of output.

Why is the unit isoquant shaped as it is? Note first that no point to the northeast of A can be on the unit isoquant, because any such point (like B) is technologically inefficient. For the same reason, no point to the north-

---

[1]Later in this book we shall adopt a more general definition.

Exhibit 6–1   The Unit Isoquant

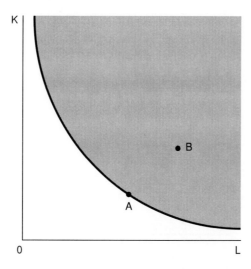

The shaded region represents all of the different baskets of capital and labor that can be used to produce one unit of X. Baskets that are off the boundary, like B, are technologically inefficient, in that a unit of X can be produced by a different basket (like A) containing smaller quantities of both inputs. The technologically efficient baskets for producing a unit of X are those on the unit isoquant, which is the heavy curve that bounds the shaded region.

east of *any* point on the unit isoquant can also lie on the unit isoquant. It follows that the points on the isoquant must all be to either the northwest or the southeast of each other. Another way to say this is:

The unit isoquant is downward sloping.

The Marginal Rate of Technical Substitution

Suppose that each day a firm uses the basket of inputs A to produce one unit of X. One day an employee calls in sick, making it necessary to get by with one less unit of labor. How much additional capital will the firm have to use in order to maintain the daily output level? The answer is shown in Exhibit 6–2. Reducing labor input by one unit corresponds geometrically to moving one unit to the left; maintaining an output level of one unit of X corresponds geometrically to staying on the isoquant. Taken together, these requirements mandate that the firm move to point A′. The vertical distance between A and A′ is the additional capital that must be added to the usual daily ration. That vertical distance has been labeled ΔK in Exhibit 6–2.

Exhibit 6–2   The Marginal Rate of Technical Substitution

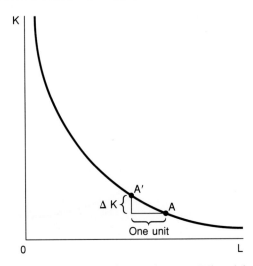

The firm produces one unit of X per day using basket A of inputs. When labor input is reduced by one unit, capital input must be increased by ΔK units in order for the firm to remain on the isoquant and maintain its level of output. The number ΔK is the marginal rate of technical substitution of labor for capital.

Marginal rate of technical substitution of labor for capital The amount of capital that can be substituted for one unit of labor, holding output constant.

For all practical purposes, the distance ΔK is equal to the slope of the isoquant at the point A.[2] The absolute value of this slope is called the **marginal rate of technical substitution of labor for capital,** abbreviated $MRTS_{LK}$; it is the amount of capital necessary to replace one unit of labor while maintaining a constant level of output.

▷ *Exercise 6.1* Give a definition and a geometric interpretation for the marginal rate of technical substitution of *capital* for *labor.*

Suppose that a construction firm produces one house per day by employing 100 carpenters and 10 power tools. Then it is reasonable to think that when a carpenter calls in sick, the firm can maintain its level of production through a small increase in power tool usage. On the other hand, if the same firm produces the same one house per day by employing 10 carpenters and 100 power tools, we expect it to need a much larger increase in tool usage to compensate for the same absent carpenter. In other words, when much labor and little capital are employed to produce a unit of output, the $MRTS_{LK}$ is small, but when little labor and much capital are employed to produce the same unit of output, the $MRTS_{LK}$ is large.

---

[2]The line through A and A′ is nearly tangent to the isoquant, and can be made more nearly tangent by measuring labor in smaller units when it is desirable to do so. Its slope is equal to the rise over the run, which is $-\Delta K\,/\,1$, or $-\Delta K$.

Exhibit 6–3 **The Production Function**

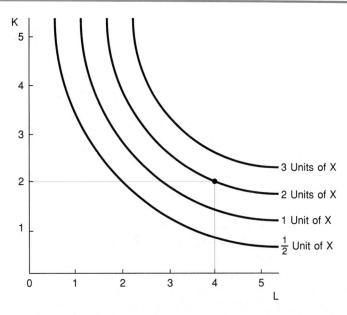

The family of isoquants can be used to determine the maximum level of production that can be attained with any given level of inputs. For example, if the firm uses 4 units of labor and 2 of capital, then it can produce 2 units of output and no more. This rule for calculating the output that can be produced from a given basket of inputs is the firm's production function.

Geometrically, this means that at points far to the southeast the isoquant is shallow, while at points far to the northwest it is steep. That is, the isoquant is convex.

The Production Function

Suppose that the firm wants to produce 2 units of X instead of one. We can draw an isoquant representing all of the technologically efficient input combinations that the firm can use. This "2-unit" isoquant lies above and to the right of the original "one-unit" isoquant. We can go on to draw isoquants for any given level of output, generating a family of isoquants such as the one shown in Exhibit 6–3.

The important facts about isoquants are these:

Isoquants slope downward, they fill the plane, they never cross, and they are convex.

You should recognize this list of properties; it characterizes families of indifference curves as well.

▷ *Exercise 6.2* Explain why isoquants never cross. Explain why they fill the plane.

Suppose that we want to know how much output the firm can produce with a given basket of inputs. We can use the family of isoquants to answer this question. For example, suppose that we want to know how much the firm can produce using 4 units of labor and 2 units of capital. From Exhibit 6–3 we see that this basket lies on the 2-unit isoquant; thus the firm can use this basket to produce 2 units of X.

Production function
The rule for determining how much output can be produced with a given basket of inputs.

The rule for determining how much output can be produced with a given basket of inputs is called the firm's **production function.** If we know the family of isoquants, then we know the production function, and vice versa. Therefore we can think of the graph in Exhibit 6–3 as providing a picture of the firm's production function.

The Choice of a Production Process

For any level of output the corresponding isoquant presents the firm with a menu of ways in which to produce that output. Each point on the isoquant should be thought of as corresponding to a different production process. Each of these processes has a cost, determined by the prices of labor and capital. Ideally, the firm would like to choose the least-cost process for producing any given level of output.

Unfortunately, changing from one production process to another is not always possible over short periods of time. Therefore, although the firm can choose any point on the isoquant in the long run, it might have much more limited choices in the short run. As a result the firm's costs might be very different depending on how long it has to make adjustments. This necessitates two separate analyses of production and costs: one in which the firm can make only limited adjustments (the short run) and one in which it can choose any point on the isoquant (the long run). These are the topics of the next two sections.

6.2 Production and Costs in the Short Run

In the short run the firm has limited options. The Chrysler Corporation cannot decide to instantly change the number of assembly lines that it operates. Union contracts might prevent immediate adjustments in the amount of labor employed. The short-run analysis of production and costs, which is the topic of this section, is designed to take account of this phenomenon.

Fixed factor of production
One that the firm must employ in a given quantity.

Fixed and Variable Factors

We say that a **factor of production** is **fixed** if the firm cannot change the quantity of that factor that it employs. A factor is **variable** when the firm can make such changes. A power plant cannot easily change the number of

Variable factor of production
One that the firm can employ in varying quantities.

dams that it operates, but it may be able to adjust the size of its work force at a moment's notice. In this case dams are a fixed factor and labor is a variable factor. To a farmer land may be a fixed factor.

The distinction between fixed and variable factors is a vague one, and a given factor may be either fixed or variable depending on the time period in which changes must be made. A new dam cannot be constructed in five minutes, but it can in five years. Over five minutes dams are a fixed factor, but over five years they are a variable factor. Given a sufficiently long time, any factor is variable.

Short run
A period of time over which some factors are fixed.

Long run
A period of time over which all factors are variable.

In many circumstances one factor is more easily variable than another over an important period of time, and much insight can be gained from a simplified model that assumes one factor completely variable and the others completely fixed. A time period in which such a model applies is referred to by economists as the **short run.** The short run is to be distinguished from the **long run,** which is a period of time sufficient for all factors to be considered variable.

Product Curves

For purposes of illustration, we shall adopt a vision of the short run in which capital is fixed and labor is variable. We will assume that the firm's employment of capital is fixed at 5 units. This is indicated in Exhibit 6–4. The firm is constrained to operate on the horizontal line corresponding to 5 units of capital. For example, if the firm wants to produce 3 units of output, it must operate at point A.

The black points in Exhibit 6–4 are typical of those available to the firm. Each corresponds to a quantity of labor (read from the labor axis) and a quantity of output X (read from the label on the corresponding isoquant). For any quantity of labor input, we can use the graph to see how much the firm can produce. For example, if the firm employs 2 units of labor, it can achieve 7 units of output at point B. If it employs 3 units of labor, it can achieve 12 units of output, at point C.

Total product
The quantity of output that can be produced with a given input.

Short-run production function
The rule for determining how much output can be produced with a given amount of labor input in the short run (with capital employment held fixed).

This information is recorded in the table and panel A of Exhibit 6–5. For a given quantity of labor, the corresponding quantity of X is called the **total product.** The curve that relates labor to output is called the firm's *total product curve.* Sometimes it is also called the firm's **short-run production function.**

Marginal product of labor
The additional output due to employing one more unit of labor (with capital employment held fixed).

We define the **marginal product of labor** (abbreviated MP_L) to be the additional output due to the last unit of labor employed. For example, when the amount of labor is increased from 5 to 6, the total product increases by 2 units (from 19 to 21), so at that point the marginal product of labor is 2 units of output per unit of labor employed.

Total product and marginal product of labor must be plotted on separate graphs because the units are different on the vertical axes. Total product is measured in units of X, whereas marginal product of labor is measured in units of X *per* unit of labor.

Exhibit 6–4   The Firm's Short-Run Production Possibilities

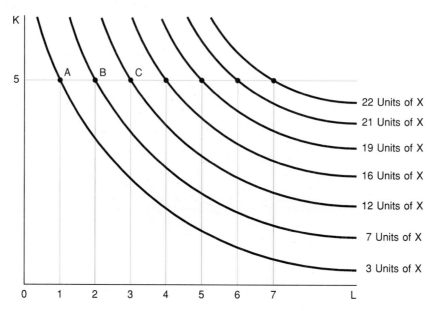

If the firm employs 5 units of capital and cannot vary this in the short run, then the only possibilities available to it are those on the horizontal line. If it wants to produce 16 units of output, the only way it can do so is by employing 5 units of capital and 4 units of labor.

The marginal product of labor can be thought of as the slope of the total product curve. When we go from 5 units of labor to 6, the amount of labor input is increased by 1 unit, while the quantity of output is increased by 2 units. The slope of the total product curve is therefore approximately 2 / 1 = 2, which is the marginal product of labor.

The Shapes of the Product Curves

We have drawn the total product curve sloping upward to indicate that increases in labor input lead to increases in output. Up to 3 units of labor, the total product curve increases in steepness (the marginal product curve is increasing); thereafter it continues to slope upward but less and less steeply (marginal product decreases).

The shape we have chosen is fairly typical. The key to understanding it is to remember that the quantity of capital is fixed at 5 units throughout the entire discussion. This means that we are assuming a fixed plant size and a fixed number of machines. When there are very few workers, they are unable to make efficient use of all this capital. As a result, 2 workers may be able to do more than twice the work of 1 worker. This is largely due to the

Exhibit 6–5   **Total and Marginal Products**

Quantity of Labor	Total Product	Marginal Product of Labor
1	3	3
2	7	4
3	12	5
4	16	4
5	19	3
6	21	2
7	22	1

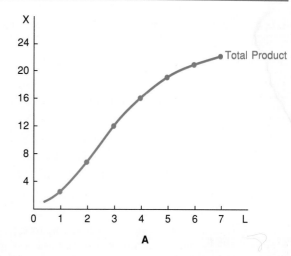

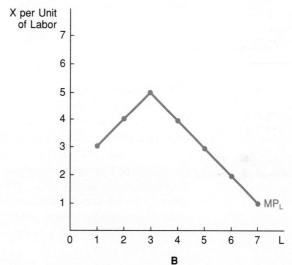

The total products in the table are taken from the graph in Exhibit 6–4. For example, the first row records the information from point A in Exhibit 6–4. The marginal product of labor (MP_L) is the additional output due to the last unit of labor employed. The MP_L is the slope of the total product curve.

advantages of *specialization*. A single worker operating an automobile assembly line will get dizzy rushing from place to place; a few workers located at strategic points along the line can each concentrate on a single task, making production much more efficient.

However, there comes a point beyond which each additional worker contributes relatively little to the enterprise. Four lumberjacks operating 1 chain saw will not cut down many more trees than 3 lumberjacks operating 1 chain saw. After enough lumberjacks have been added, the marginal product of lumberjacks could become negligible.

In fact, it could even become negative (although we haven't drawn it this way in Exhibit 6–5). It is easy to imagine that there could come a point beyond which the addition of laborers actually decreases total output. Four chefs in a crowded kitchen may bake fewer pies than 3 chefs in the same kitchen could.

▷ *Exercise 6.3* Draw the total product and marginal product of labor curves for a bakery in which additional bakers eventually begin to get in each other's way.

When the marginal product is decreasing (for example, in Exhibit 6–5, when more than 3 units of labor are employed), the firm is said to experience **diminishing marginal returns to labor.** We shall make the general assumption that beyond some level of employment, diminishing marginal returns are the rule. The level of employment at which the marginal product begins to decline is called the **point of diminishing marginal returns;** it occurs at L = 3 in our example.

Diminishing marginal returns to labor
The circumstance in which each unit of labor has a smaller marginal product than the last.

Point of diminishing marginal returns
A level of employment beyond which there are diminishing marginal returns.

Marginal Returns and the Marginal Rate of Technical Substitution

The marginal products of labor and capital determine the marginal rate of technical substitution. Suppose that labor input is reduced by one unit and that capital input is increased by ΔK units, where ΔK is just sufficient to maintain the old level of output. Then ΔK is the $MRTS_{LK}$.

Let us ask what happens to output at each of the two steps in this experiment. When the labor input is decreased by one unit, output goes down by the amount MP_L. When the capital input is increased, output goes up by MP_K units for each of the additional ΔK units of capital; thus output goes up by a total of $MP_K \cdot \Delta K$ units. The net effect is to maintain the old level of output, so that we must have

$$MP_L = MP_K \cdot \Delta K,$$

or

$$MRTS_{LK} = \Delta K = \frac{MP_L}{MP_K}.$$

This equation shows that the marginal rate of technical substitution is related to the marginal products of the factors. However, it is important to remember the conceptual distinction. When we measure the $MRTS_{LK}$, we imagine holding output fixed, varying labor input, and seeing how much capital input must vary. When we measure the MP_L, we imagine holding capital input fixed, varying labor input, and seeing how much output will vary.

Costs

In deciding how much to produce, the firm must be concerned with the costs of production. These costs are of two kinds: the cost of hiring capital (called the **rental rate** of capital) and the cost of hiring labor (called the **wage rate** of labor). The price per unit of capital is usually denoted P_K and the price per unit of labor is denoted P_L.

Rental rate
The price of hiring capital.

Wage rate
The price of hiring labor.

For example, suppose that The Dryden Press produces books by using printing presses that it rents for $10 per hour and typesetters whom it hires at a wage of $15 per hour. The printing presses are capital and the typesetters are labor, so we write P_K = $10 per hour and P_L = $15 per hour.

Suppose that The West Publishing Company also hires typesetters at $15 per hour but owns its own printing presses. Now you might be tempted to think that P_K is zero, or equal to the cost of maintaining and cleaning the presses. This is not correct. When West uses its own printing presses, it forgoes the opportunity to rent them to Dryden, or to some other publisher, at the market rate of $10 per hour. This is every bit as much a cost as Dryden's. Therefore West's rental rate on capital is exactly the same as Dryden's: $10 per hour.

 As the preceding paragraph illustrates, when the firm uses factors of production that it owns, we must be sure to include the associated opportunity costs in reckoning its costs.

For purposes of our example, we will continue to assume P_K = $10 and P_L = $15 and that the product curves are as given in Exhibit 6–5. Because the firm's use of capital is fixed at 5 machines in the short run, its daily expenditure on capital is the rental rate per machine multiplied by 5, in this case $10 · 5 = $50. This portion of the cost, which is a given number unaffected by the level of output chosen, is a **fixed cost.** Expenditure on labor is $15 · L, where L is the quantity of labor hired by the firm. This number depends on L, which the firm can choose. It is referred to as a **variable cost.**

Fixed cost
The cost of hiring fixed factors.

Variable cost
The cost of hiring variable factors.

The Variable Cost Curve

The firm's variable cost (VC) curve displays various quantities of X on the horizontal axis and their variable costs on the vertical axis. Given the wage rate of $15, the total product curve determines the VC curve. Both curves are shown in Exhibit 6–6. For example, we see from point C on the total product curve that 3 units of X require 1 unit of labor. Since 1 unit of labor can be hired for $15, the variable cost of producing 3 units of output is exactly $15. This is shown by point C' on the VC curve. Similarly, point D shows that 7 units of X can be produced with 2 units of labor, which can be purchased for $30. Therefore the variable cost of producing 7 units is $30, as shown by point D'.

Exhibit 6–6   The Variable Cost Curve

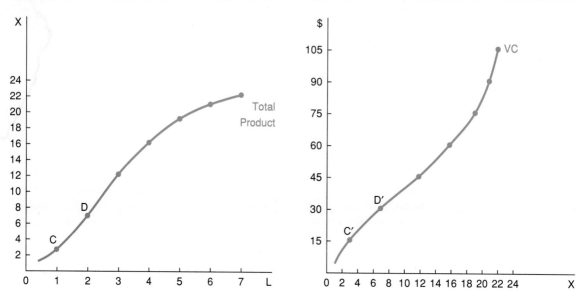

The total product curve is reproduced from Exhibit 6–5. The variable cost (VC) curve can be derived from the total product curve. For example, point C reveals that 3 units of X can be produced with 1 unit of labor, so the variable cost of producing 3 units of X is the cost of hiring 1 unit of labor. Assuming P_L = $15, this gives point C′.

▷ *Exercise 6.4* Suppose that the wage rate of labor changes to $20. Draw the new variable cost curve.

▷ *Exercise 6.5* What is the geometric relationship between the total product curve and the variable cost curve? In other words, what combination of flippings, reflections, and the like will convert one into the other?

The shape of the VC curve is determined by the shape of the total product curve. It is always increasing (producing more output is always costlier), but the rate of increase falls off at first, reflecting the gains from specialization as more labor is added. Eventually, the point of diminishing marginal returns is reached and the curve begins to get steeper, reflecting the fact that it takes more additional workers to produce a unit of X than it did before. Recall from Exhibit 6–5 that in our example the point of diminishing marginal returns is at L = 3, where X = 12; therefore X = 12 is the point where the slope of the VC curve begins to increase.

Exhibit 6–7 **The Total Cost Curve**

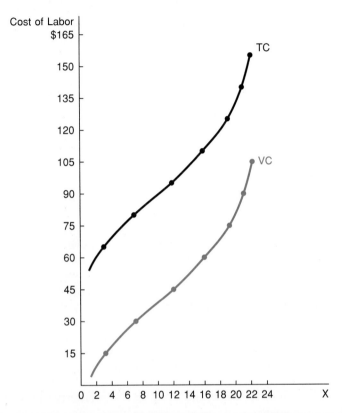

The variable cost (VC) curve is reproduced from Exhibit 6–6. The total cost (TC) curve is obtained by adding the fixed cost (in this example $50) to the VC curve. Thus the TC curve is always a parallel upward shift of the VC curve.

The Total Cost Curve

Total cost
The sum of fixed cost and variable cost.

The firm's **total cost** (TC) is the sum of its fixed cost (FC) and its variable cost (VC). In our example we have assumed that capital is a fixed factor and labor a variable one; therefore the firm's expenditure on capital is a fixed cost and its expenditure on labor is a variable cost. We have assumed that the firm rents 5 units of capital at a price of $10 per unit, so that in our example FC = $50. Exhibit 6–7 shows the variable cost curve (reproduced from Exhibit 6–6) and the total cost curve, which is obtained by shifting the variable cost curve vertically upward a distance $50.

Since the total cost curve is always obtained by shifting the variable cost curve vertically by a fixed amount, it has the same shape as the variable cost curve: increasing, at a rate that falls off at first and then begins to increase sharply.

Average and Marginal Cost Curves

In Exhibit 6–8 we have displayed the costs of producing various quantities of X, with all information taken from the graph in Exhibit 6–7. **Average cost** (AC) is the firm's average cost per item when a given quantity is produced; it is defined by the equation

Average cost
Total cost divided by quantity.

$$AC = \frac{TC}{Q} = \frac{FC}{Q} + \frac{VC}{Q},$$

Average variable cost
Variable cost divided by quantity.

where Q is the quantity of X being produced. **Average variable cost** (AVC) is just that portion of average cost that is attributable to variable costs. It is defined by the equation

$$AVC = \frac{VC}{Q}.$$

We have also displayed the firm's marginal cost (MC) for each quantity of X; as in Chapter 5, it is defined to be the additional cost associated with the last increment of X. Thus, for example, at a quantity of 6, the total cost is $76.58, whereas at a quantity of 5 it is $72.97; therefore the marginal cost at a quantity of 6 is $76.58 − $72.97 = $3.61. As we observed in Chapter 5, marginal cost is the slope of total cost.

▷ *Exercise 6.6* Which of the numbers in Exhibit 6–8 could be calculated directly from the numbers in Exhibit 6–5? Which could be calculated directly from the graph in Exhibit 6–7?

Here are the key facts about the geometry of the average and marginal cost curves:

1. The marginal cost curve is U-shaped. This reflects the shape of the total cost curve in Exhibit 6–7. Where the total cost curve is steep, marginal cost is high. This occurs both at low and high levels of output. At low levels of output, marginal cost is falling because of the advantages gained from specialization. At high levels of output, marginal cost is increasing because diminishing marginal returns have set in.

2. The average cost and average variable cost curves are also U-shaped.

3. When marginal cost is below average cost, average cost is falling. In Exhibit 6–8 this refers to the region in which the quantity of X is less than 20. To see why, consider, for example, the situation when 10 items have been produced. The average cost of producing each of those 10 items is $8.94. The last item is produced at a marginal cost of $2.98, which is below this average; therefore producing it has the effect of bringing the average down (from $9.60 to $8.94).

4. When marginal cost is above average cost, average cost is rising. In Exhibit 6–8 this refers to the region in which the quantity of X is greater than 20.

Exhibit 6–8   The Firm's Short-Run Cost Curves

Quantity	Variable Cost	Fixed Cost	Total Cost	Average Variable Cost	Average Cost	Marginal Cost
1	$ 5.58	$50	$ 55.58	$5.58	$55.58	$ 5.58
2	10.52	50	60.52	5.26	30.26	4.94
3	15	50	65	5.00	21.67	4.48
4	19.12	50	69.12	4.78	17.28	4.12
5	22.97	50	72.97	4.59	14.59	3.85
6	26.58	50	76.58	4.43	12.76	3.61
7	30	50	80	4.29	11.43	3.42
8	33.25	50	83.25	4.16	10.41	3.25
9	36.37	50	86.37	4.04	9.60	3.12
10	39.35	50	89.35	3.94	8.94	2.98
11	42.23	50	92.23	3.84	8.38	2.88
12	45	50	95	3.75	7.92	2.77
13	48.42	50	98.42	3.72	7.57	3.42
14	52.03	50	102.03	3.72	7.29	3.61
15	55.88	50	105.88	3.73	7.06	3.85
16	60	50	110	3.75	6.88	4.12
17	64.48	50	114.48	3.79	6.73	4.48
18	69.42	50	119.42	3.86	6.63	4.94
19	75	50	125	3.95	6.58	5.58
20	81.58	50	131.58	4.08	6.58	6.58
21	90	50	140	4.29	6.67	8.42
22	105	50	150	4.77	7.05	15.00

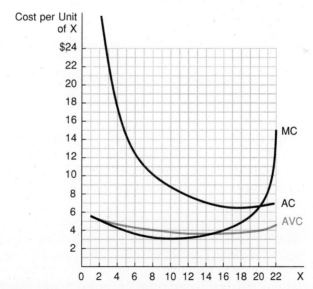

The table and the graph show the firm's average cost, average variable cost, and marginal cost at each level of output. All of this information can be calculated on the basis of knowing the firm's fixed and variable costs. The variable costs are displayed in Exhibit 6–6. The highlighted rows correspond to the darkened points in Exhibit 6–6, which come from the table in Exhibit 6–5.

5. Marginal cost crosses average cost at the point where average cost is minimized (that is, at the bottom of the average cost "U"). This is a geometric consequence of points 3 and 4. When marginal cost just equals average cost, average cost is just changing from falling to rising.

6. The analogues of points 3, 4, and 5 hold when average cost is replaced by average variable cost. When marginal cost is below average variable cost, average variable cost is falling; when marginal cost is above average variable cost, average variable cost is rising, and marginal cost crosses average variable cost when average variable cost is at a minimum.

The moral of this section is that all of the firm's short-run cost curves can be derived from knowledge of the firm's production function (that is, knowledge of the isoquants) and the prices of the factors of production. In later chapters we will see how all of the firm's supply behavior can be derived from knowledge of its cost curves. Therefore, just as the consumer's tastes, encoded in his indifference curves, are the key to understanding demand, so the firm's technology, encoded in its isoquants, is the key to understanding supply.

6.3 Production and Costs in the Long Run

In this section we will develop the long-run cost curves, which we will need when we study the firm's supply decisions in the long run. We shall see that the long-run cost curves, like the short-run cost curves, depend only on technology and factor prices.

Choosing a Production Process

In the long run no factor of production is fixed, and the firm is free to use any production process. In making its choice, the firm will be guided by the costs of the various processes. We will begin by developing a geometric device for keeping track of these costs.

Isocosts and Output Maximization

Suppose that the firm can hire labor at a going wage rate of P_L and can hire capital at a going rental rate of P_K. Suppose also, for the moment, that the firm spends an amount E on inputs. Then the firm will be able to purchase L units of labor and K units of capital if and only if L and K satisfy the equation

$$P_L \cdot L + P_K \cdot K = E.$$

Isocost
The set of all baskets of inputs that can be employed at a given cost.

The collection of pairs (L,K) that satisfy this equation form a straight line with slope $-(P_L/P_K)$. That line, called an **isocost,** is shown in Exhibit 6–9.

Exhibit 6–9 **Maximizing Output for a Given Expenditure**

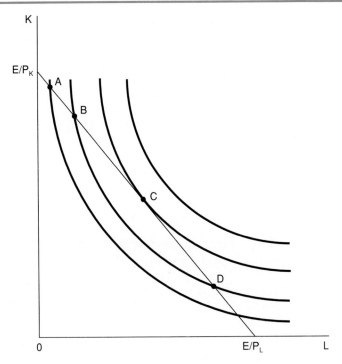

If the firm spends the amount E to hire inputs, it can choose any production process along the isocost line, such as A, B, C, or D. Of these it will choose the one that yields the greatest output, which is the point of tangency C.

Given the level of expenditure E, the firm can choose any point on the pictured isocost. For example, the firm can choose any of points A, B, C, or D. Because it is always better to have more output than less, the firm will choose the point on the highest possible isoquant. This occurs at the tangency C.

In order to maximize output for a given expenditure on inputs, the firm will always choose to operate at a point of tangency between an isocost and an isoquant.

Output Maximization and the Equimarginal Principle

There is another way to reach the same conclusion. Suppose that the firm considers spending an additional dollar to hire more labor. What are the marginal benefit and marginal cost of doing so?

By spending an extra dollar, the firm will be able to hire an additional $1/P_L$ units of labor, each of which will increase output by the amount MP_L. Therefore the marginal benefit of spending a dollar on labor is that output will increase by MP_L/P_L. However, the extra dollar spent hiring labor means that the firm must spend a dollar less on capital (this is because we are holding total expenditures fixed in this discussion). Therefore the firm must hire $1/P_K$ fewer units of capital, each of which would have increased output by MP_K. So the marginal cost of spending another dollar on labor is a reduction in output by MP_K/P_K.

We know from the equimarginal principle that the firm should choose a point where marginal benefit and marginal cost are equal. In other words, it should seek to set

$$\frac{MP_L}{P_L} = \frac{MP_K}{P_K}.$$

Rearranging terms, this is the same as

$$\frac{MP_L}{MP_K} = \frac{P_L}{P_K}.$$

The left side of this equation is equal to the $MRTS_{LK}$, which is the absolute value of the slope of the isoquant. The right side is the absolute value of the slope of the isocost. So the equimarginal principle dictates that the firm should operate where the slope of the isoquant and the slope of the isocost are equal, which occurs at the point of tangency.

What if the firm makes the mistake of operating at point A in Exhibit 6–9? At A the isoquant is steeper than the isocost, so we can write

$$\frac{MP_L}{MP_K} = MRTS_{LK} > \frac{P_L}{P_K}$$

and rearrange terms to get

$$\frac{MP_L}{P_L} > \frac{MP_K}{P_K}.$$

Now suppose that the firm considers spending a dollar more on labor and a dollar less on capital. Under this policy, output would increase by MP_L/L as a result of the additional labor input and decrease by MP_K/P_K as a result of the reduction in capital input. According to the inequality, the first effect is greater, so output increases. Therefore the firm will adopt this policy, moving down and to the right along the isocost to a point like B. This will continue until MP_L/P_L and MP_K/P_K become equal at the tangency C.

▷ *Exercise 6.7* Give a similar description of the adjustment process that takes place if the firm starts at point D.

The Expansion Path

All of this should have a familiar ring to it; it is reminiscent of the way in which consumers choose bundles of output goods to purchase. However, the analogy is less close than it first appears. There is one critical difference

Exhibit 6–10 **The Expansion Path**

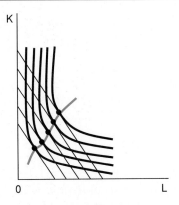

Unlike the consumer, who is constrained to his budget line, the firm can choose any level of expenditure on inputs. That is, it can choose to be on any isocost. It will always want to be at a point where the isocost is tangent to an isoquant. Thus the firm might choose any of the darkened points in the diagram. The curve through these points is the firm's expansion path. In order to determine which of the points on the expansion path the firm will choose, it is necessary to take account of the firm's marginal revenue curve. This requires additional information that is not shown in this diagram.

between the consumer, who seeks a tangency between his budget line and an indifference curve, and the firm, which seeks a tangency between an isocost and an isoquant.

The difference is this: A consumer has a *given* income to divide among consumption goods, whereas a firm can *choose* its level of expenditure on inputs. Put another way, a consumer is constrained to only one budget line, whereas a firm has a whole *family* of isocosts (one for each level of expenditure) from which it can choose.

Unlike an individual, a firm has no budget constraint. The reason is that individuals pursue consumption, whereas firms pursue profits. As a result, the firm can "afford" to spend any amount on inputs that is appropriate to its goal. Even when there is a limited amount of cash on hand, a profit-maximizing firm can borrow against its future profits to achieve whatever is the optimal level of expenditure and output. The same borrowing opportunities are not available to an individual who decides he wants to visit Hawaii.

In terms of our graphs, the consequence of all this is that we must consider the entire family of isocost lines available to the firm. They will all be parallel, since they all have the same slope $-(P_L/P_K)$, but those reflecting higher levels of expenditure will be farther out than others.[3] This is shown in Exhibit 6–10.

[3] We are assuming that P_L and P_K are not affected by the actions of the firm. This assumption would fail only if the firm in question hired a significant proportion of either all the labor or all the capital in the economy.

Expansion path
The set of tangencies
between isoquants and
isocosts.

The tangencies between isocosts and isoquants lie along a curve called the firm's **expansion path.** We know that the firm will choose one of these tangencies. However, we have not yet said anything that allows us to determine which tangency the firm will choose. In order to fully predict the firm's behavior, we know from Chapter 5 that we need to take account of the marginal revenue curve, which is derived from the demand for the firm's output. Since this information does not appear in the expansion path diagram, it is not surprising that we cannot use the diagram to predict the firm's behavior.

Cost Minimization

We have spoken of the firm as first determining a level of expenditure (choosing an isocost) and then maximizing output for that expenditure (which occurs at a tangency with an isoquant). There is also a different way to view the firm's problem. We can think of the firm as first deciding how much to produce (choosing an isoquant) and then producing that output in the least expensive way possible. Exhibit 6–11 shows the isoquant the firm has chosen, together with several isocosts. In order to stay on the isoquant and minimize costs, the firm must choose that point on the isoquant that is on the lowest possible isocost. This occurs at the tangency F.

Exhibit 6–11   **Cost Minimization**

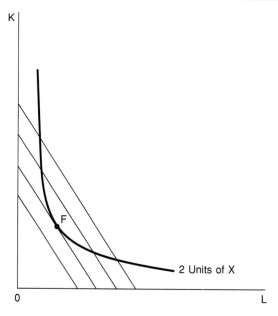

In order to produce 2 units of X, the firm must select a production process on the 2-unit isoquant. Of these processes, it will choose the one that is least costly, which is to say the one on the lowest isocost, namely F.

Exhibit 6–12   **Short-Run versus Long-Run Production**

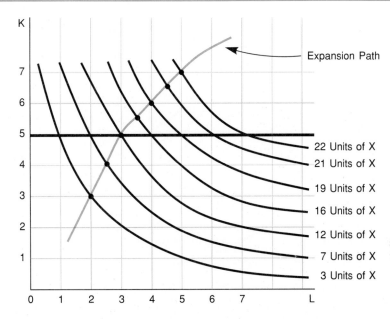

In the short run, the firm is committed to using 5 units of capital. Therefore if it wants to produce 19 units of output, it must select the production process where the 19-unit isoquant meets the horizontal line K = 5. There it employs 5 units of labor and 5 units of capital. In the long run, the firm can adjust its capital usage and can pick the least expensive production process on the isoquant, which occurs on the expansion path at (4,6). In the long run, the firm employs 4 units of labor and 6 units of capital.

In summary, there are two ways to look at the firm's problem, both leading to the same conclusion. We can think of choosing a level of expenditure and then maximizing output, or we can think of choosing a level of output and then minimizing expenditure. From either point of view, the solution is to choose a tangency between an isocost and an isoquant, that is, a point on the firm's expansion path.

The Long-Run Cost Curves

We can use the firm's expansion path to construct its long-run cost curves. The isoquants of Exhibit 6–12 are identical to those of Exhibit 6–4. We are continuing to assume input prices of P_K = $10 and P_L = $15. These input prices determine the isocosts, which determine the firm's expansion path. The expansion path is shown in the exhibit.

Suppose that the firm wants to produce 19 units of X per day and expects to continue doing so. What production process will it use? In the short run, capital usage is fixed, say at 5 units. Therefore the firm must

Exhibit 6–13 Short-Run and Long-Run Total Cost Curves

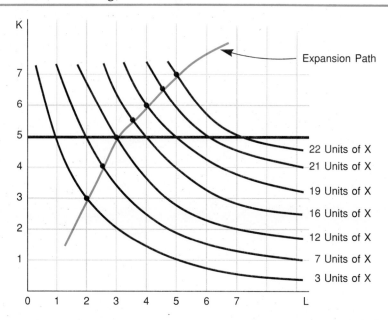

	Short Run					Long Run			
	Factors Employed		**Cost of Factors**		**Total Cost**	**Factors Employed**		**Cost of Factors**		**Total Cost**
Quantity of Output	**K**	**L**	**K**	**L**		**K**	**L**	**K**	**L**	
3	5	1	$50	$ 15	$ 65	3	2	$30	$30	$ 60
7	5	2	50	30	80	4	2.5	40	37.50	77.50
12	5	3	50	45	95	5	3	50	45	95
16	5	4	50	60	110	5.5	3.5	55	52.50	107.50
19	5	5	50	75	125	6	4	60	60	120
21	5	6	50	90	140	6.5	4.5	65	67.50	132.50
22	5	7	50	105	155	7	5	70	75	145

Long-run total cost
The cost of producing a given amount of output when the firm is able to operate on its expansion path.

operate on the horizontal line where K = 5, so the only way to produce 19 units of output is by hiring 5 units of capital and 5 units of labor. But in the long run, the firm is free to vary its employment of both factors and will adopt the production process that produces 19 units of X at the lowest cost. This occurs where the 19-unit isoquant is tangent to an isocost, at the point (4,6) on the expansion path. Therefore in the long run, the firm will use 4 units of labor and 6 units of capital to produce 19 units of output.

The short-run total cost of producing 19 units of X is equal to the price of hiring 5 units of capital and 5 units of labor. Given our assumed input prices, this comes to $10 · 5 + $15 · 5 = $125. The **long-run total cost** of producing 19 units of X is the cost of producing those units after the firm has made its long-run adjustment to 6 units of capital and 4 units of labor; this comes to $10 · 6 + $15 · 4 = $120.

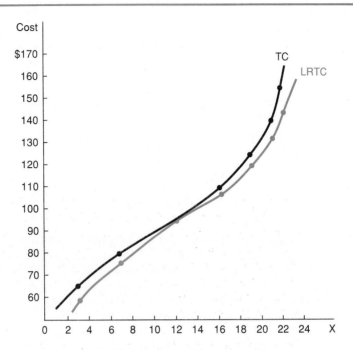

With P_K = \$10 and P_L = \$15, the isoquant diagram gives rise to the table. Points from the table are plotted on the graph. The short-run total cost (TC) curve is drawn on the assumption that capital employment is fixed at 5 units. It is the same curve that was constructed in Exhibit 6–7.

Because the firm always chooses the least expensive production process in the long run, long-run total cost is never greater than short-run total cost. If the firm happens to want to produce exactly 12 units of output, then its desired long-run capital employment is equal to its existing capital employment of 5 units. In this fortunate circumstance, the firm can produce at the lowest possible cost even in the short run. For any other level of output, short-run total cost exceeds long-run total cost.

The long-run total cost can never be greater than the short-run total cost, because in the long run the firm always chooses the least expensive production process.

▷ *Exercise 6.8* On the basis of Exhibit 6–12, what is the one level of output at which short-run and long-run total costs are equal? How can you tell?

In Exhibit 6–13 we show the firm's short-run total cost (TC) curve (this is the same TC curve that was constructed in Exhibit 6–7) and its long-run total cost (LRTC) curve. The data in the table are taken from the isoquant diagram, which is reproduced from Exhibit 6–12. The graphs display these same data.

A Multitude of Short Runs

Until now, we have held the firm's use of capital fixed at 5 units in the short run. In other short-run situations the firm may find its use of capital fixed at some other level. If so, the firm's short-run total cost curve will be different, although its long-run total cost curve will remain unchanged. It will still be true that the firm's short-run total cost curve will lie above its long-run total cost curve, touching it only at the one point where the fixed capital stock happens to be optimal.

▷ *Exercise 6.9* Suppose that the firm's capital stock is fixed at 4 units. Continue to assume prices of $10 for labor and $15 for capital and compute some points on the new short-run total cost curve (you will have to use the graph in Exhibit 6–12, and you may have to approximate some numbers). At what level of output does the new short-run total cost curve touch the long-run total cost curve?

Exhibit 6–14 shows the long-run total cost curve together with several short-run total cost curves corresponding to different fixed quantities of capital. Each quantity of capital yields a short-run total cost curve, so that the curves in Exhibit 6–14 are only part of an infinite family of such curves. The long-run total cost curve is the lower boundary of the region in which those short-run total cost curves live.

Long-Run Average and Marginal Costs

In Exhibit 6–8 we constructed the (short-run) average cost and (short-run) marginal cost curves from our knowledge of the short-run total cost curve. We can follow exactly the same procedure with long-run costs. The long-run total cost curve of Exhibit 6–13 gives rise to long-run average cost (LRAC) and long-run marginal cost (LRMC) curves. **Long-run average cost** is given by the equation

Long-run average cost
Long-run total cost divided by quantity.

$$LRAC = \frac{LRTC}{Q}$$

Long-run marginal cost
That part of long-run total cost attributable to the last unit produced.

and **long-run marginal cost** is the part of long-run total cost attributable to the last unit produced. For example, at a quantity of 22 units, we have LRAC = TC/(22 units) = $145/(22 units) = $6.59 per unit. At the same quantity, we have LRMC = ($145 – $132.50) per unit = $12.50 per unit. (All of the numbers here are taken from Exhibit 6–13.) The long-run average and marginal cost curves are depicted in Exhibit 6–15.

Comparing the long-run Exhibit 6–15 with the short-run Exhibit 6–8, you will find one less curve in Exhibit 6–15. That is because there is no distinction between long-run average cost and long-run average variable cost, since all costs are variable in the long run.

Exhibit 6-14   **Many Short-Run Total Cost Curves**

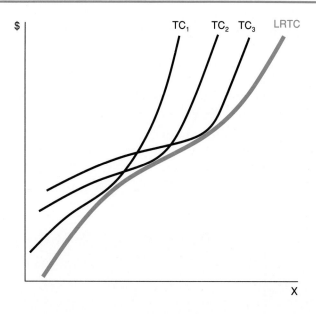

When we draw a short-run total cost curve, we assume a fixed level of capital employment. If we assume a different fixed level of capital employment, we get a different short-run total cost curve. The graph shows the short-run total cost curves that result from various assumptions.

Each total cost curve touches the long-run total cost curve in one place, at that level of output for which the fixed capital stock happens to be optimal. In that case the firm's long-run and short-run choices of production process coincide. The long-run total cost curve is the lower boundary of the region in which the various short-run total cost curves live.

Returns to Scale

The firm's long-run average cost and marginal cost curves are derived from its long-run total cost curve, which in turn is determined by factor prices and the firm's production function. In order to study the shapes of the long-run average cost and marginal cost curves, we must examine the production function further.

Here is an important question about the production function: When all input quantities are increased by 1%, does output go up by (1) more than 1%, (2) exactly 1%, or (3) less than 1%? Depending on the answer to this

Exhibit 6–15   **Long-Run Average and Marginal Costs**

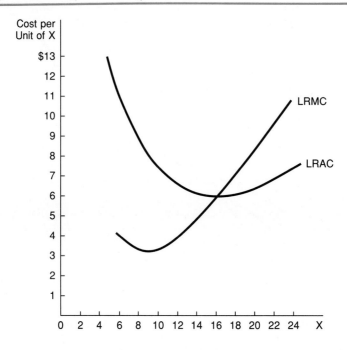

The graph shows the long-run average cost (LRAC) and long-run marginal cost (LRMC) curves associated with the long-run total cost curve of Exhibit 6–13.

Increasing returns to scale
A condition where increasing all input levels by the same proportion leads to a more than proportionate increase in output.

Constant returns to scale
A condition where increasing all input levels by the same proportion leads to a proportionate increase in output.

question, we say that the production function exhibits (1) **increasing returns to scale,** (2) **constant returns to scale,** or (3) **decreasing returns to scale.**

Students often confuse the concepts of diminishing marginal returns on the one hand and decreasing returns to scale on the other. The two concepts are entirely different, and they are entirely different in each of two ways. The most important difference is that diminishing returns to scale is a short-run concept that describes the effect on output of increasing one input while holding other inputs fixed. Decreasing returns to scale is a long-run concept that describes the effect on output of increasing all inputs in the same proportion. The other difference is that the concept of diminishing marginal returns deals with marginal quantities, whereas the concept of decreasing returns to scale deals with total and average quantities. When we ask about diminishing

Decreasing returns to scale
A condition where increasing all input levels by the same proportion leads to a less than proportionate increase in output.

marginal returns, we ask: "Will the next unit of this input yield more or less output at the margin than the last unit did?" When we ask about decreasing returns to scale, we ask: "Will a 1% increase in all inputs yield more or less than a 1% increase in total output?"

For given input prices, diminishing marginal returns are reflected by an increasing short-run marginal cost curve. Decreasing returns to scale, as we shall soon see, are reflected by an increasing long-run average cost curve.

Increasing Returns to Scale

Increasing returns to scale are likely to result when there are gains from specialization or when there are organizational advantages to size. Two men with two machines might be able to produce more than twice as much as one man with one machine, if each can occasionally use a helping hand from the other. At low levels of output, firms often experience increasing returns to scale.

Constant and Decreasing Returns to Scale

At higher levels of output, the gains from specialization and organization having been exhausted, firms tend to produce under conditions of constant or even decreasing returns to scale. Which of the two, constant or decreasing returns, is more likely? A good case can be made for constant returns. When a firm doubles all of its inputs, it can, if it chooses, simply set up a second plant, identical to the original one, and have each plant produce at the original level, yielding twice the original output. This strategy generates constant returns to scale, and suggests that the firm should never have to settle for decreasing returns. This argument is often summed up in the slogan "What a firm can do once, it can do twice."

Students sometimes object to this argument for constant returns. They argue that doubling the number of men and the number of machines can lead to congestion in the factory and consequently to less than a doubling of output. This objection overlooks the fact that factory space is itself a productive input. When we measure returns to scale, we assume that *all* inputs are increased in the same proportion. In particular, we must double the space in the factory as well as the numbers of men and of machines.

A related objection is that when the scale of an operation is doubled, the owners can no longer keep as watchful an eye on the entire enterprise as they could previously. But if we view the owners' supervisory talents as a productive input, this objection breaks down as well. Any measurement of returns to scale must involve increasing these talents in the same proportion as all other productive inputs.

As long as *all* productive inputs are truly variable, the argument for constant returns is a convincing one. However, if there are some inputs (such as managerial skills or the owner's cleverness as an entrepreneur) that are truly *fixed even in the long run,* then there may be decreasing returns to scale with respect to changes in all of the variable inputs. As a result, most economists are comfortable with the assumption that firms experience decreasing returns to scale at sufficiently high levels of output.

Returns to Scale and the Average Cost Curve

Under conditions of increasing returns to scale, the firm's long-run average cost curve is decreasing. This is because a 1% increase in output can be accomplished with less than a 1% increase in all inputs. It follows that an increase in output leads to a fall in the average cost of production.[4]

Under conditions of decreasing returns to scale, the firm's long-run average cost curve is increasing. Under conditions of constant returns to scale, the firm's long-run average cost curve is flat.

▷ *Exercise 6.10* Justify the two assertions in the preceding paragraph.

If we assume that firms experience increasing returns to scale at low levels of output and decreasing returns thereafter, the firm's long-run average cost curve is U-shaped, as in Exhibit 6–15. Only at one level of output (the quantity at which long-run total cost is minimized) does the firm face constant returns to scale.

When long-run marginal cost is below long-run average cost, long-run average cost is decreasing, and when long-run marginal cost is above long-run average cost, long-run average cost is increasing. Consequently, when long-run average cost is U-shaped, it is cut by long-run marginal cost at the bottom of the U. This is true in the long run for the same reason that it is true in the short run.

In general, the upward-sloping part of the firm's long-run marginal cost curve will be much more elastic than the upward-sloping part of its short-run marginal cost curve. Marginal cost rises much more quickly when the firm is constrained not to vary certain inputs (in the short run) than when it can vary all inputs to minimize costs for each level of output (in the long run).

Summary

The role of the firm is to convert inputs into outputs. The cost of producing a given level of output depends on the technology available to the firm (which determines the quantities of inputs the firm will need) and the prices of the inputs.

In the short run the firm is committed to employing some inputs in certain fixed amounts. In the long run it is free to vary its employment of every input, allowing it to produce any given level of output at the lowest possible cost.

---

[4]This argument assumes that the firm can hire all of the inputs that it wants to at a going market price. Without this assumption, the long-run average cost curve could be increasing even with increasing returns to scale. The same caveat applies to all of our arguments in this subsection.

The firm's technology is embodied in its production function, which is illustrated by the isoquant diagram. The slope of an isoquant is equal to the marginal rate of technical substitution between labor and capital. We expect the $MRTS_{LK}$ to decrease as we move down and to the right along the isoquant, with the result that isoquants are convex.

We assume that capital is the factor that is fixed in the short run. This constrains the firm to operate along some horizontal line in the isoquant diagram. To find the total product associated with L units of labor, we can look at the point corresponding to L on this horizontal line and determine which isoquant passes through that point.

From the total product we can compute the marginal product. The marginal product of labor is assumed to decrease after a certain point, known as the point of diminishing marginal returns.

The total cost of producing Q units of X is the sum of fixed cost (the cost of capital) and variable costs (the cost of labor). The fixed cost is $P_K \cdot K$, where K is the fixed quantity of capital. To compute the variable cost, we find the point where the Q-unit isoquant crosses the horizontal line at K. This shows how much labor the firm must use; variable cost is the quantity of labor times the wage rate.

From total costs we can compute average, average variable, and marginal costs. All three curves are typically U-shaped, with marginal cost cutting average variable cost and average cost at the bottoms of the U's. These shapes are consequences of diminishing marginal returns to labor.

In the long run the firm will maximize output for any given level of expenditure, which leads it to choose a point of tangency between an isocost and an isoquant. Alternatively, we can think of the firm as minimizing cost for any given level of output; this reasoning also leads to the conclusion that the firm will operate at a tangency. The set of all such tangencies forms the firm's expansion path.

The long-run total cost of producing Q units of X is the cost of the input basket where the expansion path meets the Q-unit isoquant.

Long-run total cost is never more than short-run total cost. The two are equal only for that quantity where the firm's existing plant size is optimal.

The shape of the long-run average cost curve depends on whether the production function exhibits decreasing, constant, or increasing returns to scale. When returns to scale are increasing, average cost is increasing, and vice versa. We expect increasing returns (decreasing average cost) at low levels of output due to the advantages of specialization. At higher levels of output there will be constant returns to scale unless some factor is fixed even in the long run; however, this case is very common due to limits on the skills and supervisory ability of the entrepreneur. Therefore we usually draw the long-run average cost curve increasing at high levels of output, making the entire curve U-shaped. Long-run marginal cost cuts through long-run average cost at the bottom of the U.

Review Questions

R1. Define the marginal rate of technical substitution.

R2. What are the geometric properties of isoquants? Why do we expect these properties to hold?

R3. Explain how to derive the firm's (short-run) total product and total cost curves from the isoquant diagram. How would these curves be affected by a change in the rental rate on capital? How would they be affected by a change in the wage rate of labor?

R4. What is the relationship between the marginal products of the factors of production and the marginal rate of technical substitution?

R5. Define the average, average variable, and marginal cost curves. What geometric relationships hold among them?

R6. What is the firm's expansion path? Why does the firm want to operate on the expansion path in the long run?

R7. Explain how to derive the firm's long-run total cost curve. How does it compare with the short-run total cost curve?

R8. What are increasing, constant, and decreasing returns to scale? Under what circumstances would you expect to observe each? What are the implications for the shape of the long-run average cost curve?

Numerical Exercise

N1. A firm discovers that when it uses K units of capital and L units of labor, it is able to produce $\sqrt{KL}$ units of output.

    a. Draw the isoquants corresponding to 1, 2, 3, and 4 units of output.

    b. Suppose that the firm produces 10 units of output using 20 units of capital and 5 units of labor. Compute the $MRTS_{LK}$. Compute the MP_L. Compute the MP_K.

    c. On the basis of your answers to part b, is the equation $MRTS_{LK} = MP_K/MP_L$ approximately true? (It would become closer to being true if we measured inputs in smaller units.)

    d. Suppose that capital and labor can each be hired at $1 per unit and that the firm uses 20 units of capital in the short run. What is the short-run total cost to produce 10 units of output?

    e. Continue to assume that capital and labor can each be hired at $1 per unit. Show that in the long run, if the firm produces 10 units of output, it will employ 10 units of capital and 10 units of labor. (*Hint:* Remember that in the long run the firm chooses to set $MP_K/P_K = MP_L/P_L$.) What is the long-run total cost to produce 10 units of output?

    f. Does this production function exhibit constant, increasing, or decreasing returns to scale?

Problem Set

1. Terry's Typing Service produces manuscripts. The only way to produce a manuscript is for one secretary to use one typewriter for one day. Two secretaries with one typewriter or one secretary with two typewriters can still produce only one manuscript.

    a. Draw Terry's one-unit isoquant.

    b. Assuming that Terry's technology exhibits constant returns to scale, draw several more isoquants.

    c. Assuming that Terry rents typewriters for $4 apiece per day and pays secretaries $6 apiece per day, draw some of Terry's isocosts. Draw the expansion path.

    d. Terry has signed a contract to rent exactly 5 typewriters. Illustrate the following, using tables, graphs, or both: the total product and marginal product of labor; the short-run total cost, variable cost, average cost, average variable cost, and marginal cost; the long-run total cost, long-run average cost, and long-run marginal cost.

2. The desert town of Dry Gulch buys its water from LowTech Inc. LowTech hires residents to walk to the nearest oasis and carry back buckets of water. Thus the inputs to the production of water are workers and buckets. The walk to the oasis and back takes one full day. Each worker can carry either one or two buckets of water but no more.

   a. Draw some of LowTech's isoquants. With buckets renting for $1 a day and workers earning $2 per day, draw some of LowTech's isocosts. Draw the expansion path.

   b. LowTech owns 5 buckets. It could rent these out to another firm at $1 per day, or it could rent additional buckets for $1 per day, but neither transaction could be arranged without some delay. Illustrate the following, using tables, graphs, or both: the total product and marginal product of labor; the short-run total cost, variable cost, average cost, average variable cost, and marginal cost; the long-run total cost, long-run average cost, and long-run marginal cost.

3. *True or false:* In an isolated town with one major employer, that employer's isocosts are likely to be curves rather than straight lines.

4. *True or false:* A wise entrepreneur will minimize costs for a given output rather than maximize output for a given cost.

5. *True or false:* You should quit studying when you reach the point of diminishing marginal returns.

6. *True or false:* Diminishing marginal returns to labor need not imply decreasing returns to scale. However, increasing marginal returns to labor *would* imply increasing returns to scale.

7. *True or false:* If in agriculture there were increasing marginal returns to labor and constant returns to scale, then it would be possible for one farmer to feed the world from a flowerpot. (*Hint:* The inputs are labor and land. Start with one farmer and one full-sized farm. Imagine the experiment of first doubling the number of workers, then halving both the number of workers and the amount of land.)

Refer to Answers to Problem Sets for solution to problem 1.

Diminishing Returns, Production, and Exchange

A society that decides to produce more wheat must also decide to produce less of something else. This is because the factors of production that are employed in farming are no longer available to other industries. If growing more wheat means employing more people as farmers, it also means employing fewer people in factories.

What determines how resources are allocated across various industries? If more wheat means fewer cars, what determines the production levels of wheat and of cars? The answer involves the production process, which we have just finished studying. In this appendix we will see how the production process determines the available opportunities and how one of these opportunites is selected. We will do so in the context of a very simple society, one consisting of a single castaway on an island. However, we will also see that much of what we discover is applicable in a far more general setting.

We shall begin by considering a completely isolated castaway and then turn to consider a castaway who is able to trade with the natives of neighboring islands. We will be able to see precisely how the castaway gains from trade, and by analogy we will be able to see how countries gain from trading with one another. Finally, we will make the remarkable discovery that, as a general rule, small countries gain more from international trade than large ones do.

Robinson Crusoe

Robinson Crusoe lives alone on an island where all he can produce are tomatoes and cooked fish. Tomatoes are produced using labor and land, and cooked fish are produced using labor and fish. Each resource is available to Robinson in fixed supply: He can farm no more land than there is on the island, harvest no more fish than live in the surrounding waters, and work no more than eight hours per day.

Although Robinson has a fixed amount of labor available to him, labor is a variable factor in both the fishing and tomato-growing industries. As long as Robinson engages in both activities, it is always possible for him to devote more time to one and less to the other.

We view Robinson as analogous to an entire society, in which there are many industries. The factors of production that we treat as variable from the point of view of any given firm can still be fixed over long periods of time from the point of view of society as a whole.

Because Robinson has a fixed amount of land to farm, there are diminishing marginal returns to labor in tomato growing. Similarly, there are diminishing marginal returns to labor in fishing. The curve in Exhibit 6A–1 shows the various combinations of tomatoes and fish dinners that Robinson could choose to produce. For example, if he grows no tomatoes, Robinson can produce 15 fish dinners per week, whereas if he catches no fish, he can produce 18 tomatoes per week. The curve is called Robinson's **production possibility curve.**

Production possibility curve
A curve showing all of the combinations of outputs that a society could produce.

Suppose that Robinson is currently at point E in Exhibit 6A–1, so that he produces T tomatoes and F fish dinners per week. If Robinson produces one fewer tomato, how many additional fish dinners can he produce? The answer is given by the distance ΔF, which is also the absolute slope of the production possibility curve. When Robinson is at point E, we can think of ΔF as the price of tomatoes in terms of fish dinners, since Robinson can effectively "trade" one tomato for ΔF fish dinners by varying his work habits. Should we expect ΔF to be large or small?

To answer this question, begin by noting that point E is quite far to the southeast on the production possibility curve. At this point Robinson produces lots of tomatoes and very few fish dinners. Since he devotes a lot of labor to his tomato production, the marginal product of his labor there is very low. The last tomato grown requires a lot of additional labor. When Robinson forgoes that last tomato, he frees up a lot of additional labor for fishing. Moreover, since he currently fishes very little, the marginal product of his labor in fishing is quite high. In summary, one less tomato means a lot of additional time spent fishing, where labor is very productive at the margin. One less tomato means a lot more fish. Thus ΔF is very large.

This means that far to the southeast the production possibility curve is very steep. A similar argument shows that far to the northwest the curve is very shallow. Taken together, these two observations imply that, as shown in Exhibit 6A–1:

The production possibility curve bows outward from the origin.

To complete the analysis, we must bring Robinson's preferences into the picture. Exhibit 6A–2 shows both the production possibility curve and Robinson's indifference curves between tomatoes and fish dinners. Robinson may choose any point on the production possibility curve, and he will

Exhibit 6A–1   **The Production Possibility Curve**

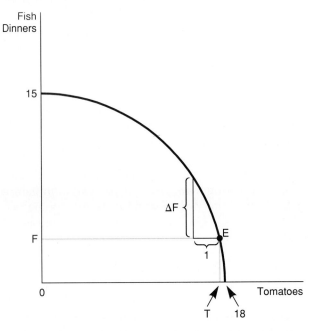

The curve shows the various combinations of tomatoes and fish dinners that Robinson can produce. If Robinson is at point E and produces one less tomato, he can produce ΔF more fish dinners, where ΔF is the absolute slope of the curve. This slope can be thought of as the price of tomatoes in terms of fish dinners.

Since point E is far to the southeast along the curve, Robinson produces many tomatoes and few fish dinners. Thus he devotes many hours to tomato growing and few hours to fishing, so that the marginal product of his labor is low in tomato growing and high in fishing. One less tomato grown will mean many fewer hours spent growing tomatoes (because of the low marginal product), and each of these hours will add a lot to the fish harvest (because of the high marginal product). On both counts, one less tomato grown will mean many more fish caught, so the absolute slope ΔF is large.

Similarly, far to the northeast along the curve, the absolute slope is small. Taken together, these observations imply that the curve bows outward from the origin.

choose so as to achieve the highest possible indifference curve. That is, he selects point B.

At point B Robinson has equated the relative price of tomatoes in terms of fish dinners (the slope of the production possibility curve) to his marginal rate of substitution between tomatoes and fish dinners (the slope of the indifference curve). This makes good economic sense, just as it did in Chapter 3.

Robinson Crusoe and Foreign Trade

Now suppose that Robinson establishes contact with the natives of nearby islands. He discovers that the residents of these islands often trade fish

Exhibit 6A–2   **Robinson Crusoe's Optimum**

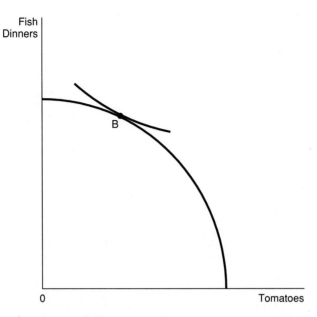

From the points on his production possibility curve, Robinson chooses point B, where he is on the highest possible indifference curve. At such a tangency the slopes of the production possibility curve and of the indifference curve are equal. That is, the relative price of tomatoes in terms of fish dinners is equal to Robinson's marginal rate of substitution between tomatoes and fish dinners.

dinners and tomatoes among themselves, at a going price of P fish dinners per tomato.

Robinson now faces two separate decisions: How much of each commodity should he produce, and how much of each should he consume? Without trade, these were different ways of asking the same question. With trade, they are not.

We already know, on the basis of Chapter 3, how Robinson makes his consumption decision: He selects the point where his budget line is tangent to an indifference curve. What is his budget line? It is a line with absolute slope P (where P is the going relative price of tomatoes). Moreover, it must pass through the basket that Robinson produces. This is because the basket that he produces is certainly available to him (he can simply consume it and refuse to trade) and so must be on his budget line.

Panel A of Exhibit 6A–3 shows several lines with absolute slope P. If Robinson produces either basket A or basket E, the lightest of these lines will be his budget line. If he produces either basket B or basket D, the middle line will be his budget line. If he produces basket C, the dark line will be his budget line. Clearly, the last is the best choice. Robinson produces basket C.

Exhibit 6A–3   **Production and Consumption with Foreign Trade**

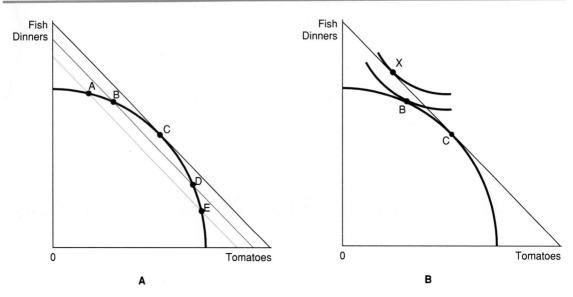

A   B

When Robinson can trade with his neighbors at a relative price of P fish dinners per tomato, he faces a budget line of absolute slope P. All of the lines in panel A have that slope. By choosing a basket to produce, Robinson can choose his budget line from among the lines pictured. If he produces basket A or basket E, he has the light budget line; if he produces basket B or basket D, he has the middle budget line; if he produces basket C, he has the dark budget line. The dark budget line is the best one to have, so Robinson produces basket C. He then trades along the budget line to his optimal basket X, shown in panel B. Without trade, Robinson would choose basket B. Since basket X is preferred to basket B, Robinson gains from trade.

The key to understanding this is to remember that *deciding what to produce is tantamount to choosing a budget line.* Because it is always desirable to have a budget line as far out as possible, it follows that:

Production occurs at the point where the production possibility curve is tangent to a line of slope P.

Panel B of Exhibit 6A–3 shows Robinson's consumption choice. Having produced basket C, his budget line is the one shown in panel B. His optimal basket on this budget line is X, which he can now trade for. Notice that X is outside Robinson's production possibility curve, which means that he could never have produced this basket for himself. Without foreign trade, Robinson would have chosen basket B, which he likes less than X.

The Gains from Trade

We have seen that Robinson can benefit from trade with his neighbors. How much does he benefit?

Exhibit 6A–4   **Autarkic versus World Relative Prices**

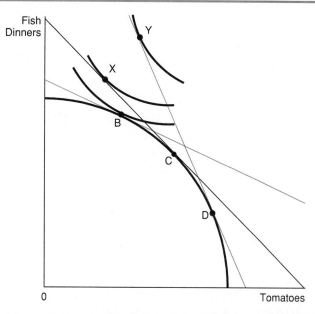

The slope of the blue line represents the autarkic relative price on Robinson's island. If the world relative price is the same as the autarkic relative price, then Robinson both produces and consumes basket B, just as he would with no opportunity to trade.

If, instead, the world relative price is given by the slope of the black line, then Robinson produces basket C and consumes basket X, which is an improvement over basket B. If the world relative price goes up to the slope of the gray line, then Robinson produces basket D and consumes basket Y, which is a further improvement.

The more the world relative price differs from the autarkic relative price, the more Robinson can gain from trade.

Autarkic relative price
The relative price that would prevail if there were no foreign trade.

World relative price
The relative price that prevails when there is trade among countries.

To answer this question, we must compare two different relative prices. One is the **autarkic relative price** that would prevail on Robinson's island if there were no trade. The other is the **world relative price** at which Robinson trades with his neighbors.

In Exhibit 6A.4 the slope of the blue line is the autarkic relative price, since Robinson would choose point B in the absence of trade. The slopes of the other lines represent possible world relative prices.

First suppose that the world relative price happens to be the same as the autarkic relative price. In that case Robinson must select a budget line parallel to the blue line, and the blue line itself is the one that he selects (since it is tangent to the production possibility curve). He selects this budget line by producing basket B. The optimal consumption basket on this budget line is also basket B. Thus Robinson chooses not to trade. He consumes the same basket whether or not he has the opportunity to trade.

Suppose, alternatively, that the world relative price is given by the slope of the black line. In that case Robinson produces basket C and trades for basket X. This makes him better off than if the world relative price and the autarkic relative price were equal.

Now suppose that the world relative price is given by the slope of the gray line. In this case Robinson produces basket D and trades for basket Y, which is even better than basket X.

The more the world relative price deviates from the autarkic relative price, the more Robinson gains from trade.

The black and gray lines in Exhibit 6A–4 represent world relative prices that are higher than the autarkic relative price. You should be able to draw a picture that illustrates the same phenomenon for world relative prices that are lower than the autarkic relative price: The greater the *difference* between the autarkic and world relative prices, the more Robinson is able to gain from the trade.

What determines the world price? The answer is: supply and demand by everyone in the world, including Robinson. Thus the world price is a sort of average of the autarkic relative prices on all of the various islands that make up Robinson's trading group. If Robinson's supply and demand are a large percentage of the world's supply and demand, then his own autarkic relative price will count quite heavily in this average, which makes it likely that his autarkic relative price and the world relative price will be very similar. If on the other hand, Robinson is an insignificant player in the world market, there is a much greater chance that the world relative price will be quite different from his autarkic one.

From this reasoning we conclude that small countries generally have more to gain from international trade than large ones do. For many goods, world relative prices do not differ drastically from U.S. autarkic relative prices, so the United States has relatively little to gain from trade in these goods. But New Zealand, for example, where the autarkic relative price of wool is quite low, benefits greatly from being able to trade its wool for other goods at the comparatively high world relative price.

Chapter Seven

Competition

In the first chapter of this book we saw some of the power of supply and demand analysis. That analysis can be greatly strengthened and refined when we understand the sources of supply and demand. From that knowledge we can draw inferences about when supply and demand curves are likely to be more or less elastic, what will or will not cause them to shift, and when those shifts are likely to be relatively large or small.

Demand, as we saw in Chapter 4, arises from tastes. Supply, as we began to see in Chapter 5, arises from costs. In this chapter we will see exactly how information about costs can be used to derive the supply curves of a competitive firm and a competitive industry. We will study how prices and quantities are determined in such an industry and the circumstances under which those prices and quantities might change.

7.1 The Competitive Firm

A firm is said to be **perfectly competitive** if there is a market price at which consumers will buy whatever quantity the firm offers for sale. (Sometimes we abbreviate the phrase *perfectly competitive* to simply *competitive*.) The

Perfectly competitive firm
One that can sell any quantity it wants to at some going market price.

Tailor Dress Company, which we studied in Chapter 5, is not perfectly competitive because it faces a downward-sloping demand curve for its product. To increase sales, it must lower its price. A perfectly competitive firm, by contrast, faces a *horizontal* (infinitely elastic) demand curve, reflecting the fact that at the market price demanders will buy any quantity that the firm wants to sell.

This situation is most likely to occur when the firm is very small relative to its industry. No matter how much the firm produces, its productivity will not significantly affect the industry's total output. Therefore there will be no significant effect on the price at which that output can be sold.

The best example to keep in mind is that of a wheat farmer, who provides a minuscule percentage of the wheat grown in the world. Regardless of whether he produces 10 bushels or 1,000, he remains too small to have any impact on the going market price. The demand curve for his wheat is horizontal, because the market will absorb whatever quantity he provides at the going price. If he tries to charge even a fraction of a penny more, he will sell no wheat, because buyers can just as easily buy from someone else. If he charges even a fraction of a penny less, the public will demand more wheat from him than he can possibly produce—effectively, an infinite quantity.

Of course, the demand curve for *wheat* is still downward sloping; it is just the demand for *Farmer Ryan's wheat* that is horizontal. To see how this can be, look at the two demand curves depicted in Exhibit 7–1. Notice in particular the units on the quantity axis. When Farmer Ryan increases output from 1 bushel to 10 bushels, he is moving a long distance to the right on his quantity axis. At the same time he has moved the wheat *industry* a practically infinitesimal distance to the right, say from 10,000,000 bushels to 10,000,009 bushels. This tiny change in the industry's output requires essentially no change in price.

Farmer Ryan's horizontal demand curve results from his being a very small part of a very large industry, in which all of the products produced are interchangeable and buyers can quite easily buy from another producer if Farmer Ryan tries to raise his price. All of these conditions tend to lead to perfect competition, but perfect competition can happen even without them. The only requirement for a firm to be called perfectly competitive is that the demand curve for its product be horizontal (for whatever reason).

Revenue

A perfectly competitive firm faces a particularly simple total revenue curve and marginal revenue curve. If the going price for wheat is $5 per bushel, Farmer Ryan's total revenue and marginal revenue are as shown in Exhibit 7–2.

When Farmer Ryan sells Q bushels of wheat, his total revenue is $5 × Q. The graph of this total revenue function is a straight line through the origin, shown in panel A of Exhibit 7–2.

Exhibit 7–1   **The Demand Curve for Wheat**

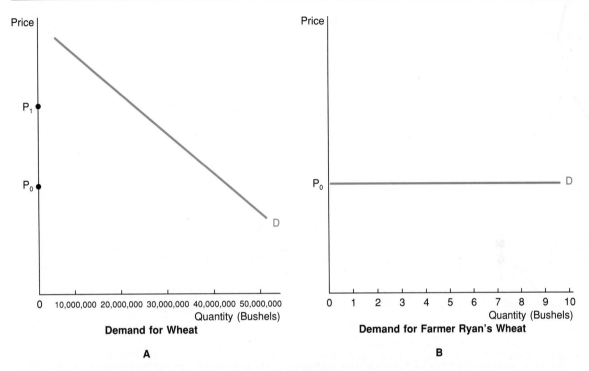

Panel A shows the downward-sloping demand curve for wheat. Panel B shows the horizontal demand curve for Farmer Ryan's wheat. If the price of all wheat goes up from P_0 to P_1, consumers will buy less wheat. If the price of just Farmer Ryan's wheat goes up from the market price of P_0 to P_1, consumers will buy none of it at all; they will shop elsewhere.

Farmer Ryan's marginal revenue is the same at every quantity; it is always equal to the going market price of $5 per bushel. Whenever he sells an additional bushel, he collects an additional $5. In general, for any competitive firm, we have the equation:

Marginal Revenue = Price.

Farmer Ryan's marginal revenue curve is a horizontal line at the level of $5 per bushel. In other words, it looks exactly like the demand curve for Farmer Ryan's wheat, which is also flat at the market price. The (identical) demand and marginal revenue curves are both shown in panel B of Exhibit 7–2.

The marginal revenue curve of a competitive firm is a horizontal line at the market price.

Exhibit 7–2   Total and Marginal Revenue at the Competitive Firm

Quantity	Total Revenue	Marginal Revenue
1	$ 5	$5/item
2	10	5
3	15	5
4	20	5

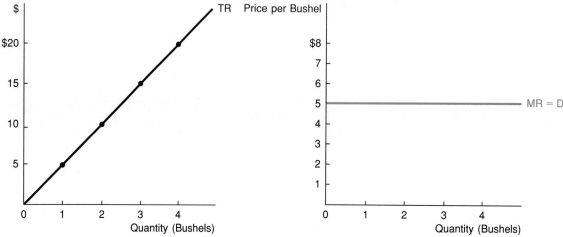

If the going price of wheat is $5 per bushel, then Farmer Ryan's total revenue is given by the equation TR = $5 × Q. The graph of this equation is a straight line through the origin. No matter what quantity he sells, his marginal revenue is $5 per bushel. The graph of marginal revenue is a horizontal line at $5, identical to the graph of the demand curve for Farmer Ryan's wheat.

Short-Run Costs and Supply

Short-run supply curve
A curve that shows what quantity the firm will supply in the short run in response to any given price.

Long-run supply curve
A curve that shows what quantity the firm will supply in the long run in response to any given price.

We have seen in Chapter 6 that a firm's cost curves are different in the short run (when some factors of production are fixed) than they are in the long run (when all factors are variable). Consequently, the firm's supply responses will differ in the short run and long run. Suppose that you run a pizza restaurant, employing both labor and pizza ovens. If the price of pizza goes up, you can increase your output in the short run by hiring more workers. In the long run you can build additional pizza ovens as well. In the long run you will produce more pizzas.

Therefore we must distinguish two supply curves. For any given price, the **short-run supply curve** shows how the firm would respond to that price in the short run, and the **long-run supply curve** shows how the firm would respond to that price in the long run. We will study the short-run supply curve first. For this we must begin by considering the firm's short-run cost curves.

Exhibit 7–3   **The Optimum of the Competitive Firm**

Quantity	Marginal Cost	Marginal Revenue
1	$2/item	$5/item
2	3	5
3	4	5
4	5	5
5	6	5
6	7	5

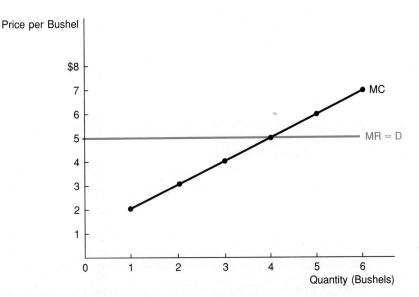

Farmer Ryan, like any profit-maximizing producer (competitive or not) produces at the point where marginal cost equals marginal revenue. Because he is a competitive producer, Farmer Ryan's marginal revenue curve is a horizontal line at the going market price. Thus it is equally correct to say that he operates where marginal cost equals price. In this case he produces 4 bushels of wheat at the market price of $5 per bushel.

The Supply Decision When Marginal Cost Is Increasing

Suppose that Farmer Ryan's (short-run) marginal costs are as shown in Exhibit 7–3. Maximizing profits by equating marginal cost with marginal revenue (which we called Method 2 in Chapter 5), we see that Farmer Ryan wants to produce 4 items and sell them at the market price of $5 per item.

▷ *Exercise 7.1* What is Farmer Ryan's total revenue? If his fixed costs are $2, what is the total cost of producing 4 items? What is his profit?

Any firm, competitive or not, chooses its quantity according to the rule:

Marginal cost = Marginal revenue.

For a competitive firm the marginal revenue is equal to the market price. Thus for a competitive firm (and only for a competitive firm) it is equally correct to say:

The competitive firm chooses its quantity according to the rule:

Marginal cost = Price.

This rule for choosing quantities should make good intuitive sense. The firm faces a market price at which it can sell its goods. It produces goods as long as it can do so at a marginal cost that is lower than the market price. When marginal cost exceeds the market price, any additional items produced would subtract from the firm's profits. The time to stop producing is just before that happens, when the marginal cost of producing an item is exactly equal to the price at which that item can be sold.

Suppose that the market price of wheat were to rise to $6 a bushel. From the marginal cost curve in Exhibit 7–3, we see that Farmer Ryan would now provide 5 bushels of wheat, the quantity at which marginal cost equals $6 per bushel. If the market price were to rise to $7, Farmer Ryan would provide 6 bushels.

These facts are illustrated in Exhibit 7–4. Table A is Farmer Ryan's marginal cost curve, reproduced from Exhibit 7–3. Table B shows the quantities Farmer Ryan would produce at each price. We have already observed, and the graph illustrates, that at a price of $5 he would supply 4 bushels, at a price of $6 he would supply 5 bushels, and at a price of $7 he would supply 6 bushels. These observations are recorded in the last three rows of Table B. The other rows are deduced similarly.

▷ *Exercise 7.2* At a price of $4, how much wheat will Farmer Ryan supply? Explain why.

At each given price Table B tells us what quantity Farmer Ryan will supply. We have a name for such a table. It is none other than Farmer Ryan's supply schedule, and if we plot the same information on a graph we will get a picture of his supply curve!

In fact, we already have a picture of his supply curve. It is identical in appearance to his marginal cost curve, illustrated in Exhibit 7–4. The curves must be identical, because all of the numbers in Table B are the same as those in Table A.

Although Farmer Ryan's supply and marginal cost curves appear identical, there is still an important conceptual difference between them. To use the marginal cost curve, you "input" a quantity (on the horizontal axis) and read off the corresponding marginal cost in dollars per item (on the vertical axis). To use the supply curve, you "input" a price (on the vertical axis) and read off the corresponding quantity (on the horizontal axis). However, despite this conceptual difference, the fact that the curves are identical in appearance will prove to be very important.

Exhibit 7–4   Marginal Cost and Supply

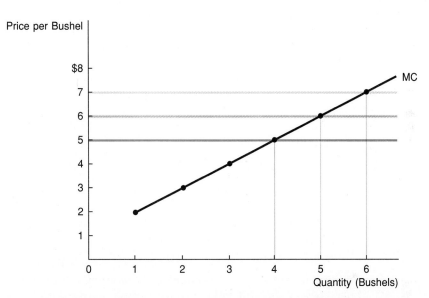

Table A	
Quantity	**Marginal Cost**
1	$2/item
2	3
3	4
4	5
5	6
6	7

Table B	
Price	**Quantity**
$2/item	1
3	2
4	3
5	4
6	5
7	6

Table A is Farmer Ryan's marginal cost schedule; the graph shows his marginal cost curve.

Table B shows the quantity Farmer Ryan would supply at each price. Each entry is obtained by reading the marginal cost curve backward—we imagine a price, look for that price in the right-hand column of Table A (or on the vertical axis of the graph), and observe that the corresponding quantity is what Farmer Ryan would produce at that price.

The horizontal lines in the graph represent hypothetical market prices of $5, $6, and $7. At these prices the quantities supplied, read off the marginal cost curve, are 4, 5, and 6. These are entered as the last three rows of Table B.

If we plot a graph of Farmer Ryan's supply curve using the data points from Table B, it will look exactly like his marginal cost curve, because all of the numbers in Table B are the same as those in Table A.

The Irrelevance of Fixed Costs

In the short run, fixed costs are unavoidable. As a result, they have no bearing on any economic decision.

Exhibit 7–5   The Irrelevance of Fixed Costs

Quantity	Total Revenue	Marginal Revenue	Total Cost	Marginal Cost	Profit
1bu	$ 5	$5/bu	$ 4	$2/bu	$1
2	10	5	7	3	3
3	15	5	11	4	4
4	20	5	16	5	4
5	25	5	22	6	3
6	30	5	29	7	1

Example 1: Fixed Cost = $2

Quantity	Total Revenue	Marginal Revenue	Total Cost	Marginal Cost	Profit
1bu	$ 5	$5/bu	$22	$2/bu	−$17
2	10	5	25	3	−15
3	15	5	29	4	−14
4	20	5	34	5	−14
5	25	5	40	6	−15
6	30	5	47	7	−17

Example 2: Fixed Cost = $20

In the first example we assume fixed costs of $2, and in the second example we assume fixed costs of $20. Marginal costs and marginal revenues are the same in each case. Consequently, optimal output is the same in each case: the quantity at which marginal cost equals marginal revenue, which is 4. In the first example the maximum attainable profit is $4, and in the second it is −$14, which is better than any of the alternatives.

Exhibit 7–5 shows the conditions on Farmer Ryan's farm under two different assumptions about his fixed costs. In the first example we assume fixed costs of $2, and in the second example we assume fixed costs of $20. In either case he will produce at the point where marginal cost is equal to the market price of $5; that is, he will produce 4 bushels of wheat.

In Example 1 Farmer Ryan maximizes his profit at $4; in Example 2 he maximizes it at −$14. Even though −14 is a negative number (so that the farmer is suffering losses), he is still maximizing profits in the sense that any other level of output would lead to an even larger negative number.

A natural question now is this: In the second example wouldn't Farmer Ryan quit farming altogether rather than continue to take losses? If we were examining his long-run behavior, the answer would be yes, but in the short run the answer is no. In the short run Farmer Ryan is saddled with $20 in fixed costs, which he cannot avoid even if he stops farming altogether. For example, the fixed factor of production might be the farm itself, which he leases on a yearly basis. Until the lease is up, there is nothing he can do about his fixed costs. If he decides not to plant crops at all, his profits will be −$20 instead of −$14.

Because sunk costs are sunk, and because the firm's fixed costs are sunk in the short run, it follows that fixed costs are irrelevant to the firm's

Exhibit 7–6   **The Supply Decision with a U-Shaped Marginal Cost Curve**

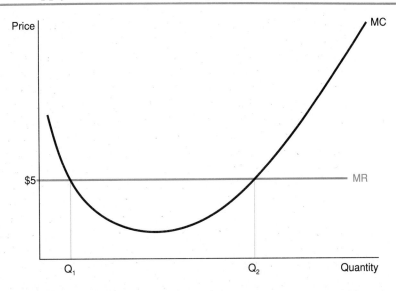

At a market price of $5 the firm produces Q_2 items (assuming it produces at all). It takes losses on the first Q_1 of these, all of which are produced at a marginal cost of more than $5, and it earns positive profits on the others. If those positive profits fail to outweigh the losses on the first Q_1 items, the firm will shut down.

short-run supply decisions, including the decision about whether to shut down.

▷ *Exercise 7.3* Suppose that the price of wheat goes up to $6 per bushel. Construct new tables to replace those in Exhibit 7–5. How much wheat will Farmer Ryan produce, and what will his profit be, with fixed costs of $2? With fixed costs of $20?

The Supply Decision with a U-shaped Marginal Cost Curve

Farmer Ryan has a marginal cost curve that is everywhere upward sloping. We saw in Chapter 6, however, that the firm's short-run marginal cost curve is typically U-shaped. We will now examine the supply decision for such a firm.

Exhibit 7–6 shows the U-shaped marginal cost curve of a competitive firm facing a market price of $5. We know that such a firm, if it produces at all, will produce a quantity at which marginal cost and the market price are equal. We can see from the graph that there are two quantities at which this occurs: Q_1 and Q_2. Which will the firm choose?

Suppose that it produces Q_1 items. In that case it is possible to produce an additional item at a marginal cost that is less than the market price. This is because the marginal cost curve is downward sloping in the vicinity of Q_1. It follows that the firm can do better by producing another item. It will continue to produce as long as price exceeds marginal cost, and then it will stop; that is, it will produce Q_2 items.

▷ *Exercise 7.4* Consider the firm described in Exhibit 6–8. If this firm faces a market price of $5.58, how much will it produce? How much profit will it earn? How much profit would it earn if it produced only one unit?

A competitive firm, if it produces at all, will always choose a quantity where price equals marginal cost *and* the marginal cost curve is upward sloping. Only the upward-sloping part of the marginal cost curve is relevant to the firm's supply decisions.

The Shutdown Decision

We now know how much the firm will produce if it produces at all. We still must ask how the firm decides between remaining in operation and shutting down.[1]

In order to make this decision, the firm's owner must compare the profit to be earned from continuing to operate with the profit to be earned from shutting down. If the firm shuts down, it will still have to meet its fixed costs, while earning no revenue. Therefore its profit will be the negative number $-FC$, where FC stands for fixed costs. If the firm stays in business, producing a quantity Q, its profits will equal $TR - TC$, where TR is total revenue and TC is total cost. If $TR - TC$ is positive, it is certainly best to keep the business operating. Even if $TR - TC$ is negative, it might be better to operate than to shut down. The firm will want to operate if and only if

$$TR - TC > -FC.$$

Substituting the identity $TC = FC + VC$, this condition becomes

$$TR - FC - VC > -FC,$$

or

$$TR > VC.$$

The latter inequality should make good intuitive sense. Because the fixed costs of the firm are unavoidable in the short run, they are irrelevant to the decision of whether to shut down. The variable costs are the additional costs that the firm will incur if it continues to operate; they are avoidable and so are relevant to the shutdown decision. Staying in operation is a good idea precisely if the total revenue that the firm will earn outweighs these additional costs.

---

[1]We consider only temporary shutdowns, because we are considering only the short-run behavior of the firm. Permanent shutdowns (that is, exits from the industry) are usually treated as a long-run phenomenon.

Exhibit 7–7   **The Competitive Firm's Supply Responses**

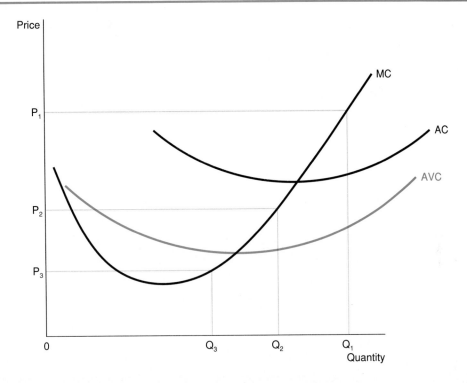

At price P_1, optimal output is Q_1. At Q_1, the average cost of production is less than P_1, so the firm earns positive profits.

At price P_3, the quantity Q_3 equates price with marginal cost. However, at this quantity the average variable cost is greater than the price P_3. Therefore it is best for the firm to shut down.

At price P_2, optimal output is Q_2. Here the price exceeds average variable cost, so the firm earns more by producing than it does by shutting down. However, the price is less than average cost, so that the firm is earning negative profits.

Remembering that TR $= P \cdot Q$ (P is price and Q is quantity), we can rewrite our inequality as

$$P \cdot Q > VC.$$

Then if we divide each side by Q, the inequality becomes

$$P > AVC.$$

In other words, the firm will stay in operation if, after choosing the optimal quantity to produce, it finds that the price of a unit of output exceeds the average variable cost of producing a unit of output. We reiterate that only variable costs are relevant to the decision.

The Short-Run Supply Curve

In Exhibit 7–7 we see three possible market prices that a competitive firm might face. At a price of P_1, the firm will produce a quantity of Q_1. At this quantity P_1 is greater than both average cost and average variable cost. The firm will stay in operation, producing Q_1 items and earning positive profits.

At a price of P_3, the firm's optimal output is Q_3. However, here the average variable cost of production exceeds P_3. Remaining in business will lead to a net reduction in profits, so the firm shuts down.

At a price of P_2, the firm's optimal output is Q_2. Here the average variable cost is less than P_2, so the firm stays in business. However, the average cost of production (including fixed costs) is *greater* than P_2, so the firm's profits are negative. Nevertheless, the firm loses less by continuing to produce than it would by shutting down.

▷ *Exercise 7.5* Consider the example of Exhibit 6–8. Suppose that the market price of X is $9. Adjoin columns to the table for Total Revenue, Marginal Revenue, and Profit. How much does the firm produce and why?

Repeat with a market price of $6. How much will the firm produce? How much profit will it earn? How much would it earn if it shut down? Will the firm remain in operation? Does price exceed average variable cost?

Repeat the last paragraph with a market price of $3.50.

Shutdown price
The output price below which the firm could no longer cover its average variable costs and would therefore shut down.

The price P at which the marginal cost curve crosses the average variable cost curve is called the **shutdown price** of the firm. It is shown in Exhibit 7–8. When price is above the shutdown price, the firm produces a quantity read off the marginal cost curve. At prices lower than the shutdown price, the firm shuts down and produces nothing.

We conclude that:

The competitive firm's short-run supply curve is identical to that part of its marginal cost curve that lies above its average variable cost curve.

In Exhibit 7–8 this is the heavy portion of the marginal cost curve. A more complete description of the short-run supply curve is that it consists of two disconnected pieces, namely the two heavy segments in Exhibit 7–8.

Why Supply Curves Slope Up

When the competitive firm's marginal cost curve is U-shaped, its supply curve consists of that part of the marginal cost curve that lies above average variable cost. Since the marginal cost curve cuts the average variable cost curve from below, the entire supply curve is upward sloping.

To the question "Why do supply curves slope up?" we can answer "Because average and marginal cost curves are U-shaped." This is correct, but it raises another question: Why are the cost curves U-shaped? The

Exhibit 7–8   **The Competitive Firm's Short-Run Supply Curve**

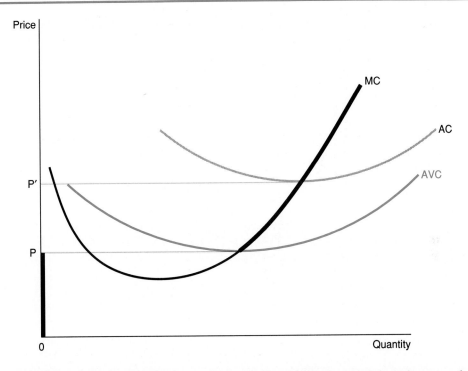

At prices below the shutdown price P, the firm cannot cover its variable costs and shuts down, producing zero output. At prices above P, it produces the quantity that equates price with marginal cost; this quantity can be read off the marginal cost curve. Thus the two heavy segments constitute the firm's short-run supply curve. At prices above P', the price of an item exceeds the average cost of production, so the firm earns positive profits. At prices below P', profits are negative.

answer, as we saw in Chapter 6, is that this is a consequence of diminishing marginal returns to the variable factors of production.

The technological fact of diminishing marginal returns suffices to account for the upward-sloping supply curves of competitive firms.

Using the Short-Run Supply Curve

The short-run supply curve reflects the firm's supply responses in situations where some factor of production is fixed. This is likely to be the case when price changes are expected to be temporary. It is often infeasible to alter things like plant size in response to day-to-day price fluctuations. If we want to know how a firm will respond to such fluctuations, we think of the plant size as fixed and use the short-run supply curve.

Even if price changes are expected to be permanent, it may not be possible to respond to them immediately. If the price of cars goes up and is

Exhibit 7–9   **The Competitive Firm's Long-Run Supply Curve**

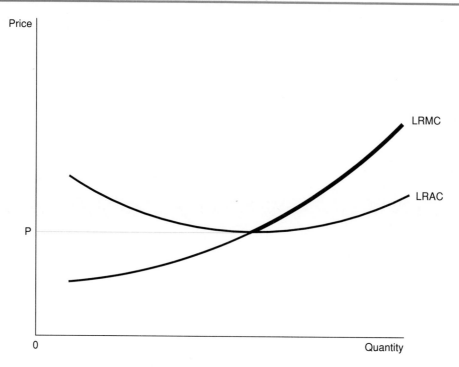

Unless the price is high enough to cover all of its costs, the firm will leave the industry in the long run. Therefore the long-run supply curve is that portion of the long-run marginal cost curve that lies above the long-run average cost curve. At prices below P, the firm leaves the industry and produces zero.

expected to stay up, General Motors will build more plants, but it will take time to build them. Therefore the immediate effect on quantity can be read off the short-run supply curve. After the new plants are constructed, quantity will change again in ways that are reflected by the long-run supply curve.

Long-Run Costs and Supply

In the long run a firm that is earning negative profits will leave the industry. Thus firms will not produce when price is below long-run average cost (remember that in the long run there is no distinction between average cost and average variable cost). When a firm does produce, it will produce the quantity that equates price with long-run marginal cost. Therefore when the long-run cost curves are U-shaped, the competitive firm's long-run supply curve is the heavy segment of the curve in Exhibit 7–9.

Exhibit 7–10   **Long-Run and Short-Run Supply Responses**

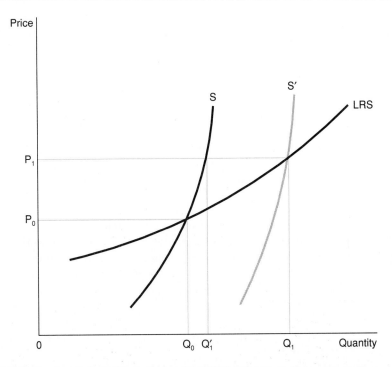

In long-run equilibrium at P_0, the firm is both on its long-run and short-run supply curves. A change in price, to P_1, has the immediate effect of causing the firm to move along its short-run supply curve S to the quantity Q_1'. In the long run, the firm can vary its plant capacity (for example, a hamburger stand can install more grills) and move along its long-run supply curve LRS to Q_1. With the new plant capacity, the firm has a new short-run supply curve S'. In the new equilibrium at price P_1 and quantity Q_1, the firm is again on both its long-run and short-run supply curves.

Comparing Short-Run and Long-Run Supply Response

The competitive firm's long-run supply curve tends to be much more elastic than its short-run supply curve. This is because in the long run it is able to respond more flexibly to price changes by varying those factors that are fixed in the short run.

Consider, for example, a hamburger stand that produces hamburgers using inputs that include grills, ground beef, and short-order cooks. In the short run the quantities of beef and of cooks are variable, but the number of grills is not. The stand has been selling hamburgers at the going price of P_0 (in Exhibit 7–10) for a very long time, and thus has adjusted the number of grills so as to produce Q_0 hamburgers at the lowest possible cost. The quantity Q_0 is chosen by using the long-run supply curve, and, because all capital adjustments have been made, Q_0 corresponds to P_0 on the short-run supply curve as well.

Now suppose that the price rises to P_1. In the long run the stand will want to expand the number of grills, but in the short run it cannot. Therefore quantity goes up to Q_1', read off the short-run supply curve. In the long run, after the facilities have been expanded, quantity will rise to Q_1, and the new scale of operations will lead to new short-run total cost, average cost, marginal cost, and supply curves. The new short-run supply curve is the curve S' in Exhibit 7–10.

Supply, Demand, and Equilibrium

We know from Chapter 5 that any supplier, if he produces at all, chooses to operate where marginal cost is equal to marginal revenue. In this section we have learned that for a competitive producer the marginal revenue curve is the same as the demand curve, and, in the region where he produces at all, the marginal cost curve is the same as the supply curve. Therefore we can just as well say that a competitive supplier chooses to operate at the point where supply is equal to demand.

In an industry in which all of the firms are competitive, each individual firm operates where supply equals demand, and so the industry-wide supply (which is the sum of the individual firms' supplies) must equal the industry-wide demand (which is the sum of the demands from the individual firms). In other words, such an industry will be at equilibrium, simply as a consequence of optimizing behavior on the part of individuals and firms.

In Chapter 1 we gave some "plausibility arguments" for the notion that in many industries prices and quantities would be determined by the intersection of supply and demand. Now we have a much stronger reason to believe the same thing. If an industry is competitive, profit-maximizing firms will be led to the equilibrium outcome as if—by an invisible hand.

7.2 The Competitive Industry

Competitive industry
An industry in which all firms are competitive and any firm can freely enter or exit.

A **competitive industry** is one in which all firms are competitive, and any firm that wants to can freely enter or exit from the industry in the long run. As we have just seen, the market for the product of any firm in such an industry will be in equilibrium, as will the market for the product of the entire industry.

In Section 7.1 we studied the firm's supply curves. In this section we will study the industry's supply curve. Then we will examine the interplay between the supply and demand curves for the industry and the supply and demand curves for the firm. This will enable us to understand how firms in a competitive industry react to changes in things like taxes, demand, costs, and the like.

Exhibit 7–11 **The Industry Supply Curve**

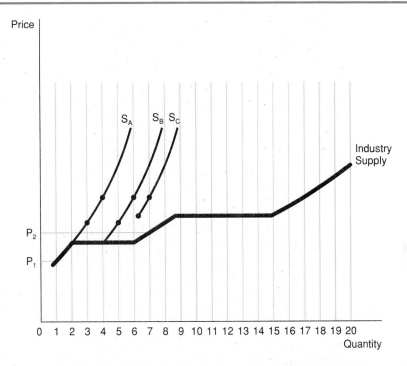

As the price goes up, two things happen. First, each firm that is producing increases its output. Second, firms that were not previously producing start up their operations. As a result, industry output increases more rapidly than that of any given firm, so the industry supply curve is more elastic than that of any given firm.

The Short-Run Supply Curve of the Competitive Industry

Given the short-run supply curves of competitive firms, we can construct the short-run supply curve for a competitive industry. In the short run we assume that there is a fixed number of firms in the industry.[2] To get the industry supply curve, we begin by summing the supply curves of these individual firms. At a given price, we ask what quantities each of the firms will provide; then we add these numbers to get the quantity supplied by the industry.

Because different firms have different shutdown prices, the number of firms in operation will tend to be small at low prices and large at high

[2]Thus the short-run supply curve does not consider the possibility of entry or exit from the industry. We usually treat these as long-run phenomena and will incorporate them in the long-run supply curve.

prices. As a result, the industry supply curve will tend to be more elastic than the supply curves of the individual firms. This can be seen in Exhibit 7–11. Here firms A, B, and C have the individual supply curves shown. At price P_1, only firm A produces, so the quantity supplied by the industry is the same as the quantity supplied by firm A. At the higher price P_2, firm B produces as well, and the industry supplies the sum of firm A's output and firm B's output. At prices high enough for firm C to produce, industry output is correspondingly greater.

The industry supply curve in Exhibit 7–11 jumps rightward each time it passes a firm's shutdown price. In an industry with many firms, the effect of this is to greatly flatten the industry supply curve relative to those of the individual firms.

The phenomenon of additional firms starting production as prices go up is not the same as the entry of new firms into the industry. In the short run we assume that firms cannot move from one industry to another. All of the firms discussed in this section are already in the industry. Their only choice is between producing and shutting down. The process of entry, which actually brings new firms into an industry, is a long-run phenomenon that we will discuss in Section 7.3.

The Factor-Price Effect

Factor-price effect
The effect that an expansion of industry output has on the price of a factor of production, thereby raising marginal costs in the industry.

We have said that the supply curve of a competitive industry is obtained by summing the supply curves of the individual firms. It is sometimes necessary to modify this statement to take account of the **factor-price effect.** This occurs when the industry in question represents a substantial fraction of the demand for the variable factor of production. For example, the steel industry represents a substantial fraction of the demand for iron. In this case a rise in the price of output causes an increase in production, which raises the industry's demand for the variable factor. Because this is a significant fraction of overall demand for the variable factor, that factor's price goes up. This factor price increase raises the marginal cost curve of every firm in the industry, causing them to produce less than they otherwise would have.

In the presence of a factor-price effect, a rise in price will increase industry output, but by less than you might think if you naively added the individual firms' supply curves. Similarly, a fall in price will decrease industry output, but by less than might naively be expected.

▷ *Exercise 7.6* Explain carefully what happens to industry output when there is a factor-price effect and the output price falls.

Exhibit 7–12 contrasts the sum of the individual firms' supply curves with the industry supply curve in the presence of a factor-price effect. The factor-price effect tends to make the industry supply curve steeper (less elastic) than it would otherwise be.

Exhibit 7–12 The Factor-Price Effect

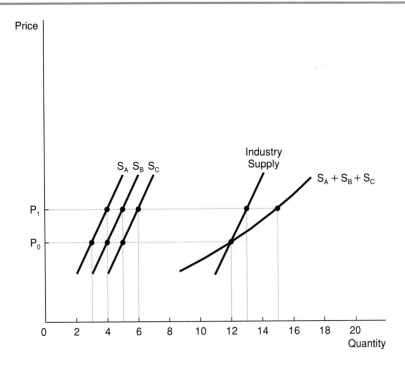

Firms A, B, and C are steel producers. At the current price P_0, they supply 3, 4, and 5 tons of steel, so that the industry supplies 12 tons. If the price were to rise to P_1, then under current cost conditions the firms would supply 4, 5, and 6 tons of steel for an industry total of 15 tons. However, when all of the firms increase output simultaneously, they drive up the price of iron, which is used in making steel. As a result, each firm's marginal cost curve moves back (the new marginal cost curves of the firms are not shown) and they produce less than they would otherwise. Therefore, at a price of P_1, the industry supplies only 13 tons instead of 15.

There is a factor-price effect when the industry in question represents a substantial fraction of the demand for one of its inputs. It causes the industry supply curve to be less elastic than the sum of the individual firms' supply curves.

The Industry's Costs

In the short run the competitive industry consists of a fixed number of firms. These firms collectively produce some quantity of output. The total cost of producing that output is the sum of the total costs of all of the individual firms.

Suppose that you were appointed the czar of American agriculture and given the power to tell each farmer how much to produce. You would like to maintain the production of wheat at its current level of 1,000,000 bushels per year, but you would like to do this in such a way as to minimize the total costs of the industry. How would you go about this?

The equimarginal principle points the way to the answer. Suppose that the marginal cost of growing wheat is $5 per bushel at Farmer Black's farm and $3 per bushel at Farmer White's. Then you can maintain industry output while reducing total cost by $2 if you order Black to produce one less bushel and White to produce one more bushel. You should continue to do this until the marginal costs of production are just equal at both farms.

Indeed, as long as any two farms have differing marginal costs, you can reduce total costs in the same way. Total costs are minimized when marginal cost is the same at every farm.

Now, the miracle: In competitive equilibrium every farmer chooses to produce a quantity at which price equals marginal cost. Since all farmers face the same market price, it follows that all farmers have the same marginal cost. From this we have the following result:

In competitive equilibrium, the industry automatically produces at the lowest possible total cost.

Students sometimes think that this result follows from the attempts of firms to minimize their costs. But no firm has any interest in the costs of the industry as a whole. The minimization of industry-wide costs is a feature of competitive equilibrium that is not sought by any individual firm.

What is the marginal cost to the industry of producing a unit of output? You might think that this question is unanswerable, because the industry consists of many firms, each with its own marginal cost curve. How are we to decide which firm to think of as producing the "last" unit of output in the industry?

The answer to the last question is that it doesn't matter. We have just seen that in competitive equilibrium, the cost of producing the last unit of output is the same at every firm. That cost is the industry's marginal cost of production.

At each point along its supply curve, the competitive industry produces a quantity that equates price with marginal cost. Therefore the industry's supply curve is identical to the industry's marginal cost curve, just as each individual firm's supply curve can be identified with its own marginal cost curve.

Competitive Equilibrium

Exhibit 7–13 illustrates the relationship between the competitive industry and the competitive firm. The industry faces a downward-sloping demand curve for its product. The price P_0 is determined by industry-wide equilibrium, and this same price P_0 is what appears to the individual firm as the "going market price," at which it faces a flat demand curve. The firm then

Exhibit 7–13   **The Competitive Industry and the Competitive Firm**

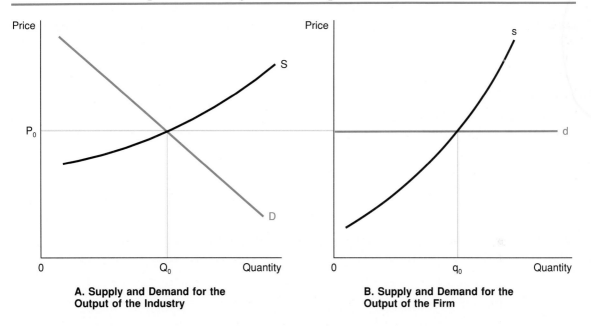

**A. Supply and Demand for the
Output of the Industry**

**B. Supply and Demand for the
Output of the Firm**

The equilibrium price P_0 is determined by the intersection of the industry's supply curve with the downward-sloping demand curve for the industry's product. The firm faces a horizontal demand curve at this going market price and chooses the quantity q_0 accordingly. The industry-wide quantity Q_0 is the sum of the quantities supplied by all of the firms in the industry.

produces the quantity q_0, at which its supply curve S (that is, its marginal cost curve) crosses the horizontal line at P_0.

Changes in Fixed Costs

Now we can investigate the effect of a change in costs. Suppose, first, that there is a rise in fixed costs, such as a general increase in the cost of large machinery or a new licensing fee for the industry. What happens to an individual firm's supply curve? Nothing, because marginal cost is unchanged. What about the industry's supply curve? It remains unchanged also, because industry supply is the sum of the individual firms' supplies and these remain fixed. Thus no curves shift in Exhibit 7–13, so both price and quantity remain unchanged.

Although this analysis is both correct and complete in the short run, it would be misleading to leave this example without mentioning an important long-run effect. Some firms might find themselves earning negative profits as a result of the rise in fixed costs, and those firms will leave the industry as soon as it is feasible to do so. The new industry supply curve is

Exhibit 7–14   A Rise in Fixed Costs

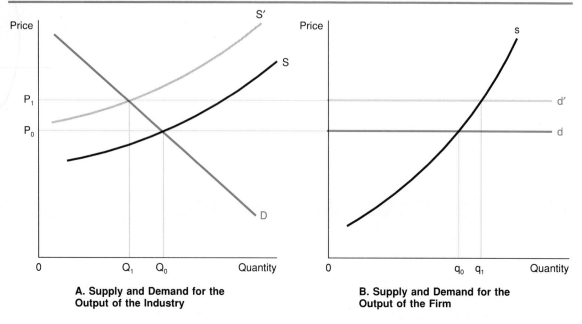

A. Supply and Demand for the Output of the Industry

B. Supply and Demand for the Output of the Firm

A rise in fixed costs leaves the firm's marginal costs, and hence its supply curve, unchanged. Thus the industry supply curve is unchanged, and both price and quantity are unchanged in the short run. Eventually, however, some firms will be driven from the industry by the increase in costs. The industry supply curve will now be the sum of fewer individual firm supply curves than before, so it shifts back to S'. The firm now faces a going market price of P_1 instead of P_0 and increases its quantity to q_1 from q_0.

---

the sum of a reduced number of individual firm supply curves. As a result, it is situated to the left of the previous industry supply curve, at S' in Exhibit 7–14.

▷ *Exercise 7.7* Draw graphs illustrating the effect of a fall in fixed costs. Distinguish the immediate effect from the effect after there has been time for new firms to enter the industry.

Prior to the change in costs, the firm produces q_0 at the market equilibrium price (P_0). After the change and after enough time for exit to take place, if our firm is one of those that remain in the industry, it will face a new, higher market price (P_1). At this price the firm increases its output to q_1.

A Change in Marginal Costs

Next consider the case of a rise in marginal costs, such as a rise in the price of raw materials or the imposition of an excise tax. This will immediately raise each firm's marginal cost curve and will also cause some firms to shut

Exhibit 7–15   **A Rise in Marginal Costs**

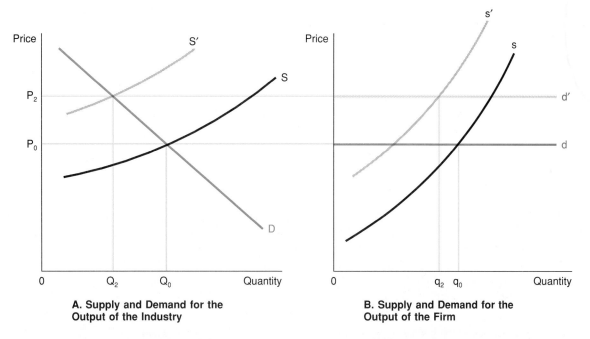

**A. Supply and Demand for the
Output of the Industry**

**B. Supply and Demand for the
Output of the Firm**

A rise in marginal costs causes the firm's supply curve to shift left from s to s' in panel B. The industry supply curve shifts left from S to S' in panel A, both because each firm's supply curve does and because some firms may shut down. The new market price is P_2. The firm operates at the intersection of s' with its new horizontal demand curve at P_2. Depending on how the curves are drawn, the firm could end up producing either more or less than it did before the rise in costs. (That is, q_2 could be either to the left or to the right of q_0.)

down. The industry supply curve moves leftward for both of these reasons, and we get a new market equilibrium price of P_2, shown in Exhibit 7–15. Depending on the shapes of the curves, the individual firm's output could go either up or down.

▷ *Exercise 7.8* Draw graphs illustrating the effect of a fall in marginal costs.

Changes in Demand

Exhibit 7–16 shows the effect of an increase in the demand for the industry's output. The new market equilibrium price of P_3 is taken as given by the firm, which increases its output to q_3.

▷ *Exercise 7.9* Draw graphs illustrating the effect of a fall in demand for the industry's output.

Exhibit 7–16   A Change in Demand

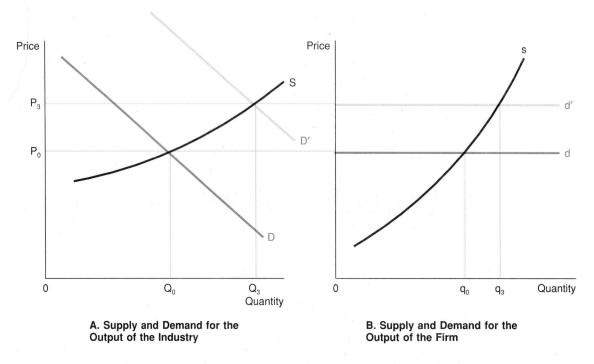

A. Supply and Demand for the
Output of the Industry

B. Supply and Demand for the
Output of the Firm

An increase in the demand for the industry's output raises the equilibrium price to P_3 and the firm's output to q_3.

7.3 The Competitive Industry in the Long Run

When we studied the short-run supply curve of a competitive industry, we began by adding up the supply curves of a given number of individual firms. In the long run we must take account of another factor: The number of firms can change due to the possibilities of entry and exit. Understanding entry and exit is the key to understanding long-run supply. Firms enter when there is an opportunity to earn positive profits, and they exit when profits are negative. Therefore our analysis of long-run supply must begin with a discussion of profits.

Profits in a Competitive Industry

How much profit is earned by a profit-maximizing firm in a competitive industry? In long-run equilibrium the surprising answer is zero! When profits are calculated correctly, the firms in a competitive industry must be earning zero profits. This is because if profits were positive, other firms would enter the industry, driving prices down. This process would continue until profits had fallen to zero.

Does this mean that firms are unsuccessful at choosing quantities so as to maximize profits? Not at all—they *are* maximizing profits, and the largest profit available to them is zero. If they produced a different quantity, their profits would be negative.

The key to understanding this apparently strange result is to keep in mind that an economist's definition of profit is very different from an accountant's definition. Imagine a paperboy who buys 100 papers at 20¢ apiece and sells each of them for a quarter. At the end of the day he visits his accountant and is informed that he has earned a profit of $5 ($25 in revenue minus $20 in costs). Later in the day he encounters an economist and boasts about the big profits he is making in the newspaper delivery industry. How will the economist respond?

The economist certainly agrees that the paperboy has earned $25 in revenue. But on the subject of costs, he argues that the $20 outlay for newspapers is only the beginning. He asks the paperboy what he would have been doing if not delivering papers. The boy responds, "Running a lemonade stand." "And what would you have earned," asks the economist, "if you'd worked as hard at running that lemonade stand as you did at delivering papers?" "Probably about $4.50," says the boy, beginning to suspect what the economist is up to. "I see," says the economist. "And by delivering papers, you gave up a chance to earn that $4.50. That forgone opportunity was part of the cost of delivering newspapers, wasn't it? I guess your profits were really only 50 cents." The boy, sadder and wiser, goes home, vowing to give up boasting to economists.

Or perhaps not. Perhaps the boy is an optimistic sort who digests the economist's argument and then says, "Well, at least I did make a positive profit of 50¢—thanks to the fact that the kids running lemonade stands are all bringing home about $4.50, and the kids selling newspapers are bringing home $5 for the same amount of work."

Now the economist should suspect very strongly that the boy is lying—or at least misinformed. If all the paperboys are earning $5, and all the kids running lemonade stands are making $4.50, what will happen? Some of the kids selling lemonade will decide to sell newspapers—they will exit the lemonade industry and enter the delivery industry. This will tend to drive down the returns to newspaper delivery and raise the returns to selling lemonade. How long will this process continue? Until returns are equalized across the two industries. That is, until profits in each industry are zero.

Now we can understand better what is meant by the statement "When profits are calculated correctly, the firms in a competitive industry must be earning zero profits." *Calculated correctly* means "calculated as an economist would calculate them," as total revenue minus the total of *all* costs, including the opportunity costs that your accountant won't let you claim on your tax return.

Let's give the paperboy one more chance. Perhaps he wants to argue as follows: "All those kids running lemonade stands earn only $4.50. You claim that if I were making $5 selling newspapers, they would all switch to selling newspapers. But that's not true, because in fact most paperboys only make $4.50, and that's all that the lemonade sellers could make if they switched. I just happen to be one of the few paperboys making *more* than $4.50. I make $5 because I'm an exceptionally talented paperboy. I have extra-strong muscles in my legs, so I can pedal my bicycle and deliver papers twice as fast as anyone else. I have uncanny intuition about who will be interested in buying a paper and know just which doors to knock on soliciting new subscriptions. As a result, I can earn far more in the field of newspaper delivery than I can running a lemonade stand or anything else. *Now* will you admit that my profits are positive?"

No, he won't. (Economists are an obstinate lot.) "Well, I'm thinking about those kids in the lemonade business," he'll say. "They're all sitting there making $4.50 and they see you making $5. They're all thinking, 'I really ought to get into selling newspapers, so I can make more money too.' But they realize they can't do it on their own. They're just not as good at it as you are. So the clever ones are thinking, 'I should start a newspaper delivery business and hire that kid who's always arguing with the economist to run it for me.' Since you can bring in $5 a week for them, they'll be willing to pay you up to $5 a week to do the job. By staying in business for yourself, you're forgoing that $5 a week. Now let's figure out your profits. Revenue of $25 minus $20 to buy the newspapers minus $5 you could have made running the same business for someone else—this comes to a profit of just about—" (here he pushes a few buttons on his calculator) "zero."

The economist is making a subtle but crucial distinction. He distinguishes between the newspaper delivery firm that the boy owns and operates and the boy himself. He thinks of the firm as renting the boy's special skills from him at a rate of $5 per year. (This is the rate those skills command on the open market.) The boy earns a **rent** of $5 per year, whereas the firm earns a profit of zero.

Rent
A payment made by the firm to hire a factor of production. When the firm and the factor are owned by the same person, we imagine the firm paying the factor its opportunity cost and count this as a rent.

In general, *firms earn profits whereas individuals earn rents*. Profits are equal to revenues minus costs. The costs to be counted are both explicit (wages, equipment rental, and the like) and implicit (the rents paid by the firm to its owners for the use of their special skills). The latter rents must be sufficient to induce the owners not to sell their skills elsewhere, and so must be equal to what somebody else would pay to hire those skills.

Different economists have different preferences about how to treat especially productive inputs, such as the paperboy's skills or the exceptionally fertile land on some particular farm. We have taken the view that the firm hires the input from its owner and pays him a rent equal to its opportunity cost, leaving the firm with a profit of zero. The payments are often implicit, because the owner of the input and the owner of the firm might be the same person—so we have to imagine Young Jeeter the delivery firm owner paying rent to Young Jeeter the good bicyclist for delivering his papers, or Farmer Ryan the owner of the farm paying rent to Farmer Ryan the owner of the land in exchange for its use.

Some economists would prefer to say that when a firm has access to especially productive inputs, we should not maintain this fiction about rents being paid, but should instead say that the firm is earning positive profits.

It doesn't matter what we call a profit and what we call a rent, as long as we are consistent in our use of language. In this book we will consistently use language as the economist used it in his dialogue with the paperboy. What *does* matter is the idea underlying this terminology: If all firms are identical, then they will enter an industry until each firm is indifferent between being in that industry and the next best alternative. If there are differences among firms, then the more efficient firms will enter the industry first, followed by slightly less efficient firms, and so on until the last firm to enter is indifferent between being in the industry and the next best alternative. We are then free to say either that the more efficient firms are earning profits or (as we will do in this book) that their owners are earning rents on whatever resource it is that makes them more efficient.

With the definitions we are using, the following must be the case:

All firms earn zero profits in long-run competitive equilibrium.

This statement must be interpreted with care. The word *profits* is being used to mean **economic profits,** which is to say the difference between revenues and all costs, inclusive of the opportunity costs of resources owned by the firm. These are to be distinguished from **accounting profits,** which are calculated without subtracting those opportunity costs. Accounting profits are of little interest in economics, but they are what most noneconomists are referring to when they use the word *profit*.

Economic profits
Total revenue minus total cost.

Accounting profits
Total revenue minus those costs that an accountant would consider; this excludes the opportunity costs of resources owned by the firm.

You might wonder why firms bother to operate at all if they earn zero profits. The answer is that if they failed to operate (and if they failed to operate in a profit-maximizing way), they would earn negative profits and be worse off. If the firm did not operate at all, it would forgo the opportunity to earn positive accounting profits, and the economist would reckon this forgone opportunity as a loss.

An example might help: Suppose that you have the choice between working at McDonald's, working at Burger King, or staying home, which you find no more or less pleasant than working. At either McDonald's or Burger King you could earn $50 a week. By the accountant's reckoning, your profits from working at either place are $50 a week and your profits if you stay home are zero. By the economist's reckoning, your profits from working at either place are zero, since you have forgone the opportunity to work at the other place, and your profits from staying home are -50, due to the forgone opportunity to work. Both will agree that you maximize profits by working rather than staying home.

Exhibit 7–17   **Long-Run Zero-Profit Equilibrium**

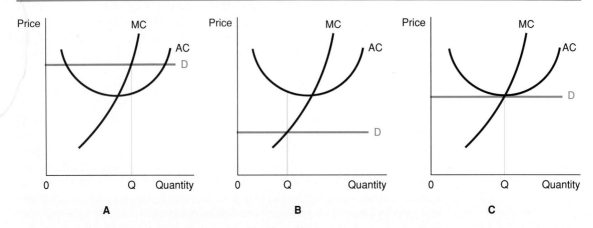

In each panel the firm produces quantity Q, where marginal cost equals price, so that profits are maximized. (Q is different in each panel.) In panel A price exceeds average cost at Q, so that the firm earns positive profits. This will attract entry, driving down the price. In panel B average cost exceeds price at Q, so that the firm earns negative profits. This leads to exit, driving up the price. In panel C price equals average cost, so that profits are zero. Panel C is the only correct depiction of a long-run zero-profits equilibrium.

Average Cost in the Long Run

The long-run situation of the competitive firm is completely summarized by three curves: the firm's long-run marginal and average cost curves and the flat demand curve for its product. In order to draw the three curves on the same diagram, we must understand the relationships among them. We already know from Section 6.3 that when long-run average cost is U-shaped, long-run marginal cost cuts through at the bottom of the U. This leaves three possible configurations, shown in the three panels of Exhibit 7–17. We can use the zero profits condition to show that only panel C can be correct.

We need three observations:

1. The firm produces that quantity Q at which marginal cost equals marginal revenue. This just says that the firm maximizes profits.

2. Marginal revenue = Price. This just says that the demand curve is flat, or, in other words, that the firm is competitive.

3. Profits are zero. In other words,

$$\text{Total revenue} = \text{Total cost.}$$

Since Total revenue = P × Q, we can divide each side by Q to get

$$P = \frac{TC}{Q} = AC.$$

Putting these facts together, we discover that at quantity Q we have MC = MR = P = AC. That is, Q must be the quantity at which marginal and average costs are equal, and we know that this happens at the bottom of the U. Thus only panel C in Exhibit 7–17 can be correct.

We conclude that a firm in long-run competitive equilibrium produces at the lowest point on its average cost curve.

In long-run competitive equilibrium, firms produce at the lowest possible average cost.

It is not correct to say that firms seek to minimize average costs. Firms seek to maximize profits, which is not at all the same thing. The fact that firms minimize average costs in the long run is as much a consequence of the zero profits condition as it is of profit maximization. If entry were prohibited, firms might very well be in the situation depicted by panel A in Exhibit 7–17, where price exceeds average cost at the quantity Q and average cost is not minimized.

Long-Run Supply with All Firms Identical

A firm decides whether to enter an industry on the basis of what it can earn in that industry and what it can earn elsewhere. An important consideration is whether the firm has access to specialized skills or factors of production that are especially valuable in one particular industry. We shall begin by analyzing an industry in which there are no such firms. Then we shall relax this assumption to get a more complete picture of the possible structures that a competitive industry could have.

The Entry Decision and the Long-Run Supply Curve

How does a firm decide whether to become a barbershop? The answer must depend partly on what alternatives it has. Suppose, for simplicity, that the only alternative to becoming a barbershop is for the firm to remain what it is now, namely a gas station. (Imagine an entrepreneur who owns a piece of land and a building that can be used for either purpose.) Suppose, also for simplicity (though we shall relax this later), that all firms are identical in the sense that they have access to identical resources and no firm has any comparative advantage in either industry.

The owner of the firm can begin by observing the accounting profits of the gas station owners. Suppose that each gas station earns $100 per year by this reckoning. Then the firm will become a barbershop if barbershops earn more than $100, will remain a gas station if barbershops earn less than $100, and will be just indifferent between the two if barbershops earn exactly $100.

Now, what determines how much barbershops earn? Taking input costs as given, the only variable that affects the earnings of barbershops is the price of haircuts. Let us suppose that barbershops can earn $100 per year when the price of haircuts is $2. They can earn more than $100 per year

Exhibit 7–18   **The Long-Run Industry Supply Curve with All Firms Identical**

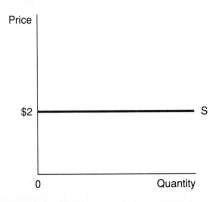

There is exactly one price of haircuts that will allow firms to earn zero economic profits in the barbershop industry. That price is known as the entry price. On the assumption that all firms are identical, all will have the same entry price. Here we assume that price to be $2. At any higher price, every firm in the world would enter the industry, yielding an effectively infinite quantity supplied. At any lower price, every firm would exit, yielding zero quantity supplied. At a price of $2, selling haircuts is exactly as attractive as the alternative of selling gasoline, so firms are indifferent about entry. Any number of firms might enter and any quantity might be supplied. Therefore the long-run supply curve for haircuts is flat at a price of $2.

Entry price
The minimum output price that would cause a firm to enter a given industry.

when the price of haircuts is more than $2, and they can earn less than $100 per year when the price of haircuts is less than $2.

We say that $2 is the **entry price** in the barbershop industry. It is the price of output at which firms will be just indifferent about entering the industry.

At prices above the entry price of $2, there will be an opportunity to earn positive economic profits in the barbershop industry, and every firm in the world will choose to enter. The quantity of haircuts supplied by the industry will be effectively infinite. At prices below the entry price of $2, barbershops earn negative economic profits, and all exit to become gas stations. The quantity of haircuts supplied will be zero. At the price of $2 each firm is indifferent between becoming a barbershop and not becoming a barbershop. The industry could supply any quantity of haircuts at all, depending on what firms do.

It follows that the industry supply curve for haircuts is flat at the price of $2, as shown in Exhibit 7–18.

An Exception: The Factor-Price Effect

In the long run, as in the short run, there is potentially a factor-price effect. When firms purchase variable inputs, we usually assume that they do so at a going market price, and that this price is unaffected by how much the firm purchases. This assumption is justified if the firm's demand for the input is a small part of the market's demand.

Exhibit 7–19   **The Long-Run Factor-Price Effect**

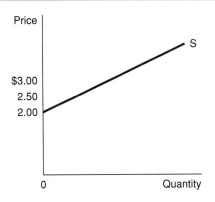

The initial entry price is $2. When there are no firms in the industry, every firm is willing to enter at this price. However, as soon as a few firms do enter, input prices are bid up, making entry less attractive. Now a higher output price, say $2.50, is necessary to attract more firms to the industry. This continues, so that after a little more entry, the output price must be $3, and so on. Ever-higher output prices are necessary to call forth higher quantities supplied. Therefore the long-run supply curve can slope upward, even with all firms identical.

When the entire industry expands, however, we face the possibility that the price of an input could be bid up, raising the costs and thereby changing the entry prices of the individual firms.

Let us take a very simple numerical example. Suppose that gas stations all earn accounting profits of $100. A gas station can become a barbershop by purchasing a razor for $8. Any barbershop can sell exactly 54 haircuts, and has no costs other than the purchase of the razor.

If the price of haircuts is $2, each barbershop will have revenues of $108. Subtracting the $8 cost of the razor, the shop is left with $100, which is the same as what it could earn as a gas station. Therefore $2 is the entry price to the barbershop industry. At this price every firm is indifferent about entry.

Now suppose that many gas stations do become barbershops. They each buy a razor, and in doing so they bid the price of razors up to $35. At a price of $2 per haircut, a barbershop can now earn only $2 × 54 − $35 = $73, so that no firms will enter. However, at a price of $2.50 per haircut, a barbershop can earn exactly $2.50 × 54 − $35 = $100. Therefore $2.50 is the new entry price.

As even more firms enter, the price of razors will go up yet again, and the entry price will be bid up even further.

▷ *Exercise 7.10* Suppose that the price of a razor gets bid up to $116. What will be the new entry price in the barbershop industry?

The result of this is that even though all firms are identical, the industry's long-run supply curve will still slope upward. As firms enter and input prices are bid up, higher output prices are necessary to attract additional supply.

The long-run factor-price effect is illustrated in Exhibit 7–19.

Long-Run Supply with Not All Firms Identical

Now let us relax our assumption that all firms are identical. Some firms might be more efficient than others because they own specialized resources, such as talent, patent rights, confidential information about the market, or high-quality equipment that is not readily available to others.

If these resources cause firms to have different cost curves (the paper-boy with strong legs delivers papers at a lower marginal cost than the paperboy who has to struggle to get uphill), then they will have different entry prices. The most efficient firm will have the lowest entry price. Remember that the "most efficient" firm is the one with the comparative advantage. A boy with low opportunity costs (one who can only earn $1 per year selling lemonade) will switch to selling newspapers as soon as the price of newspapers is high enough to allow him to earn $1.01 by doing so. A boy who is more talented in both industries might or might not have a comparative advantage delivering newspapers. His entry price could be either higher or lower.

▷ *Exercise 7.11** Consider the electrician and the carpenter described in Exhibit 2–2. Suppose that the market wage for paneling is $9 per job. What is each worker's entry price in the rewiring industry? Suppose that the market wage for rewiring is $10 per job. What is each worker's entry price in the paneling industry?

In an industry where not all firms are identical, the long-run supply curve is upward sloping because different firms have different entry prices. As the price goes up, successively less efficient firms are tempted into the industry, thereby increasing quantity supplied.

An Intermediate Case: A Few Efficient Firms

One case of interest is that in which there are a few firms with access to special resources that are useful in the industry, and then a great number of other firms that are essentially identical. In this case the few efficient firms will be willing to enter the industry at low output prices, yielding a small but nonzero quantity supplied. At the entry price of the nonefficient firms, any number can enter and any quantity can be supplied. Thus the supply curve could be as shown in Exhibit 7–20. In such an industry, when there is sufficient demand for equilibrium to occur on the flat part of the supply curve, it is usually harmless to assume (for simplicity) that the entire supply curve is flat.

Exhibit 7–20   **Long-Run Supply with a Few Efficient Firms**

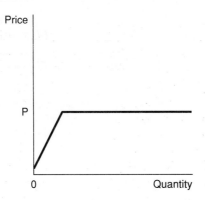

Suppose that there are a few exceptionally efficient firms and a great number of other identical firms. At low prices, the efficient firms enter and supply small quantities of output. At the entry price of the less efficient firms (P), the supply curve becomes flat.

Long-Run Industry Costs

There is a close analogy between the shapes of the individual firm's long-run cost and supply curves and the competitive industry's long-run cost and supply curves. The shapes of the firm's long-run cost and supply curves are determined by whether the firm experiences increasing, decreasing, or constant returns to scale. The same is true at the industry level, as discussed below.

Constant Cost Industries

Recall that if the firm experiences constant returns to scale, then its long-run average cost curve and long-run supply curve are flat. This occurs when it is true that "what the firm can do once, it can do twice." In other words, if all inputs are truly variable, the firm can double its output by doubling its inputs, thereby doubling its costs. Each unit of output is produced at the same average cost and same marginal cost as any other.

From the industry's point of view, firms are like an input into the production function, in the sense that the industry uses firms to produce output. When firms are truly a variable input, in the sense that any number of identical firms can enter the industry, and when all other resources are truly variable, in the sense that the industry can acquire them in unlimited quantities at a given price, then the industry's long-run average cost curve is flat. The industry can double its output by simply doubling the number of firms and having each new firm behave like each of the old firms.

Another way to say this is: "What the industry can do once, it can do twice."

An industry with a flat long-run average cost curve (and consequently a flat long-run supply curve) is called a **constant cost industry.**

Increasing Cost Industries

An industry fails to have constant costs only when some part of the production process cannot be perfectly replicated. This occurs either when there are differences among firms or when a factor-price effect makes it impossible to acquire an unlimited quantity of some input at a given cost. Either of these phenomena leads to decreasing returns to scale in the industry, causing the industry's long-run average cost curve to eventually slope upward. Consequently, the industry's long-run supply curve eventually slopes upward. Such an industry is called an **increasing cost industry.**

Agriculture is a good example of an increasing cost industry. The quality of land varies significantly from farm to farm. The 200 most efficient farms can produce less than twice the output of the 100 most efficient farms.

Decreasing Cost Industries

There is also the possibility that the industry's long-run average cost curve slopes downward over the entire range of market demand. This is the case of a **decreasing cost industry.** Imagine a community with a small number of printers, each of whom makes his own ink. When the number of printers increases, an ink-making industry arises to serve them. Now each printer can buy ink from a specialist at a lower cost than making it himself. Because the ink industry can arise only when there are enough printers to support it, the entry of new printers drives down costs for existing printers. Twice the number of printers can produce more than twice the number of printed pages. There are increasing returns to scale in the industry, and consequently decreasing long-run average costs and a decreasing long-run supply curve.

In Chapter 2 we discussed the gains from trade due to comparative advantage. Decreasing cost industries present an example of a different kind of gain from trade, one that is not due to comparative advantage on the part of the traders. Suppose that each of two different isolated countries has a small number of printers, insufficient to support an ink maker. If these two countries begin to trade with each other, the combined number of printers could suffice to bring an ink maker into the market. Residents of both countries would gain from the reduced cost of producing pamphlets.

How Long Is the Long Run?

To the question "How long is the long run?" the quick answer is that it is the amount of time necessary for all firms to adjust completely to a change

Constant cost industry An industry in which the long-run average cost curve is flat; that is, an industry that produces subject to constant returns to scale.

Increasing cost industry An industry in which the long-run average cost curve is eventually upward sloping; that is, an industry that produces subject to eventually decreasing returns to scale.

Decreasing cost industry An industry in which the long-run average cost curve is downward sloping; that is, an industry that produces subject to increasing returns to scale.

in price, where adjustments can include entering or exiting from the industry. In practice, this length of time can vary considerably from industry to industry. In an industry where capital is relatively unimportant, such as sidewalk flower vending, adjustments can occur very quickly. In an industry that relies heavily on its physical plant, such as publishing, adjustments take longer.

When we make arguments that rely on entry and exit, we should remember that we are dealing with processes that take time. In the real world a firm cannot instantly convert itself from a dress shop to a cafeteria. If the demand for cafeteria services rises, cafeteria owners may indeed find themselves earning positive profits—*until* other firms have had a chance to enter the industry. It is only after the smoke has cleared and firms have moved into the industry that profits return to zero. Notice that this means that over any length of time too short to allow for entry, the supply curve of any competitive industry is upward sloping.

Many economists argue that the long-run zero profits equilibrium is never reached, because demand curves and cost curves shift so often that the entry and exit process never settles down. Although this is arguably true in many industries, the zero profits condition is often a very useful approximation to the truth.

Long-Run Competitive Equilibrium

The relationship between the competitive industry and the competitive firm is the same in the long run as it is in the short run: The market price is determined by the intersection of the industry-wide supply and demand curves, and firms face flat demand curves at the level of this market price. This is the same relationship that is illustrated in Exhibit 7–13 for the short-run case.

However, the analysis of *changes* in equilibrium is not the same in the long run as in the short run. This is primarily because the long-run and short-run industry supply curves move differently in response to various changes in the economic environment. Anything that affects the profitability of firms can lead to entry or exit from the industry and hence to a shift in the long-run industry supply curve. However, changes in profits do not affect anything in the short run, because in the short run there can be no entry or exit.

 Entry and exit due to changes in the price of output are reflected by movements *along* the long-run supply curve. Entry and exit due to things other than the price of output are reflected by movements *of* the long-run supply curve.

Changes in Fixed Costs

Suppose that new legislation is passed requiring each amusement park to carry $100 million worth of liability insurance, which is more than amusement parks now carry. This does not affect any firm's marginal cost curve, either in the short run or in the long run. In the short run, it also does not affect the industry supply curve, since there are a fixed number of amusement parks, and no park's supply curve shifts. Thus, in the short run there is no change in price or quantity. However, since amusement parks earn zero profits before the law is passed, they must earn negative profits after the law is passed. Therefore there will be exit from the industry, which is illustrated by a shift in the long-run industry supply curve. Exhibit 7–21 illustrates the old and new equilibria, first under the assumption that amusement parks are a constant cost industry and then under the assumption that they are an increasing cost industry.

In Chapter 6 we argued that in the long run, firms have no fixed costs because they can vary their employment of any factor of production. As long as a firm's costs consist entirely of payments to factors, it is correct to say that the firm has no fixed costs. However, the insurance requirement that we have just considered, because it can not be avoided and does not vary with output, is a fixed cost even in the long run.

It is important to distinguish a fixed cost from a sunk cost. Although the insurance payment is a fixed cost for any firm that decides to remain in the industry, it is not yet a sunk cost at the point when the entry/exit decision is being made. Thus, it is relevant to the decision. A cost that is truly sunk, in the sense that it can not be avoided even by leaving the industry, will not affect anything.

Changes in Marginal Costs

An increase in the variable costs of production causes the firm's average and marginal cost curves to shift upward. The industry supply curve shifts leftward, both because each firm's supply curve shifts and because some firms leave the industry. The new equilibrium for an increasing-cost industry is illustrated in Exhibit 7–22. The picture for a constant-cost industry is similar.

Changes in Demand

The panels of Exhibit 7–23 show the effect of an increase in demand in a constant-cost, increasing-cost, and decreasing-cost industry. Only the industry-wide picture is shown. Both the short-run and the long-run effects are illustrated.

Initially the industry is in both short-run and long-run equilibrium at the price P_0 and quantity Q_0. An increase in demand, from D to D', initially leads to a movement along the short-run supply curve S to a higher price P_1 and a higher quantity Q_1. In the long run, after the higher price attracts entry, the industry moves to the intersection between the long-run supply curve LRS and the new demand curve D'. There is now a new short-run industry supply curve S'.

Exhibit 7–21   **A Rise in Fixed Costs**

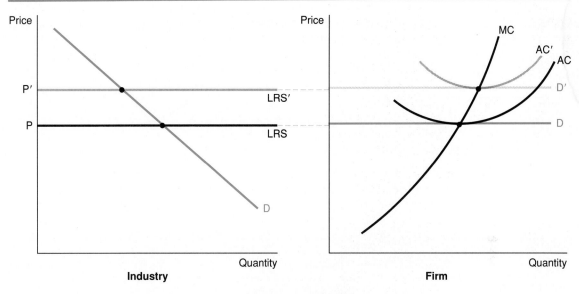

A. Constant Cost Industry

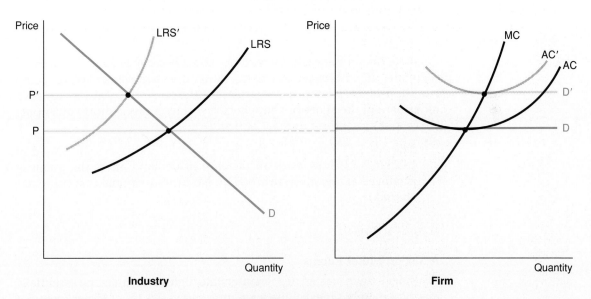

B. Increasing Cost Industry

Suppose that there is an increase in some cost that is a fixed cost for firms even in the long run. The top graphs show the effect on long-run competitive equilibrium in a constant cost industry and the bottom graphs show the effect on long-run competitive equilibrium in an increasing cost industry. In each case, the firm's average cost curve rises from AC to AC', without any change in marginal cost. Now existing firms earn negative profits, so long-run industry supply shifts from LRS to LRS', which is just far enough so that at the new equilibrium price P' firms can earn zero profits again.

Exhibit 7–22   A Change in Marginal Cost

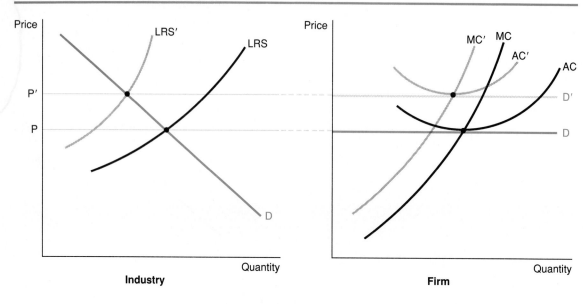

An increase in marginal cost raises the firm's marginal and average cost curves to MC' and AC'. Industry supply moves back to LRS', so that price rises to P' where firms can once again earn zero profits.

Note that in this case, entry comes about because of a rise in price and therefore causes a movement along, rather than a movement of, the long-run supply curve. However, regardless of the cause, entry always causes a movement of the short-run supply curve, since a given short-run supply curve assumes a fixed number of firms.

▷ *Exercise 7.12* For each of the three types of industries illustrated in Exhibit 7–23, how does an increase in demand affect the quantity produced at any given firm? (*Hint:* No firm's marginal cost curve has shifted.)

Applications

A Tax on Motel Rooms

Consider a town located near an interstate highway, with many essentially identical motels. One day the town imposes a sales tax of $5 per room per night. Who pays the tax?

By far the most important input in the provision of motel services is the physical motel rooms. However, it is not the only input. By hiring a larger maintenance staff, for example, a motel owner may be able to increase the number of rooms he has available on the average night. In the short run motel rooms are a fixed input and maintenance staff is a variable input.

Exhibit 7–23   Constant Cost, Increasing Cost, and Decreasing Cost Industries

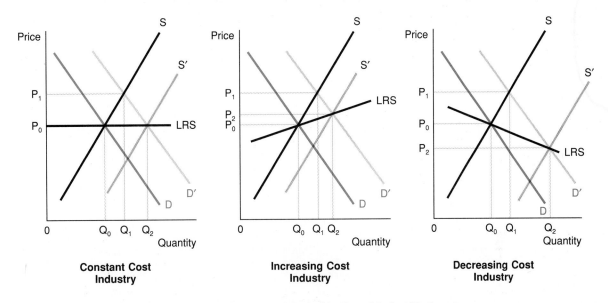

Constant Cost Industry

Increasing Cost Industry

Decreasing Cost Industry

The graphs show the long-run effects of a rise in demand in three kinds of industries.

In the constant cost case, the industry is initially in long-run equilibrium at a price of P_0. An increase in demand has the immediate effect of bidding up price to P_1 and output to Q_1 as the industry moves along its short-run supply curve S. At the new price of P_1, firms earn positive profits, so there is entry until the price is driven back down to P_0. The industry now produces Q_2 on its new short-run supply curve S'.

In the increasing cost case, the industry is initially in long-run equilibrium at a price of P_0. An increase in demand has the immediate effect of bidding up price to P_1 and quantity to Q_1 as the industry moves along its short-run supply curve S. At the new price of P_1, firms earn positive profits, so there is entry. Price is driven back down, but costs are driven up, either because the new firms are less efficient than the old ones or because of the factor-price effect. Therefore profits are driven to zero at a price higher than the original price P_0. That price is P_2, and industry output is Q_2 on its new short-run supply curve S'.

In the decreasing cost case, the industry is initially in long-run equilibrium at a price of P_0. An increase in demand has the immediate effect of bidding up price to P_1 and quantity to Q_1 as the industry moves along its short-run supply curve S. At the new price of P_1, firms earn positive profits, so there is entry. This entry reduces costs at the existing firms (as in the example of the printing industry described in the text). As the existing firms' marginal cost curves fall, a new short-run industry supply curve is established at S' and the price drops to P_2, with industry output at Q_2.

Because of the importance of the fixed input, the short-run supply curve for motel rooms is nearly vertical. Consequently, the tax will be paid mostly by suppliers (motels), as shown in panel A of Exhibit 7–24, where the price falls from P to P', almost the entire amount of the tax.

In the long run, however, the number of motel rooms is variable, because individual motels can expand or contract, because new motels can appear, and because existing motels can convert to other enterprises, say by becoming coffee shops. Therefore the long-run industry supply curve is much flatter than the short-run industry supply curve. Is it perfectly flat?

Exhibit 7–24   A Tax on Motel Rooms near a Highway

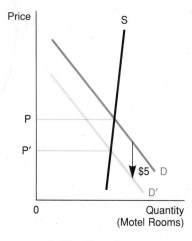

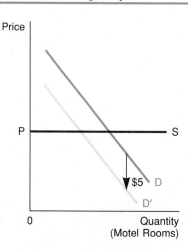

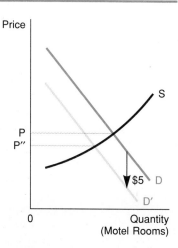

A. The Short Run

B. The Long Run If Motels Use
a Small Percentage of the
Land near the Highway

C. The Long Run If Motels Use a
Large Percentage of the Land
near the Highway

In the short run the number of motel rooms is nearly fixed. (It is not entirely fixed, because the number of rooms available on a given night can be stretched by the use of additional maintenance staff or other means.) As a result, the short-run supply curve is nearly vertical, so a sales tax lowers the price of rooms by almost the full amount of the tax, from P to P′ in panel A. The tax burden falls almost entirely on suppliers.

In the long run the lowered price leads to exit from the industry, causing prices to rise until profits are zero again. If the marginal cost of building motels is constant, then price must be bid up to its original level P, as in panel B. Now demanders pay the full burden of the tax.

If, on the other hand, motels use a significant proportion of the land near the highway, then exit will drive down land prices and so drive down the cost of owning a motel. As a result, the new zero profits price will be lower than the original price, at P″ in panel C, though the price does not fall by as much as in the short run.

Suppose for the moment that the motel industry uses only a small portion of the land near the highway. In this case there is no reason for the construction of the thousandth motel to cost more than the construction of the first motel. Motel rooms are provided by the industry at constant marginal cost, so that there is a flat long-run industry supply curve, as shown in panel B of Exhibit 7–24. In the long run firms exit from the industry until the price of motel rooms is bid back up to P, and the tax is paid entirely by demanders (travelers).

Suppose, on the other hand, that the motel industry demands a significant fraction of the land near the highway. Then when the industry contracts, the price of land decreases, reducing the marginal cost of owning a motel room. The industry's long-run marginal cost curve is upward sloping (though not as steeply as its short-run marginal cost curve), as shown in panel C of Exhibit 7–24. Therefore price is bid up from P′ in the short run to P″ in the long run, but not all the way back up to P. The tax will be split between suppliers and demanders, with demanders paying much more than they did in the short run.

▷ *Exercise 7.13* Illustrate the short-run and long-run effects of a government program that subsidizes motel visits.

Tipping the Busboy

In Carmel, California, there is an organization called the Brotherhood for the Respect, Elevation, and Advancement of Dishwashers. The organization's purpose is to encourage people to give tips to busboys. Who will benefit if they succeed in establishing this custom?

A partial answer is: not busboys. The talents required of a busboy are reasonably widespread in society. A grocery bagger or a parking lot attendant can easily decide to become a busboy. Because there are no (or very few) individuals with special "busboy skills," busboys' services are provided at a constant cost.

It follows that the total compensation of busboys cannot change. If tips increase, wages must decrease by the same amount. The increase in tips causes positive profits; the positive profits cause grocery baggers to become busboys; the entry of the grocery baggers causes wages to fall; and the whole process continues until grocery bagging and bussing tables are again equally attractive.

Students sometimes argue that as grocery baggers leave their own industry to become busboys, the wage of baggers will rise. This would be true if bagging were the only other unskilled occupation. But since the new busboys come from *many* other industries, the number coming from any *one* other industry is negligibly small.

Another way to make the same point is this: Since potential busboys are all pretty much identical, the supply curve of busboys is a horizontal line at the entry price determined by the condition that bussing be just as attractive as bagging. If the supply curve for a good is horizontal, then changes in demand cannot change its price.

If busboys don't gain, who does? Tipping reduces the costs of restaurant owners, who now pay lower wages. Suppose that customers leave a tip of size T at each meal. Then busboys' wages are reduced by T per meal served, which lowers the industry's supply curve by the amount T. The short-run effect is illustrated in panel A of Exhibit 7–25. The fall in costs leads to a fall in the price of restaurant meals, to P_1. Who benefits? The restauranteurs and, ironically, the customers themselves.

In the long run there are two possibilities to consider, both of which are shown in Exhibit 7–25. In each case the long-run supply curve falls by T. If the restaurant industry has constant costs, as in panel B, then the price of a meal drops by exactly T, the full amount of the tip. Although the customers would like to tip the busboys, the entire value of their tips is returned to them in the form of lower meal prices!

Exhibit 7–25   **Tipping the Busboy**

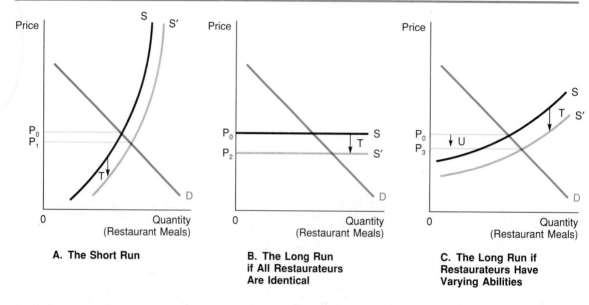

| A. The Short Run | B. The Long Run if All Restaurateurs Are Identical | C. The Long Run if Restaurateurs Have Varying Abilities |

Suppose that people decide to start tipping busboys. Because bussing services are provided at constant cost (there are many essentially identical busboys), the total compensation of busboys cannot change. Therefore wages are reduced by the amount of the tip, T. The marginal cost of serving meals falls by this amount.

In the short run (panel A), price falls, but by less than T. Part of the tip is returned to the customer through the lower price, and the rest goes to the restaurant owner.

In the long run, if all restauranteurs are identical (panel B), entry bids profits back down to zero only when the price of meals falls by the full amount T. We can see this geometrically: The horizontal supply curve falls by T, and the price falls by this full amount.

If not all restauranteurs are identical, then entry by less efficient firms can drive profits to zero even though the price is reduced by less than the full amount of the tip. This is shown in panel C, where the upward-sloping long-run supply curve drops by the amount T, but the price of meals falls by something less, which we label U. Those restauranteurs who were in the industry originally gain rents equal to T − U per meal served (their marginal costs fall by T but their price falls by U, so they gain the difference), while customers get back U in the form of a lower price. The tip is split between the restauranteur and the customer; the busboy gets nothing.

The other possibility is that there are increasing costs in the restaurant industry. This would be the case, for example, if the potential entrants have varying aptitudes for restaurant management. That case is shown in panel C. Here the price of restaurant meals drops, but not by the full amount of the tips. The tips are split between the restauranteurs and their customers, with the customers getting back more in the long run than they do in the short run.

Summary

A perfectly competitive firm is one that faces a horizontal demand curve for its product; that is, it can sell any quantity it wants to at the going market price. The total revenue curve for such a firm is a straight line through the origin, and the marginal revenue curve is a horizontal line at the going market price. Thus the marginal revenue curve is identical with the demand curve.

Like any producer, competitive or not, the competitive firm produces, if it produces at all, where marginal cost equals marginal revenue. Since marginal revenue equals price for a competitive firm, we can say that such a firm produces, if it produces at all, where marginal cost equals price. To see what the firm will produce in the short run, we use its short-run marginal cost curve, and to see what it will produce in the long run, we use its long-run marginal cost curve.

In the short run the firm will produce precisely if its revenue exceeds its variable costs. This is the same as saying that the firm will produce precisely if the market price exceeds its average variable cost. In the long run the firm has no fixed costs, so it will produce precisely if the market price exceeds its full average cost. Thus the firm's short-run supply curve is that portion of its marginal cost curve that lies above average variable cost, and its long-run supply curve is that portion of its long-run marginal cost curve that lies above long-run average cost.

A competitive industry is one in which all firms are competitive and any firm can freely enter or exit in the long run.

To derive the short-run industry supply curve, we assume a fixed number of firms and add their quantities supplied at each price. It might then be necessary to modify the industry supply curve to take account of the factor-price effect.

The competitive industry operates at the point where supply and demand are equal, because each individual firm maximizes profits at this point. In competitive equilibrium the total cost of producing any quantity of output is minimized. This is because each firm has the same marginal cost (equal to the market price).

To study long-run equilibrium, we must take account of the possibility of entry and exit. This is governed by the zero profits condition. There are several cases to consider.

One possibility is that all firms are identical and the industry produces according to constant returns to scale (so that doubling the number of identical firms will double industry output). In this case there is only one price that can prevail: the one at which each firm earns exactly zero profits. Any higher price would bring entry, bidding the price back down, and any lower price would bring exit, bidding the price back up. Here the industry long-run supply curve is flat, and the industry is known as a constant cost industry.

A second possibility is that all firms are identical but that nevertheless there are decreasing returns to scale. Doubling the number of firms will less than double output, because of the factor-price effect. In this case firms might earn zero profits at a low price when there are few firms but will earn zero profits only at a higher price when there are many firms. As a result, price must rise as the industry expands. The industry long-run supply curve is upward sloping. This is an example of an increasing cost industry.

A third possibility is that there are differences among firms. At a low price only the most efficient firms will want to enter. At higher prices more firms will enter, always to the point where the last firm is just indifferent between remaining in the industry and its next best alternative. At these higher prices the owners of the more efficient firms will earn rents, which we think of as paid by the firm to the owner of the superior resource that makes it more efficient. Once again the industry experiences decreasing returns to scale (doubling the number of firms reduces the average efficiency of firms and less than doubles output) and has an upward-sloping long-run supply curve. This is another example of an increasing cost industry.

A final possibility is that the act of entry by some firms reduces the costs of production. For example, when the industry reaches a certain size, specialized subindustries can be formed. In this case there are increasing returns to scale, and a downward-sloping long-run supply curve. We call this a decreasing cost industry.

Review Questions

R1. For a competitive firm with an upward-sloping marginal cost curve, explain carefully why the marginal cost curve and supply curve are identical.

R2. When a competitive firm has a U-shaped marginal cost curve, what is its supply curve in the short run? In the long run? Explain why.

R3. What is the smallest profit that a competitive firm can earn in the short run? In the long run?

R4. Explain the marginal condition for minimizing the industry's total costs. Explain why this condition is satisfied in a competitive industry.

R5. What is the relationship among the following concepts: (a) the returns to scale experienced in a competitive industry, (b) the shape of the average cost curve in that industry, and (c) the shape of the long-run supply curve in that industry. Explain.

R6. If all firms earn zero profits in long-run equilibrium, why do any firms exist?

R7. In what kinds of industries are all firms indifferent about being in the industry? In what kinds are some firms not indifferent?

Numerical Exercises

N1. Kites are manufactured by identical firms. Each firm's long-run average and marginal costs of production are given by

$$AC = Q + \frac{100}{Q} \quad \text{and} \quad MC = 2Q,$$

where Q is the number of kites produced.
  a. In long-run equilibrium, how many kites will each firm produce? Describe the long-run supply curve for kites.
  b. Suppose that the demand for kites is given by the formula

$$Q = 8000 - 50P,$$

where Q is the quantity demanded and P is the price. How many kites will be sold? How many firms will there be in the kite industry?
  c. Suppose that the demand for kites unexpectedly goes up to

$$Q = 9000 - 50P.$$

In the short run it is impossible to manufacture any more kites than those already in existence. What will the price of kites be? How much profit will each kite maker earn?
  d. In the long run, what will the price of kites be? How many new firms will enter the kite-making industry? How much profit will they earn?

N2. Suppose that a law is passed requiring each kite maker to have one fire extinguisher on the premises. (These are the same kite makers we met in the preceding exercise.) The supply curve of fire extinguishers to the kite makers is

$$Q = P.$$

For example, at a price of $3, 3 fire extinguishers would be provided. Suppose that the kite industry reaches a new long-run equilibrium.

a. Let F be the number of firms in the kite industry. Explain why each now has long-run cost curves given by

$$AC = Q + \frac{100}{Q} + \frac{F}{Q} \quad \text{and} \quad MC = 2Q.$$

b. How many kites will each firm produce? (You will have to express your answer in terms of F.) How many kites will the entire industry produce? (Again, you will have to express your answer in terms of F.) What will the price of kites be?

c. If the price of kites is P, what is the number of firms F? How many kites will the industry produce in terms of P? Write a formula for the long-run industry supply curve.

d. Suppose, as in Exercise 1, that the demand for kites is

$$Q = 8000 - 50P.$$

What will be the price of kites? How many kites will be produced? By how many firms? How much profit does each firm earn?

Problem Set

1. *True or false:* If one firm in a competitive industry discovered a cheaper manufacturing process for its product, it could lower its prices, steal its competitors' customers, and be better off.

2. *True or false:* If the price of fire insurance for department stores goes up, the increase will be passed on to consumers if there is only one department store in town, but not if there is heavy competition among department stores.

3. Suppose that the price of beer goes up due to a change in demand. *True or false:* Not only will the total profits of beer makers go up, but so will their average profit per can of beer sold.

4. Suppose that a series of bombings eliminates a number of video stores in your neighborhood. What will happen to the number of tapes sold at one of the surviving stores in the short run? In the long run? Illustrate your answer with graphs.

5. Books with many mathematical formulas in them are generally more expensive than similar books written entirely in prose. *True or false:* Because typesetting is not part of the marginal cost of producing a book, the cost of typesetting mathematics cannot be used to explain this phenomenon.

6. *True or false:* The number of meals served by a restaurant today depends on the demand curve that it faces today; the demand curve that it faced in the past is irrelevant.

7. Suppose that the demand for seafood increases one year and then unexpectedly returns to its original level the following year. *True or false:* Once the demand returns to its original level, the price and quantity will return to their original levels as well.

8. Suppose that gas station owners can buy all of the gasoline they want at a going price of P_w, so that P_w is part of the marginal cost of

providing gasoline to their customers. Suppose that P_w falls, bringing entry to the gas station industry. Do existing gas station owners benefit in the short run? In the long run? Could they actually be made worse off as a result of the fall in price and the entry?

9. In the Woody Allen film *Radio Days*, a character who has never been able to succeed in the world of business decides to begin a career engraving gold jewelry. He argues that this should be especially lucrative because the engraver gets to keep the gold dust from other people's rings. Comment on his reasoning.

10. *True or False:* An excise tax on the product of a decreasing cost industry would raise the price by *more* than the amount of the tax.

For each of the following phrases or statements, decide how the circumstance being described might affect the price and quantity of drinks sold at the Airliner Bar. Answer (a) in the short run, assuming perfect competition, (b) in the long run, assuming that bars are a competitive increasing cost industry, (c) in the long run, assuming that bars are a competitive constant cost industry, and (d) assuming that the Airliner Bar is the only bar in town.

11. A rise in the wholesale price of liquor.

12. The owner recalculates and discovers that the redecoration he completed last month actually cost 15% more than he thought it did.

13. The need to deal with a disgruntled customer who threatens to sue after being mistakenly served *lye* instead of *rye*. In exchange for a large payoff, he offers not only to withhold suit, but also to keep his mouth (or what is left of it) shut about the incident.

14. The same incident, except that the newspapers have already found out about it.

15. A rise in the yearly price of liquor licenses.

16. The City Council passes a one-time emergency tax measure, requiring every local tavern owner to immediately contribute $30 to the town treasury.

17. The owners of a neighboring establishment complain about the noise from the Airliner Bar, and they win a court order requiring the bar to compensate them. The court rules that the Airliner Bar must pay the neighbors 5¢ for each drink it serves.

18. A general breakdown of family life leads to a lot more people going out to bars.

19. It is discovered that all of the land in town has oil under it.

20. It is discovered that the land under the Airliner Bar has oil under it.

Refer to Answers to Problem Sets for solutions to problems 3 and 8.

Chapter Eight

Welfare Economics and the Gains from Trade

We now know a great deal about what determines the prices and quantities of goods traded in the marketplace. We learned about the sources of demand curves in Chapters 3 and 4 and about the sources of supply curves in Chapters 5, 6, and 7. We know that a competitive market operates at the point where the supply and demand curves cross.

All of the theory we have developed involves the efforts of individuals and firms to make themselves as well off as possible: Individuals seek the highest possible indifference curve and firms seek the maximum possible profit. These efforts constitute the reason why trade takes place.

In this chapter we will develop a way to measure the gains from trade. When a consumer purchases a dozen eggs from a farmer, each is better off (or at least not worse off)—otherwise no trade would have occurred in the first place. The question we will address is: How *much* better off are they?

Once we know how to measure the gains from trade, we will be able to study the ways in which these gains are affected by various changes in market conditions. Such changes include taxes, price controls, subsidies, quotas, rationing, and so forth. We will be able to see who gains and who loses from such policies and to evaluate the size of these gains and losses.

Finally, we will learn one of the most remarkable facts in economics: In a competitive equilibrium the sum of all the gains to all the market participants is as large as possible. This fact, called the *invisible hand theorem*, suggests a normative standard by which market outcomes can be judged. We will examine this normative standard and compare it to some alternatives. In particular, we will study the goals of economic efficiency and of fairness in income distribution. We will see some of the senses in which these goals conflict and others in which they are compatible.

8.1 Measuring the Gains from Trade

When a consumer buys eggs from a farmer, each one gains from the trade. Our first task is to devise a method for measuring the extent of these gains.

Consumer's and Producer's Surplus

We begin by considering the gains to the consumer. First, we develop a geometric measure of the value that the consumer places on his purchases.

Marginal Value and Demand

Value
The maximum amount that a consumer would be willing to pay for an item.

Consider the buyer of eggs. We begin by asking him how much he values one egg. The **value** of an egg to a consumer is defined to be the maximum amount that the consumer would be willing to pay to acquire that egg. Let us suppose that our (very hungry) consumer would be willing to pay up to $15 in exchange for an egg.[1] In this case the value of one egg to this particular consumer is $15.

How much, then, would the consumer value 2 eggs? Presumably more than $15. But we expect him to value 2 eggs at something less than $30, because somebody who already has an egg will place less value on a second egg than on the first. In other words, the *marginal* value of the second egg is something less than $15, and so the total value of the first 2 eggs is something less than $30.

Why does marginal value decrease as the consumer acquires more eggs? Because when he has only one egg, he uses it in the one way in which he would most like to use an egg. Perhaps that means that he fries it for breakfast. When he has 2 eggs, he fries the first one and uses the second for whatever he considers to be an egg's second most important use (maybe egg salad for lunch). Even if he uses the second egg together with the first

---

[1]Of course, if the consumer can buy eggs in the marketplace for less than $15 apiece, then he will never pay more than the market price for an egg. When we say that he "would be willing" to pay up to $15 for an egg, we mean that if the market price were anything less than $15, he would purchase the egg, but if it were anything more than $15, he would choose not to purchase it.

Exhibit 8–1 **Demand and Marginal Value**

Table A: Total and Marginal Value

Quantity	Total Value	Marginal Value
1	$15	$15/egg
2	28	13
3	38	10
4	45	7
5	50	5
6	52	2

Table B: Demand

Price	Quantity
$15/egg	1
13	2
10	3
7	4
5	5
2	6

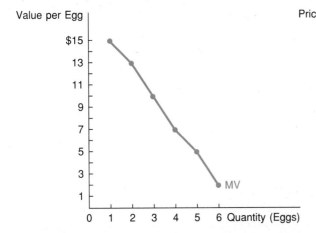

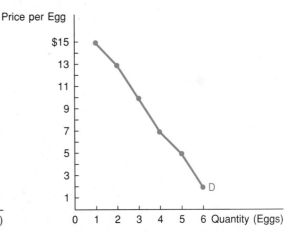

At a given market price the consumer will choose a quantity that equates price with marginal value. As a result, his demand curve for eggs is identical with his marginal value curve.

egg to make an omelet, it is reasonable to assume that the second half of his omelet is less valuable to him than the first half.

As the consumer acquires more eggs, their marginal value continues to decrease. Let us assume that these marginal values are as given in Table A in Exhibit 8–1. How many eggs will this consumer buy if the market price is $7/egg? He will certainly buy a first egg: He values it at $15 and can get it for $7. He will also buy a second egg, which he values at $13 and can also get for $7. Likewise, he will buy a third egg. The fourth egg, which he values at $7 and can purchase for $7, is a matter of indifference; we will assume that the consumer buys this egg as well. The fifth egg would be a bad buy for our consumer; it provides only $5 worth of additional value and costs $7 to acquire. The number of eggs purchased is 4.

▷ *Exercise 8.1* Add to Table A in Exhibit 8–1 a "net gain" column displaying the difference between total value and total cost. Verify that the
consumer is best off when he purchases 4 eggs.

▷ *Exercise 8.2* How many eggs will the consumer purchase when the
market price is $5 per egg? Explain why.

There is nothing new in this reasoning; it is just an application of the
equimarginal principle. The consumer buys eggs as long as the marginal
value of an egg exceeds its price, and stops when the two become equal. In
other words, he chooses that quantity at which price equals marginal
value. In Table B of Exhibit 8–1 we record the number of eggs the consumer
will purchase at each price. Table B is the consumer's demand schedule,
and the corresponding graph is a picture of his demand curve for eggs.[2]
(Compare this reasoning with the derivation of Farmer Ryan's supply
curve in Exhibit 7–4.)

The graphs in Exhibit 8–1 display both the consumer's marginal value
curve and his demand curve for eggs. The curves are identical, although
they differ conceptually. To read the marginal value curve, take a given
quantity and read the corresponding marginal value off the vertical axis.
To read the demand curve, take a given price and read the corresponding
quantity off the horizontal axis.

In fact, what we have learned is not new. The marginal value of an egg,
measured in dollars, is the same thing as the consumer's marginal rate of
substitution between eggs and dollars: It is the number of dollars for which
he would be just willing to trade an egg. In an indifference curve diagram
between eggs and dollars, the marginal value is the slope of an indifference
curve and the price is the slope of the budget line. We saw in Section 3.2
that the consumer's optimum occurs at a point where the marginal value is
equal to the price, and that this is the source of the consumer's demand
curve.

Total Value as an Area

Suppose that the consumer of Exhibit 8–1 acquires 4 eggs. We would like to
depict geometrically the total value that he derives from them. We begin by
depicting the $15 in value represented by the first egg. This $15 is the area of
rectangle 1 in panel A of Exhibit 8–2. The height of the rectangle is 15, and
the width of the rectangle (which stretches from a quantity of 0 to a
quantity of 1) is 1. Thus the area is $15 \times 1 = 15$. The $13 in value that the
consumer receives from the second egg is represented by rectangle 2 in the
same graph. The height of this rectangle is 13 and its width is 1, so its area is
$13 \times 1 = 13$.

---

[2]More precisely, the graph is a picture of his *compensated* demand curve. When we talk about "willingness
to pay" for an additional egg, we are asking what number of dollars the consumer could sacrifice for that
egg and remain equally happy. The points on the marginal value curve all represent points on the same
indifference curve for the consumer.

 All of the demand curves in this chapter are really compensated demand curves. However, the
compensated and uncompensated demand curves coincide when income effects are small, so measurements using the ordinary (uncompensated) demand curve are good approximations for most purposes.

Exhibit 8–2   **Total Value**

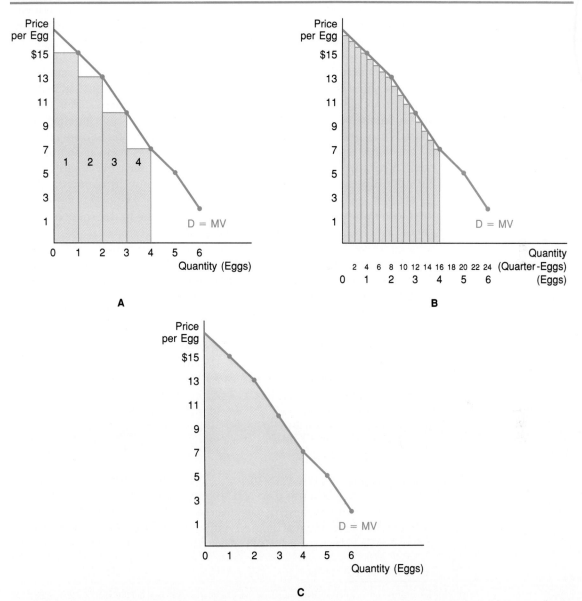

A

B

C

When the consumer buys 4 eggs, their marginal values ($15, $13, $10, and $7) can be read off the demand curve. Their values are represented by the areas of rectangles 1 through 4 in panel A. Therefore their total value is the sum of the areas of the rectangles.

We can get a more accurate estimate of total value if we measure eggs in smaller units. Panel B shows the calculation of total value when we measure by the quarter-egg instead of by the whole egg. As we take smaller and smaller units, we approach the shaded area in panel C, which is the exact measure of total value when the consumer buys 4 eggs.

The area of rectangle 3 is the marginal value of the third egg purchased, and the area of rectangle 4 is the marginal value of the fourth egg purchased. The total value of the 4 eggs is the sum of the 4 marginal values, or the total area of the 4 rectangles.

Actually, what we have done is only approximately correct. The reason is that the marginal value table in Exhibit 8–1 omits some information. It does not show the value of 1½ eggs or 3¼ eggs, for example.[3] In order to consider such quantities, we might make our measurements not in "eggs," but in "quarter-eggs." If we do so, the quantity of "quarter-eggs" purchased is 16, and the four rectangles of panel A of Exhibit 8–2 are replaced by the 16 rectangles of panel B, each one-quarter as wide as the original ones. Refining things even further, we could measure quantities in "hundredth-eggs," making 400 rectangles. As our fundamental units get smaller, our approximation to the total value of 4 eggs gets better. The total value of the consumer's 4 eggs is exactly equal to the shaded area in panel C.

The total value of the consumer's purchases is equal to the area under the demand curve out to the quantity demanded.[4]

The total value of 4 eggs is completely independent of their market price. Imagine offering the consumer a choice of living in two worlds, both identical except for the fact that in one world he has no eggs and in the other he has 4. Ask him what is the most he would be willing to pay to live in the second world rather than the first. His answer to that question is the total value that he places on 4 eggs.

The Consumer's Surplus

Suppose that the market price of an egg is $7. The consumer of Exhibit 8–1 will purchase 4 eggs at this price. His expenditure totals $7 \times 4 = $28. This number can also be represented by an area. It is the area labeled B in Exhibit 8–3, which is a rectangle of height 7 and width 4. The area of this rectangle is $7 \times 4 = 28$. The total value of the consumer's eggs is equal to the entire

---

[3]You might think it is impossible to purchase just one-quarter of an egg, but this is not so. Remember that every demand curve has a unit of time implicitly associated with it. If our demand curves are "per week," then the way to purchase exactly one-quarter of an egg per week is to buy one every four weeks.

[4]If you have had a course in calculus, you might be interested to know that we have just "proven" the fundamental theorem of calculus! Think of total value as a function (where quantity is the variable). The marginal value is the addition to total value when quantity is increased by one small unit. In other words, marginal value is the derivative of total value. The area under the marginal value curve out to a given quantity is the integral of marginal value from zero out to that quantity. We have argued that this integral is equal to the total value associated with that quantity. In other words, integrating the derivative brings you back to the original function.

Perhaps you knew the fundamental theorem of calculus but always accepted it as a mysterious fact of nature. If so, thinking about the economics of total and marginal values should give you some real insight into why the fundamental theorem is true.

Exhibit 8–3   **The Consumer's Surplus**

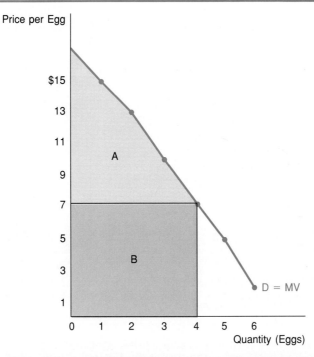

In order to acquire 4 eggs, the consumer would be willing to pay up to the entire shaded area, A + B. At a price of $7 per egg, his actual expenditure for 4 eggs is $28, which is area B. The difference, area A, is his consumer's surplus.

Consumer's surplus
The consumer's gain from trade; the amount by which the value of his purchases exceeds what he actually pays for them.

shaded area, and the cost to him of acquiring those eggs is the area labeled B. The gain to the consumer is the remainder, namely area A.

Area A is called the **consumer's surplus** in the market for eggs. It is the total value (to him) of the eggs he buys, minus what he actually pays for them.

The consumer's surplus is the area under the demand curve down to the price paid and out to the quantity consumed.

▷ *Exercise 8.3* Suppose that for some reason the consumer can buy eggs only once in his life. In this case he can only purchase a whole number of eggs, and panel A of Exhibit 8–1 shows the correct total value, not just an approximation. Depict the area representing the consumer's surplus in this situation. Use geometry to measure this area. How does it compare with the "net gain" you calculated in Exercise 8.1? Explain why this result is to be expected.

The Producer's Surplus

The consumer is not the only party to a transaction, and he is not the only one to gain from it. There is a producer as well, and we can also calculate *his*

Exhibit 8–4   **The Producer's Surplus**

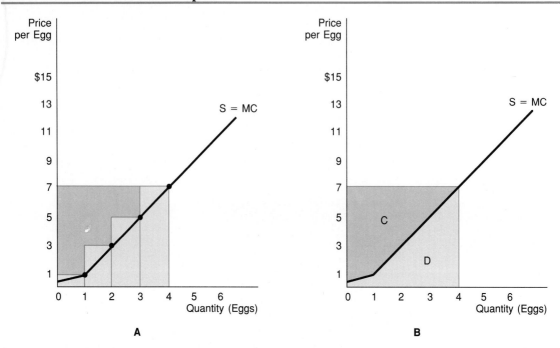

If the producer supplies 4 eggs, his cost is the sum of the 4 marginal costs, which are represented by the rectangles in panel A. If we measure eggs in very small units, we find that an exact measure of his cost is area D in panel B. At a market price of $7, his revenue is $7 × 4 = $28, which is the area of rectangle C + D. Thus his producer's surplus is area C.

gains from trade. Imagine a producer with the marginal cost curve shown in Exhibit 8–4. Suppose that this producer supplies 4 eggs to the marketplace. What is the cost of supplying these 4 eggs? It is the sum of the marginal cost of supplying the first egg ($1), the marginal cost of the second ($3), the marginal cost of the third ($5), and the marginal cost of the fourth ($7). These numbers are represented by the 4 rectangles in panel A of Exhibit 8–4. Their heights are 1, 3, 5, and 7, and they all have width 1.

As with the consumer's total value, we must realize that the rectangles of panel A provide only an approximation, because we are making the faulty assumption that eggs can be produced only in whole-number quantities. A more accurate picture would include many very thin rectangles, and the sum of their areas would be the area labeled D in the second panel. This is the cost of providing 4 eggs.[5]

---

[5]By adding up the producer's marginal costs, we are excluding any fixed costs that the producer might have. This is because we are considering only how the producer is affected by trade, whereas he would incur his fixed costs whether or not he traded. This makes the fixed costs irrelevant to the discussion.

Next we depict the producer's total revenue. This is easy: He sells 4 eggs at $7 apiece, so his revenue is 4 × $7, which is the area of the rectangle C + D in Exhibit 8–4.

Now we can compute the producer's gains from trade: His total revenues are C + D and his costs of production are D. The difference, area C, is called the **producer's surplus** and represents the gains to the producer as a result of his participation in the marketplace.

Producer's surplus
The producer's gain from trade; the amount by which his revenue exceeds his variable costs of production.

If the producer is competitive, his marginal cost curve can be identified with his supply curve. Therefore:

The producer's surplus is the area above the supply curve up to the price received and out to the quantity supplied.

For a noncompetitive producer, we would want to change *the supply curve* to *the marginal cost curve* in the preceding sentence, but for a competitive producer these are the same thing.

Social Gain

In panel A of Exhibit 8–5 we have drawn both the supply and the demand curve on the same graph. The consumer's surplus is taken from Exhibit 8–3 and the producer's surplus is taken from Exhibit 8–4.

Social gain or **welfare gain**
The sum of the gains from trade to all participants.

The consumer's and producer's surpluses depicted in Exhibit 8–5 provide a measure of the gains to both parties. Their sum is called the **social gain,** or **welfare gain,** due to the existence of the market. Students sometimes want to know where these gains are coming from: If the consumer and the producer have both gained, then who has lost? The answer is *nobody*. The process of trade creates welfare gains, which simply did not exist before the trading took place. The fact that the world as a whole can be made better off should not strike you as surprising: Imagine the total value of all the goods in the world 100 years ago and compare it with the value of what you see around you today. In a very real sense, the difference can be thought of as the sum of all the little triangles of surplus that have been created by consumers and producers over the passage of time.

There is another way to measure the welfare gains created by the marketplace. Rather than separately computing a consumer's surplus and a producer's surplus, we can calculate the total welfare gain created by each egg. This is shown in panel B of Exhibit 8–5. The first rectangle represents the difference between the marginal value of the first egg and the marginal cost of producing it, which is precisely the welfare gain due to that egg. The height of the rectangle is 15 − 1 = 14, and its width is 1, giving an area of 14. Similarly, the second rectangle has a height of 13 − 3 = 10 and a width of 1, giving an area of 10, which is the welfare gain from the second egg. The welfare gain due to the exchange of 4 eggs is the sum of the 4 rectangles (the fourth "rectangle" has height zero!). As usual, our focus on whole numbers has forced us to approximate: The total welfare gain is actually the entire shaded area between the supply and demand curves out to the equilibrium point.

Exhibit 8–5   **Welfare Gains**

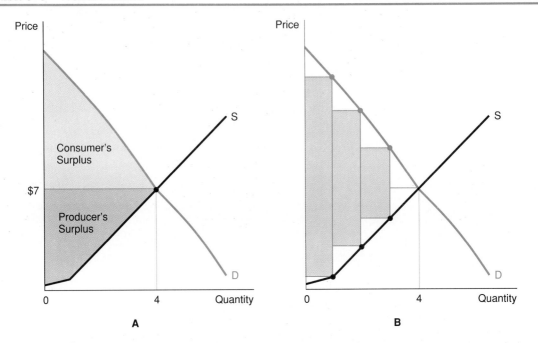

Panel A shows the consumer's surplus and the producer's surplus when 4 eggs are sold at a price of $7. The sum of these areas is the total welfare gain. The second panel shows another way to calculate the welfare gain. The first egg creates a gain equal to the area of the first rectangle, the second creates a gain equal to the area of the second rectangle, and so on. When units are taken to be small, the sum of these areas is the shaded region, which is the sum of the consumer's and producer's surpluses.

Notice that the total welfare gain (shown in panel B) is the sum of the consumer's and producer's surpluses (shown in panel A). This is as it should be: All of the gains have to go somewhere, and there are only the consumer and the producer to collect them.

Social Gains and Markets

Next we want to consider markets with more than one consumer and with more than one producer. It turns out that consumers' and producers' surpluses can again be computed in exactly the same way.

Imagine a world with three consumers: Larry, Moe, and Curly. Exhibit 8–6 displays each man's marginal value schedule for eggs. In this world, when the price is $15, Larry buys 1 egg and Moe and Curly each buy 0 eggs. The total quantity demanded is 1. At a price of $13, Larry and Moe buy 1 each and Curly buys 0; the quantity demanded is 2. At a price of $11, Larry buys 1, Moe buys 2, and Curly buys 0 for a total of 3, and so on. The resulting demand curve is also shown in Exhibit 8–6.

Exhibit 8–6   Consumers' Surplus in the Market

Larry			Moe			Curly	
Quantity	**Marginal Value**		**Quantity**	**Marginal Value**		**Quantity**	**Marginal Value**
1	$15/egg		1	$13/egg		1	$7/egg
2	8/egg		2	11/egg		2	3/egg

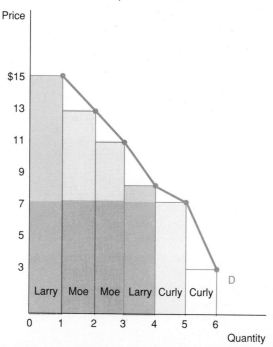

The demand curve is constructed from the marginal value curves of the three individuals. At a price of $7, Larry buys 2 eggs that he values at $15 and $8, Moe buys 2 that he values at $13 and $11, and Curly buys 1 that he values at $7. These marginal values are represented by the first 5 rectangles under the demand curve, each labeled with the appropriate consumer's name. The total value of the 5 eggs to the consumers is the sum of the areas of the first 5 rectangles. The cost to the consumers is the darker area. The consumers' surplus is what remains; it is the area under the demand curve down to the price paid and out to the quantity purchased.

The rectangles below the demand curve represent the marginal values of the eggs that are purchased. Each rectangle is labeled with the name of the man who consumes the corresponding egg: the first egg sold is bought by Larry, the second and third by Moe, the fourth by Larry, the fifth and sixth by Curly.

Now suppose that the price of eggs is $7. How many eggs are sold, and what is their total value? Larry buys 2 (the first and fourth), Moe buys 2 (the second and third), and Curly buys 1 (the fifth). The values of these eggs are given by the areas of the corresponding rectangles, and the total value to the consumers is the sum of the 5 areas, which are shaded in Exhibit 8–6. From this must be subtracted the total amount that the consumers pay for the 5 eggs, which is represented by the darker, lower

Exhibit 8–7   Producers' Surplus in the Market

Firm A		Firm B		Firm C	
Quantity	**Marginal Cost**	**Quantity**	**Marginal Cost**	**Quantity**	**Marginal Cost**
1	$1	1	$5	1	$6
2	3	2	11	2	7

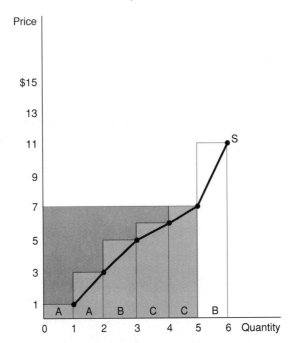

The market supply curve is the industry's marginal cost curve. When the price is $7, Firm A produces 2 items at marginal costs of $1 and $3, Firm B produces 1 at a marginal cost of $5, and Firm C produces 2 at marginal costs of $6 and $7. These costs are represented by the darker rectangles below the supply curve. The revenue earned by producers is the entire shaded region. The portion of that region above the supply curve is the producers' surplus.

portions of the rectangles. The remaining portion, above the $7 price line, is the consumers' surplus. The consumers' surplus is composed of many rectangles, and each consumer receives some of these rectangles as his share of the welfare gain. But, just as before, the total consumers' surplus is represented by the area under the demand curve down to the price paid and out to the quantity purchased.

An analogous statement holds for producers' surplus. Suppose that three different firms have the marginal cost schedules shown in Exhibit 8–7. The total supply curve is then given by the graph. The dark rectangles corresponding to individual eggs are labeled with the names of the firms that produce them. Producers' surplus is given by total revenue (the entire shaded region) *minus* the sum of the areas of these rectangles, out to the quantity produced. That is, the producers' surplus is the light part of the shaded region in the exhibit. This surplus is divided up among the producers, but the total of all the producers' surplus is still given by the area above the supply curve up to the price received and out to the quantity supplied.

Changes in Consumers' and Producers' Surplus

The Effect of a Sales Tax

Panel A of Exhibit 8–8 shows the supply and demand for coffee. Panel B shows the same market after a 5¢ per cup sales tax is placed on consumers. As we know from Chapter 1, this has the effect of lowering the demand curve vertically a distance 5¢.

Before the sales tax is imposed, the consumers' and producers' surpluses are as shown in panel A. The sum of these is the total welfare gained by all members of society, and we will refer to it as the "social gain." In terms of the areas in panel B, we have:

> **Consumers' surplus** = A + B + C + D + E
> **Producers' surplus** = F + G + H + I
> _____
> **Social gain**   = A + B + C + D + E + F + G + H + I

Once the sales tax is imposed, we need to recompute the consumers' and producers' surpluses. The consumers' surplus is the area below the demand curve down to the price paid and out to the quantity consumed. The question now arises: Which demand curve? The answer is: The original demand curve, because this is the curve that reflects the consumers' true marginal values. Which price? The price paid by demanders—P_d. Which quantity? The quantity that is sold when the tax is in effect—Q'. The consumers' surplus is area A + B.

What about producers' surplus? We need to look at the area above the supply curve up to the price received and out to the quantity supplied. The relevant price to suppliers is P_s and the relevant quantity is the quantity being sold in the presence of the sales tax—Q'. The producers' surplus is I.

We can now make the following tabulation:

	Before Sales Tax	After Sales Tax
Consumers' Surplus	A+B+C+D+E	A+B
Producers' Surplus	F+G+H+I	I
Social Gain	A+B+C+D+E+F+G+H+I	?

What about the social gain after the sales tax is imposed? Can't we find it by simply adding the consumers' and producers' surpluses? The answer is no, because there is now an additional component to consider. We must ask what becomes of the tax revenue that is collected by the government.

Exhibit 8–8   **The Effect of a Sales Tax**

	Before Sales Tax	After Sales Tax
Consumers' Surplus	A+B+C+D+E	A+B
Producers' Surplus	F+G+H+I	I
Tax Revenue	—	C+D+F+G
Social Gain	A+B+C+D+E+F+G+H+I	A+B+C+D+F+G+I
Deadweight Loss		E+H

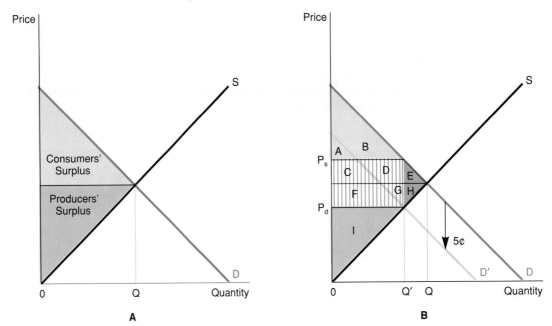

Before the sales tax is imposed, consumers' and producers' surpluses are as shown in panel A. The first column of the chart shows these surpluses in terms of the labels in panel B. The second column shows the gains to consumers and producers after the imposition of the sales tax, and includes a row for the gains to the recipients of the tax revenue. The total social gain after the tax is less than the social gain before the tax. The difference between the two is area E + H, the deadweight loss.

The simplest assumption is that it is given to somebody (perhaps as a welfare or social security payment). Alternatively, it might be spent to purchase goods and services that are then given to somebody. In some form or another, some individual (or group of individuals) ultimately collects the tax revenue, and that individual is part of society. The revenue that he collects is welfare gained.

How much tax revenue is there? The answer: It is equal to the tax per cup (5¢) times the number of cups sold (Q'). Since the vertical distance between the two demand curves is 5¢, the amount of this revenue is equal to the area of the rectangle C + D + F + G (height = 5¢, width = Q′). The final version of our table is this:

	Before Sales Tax	After Sales Tax
Consumers' Surplus	A+B+C+D+E	A+B
Producers' Surplus	F+G+H+I	I
Tax Revenue	—	C+D+F+G
Social Gain	A+B+C+D+E+F+G+H+I	A+B+C+D+F+G+I

The social gain entry is obtained by adding the entries in the preceding three rows. Even after the tax revenue is taken into account, the total gain to society is still less after the tax than it was before. The reduction in total gain is called the **deadweight loss** due to the tax. In this example the deadweight loss is equal to the area E + H. Other terms for the deadweight loss are *social loss, welfare loss,* and *efficiency loss.*

Deadweight loss
A reduction in social gain.

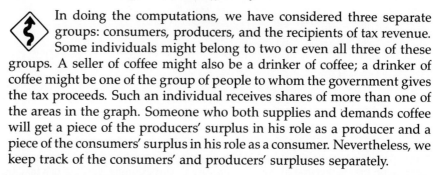 In doing the computations, we have considered three separate groups: consumers, producers, and the recipients of tax revenue. Some individuals might belong to two or even all three of these groups. A seller of coffee might also be a drinker of coffee; a drinker of coffee might be one of the group of people to whom the government gives the tax proceeds. Such an individual receives shares of more than one of the areas in the graph. Someone who both supplies and demands coffee will get a piece of the producers' surplus in his role as a producer and a piece of the consumers' surplus in his role as a consumer. Nevertheless, we keep track of the consumers' and producers' surpluses separately.

Understanding Deadweight Loss

Exhibit 8–9 presents another view of the deadweight loss. The prices and quantities are the same as in panel B of Exhibit 8–8. At the original equilibrium quantity Q, the social gain is the sum of all the rectangles. At Q′, which is the quantity with the tax, the social gain consists of only the blue rectangles. The next cup of coffee after Q′ would increase welfare if it were produced, because the marginal value it provides (read off the demand curve) exceeds the marginal cost of producing it (read off the supply curve). However, that cup is not produced and an opportunity to add to welfare is lost.

The deadweight loss calculated in Exhibit 8–9 is the same as the deadweight loss calculated in Exhibit 8–8, where it corresponds to the area E + H.

If we think of the social gain as a pie divided among various groups, then a tax has two effects: It changes the way the pie is distributed, and it simultaneously changes the size of the entire pie. Thus, in Exhibit 8–8, the pie originally consists of all the lettered areas. The tax reduces the consumers' and producers' pieces. On the other hand, the recipients of the tax revenue, who get nothing in the absence of the tax, do now receive a piece

Exhibit 8–9   **Deadweight Loss**

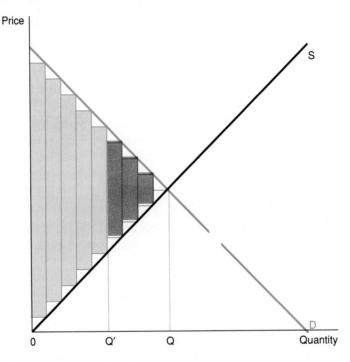

If the market operates at the equilibrium quantity Q, all of the rectangles are included in the social gain. If for any reason the market operates at the quantity Q' (for example, because of a tax), then only the blue rectangles are included. The units of output that could create the gray rectangles are never produced, and those rectangles of gain are never created. The gray rectangles, representing gains that could have been created but weren't, constitute the deadweight loss.

of the pie. After adding up everyone's pieces, we find that the total pie has shrunk; the losses to the losers exceed the gains to the winners. The shrinkage in the pie is the deadweight loss.

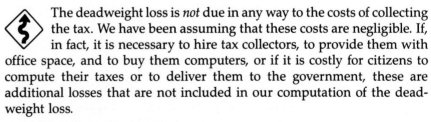

The deadweight loss is *not* due in any way to the costs of collecting the tax. We have been assuming that these costs are negligible. If, in fact, it is necessary to hire tax collectors, to provide them with office space, and to buy them computers, or if it is costly for citizens to compute their taxes or to deliver them to the government, these are additional losses that are not included in our computation of the dead-weight loss.

▷ *Exercise 8.4* In Exhibit 8–9 how much does each group of losers lose? How much does each group of winners win? Is the excess of losses over gains equal to the deadweight loss?

A moral of this story is that "taxes are bad"—though not in the sense you might think. You might think that taxes are bad because paying them makes you poorer. True, but collecting them makes somebody else richer. In Exhibit 8–8 the areas C + D + F + G that are paid in taxes do end up in somebody's pocket. Whether this is a good thing or a bad thing depends on whose pocket you care about most. The aspect of the tax that is unambiguously "bad" is the deadweight loss. This is a loss to consumers and producers that is not offset by a gain to anybody.

▷ *Exercise 8.5* Work out the effects of an *excise* tax of 5¢ per cup of coffee. (*Hint:* We already know that an excise tax has exactly the same effects as a sales tax, so you will know your answer is right if it gives exactly the same results as in Exhibit 8–8.)

Whenever a policy creates a deadweight loss, it is possible to imagine an alternative policy that would be better for everybody. Exhibit 8–10 illustrates such a policy. The graph in the exhibit is the same as panel B of Exhibit 8–8. Suppose that instead of a 5¢ sales tax, we adopt the following plan: One night, without warning, the tax collector breaks into the homes of the consumers and steals an amount of wealth equal to the area C + D + ½E. Then he breaks into the homes of the producers and steals the area F + G + ½H. Finally, like Robin Hood, he gives all the proceeds to the people who would have been receiving the tax revenue.

The table in Exhibit 8–10 compares the effects of three different policies. The first and second columns are taken from Exhibit 8–8 and show the welfare gains before and after a tax is imposed. The third column shows the effect of eliminating the tax and instituting the Robin Hood policy.

Compare the second and third columns of the table. You will find that all three groups—consumers, producers, and tax recipients—are happier in the Robin Hood world than in a world with a sales tax. This is possible because the Robin Hood policy creates no deadweight loss; it results in a social gain as great as in the world without taxes. Because there is more surplus to go around, it's not surprising that we can find a way to increase everyone's share. When the pie is bigger, you can always give everyone a bigger piece.

An important feature of the Robin Hood policy is that it is totally unexpected and nobody can do anything to avoid it. If people know in advance, for example, that Robin Hood will be stealing from all producers of coffee, the producers will react to this as they would to a tax, and produce less. Their exact reaction will depend on Robin's exact policy: If he steals more from those who produce more, he is effectively imposing an excise tax, which causes each firm to reduce its quantity. If he steals equally from all producers, the main effect will be to drive some producers out of the industry altogether.

Exhibit 8–10   **The Tax Collector versus Robin Hood**

	Before Taxation	With Sales Tax	With Robin Hood Policy
Consumers' Surplus	A+B+C+D+E	A+B	A+B+½E
Producers' Surplus	F+G+H+I	I	½H+I
Tax Revenue	—	C+D+F+G	C+D+½E+F+G+½H
Social Gain	A+B+C+D+E+F+G+H+I	A+B+C+D+F+G+I	A+B+C+D+E+F+G+H+I
Deadweight Loss		E+H	

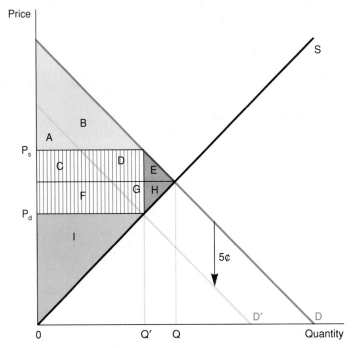

The table shows the effects of three different policies. In the first column there is no tax, in the second column there is a sales tax, and in the third column there is a Robin Hood policy whereby the tax collector unexpectedly takes C + D + ½E from the consumers, takes F + G + ½H from the producers, and gives all of the proceeds to the same group that gets the revenue from the sales tax.

Every member of society prefers the Robin Hood policy to the sales tax. Because the Robin Hood policy creates no deadweight loss, it makes it possible to give everyone a bigger share of the social pie.

When people anticipate Robin's actions, they will take steps to avoid them. These steps will include producing and consuming less coffee, and this will create a deadweight loss. The only way to avoid a deadweight loss is for the market to produce the equilibrium quantity of coffee, and this happens only if nobody is given a chance to alter his behavior in order to reduce his tax burden.

As with the tax policy, we are ignoring any costs involved with implementing the Robin Hood policy (such as Robin's expenditure on burglar tools or the value of his time). Any such costs would lessen the social gain.

Normative Criteria

Which policy is better: to tax or not to tax? If these are the only two options, economics has no answer. Clearly, consumers and producers prefer no tax, and the revenue recipients prefer a tax. However, our analysis has revealed two very important points. First: *If* your goal is to maximize the total gains to all members of society, *then* it is better not to tax. Second: There is another policy (namely Robin Hood's) that *everyone* would prefer over taxation. If this other policy is available, it is surely "better" than taxation in any reasonable sense. Of course, as this example illustrates, the alternative policy might not be available for political or technological reasons.

There are a number of different normative criteria that can be used to rank the desirability of various policies. The choice of a normative criterion is at least partly, and perhaps entirely, a matter of personal taste. However, economics can help us understand the implications of various criteria.

One choice is the **Pareto criterion,** according to which policy A can be called better than policy B only when every individual prefers policy A to policy B. In this case we say that policy A is **Pareto-preferred** to policy B. Of the policies considered in Exhibit 8–10, the Robin Hood policy is Pareto-preferred to the sales tax policy. However, the Pareto criterion cannot be used to choose between the no-tax policy and the sales tax policy, since consumers and producers prefer one and tax recipients prefer the other. For the same reason, the Pareto criterion provides no basis on which to choose between the no-tax and the Robin Hood policy.

A policy is called a **Pareto-optimal policy** if no other policy is Pareto-preferred to it. The no-tax and Robin Hood policies are Pareto-optimal, but the sales tax policy is not. The phrase *economically efficient* is sometimes used to mean Pareto-optimal.

> *Exercise 8.6* Why is the sales tax policy not Pareto-optimal?

No policy that causes a deadweight loss can be Pareto-optimal. A deadweight loss means that the social pie is smaller than it needs to be. By enlarging the pie, it is always possible to devise a distribution that gives everyone a bigger piece, which is a Pareto-preferred thing to do.

The **efficiency criterion** is an alternative way to judge policies. According to the efficiency criterion, policy A can be called better than policy B when the welfare gains from policy A exceed those from policy B. In this case we say that policy A is **more efficient** than policy B.

Pareto criterion
A normative criterion according to which one policy is better than another only if every individual agrees that it is preferable.

Pareto-preferred
Preferred by every individual.

Pareto-optimal policy
A policy to which no other policy is Pareto-preferred.

Efficiency criterion
A normative criterion according to which one policy is better than another if it creates more social gain.

More efficient
Preferred according to the efficiency criterion.

In Exhibit 8–10 the no-tax policy is more efficient than the sales tax policy. This illustrates that the efficiency criterion allows us to make some comparisons that would not be possible according to the Pareto criterion.

Suppose that coffee is currently untaxed and that a proposal has been made to institute a sales tax on coffee. An opponent of the tax might argue that although it will create both losers and winners, the tax is bad because *the losses to the losers will exceed the gains to the winners.* This is just another way to say that the policy will create some deadweight loss. A person who is convinced by this argument is applying the efficiency criterion. A possible response is that there will nevertheless be some winners and some losers, so we have no basis for saying that the tax is either good or bad. A person who argues this way is applying the Pareto criterion.

The tax opponent can argue that the Robin Hood policy is certainly preferred to the sales tax by any reasonable criterion, making the sales tax a bad choice. But a response to this is that, although we all agree that the Robin Hood policy is better than the sales tax, the Robin Hood policy is not a viable alternative. The only proposals on the table are to tax or not to tax, and comparisons with the Robin Hood policy are beside the point.

Many economists regard the efficiency criterion as a good rough guide to policy choices, though few would defend it as the sole basis on which to make such decisions. Regardless of your feelings on this issue, calculations of social gains and deadweight losses can still be useful in understanding the consequences of various alternatives. If a policy causes a large dead-weight loss, it is at least worth considering whether there is some good way to revise the policy so that the loss can be made smaller.

Examples and Applications

The machinery of consumers' and producers' surpluses is widely applicable, as the following sequence of examples will illustrate. All of them use just one basic procedure, which is summarized in Exhibit 8–11.

Subsidies

Suppose that the government institutes a new program whereby every purchaser of home insulation receives a rebate of $50 per unit of insulation purchased. This has the effect of shifting the demand curve upward a vertical distance $50, from D to D' in Exhibit 8–12.

With the subsidy, the quantity sold is Q', at a market price of P_s. This is the price suppliers receive for insulation. However, the consumer actually pays less, because he receives a payment of $50 from the government, so that his actual cost is $P_s - \$50 = P_d$.

To calculate consumers' and producers' surpluses before the subsidy, we use the equilibrium price and quantity. This is shown in the first column of the table in Exhibit 8–12.

After the subsidy, consumers purchase quantity Q' at a price to them of P_d. Their consumers' surplus is the area under the *original* demand curve

Exhibit 8–11   Calculating the Consumers' and Producers' Surpluses

You will often be asked to calculate the effects of governmental policies on consumers' and producers' surpluses. Here are some rules to help you:

1.   Begin by drawing a supply and demand diagram showing equilibrium both before and after the policy is imposed. Draw horizontal and vertical lines from the interesting points in your diagram to the axes. After a while you will get a feel for which lines to draw and which to omit. It never hurts to draw more than you need.

2.   Before you proceed, label every area that is even possibly relevant with a letter of the alphabet.

3.   When calculating consumers' surplus, use only the demand curve and prices and quantities that are relevant to the consumer. When calculating producers' surplus, use only the supply curve and prices and quantities relevant to the producer.

4.   Remember that the demand and supply curves are relevant only because they are equal to the marginal value and marginal cost curves. If for some reason the demand curve should separate from the marginal value curve, continue to use the marginal value curve for calculating consumers' surplus. Do likewise if the supply curve should separate from the marginal cost curve.

5.   Check your work with a picture like Exhibit 8–9: Calculate the social gain directly by drawing rectangles of "welfare gains" for each item actually produced and by summing the areas of these rectangles. The sum should equal the total of the gains to all of the individuals involved.

D out to this quantity and down to this price. We use the original demand curve because it is this curve that represents the true marginal value of insulation to consumers. The intrinsic value of home insulation is not changed by the subsidy. Therefore the consumers' surplus is the area A + C + F + G, as recorded in the second column of the table.

To calculate producers' surplus, we use the quantity Q' and the producers' price P_s. This yields the area C + D + F + H, which is also recorded in the table.

We are still not finished. The subsidy being paid to consumers must come from somewhere, presumably from tax revenues. This represents a cost to taxpayers equal to the number of units of insulation sold times $50 per unit. Geometrically, this is represented by the rectangle C + D + E + F + G. This cost is a *loss* to the taxpayers, and so must be *subtracted* in the computation of social gain. The deadweight loss of E is the difference between social gain before and after the subsidy.

▷ *Exercise 8.7* Verify the calculation of social gain in Exhibit 8–12.

Exhibit 8–12   **The Effect of a Subsidy**

	Before Subsidy	After Subsidy
Consumers' Surplus	A + C	A + C + F + G
Producers' Surplus	F + H	C + D + F + H
Cost to Taxpayers	—	C + D + E + F + G
Social Gain	A + C + F + H	A + C + F + H − E
Deadweight Loss		E

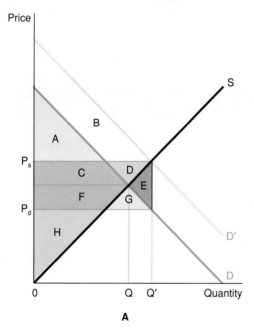

A

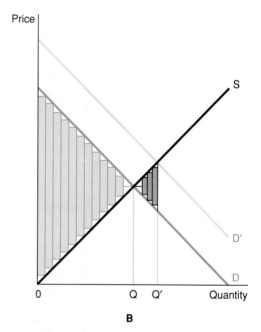

B

The table shows the gains to consumers and producers before and after the institution of a $50-per-unit government subsidy to home insulation. With the subsidy in effect, there is a cost to taxpayers that must be *subtracted* when we calculate the social gain. We find that the social gain with the subsidy is lower by E than the social gain without the subsidy. E is the deadweight loss.

To check our work, we can consider the social gain created by each individual unit of insulation, shown in panel B. Each unit up to the equilibrium quantity Q creates a rectangle of social gain. After Q units have been produced, we enter a region where marginal cost exceeds marginal value. Each unit produced in this region creates a social *loss* equal to the excess of marginal cost over marginal value; these losses are represented by the gray rectangles, which stop at the quantity Q′ that is actually produced. The social gain is equal to the sum of the blue rectangles minus the sum of the gray ones. Since the social gain without the subsidy is just the sum of the blue rectangles, the gray rectangles represent the deadweight loss.

Students often want to know how areas C and F can be part of both the consumers' surplus and the producers' surplus. The answer is that surplus is not an area at all—the area is just a *measure* of surplus. The fact that you have 12 yards of carpet and your friend has 12 yards of carpet does not mean that you both own the same "yards," only

Exhibit 8–13   **Another Way to Do It**

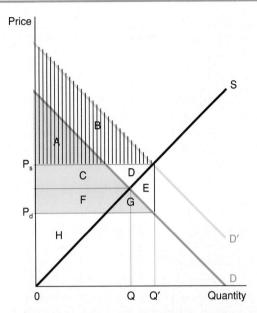

The method that we have been using to calculate social gain is adequate for most problems. However, there is an alternate method that may occasionally be more convenient.

We illustrate with the "subsidy" example from Exhibit 8–12. The graph here is identical to panel A in that exhibit. There are two ways of viewing a $50 rebate for home insulation. The first way, which we adopted in Exhibit 8–12, is to say that the rebate does not alter the value of home insulation. Consumers benefit from the subsidy by being able to buy insulation at a lower price. This is why we use the *old* demand curve (the true marginal value curve) and the price paid by consumers (P_d) as boundaries for the area of consumer surplus. This gives the shaded area A + C + F + G.

An alternative and *equally valid* point of view is to say that a subsidy is like a $50 bill taped to each unit of insulation. This raises the marginal value of the insulation by $50. However, we now have to view the insulation as being purchased at the market price P_s. If we said that the insulation has increased in value *and* that the consumer is paying less than market price for his insulation, we would be wrongly double-counting the $50 rebate.

From the alternative point of view, the consumer surplus is the area under the *new* demand curve down to the *market* price P_s and out to the quantity Q′. That is, the striped area A + B.

If both points of view are equally valid, how can they give different answers? The answer is: They don't. In fact, area A + B is equal to area A + C + F + G. They have to be equal, because each represents the consumers' surplus calculated correctly, and there can be only one consumers' surplus. If you find that argument unconvincing, try proving directly that the two areas are equal. This is an exercise in high school geometry if you assume all curves are straight lines; it is an exercise in calculus otherwise.

that each of you owns carpeting that can be measured by the same yardstick. The areas of surplus are yardsticks by which we measure different individuals' gains from trade.

Panel B in Exhibit 8–12 provides a way to check our work. The blue rectangles to the left of equilibrium represent gains to social welfare just as in Exhibit 8–9. In this case, however, *more* than the equilibrium quantity is produced. Consider the first item produced after equilibrium. The marginal value of this item to consumers (read off the original demand curve) is *less* than the marginal cost of producing it. The difference between the two is the area of the first gray rectangle. This area therefore represents a net welfare *loss* to society. Similarly, the next item produced represents a welfare loss in the amount of the area of the second gray rectangle, and so on out to the quantity Q'. The total welfare loss is the sum of these rectangles, which is equal to the area E in panel A. Therefore area E should be the deadweight loss, and the calculation in the table is confirmed.

An alternative way to calculate the consumers' surplus is shown in Exhibit 8–13. For most purposes, it suffices to use either the method of Exhibit 8–12 or that of Exhibit 8–13. Since both always lead to the same answers, you need to master only one of them. However, there will be a few occasions later on in this book where you will find it much easier to use the alternative method of Exhibit 8–13.

Price Ceilings

Price ceiling
A maximum price at which a product can be legally sold.

Effective price ceiling
A price ceiling set below the equilibrium price.

A **price ceiling** is a legally mandated maximum price at which a good may be sold. The effect of a price ceiling depends on its level. If the legal maximum is above the equilibrium price that prevails anyway, then the price ceiling has no effect (a law forbidding any piece of bubble gum to sell for more than $2,000 will not change anyone's behavior). An **effective price ceiling** is one set below the equilibrium price, like the price P_0 in Exhibit 8–14.

At the price P_0, producers want to sell the quantity Q_s and consumers want to buy the quantity Q_d. What quantity will actually be traded? The answer is Q_s, because as soon as Q_s units are sold, the sellers will pack up and go home. When buyers and sellers disagree about quantity, the group wanting to trade fewer items always wins, because trading stops as soon as either party loses interest.

Another, and very real, possibility must be considered: Since buyers are frustrated, they will be willing to offer prices higher than P_0, and sellers may accept these prices in violation of the law. For purposes of our simple analysis, we will assume that the law is perfectly enforced and this does not occur. We will also assume that the enforcement is costless (otherwise the cost of enforcement would have to be subtracted from social gain).[6]

The quantity sold is Q_s. What price do consumers pay? You may think the answer is obviously P_0, but this is incorrect. At a price of P_0, consumers

---

[6]Here is an interesting puzzle: Why is it that in "victimless crimes" like prostitution and the sale of drugs, both parties are held criminally liable, whereas in the equally "victimless" crime of violating a price control, only the seller faces legal consequences? For an interesting discussion of this puzzle, see J. Lott and R. Roberts, "Why Comply: The Political Economy of Enforcing Price Controls and Victimless Crime Laws," 1987.

Exhibit 8–14 **A Price Ceiling**

	Before Ceiling	After Ceiling
Consumers' Surplus	A+B+C	A
Producers' Surplus	D+E+F	F
Social Gain	A+B+C+D+E+F	A+F
Deadweight Loss		B+C+D+E

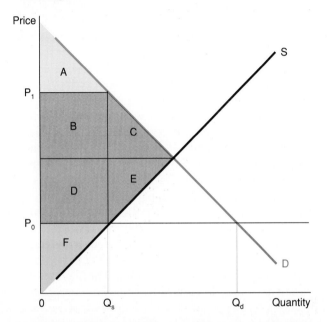

At a maximum legal price of P_0, demanders want to buy more than suppliers want to sell. Therefore they compete against each other for the available supply, by waiting in line, advertising, and so forth. This increases the actual price to consumers. The full price to consumers must be bid all the way up to P_1, since at any lower price the quantity demanded still exceeds the quantity supplied, leading to increases in the lengths of waiting lines.

The deadweight loss comes about for two reasons. First, there is the reduction in quantity from equilibrium to Q_s. This loss is the area C + E. Second, there is the value of the consumers' time spent waiting in line. This is equal to $P_1 - P_0$ times the quantity of items purchased, which is the rectangle B + D.

want to purchase more goods than are available. Therefore *they will compete with each other* to acquire the limited supply. Depending on the nature of the good, this may take the form of standing in line, searching from store to store, advertising, or any of a number of other possibilities. All of these activities are costly, in time, gasoline, energy, and other currency, and these costs must be added to the "price" that consumers actually pay for the item.

How high will the price go? It must go to exactly P_1 in Exhibit 8–14. At any lower price the quantity demanded still exceeds Q_s, and consumers will intensify their efforts. Only when the "price" reaches P_1 will the market equilibrate.

Of course, even though P_1 is the price paid by consumers, the price received by suppliers is still P_0. Therefore we use P_1 to calculate consumers' surplus and P_0 to calculate producers' surplus. In each case the appropriate quantity is Q_0, the quantity actually traded. The computations are shown in Exhibit 8–14.

▷ *Exercise 8.8* Verify the correctness of the table in Exhibit 8–14.

The deadweight loss calculated in Exhibit 8–14 comes about for two reasons. First, there is the reduction in quantity from Q to Q_s, which leads to a social loss of $C + E$ just as in the case of a tax. However, now there is another sort of loss as well. The value of the time people spend waiting in lines is equal to the value of the time-per-unit-purchased ($P_1 - P_0$) times the quantity of units purchased (Q_s), which is the rectangle $B + D$. Taken together, these effects account for the entire deadweight loss.

Notice that from a social point of view there is a great difference between a *price control* that drives the demanders' price up to P_1 and a *tax* that drives the demanders' price up to P_1. Because the revenue from a tax is wealth transferred from one individual to another, it is neither a gain nor a loss to society as a whole. But the value of the time spent in waiting lines is wealth lost and never recovered by anyone.

Some of the deadweight loss can be avoided if there is a class of people in society with a relatively low value of time. Suppose, for simplicity, that some people's time has zero value. These people will offer their services as "searchers" or "line-standers," and consumers will be willing to pay them up to $P_1 - P_0$ per unit purchased for these services. The line-standers will earn ($P_1 - P_0$) times Q_s, which is represented by rectangle $B + D$. This gain comes at no expense to anybody, so $B + D$ is added to society's welfare and the deadweight loss is now only $C + E$.

If, more realistically, nobody's time has zero value, but some people's time is worth less than $P_1 - P_0$, then that group of people will still be able to serve as line-standers, earning a net gain of $B + D$ *minus* the value of their time. Thus $B + D$ is the most that can be recovered through the use of line-standers.

Of course, some consumers whose time has low value might stand in line to make their own purchases. We view these consumers as having purchased line-standing services from themselves at the going price of $P_1 - P_0$. Such a consumer earns part of area A as a consumer, and part of area $B + D$ as a line-stander.

Tariffs

Suppose that Americans buy all of their cameras from Japanese companies. It is proposed that a tariff of $10 per camera be imposed on all such imports and that the proceeds be distributed to Americans chosen at

Exhibit 8–15   **A Tax on Imported Cameras**

	Before Tariff	After Tariff
Consumers' Surplus	$A+B+C+D$	A
Tariff Revenue	—	$B+C+E+F$
Social Gain	$A+B+C+D$	$A+B+C+E+F$

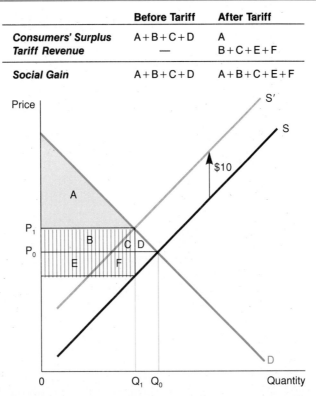

If cameras are supplied by foreigners and purchased by Americans, then a tariff affects Americans through the consumers' surplus and through the tax revenue that it generates.

random. What areas must we measure to see whether the tariff makes Americans as a whole better off?

Exhibit 8–15 shows the market for cameras, with both the original and post-tariff supply curves. The table shows the gains to Americans before and after the tariff. These gains are calculated using the pre-tariff price and quantity of P_0 and Q_0 and the post-tariff price and quantity of P_1 and Q_1. Notice that we do not include the producers' surplus, since this is earned by the Japanese companies and the question asks only about the welfare of Americans. If we had been asked about the welfare of the entire world, we would have included producers' surplus in our calculations.

▷ *Exercise 8.9* Calculate the social gains to the entire world before and after the tariff is imposed.

Now we return to the question: What areas must we measure? The answer is evidently that one must compare area D with area E + F. If D is

Exhibit 8–16   **A Tariff on Imported Cameras That Are Elastically Supplied**

	Before Tariff	After Tariff
Consumers' Surplus	A+B+C	A
Tariff Revenue	—	B
Social Gain	A+B+C	A+B
Deadweight Loss		C

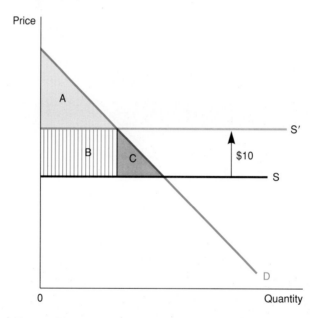

If the United States is a small part of the market to which the Japanese sell cameras, then Americans will face a flat supply curve. In this case a tariff always reduces the welfare of Americans.

bigger, the tariff improves the welfare of Americans; otherwise it reduces their welfare.

In practice, these areas can be estimated if the supply and demand curves can be estimated, and, as we remarked in Chapter 1, there are econometric methods available for this. Therefore an economist can contribute meaningfully to a debate about tariffs by computing the relevant areas and reporting which policy is better—*provided* that the goal is to maximize Americans' welfare.

It is often a reasonable assumption that a country faces flat supply curves for imported items. The reason for this is that Japanese firms sell cameras in many foreign countries, and the United States is only a small part of their market. Thus changes in quantity that appear big (from our point of view) may in fact correspond only to very small movements along the Japanese supply curves and hence to small changes in price. Exhibit 8–16 shows the analysis of a tariff when the supply curve is flat. In this case you can see that the tariff always reduces Americans' welfare.

Tariffs and Domestic Industries

A more interesting example involves tariffs on a product that is produced both domestically and abroad. Suppose that Americans purchase cars from Japan subject to a flat Japanese supply curve at price P_0, and that domestic car manufacturers have the upward-sloping supply curve shown in panel A of Exhibit 8–17. Assuming that all cars are identical, no consumer will be willing to pay more than P_0 for a domestic car, since he can always buy an import instead. Therefore all cars sell at a price of P_0. At this price the number of cars produced by domestic manufacturers is Q_0, and the number purchased by domestic consumers is Q_1. The difference, $Q_0 - Q_1$, is the number of imports. Table A in Exhibit 8–17 shows the consumers' and producers' surpluses.

Now suppose that we impose a tariff of $500 on each imported car. This raises the foreign supply curve $500 to a level of $P_0 + \$500$. The price of cars goes up to $P_0 + \$500$, the quantity supplied domestically goes up to Q'_0 (in panel B of Exhibit 8–17), and the quantity demanded falls to Q'_1. The quantity imported falls to $Q'_1 - Q'_0$.

In Exhibit 8–17 Table B shows the consumers' and producers' surpluses both before and after the tariff. (The "before" column, of course, simply repeats the calculation from Table A.) What about revenue from the tariff? The number of imported cars is $Q'_1 - Q'_0$, and the tariff is $500 on each of these. Thus the tariff revenue (which ends up in American pockets) is $(Q'_1 - Q'_0) \times \$500$, and this is the area of rectangle I. This is recorded in Table B, along with a comparison of social gains.

We can see that even when there is a domestic industry that benefits from the tariff, and even though the tariff revenue is a gain to the country, tariffs still cause a deadweight loss (we say that they are *inefficient*) because consumers lose more than all other groups gain.

▷ *Exercise 8.10* Suppose that the government wants to benefit domestic auto producers and the recipients of tax revenue at the expense of car buyers. Devise an efficient (though perhaps impractical) way of doing this that makes everybody happier than a tariff does.

Robbery

From the point of view of economic efficiency (that is, the maximization of the total gains to all members of society), a loss to one group that is exactly offset by a gain to another group is a "wash." To one who is interested only in maximizing social gain, such a transfer is neither a good thing nor a bad thing. How, then, should such a one feel about *robbery*?

Many people think that robbery constitutes a social loss equal to the value of what is stolen. Their reasoning is simple but faulty: They notice the loss to the victim without noticing the offsetting gain to the robber. A more sophisticated answer would be to say that robbery is a matter of

Exhibit 8–17   A Tariff When There Is a Domestic Industry

Table A

Consumers' Surplus	A+B
Producers' Surplus	C
Social Gain	A+B+C

Table B

	Before Tariff	After Tariff
Consumers' Surplus	E+F+G+H+I+J	E+F
Producers' Surplus	K	G+K
Tax Revenue	—	I
Social Gain	E+F+G+H+I+J+K	E+F+G+K+I
Deadweight Loss		H+J

A

B

We assume that Americans can buy any number of cars from Japan at the price P_0. The supply curve S shows how many cars American manufacturers will provide at each price. At the price P_0, American producers supply Q_0 cars and American consumers purchase Q_1 cars. The difference, $Q_1 - Q_0$, is the number of cars imported. Table A shows the gains to Americans.

In panel B we see the effect of a $500 tariff on imported cars. The price of a foreign car rises to $P_0 + \$500$, and the number of imports falls to $Q'_1 - Q'_0$. Table B compares gains before and after the tariff. Note that the first column of Table B is identical to Table A except that it uses the labels from panel B rather than panel A. The tariff revenue is computed by observing that the area of rectangle I is $(Q'_1 - Q'_0) \times \$500$.

indifference, because stolen goods do not disappear from society; they only change ownership.

However, this more sophisticated answer is also wrong. There *is* a social cost to robbery. It is the opportunity cost of the robber's time and energy. The robber who steals your bicycle could, perhaps, with the same expenditure of energy, be building a bicycle of his own. If he did, society would have two bicycles; when he steals yours instead, society has only one. The option to steal costs society a bicycle.

Exhibit 8–18   **The Social Cost of Robbery**

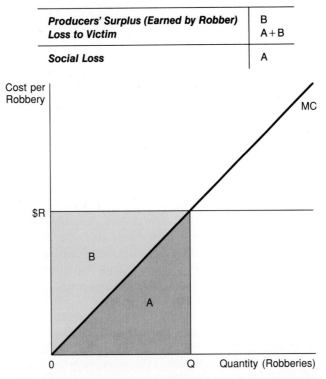

Producers' Surplus (Earned by Robber)	B
Loss to Victim	A + B
Social Loss	A

We suppose that a robber can expect to earn $R for each robbery he commits. Then robberies will take place until the robbers' marginal cost (the opportunity cost of their time, energy, and so on) equals $R. The number of robberies committed is Q, and robbers earn a producers' surplus of B. However, victims lose the amount stolen, which is A + B. There is a net social loss of A. If society pursues economic efficiency, A is the maximum amount it would be willing to spend to prevent all robberies.

This shows that robbery is socially costly; we still have to ask: *How costly?* To answer this, it is reasonable to treat robbery as a competitive industry: Robbers will continue to rob until the marginal cost (in time, energy, and so on) of committing an additional crime is equal to the marginal revenue (in loot). The cost is what interests us, the loot is observable, and we know that the two are equal. So, at the margin, we can reckon the cost of a robbery as approximately equal to the value of what is stolen.

This tells us that the amount stolen is a correct measure of the cost of the last robbery committed. In Exhibit 8–18 we calculate the total social cost of all robberies. Suppose that a robber can expect to earn $R each time he commits a robbery. Then robbers will steal until the marginal cost of stealing is equal to $R; that is, they will commit Q robberies. The amount stolen is $R × Q, the area A + B. However, the robbers' total costs are given by the area under the supply curve, A. This cost to the robbers is society's cost as well. Therefore the total social cost of all robberies (A) is less than the value of what is taken (A + B).

This analysis ignores the very real possibility that people will take costly steps to protect themselves from robbery—installing burglar alarms, deadbolt locks, and the like. These additional costs are also due to the existence of robbery and must be added to area A in order to calculate the full social cost of robberies.

The more general lesson of this example is that effort expended in nonproductive activity is social loss. Accountants devising new methods of tax avoidance, lawyers in litigation, lobbyists seeking laws to transfer wealth to their clients, and all of the resources that they employ (secretaries, file clerks, Xerox machines, telephone services, and so on) are often unproductive from a social point of view. Whatever they win for their clients is a loss for their adversaries. In the absence of this activity, all of these resources could be employed elsewhere, making society richer.

On the other hand, some of this seemingly unproductive activity serves hidden and valuable purposes. Suppose that a law is passed requiring that all owners of apple orchards donate $5,000 each to the president's brother. The owners of apple orchards might hire a lobbyist to assist them in having this law overturned. If the effort is successful, apple growers will win only what the president's brother loses, and so at one level of analysis the lobbyist's time contributes nothing to the welfare of society. On the other hand, if all of the orange growers were made very nervous by this law and planned to burn down their orange trees as a precaution against their being next, then the lobbyist saves a lot of valuable orange trees through his efforts. Insofar as redistributing income affects the incentives to engage in productive activities, it can indirectly affect society's welfare.

Theories of Value

We have defined value in terms of consumers' willingness to pay, and we have discovered that the price of an item is equal to its marginal value. Other theories of value have arisen in the history of economics, only to be abandoned when careful analysis revealed them as erroneous. Because such errors are still common in much discussion by noneconomists, it is worth examining them to see why they should be avoided.

The Diamond–Water Paradox

Many classical economists were puzzled by the so-called "diamond–water paradox." How can it be that water, which is essential for life and therefore as "valuable" a thing as can be imagined, is so inexpensive relative to diamonds, which are used primarily for decoration and the production of nonessential goods? If price reflects value, shouldn't a gallon of water be worth innumerable diamonds?

The paradox is resolved when you realize that price reflects not *total*

Exhibit 8–19   **The Diamond–Water Paradox Resolved**

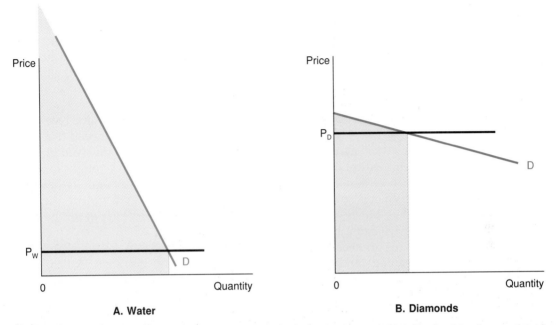

A. Water   **B. Diamonds**

If you had no water and no diamonds, you would be willing to pay far more for a first bucket of water than for a first diamond. Therefore your marginal value (= demand) curve for water starts out much higher than your marginal value curve for diamonds. At the market prices P_W and P_D, you consume Q_W buckets of water and Q_D diamonds, so that the marginal value of a bucket of water (P_W) is much less than the marginal value of a diamond (P_D).

It is true that the total value of all your water (the shaded area in panel A) is greater than the total value of all your diamonds (the shaded area in panel B). The graphs show that this is perfectly consistent with a low marginal value for water and a high marginal value for diamonds. The price, which is equal to the marginal value, should not be expected to reflect the total value.

value, but *marginal* value. Exhibit 8–19 depicts the demand curves for water and for diamonds, together with their market prices and the corresponding consumers' surpluses. The marginal value of your first gallon of water is indeed much higher than the marginal value of your first diamond, and this is reflected by the heights of the demand curves at low quantities. But this has nothing to do with the *price* of water; the price is equal to the marginal value of the last bucket consumed, and this may be very low if you consume many gallons.

Notice that the total value (the colored area) in the market for water is much higher than in the market for diamonds: If you lost all of your water and all of your diamonds, you would be willing to pay more to retrieve the water than to retrieve the diamonds. In consequence, the consumers' surplus is much higher in the market for water than in the market for diamonds. Exhibit 8–19 shows that there is nothing paradoxical about a low price and a large consumers' surplus existing simultaneously.

The Labor Theory of Value

The **labor theory of value** is an error that deceived such diverse economists as Adam Smith and Karl Marx. In its simplest form it says that the price of an item is determined by the amount of labor used in its production.[7] In this form it is clearly false: You can expend an enormous quantity of labor digging a gigantic hole in your backyard, and the price that hole commands in the marketplace may be far less than the price of a short story produced by a good writer in an afternoon, sitting at a word processor in an air-conditioned house sipping lemonade.[8]

For a theory so evidently false, the labor theory of value (even in this simple form) is remarkably pervasive. You will hear it argued that doctors "ought to" earn high salaries because of all the effort involved in earning their medical degrees, or that people in occupation A "ought to" earn as much as people in occupation B because they work equally hard. Such arguments ignore the fact that value is determined not by the cost of inputs, but by demand—the consumer's willingness to pay for the good or service being offered.

Another common belief that embodies the labor theory fallacy is that a meaning can be attached to the "book value" of a firm. A firm's "book value" is a measure of what it would cost to produce the actual physical assets of the firm. It is computed, for example, by adding up the cost of the bricks used to build the firm's plants and office buildings, the desks and chairs in the executive offices, the machines along the assembly line, and the letterhead stationery in the cabinets. This book value can be compared to the actual price at which one could acquire the entire firm (say, by purchasing all of its stock). It sometimes happens that a firm can be acquired for less than book value, and it is widely believed that this represents a bargain.

Not so. The fact that a factory is built from $1 million worth of bricks does not make that factory worth $1 million, any more than your application of $1 million worth of labor would make a hole in your backyard worth $1 million. If your labor is devoted to the production of something that nobody wants, or if the bricks are glued together to form a factory that produces nothing useful, this will be reflected in the price. What we have here is a "brick theory of value," different perhaps from the labor theory of value, but perfectly analogous and just as false.

A final example illustrates both the diamond–water and the labor

---

[7]Of course, this is a simpler form than economists have ever believed; typical versions restrict attention to "socially necessary" labor and include the labor of previous generations who built machines used in current production.

[8]It *is* true, of course, that in a competitive market, price will be equal to marginal cost (and a competitive producer will not choose to dig a hole in his backyard for sale in the marketplace). But marginal cost is not labor cost. Some labor costs may be sunk (and therefore irrelevant), and many relevant costs have nothing to do with labor. The relevant costs, as always, are the opportunity costs—the writer with his word processor could be writing a movie script instead.

theory paradoxes. It is sometimes argued that something must be wrong with society's values when a baseball player (for example) earns a salary in the high six figures for playing a game that (1) he enjoys anyway and (2) produces little social value compared to something like teaching elementary school, which is far less lucrative. The first point is the labor theory of value again. It errs by assuming that how hard the baseball player works determines the value of what he produces. The second point uses the erroneous reasoning that underlies the diamond–water paradox. It may very well be that teachers (like water) produce far more total social value than star baseball players. It may also be true that *one additional teacher* produces less social value than one additional star baseball player. This can be true, for example, if there are many teachers and few star baseball players. We should not expect the price of a teacher or a baseball player to tell us anything about the total value to society of the two professions.

8.2 The Invisible Hand

Based on the examples in Section 8.1, you might have begun to suspect that any deviation from competitive equilibrium leads to a reduction in social gain. In this section we will see that this is, in fact, the case.

The Fundamental Theorem of Welfare Economics

Exhibit 8–20 shows the competitive market for potatoes. We can ask two questions about this market, ostensibly as different as questions can be:

1. What is the quantity of potatoes actually produced and sold?

2. Suppose you were a benevolent dictator, concerned only with maximizing the total welfare gains to all of society. What quantity of potatoes would you *order* produced and sold?

Note well the dissimilarity between these questions. One is a question about what *is;* the other is a question about what *ought* to be.

We know the answers to each of these questions. They are:

1. The quantity of potatoes produced and sold is at Q_0, where supply equals demand. We have seen that individual suppliers and demanders, seeking to maximize their own profits and their own happiness, will choose to operate at this point.

2. To maximize social gains, you would continue ordering potatoes to be produced as long as their marginal value exceeds the marginal cost of producing them. You would stop when marginal cost equals marginal value, that is, at Q_0.

    The choice of Q_0 yields a social gain of A + B in Exhibit 8–20. A despot who made the mistake of ordering only Q_1 potatoes produced would limit social gain to area A. If he made the mistake of ordering Q_2, area C would be subtracted from the social gain, since it is made up

Exhibit 8–20   **The Invisible Hand**

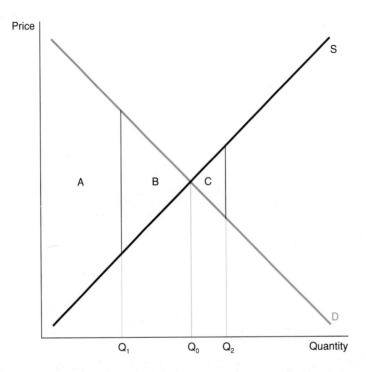

Under competition, the quantity produced is Q_0, where supply equals demand. A benevolent dictator who wanted to maximize social gain would employ the equimarginal principle and order potatoes to be produced to a quantity where marginal cost equals marginal value. This also occurs at quantity Q_0.

If the dictator ordered Q_1 potatoes produced, social gain would be area A; if he ordered Q_2, social gain would be A + B − C. The maximum social gain, at Q_0, is A + B.

of rectangles whose areas represent an excess of marginal cost over marginal value.

It is an astounding fact that the two questions have identical answers. The coincidence results from the prior coincidences of the supply curve with the marginal cost curve, and of the demand curve with the marginal value curve.

The fact is not only astounding, but fortunate. It means that people living in a competitive world will achieve the maximum possible social gain without any need of a benevolent despot. The market alone achieves an outcome that is economically efficient. To say the same thing in different words, competitive equilibrium is Pareto optimal.

The eighteenth-century economist Adam Smith was so struck by this observation that he described it with one of the world's most enduring metaphors. Of the individual participant in the marketplace, he said:

He intends only his own gain, and he is . . . led by an invisible hand to promote an end which was no part of his intention.[9]

Noneconomists frequently misunderstand what Smith meant by the "invisible hand." Some think it is a metaphor for an ideology or a philosophical point of view; the notion has even been described as a theological one! In fact, the *invisible hand* expresses what is at bottom a mathematical truth. The point of equilibrium (where competitive suppliers will operate "intending only their own gain") is also the point of maximum social gain (an end that is no part of any individual participant's intention).

The Idea of a General Equilibrium

The preceding analysis is striking, but it is incomplete. By participating in the potato market, people change conditions in other markets as well. When he grows more or fewer potatoes, a farmer consequently grows less or more of something else. The amount of labor that he hires changes. When a consumer changes his potato consumption, he probably also changes his consumption of rice, and of butter. At one further remove, any change in the potato market affects the potato farmer's income, which affects his purchases of shoes, which affects the market for leather, which affects the market for something else, ad infinitum.

If we really want to understand the welfare consequences of competitive equilibrium in the potato industry, we need to consider its effects in all of these other markets as well. Could it be that by maximizing welfare gains in one market, we are imposing a net welfare *loss* in the totality of all other markets?

It was not until the 1950s, nearly 200 years after Adam Smith, that economists developed the mathematical tools necessary to deal fully with this complicated question. In that decade economists such as Kenneth Arrow, Gerard Debreu, and Lionel McKenzie devised techniques that make it possible to study all of the markets in the economy at one time. In this they were advancing a subject called **general equilibrium analysis,** first invented by the nineteenth-century economist Léon Walras. One of the great and powerful results of general equilibrium theory is that even in view of the effects of all markets on all other markets, competitive equilibrium is still Pareto optimal. This discovery is usually called the *First Fundamental Theorem of Welfare Economics,* or the *Invisible Hand Theorem.*

If the Invisible Hand Theorem seems obvious to you, you almost surely do not understand it. The Pareto optimality of competitive equilibrium is a deep and wondrous fact about the price system. We shall see repeatedly in later chapters (especially Chapters 10, 11, and 12) that no analogous statement need be true in the absence of competition or in the absence of prices. The statement is neither a trivial observation nor a philosophical speculation. It is a truth, and a surprising one.

General equilibrium analysis
A way of modeling the economy so as to take account of all markets at once, and of all the interactions among them.

---

[9]From Book 4 of Smith's monumental work *The Wealth of Nations,* first published in 1776.

An Edgeworth Box Economy

The Invisible Hand Theorem is true in very complex economies with many participants and many markets, but we will illustrate it (and the basic ideas of general equilibrium analysis) only in the simplest possible case. Assume a world with two people (Aline and Bob) and two goods (food and clothing). We will simplify further by assuming that there is no production in this world; Aline and Bob can only trade the goods that already exist. These assumptions will enable us to present a complete general equilibrium model and to illustrate the Invisible Hand Theorem.

Edgeworth box
A certain diagrammatic representation of an economy with two individuals, two goods, and no production.

Since there is no production in this world, there is only a fixed, unchangeable amount of food and clothing. In panel A of Exhibit 8–21 we draw a box that has a width equal to the amount of food in existence, and a height equal to the amount of clothing. Such a box is called an **Edgeworth box.**[10] Using the lower left-hand corner as the origin, we draw Aline's indifference curves between food and clothing. We also mark one point of special interest: It is Aline's **endowment point,** O, representing the basket of food and clothing that she owns at the beginning of the story.

Endowment point
The point representing the initial holdings of an individual in an Edgeworth box.

In panel B we do a strange thing: We turn the entire page upside down, and we draw Bob's (black) indifference curves in the same box. For him, the food axis is the line that Aline views as the top of the box, and the clothing axis is the line that Aline views as the right side of the box.

To plot Bob's endowment point, remember that the width of the box is equal to the sum of Bob's and Aline's food endowments, and that the height is equal to the sum of their clothing endowments. A moment's reflection should convince you that Bob's endowment point (measured along *his* axes) is the same as Aline's endowment point (measured along *her* axes).

Panel C shows a piece of panel B: All but two indifference curves have been eliminated. We have retained only those indifference curves (one of Aline's and one of Bob's) that pass through the endowment point.

Now suppose that Bob and Aline discuss the possibility of trade. Aline will veto any trade that moves her into region A, C, or E, since these all represent moves to lower indifference curves from her point of view. Similarly, Bob will veto any trade that moves him into region A, B, or E. (Hold the book upside down for help in seeing this!) However, a movement anywhere inside region D will make both parties better off. For this reason

Region of mutual advantage
The set of points that are Pareto-preferred to the initial endowment.

region D is called the **region of mutual advantage,** and Aline and Bob can arrange a trade that will move them into this area.

After moving to a new point inside the region of mutual advantage, Aline and Bob face a new, smaller region of mutual advantage, as shown in panel D. They will move to a new point in this new region and will continue this process until no region of mutual advantage remains. This occurs precisely when they reach a point where their indifference curves are tangent to each other, such as the point P in panel D.

[10]After the nineteenth-century British economist F. Y. Edgeworth.

Exhibit 8–21   **Trade in an Edgeworth Box Economy**

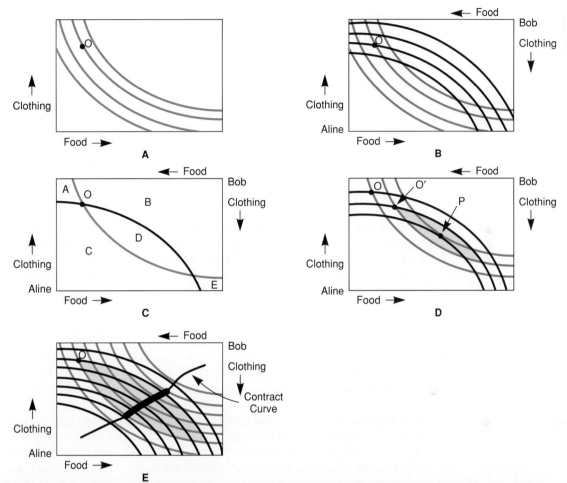

Panel A shows Aline's indifference curves and her endowment point O. Panel B adds Bob's (black) indifference curves, using the northeast corner of the box as origin. Measuring along Bob's axes, his endowment point is also O.

Panel C shows only those indifference curves that pass through the endowment point. Movements into the region of mutual advantage, D, benefit both parties. Moves into any other region will be vetoed by one or both of the parties.

Panel D shows the situation after Aline and Bob make the mutually beneficial trade to point O'. The shaded region is the new region of mutual advantage. Trade will continue until they reach a point like P in panel D, where there is no region of mutual advantage. Such points are on the contract curve, consisting of the tangencies between Aline's and Bob's indifference curves. The points on the contract curve are precisely those that are Pareto-optimal.

In panel E the shaded region is the original region of mutual advantage. Trade leads to the choice of a point on the contract curve in this region. The darker segment of the contract curve is the set of possible outcomes.

A point of tangency between Aline's and Bob's indifference curves is a point from which no further mutually beneficial trade is possible. In other words, such a point is Pareto optimal; from that point no change

Contract curve
The set of Pareto-optimal points.

can improve both parties' welfare. The collection of all Pareto-optimal points forms a curve, which is called the **contract curve** and is illustrated in panel E.

We do not know in advance exactly what point Aline and Bob will reach through the trading process. We know only that it will be somewhere within the original region of mutual advantage, and that it will be on the contract curve. The set of possible outcomes is the darker segment of the contract curve shown in panel E.

Competitive Equilibrium in the Edgeworth Box

Our analysis has revealed an infinite variety of possible outcomes for the bargaining process. Next we ask what can happen if Aline and Bob play according to a far more restrictive set of rules. Instead of letting them bargain in whatever way they choose, we require them to bargain through the mechanism of a price system.

The new rules of the game work this way: Aline and Bob decide on a relative price for food and clothing. At this price, each decides how much of each commodity he or she would like to buy or sell. If their desires are compatible (that is, if Aline wants to buy just as much food as Bob wants to sell), they carry out the transaction. If their desires are not compatible, they decide on a new relative price and try again. This process continues until they find a relative price that "clears the market" in the sense that quantities demanded equal quantities supplied.

Why would Aline and Bob ever agree to such a strange and restricted set of rules? They wouldn't, because two people can bargain far more effectively without introducing the artifice of market-clearing prices. But our interest in Aline and Bob is not personal; we are concerned with them only because we are interested in the workings of much larger markets, and such markets *do* operate through a price mechanism. So we shall force Aline and Bob to behave the way people in large markets behave, hoping that their responses will teach us something about those large markets.

Suggesting a relative price is equivalent to suggesting a slope for Aline's budget line. Once we know this slope, we know her entire budget line. This is because her budget line must pass through her endowment point, in view of the fact that she can always achieve this point by refusing to trade. Bob's budget line (viewed from his upside-down perspective) is the same as Aline's. In panel A of Exhibit 8–22 a relative price has been suggested that leads Aline to choose point X and Bob to choose point Y. The total quantity of food demanded is more than exists in the world; the total quantity of clothing demanded fails to exhaust the available supply. The market has not cleared and a new relative price must be tried. In view of the outcome at the current price, it seems sensible to raise the relative price of food. That is, we try a steeper budget line, as in panel B. This time Aline and Bob both choose the same point Z and the market clears.

Competitive equilibrium
A point that everyone will choose to trade to, for some appropriate market prices.

The mutually acceptable point Z in panel B is called a **competitive equilibrium** for this economy. It requires finding a budget line that goes

Exhibit 8–22 Competitive Equilibrium in an Edgeworth Box Economy

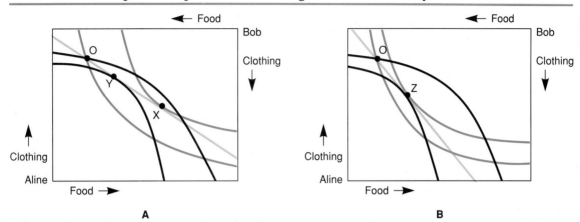

In panel A a relative price has been suggested that leads to the budget line pictured. (This is Aline's budget line from her perspective and Bob's budget line from his.) Aline chooses point X and Bob chooses point Y. But these points are not the same; the quantities that Aline wants to buy and sell are not the same quantities that Bob wants to sell and buy.

In panel B a different relative price has been suggested. At this price Aline's desires are compatible with Bob's. Point Z is a competitive equilibrium.

through the original endowment point and leads to the same optimum point for Aline that it does for Bob. It is not immediately obvious that a competitive equilibrium should even exist, but it turns out to be possible to prove this.[11]

The Invisible Hand in the Edgeworth Box

At the competitive equilibrium Z of Exhibit 8–22, Aline's indifference curve is tangent to the budget line, and Bob's indifference curve is tangent to the same budget line. It follows that Aline's and Bob's indifference curves are tangent to each other. This in turn means that the competitive equilibrium is a point on the contract curve, that is, it is Pareto optimal.

This reasoning shows that in an Edgeworth box economy, any competitive equilibrium is Pareto optimal. That is, the Invisible Hand Theorem is true.

We began this section by noticing that competitive equilibrium is Pareto optimal in the context of a single market. We have just seen that the

---

[11]In fact, *you* can prove it, if you have had a course in calculus. Define the *aggregate excess demand* for food to be the sum of the quantities demanded by Bob and Aline, *minus* the world supply of food. At a price of zero, draw the budget line and compute the aggregate excess demand. Do the same at an infinite price. Now use the Intermediate Value Theorem to complete the proof.

same is true in the context of an entire economy (albeit an extraordinarily simple economy in which no production takes place). The same is also true in far more complex models involving many markets and incorporating production, though this requires advanced mathematics to prove.

8.3 Other Normative Criteria

In their studies of normative criteria, economists have generally focused on two issues: the allocation of resources and the distribution of income. The allocation of resources concerns what shall be produced, using what inputs, and in what quantities. The distribution of income concerns who receives the output.

In principle, these issues can be completely separated. One concerns the size and type of pie we should bake and the other concerns how the pie should be divided. Thus suppose, as we did in Exhibit 8–10, that the government wants to redistribute income away from the buyers and sellers of coffee to some other group in society. If this is accomplished through the Robin Hood policy of taking, completely unexpectedly, from the consumers and producers and giving to the recipients, then there is no effect on the allocation of resources. The same amount of coffee is produced as before; the social pie is unchanged.

On the other hand, the phrase *in principle* with which we began the preceding paragraph hides a multitude of difficulties. First, there are limits to what sorts of redistribution the political system will tolerate. What these limits are and why they exist are fascinating questions that are still not well understood. More fundamentally, in order for a redistribution to have no effect on the allocation of resources, it must be entirely unexpected; otherwise the buyers and sellers of coffee will change their behavior to avoid it. In addition to its being unexpected, consumers and producers must not be allowed to suspect that it might ever be repeated; otherwise, once again, their behavior will change.

Any *realistic* attempt to redistribute income, such as the sales tax of Exhibit 8–10, will have some effect on the allocation of resources as well. The efficiency criterion asserts that policies should be evaluated only by their effects on resource allocation. However, many widespread notions of fairness suggest that considerations of income distribution should also play a part in the choice of policies.

In this section we will develop the notion of an envy-free allocation, which provides a normative criterion that attempts to capture some of these notions of fairness. With this and the efficiency criterion before us, we will be able to turn to the interesting question of when and whether it is possible to satisfy *both* criteria at the same time. Can we arrange society in such a way that we both bake the largest possible pie and see that everyone receives a fair share?

Exhibit 8–23   **Envy-Free Allocations**

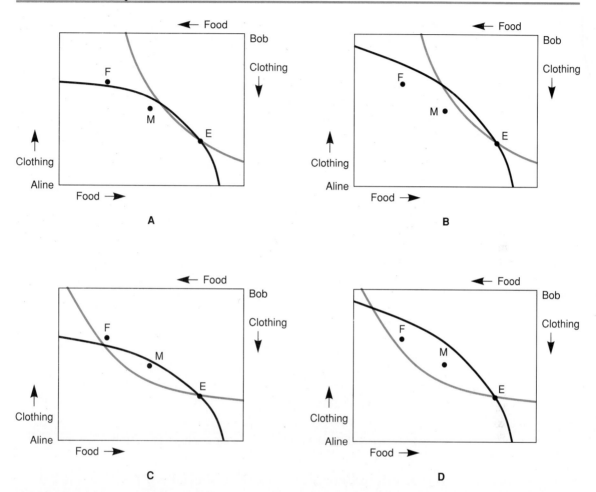

In each panel E is the point that each person views as his own endowment, and its mirror image F is the point that each person views as the other person's endowment. The allocation E is envy-free if, as in panel A, each person prefers basket E over basket F.

Envy-Free Allocations

Envy-free allocation
An outcome in which nobody would prefer to trade baskets with anybody else.

A division of the goods in society is called an **envy-free allocation** if no person would prefer somebody else's basket to his own. We shall explore this concept in the context of the Edgeworth box economy of Section 8.2. Exhibit 8–23 shows Aline's endowment point, E. Bob's endowment point, when viewed from Bob's origin in the northeast corner, is also E. However, when viewed from Aline's origin in the southwest corner, Bob's endow-

Exhibit 8–24   Trading When Everyone Starts with Equal Shares

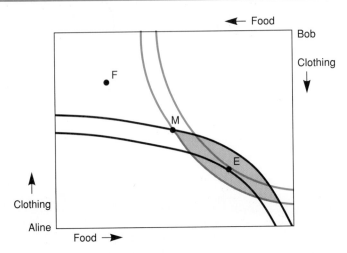

If the endowment point is the midpoint M, Aline and Bob will trade to a point like E in the (shaded) region of mutual advantage. F is the mirror image of E. The geometry forces Aline's indifference curve through E to pass above F, and Bob's indifference curve through E to pass below F. Consequently, the allocation E is envy-free.

ment is F, which is the mirror image of E through the midpoint M of the box. From Bob's origin, F is Aline's endowment.

In short, each person, viewing the situation from his own origin, regards E as his own endowment point and F as the other person's. The allocation is envy-free if, as in panel A, Aline and Bob each prefer point E to point F.

▷ *Exercise 8.11* In each of the other panels of Exhibit 8–23, who envies whom?

Now let us suppose that before trading takes place, Aline and Bob are allocated equal quantities of food and clothing. This means that the initial endowment point is the midpoint M in Exhibit 8–24. From this point Aline and Bob will trade to a new point in the region of mutual advantage, labeled E in the exhibit. Its mirror image is labeled F. Because the region of mutual advantage is bounded by the indifference curves through M, it follows that Aline's indifference curve through E passes above F, and that Bob's indifference curve through E passes below F as in panel A of Exhibit 8–23. Consequently, the allocation is envy-free.

We know that there is always a competitive equilibrium in an Edgeworth box, and that the competitive equilibrium is efficient (that is, Pareto optimal). We also know that the competitive equilibrium is inside the region of mutual advantage. We have just learned that if the initial endowment is the midpoint of the box, where everyone starts with equal shares of both goods, then any point in the region of mutual advantage is envy-free. Putting this together, we have our conclusion:

If everyone starts with equal shares, then a competitive equilibrium is both efficient and envy-free.

Like the Invisible Hand Theorem, this statement remains true in economies far more complex than that of the Edgeworth box. It shows that efficiency and fairness can be achieved simultaneously.

Summary

Consumers and producers both gain from trade. Consumers' and producers' surpluses are measures of the extent of their gains.

When the consumer buys a good X, the total value of his purchase is given by the area under his demand curve out to the quantity. This area is the most that he would be willing to pay in exchange for that quantity of X. After we subtract the total cost to the consumer, we are left with the area under his demand curve down to the price paid and out to the quantity consumed. This area is his consumer's surplus. It is the amount that the consumer would be willing to pay in exchange for being allowed to purchase good X.

The producer's surplus is the excess of the producer's revenues over his costs. It is measured by the area above the supply curve up to the price received and out to the quantity supplied.

When there is more than one consumer or more than one producer, the total surplus to all consumers is given by the area under the market demand curve down to the price paid and out to the quantity purchased. The total surplus to all producers is given by the area above the market supply curve up to the price received and out to the quantity sold.

Policies such as taxes or price controls can change prices and quantities and consequently change the consumers' and producers' surpluses. They also sometimes generate tax revenue (which is a gain to somebody) or impose a cost on taxpayers (which is a loss). Social gain is the sum of consumers' and producers' surpluses, plus any other gains, minus any losses. If a policy reduces social gain below what it might have been, the amount of the reduction is known as a deadweight loss.

Whenever there is deadweight loss, it is possible to devise an alternative policy that is Pareto-preferred (that is, preferred by everybody) to the current policy. A policy is said to be Pareto-optimal, or efficient, if no other policy is Pareto-preferred.

The efficiency criterion is a normative criterion which asserts that we should prefer policies that maximize social gain, or equivalently, minimize deadweight loss. Few (if any) would argue that the efficiency criterion should be the sole guide to policy, but many economists consider it reasonable to use as a rough guideline. When a policy creates large deadweight losses, there may be a Pareto-preferred policy that is actually possible to implement.

The Invisible Hand Theorem states that competitive equilibrium is Pareto optimal. That is, in a competitive market where each individual seeks only his own personal gains, it turns out to be the case that social gains are maximized. This is true in individual markets, and remains true when the entire economy is taken into account. The Edgeworth box presents an example of a complete economy that can be used to illustrate the workings of the Invisible Hand.

The Edgeworth box can be used to illustrate other normative criteria as well, such as the notion of envy-freeness, which is a sort of fairness notion. It turns out that if everyone starts out with equal assets, any competitive equilibrium is both efficient and envy-free.

Review Questions

R1. Explain why a consumer's demand curve is identical with his marginal value curve.

R2. What geometric areas represent the value of the goods that a consumer purchases and the cost of producing those goods? What geometric area represents the social gain from the goods' production, and why?

R3. What geometric areas represent the consumers' and producers' surpluses, and why?

R4. Analyze the effect on social welfare of a sales tax.

R5. Analyze the effect on social welfare of a subsidy.

R6. Analyze the effect on social welfare of a price ceiling.

R7. Analyze the effect on social welfare of a tariff, assuming that the country imposing the tariff constitutes a small part of the entire market. First answer assuming that the good in question is available only from abroad, then repeat your answer assuming that there is a domestic industry.

R8. "The fact that secretaries are paid less than corporate executives shows that society values secretarial services less than it values the work of executives." Explain why this statement is false.

R9. State the Invisible Hand Theorem. Illustrate its meaning using supply and demand curves.

R10. Explain the difference between the allocation of resources and the distribution of income. With which is the efficiency criterion concerned?

R11. Using an Edgeworth box, illustrate the region of mutual advantage and the contract curve. Explain why trade will always lead to a point that is both in the region and on the curve.

R12. Using an Edgeworth box, illustrate the competitive equilibrium. Explain how you know that the competitive equilibrium is on the contract curve. How does this illustrate the Invisible Hand Theorem?

R13. Using an Edgeworth box, illustrate the notion of an envy-free allocation. Explain why we know that it is always possible to find an allocation that is both efficient and envy-free.

Problem Set

1. *True or false:* If Jack Daniels whiskey sells for $10 per bottle and if 1,000 bottles were sold last year, then the total value of those bottles to consumers was $10,000.

2. Suppose that your demand curves for gadgets and widgets are both straight lines but your demand curve for gadgets is much more elastic than your demand curve for widgets. Each is selling at a market price of $10, and at that price you choose to buy exactly 30 gadgets and 30 widgets.
   a. From which transaction do you gain more surplus?
   b. If forced at gunpoint to buy either an extra gadget or an extra widget, which would you buy?
   c. Illustrate the change in your consumer's surplus as a result of the forced transaction of part b.

3. Pablo Picasso frequently "paid" for restaurant meals by quickly drawing a picture, consisting of a few lines, on a napkin and signing it. Was he eating for free? If so, who was paying for his meals, and why did restaurant owners allow it?

4. *True or false:* If there is a fixed amount of land in Wyoming, then a sales tax on Wyoming land will have no effect on social welfare.

5. *True or false:* Because time is valuable, it is just as expensive for society to have people wait in long lines for gasoline as to have them pay high prices.

6. *True or false:* A sales tax on a price-controlled item can improve social welfare.

7. Suppose that an effective price *floor* is established in the market for oranges and that the government agrees to buy any oranges that go unsold at this price. The oranges purchased by the government are discarded.
   a. Show the number of oranges purchased by the government.
   b. Show the consumers' surplus, the producers' surplus, the cost to the taxpayers, and the social gain both before and after the program is introduced.
   c. What is the deadweight loss from this program?

8. Suppose that a law is passed requiring each purchaser of gasoline to present one ration ticket per gallon purchased. A ration ticket cannot be reused. A quantity of ration tickets (*less* than the equilibrium quantity of gasoline) is printed and distributed randomly to citizens, who may buy and sell them freely. Assume that it costs nothing to print and distribute ration tickets. Show on a graph (a) the price of the ration tickets, (b) the consumers' surplus, (c) the producers' surplus, (d) the value of the ration tickets that people receive, and (e) the deadweight loss.

9. Suppose that South Molucca is willing to supply any number of birdcages to Americans at a price of P_0. American birdcage manufacturers have an upward-sloping supply curve that intersects demand at a price above P_0.

    a. Explain why the market price for birdcages is P_0. Show how many birdcages Americans buy at this price. Show how many are provided domestically and how many are imported from South Molucca.

    b. Show the welfare gain to Americans from the existence of the birdcage market, and show how it is distributed between consumers and producers.

    c. Now suppose that a quota is enacted that permits the South Moluccans to sell only Q_0 birdcages per year in America, and that Q_0 is less than the quantity they have been selling to us up until now. Show that there is only one price consistent with Americans wanting to import exactly Q_0 birdcages, and explain why the price of birdcages will rise to that level.

    d. Show the new gains to American producers and consumers. Who wins and who loses as a result of the quota? Which is greater—the amount the winners win or the amount the losers lose? Show on your graph the difference between these two quantities.

    e. Suppose that the quota is abolished and replaced by a tariff that causes the number of imported birdcages to fall to Q_0. Which Americans prefer the tariff to the quota, and which prefer the quota to the tariff? Which do the South Moluccans prefer—the tariff or the quota?

10. Suppose that it is now between harvests, so that the number of avocados is in fixed supply. There are equal numbers of avocados available in Los Angeles and San Francisco, but the demand curve is much higher in Los Angeles.

    a. Compare the prices and quantities of avocados in the two locations.

    b. In view of your answer to part a, what will avocado suppliers begin to do? If it is costless to ship avocados, when will this process stop? Why?

    c. Draw the demand and supply curves for avocados in the two cities both before and after the process you described in part b. Compare consumers' and producers' surpluses before and after the process takes place.

    d. Suppose that it were made illegal to transport avocados from one city to another. Could this benefit consumers? Producers? Society as a whole? What areas would you have to measure to get definitive answers to these questions?

11. Popeye and Wimpy trade only with each other. Popeye is endowed with 8 hamburgers and 2 cans of spinach, and Wimpy is endowed with 2 hamburgers and 8 cans of spinach. Their indifference curves, somewhat unusually, are all straight lines, Popeye's being much steeper than Wimpy's:

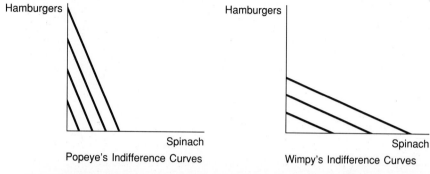

Popeye's Indifference Curves   Wimpy's Indifference Curves

In an Edgeworth box, show the initial endowment, the region of mutual advantage, the contract curve, and the competitive equilibrium.

12. Adam and Eve consume only apples. Of the following allocations of apples, which are preferred to which others according to (a) the Pareto criterion, (b) the efficiency criterion? Which allocations are envy-free?

   (i)   Adam has 10 apples and Eve has 0 apples.
   (ii) Adam has 8 apples and Eve has 2 apples.
   (iii) Adam has 5 apples and Eve has 5 apples.
   (iv) Adam has 0 apples and Eve has 10 apples.
   (v)   Adam has 4 apples and Eve has 4 apples.

Refer to Answers to Problem Sets for solutions to problems 2a, 2b, 5, and 9.

Chapter Nine

Knowledge in Society

Every night the 1.5 million residents of Manhattan Island go to bed confident that when they awake, they will be able to purchase food, clothing, gasoline, and dozens of other items that are sent to New York City from thousands of miles away. How can Iowa farmers and Texas oil producers know what products to ship to Manhattan and in what quantities? Since each individual supplier makes an independent decision about how much to send, why do residents of the city not find all the stores nearly empty on some days or full to overflowing on others? When New Yorkers want more pork, how do the suppliers of feed corn know to increase production so that the hog farmers can raise more hogs? How is this activity coordinated with the activities of the butchers and truck drivers and refrigerator repairmen who are the hog farmers' partners in the production of pork chops? How *can* it be coordinated when all of these producers are unknown to each other?[1]

In this chapter we will see how prices serve to convey information so that complex social activities can be organized and implemented. This will

---

[1]Such questions were raised by the nineteenth-century French economist Frederic Bastiat in his book *Economic Sophisms*, 1873.

extend our understanding of the social role of prices that was developed in Chapter 8. There we saw how the price system acts to allocate resources efficiently by ensuring that appropriate quantities will be produced. Here we will focus on how prices contribute to the efficient production and distribution of those quantities by embodying vast amounts of knowledge not available to any individual. The two effects work together—hand in Invisible Hand—to lead to social outcomes that take account of producers' costs and consumers' preferences in ways that no individual planner could hope to accomplish.

9.1 The Informational Content of Prices

Prices and Information

In February 1976 the prestigious journal *Science* carried an article titled "Limits to Exploitation of Nonrenewable Resources." It contained this passage:

> To society . . . the profit from mining (including oil and gas extraction) can be defined either as an energy surplus, as from the exploitation of fossil and nuclear fuel deposits, or as a work saving, as in the lessened expenditure of human energy and time when steel is used in place of wood in tools and structures.[2]

Presumably the "energy surplus" associated with, say, a coal deposit refers to the difference between the energy that can be extracted from the coal deposit on the one hand, and the energy required to excavate it on the other.

By this accounting, a society's choice of energy sources becomes a matter of simple arithmetic. Suppose, for simplicity, that it is necessary to choose between two projects: mining coal (which is located in the eastern half of the United States) and drilling for oil (which is located in the West). Coal mining yields sufficient fuel to provide 1,000 British thermal units[3] of energy per month, but the mining process itself consumes 500 BTU's in the same time period. Oil drilling yields 800 BTU's per month but consumes 200 BTU's. Because the "social profit" from oil (600 BTU's per month) exceeds that from coal (500 BTU's), society should choose to drill for oil.

Alas, the world is not so simple. A subsequent issue of the same journal carried a letter from Harvard economist Robert Dorfman, who elucidated the fallacy. Suppose that the land in the West is the only land suitable for growing hops. A society that drills for oil will then be a society without beer.

---

[2]E. Cook, "Limits to Exploitation of Nonrenewable Resources," *Science* 191 (1976), 677–682.

[3]British thermal units, or BTU's, are the basic units in which energy is measured.

Exhibit 9–1   **Information and Prices**

WESTERN U.S.

Land suitable for:
Oil Drilling
Growing Hops
Attractive Housing

EASTERN U.S.

Land suitable for:
Coal Mining
Raising Cattle

Even if we know that oil drilling produces more energy than coal mining, we still do not have enough information to choose between the two projects. If we drill for oil, we must do without beer and attractive housing, while if we mine coal we must do without beef. The desirability of either alternative depends on the availability of substitutes for beer, western housing, and beef. A blue-ribbon commission can make a disastrously wrong decision if it is missing just one fact. For example, if the commission is unaware of a new breed of cattle that thrives in the West, it might rule out coal mining in the mistaken belief that eastern land is the only source of beef.

However, prices convey the relevant information. The existence of the new breed of cattle drives up the price of western land and drives down the price of eastern land. Although the prices do not reveal the existence of the new breed of cattle, they do reveal that *something* has raised the value of western land and lowered the value of eastern land. This is precisely the kind of information that is needed to choose between the two energy sources.

Then perhaps it is best to mine coal instead. Or perhaps not—the Eastern land might be the best place to raise cattle. On the other hand, the West might be where everyone wants to live, because of its better climate and greater scenic beauty. (See Exhibit 9–1.) What should society do?

A rational choice involves weighing the importance of the alternative uses of land in the different regions of the country. Essentially, there are two ways to do this. One is to empanel a blue-ribbon commission, peopled by experts in mining, agriculture, ranching, housing, and other fields, and to empower this commission to collect evidence about public desires and technological constraints. The panel would inquire into how the Eastern land might be made suitable for the growing of hops, and at what cost. It would ask whether there is a way to make beer without hops, or whether beer can be adequately imported, or whether there is some other beverage that might easily take the place of beer. Having settled these questions, it would move on to analogous questions about housing. At some point the commission would issue a report, making the best recommendation it can on the basis of the information it has been able to acquire.

An alternative is to observe the *price* of land in each region.

The price of a parcel of land is equal (under competition) to the marginal cost of providing that parcel. Since a cost is nothing but a forgone opportunity, the price is a measure of the value of the land in the most valuable of its alternative uses.

When we observe that an acre of land in the West sells for $1,000 and that an acre in the East sells for $800, we know that someone values the Western land at $1,000 per acre and that no one values the Eastern land at more than $800 per acre. The price alone does not reveal the most valuable use of the Western land, but it does reveal how much the land is worth in that use.[4]

Which method is more informative? The commission's report, which may fill three bound volumes and represent two years' work, can be worse than useless if the panelists fail to take account of even one important fact. Not knowing about a new breed of cattle that thrives in the West, they recommend that the East be reserved for the vital role of producing beef, and that the West be exploited for energy—sacrificing both beer and good living and unnecessarily impoverishing society.

Had the commissioners observed the high price of land in the West, they would have known that something was afoot—in this case the owners of the new breed of cattle bidding up the price of land. While an observer of the price might know less about ranching than the commissioners do, he will know more about how to extract energy efficiently.

Prices convey information. They reflect the information available to all members of society (in this case the small number who know about the new cattle reveal the relevant part of their knowledge through the price of land). The commissioners, no matter how wise and how benevolent, can never gather more than a fraction of the information that may be relevant to their decision—but *all* of that information is reflected in the price.

---

[4]There are exceptions to this rule, as we shall see in Chapter 12.

Prices have at least two other advantages over expert panels. One is that observing prices is free. Expert panels consume resources—lots of resources if they do their jobs well.

The other advantage of prices is that in addition to conveying information, they also provide appropriate incentives to act on that information. When a price tells you (by being high) that Western land is valuable to someone, you will not choose to use it yourself unless it is even more valuable to you.

Here is Dorfman again:

> Clearly, then, social costs cannot be measured in . . . simple physical units. The only adequate measure is what economists call "social opportunity costs," meaning the social value of the alternative commodities that have to be forgone in order to obtain the commodity being produced. Under certain idealized conditions this opportunity cost is measured by the dollars-and-cents cost of producing the commodity. Under realistic conditions the dollars-and-cents production cost is a fair approximation to the social cost. Under almost any conceivable conditions the dollars-and-cents cost is a much better approximation to social cost than the amounts of energy expended or any other simple physical measure.
>
> Energy is indeed a scarce and valuable resource; but . . . there is a good deal more to life . . . than British thermal units.[5]

The Problem of the Social Planner

Try the following experiment: Ask your friends to name the two ways to get a chicken to lay more eggs. Few will know. The two ways to get a chicken to lay more eggs are to feed it more or to provide it with more hours of "daylight" in the form of fluorescent fixtures that are usually powered by natural gas. In chicken farming natural gas and chicken feed are close substitutes.

Imagine a chicken farm next door to a steel mill. In a typical week each consumes 100 cubic feet of natural gas. The steel mill has no economical alternative production process, and it would have to curtail its operation significantly if natural gas became unavailable. The chicken farmer, at an additional cost of a few cents per day, could switch off the lights and use more chicken feed.

One day it transpires that only 100 cubic feet of natural gas per week will be available in the future. A benevolent economic planner, seeking only to benefit society, must decide how to allocate this natural gas. Perhaps he observes that the steel mill and the chicken farmer have historically used natural gas in equal quantities, and on this basis he decides that their "needs" for natural gas are roughly equal. He assigns 50 cubic feet per week to the steel mill and 50 cubic feet to the chickens.

---

[5]From *Science*, letter to editor by R. Dorfman, 1976.

As a result, there is a substantial cutback in steel output, to society's detriment. If all 100 cubic feet had been assigned to the steel mill, production would have continued about as before, with the chicken farmer having slightly higher costs and perhaps cutting egg production by a small amount.

Why does this benevolent planner not recognize his mistake? Because he—like the friends you were invited to poll on this question, and almost everybody else except for chicken farmers and the readers of this book—has never remotely suspected that chicken feed can be substituted for natural gas. Why doesn't the chicken farmer tell him? If he did, he would lose his natural gas allocation and his costs would go up—only slightly, to be sure, but the incentive is still to keep mum.

An alternative social arrangement is to abolish the planner and to allocate the gas via the price system. Now when natural gas becomes more scarce, the price gets bid up. This has two effects on the chicken farmer: He acquires the information that the available natural gas is more valuable to someone else than it is to him, and he acquires an incentive to react accordingly. He puts in an order for some chicken feed.

The Use of Knowledge in Society

In 1945, Friedrich A. Hayek (later a Nobel Prize winner) addressed the American Economic Association on the occasion of his retirement as its president. The title of his address was "The Use of Knowledge in Society." In it he called attention to the social role of prices as carriers of information, allowing the specialized knowledge of each individual to be fully incorporated in decisions concerning resource allocation. He contrasted this knowledge with so-called "scientific knowledge" and found it unjustly underrated by comparison:

> A little reflection will show that there is beyond question a body of very important but unorganized knowledge which cannot possibly be called scientific in the sense of knowledge of general rules: *the knowledge of the particular circumstances of time and place.* It is with respect to this that practically every individual has some advantage over all others in that he possesses unique information of which beneficial use might be made, but of which use can be made only if the decisions depending on it are left to him or are made with his active cooperation. We need to remember only how much we have to learn in any occupation after our theoretical training, how big a part of our working life we spend learning particular jobs, and how valuable an asset in all walks of life is knowledge of people, of local conditions, and special circumstances. To know of and put to use a machine not fully employed, or somebody's skill which could be better utilized, or to be aware of a surplus stock which can be drawn upon during an interruption of

supplies, is socially quite as useful as the knowledge of better alternative techniques.[6] (*Emphasis added*)

The special knowledge of the chicken farmer is a sort of knowledge of the particular circumstances of time and place. But Hayek is referring here to knowledge even much more specialized (and inaccessible to the planner) than that: the knowledge of the foreman that a leak in a certain machine can be plugged with chewing gum; the knowledge of a manager that one of the file clerks has a knack for plumbing repairs; the knowledge of a shipper that a particular tramp steamer is half-full. No planner can have access to this knowledge:

> The sort of knowledge with which I have been concerned is knowledge of the kind which by its nature cannot enter into statistics and therefore cannot be conveyed to any central authority in statistical form. The statistics which such a central authority would have to use would have to be arrived at precisely by abstracting from minor differences between the things, by lumping together, as resources of one kind, items which differ as regards location, quality, and other particulars, in a way which may be very significant for the specific decision.

Suppose that you and your friends discover a new science fiction writer whose works you all rush out to buy. It may not occur to you that this requires more linseed plants to be grown in Asia, but it does, because the oil from those plants is used to make the ink to print the books that the stores now want to restock. The Asian linseed farmer is no more aware of the change in your reading habits than you are of your need for his services, but he nevertheless responds by increasing his output. Your increased demand for books causes a rise in the price of linseed and informs the farmer that someone, somewhere, wants more linseed for some reason.

A competing economics textbook begins its first chapter by observing that "the rest of us people" (together with nature) "dominate your life and prevent you from having all you want."[7] However, the authors warn:

> Do not suppose that if we were less greedy, more would be within your grasp. For greed impels us to produce more, not only for ourselves, but, miraculously, more for you too . . . .

What the authors have in mind is that other people's greed enables you to offer them incentives to act as you want. It is because the carpenter is

---

[6]F. A. Hayek, "The Use of Knowledge in Society," *American Economic Review* 35 (September 1945), 519–530.

[7]A. Alchian and W. Allen, *Exchange and Production: Theory in Use* (Belmont, CA: Wadsworth, 1969).

"greedy" that you can hire him to build your house.[8] In fact, we can say more. While greedy neighbors are more likely than apathetic neighbors to respond to your desires, you might imagine that the best possibility is a third one that the authors did not consider: What if the rest of the world were neither greedy nor apathetic, but actively altruistic, attempting to cater to all of your wishes?

While such a world would have obvious advantages, it would also have a less obvious disadvantage: In the absence of a price system, you would be severely limited in your ability to communicate your desires. The farmer in Asia, wanting only to make your life more pleasant, has no criterion by which to choose between producing more linseed or more of some other crop. You have no way of informing him, because you don't realize that a yen for science fiction creates a need for more linseed oil—or if you do realize this, then you don't realize that you also need more glycerin, to make the glue with which the books are bound.

Your need for the selfishness of others stems not just from the fact that it motivates them to respond to your desires—altruism on their part would serve that purpose even better. It also stems from your need to *communicate* those desires. Students—and others who have not previously encountered the idea—generally find it quite surprising that a major role of prices in society is to fulfill this need.

The Costs of Misallocation

We now want to explicitly relate the "informational" aspect of prices to the "equilibrating" aspect that has been stressed in previous chapters. Exhibit 9–2 displays the marginal value curves of three consumers in the market for eggs and the corresponding market demand curve. (The graph and tables are identical to those of Exhibit 8–6.)

The rectangles represent marginal values associated with individual eggs, each labeled with the name of the man who buys the corresponding egg and receives the corresponding value. When the market price is $7 per egg, 5 are sold and the top parts of the shaded rectangles constitute the consumer's surplus.

▷ *Exercise 9.1* Assume a flat supply (= marginal cost) curve at $7 and calculate the total value of the eggs produced, the total cost of producing them, and the social gain. (Assume that eggs can be consumed only in "whole number" quantities for this calculation.)

Now let us reintroduce our benevolent social planner. Although the price system has been abolished, he has managed through painstaking research to discover the demand and supply curves for eggs. Plotting both of these on the same graph, he discovers that equilibrium occurs at a

---

[8]Adam Smith put this very well. In *The Wealth of Nations* he said, "It is not from the benevolence of the butcher, the brewer, or the baker that we expect our dinner, but from their regard to their own interest. We address ourselves not to their humanity but to their self-love."

Exhibit 9–2   **The Costs of Misallocation**

Larry		Moe		Curly	
Quantity	**Marginal Value**	**Quantity**	**Marginal Value**	**Quantity**	**Marginal Value**
1	$15/egg	1	$13/egg	1	$7/egg
2	8	2	11	2	3

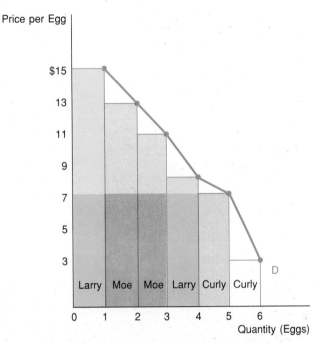

When the market price is $7 per egg, 5 eggs are sold (2 to Larry, 2 to Moe, and 1 to Curly) and their total value (the sum of the shaded rectangles) is $54. If the same 5 eggs were distributed by a mechanism other than the market, the total value might be less. For example, if a social planner gave 2 eggs to Larry, 1 to Moe, and 2 to Curly, the total value would be only $46. In this case, therefore, the usual measures of social gain would overstate the true social gain by $8.

quantity of 5. Wishing to maximize social gain and realizing that this is accomplished at equilibrium, he orders 5 eggs to be produced and distributed to consumers.

It appears that the social planner has succeeded in duplicating the workings of a competitive market, but this need not be true and, in fact, is not likely to be. Suppose that the planner orders the 5 eggs to be distributed as follows: 2 to Larry, 1 to Moe, and 2 to Curly. The marginal values of these eggs are equal to the areas of the first, second, fourth, fifth, and sixth rectangles in Exhibit 9–2. In comparison with competition, Moe has lost his second egg (worth $11 to him), and Curly has gained a second egg (worth only $3 to him). There is a net social loss of $8.

Exhibit 9–3   **Planning versus Markets**

Firm A		Firm B		Firm C	
Quantity	**Marginal Cost**	**Quantity**	**Marginal Cost**	**Quantity**	**Marginal Cost**
1	$1	1	$ 5	1	$6
2	3	2	11	2	7

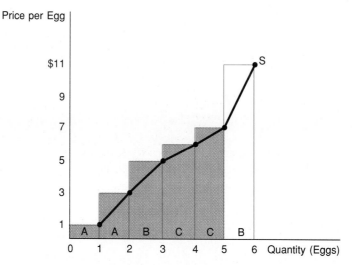

At a market price of $7, 5 eggs are produced in the least costly way possible. If a social planner orders 5 eggs to be produced and fails to realize that the low-cost producer is Firm A, then the total cost of production will be higher than necessary.

▷ *Exercise 9.2* Calculate the total value and total cost of the 5 eggs distributed by the planner. Compare these with your answer to Exercise 9.1.

In attempting to justify his actions, the social planner might look at the graph in Exhibit 9–2 and argue: "It is clear from this graph that social gain is maximized at a quantity of 5. That is the quantity I ordered produced. Therefore social gain is maximized." But in actuality the social gain is a sum of 5 rectangles. We compute it by looking at the area under the demand curve out to a quantity of 5, implicitly assuming that it is the sum of the *first* 5 rectangles. This in turn assumes that the 5 eggs are distributed where they will be valued the most. In a competitive market this assumption is justified (Curly simply won't buy a second egg at $7, whereas Moe will). In the absence of a price system, it is not.

What must the social planner do to really maximize welfare? He must give Curly's second egg to Moe instead. (Of course, by doing this, he increases welfare and so can make both parties better off.)

▷ *Exercise 9.3* Describe explicitly how the social planner can make both Curly and Moe better off.

Now we return to the problem that is the theme of this chapter: How is the planner to *know* that Moe values a second egg more than Curly does? This information is available only to Moe and Curly. Its inaccessibility to the social planner renders him powerless to make improvements.

We can summarize as follows:

> **When allocation decisions are not made on the basis of price, the traditional measures of social gain (via areas) overstate the actual gains to society. Equivalently, the traditional measures of dead-weight loss underestimate the losses.**

▷ *Exercise 9.4* Suppose that the supply curve for eggs is as given in Exhibit 9–3 (which is identical to the curve in Exhibit 8–7). A social planner orders 5 eggs to be produced, one by firm A and two each by firms B and C. What is the extent of the social loss due to the social planner's failure to perceive that A is the low-cost producer?

Example: A Military Draft

Society, through its armed forces, demands military services that are supplied by Young Men Between the Ages of 18 and 26. Suppose that the armed forces are able to set a maximum price (below equilibrium) that they will pay for military services, and suppose that they can *compel* Young Men to supply the quantity of military services that is demanded at that price (Q_d in Exhibit 9–4). The "draft" column of the table in Exhibit 9–4 shows the distribution of gains; the "volunteer army" column shows the gains in equilibrium for comparison.[9]

Exhibit 9–5 elaborates on the reason why the producers' surplus is F − C − D − E in the presence of a draft. Panel A of Exhibit 9–5 reproduces the relevant part of the graph in Exhibit 9–4. Revenue to producers (that is, the wages paid to soldiers) is given by price times quantity, that is, the rectangle X + Z. The sum of the marginal costs to producers is the sum of the rectangles in panel B, which is the same as area Y + Z in panel A. The difference is $(X + Z) − (Y + Z) = X − Y$, which is the same as F − C − D − E in Exhibit 9–4.

▷ *Exercise 9.5* Verify the deadweight loss in Exhibit 9–4 by calculating social gain directly (that is, using rectangles representing marginal value minus marginal cost, without breaking things down into consumers' and producers' surpluses).

---

[9]By drawing one graph, we are implicitly assuming that all Young Men would make equally good soldiers. To dispense with this assumption, we could draw several graphs, each showing the demand for soldiers of a different level of quality. None of our conclusions would be substantially altered.

Exhibit 9–4   **A Military Draft**

	Volunteer Army	Draft	Limited Draft
Consumers' Surplus	A	A+B+C+D	A+B+C
Producers' Surplus	B+F	F−C−D−E	F−C
Social Gain	A+B+F	A+B+F−E	A+B+F
Deadweight Loss		E	

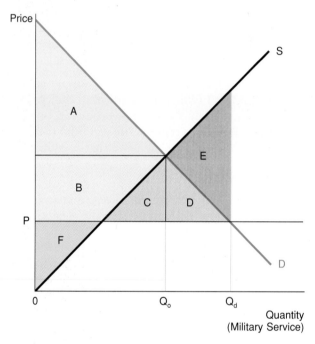

Military services are supplied by Young Men and demanded by society through the armed forces. The first column shows the gains at equilibrium, with a volunteer army. We assume that the wage rate is set at P, so that more Young Men are demanded than will volunteer. If the army can draft as many Young Men as it wants to at the price P, it will choose the quantity Q_d and social gains will be as depicted in the second column. If, on the other hand, the army is permitted to hire only Q_0 Young Men, social gains will be as in the third column, seemingly eliminating the deadweight loss. This leads to the apparent conclusion that the limited draft is as efficient as the volunteer army. As explained in the text, however, this conclusion is misleading.

Now consider an alternative policy. Suppose that at the same controlled price P, the armed forces can compel services only from that number of Young Men who would have enlisted voluntarily at the equilibrium price. In Exhibit 9–4 the number of soldiers is Q_0 and the social gains are computed in the "limited draft" column of the table. Notice that the measured deadweight loss becomes *zero*.

Exhibit 9–5   **Computing Producers' Surplus with a Draft**

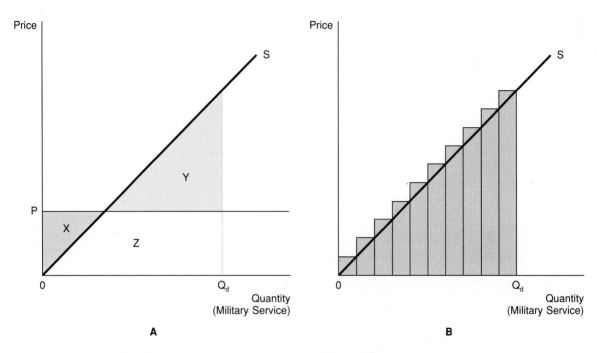

A   **B**

If the army forcibly hires Q_d soldiers at the price P, then soldiers will earn $P \times Q_d = X + Z$ in wages. Their opportunity cost of being in the army is the sum of all the rectangles in panel B, which is the same as area $Y + Z$ in panel A. This leaves a producers' surplus of $(X + Z) - (Y + Z) = X - Y$.

▷ *Exercise 9.6* Verify all of the entries in the "limited draft" column of the table. Recompute the deadweight loss by a different method and make sure the answers coincide.

Notice that, compared to the volunteer army, the new "limited" version of the draft transfers the amount B + C from Young Men to the other members of society.

▷ *Exercise 9.7* Give an economic interpretation of the area B + C in Exhibit 9–4.

Now we are closing in on the main point: Even though the computed deadweight loss is zero, the limited draft is still inferior to the volunteer army from the point of view of economic efficiency. There are social costs associated with the draft that are not captured in our representation of deadweight loss.

Exhibit 9–6   **Underestimating Deadweight Loss**

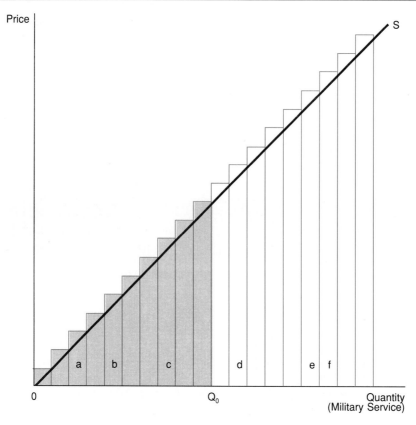

Q_0 is the number of Young Men who would join a volunteer army. Each of these Young Men has an opportunity cost of joining that is represented by one of the shaded rectangles. When we compute producers' surplus, we take the total revenue earned by Young Men and subtract this shaded area.

   Under a limited draft, the same number of Young Men enter the army. However, those who are drafted are not identical to those who would have volunteered. Suppose that the draft board selects the Young Men represented by rectangles d, e, and f instead of rectangles a, b, and c. In that case, social welfare is reduced by the area (d + e + f) − (a + b + c), even though this reduction is ignored in the usual welfare computations. Hence the measured deadweight loss is overly optimistic.

Consider the calculation of producers' surplus, which is illustrated anew in Exhibit 9–6. We begin with the total revenue of soldiers and subtract from it the sum of the shaded rectangles. These rectangles are the costs of joining the army for the Q_0 Young Men who would volunteer at the equilibrium price. But it is unlikely that these are the very Young Men who are drafted. Instead of drafting the Young Men represented by rectangles a, b, and c, the authorities may draft those represented by rectangles d, e, and f. The true producers' surplus is reduced by the area (d + e + f) − (a + b +

c). The measured producers' surplus and consequently the measured deadweight loss are too optimistic.

In concrete terms, what this means is that the Selective Service Board will draft Young Men who are potentially brilliant brain surgeons, inventors, and economists—Young Men with high opportunity costs of entering the service—and will leave undrafted some Young Men with much lower opportunity costs. The social loss is avoided under a voluntary system, in which precisely the men with the lowest costs will volunteer.

What if the authorities choose to draft only the low-cost Young Men? Here, of course, the problem of knowledge becomes insurmountable. Information about individual opportunity costs, available for free under a voluntary system, is available only at high cost and with great uncertainty in the absence of prices. The Selective Service authorities can pass out questionnaires—but who will freely reveal that his costs are low? They can observe people's behavior—but who can observe the difference between two starving novelists in garrets, one with a brilliant vision that needs only careful nurturing to become great literature, the other barren of ideas, frustrated, and ready to quit?

It is often argued that the draft is better for society than a volunteer army because it is less costly. This argument is wrong.[10] The cost of maintaining an army is the sum of the opportunity costs of its soldiers and is independent of the wages paid to those soldiers. Higher wages mean less wealth for taxpayers and more for soldiers, but no more or less for society, to which taxpayers and soldiers equally belong. There are two ways in which an army can be unnecessarily costly: It can be the wrong size or it can consist of the wrong people. Exhibits 9–4 and 9–6 illustrate these two mistakes.

The Social Role of Rent

An issue of great importance in the history of economic thought has been the social function of the rent on land. The nineteenth-century English economist Henry George argued in his book *Progress and Poverty* that because the quantity of land is fixed, the payment of rent to landlords serves no economic purpose. Increased demand for land (which, he argued, is an inevitable consequence of population growth) bids up prices, but, unlike in other markets, this increased price calls forth no additional output. Landlords are enriched to no social end.

This analysis, applied to a more general notion of "rent," was a recurrent theme in the writings of Fabian socialism.[11] The **rent** earned by a factor of production is the excess of payments received by that factor over the

Rent
Payments to a factor of production in excess of the minimum payments necessary to call it into existence. In other words, the producer's surplus earned by the factor.

---

[10]Of course, there are many other arguments for and against the draft, but their validity does not concern us here.

[11]The Fabian Society was a major contributor to British political discourse in the early part of this century. Its most prominent spokesmen were the economists Sidney Webb and George Bernard Shaw.

minimum payments necessary to call it into existence. When Clint East-wood earns $1,000,000 a year for starring in movies that he would be willing to star in for $50,000, the difference ($950,000) is rent. In other words, rent is producers' surplus. The lowest annual income that would induce Eastwood to become a movie star is equal to the area under his supply curve out to the quantity of movies he appears in each year. His revenue is a rectangle representing the quantity of movies times the wage per movie. The difference is producers' surplus, or rent.

Exhibit 9–7 shows the markets for land and for Clint Eastwood. We adopt, for the sake of argument, George's assertion that the supply curve for land is vertical.[12] In this case all of the revenue collected by landlords is rent (the shaded area in panel A of Exhibit 9–7). Eastwood's supply curve becomes essentially vertical above a certain price; there is a limit to the number of movies that a person can make in a year. As a result, his revenue (area A + B in panel B) consists almost entirely of rent (the shaded area A). In general:

> **When a factor is in fixed (or nearly fixed) supply, the revenue it earns will consist entirely (or almost entirely) of rent.**

▷ *Exercise 9.8* Explain why the "rents" described in Section 7.3 are the same as those described here.

The Fabians argued that there would be no social cost associated with the appropriation of rents by the government. Suppose that landlords were not permitted to collect rent, but were told by the government to allow designated individuals to use their land at a price of zero. Suppose that Eastwood, who now makes two movies per year, were given a govern-ment salary equal to area B in panel B of Exhibit 9–6 and ordered to continue making two movies per year. Such confiscation of rents (the Fabians argued) would not affect social welfare.

▷ *Exercise 9.9* Compute consumers' and producers' surpluses in the markets for land and for Clint Eastwood's services, both before and after the confiscation of rents. Verify that there is no deadweight loss.

The fly in the Fabian ointment is that land is not equally valuable in all uses, and Clint Eastwood is not equally valuable in all movies. Exhibit 9–8 shows the sort of error that can arise in the allocation of land. When landlords earn rents, they let their land to the people who will pay the most for it: those represented by the shaded rectangles. If land is not allocated to precisely those people, there is a diminution in social welfare. If land is not allocated by price, there is no way to identify those people.

Similarly, it matters not only that Clint Eastwood makes two movies per year; it matters *which* movies he makes. Those movie producers who

---

[12]In fact, this is probably false in any reasonable sense. The relevant market for a given purpose is not land, but "agricultural land" or "land suitable for building," and the like. Such things *can* be created: Irrigation converted the Negev Desert to productive farmland, for example.

Exhibit 9–7   **The Rent on Land and the Rent on Clint Eastwood**

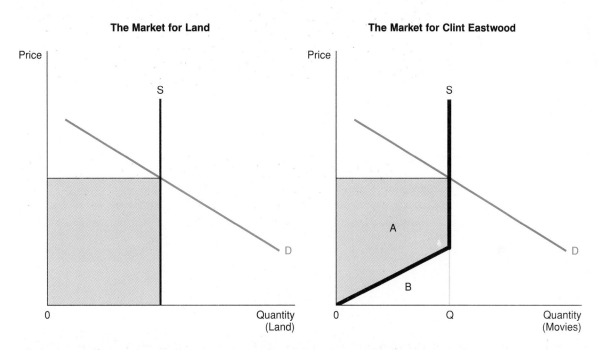

If the supply curve for land is vertical, then all of the revenue earned by landowners is producers' surplus, or rent (the shaded area in panel A). If the supply curve for Clint Eastwood's services becomes vertical at a quantity where the demand price is still very high, then almost all of his income is rent (the shaded area A in panel B). Rent can be interpreted as the amount by which a factor's income exceeds what is necessary to call it into existence. Because the land would exist even if its owners earned no income, all of their income is rent. Because Clint earns A + B for making Q movies, but would be willing to make Q movies if he were paid B to do so, his rent is A.

will pay him the highest salary are those who value his talents most highly; that is, those who think that his presence will most enhance people's desire to see their movies. If he works on projects where his talents contribute less, efficiency is lost. Notice that even if Clint is given the freedom to choose his acting assignments, and even in the event that he is entirely altruistic and wants to work only where he is most valuable, he is unlikely to *know* where he is most valuable if the studios cannot bid for his services.

The Fabian literature contains much interesting economic argument, some of it correct, and the tracts by Shaw are both readable and highly entertaining. His *Intelligent Woman's Guide to Socialism and Capitalism* is a rare phenomenon: economic writing by a master of English prose. It is a fertile source of propositions on which you can test out the analytic skills you have been developing in this course. It's also fun to read.

Exhibit 9–8   **The Social Role of Rent**

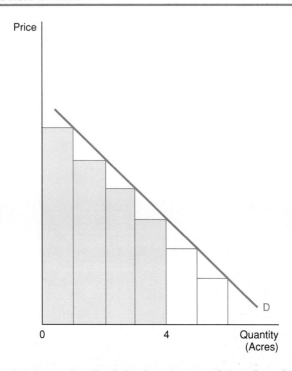

With the supply of land fixed at 4 acres, landlords let those acres to those who value them the most. The total value of the land to its users is the sum of the 4 shaded rectangles. If all rent were confiscated, the 4 acres of land would still exist, which led some thinkers to believe that no social harm would be done. But in fact the confiscation of rents leaves landlords with no incentive to seek out the users represented by the 4 shaded rectangles. Land will be used for less valuable projects, represented by the unshaded rectangles, and social welfare will be diminished.

9.2 The Informational Content of Prices: Applications

Hayek's 1945 article was prescient. Since that time the vision of prices as carriers of information has become ubiquitous in economics. In this section we will discuss two of the most important applications of this point of view. First, we will examine the informational content of prices in the markets for financial securities, such as stock exchanges. Then we will see how the informational role of prices in the labor market can be used to explain the relationship between unemployment and inflation.

Efficient Markets for Financial Securities

Efficient market
A market in which prices fully reflect all available information.

An **efficient market** is one in which prices fully reflect all available information. Here we shall be interested in the markets for financial securities, such as the shares of corporate stock that are traded on stock exchanges.

The owner of a share of stock owns a fraction of the corporation and participates fully in its profits and losses.

Efficient securities markets serve an important social function, since they allow firms to make appropriate decisions regarding the allocation of resources (how much to produce, how much to invest in future growth, and so on) and assure investors that the prices they are paying for assets are meaningful indications of those assets' actual value. However, many noneconomists believe that asset markets in general and the stock market in particular are inefficient.

Technical Analysis

The most extreme believers in inefficient markets are the so-called "chartists," or "technical analysts." They argue that a careful study of the past prices of a given stock conveys useful information about future prices.

It is easy to see why this analysis cannot be correct if markets are efficient. Suppose that the past behavior of the stock of XYZ Corporation exhibits a pattern that indicates a probable price rise in the near future. That probable price rise is an important feature of XYZ stock, making it more valuable to hold. In an efficient market that higher value will already be reflected in the *current* price. (It is also easy to see the mechanism by which this would occur: Smart investors, observing the pattern, expect a price rise tomorrow and rush out to buy the stock today. This bids up *today's* price.) If the market is perfectly efficient, the chartist cannot expect to profit, because any stock that can be identified as a "good buy" will be expensive—and therefore *not* such a good buy!

There is overwhelming evidence against the chartists.[13] Hundreds of careful statistical studies indicate that knowledge of past price changes contributes nothing to the prediction of future price changes. All of the information contained in the past history of the stock is already embedded in a single number—the current price.

Analysis of Market Conditions

Some dissenters from the efficient-markets hypothesis are less extreme. While admitting the unprofitability of technical analysis, they claim that a more general analysis of market conditions (still making use only of publicly available information) can provide important clues to the savvy investor. This proposition is harder to test than the claims of the chartists, and the empirical evidence is correspondingly less definitive. Nevertheless, the overwhelming majority of researchers in the field, basing their conclusions on decades of empirical work, reject this claim as well. The theoretical basis for this rejection is the same as that for rejecting chartism: Any publicly available information indicating that a stock will soon go up (or down) will cause an immediate shift in demand and an immediate price adjustment, leaving no opportunity for profit.

---

[13]See E. Fama, "Efficient Capital Markets: A Review of Theory and Empirical Work," *Journal of Finance* 25 (May 1970), 383–417 for an overview.

There is still room for argument over the meaning of the word *immedi-ate*. How quickly do prices adjust to new information? If the adjustment process takes sufficiently long, an observant investor may have time to cash in.

To put the question another way: Prices reflect all available information in the long run, but how long is the long run? Recent evidence supports the hypothesis that the long run is shorter than 30 seconds—that is, all information entering the marketplace is fully incorporated into prices within 30 seconds of its arrival.[14] Hardly comforting news to the investor who analyzes patterns at leisure over a cup of coffee and the daily business page.

Asset Markets and the Royal Head-Flipper

Does this mean that no technical analyst will ever succeed in the stock market? Of course not; some will do well, for the same reasons that some people do well at the roulette wheel. If there are enough such analysts (and there are), a few will even win consistently, by the simple laws of proba-bility. All of these will attribute their success to their singular talents. To them we dedicate a bit of economic folklore: the Fable of the Royal Head-Flipper.

In a faraway land with 64 million inhabitants, the king wished to appoint a royal head-flipper. Calling all of his subjects before him, he gave each one a coin and ordered all to flip. Thirty-two million came up heads and 32 million came up tails. Those who flipped tails were obviously no good at flipping heads and were eliminated from the competition. The remaining 32,000,000 flipped again. When 16 million failed, they too were sent home. On the twenty-fifth trial, only 2 remained. They each flipped, and one prevailed. He was appointed the royal head-flipper by the king, who congratulated him with a toast: "Here's to the royal head-flipper, whose prowess has enabled him to flip heads 26 times in a row. According to the royal statistician, the odds against such a feat occurring by chance are a staggering 64 million to one!"

A Theory of Unemployment

For many decades prior to the 1970s, economists observed a correlation between the rate of inflation and the level of employment. When inflation (the rate of increase in absolute prices) was higher than usual, employment tended to be high also. In periods of low inflation, employment was low. More recently, this relationship has broken down. Many explanations have been offered for these phenomena, although there is no consensus among economists as to which come closest to the truth. Here we will present one

---

[14]See L. J. Feinstone, "Minute by Minute: Efficiency, Normality and Randomness in Intra-Daily Asset Prices," *Journal of Applied Econometrics* 2 (1987), 193–214.

possible explanation, of particular interest because it focuses on the informational content of prices. The version we will present is a caricature; a fully articulated model is more appropriate for a course in macroeconomics. In its general outlines, however, the theory we will present has been a highly influential one and has occupied a central role in macroeconomic thinking for the last 15 years.[15]

We know from Chapter 2 that only relative prices are relevant to the determination of equilibrium. If all prices (including wages) were to double tomorrow, markets could remain in equilibrium without any quantity adjustments. If it were known that such a doubling occurred every Wednesday, nothing of any real economic significance would be affected.[16]

Now imagine an unemployed worker. He is unemployed not because there are no jobs available to him, but because the only available jobs pay wages lower than he is willing to accept. The highest wage offer he has received has been $8,000 a year, but he is not willing to work for less than $10,000.

One night, while our worker is sleeping, all prices and all wages double. He is awakened the next morning by a telephone call from an employer who says, "I am now prepared to offer you an annual salary of $16,000." Of course, $16,000 today will buy only what $8,000 bought yesterday, so the worker, if he is fully informed, will not accept the position.

But what if he is *not* fully informed? What if he went to sleep unaware of the changes that were to take place in the middle of the night, and having just been awakened by a telephone call is still unaware of them? In that case he will accept the job, convinced that he will be earning far more than his minimum requirement of $10,000.

Now, after a day on the job, our hero is likely to stop at the supermarket to indulge the temptations of his new economic status. When he sees the prices on the items, he will recognize himself to be the victim of a cruel hoax, and begin the mental task of composing a letter of resignation.

This story suggests a reason why an increase in inflation could lead to an increase in employment. It also suggests that the effect is ephemeral. More importantly, it implies that employment is affected only by *unexpected* inflation. When inflation becomes the norm (as it did in the 1970s), workers can no longer be "fooled" by high absolute wages.

Another important implication is that the increase in employment resulting from an unexpected inflation is not socially beneficial—it is a consequence of deceiving people into working more than they would choose to if they were fully aware of their economic environment.

---

[15]The broad outlines of this theory were sketched around 1968 by Milton Friedman and Edmund Phelps (working independently). The first careful development was by Robert E. Lucas, Jr., in "Expectations and the Neutrality of Money," *Journal of Economic Theory* 4 (1972), 103–124.

[16]We will see in Chapter 18 that there is one important exception to this statement. Briefly, a rise in absolute prices reduces the purchasing power of money, so an expected rise in absolute prices makes it more desirable to hold nonmonetary assets, such as real estate. The increase in demand for these "inflation-proof" assets has real effects. For the present discussion, those effects are irrelevant.

The fundamental role of inflation in this model is to dilute the informational content of prices. A rise in the nominal wage rate for plumbers may indicate either an increase in demand for plumbers' services or a rise in the general price level. If plumbers know the inflation rate, they can make the distinction. An increased demand for plumbers will lead to a higher relative price for their time and call forth more plumbing services—an example of prices transmitting the necessary information to the appropriate parties. If plumbers are uncertain of the inflation rate, they will be uncertain of the real value of their wages and may provide the "wrong" amount of service from a social point of view. If they underestimate the rate of inflation, they will provide too much plumbing; if they overestimate, they will provide too little.

▷ **Exercise 9.10** Explain in detail why a plumber who has overestimated the rate of inflation will provide less plumbing service as a result.

Macroeconomists have devoted considerable effort to understanding the ways in which uncertainty about inflation introduces "static" into the price signals that people use to make economic decisions. Much research is devoted to the methods that people use to disentangle valuable information from this static, and to the consequences of the necessary imperfections in these methods. An underlying theme is that society is best served by the accurate dissemination of knowledge, and that prices are the most effective known tool for accomplishing this task.

Summary

The price of an item reflects the value of that item to some potential user. It also provides an incentive for others to act on that information. If the item is valuable elsewhere, the high price will tell potential users to search for substitutes.

Prices allow complex economies to be coordinated in ways that take account of vast amounts of knowledge. This knowledge includes what Hayek called the "particular circumstances of time and place." Each individual producer and consumer has access to special information that is not available to anyone else, and prices lead him to use this information in deciding how to allocate resources. A social planner without access to all of this information will allocate resources less efficiently.

The conventional measures of social welfare that were introduced in Chapter 8 make the implicit assumption that all goods are produced by the low-cost producers and distributed to the consumers who value them the most. In the absence of a price system, this assumption may be unjustified, in which case the usual measures of social welfare are overly optimistic.

An efficient market is one in which prices fully reveal all available information. Markets for financial assets appear to provide examples.

When the informational content of prices is diluted, as by an inflation that makes it difficult for people to distinguish absolute from relative price changes, resources are allocated less efficiently. This provides one possible explanation of why the level of employment will change in response to an unexpected inflation but not to an expected one.

Review Questions

R1. A social planner equipped with knowledge of all market supply and demand curves would still lack much of the knowledge necessary to duplicate the functioning of the price system. Give some examples of the knowledge that he would lack. How is this knowledge taken into account when prices are used to allocate resources?

R2. Explain why a rise in soldiers' wages does not increase the cost of maintaining an army.

R3. What is the social role of rent? If all rents were confiscated, would there be a consequent loss of efficiency? Why or why not?

R4. What is an efficient market?

R5. "If it is well-known that IBM will soon release a new and highly desirable product, then it is a good idea to buy IBM stock." Explain why this statement is wrong.

Problem Set

1. A race of timid elves passes the time by sneaking out at night, locating machinery that is in disrepair, and fixing it while people are sleeping. The human beneficiaries of this largesse are, of course, surprised and delighted when they discover the elves' handiwork the following morning. *True or false:* If the elves were to start charging for their services, humans would certainly be made worse off.

2. A chemical company is considering locating a plant on the outskirts of a certain town. Although the town welcomes the benefits that this plant will bring, some residents have expressed concern about the possibility of an accident involving toxic chemicals. The city council has met to discuss the matter. Although none of the councilmen has any background in chemistry or engineering, many have strong opinions (some pro and some con) about whether a building permit should be issued. One councilman, who has remained neutral throughout, suggests that the permit be issued if and only if the chemical company can demonstrate the ability (either through its own assets or an adequate insurance policy) to reimburse the townspeople for any damage caused by its factory. Explain his reasoning. Explain why his policy might be expected to lead to a socially optimal decision.

3. *True or false:* In a large corporation it is usually better for the central management to make decisions rather than divisional managers, because the central management has access to a wider range of information.

4. Aramis, Porthos, and Athos have the following marginal value schedules for swords:

Number of Swords	Aramis's MV	Porthos's MV	Athos's MV
1	$10	$7	$9
2	8	5	6
3	0	4	2
4	0	3	0

Aramis, Porthos, and Athos are the only buyers of swords in the community, and swords are produced at a constant marginal cost of $6 per sword.

a. If the industry is competitive, how many swords will be produced and at what price will they be sold? Justify your answer.

b. Suppose that a social planner orders 5 swords to be produced, with 4 distributed to Porthos and 1 to Athos. What is the social loss in this situation (compared with competitive equilibrium)? Justify your answer.

5. Evaluate the following methods of providing an army. Rank them in order of preference from the point of view of (a) Young Men, (b) consumers of military service, (c) economic efficiency. Assume that the army will be of the same size in all cases.

(1) A volunteer army, financed by a tax on all citizens.

(2) A draft, with soldiers paid a wage of zero.

(3) A volunteer army, financed by a tax on Young Men.

(4) A draft, with soldiers paid a wage of zero but with the proviso that draftees may hire other Young Men to take their place.

6. Suppose that the supply of land is vertical and that the government imposes a 50% tax on land rents. *True or false:* There would be no social loss as a result of this tax.

7. The University of Rochester has a fixed number of parking spaces for students on campus. They are currently sold at a price that clears the market. It has been proposed that the price should be lowered and a lottery held to determine who may park on campus. Each winner of the lottery would receive a ticket entitling him to purchase a parking space, and these tickets could be freely bought and sold. The number of winners would be equal to the number of parking spaces.

a. Graph the supply and demand for parking spaces. Show on your graph the price of a ticket. Show the consumers' surplus (earned by parkers), the producers' surplus (earned by the university), and the total value of the tickets to the winners of the lottery. Who gains, who loses, and who is unaffected if this plan is adopted?

b. The nearby University of Retsehcor is identical to the University of Rochester in every way except two. First, nobody at Retsehcor has proposed a lottery plan as at Rochester. Second, someone at Retsehcor has proposed that the university hold a lottery and give cash gifts to randomly chosen students. (An alternative proposal is to simply randomize tuition.) Compare the effects of the Retsehcor plan with those of the Rochester plan.

c. An alternative proposal at the University of Rochester would institute the lottery without allowing the resale of tickets. The university would carefully monitor compliance, expelling any lottery winner who allowed his parking spot to be used by anybody else. How would this revision affect welfare if the enforcement mechanism were successful? If it were unsuccessful?

Refer to Answers to Problem Sets for solutions to problems 1 and 2.

Chapter Ten

Monopoly

Market power or **monopoly power**
The ability of a firm to affect market prices through its actions. A firm has monopoly power if and only if it faces a downward-sloping demand curve.

A firm that is not perfectly competitive is said to have **market power.** The decisions of such a firm affect the market price of its output. Another name for market power is **monopoly power.** This term can be misleading, because etymology suggests (and popular usage affirms) that a monopoly is a "single seller," the only firm in its industry. Indeed, many textbooks adopt this definition. However, the condition of being a single seller is difficult to make precise. Coca-Cola Inc. is the only producer of Coca-Cola, but it is not the only producer of cola beverages. Is it a single seller? You might answer this question one way if you think that Pepsi is basically indistinguishable from Coke, and another way if you have a strong preference for one or the other.

We would prefer to avoid having to deal with such difficult questions. Therefore, although the single seller is a good example to keep in mind, we shall use the word *monopoly* in reference to any firm that faces a downward-sloping demand curve for its output.

In the first section of this chapter we will learn how prices and quantities are determined under monopoly, we will explore the welfare consequences of monopoly pricing, and we will see how these welfare

289

consequences can be affected by government policies. In the second section we will study some of the sources of monopoly power. In the third section we will learn about a variety of profitable pricing strategies that are available to a monopolist but not viable under perfect competition.

10.1 Price and Output under Monopoly

In this section we will learn how a monopolist chooses price and quantity, and will examine the welfare consequences of these choices.

Monopoly Pricing

The Tailor Dress Company, which we first met in Chapter 5, is a monopolist. The demand curve for its product, displayed in Exhibit 10–1, is downward sloping. The exhibit also displays Tailor's marginal revenue curve (which can be computed from the demand curve) and its marginal cost curve.

Like any firm, Tailor operates at the point where marginal cost equals marginal revenue; that is, it produces 3 dresses. The price that it charges is the highest price at which demanders will purchase those 3 dresses. This price is $8 per dress, which can be read off the demand curve at a quantity of 3.

The Monopolist's Marginal Revenue Curve

In Exhibit 10–1 the marginal revenue curve lies everywhere below the demand curve. To understand why, let us compute the marginal revenue when the Tailor Dress Company produces 3 dresses. Suppose that the company has already produced 2 dresses, which can be sold for $9 each, yielding a total revenue of $18. When it makes a third dress, two things happen. First, since the price of dresses is now $8, and since Tailor is making one more dress, total revenue goes up by $8. Second, the first 2 dresses, which could have been sold for $9 each, can now be sold for only $8 each, reducing total revenue by $2. The marginal revenue derived from the third dress is $8 − $2 = $6. The marginal revenue is less than the demand price of $8.

In general, there are two components to a monopolist's marginal revenue: There is the *price* at which he can sell an additional item (an increment to revenue) and the *price reduction* on earlier items that will now have to be sold at a lower price in order to induce demanders to accept the new quantity (a decrement). Combined, these yield a marginal revenue that is less than the demand price.[1]

---

[1]If you have had calculus, you may recognize this as an application of the product rule for differentiation. Since Total revenue = Price × Quantity, we can write

$$MR = \frac{dTR}{dQ} = P + Q\frac{dP}{dQ}.$$

The term dP/dQ, being calculated along the downward-sloping demand curve, is negative.

Exhibit 10–1   **Monopoly Price and Output**

Quantity	Price	Total Revenue	Marginal Revenue	Total Cost	Marginal Cost
1 dress	$10/dress	$10	$10/dress	$ 5	$4/dress
2	9	18	8	10	5
3	8	24	6	16	6
4	7	28	4	23	7
5	6	30	2	31	8
6	5	30	0	40	9
7	4	28	−2	50	10
8	3	24	−4	61	11

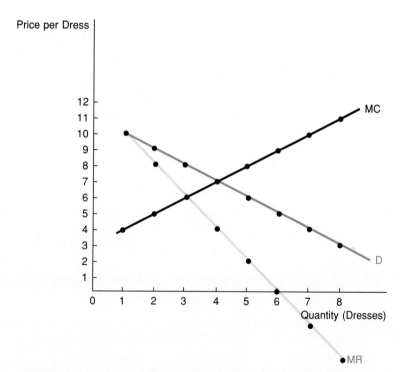

The Tailor Dress Company produces 3 dresses (the quantity at which marginal cost equals marginal revenue) and sells them at a price of $8 apiece. The price is read off the demand curve at a quantity of 3.

▷ *Exercise 10.1* Compute the two components of marginal revenue at a quantity of 4. Do they add up to the number in the table in Exhibit 10–1?

Notice that a competitive producer faces only the first component of marginal revenue. Because he can sell any quantity at the market price, he does not need to reduce his price when he increases his output. This is why marginal revenue is equal to (demand) price for a competitive producer, although it is always less than that for a monopolist.

Elasticity and Marginal Revenue

A producer facing a downward-sloping demand curve can increase his sales only if he lowers his price. A 1% increase in quantity requires a $(1/|\eta|)\%$ decrease in price, where η is the price elasticity of demand. A one *unit* increase in quantity, from Q to $Q + 1$, increases quantity by the fraction $1/Q$, and so decreases price by the fraction $(1/|\eta|) \cdot (1/Q)$. Since this is the *fraction* by which price falls, the *amount* by which price falls must be $P \cdot (1/|\eta|) \cdot (1/Q)$.

Using this observation, we can derive a formula for the monopolist's marginal revenue. When he produces one more item, two things happen. First, he collects the price P for that item. Second, he must sell the preceding Q items at a price that is reduced by $P \cdot (1/|\eta|) \cdot (1/Q)$ per item; this reduces his revenue by $[P \cdot (1/|\eta|) \cdot (1/Q)] \cdot Q = P \cdot (1/|\eta|)$. Combining the two effects, we find that marginal revenue is given by

$$MR = P - P \cdot \frac{1}{|\eta|} = P \cdot \left(1 - \frac{1}{|\eta|}\right).$$

From this formula we see that if $|\eta| > 1$, then marginal revenue is positive, whereas if $|\eta| < 1$, then marginal revenue is negative. This makes good sense. For $|\eta| > 1$, a 1% increase in quantity requires a less than 1% increase in price, so that total revenue increases. Since total revenue is increasing, marginal revenue is positive. When $|\eta| < 1$, the opposite is true. Since a typical (downward-sloping) demand curve yields a marginal revenue curve that is positive for small quantities and negative for large quantities (see Exhibit 10–1), we can conclude that a downward-sloping demand curve is elastic when quantity is small and inelastic when quantity is large.

▷ *Exercise 10.2* In Exhibit 10–1 which is the elastic portion of the demand curve? Which is the inelastic portion?

Because the monopolist chooses the quantity where marginal revenue equals marginal cost and because marginal cost is positive, it follows that at the chosen quantity marginal revenue is positive. Therefore the monopolist always operates on the elastic portion of the demand curve.

Example: Price Increases and Monopoly Power

Several years ago, an unexpected frost killed a substantial portion of the Florida orange crop. The price of oranges rose by so much that the total revenue of orange growers actually increased. At the time, many news reporters and editorialists argued that such a large price increase must be evidence of monopoly power in the orange-growing industry.

Using economic analysis, we can show not only that the conclusion is wrong, but that the exact opposite is true: The increase in total revenue demonstrates that the orange-growing industry can not possibly be monopolized. Because the fall in quantity led to increased total revenue, it follows that the industry's marginal revenue was negative. Suppose for example that the total revenue associated with 100 bushels of oranges is $1,000, but the total revenue associated with 99 bushels of oranges is $1,020. Then the marginal revenue from the hundredth bushel is *minus* $20.

However, we have just seen that no monopolist would operate where marginal revenue is negative. It follows that the orange-growing industry can not be controlled by a monopolist.

To make the same point in different terms: If a decrease in quantity yields an increase in total revenue, then a monopolist who controlled the industry would not have waited for a frost before decreasing quantity. He would long ago have restricted the production of oranges to a point where any further reductions would reduce his profits.

The Monopolist Has No Supply Curve

Where is the monopolist's supply curve? Points on the supply curve answer questions such as: "How much would you produce at a going market price of $1?", and "How much would you produce at a going market price of $2?" and so on. These are questions that a monopolist is never asked, because he never faces a going market price. The price is a consequence of the monopolist's actions, rather than a datum to which he must react. Therefore a monopolist has no supply curve; a supply curve presumes the existence of a going market price.

Welfare

Suppose that the shoe industry is dominated by a monopoly supplier of the "single seller" breed. Suppose also that a competitive shoe industry would produce with the same (industry-wide) marginal cost curve as the monopolist's. Exhibit 10–2 shows the quantities produced by the monopolist (Q_M) and the competitive industry (Q_C) and the prices that they charge. The table shows consumers' and producers' surpluses in each case.

▷ *Exercise 10.3* Verify the entries in the table in Exhibit 10–2.

From Exhibit 10–2 it is clear that consumers' surplus is reduced by the existence of the monopoly. It is less obvious, but nonetheless true, that producers' surplus is increased. The monopoly producer's surplus exceeds the competitive producers' surplus by the amount $C + D - H$, and your first thought might be that it would be necessary to measure areas in order to determine whether this is positive or negative. Recall, however, that the monopolist is choosing the strategy that will benefit him the most. Since the monopolist could choose the competitive output Q_C but prefers the smaller output Q_M instead, we infer that the producer's surplus is higher at Q_M than at Q_C. In other words, $C + D + F + G > F + G + H$.

Exhibit 10–2 also shows a social welfare loss of $E + H$ due to the existence of the monopoly. This is the amount by which the consumers'

Exhibit 10–2   **Monopoly versus Competition**

	Competition	Monopoly
Consumers' Surplus	A+B+C+D+E	A+B
Producers' Surplus	F+G+H	C+D+F+G
Social Gain	A+B+C+D+E+F+G+H	A+B+C+D+F+G
Deadweight Loss		E+H

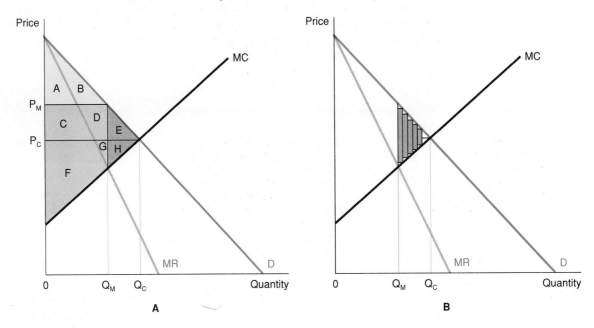

The table assumes that a monopoly and a competitive industry would have the same marginal cost curve. The competitive industry produces the equilibrium quantity Q_C and the monopolist produces its profit-maximizing quantity Q_M. Since marginal value still exceeds marginal cost at Q_M, it would be efficient for additional units to be produced. The social gains from additional units after Q_M are represented by the rectangles in panel B. Since the monopolist does not produce those units, those social gains are sacrificed, giving a deadweight loss of E + H.

losses exceed the producer's gains. It is easy to see the reason for this welfare loss: When output is at Q_M, marginal value still exceeds marginal cost. It is socially beneficial to produce another pair of shoes, creating the first rectangle of social gain shown in panel B of the exhibit. From the viewpoint of efficiency, additional pairs of shoes should be produced, as they would be under competition.

When an item's marginal value exceeds its marginal cost, the competitive producer will always choose to provide it, because he can sell the item for more than it will cost him to produce it. However, the monopolist will not always make the same choice. The monopolist must reason as follows: "It is true that I can sell the next item for more than it will cost me to produce it. But it is also true that producing this item will reduce the price at which I can sell all of the items I've already decided to produce. I have to weigh both of these considerations before deciding to proceed." The second consideration is, of course, irrelevant to the competitor, whose actions do not affect the market price.

Monopoly and Public Policy

What can be done to reduce the efficiency loss due to monopoly? Since the inefficiency results from a reduction in output caused by the monopolist's pursuit of high profits, some might argue that the government should tax away the monopolist's ill-gotten gains. However, this "solution" only reduces efficiency still further. The original problem is that production is less than it should be from a social viewpoint, and the effect of a tax is to lower production still further. The tax increases the deadweight loss.

▷ *Exercise 10.4* Draw the monopolist's demand, marginal revenue, and marginal cost curves both before and after the imposition of an excise tax on his output. Label the areas of deadweight loss both before and after the tax.

Subsidies

The preceding observation suggests that the real solution might be to give the monopolist a *subsidy* per unit of output.

Exhibit 10–3 shows the effect of an "ideal" subsidy, that is, one of exactly the right size to induce the monopolist to supply the competitive quantity Q_C. We know that this quantity maximizes social gain, so the deadweight loss is reduced to zero.

To see how the gains and losses are distributed over society, notice that the ideally subsidized monopolist produces the same quantity at the same price as does a competitive market. Therefore the consumers' surplus is the same in either case. The monopolist earns both the competitive producers' surplus and the revenue from the subsidy; the latter, of course, comes from the taxpayers.

We can see this distribution in Exhibit 10–3. In the presence of the $S-per-unit subsidy, the monopolist chooses the quantity Q_C and the price P_C. Therefore the consumers' surplus is A + B + C + D + E, just as in competition. To compute the producers' surplus by our usual methods, we would have to draw a horizontal line at the "price received by suppliers," a distance $S above the price charged in the marketplace. This would clutter the diagram beyond all redemption, so we resort to an alternative method, which was introduced in Exhibit 8–13. According to this method, we calculate using the price charged in the marketplace and the new, lower marginal cost curve. This gives a producers' surplus of F + G + H + I + J

Exhibit 10–3　A Subsidized Monopolist

	Competition	Unsubsidized Monopoly	Subsidized Monopoly
Consumers' Surplus	A+B+C+D+E	A+B	A+B+C+D+E
Producers' Surplus	F+G+H	C+D+F+G	F+G+H+I+J+K
Cost to Taxpayers			I+J+K
Social Gain	A+B+C+D+E+F+G+H	A+B+C+D+F+G	A+B+C+D+E+F+G+H

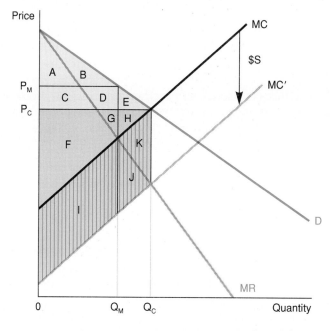

An unsubsidized monopolist produces the quantity Q_M. The subsidy of $S per unit of output, which lowers the marginal cost curve to MC', is chosen to be of just the right size so that the monopolist will now produce the competitive quantity Q_C. Since the competitive quantity maximizes social gain, the deadweight loss is eliminated.

The table confirms that social gain is the same as it would be under competition.

+ K. By elementary geometry, the cost to taxpayers, $S $\times$ Q_C, is represented by the area of the trapezoid I + J + K. These calculations are shown in the third column of the table in Exhibit 10–3. The social gain is just what it would be under competition, so the deadweight loss is zero, as we have already argued that it must be.

Of course, this analysis assumes an "ideal" subsidy, which in turn assumes that policymakers are able to discern both the competitive equilibrium quantity and the size of the subsidy needed to call forth that quantity from the monopolist. A more reasonable expectation is that the

Exhibit 10–4   **A Price Ceiling**

If a monopolist is required by law to charge no more than the competitive price P_C, then he effectively faces the demand and marginal revenue curves shown in panels B and C. He produces at the point Q_C, where marginal cost and marginal revenue are equal.

subsidy will either be too small or too large. If it is too small, it is still certain to be welfare-improving, but perhaps by less than we might hope. If it is too large, it will encourage overproduction. Depending on the size of the subsidy, this could be either less or more detrimental than the under-production it was designed to replace.

▷ *Exercise 10.5* Draw diagrams depicting the effects of subsidies that are smaller or larger than the optimal one. Indicate the areas of dead-weight loss in each. Compare these areas with the areas of deadweight loss from an unsubsidized monopoly.

Price Ceilings

From an efficiency standpoint, it is desirable to subsidize a monopolist, although the size of the optimal subsidy may be difficult to determine. From a political viewpoint, it can be difficult to generate support for subsidies to a firm or an individual who is already perceived as wealthier than he "deserves" to be. There is, however, another approach to the "problem" of monopoly.

Consider a price ceiling imposed on a monopolist, at the level of the competitive price. This is shown in panel A of Exhibit 10–4. If the price ceiling is perfectly enforced, the monopolist effectively faces a flat demand curve at the price P_C out to the quantity Q_C. This is because no demander can ever offer a price higher than P_C, so that portion of the demand curve that lies above P_C becomes irrelevant to the monopolist's calculations. The new demand curve is as shown in panel B of Exhibit 10–4; it is flat out to Q_C

and becomes identical with the old demand curve thereafter. The new marginal revenue curve is shown in panel C of the exhibit: In the region where demand is flat at P_C, we always have marginal revenue equal to P_C (just as in the competitive case). In the region of downward-sloping demand, the original marginal revenue curve is still in effect; thus the new marginal revenue curve jumps downward at the quantity Q_C.

The monopolist produces the quantity where his new marginal revenue curve meets his marginal cost curve, that is, the competitive quantity Q_C. (Refer to panel A to see this.) Consumers' surplus and producers' surplus are what they would be under competition, and there is no deadweight loss.

▷ *Exercise 10.6* Give the reasons for the assertions made in the preceding paragraph. In a competitive market, price controls caused social loss due to time spent waiting in line and so on, yet no such social loss takes place in the market pictured in Exhibit 10–4. Why not?

Unfortunately, finding the optimal price ceiling may be no easier for the policymaker than finding the right level of subsidy. In the absence of a competitive market, it is difficult to determine what the competitive price would be. It is therefore possible to set the price ceiling either too high or too low. If it is set too high, its effect will be diminished. Deadweight loss will be reduced but not eliminated altogether. If it is set too low, there will be deadweight loss due to underproduction. If it is set very low, the deadweight loss can be greater than with an unregulated monopoly.

▷ *Exercise 10.7* Draw diagrams depicting price ceilings that are higher or lower than the optimal one. Show the areas of deadweight loss and compare them with the deadweight losses in the absence of a price control.

Rate-of-Return Regulation

In practice, many monopolists (such as public utility companies) are required to set prices in such a way that they will earn no more than a "normal" rate of return on their capital investment. That is, they must earn no more than they could by investing the same amount of capital in some other industry; they are required to earn zero economic profits.

It is sometimes argued that this policy is desirable because the goal is to make monopolists behave more like competitors, and competitors earn zero profits in long-run equilibrium. The problem with this argument is that it is not the zero profits aspect of competition that one wishes to reproduce; it is the efficiency aspect. Although efficiency and zero profits are compatible under competition, they are very unlikely to be compatible under monopoly.

Exhibit 10–5 shows two possible configurations of demand, marginal revenue, marginal cost, and average cost curves. In each case the monopolist earns zero profits when he produces the quantity Q_Z and sells at the

Exhibit 10–5   **Zero Profits Regulation of Monopoly**

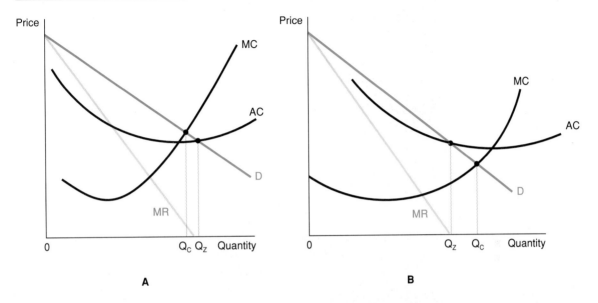

The two panels show two possible configurations of demand, marginal revenue, marginal cost, and average cost curves for a monopolist. If the monopolist is required by law to earn zero profits, he will produce that quantity Q_Z at which the demand price is equal to average cost. The efficient level of output is Q_C, where marginal cost equals demand. As the two panels show, Q_Z could be either greater or less than Q_C.

price P_Z. At this point price exactly covers average cost. However, in each case the efficient level of output is Q_C, where a competitive industry would produce. In panel A, a monopolist who is required to earn zero profits will produce too much from the viewpoint of efficiency. In panel B he will produce too little.

There are additional problems with regulation requiring the monopolist to earn zero profits. One is that such regulation provides the monopolist with no incentive to seek more efficient methods of production. If a new technology would lower the average cost and if the result of this is that the monopolist must lower his price accordingly, then there is no reason for him to adopt the new technology.

A closely related problem is that the owners and managers of the monopoly firm are given an incentive to adopt inefficient policies that benefit themselves personally. Suppose that the president of an electric utility company must decide whether to undertake an expensive redecoration of his office. Ordinarily, he would weigh the costs and benefits before proceeding. But if a regulatory agency always constrains the firm to earn zero profits, then the firm will be allowed to raise prices in order to cover the increased costs due to the redecoration. The president will certainly choose to undertake the project, even though it might be socially inefficient.[2]

10.2 Sources of Monopoly Power

We turn now to the question of why monopolies arise in the first place. We will discover that the answers make it necessary to modify our welfare analysis in certain cases.

Natural Monopoly

In some industries fixed costs are high and marginal costs are low. An example is the electric power industry, where the construction of even a small hydroelectric dam represents a substantial investment, but where electricity is supplied at very low marginal cost once the dam is built.

If such an industry were competitive, price would be equal to marginal cost and hence very low. Anticipating this, firms would not be willing to incur the high fixed costs associated with entry. Thus we might expect such an industry to be a good candidate for the emergence of a monopoly.

Let us be more precise about what we mean by "high" fixed costs and "low" marginal costs. Recall that

$$\text{Average cost} = \text{Fixed-cost/Quantity} + \text{Variable cost}.$$

When variable cost (that is, the sum of marginal costs) is small relative to the firm's fixed costs, this equation can be approximated by

$$\text{Average cost} \approx \text{Fixed-cost/Quantity}$$

and the term on the right decreases as quantity increases.

This calculation shows that the condition of high fixed costs and low variable costs implies that average cost decreases with quantity. More generally, we say that a condition of **natural monopoly** exists when the firm's average cost curve is decreasing at the point where it crosses market demand, as in Exhibit 10–6.[3]

If the firm in Exhibit 10–6 were forced to set prices and quantities as if the industry were competitive, it would produce the quantity Q_C at the price P_C. However, at this point average cost is greater than P_C, so the firm

Natural monopoly
An industry in which each firm's average cost curve is decreasing at the point where it crosses market demand.

---

[2]If a period of time elapses between the increase in costs and the firm's securing permission from the regulatory authority to increase its prices, then the firm still has some incentive to keep its costs down.

[3]Thus a firm with high fixed costs and low marginal costs is a natural monopoly, but by this definition there are other ways in which a firm could be a natural monopoly as well. For example, even with no fixed costs, if there are increasing marginal returns over a wide range of output, then average cost will still be declining at the point where it crosses demand.

Exhibit 10–6   **Natural Monopoly**

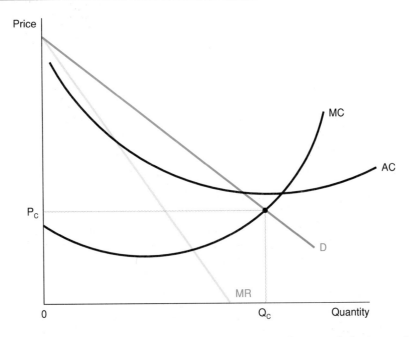

A natural monopoly occurs when each firm's average cost curve is downward sloping at the point where it crosses industry demand. Since marginal cost crosses average cost at the bottom of the U, marginal cost must cross demand at a point where price is below average cost. Thus if the firm priced competitively, it would earn negative profits.

will earn negative profits. Therefore no firm will remain in the industry if it must price competitively.

In fact, if the industry were competitive, the situation would be even worse than we have just described, because the industry supply curve, being the sum of all of the firms' supply curves, would lie to the right of the marginal cost curve shown in the exhibit. Therefore the equilibrium price would be even lower than P_C.

This shows that under conditions of natural monopoly a competitive industry cannot survive. At the competitive price no firm can cover its high fixed costs. A monopoly producer, however, may be able to enter the industry and prosper. The industry can survive only if it is monopolized.

Example: A Hamburger Machine

We can understand natural monopoly better through the use of an extreme example. Imagine a machine that can produce any number of hamburgers at zero marginal cost. The machine itself costs $100. How will price and quantity be determined in a competitive hamburger industry?

Exhibit 10–7   **Competition and Monopoly with Zero Marginal Cost**

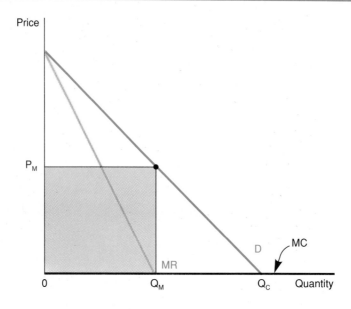

If hamburgers are produced by a hamburger machine at zero marginal cost, then the only possible competitive equilibrium price is zero, with a quantity of Q_C. Foreseeing this, no producer would be willing to purchase the machine that is necessary to enter the industry. Therefore no hamburgers are produced under competition. A monopoly producer, however, will produce quantity Q_M and sell at a price of P_M, earning revenue equal to the shaded area. If this area is greater than the cost of a hamburger machine, a monopolist will be willing to enter the industry.

At any positive price, a competitive producer with a hamburger machine will want to produce an unlimited quantity of hamburgers. Each hamburger that he sells yields positive marginal revenue at zero marginal cost. At a price of zero, the producer will supply whatever quantity of hamburgers demanders want to buy. In other words, his supply curve lies directly on top of the quantity axis.

Exhibit 10–7 shows the market demand curve for hamburgers and the (flat) marginal cost curve. Under competition the market price will be *zero*, and demanders will purchase Q_C hamburgers.

However, faced with the prospect of selling hamburgers at a price of zero, no potential producer will invest $100 in a hamburger machine in the first place. If the market is expected to be competitive, there will be no entrants and no hamburgers will be produced.

There may be room for a monopoly producer, however. In Exhibit 10–7 Q_M and P_M are the quantity and price of hamburgers produced by a monopolist with a hamburger machine. He earns the shaded area as producer's surplus. If this area is large enough, it will justify the initial $100 investment and the monopolist will set up shop.

▷ *Exercise 10.8* In a graph like that of Exhibit 10–7, draw in the firm's average cost curve. (*Hint:* It is given by the equation AC = $100/Q. Explain why this is true!) Do this exercise first under the assumption that the shaded region is greater than $100, and then under the assumption that it is less than $100. In the second case, will any firm enter the hamburger industry?

If there is additional entry, the original monopolist's revenues will be adversely affected, but each firm must still earn enough to cover the $100 "entry fee" to the industry. This means that each firm must retain some monopoly power, because we have already seen that under competition total revenue is zero.

The Welfare Economics of Natural Monopoly

In Section 10.1 we computed the welfare loss due to monopoly by comparing the social gain from a monopolized industry with the social gain available if the same industry were competitive. Now we see that in the case of a natural monopoly the comparison is unfair. It is unfair because such an industry could never survive under competition.

It is true that a hypothetical competitive electric power industry would be more socially efficient than the real electric power industry, which has monopoly characteristics. But it is also true that the competitive industry can never be more than hypothetical. The welfare that we refer to as "lost" due to the absence of competition actually never had a chance to be created in the first place.

Patents

Patents are another source of monopoly power with ambiguous welfare consequences. A patent confers a legally protected monopoly for a period of 17 years after the development of a new invention. In the absence of this monopoly the invention could be copied by others and produced competitively. On the other hand, if there were no patents the incentive to invent would be much reduced and many inventions might not come into being in the first place. In deciding on the optimal length of a patent, it is necessary to weigh the losses from monopoly production against the gains from promoting inventive activity.

Keep in mind, though, that there is an optimal quantity of inventive activity, and that it is socially undesirable to grant incentives for people to be inventive past the point where the marginal benefits of inventions exceed the marginal gains from inventors' alternative employment. Another factor often ignored is that patents divert creative individuals *away* from making socially valuable innovations that are not patentable. The inventors of the Macintosh computer received many valuable patents; the inventor of the supermarket received none. If the length of patent protection is increased, society will have more inventions like the Macintosh and fewer like the supermarket; it is very hard to judge the optimal mix.

With all of these uncertainties in mind, you should be somewhat skeptical of attempts to estimate the optimal life of patents, but such attempts have been made.[4] Although the results necessarily depend on a number of ad hoc assumptions, they tend to suggest that the existing 17-year limit is a reasonable one.

Resource Monopolies

Monopolies occasionally result when a single firm gains control of a productive input that is necessary to the industry. The most commonly cited example is Alcoa (Aluminum Company of America), which completely dominated the market for aluminum in the first 40 years of this century. Alcoa initially established its monopoly position by acquiring critical patents, but it was able to maintain its position long after the patents expired largely by virtue of owning essentially all of the sources of bauxite (the ore from which aluminum is derived) in the United States.

Legal Barriers to Entry

In many industries legal barriers to entry constitute a source of monopoly power. We will have more to say on this topic in Section 11.2. Here we will give one brief example. In many states travelers on limited-access highways can visit restaurants and gas stations at "oasis stops" without having to leave the highway. The number of oases is determined by an agency of the state government, which also decides which restaurants will be granted the rights to do business there. Because entry is restricted, these rights confer considerable monopoly power. (In many states the restaurants are subject to price controls, but they still appear to price higher than competitively.) There is a great deal of competition among restaurants to acquire these rights, much of which takes the form of lobbying appropriate government officials and applying other forms of political pressure. This lobbying process itself can consume valuable resources (lobbyists' time, for example) without producing offsetting social gains. The concomitant losses should be *added* to the welfare cost of monopoly, which is therefore underestimated by the methods of Section 10.1.

▷ *Exercise 10.9* Explain why it would be socially more efficient to legalize bribery of state officials who decide on the placement of roadside restaurants.

Some economists have used the observation of Exercise 10.9 to explain the preponderance of lawyers as members of state and federal legislative

---

[4]One of the most famous attempts is by William Nordhaus, *Invention, Growth and Welfare* (Cambridge, MA: MIT Press, 1969).

bodies. The reason is that it is easier to bribe a lawyer than (for example) a medical doctor. This is not because of any moral superiority on the part of physicians; it is a purely technological phenomenon. Many of the firms that seek favors from legislators have considerable need for legal services, and they can contrive to hire those services from favored lawyer–legislators at inflated fees. A number of U.S. congressmen from widely scattered parts of the country are associated with previously undistinguished law firms whose business has thrived since one of the partners went to Washington. A small-town medical practice would find it far more difficult to plausibly collect million-dollar fees for services rendered to large corporations thousands of miles away.

10.3 Price Discrimination

The analysis of monopoly pricing in Section 10.1 assumes that the monopolist will sell all of his output at a single price. In this section we will see that, unlike a competitor, a monopolist can benefit by charging different prices for identical items.

Example: Monopoly in the Pie Market

Exhibit 10–8 shows the market for Mrs. Lovett's pies. Mrs. Lovett faces a downward-sloping demand curve, so she acts as a monopolist. That is, she produces the quantity Q_0 where marginal cost = marginal revenue and charges $10 per pie, read off the demand curve.

Mrs. Lovett could sell additional pies if she charged any price less than $10. For example, some customers may approach Mrs. Lovett and offer to buy additional pies at the competitive price of $7. Since this price exceeds Mrs. Lovett's marginal cost, both she and her customers would benefit from such a transaction. That is to say, both producer's and consumers' surpluses will be increased. Each additional pie beyond Q_0 creates a rectangle of social gain as in the exhibit. Mrs. Lovett earns the lower portions of these rectangles as additional producer's surplus. Her customers gain the upper portions.

Although the transaction would benefit everyone, it still might not take place. Why not? Because Mrs. Lovett will be willing to market additional pies at the lower price of $7 only on the condition that her customers continue to buy Q_0 high-priced pies. Ideally, Mrs. Lovett would like to market some pies at $10 and other identical pies at $7, and then post a sign in her shop reading: "Please buy as many $10 pies as you are willing to before purchasing any $7 pies." Realistically, she fears that her customers will not cooperate. This fear leads her to produce only Q_0 pies at a single monopoly price of $10.

Conceivably, Mrs. Lovett could attempt some approximation to the scheme she has just rejected. If she believes that the typical customer is

Exhibit 10–8   **Mrs. Lovett's Pies**

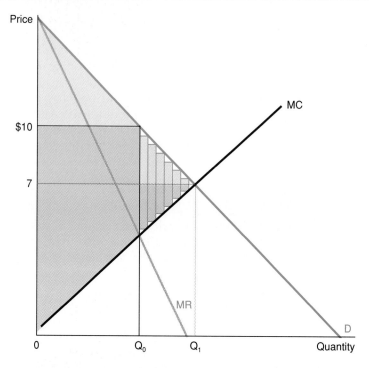

Mrs. Lovett, as a monopolist, produces Q_0 pies and sells them at a price of $10. Once she has done so, she can still sell additional pies at prices that exceed her marginal cost. For example, at the competitive price of $7, she could sell an additional $Q_1 - Q_0$ pies, creating additional social gains represented by the rectangles. The upper portions of the rectangles represent additions to consumers' surplus, and the lower portions represent additions to Mrs. Lovett's producer's surplus.

willing to buy two pies at $10 each, she can sell pies at "$10 each, 3 for $27." This effectively enables her to sell each customer a third pie for $7 without cutting into the sales of $10 pies.

But this plan, too, has its flaws. First, some of her customers might in fact have been willing to pay $10 for a third pie. A more important (and perhaps fatal) flaw is this: Some customers may buy a third pie for $7, then resell the pie for $9 to somebody else who would have been willing to buy it from Mrs. Lovett for $10. In effect, she makes it possible for her own customers to go into competition with her! We will return to these problems later in this section.

The act of charging different prices for identical items is known as **price discrimination.** Any monopolist faces the temptation to price discriminate, because he produces where marginal value exceeds marginal cost. Consequently, he can always sell additional items at a price higher than the marginal cost of producing them.

Price discrimination
Charging different prices for identical items.

Exhibit 10–9   **First-Degree Price Discrimination**

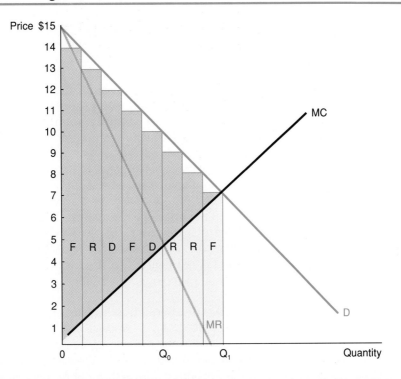

The rectangles show the marginal values of pies to Mrs. Lovett's customers, with each labeled by the initial of the corresponding customer. If she charges each customer the maximum amount that she is willing to pay for a pie, Flicka will have to pay $14 for her first pie, Ricka will pay $13 for her first pie, and so on. Since each consumer pays her marginal value for each pie, there is no consumers' surplus. All of the surplus is earned by Mrs. Lovett, who gains the entire shaded area.

A competitive producer, by contrast, faces no temptation to price discriminate. This is because he can sell any quantity he wants to at the going market price, so there is never any reason for him to sell for less.

In order to price discriminate successfully, a monopolist must be able to prevent the low-priced units from being resold, undercutting his own higher-priced sales. This is easier in some industries than in others. Utility companies offer quantity discounts, for example, because technological barriers prevent a customer from buying lots of cheap electricity and reselling it to his friends at a profit.

First-Degree Price Discrimination

Returning to Mrs. Lovett, we find that there is yet another pricing policy with even greater potential to increase her revenue. Exhibit 10–9 shows again the market for Mrs. Lovett's pies; the curves are exactly as in Exhibit

10–8. The rectangles represent the marginal values that her customers place on pies. Each rectangle is labeled with the initial of the corresponding customer. Flicka has the highest marginal value, valuing her first pie at $14. Ricka values her first pie at $13, Dicka values her first pie at $12, Flicka values her second pie at $11, and so on. If Mrs. Lovett knows all this, she can price her pies as follows: To Flicka the first pie is $14 and the second is $11. To Ricka the first pie is $13. To Dicka . . . and so on.

This scheme allows Mrs. Lovett to capture all of the social gains for herself. Each customer pays the maximum amount she would be willing to pay for each pie, so that she earns no surplus, while Mrs. Lovett gains the shaded areas shown in the exhibit. Mrs. Lovett will sell pies as long as she can collect prices higher than her marginal cost, so she will produce the competitive quantity Q_1. Therefore there is no deadweight loss.

This scheme is called **first-degree price discrimination,** to distinguish it from the **second-degree price discrimination** that Mrs. Lovett practiced when she offered quantity discounts. In second-degree price discrimination each customer is offered the same set of prices, although the price may depend on the quantity purchased. In first-degree price discrimination each individual customer is charged the highest price he is willing to pay for each item.

Either form of price discrimination leads to an increase in output and an increase in welfare. Second-degree price discrimination benefits both the producer and the consumers. First-degree price discrimination benefits the producer in two ways. First, it allows him to appropriate the consumers' surplus. Second, it allows him to produce out to the competitive quantity, creating additional welfare gains, all of which go to the producer.

First-degree price discrimination
Charging each customer the most he would be willing to pay for each item that he buys.

Second-degree price discrimination
Charging the same customer different prices for identical items.

Example: The Market for Computer Cards

Perfect first-degree price discrimination requires more knowledge than any producer can ever have. However, this knowledge can sometimes be approximated. In the ancient days when people spoke with their computers through the medium of gigantic stacks of "computer cards," IBM required users of its computers to buy all of their cards from IBM. The cards were priced above marginal cost. This strategy was widely misinterpreted as an attempt to extend IBM's monopoly power from the market for computers to the market for cards. However, this explanation makes no sense. If buyers of computers are required to pay more for cards, their willingness to pay for computers is reduced and IBM loses on the computers what it makes on the cards.[5] In actuality, *the card strategy enabled IBM to charge different prices to different customers.* In effect, those who used more cards were charged more for their computers.

---

[5]We will return to this point in the subsection on two-part tariffs later in the chapter.

IBM's ideal strategy was to require each buyer of a computer to pay the amount that a computer was worth to him. This was well approximated by charging a higher price to the heavier users. The card strategy accomplished this.

IBM found a way to approximate individual users' demand for computers. Sometimes this knowledge can be approximated by knowledge of consumers' incomes and the alternatives they have available. As with second-degree price discrimination, it is necessary (and not always possible) to prevent resales in order to succeed.

Example: Price Discrimination in Medicine

Perhaps the most successful practitioners of first-degree price discrimination in America are physicians. Medical services are generally unsusceptible to resale: the recipient of low-priced open heart surgery can hardly undercut his doctor by reselling the operation to someone else. The other important ingredient in price discrimination is knowledge of how much each consumer is willing to pay. Doctors often have access to detailed information on the incomes of their patients. The reasonable expectation is that wealthier patients will be charged more, and this expectation is fulfilled in practice.

It is sometimes argued that doctors charge poor patients less than they charge wealthy ones because their concern for the sick outweighs their desire to maximize profits. On the other hand, we have seen that this pricing policy is also to be expected from a profit-maximizing doctor with monopoly power. ("Charging poor patients less" is of course the same as "charging rich patients more," though the two phrases often evoke different reactions.) Is differential pricing by doctors an exercise of monopoly power, or is it an indication that doctors are essentially administering private charitable organizations?

In a famous essay Professor Reuben Kessel considered both hypotheses and argued that price discrimination was the more plausible answer to this question.[6] The "charity" hypothesis asserts that doctors in effect tax the rich and donate the proceeds to the poor. (Actually, it argues that they tax just those who are both rich and sick, leaving the rich and well untaxed. It is hard to think of other taxes that redistribute wealth in such a curious way.) Kessel asked why it is plausible that doctors should be so singularly altruistic. Grocers, who function in a competitive market, do not charge different prices to different customers; this is so even though food is even more of a "necessity" than medical care. In any event, differential pricing is an inefficient form of charity; charitable grocers simply donate food to the poor. Doctors could do the same with medical care. Kessel argued that the charity hypothesis is inconsistent with the observation that doctors do not charge each other for services, even though doctors' incomes are relatively

---

[6]Reuben Kessel, "Price Discrimination in Medicine," *Journal of Law and Economics,* 1958.

high. Finally, he pointed out that one would expect to see more charitable activity in times of widespread economic hardship, but medical price differentials do not appear to follow such a pattern.

There is yet another possible explanation that Kessel did not consider. Conceivably, it is more expensive for doctors to treat rich patients than to treat poor ones. Rich patients may be more demanding of the doctor's time and attention, and also may be more likely to sue for malpractice when something goes wrong. According to this explanation, rich and poor patients purchase different services from doctors, and these services are provided at different marginal costs.

What evidence can you think of that would help determine whether this explanation is more or less plausible than either of those considered by Kessel?

Third-Degree Price Discrimination

Third-degree price discrimination
Charging different prices in different markets.

The third and most common form of price discrimination is called **third-degree price discrimination.** This occurs when a seller faces two identifiably different groups of buyers having different (downward-sloping) demand curves. Such a seller can increase his profits by setting different prices for the two groups, provided resales can be prevented.

Example: Two Markets for Pies

Consider again Mrs. Lovett, who has discovered a second market for her pies. A grocery store in a large city 200 miles away is willing to buy as many pies as Mrs. Lovett wants to sell at a price of $7 each.[7]

What quantity of pies will Mrs. Lovett provide to her local customers? The ordinary monopoly quantity is Q_0 in Exhibit 10–10. At this quantity her marginal revenue is $5 per pie. But Mrs. Lovett can always sell pies to the big-city grocery store at a marginal revenue of $7 per pie. Given this, it pays to sell fewer pies locally and more in the big city. Mrs. Lovett will keep transferring pies from the local market to the big-city market as long as the local marginal revenue is less than $7. This will reduce the local quantity to Q_2 in Exhibit 10–10.

In general:

> **Any producer selling in two different markets will choose quantities so that his marginal revenue is the same in each market.**

The reason is that if marginal revenue in Market 1 were higher than marginal revenue in Market 2, the producer could increase his profits by selling one more item in Market 1 and one less in Market 2.

---

[7]By coincidence, $7 is also the competitive price in Mrs. Lovett's own hometown. Such remarkable coincidences are not to be expected. We make the assumption for purposes of this example only, and only because it helps to keep the graph readable. None of the ideas that we will stress depend on this assumption.

Exhibit 10–10   Third-Degree Price Discrimination with Monopoly in One Market and Competition in the Other

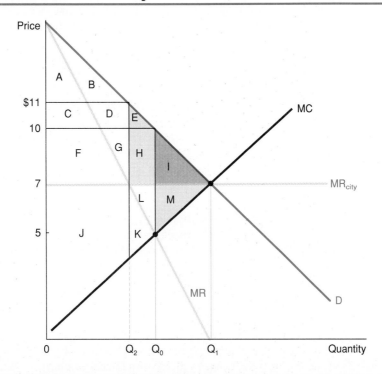

The demand and marginal revenue curves are from Mrs. Lovett's hometown market. In the distant city she can sell all of the pies she wants to at the competitive price of $7. In that case she will sell only Q_2 pies at home, as opposed to the ordinary monopoly quantity Q_0. The reason is that she can always earn $7 marginal revenue by selling pies in the city, so that she will not sell pies at home when her marginal revenue there falls below $7. When she sells Q_2 pies at home, she sets a price of $11, higher than the ordinary monopoly price of $10. The table shows what social gains would be if the pie industry were competitive, if Mrs. Lovett were an ordinary monopolist, and when Mrs. Lovett is able to sell pies in both markets at different prices.

In each case the consumers' surplus comes entirely from the local market. There is no consumers' surplus in the city market, because the demand curve there for Mrs. Lovett's pies is flat.

	Competition	Ordinary Monopoly	Price-Discriminating Monopoly
Consumers' Surplus	A+B+C+D+E+F+G+H+I	A+B+C+D+E	A+B
Producer's Surplus (Local)	J+K+L+M	F+G+H+J+K+L	C+D+F+G+J
Producer's Surplus (City)			K+L+M
Social Gain	A+B+C+D+E+F+G+H +I+J+K+L+M	A+B+C+D+E+F +G+H+J+K+L	A+B+C+D+F+G+J +K+L+M
Deadweight Loss		I+M	E+H+I

Because Mrs. Lovett sells only Q_2 pies at home, she is able to command a price of $11 for them. Then she will turn to the big-city market and will sell pies there as long as her marginal revenue ($7 per pie) exceeds her marginal cost. That is, she will produce Q_1 pies altogether, selling Q_2 of them at home for $11 each and $Q_1 - Q_2$ of them in the big city for $7 each.

The table in Exhibit 10–10 shows social gains in three situations: Mrs. Lovett as a competitor, Mrs. Lovett as an ordinary monopolist, and Mrs. Lovett as a price-discriminating monopolist.

If Mrs. Lovett sold only in the local market, the deadweight loss would be I + M. When she can sell in both markets and price discriminate, the deadweight loss is E + H + I. E + H can be either greater or less than M; therefore Mrs. Lovett's price discrimination can be either beneficial or detrimental to welfare. On the other hand, it certainly hurts the local consumers.

Of course, like all price discriminators, Mrs. Lovett has to worry about resale. One of her neighbors may get the idea to drive to the city, buy a truckload of pies at $7 apiece, bring them back and sell them locally for $10.50. Before long Mrs. Lovett may find that she is no longer a monopolist in her hometown.

A Monopolist in Two Markets

If Mrs. Lovett sells pies both in her hometown and in the big city, then she is a monopolist in one market and a competitor in another. Sometimes a producer is a monopolist in two markets. His behavior will be essentially the same as Mrs. Lovett's. Benjamin Barker is a barber who cuts the hair of both adults and children. Adults have one demand curve and children have another.

Benjamin wants to decide how many haircuts to sell to adults and how many to sell to children. We will call these quantities Q_A and Q_C. Then Benjamin wants to choose Q_A and Q_C so that his marginal revenue in the adult market, his marginal revenue in the children's market, and the marginal cost to him of producing $Q_A + Q_C$ haircuts are all equal.

▷ *Exercise 10.10* Explain why Benjamin wants all three of these numbers to be equal. If any two were not equal, how could he alter his behavior to make himself better off? How would this change in his behavior tend to equalize the three quantities?

Exhibit 10–11 shows a graphic method for determining how many haircuts Benjamin will sell to each group. The MR_A and MR_C curves are the marginal revenue curves that he faces in the adults' and children's markets. The **MR** curve is obtained by summing MR_A and MR_C horizontally. That is, for any price, read the corresponding quantities off MR_A and MR_C; then add these to get the corresponding quantity on **MR**.

Benjamin can equalize his marginal cost and both marginal revenues by choosing the quantity where his marginal cost curve MC crosses the **MR** curve. In the exhibit this means that he produces a total of $Q_A + Q_C$

Exhibit 10–11   Third-Degree Price Discrimination by a Monopolist in Two Markets

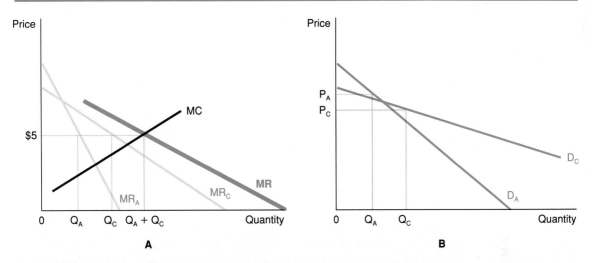

Benjamin Barker sells haircuts to adults and to children. The two groups have different marginal revenue curves, labeled MR_A and MR_C in panel A. The heavier curve **MR** is obtained by horizontally summing the curves MR_A and MR_C. Benjamin produces the quantity $Q_A + Q_C$ where MC crosses **MR**, selling Q_A haircuts to adults and Q_C to children. He chooses the corresponding prices of the adults' and children's demand curves, which are shown in panel B.

haircuts, so that his marginal cost is $5 per haircut. He sells Q_A of these haircuts to adults and Q_C to children, so that his marginal revenue is $5 per haircut in each market.

Once Benjamin has chosen the quantities Q_A and Q_C, he reads prices off the adults' and children's demand curves, just like any good monopolist. These prices, P_A and P_C, are shown in panel B of the exhibit.

Elasticities and Price Discrimination

There is an interesting relationship between the prices P_A and P_C in Exhibit 10–11. Write η_A for the elasticity of the adults' demand curve at P_A and η_C for the elasticity of the children's demand curve at P_C. Since the marginal revenue is $5 in each market, the equation that relates price to marginal revenue says that

$$P_A\left[1 - \left(\frac{1}{|\eta_A|}\right)\right] = \$5 \quad \text{and} \quad P_C\left[1 - \left(\frac{1}{|\eta_C|}\right)\right] = \$5.$$

It follows that

$$P_A\left[1 - \left(\frac{1}{|\eta_A|}\right)\right] = P_C\left[1 - \left(\frac{1}{|\eta_C|}\right)\right].$$

From this equation we can see that

$$\text{if } |\eta_C| > |\eta_A|, \text{ then } P_C < P_A,$$

whereas   if $|\eta_A| > |\eta_C|$, then $P_A < P_C$.

In other words:

The group with the more elastic demand is charged the lower price.

Roughly, this means that the monopolist will charge less in the market where he is closer to being a competitor.

Movie theaters that offer discounts to students and senior citizens are engaging in third-degree price discrimination. So are railroads that sell special "youth passes." In each case a lower price is offered to those customers who are more sensitive to price, which is to say, to those with the more elastic demand. A possible reason for this more elastic demand is that students and senior citizens have either below-average incomes or low values of time. In either case they will be more likely than others to shop around for alternatives when prices go up. This makes it desirable to price discriminate in their favor.

Conditions for Price Discrimination

We can now summarize the conditions necessary to make price discrimination profitable. First, the seller must have some degree of monopoly power. (Thus wheat farmers never offer senior citizen discounts.) Second, resales must be controllable. Therefore price discrimination is most often observed in markets for goods that have to be consumed immediately upon purchase, such as education. (Does your college charge different tuitions to different students by offering scholarship aid to some and not to others?) Each of these two conditions applies to any form of price discrimination. Finally, in the case of third-degree price discrimination, some mechanism must be found for offering lower prices to precisely those demanders who are more sensitive to price. (Are those students who get scholarships by and large the ones who would be most likely to go elsewhere—or to not attend college at all—if they had to pay full tuition?)[8]

Examples

Discount coupons for supermarket shopping constitute a mechanism for offering a lower price to appropriate consumers. The shoppers who find it worth their while to clip these coupons are those with a relatively low value of time (for example, because their wages are low); by and large, these are the customers with a greater propensity for comparison shopping. The

---

[8]In 1988 MIT sent a letter to parents announcing that it was raising both tuition and the amount of scholarship aid that it would provide. Would the parents have reacted differently if MIT had announced that it was going to exercise monopoly power more fully through an increase in price discrimination?

supermarket's ideal pricing policy is "lower prices to those who would otherwise shop elsewhere." A practical approximation to this ideal is "lower prices to those with enough free time to clip coupons."

It is important to notice that there would be no point to coupons if everyone redeemed them; in this case the store could just lower its prices and have the same effect. Similarly, there would be no point to coupons if only a random set of customers redeemed them. The point of coupons is that they offer lower prices to precisely those customers who are most sensitive to price.[9]

Manufacturers' rebates (for example: Buy a coffee maker and get a coupon that can be redeemed for $5) work much the same way. They are redeemed by precisely the shoppers who are willing to devote some extra time and energy to recovering a few dollars. These are the same shoppers who are most likely to compare prices at many stores or to decide to do without a coffee maker altogether.

Promotions that require customers to save game cards, scratch off designated areas to reveal numbers, and the like serve the same purpose. These promotions may appeal primarily to families with children, who can be enlisted to paste, scratch, tear, and cut. It is reasonable to think that those with children are those most likely to be watching pennies in their food budgets.

Students sometimes reason that if grocery stores engage in price discrimination, for which monopoly power is a prerequisite, then grocery stores must be monopolies, so we should never use the competitive model when we study them. But, in fact, we use different models to describe different phenomena. Consider a simple analogy from physics: If we want to describe the interactions of several moving balls on a billiard table, it is often safe to assume there is no friction, because friction does not play an important role in the phenomenon under study. But if we want to explain why the balls roll instead of slide, friction suddenly becomes important and we switch to a description that takes account of it. Similarly, when we want to study the determination of prices and quantities in the grocery industry, the assumption of competition may be close enough to truth to yield deep and important insights. When we switch to studying a phenomenon like price discrimination, monopoly power acquires central importance and must be explicitly included in the description.

When you order a pizza and get "free delivery," you are being charged less for a pizza than somebody who picks one up at the take-out counter. (When you take out, you pay for both the pizza and for gasoline, making the effective price of the pizza higher.) People ordering pizzas by telephone have more elastic demand because they can easily hang up the phone and

---

[9]Lee Iacocca, Chairman of the Chrysler Corporation, had an income of over $20,000,000 in 1986. It is probable that he does not clip supermarket coupons.

order a pizza elsewhere. Whenever a producer offers "free extras" that only some customers take, you should ask how the extras have been designed to appeal to the more elastic demanders.

Why, for example, do coffee shops in downtown office buildings typically offer free lids? Such a coffee shop has two classes of customers: those who work in the building and those who pass by the building on their way to work elsewhere. With regard to the first group, the shop has some monopoly power (people would rather not go outside for coffee). With regard to the second, it is nearly in perfect competition (people walking by can always stop somewhere else for coffee). Therefore they would like to offer a "free extra"—such as a lid—that is taken primarily by those who are walking by.[10]

Many hotels offer rooms at two different prices. Often the only difference between a $50 room and a $60 room is $10. If you call ahead for a reservation, you will get a $50 room. If you walk in at 11 p.m. looking tired, the $50 rooms will all be filled.

Airlines charge less for travelers who are staying over a Saturday night. These are the nonbusiness travelers who are likely to find another mode of transportation, or choose not to travel, when prices are high.

Many jewelry stores will give you a discount on a new watch if you trade in your old watch. The watches they receive as trade-ins are immediately discarded. People who already have watches are effectively charged less than those who don't. Can you see why the first group has the more elastic demand?

In each of these examples you should give thought to the question of how resales are controlled. Firms have been known to get very creative about this. Many years ago the Rohm and Haas chemical company produced a compound called methyl metacrylate that was used both in dentistry and industrial production. There were few good substitutes for this compound in dentistry, but there were many in industry. As a result, dentists were charged a much higher price than industrial users; as a further result, industrial users bought cheap and sold to dentists. The marketing directors at Rohm and Haas considered many strategies to combat this activity, one of which was to add arsenic to the compound before selling it in the industrial market. This plan was never implemented, but a closely related one was: They started a *rumor* that they had added the arsenic. This had the desired effect.

Counter-Examples

Price discrimination is evidence of monopoly power, and students confronted with so many examples sometimes infer that monopoly power is ubiquitous. It is important, then, to realize that many practices having the

---

[10]This example, invented by Robert Topel of the University of Chicago, is intended to be frivolous. An alternative (and perhaps more plausible) explanation is that lids are priced at marginal cost, and the best practical approximation to a marginal cost of .001¢ is zero.

appearance of price discrimination are, in fact, something quite different. Price discrimination occurs when the same product is sold at two different prices. Often a careful examination will reveal that two apparently identical products are actually quite different.

Many restaurants offer a lower price at the salad bar to those who order an entrée. This has the appearance of price discrimination, but an alternative explanation is that people who order entrées tend to take less food at the salad bar. This would explain a lower price on the basis of a lower cost to the restaurant.

Ice cream shops usually charge less for a second scoop than for a first. Is this second-degree price discrimination? Neither the taking of the order, nor the opening of the freezer, nor the ringing of the cash register has to be repeated for the second scoop of ice cream. Such factors make serving the second scoop genuinely cheaper for the ice cream shop and provide an alternative explanation.

The Two-Part Tariff

Two-part tariff
A pricing strategy in which the consumer must pay a fee in exchange for the right to purchase the product.

The **two-part tariff** is a monopoly pricing tactic that is similar to, but distinct from, price discrimination. It occurs when a firm charges an initial fee in exchange for the right to purchase its services. For example, an amusement park might charge an entrance fee, followed by a price for each ride. Private dining clubs require yearly membership fees that entitle the member to buy meals. Polaroid pictures provide a less obvious example. No consumer wants a camera for its own sake; the good that you actually purchase from the Polaroid company is Polaroid pictures. You pay for these pictures in two steps: First you pay for the camera, which then makes it possible for you to buy film and take pictures.

 The word *tariff* usually applies to a tax on imported goods. However, in the phrase *two-part tariff,* the word *tariff* simply means "price."

The firm that employs a two-part pricing strategy must make two decisions: how much to charge for the entry fee, and how much to charge per unit of the actual good. Each of these problems is easy to solve. For the first, the appropriate entry fee is, obviously, equal to the most that the consumer would be willing to pay in order to be allowed to purchase the item. But this amount is precisely equal to his consumer's surplus! Therefore the consumer's surplus is the entry fee the firm will charge.

This means that the firm earns the consumer's surplus (in the form of the entry fee) plus its own producer's surplus (when the consumer buys the item). So the firm, in order to maximize its own profits, should maximize the sum of consumers' and producer's surpluses. We know that this sum is maximized when the firm prices competitively, at the point where price equals marginal cost. As shown in Exhibit 10–12, this is exactly what the firm will do.

Exhibit 10–12   **Pricing Strategy with a Two-Part Tariff**

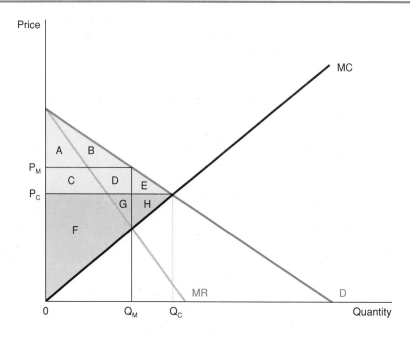

If the firm sells the monopoly quantity Q_M at the monopoly price P_M, it will earn a producer's surplus of C + D + F + G and will be able to charge the consumer A + B as an entry fee. But if it sells the competitive quantity Q_C at the lower price P_C, it will earn the smaller producer's surplus F + G + H while collecting the larger entry fee A + B + C + D + E. Under the second strategy, the firm's net earnings are increased by E + H.

With a perfect two-part tariff, the consumer gains zero (his consumer's surplus is completely eaten up by the entry fee) and all of the social gains go to the monopolist. This makes it clear why the monopolist will want to act like a competitor, since this is the strategy that maximizes social gains.

The Two-Part Tariff and Price Discrimination

If all customers have the same demand curve, a two-part-pricing monopolist maximizes profit by pricing his product at marginal cost and setting an entrance fee equal to the consumer's surplus. But if different consumers have different demand curves, they will have different consumer's surpluses, so that this strategy requires charging each consumer a different entry fee. If there is no way to distinguish one group of consumers from another, or if for some reason all consumers must be charged the same fee, then the monopolist has a more difficult problem.

To complicate his problem even further, entry fees can be used in quite a different way, as a method of price discrimination. We have already seen an example of this, namely IBM's pricing of computers and computer cards.

Since there were significant differences in demand across customers, IBM was able to price discriminate by setting a low price for computers (charging a low entry fee) and then pricing computer cards above marginal cost. This had the effect of charging a higher price to those who placed a higher value on the computer services. If there had not been much variation in these values, the optimal two-part-pricing strategy would have been a higher-priced computer and competitively priced cards.

In general, a monopolist's optimal pricing strategy depends on many factors, including the amount of diversity in his customer's demands and his ability to distinguish one kind of customer from another. Because these factors vary greatly from one industry to another, it is not surprising that pricing strategies vary greatly as well.

Example: Popcorn at the Movie Theater

An example can clarify some of the complications involved in choosing a monopoly pricing strategy. Movie theaters sell admission tickets and they also sell popcorn. How should each be priced?

If all consumers have approximately the same demand for popcorn, the best strategy is a two-part tariff in which the popcorn is priced at marginal cost and the consumer's surplus from the popcorn is added to the price of admission. On the other hand, if some moviegoers don't like popcorn, they may be driven away from the theater altogether by a high admission price. (The popcorn lovers are not driven away, since they get something in return for the high admission: the right to buy popcorn at marginal cost.) This possibility makes a two-part tariff less attractive.

An opposite strategy is to set ticket prices in whatever way is profit-maximizing at the box office, and then charge a monopoly price for popcorn. In this way the theater owner earns less from the popcorn lovers than he could have with the high admission price, but he avoids driving away his other customers.

However, there are still further considerations. Suppose that for some reason the moviegoers who like popcorn also have unusually strong preferences about what movies they see (that is, they have inelastic demand for a given movie). In this case the theater owner will want to price discriminate against them. One way to do this is to lower admission prices still further and raise the price of popcorn still higher. (This is similar to what IBM did with computer cards, but also more complicated. The reason it is more complicated is that IBM had to think only about the demand for computer services [which are produced by computers and cards working together], whereas the theater owner must concern himself with both the demand for movies and the demand for popcorn.)

If, on the other hand, the theater owner thinks that popcorn lovers are people who are relatively indifferent about what movies they see (and therefore have elastic demand for a given movie), he will want to price discriminate in their favor, perhaps by raising admission prices and then selling popcorn below marginal cost. In this way he can charge a high price to the non-popcorn eaters and a low price to the popcorn lovers who will more readily go elsewhere.

You might give thought to which of these various scenarios you find most realistic, and whether the pricing behavior it predicts is consistent with what you observe at the theaters you attend. You might also try to concoct some alternative scenarios and to think about the pricing policies they would entail. This process will begin to give you a feeling for the subtlety of the problems involved in monopoly pricing.

Summary

A firm has monopoly power when it faces a downward-sloping demand curve for its product. Such a firm also faces a downward-sloping marginal revenue curve that lies everywhere below the demand curve. Like any producer, the monopoly firm chooses the quantity where marginal cost equals marginal revenue, and then charges the price that corresponds to that quantity on the demand curve.

Because marginal revenue lies below demand, the monopolist chooses a quantity at which marginal cost is less than the consumer's marginal value. Thus he underproduces from the point of view of social welfare. Various public policies can address this problem. If the monopolist is given a subsidy per unit of output, he will increase production. If a price ceiling is set at the competitive price, the monopolist will essentially face a flat marginal revenue curve and behave like a competitor.

Monopolies arise for various reasons. An industry where each firm's average cost curve is decreasing at the point where it crosses market demand is known as a natural monopoly. If price were set equal to marginal cost in such an industry, profits would be negative and no firms would enter. A monopoly producer, however, may be able to survive since he can charge a price that is higher than marginal cost.

One common source of natural monopoly is the combination of high fixed costs and low marginal costs. However, this is not the only source.

Other sources of monopoly power include patents, the control of resources, and barriers to entry erected by the government.

Sometimes a monopolist can increase his profits by charging different prices for identical items. This practice is known as price discrimination. In first-degree price discrimination, each consumer is charged the maximum he would be willing to pay for each item. If successful, this allows the monopolist to collect all of the social gain for himself, and it provides an incentive to produce the competitive quantity. In practice, perfect first-degree price discrimination is almost never possible, but it can sometimes be approximated.

In second-degree price discrimination, each customer is offered the same set of prices, but prices vary with the items purchased. Quantity discounts can be an example of second-degree price discrimination. However, quantity discounts are not always price discrimination. They can result instead from genuine cost savings to the seller when larger quantities are exchanged.

The most common type of price discrimination is third-degree price discrimination, in which two identifiably different groups of customers are charged different prices. In this case the lower price will go to the group with the more elastic demand curve. Senior citizen discounts at movie theaters are an example.

For price discrimination to be profitable, the firm must have monopoly power, must be able to find a device that discriminates in favor of the appropriate group, and must be able to prevent resales.

Another pricing policy available to some monopolists is a two-part tariff, where the customer is charged a one-time fee for the right to buy goods from the monopolist. If the monopolist prices at marginal cost and sets an entry fee equal to the consumer's surplus, he can maximize social gain and capture all of this gain for himself. However, if different consumers have different demand curves, this strategy requires knowing each consumer's demand curve and setting his entry fee accordingly. In practice, this is usually not possible. Therefore the monopolist's pricing problem is a difficult one. Pricing at marginal cost creates more gain for him to capture through entry fees. On the other hand, in some cases (like computer cards or Polaroid film), pricing above marginal cost offers the opportunity to price discriminate. Choosing the right strategy is a complicated matter, involving both the characteristics of the product and the characteristics of the demanders.

Review Questions

R1. Why does a monopolist's marginal revenue curve lie below his demand curve? In what way does this imply that the monopolist will choose an inefficient level of output?

R2. On which part of his demand curve, the elastic or the inelastic, does a monopolist always operate? If he were operating on the other part of the demand curve, explain how he could increase his profits.

R3. Draw a graph to illustrate the effect on social welfare when a monopolist is subjected to an excise tax. Do the same when he is given an optimal subsidy.

R4. Show the effect of an optimal price ceiling on a monopolist's output.

R5. What are some of the problems with regulating a monopolist's rate of return?

R6. List some of the sources of monopoly power.

R7. How and why must the welfare analysis of monopoly be modified when there is a natural monopoly? When there is a monopoly due to the granting of a patent?

R8. Describe the three types of price discrimination. Give examples of each.

R9. Describe the conditions necessary for successful price discrimination.

R10. What is a two-part tariff?

R11. Why might a monopolist who can charge an entry fee choose to price his product at marginal cost? Why might this strategy fail?

Numerical Exercises

N1. Suppose that a monopolist faces the demand curve

$$Q = a - bP$$

where a and b are constants. Show that his marginal revenue curve is given approximately by the equation

$$MR = \frac{a - 2Q}{b}.$$

(This approximation becomes exact when very small units are chosen.)

N2. Suppose that a monopolist sells in two markets with demand curves

$$Q_A = 100 - 10P_A$$

$$Q_B = 8 - 2P_B.$$

a) Show that for any given quantity, demand is more elastic in market A than in market B.

b) Suppose that the monopolist produces at zero marginal cost. How much does he supply in each market, and what prices does he charge? (*Hint:* Use the formula for marginal revenue from the preceding problem.)

c) Suppose that the monopolist's marginal cost curve is given by

$$MC = Q/21.$$

How much does he supply in each market, and what prices does he charge?

d) Reconcile your answers to parts a), b), and c) with the statement in the text that the group with more elastic demand is always charged the lower price.

e) Suppose that the monopolist's marginal cost curve is given by

$$MC = Q/3.$$

What will the monopolist do?

Problem Set

1. *True or false:* Unlike a competitor, a monopolist can charge any price he wants to.

2. Suppose that labor costs were to rise in the automobile industry. *True or false:* A larger percentage of this increase would be passed on to consumers if the automobile industry were monopolized than if it were competitive. (For this problem, assume straight-line demand and marginal cost curves.)

3. *True or false:* An excise tax on a monopolist that causes quantity to fall by one unit is just as detrimental to social welfare as an excise tax on a competitive industry that causes quantity to fall by one unit.

4. *True or false:* If the supply of land is fixed, then it is equally efficient for land to be supplied by a monopolist or by competitors.

5. The following table shows the total cost of producing various quantities of shoehorns and the total value of those shoehorns to consumers. What are the price and quantity produced if the shoehorn industry is competitive? What are they if it is monopolized? What is the extent of the social loss due to the existence of the monopoly? (The answers to all of these questions should be *numbers.* Assume that only a whole number of shoehorns can be produced.)

Q	TC	TV	Q	TC	TV
1	$ 1	$ 9	5	15	35
2	3	17	6	21	39
3	6	24	7	28	42
4	10	30	8	36	44

6. *True or false:* The calculation of deadweight loss due to monopoly may be overly optimistic, because it does not take account of costs of misallocation à la Hayek.

7. *True or false:* The calculation of deadweight loss due to monopoly may be overly optimistic because it does not take account of resources spent in attempts to maintain the monopolists' position (such as fighting antitrust suits and the like).

8. *True or false:* When fixed costs are zero, there can be no natural monopoly.

9. *True or false:* To make a natural monopolist behave more efficiently, subsidies will work better than price controls.

10. *True or false:* If the customers of a monopolist could band together and bribe him to act like a competitor, both they and he could be better off.

11. *True or false:* If a natural monopolist is required to earn zero profits, he will produce more than is optimal, but if any other kind of monopolist is required to earn zero profits, he will produce less than is optimal.

12. *True or false:* A regulated monopoly is more likely to engage in discriminatory hiring practices than is an unregulated monopoly.

13. Many hotels allow children to stay in their parents' rooms for free. Why?

14. Some Canadian restaurants (especially in tourist areas) will accept U.S. currency at a more favorable exchange rate than the banks will give. Why?

15. In many cities, when three people share a taxicab to exactly the same address, the fare depends on whether the three were traveling together at the time they hailed the cab. Riders who know each other are charged less than those who don't. Why?

16. In Problem 5 of the Chapter 1 Problem Set, you discovered that free delivery by furniture stores makes no difference to anyone. At that time you were assuming (perhaps without being aware of it) that all customers take equal advantage of free delivery. Suppose now that only some customers accept the free delivery. What kinds of customers does this policy discriminate in favor of? Are they, in fact, the customers with the more elastic demand, and if so, why? (*Note:* The author of your textbook does not know the answer to this question.)

17. Make counterarguments to Kessel's arguments about whether doctors price discriminate to maximize profits. Which of Kessel's arguments seem to you to be the strongest and which the weakest?

18. Many cable television services will allow you to purchase viewing rights to several channels but will not allow you to purchase viewing rights to just one. Why might this be a profit-maximizing strategy for them? What determines the fee for the full cable service?

Refer to Answers to Problem Sets for solutions to problems 1 and 8.

Chapter Eleven

Market Power Further Considered

Collusion, Oligopoly, and Monopolistic Competition

Market power is an elusive goal. It is limited everywhere by the threat of entry. Even a firm producing a unique product with no close substitutes might not be able to engage in monopoly pricing, because the profits that it would earn by doing so would lure entrants and destroy its market position.

In this chapter we will study how firms attempt to acquire and exercise market power in the face of competition or potential competition from other firms. We will see that many different industry structures are possible and that no single known theory can describe them all. However, by studying a few models and a number of examples, we can develop insight into many of the issues that are involved.

11.1 Acquiring Market Power

In this section we will explore some methods that firms either use or are alleged to use in their attempts to acquire and exploit market power.

Mergers

Horizontal integration
A merger of firms that produce the same product.

Vertical integration
A merger between a firm that produces an input and a firm that uses that input.

The issue of monopoly power arises whenever two firms merge to form a larger firm. Mergers can be roughly classified into two types. **Horizontal integration** combines two or more producers of the same product. An example would be the combination of Ford, Chrysler, and General Motors into a single company. **Vertical integration** combines firms one of which produces inputs for the other's production processes. An example would be the merger of a steel plant with an auto manufacturer.

Horizontal Integration

There are essentially two different reasons why firms might want to merge horizontally. First, there may be economies of scale or other increased efficiencies associated with size, so that a larger firm can produce output at a lower average cost. Second, there may be an opportunity for the larger firm to exercise some monopoly power. Of course, both motives may be present in a single merger.

From a welfare point of view, mergers are desirable insofar as they reduce costs, and they are undesirable insofar as they create monopoly power. Exhibit 11–1 illustrates the trade-off. We assume that the industry is initially competitive, with marginal cost curve MC. (The marginal cost curve is drawn horizontal in order to simplify the diagram; nothing of importance depends on this simplification.) If the firms in the industry merge, technical efficiencies will lower the marginal cost curve to MC', but they will also enable the new, larger firm to exercise monopoly power, producing the monopoly quantity Q', where MC' crosses the marginal revenue curve MR.

The welfare consequences of the merger are ambiguous. There is a gain of F + G, representing the cost savings due to greater efficiency (the rectangle F + G has area equal to Q' times the cost savings per unit). There is also a loss of E, due to the reduction in output. Which of these is greater will vary from one individual case to another.

If MC' is very much lower than MC, then the picture will look like Exhibit 11–2. In this case the monopoly price P' is actually lower than the competitive price P, and both consumers and producers gain from the merger.

▷ *Exercise 11.1* Suppose that the merger does not reduce costs at all, so that MC = MC'. Draw the appropriate graph. In this case does the merger have an unambiguous effect on social welfare?

Exhibit 11–1   **A Horizontal Merger**

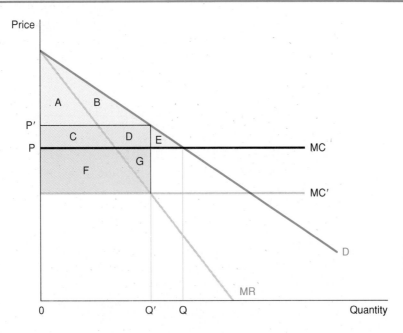

Initially, the industry's marginal cost (= supply) curve is MC. If the industry is competitive, it produces the equilibrium output Q at the price P. Because the MC curve is horizontal, there is no producers' surplus.

Following a merger, marginal cost is reduced to MC', but the newly created firm has monopoly power and so produces the quantity Q', where MC' crosses the marginal revenue curve MR. The monopoly price is P'. The table below computes welfare before and after the merger:

	Before Merger	After Merger
Consumers' Surplus	A+B+C+D+E	A+B
Producers' Surplus	—	C+D+F+G
Social Gain	A+B+C+D+E	A+B+C+D+F+G

Antitrust Policies

The Sherman Act of 1890 and the Clayton Act of 1914 give the courts jurisdiction to prevent mergers that tend to reduce competition. There has been much controversy about exactly what criteria the courts should apply in determining whether a particular merger is illegal.

One viewpoint is that mergers should be prohibited only when they reduce economic efficiency. According to this viewpoint, the court should compare areas in Exhibit 11–1 before deciding whether or not to allow a particular merger. If a merger reduces costs by enough to make the graph

Exhibit 11–2   A Horizontal Merger Leading to a Large Cost Reduction

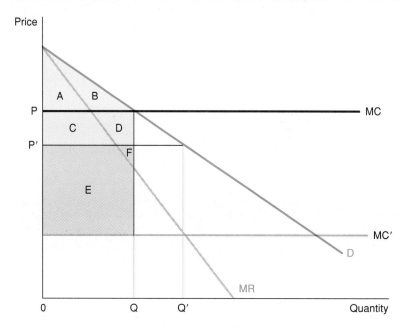

If the competitive industry's marginal cost curve is MC, and if a merger converts the industry into a monopoly with the much lower marginal cost curve MC', then price will fall from P to P', benefiting both consumers and producers.

	Before Merger	**After Merger**
Consumers' Surplus	A + B	A + B + C + D
Producers' Surplus	—	E + F
Social Gain	A + B	A + B + C + D + E + F

look like Exhibit 11–2, then according to this viewpoint the merger should certainly be allowed.

In a series of decisions beginning with *Brown Shoe v. the United States* (1962), the Supreme Court under Chief Justice Earl Warren explicitly rejected this viewpoint. Instead, the Court placed particular emphasis on the welfare of small firms that are not involved in the merger. The Court held that the Sherman and Clayton acts should be interpreted so as to protect such firms by disallowing mergers that would make it difficult for them to compete. In these cases the Court took the position that a merger could be illegal precisely *because* it would lead to a reduction in costs, lower prices, and increased economic efficiency. The reason is that smaller, less efficient firms would not be able to survive in the new environment, and the Court considered the interests of those firms to be protected by the law.[1]

The most vocal critic of the Warren Court's position has been Judge Robert Bork. In his book *The Antitrust Paradox*,[2] Bork argues forcefully that the antitrust laws should be interpreted so as to promote economic efficiency (which he calls "consumer welfare"). He argues that the interests of consumers should be given as much weight as the interests of small businesses, and that preventing mergers that would benefit consumers constitutes a misapplication of the law.

Vertical Integration

To most noneconomists, all mergers are seen as attempts to monopolize. Yet one surprising result of economic analysis is that both the intent and the effect of vertical integration can be to *reduce* monopoly power.

To see this, imagine a monopoly steel producer, Flemington Steel, which sells its product to a monopoly automobile manufacturer. In Exhibit 11–3 Flemington sets a price of Q_M and a price of P_M. Deadweight loss is $E + H$.

Suppose, however, that Flemington Steel acquires ownership of the auto manufacturer. Flemington continues to produce steel and provide it to the auto manufacturer, which is now renamed "Flemington Steel, Auto Division." Flemington earns both the producer's surplus (in its capacity as a steel maker) and the consumers' surplus (in its capacity as an automaker). Therefore Flemington will no longer be interested in maximizing just producer's surplus (at Q_M); it will instead want to maximize the sum of consumers' and producer's surpluses. Therefore it will produce at Q_C, creating more steel, more autos, lower costs in the auto industry, and ultimately lower prices to consumers.

Essentially, the effect of the vertical integration is that it enables the monopolist to profit by acting less like a monopolist and more like a competitor. Here is another way to see the same point. Suppose that the firms remained separate but that the automaker offered to pay Flemington a flat fee of $C + D$ in exchange for Flemington's behaving exactly like a competitor. This exchange would make both parties better off.

▷ *Exercise 11.2* Calculate both consumers' and producer's surpluses after the deal between Flemington Steel and the automaker is struck, and verify that both parties would benefit. What is the smallest flat fee that would make this arrangement benefit both parties? What is the largest?

[1]Among the more important of these cases were *United States v. Von's Grocery* (1966) and *Federal Trade Commission v. Procter & Gamble Co.* (1967).

[2]R. H. Bork, *The Antitrust Paradox: A Policy at War with Itself* (New York: Basic Books, 1978).

Exhibit 11–3 **Vertical Integration**

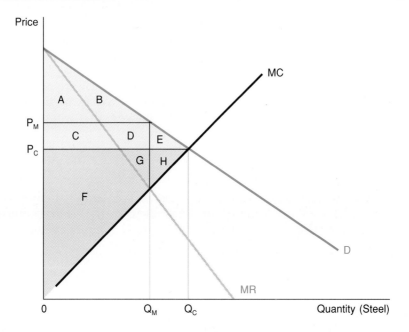

The monopolist Flemington Steel produces Q_M units of steel for sale to a monopoly automaker. This maximizes producer's surplus at C + D + F + G while restricting consumers' surplus to A + B.

If Flemington acquires ownership of the automaker, it will earn both the producer's and the consumers' surpluses and will therefore want to maximize the sum of the two. This is accomplished by producing the quantity Q_C of steel, creating a gain equal to the sum of all the lettered areas. Social gain is increased by E + H. More steel is produced, more cars are produced, and the price of cars to consumers goes down.

If such a bribe is mutually beneficial, why does it not take place? One difficulty is that there might be no way for the automaker to prevent Flemington from taking the money and then reneging on the agreement by continuing to charge monopoly prices. Some kind of enforcement mechanism is necessary in order to make the plan work.

When the two firms merge, each can continue going about its business exactly as before, except that there is now a central management with the authority to enforce mutually beneficial contracts. This enables the parties to come to an agreement that increases social gains by prohibiting the exercise of monopoly power.

Selling to Your Own Subsidiaries

It might be argued that if Flemington Steel acquires ownership of an automaker, then Flemington will be able to force the automaker to buy steel from Flemington, even if this is costlier than buying it elsewhere. According to this argument, vertical integration promotes inefficiency.

However, the argument overlooks the fact that once Flemington owns the automaker, it has every interest in that automaker's maximizing its profits. If the automaker can buy steel elsewhere more cheaply than Flemington can produce it, Flemington will happily tell the automaker to do so.

The argument that a large firm might exploit its vertically integrated subsidiaries surfaced in the Supreme Court's *Brown Shoe* decision. Brown, a shoe manufacturer, sought to merge with Kinney, which both manufactures shoes and sells them in a string of retail stores. Thus the merger had both horizontal (merging two manufacturers) and vertical (merging a manufacturer with a retailer) characteristics. The Court held that the vertical aspect of the merger would be detrimental since it would place Brown in the position of being able to force Kinney to market Brown's shoes in its retail stores. Robert Bork offered the following commentary on this reasoning:

> It completely ignores the fact that whatever considerations of price, quality, style or other matters had led Kinney not to purchase Brown's shoes before the merger would remain just as valid afterward. . . ."Forcing" Kinney to take a product inappropriate for its business would, therefore, cost Kinney at least as much as it would benefit Brown. Since Brown now owned Kinney, it could gain nothing and might well lose from this imagined maneuver.

> The problem can be stated in another way. If the Court's naive theory of "forcing" were correct, Brown would not have to acquire Kinney to employ the tactic. Since Brown, in common with almost every enterprise, was already integrated vertically, it could simply set up a separate profit and loss statement for all vertically related manufacturing operations and require each department to "force" more goods at higher prices upon the next, seriatim, all the way to the factory door. The last department might have some trouble selling all those high-priced shoes, but imagine the profits every previous department would report. Nobody has ever explained why this Rube Goldberg mechanism should suddenly become sensible if one more department, a retail outlet, is added and the shoes "forced" upon it.[3]

Predatory Pricing

Predatory pricing
Setting an artificially low price so as to damage rival firms.

Predatory pricing occurs when a firm sets prices so low as to incur losses, forcing its rivals to do the same. If the firm can outlast the competition in the resulting "price war," it may hope to be the only survivor.

Conceivably, a firm could engage in predatory pricing in some markets while continuing to charge normally in others. In this case predatory pricing becomes a form of price discrimination.

---

[3]Bork, *The Antitrust Paradox*, 213–214.

Economists disagree about how widespread this practice really is. There are a number of reasons for skepticism. First, there is nothing to prevent the reemergence of rival firms as soon as the would-be monopolist raises his prices. Second, during the period of price warfare, all sides are losing money. The predator's losses, however, are greater: It is he who is attempting to expand his market share, and therefore selling greater quantities at the artificially low price. Indeed, if the other firms "lay low" by producing very little (or even nothing) for a while, they can force the predator to take losses that are enormous compared to their own. Finally, a firm being preyed upon, if it is capable of competing successfully in the long run, can usually borrow funds to get through the temporary period of price cutting. Thus even a predator whose assets greatly outstrip his rivals' may not have any survival advantage over them.

Despite all of these arguments, there are still reasons to think that predation might sometimes be profitable. The most significant of these is that predation can serve as a warning to future entrants. By driving one rival from the marketplace, the predator can prevent many additional rivals from entering in the first place. This can make predation a sensible strategy, even when the predator's losses from underpricing far exceed his gains from the first rival's elimination.

Example: The Standard Oil Company

Historians have traditionally attributed much of the success of the Standard Oil Company to predatory price cutting. Founded in 1870 by John D. Rockefeller, Standard Oil was estimated to supply 75% of the oil sold in the United States by the 1890s. In 1911 Standard Oil (by now reorganized and called Standard Oil of New Jersey) was dissolved by order of the U.S. Supreme Court.

The role of predatory pricing in the Standard Oil case was reexamined by John McGee of the University of Washington in 1958.[4] In a widely quoted article he argued that no historical evidence supports the assertion that predatory pricing played a major role in Rockefeller's success. Instead, McGee argued, this success could be attributed primarily to a successful policy of buying out rivals. The one-time cost of such buy-outs was substantially less than the cost of predation.

Buy-outs also have the advantage of allowing the would-be monopolist to acquire the rival firm's physical plant and equipment, which at least delays the rival's ability to reconstitute himself. A firm that stops producing in response to predatory price cutting still has its factories, ready to go back into production the instant prices are raised.

On the other hand, buy-outs have the disadvantage of actually encouraging new entrants, who may be hoping to be bought out at a favorable

---

[4]John McGee, "Predatory Price Cutting: The Standard Oil (N.J.) Case," *Journal of Law and Economics* 1 (1958), 137–169.

price. And a firm that has been "bought" may soon reappear under a new name. It is said that more than a few nineteenth-century businessmen made lifetime careers out of being bought out by John D. Rockefeller.

The Robinson-Patman Act

Because of the potentially predatory nature of price discrimination, the Robinson-Patman Act of 1938 forbids price discrimination in cases where it tends to "create a monopoly, lessen competition, or injure competitors." This language is sufficiently imprecise as to invite controversy over exactly when price discrimination should be considered predatory. The most widely accepted standard (but by no means the only one) was offered in 1975 by Phillip Areeda and Donald Turner of the Harvard Law School.[5] They argue, among other things, that no price can be considered predatory unless it is below marginal cost. As long as the firm is pricing at or above marginal cost, those rivals who are more efficient (that is, have even lower costs) should be able to survive. Only when the firm prices below marginal cost is there a risk of its driving out a more efficient rival.

The Supreme Court gave its interpretation of the Robinson-Patman Act in the 1967 case *Utah Pie v. Continental Baking Company*. Utah Pie was a small local company with 18 employees marketing frozen pies in the Salt Lake City area. Continental Baking, Carnation, and Pet were large national producers of a wide variety of food products. Utah Pie alleged that these three giants price discriminated in an injurious way by selling frozen pies at a lower price in Salt Lake City than they did elsewhere. The Supreme Court agreed.

All parties to the *Utah Pie* case were in agreement that the defendants charged lower prices in Utah Pie's marketing territory than they did outside it. However, this could have resulted from the fact that elasticity of demand for Continental pies was greater in areas where Utah Pie's products were sold. In other words, Continental's actions could have been a simple case of ordinary third-degree price discrimination.

According to the Areeda–Turner rule, the price discrimination could have been considered predatory only if the defendants had priced below marginal cost in the Salt Lake City area. No evidence was offered that they had done so. Thus the Supreme Court's decision makes deviation from marginal cost an irrelevant criterion in deciding whether a pricing policy can be considered predatory. For this reason economists generally regard *Utah Pie* as a bad decision. By forbidding Continental et al. to undercut Utah Pie's prices, the Court is as likely to have created a local monopoly (in the hands of Utah Pie) as to have prevented one.

In fact, the Supreme Court essentially took the position that the mere fact that the price of pies decreased in Salt Lake City constituted a violation

[5]P. Areeda and D. Turner, "Predatory Pricing and Related Practices Under Section 2 of the Sherman Act," *Harvard Law Review* 88 (1975), 689–733.

of the Robinson-Patman act![6] This reinforced the Court's interpretation of the Sherman and Clayton acts, by reaffirming that benefits to consumers are not considered a defense against the charge of injury to other firms.

Resale Price Maintenance

Resale price maintenance, or **fair trade,** is a practice under which a monopoly supplier sets a retail price for its product and forbids retailers to undercut that price. Any retailer who sells below the set price has his supplies cut off in the future. For example, until it lost a Supreme Court case on this and other issues in 1967, the Schwinn Bicycle Company required all sellers of Schwinn bicycles to charge a price that was determined by Schwinn.

Although such a practice might at first appear to be an attempt by the manufacturer to keep prices artificially high, economic analysis suggests otherwise. The price at which consumers will buy Schwinn bicycles is determined by the quantity that Schwinn chooses to produce. If Schwinn wanted to raise prices, the most direct way for it to do so would be to restrict output. And conversely, unless Schwinn restricted output, no fair trade agreement could have enabled Schwinn to sell its bicycles at a price higher than demanders were willing to pay.

Why, then, would manufacturers choose to engage in this practice? A number of explanations have been offered.[7] One is that products like bicycles are displayed in showrooms, where people go to examine them and ask questions about them before making their purchases. If some retailers offered cut-rate prices, customers would first go to the stores with the fancy showrooms and knowledgeable sales forces, ask their questions, make their decisions, and then buy from the discounters. Eventually, those retailers who offered quality service would find that there are no rewards in that activity, and so they would eliminate all of the costly forms of assistance that customers find valuable. Consumers could find themselves worse off, and so could Schwinn, as buyers would now have a greatly reduced incentive to purchase Schwinn bicycles.

Through resale price maintenance, Schwinn ensures that its dealers, who cannot compete with each other by offering lower prices, will instead compete with each other by attempting to offer higher-quality service. Thus, according to this theory, a practice that at first seems designed to establish monopoly power at the expense of consumers can actually be more plausibly explained as a practice designed to make the product more desirable by providing consumers with services that they value.

Exhibit 11–4 illustrates the theory. Suppose that P_0 is the wholesale price at which Schwinn sells its bicycles, and suppose, for simplicity, that

Resale price maintenance or **fair trade**
A practice by which the producer of a product sets a retail price and forbids any retailer to sell below that price.

---

[6]For more on this point, see Bork, *The Antitrust Paradox,* 386–387.

[7]For an interesting discussion of this issue, see L. Telser, "Why Do Manufacturers Want Fair Trade?" *Journal of Law and Economics* 3 (1960), 86–105.

Exhibit 11–4 **Resale Price Maintenance**

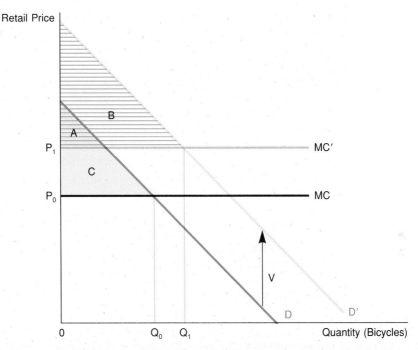

Suppose that Schwinn provides bicycles at a wholesale price of P_0 and that this is the only cost that retailers have. If the demand curve is D, then under competition the quantity sold is Q_0 and consumers' surplus is A + C.

If Schwinn maintains a retail price of P_1, dealers compete with each other by offering services that cost $P_1 - P_0$ per bicycle to provide. The value of these services to consumers is some amount V, so that the demand curve moves vertically upward a distance V to D′. The new quantity sold is Q_1.

Since Schwinn chooses to engage in the practice, we can assume that $Q_1 > Q_0$. Elementary geometry now reveals that $V > P_1 - P_0$ (the value of the dealer services exceeds the cost of producing them) and A + B > A + C (consumers' surplus is increased).

retailers have no costs other than purchasing the bicycles from Schwinn. The retailers' marginal cost curve MC is flat at P_0, and if the retail market is competitive, they sell Q_0 bicycles, where MC meets the demand curve D. Now suppose that Schwinn sets a retail price of P_1 and requires all dealers to adhere to this price. Dealers will then compete for customers by providing additional services up to the point where the cost of providing these services is $P_1 - P_0$. This raises their marginal cost curve to MC′.

▷ *Exercise 11.3* Explain why dealers provide services exactly up to the point where the cost of providing them is $P_1 - P_0$.

We assume that the dealer services add some quantity V to the value of each bicycle; thus the demand curve moves vertically upward a distance V to D′. The new quantity sold is Q_1, where MC′ meets D′.

Notice that Schwinn would engage in this practice only if Q_1 is greater than Q_0; Schwinn wants to maximize the number of bicycles it can sell at a given wholesale price. It is an easy exercise in geometry to check that if $Q_1 > Q_0$, then $V > P_1 - P_0$; that is, the value of the dealer services to consumers exceeds the cost of providing those services. This in turn, by another easy exercise in geometry, implies that area B is greater than area C, so that, for a given wholesale price P_0, the consumers' surplus with resale price maintenance (A + B) is greater than the consumers' surplus without resale price maintenance (A + C).

▷ **Exercise 11.4** Perform the easy exercises in geometry.

Do not confuse the demand curves in Exhibit 11–4, which are the demand curves facing retailers, with the demand curve facing Schwinn. The demand curve facing Schwinn passes through the point (P_0, Q_0) without resale price maintenance, and it moves out to pass through the point (P_0, Q_1) when resale price maintenance is allowed.

The analysis here is incomplete, since it takes the price P_0 as given. In fact, when resale price maintenance makes bicycles more attractive to consumers, the demand curve facing Schwinn moves out, leading Schwinn to set a new, higher price for bicycles. As a result, consumers keep only some of the increase in social welfare, and Schwinn gets the rest. Nevertheless, with the assumptions made here, it is possible to show that even after the price rises, consumers' surplus is still greater with resale price maintenance than without.

11.2 Collusion

Collusion
An agreement among firms to set prices and outputs.

Cartel
A group of firms engaged in collusion.

Collusion takes place when the firms in an industry join together to set prices and outputs. The firms participating in such an arrangement are said to form a **cartel.** By restricting each firm's production, the cartel attempts to restrict industry output to the monopoly level, allowing all firms to charge a monopoly price. This maximizes the total producers' surplus of all firms in the industry. If necessary, the resulting profits can then be redistributed among firms so that each gets a bigger "piece of the pie" than it had under competition.

Collusion is an ancient phenomenon. In the tenth century B.C. the Queen of Sheba (near what is now Yemen) held a monopoly position in the shipment of spices, myrrh, and frankincense to the Mediterranean. When Solomon, the king of Israel, entered the same market, "she came to Jerusalem, with a very great train, with camels that bear spices, and very much gold, and precious stones,"[8] which could indicate how much she valued the prospect of an amicable agreement to divide the market. More recently, Adam Smith observed:

---

[8]*1 Kings* 10:2.

Exhibit 11–5   The Prisoner's Dilemma

| | | Action of Prisoner A | |
		Confess	Not Confess
Action of Prisoner B	**Confess**	5 years each	A gets 10 years B gets 1 year
	Not Confess	A gets 1 year B gets 10 years	2 years each

Each prisoner must decide whether to confess or not to confess. Prisoner A reasons that there are two possibilities: Either B confesses, in which case A is better off confessing (so that he gets 5 years instead of 10), or B does not confess, in which case A is better off confessing (so that he gets 1 year instead of 2). Regardless of B's action, A should confess, and regardless of A's action, B should confess. As a result, they each go to jail for 5 years, whereas if neither had confessed they would only have gone to jail for 2 years.

> People of the same trade seldom meet together, even for merriment and diversion, but the conversation ends in a conspiracy against the public, or in some contrivance to raise prices.[9]

Cartels require cooperation. In order to understand the difficulties facing those who would cooperate, we will digress briefly into a topic from the Theory of Games.[10] The particular "game" we will analyze is called the "Prisoner's Dilemma."

Game Theory and the Prisoner's Dilemma

A crime has been committed and two suspects have been arrested. The suspects are taken to the police station and the district attorney meets with each one separately. To each he makes the following offer: "If you each confess, I'll send you both to jail for 5 years. If neither of you confesses, I can still get you on a lesser charge and send you to jail for 2 years each. If your buddy confesses and you don't, you'll get 10 years and he'll get 1. But if *you* are the only one to confess, you'll get off with 1 year while I put *him* away for 10. Now do you confess or don't you?" Each prisoner has to decide without conferring with the other.

Exhibit 11–5 will help you keep track of the district attorney's offer. Prisoner A, by choosing to confess or not confess, selects one of the columns in the table. Prisoner B selects one of the rows.

---

[9]Adam Smith, *The Wealth of Nations.*

[10]This theory was developed in the late 1940s by the mathematician John von Neumann and the economist Oscar Morgenstern. It has had a great deal of influence in economics and political science.

Let's evaluate the choices available to Prisoner A. What if B has confessed, thereby choosing the first row? Then A's choices are to confess and get 5 years, or to not confess and get 10 years. He should confess.

On the other hand, what if B has not confessed, thereby choosing the second row? Then A's choices are to confess and get 1 year, or to not confess and get 2 years. He should confess.

Needless to say, Prisoner A confesses. Following the same logic, so does Prisoner B. They both end up with 5 years in jail, even though they would have both been better off if neither had confessed.

It is easy to misunderstand the point of this example. Students sometimes think that Prisoner A confesses because he is afraid that Prisoner B will confess. In fact, A confesses for a much deeper reason. He confesses because it is his best strategy *regardless* of what B does. A would want to confess if he knew that B had confessed, and would also want to confess if he knew that B had not confessed. The same is true for B.

The Prisoner's Dilemma and the Invisible Hand

The Prisoner's Dilemma is an interesting case in which the Invisible Hand Theorem is not true. When each party acts in his own self-interest, the outcome is not Pareto optimal. If neither confessed, both would be better off. We saw in Chapter 8 that in competitive markets, by contrast, the equilibrium outcome is always Pareto optimal. The fact that the invisible hand can fail in a simple example like the Prisoner's Dilemma makes its success in competitive markets all the more remarkable.

Solving the Prisoner's Dilemma

How can the Prisoner's Dilemma be solved? Suppose that the prisoners of Exhibit 11–5 are members of a crime syndicate that can credibly threaten to impose severe penalties on anyone who confesses. Then the individual prisoners can be induced not to confess, and both will be better off. Contrary to what your intuition may tell you, they both benefit by being "victims" of coercion. (More precisely, each benefits from the coercion applied to the other, and this benefit exceeds the cost of the coercion applied to himself.)

Therefore it is possible that people will prefer to have their options limited in situations that resemble the Prisoner's Dilemma. In China before World War II, goods were commonly transported on barges drawn by teams of about six men. If the barge reached its destination on time (often after a journey of several days), the men were rewarded handsomely. On such a team any given member has an incentive to shirk, in the sense of working less hard than is optimal from the team's point of view. This incentive exists regardless of whether he believes that the others are shirking. Thus the situation is similar to the Prisoner's Dilemma, with the choices "Confess" and "Not Confess" replaced by "Shirk" and "Don't Shirk." As in the Prisoner's Dilemma, an outside enforcer commanding everyone not to shirk can make everyone better off. In recognition of this, it was apparently common for the bargemen themselves to hire a seventh man to whip them when they slacked off!

The Repeated Prisoner's Dilemma

The Prisoner's Dilemma becomes a far richer problem when the two players expect to meet each other repeatedly in similar situations. Even though Prisoner A can always do better in the present game by confessing, he must also worry about whether his actions today will influence Prisoner B's actions tomorrow.

Suppose that A and B plan to play the Prisoner's Dilemma on three separate occasions: Monday, Tuesday, and Wednesday. You might think that each Prisoner would have some incentive not to confess on Monday, so that he develops a reputation for reliability. Let us see whether this is true.

We begin by imagining the situation on Wednesday, which is the easiest day to think about. Since Wednesday is the last day, there are no future games to consider, and the game is just like an ordinary Prisoner's Dilemma. Regardless of what has gone before, each prisoner has the usual incentive to confess.

Now let us imagine the situation on Tuesday. Suppose that on Tuesday Prisoner A does not confess in order to convince Prisoner B that he won't confess on Wednesday. Will Prisoner B believe him? No, because Prisoner B realizes that once Wednesday arrives, Prisoner A will surely want to confess. Since he cannot convince Prisoner B of his good will anyway, Prisoner A confesses on Tuesday as well. By the same logic, so does Prisoner B.

Finally, how will the prisoners behave on Monday? Each one knows, by the logic of the preceding paragraph, that the other will confess on Tuesday. Thus there is no credibility to be gained by not confessing on Monday. Both, therefore, confess on Monday as well.

The same reasoning applies to any repeated Prisoner's Dilemma with a definite ending date. By reasoning backward from that ending date, we see that there is never any incentive to establish a good reputation, since no such attempt can ever be credible.

When there is no definite ending date, the analysis of the repeated Prisoner's Dilemma becomes a subtle and difficult problem.

Tit-for-Tat

In 1984 Professor Robert Axelrod of the University of Michigan announced the results of a remarkable experiment.[11] Axelrod had invited various experts in the fields of psychology, economics, political science, mathematics, and sociology to submit strategies for the repeated Prisoner's Dilemma. Using a computer, he invented one imaginary prisoner with

---

[11]His results are reported in a fascinating book, *The Evolution of Cooperation* (New York: Basic Books, 1984).

each strategy, and he had each prisoner play against each other prisoner in a 200-round repeated game. Each prisoner also played one 200-round game against a carbon copy of himself, and one 200-round game against a prisoner who always played randomly. The jail sentences from Exhibit 11–5 were translated into points as follows:

Sentence	Points
1 year	5
2 years	3
5 years	1
10 years	0

One of the strategies submitted was called "Tit-for-Tat." According to the Tit-for-Tat strategy, the prisoner does not confess in the first round. In future rounds he continues not confessing, except that if the opponent confesses, then the Tit-for-Tat player punishes him by confessing in the next round. In subsequent rounds, he returns to not confessing, confessing only once as punishment each time his opponent confesses.

Tit-for-Tat won the tournament decisively. Thereupon Axelrod organized a new and much larger tournament with 62 entrants. In the second tournament the lengths of games were determined randomly, rather than making them all 200 rounds. Also, all participants in the second tournament were provided with detailed analyses of the outcome of the first tournament, so that they could use these lessons in designing their strategies. Once again, Tit-for-Tat, the simplest strategy submitted, was the decisive winner.

In a final experiment, Axelrod used his computer to simulate future repetitions of the tournament. He assumed that those strategies that did well would be more widely submitted as time went on. Thus a strategy that did well in the first tournament, like Tit-for-Tat, was replicated many times in the second tournament, whereas strategies that did less well were replicated fewer times. This was intended to mimic evolutionary biology, where those animals that succeed in competition have more offspring in future generations. As the tournament was repeated, one could observe the evolution of various strategies. The chief result was that Tit-for-Tat never lost its dominance.

The success of Tit-for-Tat has a paradoxical flavor, in view of the fact that the backward reasoning of the preceding subsection suggests that there is no gain to acquiring a reputation for playing "reasonably" in a repeated Prisoner's Dilemma. The success of Tit-for-Tat seems to rely on just such reputational effects. Thus we have a puzzle. Economists don't always have all the answers.

The Prisoner's Dilemma and the Breakdown of Cartels

We now return to the topic of cartels. In a cartelized industry, price is set above marginal cost. In order to maintain this price, industry output must

Exhibit 11–6   **The Breakdown of Cartels**

		Action of Firm A	
		Cheat	**Not Cheat**
Action of Firm B	**Cheat**	$5 profit each	A gets $3 profit B gets $12 profit
	Not Cheat	A gets $12 profit B gets $3 profit	$10 profit each

Each member of the cartel must decide whether to cheat by producing more than the agreed-upon output. Cheating will increase the cheater's profits (because price is higher than marginal cost) and decrease the other firms' profits (by driving down the price of the product). It is in each firm's interest to cheat, whether it believes the other firm is cheating or not.

---

be held below the competitive level, and each firm is assigned a share of this production. Because price exceeds marginal cost, any given firm can increase its profits by selling a few more items at a slightly lower price. Of course, this increased output will tend to lower the price and to reduce industry-wide profits. For this reason, a monopolist would resist the temptation to increase output. However, a member of the cartel who "cheats" by increasing his output beyond his allotted share will reap all of the benefits from his action while bearing only some of the costs. He gets all of the additional revenue from the increment to output, whereas every-body shares the losses due to the fall in price.

It follows that a cartel member will be less mindful of the negative consequences of his actions than a single monopolist would be. He tends to cheat when he can get away with it, and so does every other member of the cartel. Eventually, output increases all the way out to the competitive level.

The breakdown of cartels is perfectly analogous to the Prisoner's Dilemma. Imagine two firms, A and B, who have formed a cartel and must decide whether to abide by the agreement or to cheat. They are confronted by the options shown in Exhibit 11–6. Reasoning exactly as in the Prisoner's Dilemma, each firm chooses to cheat, and the cartel breaks down.

If a cartel is to succeed, it needs an enforcement mechanism. That is, it needs a way to monitor members' actions and a way to punish those who cheat. Since price-fixing agreements are illegal in the United States, the enforcement must be carried out in secret. (Indeed, since the *Madison Oil* case of 1940, the courts have held that even an attempt to fix prices is illegal under the Sherman Act, regardless of whether the attempt is successful.) Whenever you hear it asserted that a cartel has been successful, your first question should be: What is the enforcement mechanism?

Example: The International Salt Case

To succeed, a cartel must know when its members are cheating. The International Salt Company may have discovered a creative solution to this monitoring problem. The company distributed a patented machine called the Lixator, which was used to dissolve rock salt. In some areas of the country Lixators were sold outright; in others they were leased subject to a requirement that the lessee agree to purchase all of its salt from International. In 1947 the Supreme Court ruled in effect that International Salt had attempted to create monopoly power in the market for salt. As in the case of IBM and its computer cards (see Section 10.3), this explanation is unlikely to be correct. Economists have generally carried the analogy further to suggest that International was price discriminating by effectively charging heavier users more for a Lixator, just as IBM effectively charged heavier users more for a computer.

In 1985 John Peterman of the Federal Trade Commission reviewed the evidence and found that the economists' explanation was also suspect.[12] He discovered a clause in the Lixator rental contract that allowed any firm to buy its salt elsewhere if it could find it at a price lower than International's. Thus International could not have charged more than the going market price for salt; if it had, it wouldn't have sold any.

What, then, could account for the structure of the Lixator contract? Here is one intriguing possibility. Suppose that salt suppliers were colluding. In that case they would have needed a way to gather information on which suppliers were undercutting the agreement, so that the cheaters could be punished. The Lixator contract, with the clause that Peterman discovered, gave International's own customers an incentive to report low salt prices to International. In this way International could be continually informed of who the price cutters were and how much they were charging.

Example: Did OPEC Ever Have Market Power?

The Organization of Petroleum Exporting Countries (OPEC) is often cited as an example of a spectacularly successful cartel. Although the organization was formed in 1960, it first appeared to flex its muscles at the time of the Arab–Israeli War in 1973. Between 1973 and 1980 the real (inflation-adjusted) price of oil increased approximately threefold. This was widely attributed to OPEC's monopoly power, and many economists, familiar with the problems of maintaining a cartel, were surprised that this monopoly power survived as long as it did.[13]

A small number of economists have taken the view that OPEC never succeeded as a cartel in the first place. They give an alternative explanation for the sharp rise in oil prices around 1973. Suppose that due to political

---

[12]John Peterman, "The *International Salt* Case," *Journal of Law and Economics* 22 (1985), 351–364.

[13]By the mid-1980s oil prices had dropped precipitously; nevertheless, by lasting a decade, the cartel far exceeded most economists' expectations.

instability in the early 1970s, foreign (mostly American) companies operating in the Middle East considered it likely that their assets would soon be confiscated. In that case the incentive would be to sell more oil in the present, because whatever is not sold now is lost forever. This would depress prices *below* the usual competitive equilibrium. With the emergence of a strong OPEC, it is argued, the rules of the game became clearer and firms were able to plan for the future with more certainty. Prices would then have risen sharply. According to this scenario, however, the price rise was not from a competitive level to a monopoly level, but instead from a subcompetitive level to a competitive one.

The evidence for this scenario is not strong. We present it not as a probable explanation of events, but rather as an instructive example of how events can admit alternative explanations. It is easy to assert that OPEC controlled oil output, and the assertion is in fact quite likely to be true. However, the mere facts that its members claimed to control output and that the price of oil did rise do not constitute a proof.

The Government as Enforcer

When cartels have been successful, the outside enforcer has often been the government. The most candid example in American history is the National Industrial Recovery Act of 1933, under the provisions of which government and industry leaders met together to plan output levels with the explicit purpose of keeping prices artificially high. The act was unanimously declared unconstitutional by the U.S. Supreme Court two years after its inception.

A more subtle channel through which government plays the role of enforcer is the apparatus of the various federal regulatory agencies. You may be surprised to learn that many industries welcome regulation. A firm that wants to be told how much to produce seems as unlikely as a bargeman who wants to be whipped. Yet, like the bargeman, the firm can find itself in a Prisoner's Dilemma where it benefits from having its actions restricted. In the next section we will explore some of the more common forms of regulatory activity.

11.3 Regulation

Much economic activity in the United States is subject to government regulation of one form or another. Regulations are highly varied in their justifications, their effects, and the institutional arrangements through which they are carried out. A variety of agencies are empowered to devise and enforce economic regulations. Some of these agencies function independently, while others are subsidiary to an executive department. Also, legislatures often pass specific statutes that are designed with regulatory intent.

All of this activity has a wide variety of effects. One of those effects can be to lessen competition in designated industries. With its power to impose legal sanctions, a government agency can reduce output below the competitive level in circumstances where any private cartel agreement would fail for lack of enforcement. In this section we will study several examples of this phenomenon. Of course, the fact that we choose to study this particular aspect of regulation does not mean that other aspects (such as the protection of consumers, the promotion of competition, or the interests of the regulators themselves) are not equally important.

Examples of Regulation

The Interstate Commerce Commission

The Interstate Commerce Commission (ICC) provides an instructive example. The ICC was created in 1887 to regulate the nation's rail system. Today its jurisdiction extends to all interstate surface transportation. Most importantly, it extends to trucking.

No trucking company is permitted to operate without the approval of the ICC. Such authority has historically been extremely difficult to obtain. Existing truckers are given the opportunity to object to new entry. When authority is granted, it specifies the routes that may be served and the type of freight that may be hauled. No trucking firm can expand its activities without ICC approval.

When deregulation of the trucking industry became a political issue in the late 1970s, the American Trucking Association lobbied vigorously to maintain the status quo. Especially since 1980 the ICC has come under continuing pressure from both parties in Congress to curtail its regulatory activities. The outcome of this political process is still unclear.

It is true, of course, that each individual trucking firm would prefer to be unregulated, provided that it could be the only unregulated firm in the industry. The realistic choice, though, is between regulation of all or of none. Given this choice, truckers prefer to be regulated.

Standards of Quality and the FDA

Regulation often takes the form of minimum *quality* standards. By preventing goods below a prescribed minimum quality from reaching the marketplace, such regulations increase the market power of those suppliers whose output meets the prescribed standards. You might think that consumers always benefit when the average quality of goods increases, but a moment's reflection will convince you that this need not be the case. Few would prefer to live in a world in which every car had the quality (and the price tag) of a Rolls Royce. Many consumers choose goods of lower quality because they would rather devote more income to other things. The poor choose goods of lower quality more frequently, and they are therefore hurt disproportionately when low-quality goods disappear from the marketplace. A poor man who is permitted to purchase steak but not hamburger might have to eat potatoes instead of meat.

There are some markets, however, in which most people will instinctively agree that minimum standards of quality are beneficial to consumers. These are the markets in which low-quality goods can be harmful or even fatal, such as the market for drugs. It is particularly revealing, then, to learn that quality standards in the drug industry may have caused more deaths than they have prevented.

This was the striking conclusion reached by Sam Peltzman in a study reported in 1973.[14] He examined the effects of the "Kefauver amendments" of 1962, which required drug manufacturers to prove both the safety and the effectiveness of their products before they could reach the market. The Food and Drug Administration (FDA) is the agency charged with enforcing this requirement.

The Kefauver amendments have saved lives by protecting consumers from harmful drugs. They have cost lives by delaying the appearance of useful drugs; people have died while the drugs that could have saved them were still in the testing process. Because the cost of testing is a disincentive to innovate, the amendments have probably cost additional lives by reducing the number of new drugs that are developed at all. They have also raised the price of existing drugs by reducing the number of substitutes. How can these effects be weighed against each other, and which are the most significant?

By comparing the rate of new-product development in the drug industry before and after 1962, Peltzman was able to estimate the costs and benefits of the Kefauver amendments to consumers. He found that the net effect was overwhelmingly negative. The amendments reduced the number of new drugs entering the marketplace from approximately 41 per year to approximately 16 per year, and they introduced an average delay of two years for a drug to reach the marketplace.

The Kefauver amendments delayed for many years the introduction in American markets of effective medications called beta blockers that can save the lives of heart attack victims and have long been available in Europe. In the AIDS epidemic of the 1980s, the FDA relaxed the rules substantially, but promising drugs such as AZT were nevertheless unavailable to victims for several months while the FDA conducted its experiments. Of course, these costs are partially offset by the FDA's successes in keeping dangerous drugs out of the marketplace, but Peltzman's study found that the costs of the Kefauver amendments still far exceed the benefits to consumers.

By restricting the supply of new drugs to the marketplace, the FDA keeps the price of many existing drugs high. Thus, regardless of its effect

---

[14]Sam Peltzman, "An Evaluation of Consumer Protection Legislation: The 1962 Drug Amendments," *Journal of Political Economy* 81 (1973), 1049–1091.

on consumers, drug safety regulation has been beneficial to many drug manufacturers.

Professional Licensing

Another area in which quality standards play a major role is professional licensing. The licensing requirements for doctors, lawyers, taxicab drivers, and cosmetologists prevent entry to these occupations and raise the prices of those who manage to obtain licenses. Many of those who are denied entry are undoubtedly charlatans; others are potentially competent practitioners who would provide service at a lower price than is now available.

The medical profession provides a particularly instructive example. State licensure began around the turn of the century at the behest of the American Medical Association (AMA). In 1910 the AMA commissioned a report (the Flexner Report) on medical education that strongly recommended that rigid and demanding standards be applied to all medical schools. The Flexner recommendations were soon enacted into law, and the AMA subsequently gained control of the process for accrediting medical school programs. As a result, the number of medical schools in the United States had fallen by more than half by 1944. Entry was (and is now) heavily restricted and under control of the AMA.

In order for physicians to retain and exercise their monopoly power, there must be an enforcement mechanism for punishing individuals who cut prices. According to Professor Reuben Kessel,[15] the AMA provides this too. Membership in county medical societies is systematically denied to price cutters. A network of regulations makes it difficult for nonmembers of these associations to practice at hospitals or to become specialists. Nonmembers are punished in other ways as well: Kessel makes the case that disgruntled patients find it far easier to find expert witnesses in a malpractice suit against a nonmember than in a suit against a member.

Although medical licensing is widely advertised as protective of the public, many aspects of the system seem to have been designed primarily to restrict entry rather than to ensure quality. Kessel calls attention to the fact that medical licenses are granted for life, whereas driver's licenses, for example, must be periodically renewed.

Restrictions on Advertising

Another way in which entry to a market can be effectively curtailed is by restricting the ability of consumers to learn about new suppliers. Suppliers who cannot make their existence known are essentially excluded from the market. In practice, this is often accomplished through restrictions on advertising. Professional societies such as the American Medical Association and the American Bar Association have gone to extraordinary lengths to restrict advertising by their members.

---

[15]Reuben Kessel, "The AMA and the Supply of Physicians," *Law and Contemporary Problems* 35 (1970), 267–283.

Many reasons have been offered to suspect that advertising raises prices. It is sometimes alleged that buyers must "pay for the advertising as well as the product." On the other hand, advertising saves the consumer the cost of having to search for information about available products. Indeed, a buyer who prefers not to pay for advertising always has the option to incur the costs of seeking out a seller who does not advertise and to buy the product at a correspondingly lower price. When buyers do not do this, they reveal that they value the informational content of advertising at a price at least equal to whatever they are paying for it.

In fact, by providing information about a wide array of sellers, advertising can promote competition and might therefore actually *reduce* prices. In 1972 Lee Benham set out to investigate this question in the market for eyeglasses.[16] This market was particularly suitable for study since there is wide variation in advertising restrictions across states. He found that in states where advertising was prohibited, the price of eyeglasses was higher by 25 to 100%. This particularly persuasive empirical study has convinced many economists that the net effect of advertising is often (though surely not always) to lower prices.

Minimum Wages

Instead of setting quality standards, the government sometimes sets minimum prices below which goods cannot be sold. This excludes the producers of low-quality goods from the marketplace, increasing the demand for those high-quality goods that are close substitutes.

By far the most important example is the federal minimum wage law. Although this law is often presented as protective of the unskilled, it is precisely they whom it excludes from the labor market. At a minimum wage of $3.35 per hour, someone who produces $3.00 worth of output per hour will not be hired to work. Overwhelming empirical evidence has convinced most economists that the minimum wage is a major cause of unemployment, particularly among the unskilled.

Among the beneficiaries of the minimum wage law are the more highly skilled workers who remain employed and who can command higher wages in the absence of less skilled competition. These more highly skilled workers tend to be represented by labor unions, which, not surprisingly, tend to support increases in the minimum wage.

Minimum wage laws also have other, less obvious effects. When the federal minimum wage was first proposed in the 1930s, it was heavily supported by the northern textile industry. The reason was that wages were lower in the South than in the North, due partly to a lower cost of living in the South. As a result, northern firms found it difficult to compete. By imposing a federally mandated minimum wage, northern producers hoped to eliminate the advantage held by their southern competi-

---

[16]Lee Benham, "The Effect of Advertising on the Price of Eyeglasses," *Journal of Law and Economics* 15 (1972), 337–352.

tion, and indeed hoped to drive the South out of textile manufacturing altogether.

Blue Laws

Laws that prohibit transactions at certain times of the day or week tend to inhibit competition and raise prices. So-called "blue laws" in many states prohibit the sale of various goods on Sunday. This solves a Prisoner's Dilemma for suppliers. Any given supplier must choose between the options "work on Sunday" and "not work on Sunday." Each will choose to work on Sunday whether his competitors are doing so or not; but each prefers to have nobody working Sunday than to have everybody working. Blue laws allow the supplier to watch football on Sunday afternoon without losing his business to a rival. Of course, this boon to suppliers comes at the expense of consumers for whom Sunday is a convenient shopping day.

An interesting variant of the blue laws was recently in effect in the city of Chicago. Until about 1980 it was illegal in Chicago to buy meat after 6 p.m. Repeal was opposed by the butchers' union.

Example: The Economics of Polygamy

The laws against polygamy provide an instructive example of the effects of output restrictions. We will consider the effect of a law that forbids any man from marrying more than one woman.

We can view men as suppliers of "husbandships," which are purchased by women at a price.[17] This price has many subtle components, including all of the agreements, spoken and unspoken, that married couples enter into. Choices about where to live, how many children to have, who will do the dishes, and where to go on Saturday nights are all contained in the price of the marriage. When husbandships are scarce, men can require more concessions on such issues as conditions of their marriages. For example, if there were only one marriageable man and many marriageable women, the man would be in a position to insist that any woman he marries must agree to attend professional wrestling with him every weeknight (assuming that this is something he values). If one woman will not agree to this price, he can probably find another woman who will.

Thus the price of a husbandship is higher when husbandships are scarce, and, similarly, the price of a husbandship is low when husbandships are abundant. If each man wanted to marry four women, the price of husbandships would be bid down (or, equivalently, the price of wifeships would be bid up) to the point where men would have to make

---

[17]Because we are examining the market for husbands, men are the producers and women the consumers. It would be equally correct to treat the marriage market as a market for wives, in which women are the producers and men the consumers. Since we are investigating the effects of a law that restricts the supply of husbands, it is more convenient to think of "husbandships" rather than "wifeships" as the commodity being traded.

considerable concessions in order to attract even one wife. It is in the interests of men as producers to restrict output so that this does not happen. Antipolygamy laws accomplish this. Thus the analysis suggests that laws against polygamy, like other laws restricting output, benefit producers (in this case men) and hurt consumers (in this case women).

Sometimes students argue that no woman in the modern world would want to be part of a multiwife marriage, and that therefore women could not possibly benefit from the legalization of polygamy. But this is incorrect, because even under polygamy those women who wanted to could demand as a condition of marriage that their husbands agree not to take any additional wives. And even if no man took more than one wife, the price of wives would still be higher.

For example, imagine a one-husband one-wife family where an argument has begun over whose turn it is to do the dishes. If polygamy were legal, the wife could threaten to leave and go marry the couple next door unless the husband concedes that it is his turn. With polygamy outlawed, she does not have this option and might end up with dishpan hands.

Another reason why students are sometimes surprised by this conclusion is that they are aware of polygamous societies in which the status of women is not high. But, of course, the difference in polygamy laws is not the only important difference between those societies and our own. The fact that polygamy is legal in many places where women are otherwise oppressed does not constitute an argument that the oppression is caused by polygamy. Our analysis compares the status of women with and without legalized polygamy on the assumption that other social institutions are held constant.

In view of our analysis, it is interesting that polygamy laws are often alleged to "protect" women. It has been observed[18] that laws prohibiting any man from marrying more than one woman are perfectly analogous to laws preventing any firm from hiring more than one black. Surely no one would be so audacious as to claim that the purpose of such a law was to protect blacks.

What Can Regulators Regulate?

In any study of the effects of regulation, it is necessary to ask what regulators actually do. In the last 25 years economists have become increasingly aware that regulators' own descriptions of their activities should not always be taken at face value.

In 1962 George Stigler and Claire Friedland examined the effects of regulation in the electric power industry.[19] They examined electric rates in the years 1912–1937. During these years some states regulated the price of

---

[18]Gary Becker, "A Theory of Marriage," *Journal of Political Economy* 81 (1973), 813–846.

[19]George Stigler and Claire Friedland, "What Can Regulators Regulate? The Case of Electricity," *Journal of Law and Economics* 82 (1974), S11–S26.

electricity and others did not. Stigler and Friedland found that the presence of regulation had no observable effect on the actual price of electricity. The evidence suggested that the regulatory commission consistently ends up setting the price that the utilities would have chosen anyway.

In 1964 Stigler applied a similar analysis to the regulation of the securities industry by the Securities and Exchange Commission (SEC).[20] The SEC requires issuers of securities (for example, corporate stocks) to make public disclosures of relevant information. If you try to sell stock in a gold mine that has never produced any gold, the SEC will require that this fact be disclosed to potential buyers. Stigler examined the performance of newly issued stocks compared to the performance of the market as a whole, before and after the formation of the SEC in 1934. He found that there was no change in the propensity of newly issued stocks to perform well. It appeared that the SEC made no real difference; there is no evidence that the mix of securities that was offered under regulation differed appreciably from the mix of securities that would have been offered in an unregulated market.

These and other studies have convinced a growing number of economists that an industry should not necessarily be considered regulated just because of the existence of an agency with the formal power to regulate it. In many cases there may be political or other considerations that prevent the agency from ever taking any steps that actually have the effect of altering economic behavior. Whether or not an allegedly "regulated" industry is really regulated in any meaningful sense is an empirical question, one that must be decided on a case by case basis.

Creative Response and Unexpected Consequences

Although it can be in the interest of an industry to be regulated, it is almost always in the interest of an individual firm to avoid the effects of regulation when possible. This often leads firms to engage in **creative response,** behaving in ways that conform to the letter of the law while undermining its spirit.

Creative response
A response to a regulation that conforms to the letter of the law while undermining its spirit.

Example: Affirmative Action Laws

Affirmative action laws provide an example where a creative response may have led to consequences directly contradictory to the intent of the original legislation. These laws and regulations arose from the observation that black workers were systematically paid less than white workers. They required employers to remedy this imbalance by paying higher wages to black workers.

However, wages are only part of the compensation that a worker receives. Typically, he receives a variety of valuable fringe benefits as well. One of the most important fringe benefits, especially in entry level posi-

---

[20]George Stigler, "Public Regulation of the Securities Market," *Journal of Business* 37 (1964).

tions, is on-the-job training. Such training enables the employee to acquire basic skills that will raise his income later in life. Its value often represents a substantial portion of the employee's total compensation.

Since on-the-job training is largely unobservable to outsiders, employers can adjust its quantity without being found guilty of violating those laws that regulate workers' compensation. Thus some employers were able to comply with the affirmative action regulations without actually changing the total value of the compensation that they offered to blacks. They simply paid a higher wage, satisfying the regulator, while compensating by offering less on-the-job training. Between the years 1966 and 1974 the *observable* wage differences between blacks and whites were essentially eliminated, but they were partially replaced by *unobservable* differences. For black workers this meant higher starting salaries, less on-the-job training, and lower future wages than before affirmative action.

The net effect of all this on the economic status of blacks could be either positive or negative. In one study[21] Professor Edward Lazear found that the relative economic status of blacks (taking account of all their expected future earnings) was not improved by the affirmative action laws. In fact, his evidence supported just the opposite conclusion—that during the period 1966–1972 the gap between black and white compensation, inclusive of the value of on-the-job training, actually widened.

Example: Reasonable Quantities of Sale Items

In the late 1970s the Federal Trade Commission (FTC), which regulates (among other things) against false and deceptive advertising, discovered that one of its regulations led to responses that were counterproductive. The FTC periodically receives complaints about the unavailability of advertised specials. Consumers travel to stores that are advertising items at unusually low prices, only to find that those items are sold out shortly after the commencement of the sale. Understandably, these consumers are annoyed. The FTC responded to these complaints in the mid-1970s by issuing a series of regulations requiring stores to have on hand a "reasonable quantity" of any item that was advertised at a sale price.

To understand the effect of these regulations, it is necessary first to understand the reasons for sales. In many (though certainly not all) cases a store will decide to discontinue stocking a certain item and will want to dispose quickly of its remaining stock. In such cases ordering sufficient additional inventory to have a "reasonable quantity" on hand would contravene the very purpose of the sale. Therefore, one effect of the regulations was that sales of this type were discontinued. In view of this effect, fewer items were offered at sale prices. At the same time, it meant that when there *were* sales, the sale items were usually available.

---

[21]Edward Lazear, "The Narrowing of Black–White Wage Differentials Is Illusory," *American Economic Review* 69 (1979), 553–564.

Throughout the late 1970s the FTC interviewed consumers about their feelings regarding the new rules. On the basis of these interviews, the FTC decided that the rules tended to benefit people with higher incomes at the expense of the poor. People with high incomes have a high value of time; they find it very costly to drive to a store only to discover that the item they are shopping for is out of stock. To them the cost of these fruitless shopping trips outweighs the benefit of having more sales to choose from. People with low incomes have a lower value of time and place greater value on being able to buy at sale prices. They prefer there to be more sales, even if the stores sometimes run out before they get there.

On the basis of this analysis, the FTC rescinded its rules on advertised specials.

Positive Theories of Regulation

Throughout this section we have examined some of the consequences of certain existing regulations. However, we have made no attempt to address the question of why some industries are regulated and others are not. We have focused primarily on ways in which regulation might act to limit competition. But we have made no attempt to formulate a general principle concerning when regulations will limit competition and when they will serve some other function, such as promoting economic efficiency.

Many economists think that there is a need for a positive theory of regulation, to predict the circumstances under which various types of regulations arise and what their effects will be. Such a theory would have to explain why the trucking industry is more heavily regulated than the airline industry, why some occupations require professional licenses while others don't, and why electricity prices seem to have been unaffected by regulation. A complete theory would begin with an explicit account of what it is that regulators are trying to accomplish. For example, regulators might be motivated by a desire to redistribute wealth in certain ways, or by a desire to protect consumers from major disasters, or even by a desire to maximize their own power. From such assumptions, one could derive conclusions about when, where, and what types of regulations are most likely to occur.

A theory of this sort might also be used to explain why regulations are selectively enforced. For example, radar detectors are legal in 48 states, despite the fact that their only purpose is to facilitate breaking the law. Why are people permitted to purchase the opportunity to violate speed limits with a reduced probability of punishment?

Various theories are consistent with this observation. If the goal of regulators is to increase economic efficiency, they might want to allow speeding by those whose time is sufficiently valuable. These would be primarily those who find it worthwhile to invest in a radar detector. An alternative theory is that regulators prefer not to antagonize the politically powerful, and that those who are wealthy enough to want radar detectors are also powerful enough to keep the regulators at bay.

Which theory seems more sensible to you? Can you think of other examples that would tend to confirm or refute one of these theories? What alternative theories can you propose?

11.4 Oligopoly

Oligopoly
An industry in which individual firms can influence market conditions.

An **oligopoly** is an industry in which the number of firms is sufficiently small that any one firm's actions can affect market conditions. Thus in an oligopoly each firm has a certain degree of monopoly power. The behavior of such firms depends on many things, including whether they are threatened by potential entry. We will first consider markets in which entry is costless (and therefore an ever-present threat) and then markets in which the number of firms is fixed.

Contestable Markets

Contestable market
A market in which firms can enter and exit costlessly.

A market in which firms can enter and exit costlessly is called a **contestable market.**[22] A commonly cited example is the market for airplane service on a particular route, say from Houston to Dallas. The owner of an airplane that is currently flying back and forth between Houston and San Antonio can easily move into the Houston-to-Dallas market if he senses a profit opportunity, and can easily return to the Houston-to-San Antonio market whenever he chooses to.

In a contestable market even a single firm producing a unique product with no close substitutes might not be able to engage in monopoly pricing, because the profits that it would earn by doing so would lure entrants and destroy its market position. Exhibit 11–7 illustrates the position of a monopolist threatened by potential entry. Assuming all firms are identical, their entry price will be P_0.

▷ *Exercise 11.5* Explain why firms would enter if the market price of output were P_0 but would not enter at any lower price.

It follows that the market price cannot be higher than P_0, since any higher price will attract entry. At this price the firm will produce the quantity Q_0. The market will demand Q_1, which may be several times Q_0. If, for example, Q_1 is twice Q_0, there will be room for a second firm to imitate exactly the actions of the first firm without exhausting market demand. If Q_1 is seven times Q_0, there will be room for seven firms altogether. In general, the number of firms that actually enter will be equal

---

[22]The study of contestable markets is a very new field in economics. The state of the art is surveyed by its founders in W. Baumol, S. Panzar, and R. Willig, *Contestable Markets and the Theory of Industry Structure* (San Diego: Harcourt Brace Jovanovich, 1982).

Exhibit 11–7   A Contestable Market

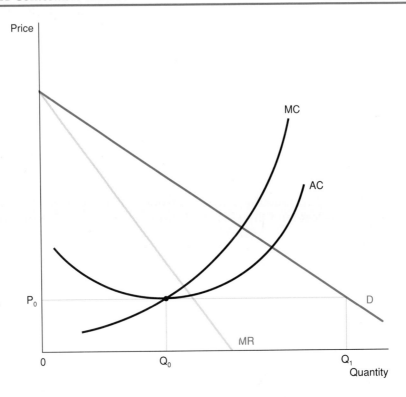

If the market is contestable, firms will enter at any price above P_0. Therefore the market price cannot be higher than P_0, because any higher price would attract entry. At this price the firm supplies Q_0 units of output and the market demands Q_1. Thus there is room in the industry for Q_1/Q_0 firms.

to Q_1/Q_0, each producing Q_0 items at a price of P_0, which equals both average and marginal cost.[23] In other words, potential entry will force firms to behave as competitors, even if there are very few firms.

> **In a contestable market with identical firms whose average cost curves cross the industry demand curve in the region where they are upward sloping, price, average cost, and marginal cost are all equal.**

Contestable Markets and Natural Monopoly

There is also the possibility of natural monopoly in a contestable market. That is, the firm's average cost curve might still be downward sloping

---

[23]There is a slight problem related to the fact that Q_1/Q_0 may not be exactly equal to an integer, in which case we expect the number of firms to be either the integer just above or just below Q_1/Q_0.

Exhibit 11–8 **Natural Monopoly in a Contestable Market**

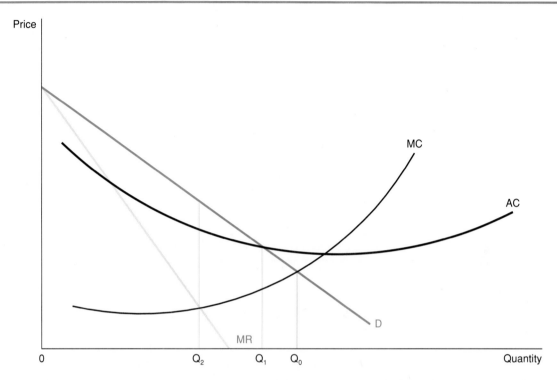

If the market is contestable, a natural monopolist must set output at Q_1 so that he earns zero profits and avoids attracting entry.

where it crosses industry demand. This is shown in Exhibit 11–8. In this case a monopoly producer cannot operate at the "competitive" point Q_0, because his profits there would be negative. On the other hand, if he follows the usual monopoly pricing rule of setting marginal cost equal to marginal revenue (producing Q_2), he may earn positive profits and lure other firms into the industry. The threat of entry forces him to operate at the zero profits point Q_1.

Oligopoly with a Fixed Number of Firms

When there is no threat of entry, the behavior of an oligopoly is more difficult to predict. One possibility is the formation of a cartel. As we have seen, the Prisoner's Dilemma guarantees that there are forces tending to undermine the success of cartels. On the other hand, cartels are really *repeated* Prisoner's Dilemmas, since firms produce output every day. We have also seen that the outcome of repeated Prisoner's Dilemmas is hard to predict.

Exhibit 11–9   The Cournot Model of Oligopoly

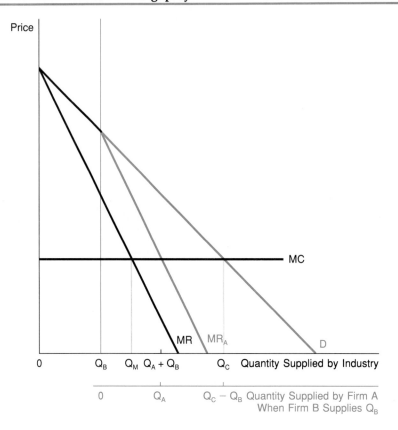

We assume that two identical firms have the flat marginal cost curve MC and face a market demand curve D. A competitive industry would produce the quantity Q_C. A monopolist would produce the quantity $Q_M = \frac{1}{2}Q_C$, where MC crosses the marginal revenue curve MR.

If Firm A assumes that Firm B will always produce quantity Q_B, then Firm A views itself as a monopolist in the market for the remaining quantity. The demand curve in that market is the blue part of the market demand curve, measured along the blue axis. The marginal revenue curve is the blue curve MR_A. Firm A produces the monopoly quantity Q_A, which is half the competitive quantity $(Q_C - Q_B)$. Combining this fact with the equation $Q_A = Q_B$ (which follows from the fact that the firms are identical), we compute that $Q_A = Q_B = \frac{1}{3}Q_C$. Thus the industry output is $\frac{2}{3}Q_C$, less than the competitive output but more than the monopoly output.

When there is no collusion, each firm's actions depend on the actions that it expects the other firms to take. Therefore the way in which firms form their expectations about each other's behavior is a crucial ingredient in modeling oligopoly. We will examine two different models that proceed

Cournot model
A model of oligopoly in which firms take their rivals' output as given.

Bertrand model
A model of oligopoly in which firms take their rivals' prices as given.

from different assumptions about expectation formation. In one, the **Cournot model,**[24] firms assume that their rivals will never change their output. In the other, the **Bertrand model,**[25] firms assume that their rivals will never change their price.

The Cournot Model

To simplify the analysis, we will assume an industry with exactly two identical firms having the flat marginal cost curve shown in Exhibit 11–9. We will also assume a straight line demand curve, so that marginal revenue has exactly twice the slope of demand. A monopoly would produce the quantity Q_M and a competitive industry would produce the quantity Q_C. Because of what we have just said about the slopes of the curves, we must have

$$Q_M = \frac{1}{2} \cdot Q_C.$$

Now let us see what the two firms will produce. Suppose that Firm B produces the quantity Q_B and Firm A makes the assumption that this quantity will never change. Then Firm A views itself as a monopolist in the market for the remaining quantity. That is, Firm A is a monopolist in a market where the zero quantity axis is the blue vertical line in Exhibit 11–9, and the demand curve is the blue part of the industry demand curve. In such a market the marginal revenue curve is the blue curve MR_A parallel to the industry marginal revenue curve MR. Firm A produces the quantity Q_A, where $MC = MR_A$. Since this is the monopoly quantity, it must lie halfway between Firm A's zero quantity axis at Q_B and the competitive point $Q_C - Q_B$. That is

$$Q_A = \frac{1}{2} (Q_C - Q_B).$$

We can also write one additional equation. Since it is assumed that Firms A and B are identical, it is reasonable to expect that they will produce equal quantities of output. This gives us the equation

$$Q_A = Q_B.$$

Putting the two equations together, we get

$$Q_A = \frac{1}{2} (Q_C - Q_A),$$

which can be solved for Q_A, giving

$$Q_A = \frac{1}{3} Q_C.$$

---

[24]For the nineteenth-century French mathematician Augustin Cournot.

[25]For the nineteenth-century French economist Joseph Bertrand.

In words, each firm produces ⅓ of the competitive quantity, so that between them they produce ⅔ of the competitive quantity. This is more than the monopoly output, which is only ½ of the competitive quantity.

The Bertrand Model

The Bertrand model has the same flavor as the Cournot model. In the Cournot model each firm assumes that its rivals will never change quantity. In the Bertrand model each firm assumes that its rivals will never change price.

As long as price exceeds marginal cost, an oligopolist in the Bertrand model will always want to undercut his rivals by offering a slightly lower price. Since he assumes that his rivals will not meet this price cut, it follows that he will be able to capture the entire market for himself. This is a profitable strategy. The tiniest of price cuts leads to a sizable increase in sales, and all of these sales are at a price that exceeds marginal cost.

Bertrand oligopolists will continue to undercut one another until price falls to marginal cost. Thus, according to Bertrand, price and output will be the same under oligopoly as they are under competition.

Criticism of the Cournot and Bertrand Models

Many economists are uncomfortable with both the Cournot and the Bertrand models of oligopoly, because each model posits that firms make incorrect assumptions about their rivals' behavior. In the Cournot model firms assume that their own choice of output will not affect their rivals' choices, despite the fact that they know that their rivals' choices are affecting their own. The same is true in the Bertrand model regarding prices instead of quantities.

This criticism highlights the major difficulty that economists face when they attempt to model oligopoly behavior. The assumptions that firms make about one another's behavior are crucial elements in the determination of their own behavior, and the economist must therefore presume to know something about those assumptions. If the assumptions turn out to be incorrect, firms should become aware of this fact over time, invalidating the model. In the real world we expect that oligopolists have at least reasonably accurate information about how their rivals behave, and we would like our models to reflect that fact. Unfortunately, satisfactory models with this property have proven difficult to construct. In much recent research, game theory has proved to be an increasingly effective tool.

11.5 Monopolistic Competition and Product Differentiation

One strategy for acquiring some degree of monopoly power in a market that is basically competitive is called **product differentiation.** As its name implies, this strategy involves producing a product that differs sufficiently

Product differentiation
The production of a product that is unique but has many close substitutes.

from the output of other producers that some consumers will have a distinct preference for it. Crest and Colgate both produce toothpaste, but they do not produce identical products. The two products are close substitutes, and neither can be priced very differently from the other without a substantial loss of market share. At the same time, there are some consumers with a very strong preference for one or the other brand, so that each firm faces a demand curve that is at least slightly downward sloping.

Products with brand names are product differentiated simply by virtue of having different brand names. But other characteristics can differentiate them as well. The location at which a product is sold can differentiate it from others. A 7–Eleven two blocks from your house is not the same to you as a 7–Eleven a mile and a half away, although they are probably close substitutes.

Monopolistic Competition

Monopolistic competition
The theory of markets in which there are many similar but differentiated products.

The theory of markets in which there are many similar but differentiated products is called the theory of **monopolistic competition.** The first panel of Exhibit 11–10 illustrates the conditions facing a monopolistically competitive firm. Suppose that the firm is currently charging price P and selling quantity Q. The demand curve d shows how much the firm can sell at any given price on the assumption that all other firms continue to charge the original price P.

▷ *Exercise 11.6* Explain why you might expect the curve d to be quite elastic compared to the demand curve facing an ordinary monopolist.

The quantity Q is determined by the condition that MC = mr, where MC is the firm's marginal cost curve and mr is the marginal revenue curve associated with d. In panel A of the exhibit, the firm is earning positive profits, since the price P exceeds average cost at quantity Q.

In the long run these profits will attract entry by other firms selling similar products. As a result, the demand curve facing the firm will shift downward, to d' in panel B of Exhibit 11–10. The firm produces quantity Q' and charges price P'. At this point price and average cost are equal, so that profits are zero and there is no further entry.

At the long-run equilibrium quantity Q', the demand curve must touch the average cost curve to give zero profits. You might wonder why we have drawn the curves tangent rather than crossing. The reason is that if the curves crossed, the firm could earn positive profits by producing a quantity slightly less than Q'. But we know that Q', the zero profits point, is also the point of maximum profits, since it is the point where MC = mr. Thus it cannot be correct to draw the average cost curve actually crossing demand.

Exhibit 11–10   Monopolistic Competition

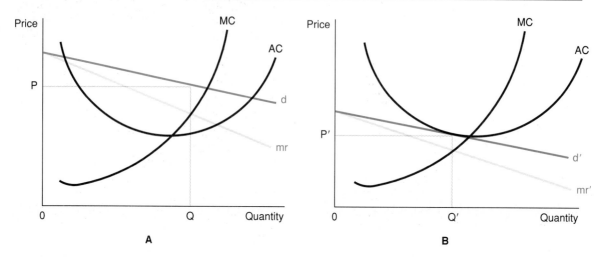

Panel A shows a short-run equilibrium in which the firm sells quantity Q at price P. Here price exceeds average cost, so the firm earns positive profits. In the long run entry drives the demand curve facing this firm down to d' in panel B, where the firm is just able to earn zero profits by selling quantity Q' at price P'.

Welfare Aspects of Monopolistic Competition

In Exhibit 11–10 we can see that price is set above marginal cost by a monopolistic competitor, so that the level of output is suboptimal. On the other hand, since we expect monopolistic competitors to face quite elastic demand curves, the deviation of output from the competitive level might not be too great.

A related issue is that a monopolistic competitor, as shown in Exhibit 11–10, does not produce at the minimum point of his average cost curve. Indeed, he cannot do so, since in long-run equilibrium he produces at a point of tangency between his average cost curve and his downward-sloping demand curve. It follows that if a monopolistically competitive industry were replaced by a competitive one, the same output could be produced at lower cost.

It is sometimes argued that monopolistically competitive firms tend to invest more in advertising and other methods of luring each other's customers than is socially optimal. Insofar as such practices simply shift customers from one firm to another without changing the nature of the products that are sold, their costs represent unnecessary social losses.

Balanced against all of this is the observation that monopolistically competitive industries do provide consumers with something that competitive industries do not, namely, differentiated products. Although Burger King and McDonald's are already similar, many people would be unhappy if one of them became exactly like the other.

Exhibit 11–11   Ice Cream Vendors on a Beach

If the vendors start out in the locations shown, each will move toward the center in an attempt to gain more customers. The equilibrium is reached when they are located right next to each other and can move no further.

How can we weigh the inefficiencies associated with monopolistic competition on the one hand against the benefits of product differentiation on the other? Although many economists have strong beliefs about the relative importance of these phenomena, there is not yet any general theory available that allows us to answer such a question in a definitive way.

The Economics of Location

Depending on market conditions, firms may choose either to exaggerate or to minimize their differences. An amusing example involves two ice cream vendors on a beach. Suppose that the beach is a straight line one mile long and that bathers are distributed evenly along it. There are two ice cream vendors, indistinguishable except for location, and each bather will patronize the vendor nearest him. Where will the vendors locate?

Exhibit 11–11 shows the initial positions of the vendors. Given these positions, vendor A will soon realize that he can have more customers if he moves to the right. As long as he stays to the left of vendor B, he will retain all of the customers to his own left, and he can acquire more by moving a bit to the right. Similarly, vendor B has much to gain and nothing to lose by shifting to the left. The only possible equilibrium is for the two vendors to locate right next to each other, exactly at the half-mile mark!

▷ *Exercise 11.7* What would happen if the vendors started out next to each other but somewhere other than at the halfway point?

Perhaps this example provides a metaphor for the behavior of the two major American political parties. With voters distributed on a continuum from left to right, and voting for the party "closest" to themselves, the parties will behave just as the ice cream vendors do. Do you believe that this metaphor captures a significant feature of reality?

Summary

This chapter surveys a number of examples and models in which firms exercise or attempt to exercise various degrees of monopoly power.

Horizontal mergers can both reduce production costs and create monopoly power, and therefore they have ambiguous welfare consequences. Vertical mergers can have the effect of reducing the exercise of monopoly power, since no monopolist would want to extract monopoly profits from one of its own subsidiaries.

In order to eliminate rivals, a firm might engage in the practice of predatory pricing, or it might attempt a strategy of buying out its rivals. Each of these strategies is severely limited. In the case of predatory pricing, there is the threat that rivals will resurface after prices are raised. In the case of buy-outs, new rivals are attracted to the industry by the prospect of being bought out.

When the firms in an industry can collude, they increase producers' surplus and thus can improve each firm's welfare through a system of side payments. However, as in the Prisoner's Dilemma, each individual firm has an incentive to cheat. The reason is that a cartel sets price higher than marginal cost, so that each firm will want to sell more than it is supposed to under the cartel agreement. Therefore cartels tend to break down unless there is a good enforcement mechanism.

In addition to its other purposes, government regulation can serve as an enforcement mechanism for a cartel. Regulations restrict output in many ways. Professional licensing, minimum quality standards, minimum prices, advertising restrictions, and blue laws can all serve to restrict output and keep prices high. However, there is some evidence that the power of regulators to alter market conditions is sometimes less than it seems.

In contestable markets, entry and exit are costless. Even when there is only one firm in a contestable market, that firm must earn zero profits because of the threat of entry.

The Cournot and Bertrand models apply to oligopolies with a fixed number of firms. In the Cournot model, firms take their rivals' output as given and end up producing more than the monopoly quantity but less than the competitive quantity. In the Bertrand model, firms take their rivals' prices as given and end up producing the competitive quantity.

Under monopolistic competition, firms produce differentiated products. Each firm's product is unique but is similar to those of other firms. Thus each firm faces a downward-sloping but nevertheless quite elastic demand curve. In the long run, entry forces profits to zero, which implies that firms must *not* be operating at the point of minimum average cost. The negative welfare consequences of this must be balanced against the gains to consumers from having a wide variety of product options, but economists have developed no good general theory of the welfare consequences of monopolistic competition.

Review Questions

R1. What is the distinction between a horizontal merger and a vertical merger?

R2. Under what circumstances is a horizontal merger welfare-improving?

R3. What are some of the advantages and disadvantages to a firm from engaging in predatory pricing? From a strategy of buying out rivals?

R4. Explain why resale price maintenance might be expected to benefit consumers.

R5. Why do both prisoners confess in the Prisoner's Dilemma? In what sense is the outcome not Pareto-optimal? How could both prisoners be made better off?

R6. Explain the analogy between the Prisoner's Dilemma and the breakdown of cartels.

R7. Why might the firms in an industry want to be regulated?

R8. What determines the number of firms in a contestable market?

R9. Explain carefully how output is determined in a Cournot oligopoly.

R10. Explain carefully how price is determined in a Bertrand oligopoly.

R11. What disturbing feature do the Bertrand and Cournot models have in common?

R12. Explain carefully how price and output are determined under monopolistic competition.

R13. Explain why, in a long-run monopolistically competitive equilibrium, average cost is never minimized.

Numerical Exercises

N1. Suppose that a monopoly steel producer produces steel at zero marginal cost, and sells to a monopoly automaker at a price P_{steel}. The automaker has no costs other than the cost of steel, which is converted into cars at the rate of one ton of steel to one car. There is no other way to produce a car than to use a ton of steel. The demand for cars is given by $Q_{cars} = 100 - P_{cars}$.

   a. For a given price of steel, what quantity of cars will the automaker produce in order to maximize profits? (*Hint:* The function $-Q^2 + kQ$, with k constant, is maximized at $Q = k/2$.)

   b. What is the equation for the automaker's demand curve for steel?

   c. How much steel is produced? At what price? How many cars are produced? At what price?

   d. If the steel producer acquires ownership of the automaker, how many cars are produced? At what price?

N2. Dr. Miles is a monopolist who sells a type of patent medicine through competitive retailers. The demand curve for this patent medicine is given by $Q = 100 - 2P$, where P is the price and Q is the number of bottles sold.

   a. If Dr. Miles has zero marginal cost, how many bottles of medicine will he sell and at what price? Calculate the consumers' surplus. Calculate Dr. Miles's producer's surplus.

   b. Now suppose that retailers are able to provide their customers with valuable services by explain-

ing how the medicine is to be used, what ailments it is effective against, and so on. By incurring a cost of C in time and effort per bottle sold, the retailer can provide services that consumers value at V per bottle sold, where V is given by $V = 5C - C^2$. What is the socially optimal amount of service per bottle for retailers to offer? What is the cost of this service?

   c. Now suppose that retailers who offer services do not sell any additional medicine, because customers accept the services and then shop elsewhere, buying from a cut-rate supplier who offers no services. To combat this, Dr. Miles institutes a fair trade agreement under which he will sell at a wholesale price of P_0 but retailers must charge a retail price of P_1. Retailers have no other costs. Explain why retailers will incur costs of service equal to $C = P_1 - P_0$. What is the socially optimal value for C?

   d. Taking C as given, write the equation of the new demand curve that retailers face after Dr. Miles institutes fair trade. Write the equation of the new demand curve Dr. Miles faces. In view of his wanting to face the highest possible demand curve, what value will Dr. Miles choose for C?

   e. Using your answers to part d, calculate the new price P_0 that Dr. Miles will charge, the new quantity sold, the new consumers' surplus, and the new producer's surplus.

Problem Set

1. *True or false:* Resale price maintenance can be good for consumers because it means there will be more dealer services. Thus if the marginal value of dealer services decreases rapidly, then the benefits of resale price maintenance are reduced.

2. Offer some alternative theories to explain why manufacturers want fair trade. How might you go about testing your theories vis-à-vis the one outlined in the text? Do they have different implications about what sorts of products might be sold under these conditions, or about what industry structures are most conducive to fair trade?

3. Many firms employ salesmen who are assigned exclusive territories. No salesman may enter another's territory and attempt to sell the manufacturer's product there. Construct a theory to explain why firms adopt this practice. Does your theory suggest what kinds of products will be sold in this way and what kinds will not be?

4. Candy makers sometimes print retail prices directly on the wrappers. Is this a form of resale price maintenance? If so, what are its benefits? If not, what is the reason for the practice?

5. In many industries workers are required to belong to a union and to pay union dues, even if they would prefer not to. *True or false:* Workers would be better off if each one could choose for himself whether to belong to the union.

6. Many bars have afternoon "Happy Hours" at which drinks are sold at a reduced price. *True or false:* Since bar owners voluntarily engage in this practice, we may infer that a law banning Happy Hours would make these bar owners unhappy.

7. Iran and Iraq, both major oil producers, have been engaged in a war for many years and have destroyed large amounts of each other's production capabilities. *True or false:* This destruction is pure social loss, and therefore both parties would surely be better off if they were not at war.

8. *True or false:* When all firms in an industry charge the same price, this is evidence of collusion.

9. Suppose that there are exactly N identical firms in an industry, all with flat marginal cost curves. Industry demand is linear. How much does each firm produce, compared to the competitive quantity, under the Cournot assumption that each takes its rivals' outputs as given? How much does the industry produce? What happens to industry output as N gets large? (*Hint:* Follow carefully the argument that is given in the text for the case N = 2.)

10. **a.** Suppose that two ice cream vendors are located on a circular beach that goes all the way around a lake. How will they locate themselves in equilibrium?

    b. Suppose instead that there are three ice cream vendors on the same circular beach. How will they locate themselves in equilibrium?

Refer to Answers to Problem Sets for solution to problem 6.

Chapter Twelve

External Costs and Benefits

External costs and benefits, or **externalities** Costs and benefits imposed on others.

Negative externalities External costs.

Positive externalities External benefits.

In previous chapters we have analyzed the gains from trade that accrue to voluntary participants in transactions. However, many transactions involve involuntary participants as well. The neighbors who breathe the smoke from a factory, the naturalist who deplores the "harvesting" of whales, the shoppers who enjoy the spectacle of department store Christmas displays—all are incurring costs or benefits from transactions that took place without their involvement. Such costs and benefits are said to be **external** and are collectively referred to as **externalities.** External costs (like the factory smoke) are called **negative externalities** and external benefits (like the pleasure from the Christmas decorations) are called **positive externalities.**

In this chapter we will study a variety of examples of externalities. We will see how externalities can be a source of economic inefficiency, and we will study some approaches to combating such inefficiencies.

12.1 Costs Imposed on Others

We will begin with a simple example of an externality: the noise from a confectioner's machinery disrupts the practice of the doctor next door. After examining the social consequences of this externality, we will present a simple policy prescription: If the confectioner is taxed for making noise, then he will produce less of it, and this can improve social welfare. In the remaining sections of the chapter we will criticize this policy prescription, and we will see that the problem is less simple than it might appear.

The Doctor and the Confectioner

Panel A of Exhibit 12–1 shows the market for Bridgman's Chocolate Confectionery, which sells candy in a competitive market at a going price of $5 per pound. In his business Bridgman uses machinery that creates noise and vibration disturbing to Doctor Sturges, a general practitioner with an office next door. The noise constitutes a negative externality imposed by the confectioner on the doctor, who is unable to consult with patients while the noise is in progress.

Private marginal costs Those costs of a decision that are borne by the decision maker.

Social marginal costs All of the costs of a decision, including the private costs and the costs imposed on others.

The curve labeled MC_P reflects Bridgman's marginal costs (cost of chocolate and other ingredients, cost of running the machinery, and so forth). Because these costs are paid by Bridgman himself, we call them **private marginal costs.** The curve MC_S includes both the private costs borne by Bridgman and the external costs imposed on Sturges. Thus it includes all costs borne by all members of society. We call these **social marginal costs.** At any given quantity the marginal external cost (Sturges's lost income, and perhaps psychological strain as well) is represented by the vertical distance between the two marginal cost curves.

Because Bridgman does not care about the costs imposed on Sturges, his supply curve is his private marginal cost curve. Equilibrium occurs at the quantity Q_E. To evaluate the welfare aspects of this equilibrium, we must measure the extent of the externalities. The externalities created by the production of successive pounds of candy are measured by the areas of the rectangles in panel B of Exhibit 12–1. The total externality is the sum of these areas; it is the area between the private and social marginal cost curves, out to the quantity produced. In panel A, this is the area B + C + D.

▷ *Exercise 12.1* Explain why the rectangles in panel B give the correct measure of the externality.

Now we can evaluate the social gain. There is no consumer's surplus because the demand curve is flat (although a similar analysis would hold without this assumption). Producer's surplus is A + C + D. Externalities detract from welfare and so must be subtracted from the social gain. The net social gain is Producer's surplus − Externalities = (A + C + D) − (B + C + D) = A − B.

Exhibit 12–1   **Private Costs versus Social Costs**

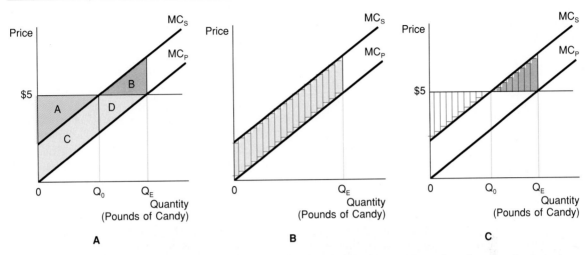

A	B	C
	Quantity (Pounds of Candy)	

Bridgman, a confectioner, has the marginal cost curve MC_P. When he produces chocolate, he also imposes external costs on Sturges. The cost to society of producing candy is the sum of Bridgman's private cost MC_P and the external costs borne by Sturges. The curve MC_S shows this full social cost.

At a market price of $5, Bridgman produces Q_E pounds of candy. Each pound produced imposes on Sturges a marginal external cost represented by one of the rectangles in panel B. The total external cost is the sum of these rectangles, which is area B + C + D in panel A.

Bridgman earns a producer's surplus equal to A + C + D. Subtracting the externality imposed on Sturges, we find a net social gain of A − B. The reason for this result is demonstrated in panel C. Each pound of candy up to Q_0 creates a social gain equal to one of the unshaded rectangles. Each pound of candy after Q_0 creates a social loss equal to one of the shaded rectangles. The net social gain is the sum of the unshaded rectangles minus the sum of the shaded ones, or A − B.

> *Exercise 12.2* Verify the last two sentences.

The social gain can also be computed directly without reference to its individual components. The demand curve depicts the marginal values of successive pounds of candy (in this case, their marginal values are all $5), and the social marginal cost curve depicts the marginal cost *to society as a whole* of providing those pounds. Part of the social marginal cost is the cost of raw materials and other factors of production; in other words, it is the private marginal cost borne by Bridgman. The remainder is noise damage to Sturges's medical practice, nerves, and psyche.

Each pound prior to Q_0 provides $5 worth of value to consumers while costing society less than $5 to produce. For each of these pounds, the excess of value over cost (that is, the social gain) is represented by one of the unshaded rectangles in panel C of Exhibit 12–1. Pounds of candy from Q_0 to Q_E cost society more than they are worth to consumers; the resulting social losses are represented by the shaded rectangles. Net social gain is the sum of the unshaded rectangles minus the sum of the shaded ones. This is the same answer we got before; it is area A − B in panel A of the exhibit.

The Pigou Tax

Society would be best off if Bridgman agreed to produce candy only as long as its marginal value exceeds its *social* marginal cost. This would lead him to produce Q_0 pounds of candy, yielding a social gain equal to area A in Exhibit 12–1. (In terms of panel C, society would gain the unshaded rectangles without losing the shaded ones.) Unfortunately, Bridgman produces candy as long as its marginal value exceeds his *private* marginal cost, which leads him to produce out to Q_E. If he could be induced to take account of the costs imposed on Sturges, he would choose the efficient level of output Q_0.

A tax can provide the appropriate incentive. Suppose that Bridgman were subject to a tax equal to the amount of the damage he imposes on his neighbor. In that case any noise-related losses to Sturges would become a part of Bridgman's private costs. We say that Bridgman **internalizes** these costs, meaning that they now fully enter his decision-making process. This would cause the private marginal cost curve MC_P in Exhibit 12–1 to move directly on top of the social marginal cost curve MC_S. With such a tax, quantity will fall to Q_0. The externality will be reduced to C (the area between the two marginal cost curves out to the new quantity produced). Tax revenue will exactly equal the amount of the costs imposed on Sturges.

> *Exercise 12.3* Explain why the tax causes the MC_P curve to coincide with the MC_S curve.

Exhibit 12–2 shows the new distribution of social gains. The graph there is identical to panel A of Exhibit 12–1, except that regions A and C have been divided into two. When Bridgman is taxed, he produces the quantity Q_0 and gains a producer's surplus of $A = A_1 + A_2$. The externality imposed on Sturges is $C = C_1 + C_2$. The tax revenue is the rectangular area $A_1 + C_1$, which is equal to the area $C_1 + C_2$. (There are two ways to verify that $A_1 + C_1 = C_1 + C_2$. The first is to use high school geometry. The second is to remember that Bridgman is being taxed an amount exactly equal to the externality that he imposes, so that the total tax revenue $A_1 + C_1$ must equal the total external cost $C_1 + C_2$.)

> *Exercise 12.4* Explain why the producer's surplus with a Pigou tax is equal to the area $A_2 + C_2$ in Exhibit 12–2. Explain why it is also equal to area A. Reconcile these facts by using geometry to show that these two areas are equal.

A tax that requires Bridgman to pay an amount equal to the externality is called a **Pigou tax** (or, sometimes, a **Pigovian tax**) in honor of the British economist A. C. Pigou, who studied such questions in his influential book

Internalize
To treat an external cost as a private cost.

Pigou tax or **Pigovian tax**
A tax equal to the amount of an externality.

Exhibit 12–2   **A Pigou Tax**

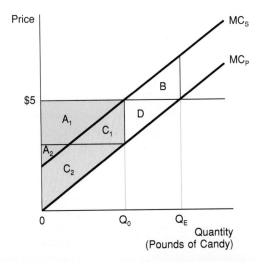

A Pigou tax would require Bridgman to pay an amount equal to the external costs that he imposes on Sturges. Since the distance between MC_P and MC_S shows the marginal external cost associated with producing a pound of candy, the Pigou tax is an excise tax equal to this distance. MC_P moves up to MC_S, Bridgman cuts back production from Q_E to Q_0, and social gains are distributed as in the table.

	Without Pigou Tax	With Pigou Tax
Gains:		
Producer's Surplus (to Bridgman):	$A + C + D$	A
Tax Revenue	—	C
Losses:		
External Costs (to Sturges)	$B + C + D$	C
Social Gain	$A - B$	A

The Economics of Welfare.[1] The Pigou tax leads to a socially optimal level of output regardless of who gets the tax revenue. One possibility, which appeals to many people's sense of fairness, is that the tax revenue could be given to Sturges. The proceeds of the tax are just sufficient to compensate him for being subjected to the noise from Bridgman's machinery.

An equivalent strategy is to institute a rule of law under which Bridgman is **liable** for his actions. This means that Sturges would have a legal right to be compensated by Bridgman for damages due to the noise. Such a liability rule is equivalent to a Pigou tax on Bridgman with the proceeds given to Sturges.

Another way to describe this liability rule is to say that Sturges is granted a **property right** to the noise-free air around his office. As the

Liable
Legally responsible to compensate another party for damage.

Property right
The right to decide how some resource shall be used.

[1]New York: Macmillan, 1920.

owner of this air, he is entitled to charge Bridgman for its use as a noise receptacle.

A Pigou tax on Bridgman with proceeds assigned to Sturges, a legal arrangement assigning liability to Bridgman, and an assignment of property rights to Sturges are three different ways of describing essentially the same thing. Regardless of how it is described, this arrangement ensures that Bridgman will consider the effects of the noise from his machinery when deciding how much to produce. The social costs of production will all become private costs; in other words, all of the externalities will be internalized. As a result, Bridgman will stop producing when marginal *social* cost equals marginal value, which is the socially efficient level of production.[2]

The Incompleteness of Pigou's Analysis

For many years all economists believed that Pigou's analysis of the problem of externalities was essentially the final word on the subject. In particular, they believed that the Pigou tax was the correct way to achieve a socially optimal outcome. However, in 1960 Ronald Coase, a law professor and legal scholar, taught economists that there is far more to say about the problem of externalities.[3] Coase demonstrated both that Pigou's analysis is incomplete and that it can lead to incorrect conclusions. There are situations in which a Pigou tax is unnecessary, and many situations in which it is actually counterproductive.

Transactions cost
Any cost of negotiating or enforcing a contract.

Coase's analysis of externalities requires the notion of **transactions costs.** A transactions cost is a cost of negotiating or enforcing a contract. If you hire someone to repair your roof, transactions costs might include the time spent locating an appropriate handyman, time or energy spent haggling over a price, the cost of hiring an inspector to make sure that the job has been done correctly, and the potential costs of filing a lawsuit if the roofer fails to make repairs as promised.

Coase's analysis of Pigou's analysis of externalities led him to two conclusions:

1.   In the absence of transactions costs, Pigou's arguments are wrong.

2.   In the presence of transactions costs, Pigou's arguments are still wrong, but for a different reason.

In Section 12.2, we will see how Coase was led to the first of these conclusions, and in Section 12.3 we will see how he was led to the second.

---

[2] The Invisible Hand Theorem tells us that competitive markets maximize social welfare. Exhibit 12–1 seems to present a counterexample. But, in fact, the reason why the equilibrium in Exhibit 12–1 is suboptimal is precisely that a market is lacking, namely, the market for air! When nobody owns the air, it can be neither bought nor sold. When Sturges acquires property rights to the air and is reimbursed for noise damage, he is "selling" the use of this air to Bridgman at a competitive price. Once again the introduction of markets leads to an optimal outcome.

[3] His arguments appear in R. H. Coase, "The Problem of Social Cost," *Journal of Law and Economics* 3 (1960), 1–44.

12.2 The Coase Theorem

In this section we will study Coase's criticism of Pigou in the case where there are no transactions costs. We will begin by reconsidering our analysis of the dispute between Sturges and Bridgman.

The Doctor and the Confectioner Revisited

Consider again the dispute between Sturges and Bridgman, and refer to Exhibit 12–1. Equilibrium output is Q_E. Optimal output is Q_0. This means that at Q_0 the social "pie" is bigger than at Q_E (in fact, it is A instead of A − B). When the pie is bigger, everyone can have a bigger piece. In the absence of transactions costs, both Sturges and Bridgman have an incentive to agree to an arrangement whereby Q_0 is produced and the "winner" reimburses the "loser" by enough to make *both parties* better off.

For example, suppose that Sturges offers Bridgman a payment equal to the area D + ½B in exchange for Bridgman's agreement to produce only Q_0 pounds of candy instead of Q_E. Then Sturges benefits, since he reduces the noise damage by D + B in exchange for a payment of only D + ½B. And Bridgman benefits, since he receives the payment of D + ½B in exchange for sacrificing only D in producer's surplus.

▷ *Exercise 12.5* What is the smallest amount Bridgman would accept in exchange for cutting output to Q_0? What is the largest amount Sturges would offer him to do so?

Side Payments

We have seen that Sturges and Bridgman both benefit when Sturges makes a one-time payment to Bridgman in exchange for his reducing output to the efficient level. Here is another example of such an agreement. Suppose that Bridgman causes $2 worth of noise damage with each pound of candy that he produces. Then Sturges will be prepared to pay Bridgman up to $2 for each pound of candy that he agrees *not* to produce. We refer to such payments as "side payments" or "bribes" (though our use of the word *bribe* is not meant to imply that the payments are in any way underhanded).

In order to evaluate the consequences of Sturges's offer, we can imagine that it takes place in two steps. First, Sturges will pay Bridgman the amount $Q_E \times \$2 = B + C + D$ (in Exhibit 12–3) if Bridgman will quit producing candy altogether. Second, he will subtract $2 from this payment for each pound of candy that Bridgman produces.

Because Bridgman can collect B + C + D from Sturges for quite literally doing nothing, this amount is a transfer of wealth from Sturges to Bridgman. Each time Bridgman produces a pound of candy, he must return $2 to Sturges. This "fee" acts exactly like a Pigou tax with the proceeds assigned to Sturges: It raises Bridgman's private marginal cost curve to the level of the social marginal cost curve, and it leads him to

Exhibit 12–3 Side Payments Cause Externalities to Be Internalized

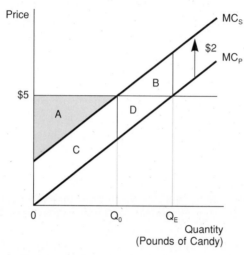

The graph is as in Exhibit 12–1. Each time Bridgman produces a pound of candy, he also imposes a $2 externality on Sturges. In the absence of transactions costs, Sturges will offer to pay Bridgman up to $2 for each pound of candy that he does *not* produce.

If Bridgman ceases production altogether, he can collect $2 \times Q_E = B + C + D$. This amount is a pure transfer of wealth from Sturges to Bridgman. Now for each pound of candy that Bridgman produces, he must return $2 to Sturges (that is, he must forgo the opportunity to collect the $2 in the first place). This forgone opportunity is exactly equivalent to a Pigou tax on Bridgman, with the proceeds assigned to Sturges. Thus Bridgman's private marginal cost curve rises to MC_S and he produces the quantity Q_0. Gains are shown in the table below.

	Original	With Pigou Tax (Proceeds to Sturges)	With Sturges Bribing Bridgman
Bridgman's Gains:			
Producer's Surplus	A + C + D	A	A
Transfer	—	—	B + C + D
Sturges's Gains:			
Tax Revenue		C	
Sturges's Losses:			
Noise Damage	B + C + D	C	—
Transfer	—	—	B + C + D
Social Gain	A − B	A	A

produce the quantity Q_0. He returns to Sturges the amount $Q_0 \times \$2 = C$, so that his net payment from Sturges is $B + D$.

Of course, the actual bribing process takes place in just one step: Bridgman cuts back production from Q_E to Q_0 and Sturges pays him $(Q_E - Q_0) \times \$2 = B + D$ for doing so. However, for the purpose of calculating gains and losses, it is convenient to imagine Sturges first paying $B + C + D$ and then having amount C returned to him.

Students sometimes point out that when Sturges bribes Bridgman, Bridgman still produces Q_0 pounds of candy, creating noise damage equal to area C. Why, then, is there no entry for "noise damage" in the third column of the table in Exhibit 12–3?

The answer is that noise damage is no longer a cost to Sturges, because he is fully compensated for it. Every time Sturges is subjected to $2 worth of nerve-wracking vibration, he subtracts $2 from his payment to Bridgman. This implicit $2 fee exactly offsets the damage from the noise.

▷ *Exercise 12.6* Consider again the arrangement described at the beginning of this section, wherein Sturges pays Bridgman $D + \frac{1}{2}B$ in exchange for his reducing output to Q_0. Explain why this can be thought of as a transfer of $\frac{1}{2}B + C + D$, followed by a $2-per-pound Pigou tax, with the proceeds assigned to Sturges.

The reduction of output from Q_E to Q_0 raises social welfare by area B. Who gets this increase? An inspection of the first and third columns of the table in Exhibit 12–3 reveals that it all goes to Bridgman. His gains increase from $A + C + D$ to $A + B + C + D$, while Sturges's losses stay fixed at $B + C + D$.

▷ *Exercise 12.7* How does the plan described in Exercise 12.6 divide the increase in social welfare between Sturges and Bridgman?

In the absence of transactions costs, Sturges and Bridgman will come to an agreement under which output is reduced to Q_0 and the welfare gain of B is divided between the two parties. The division of this gain depends on the details of the bargaining process and is difficult to predict. The example of Exhibit 12–3 illustrates the extreme case where Bridgman gets everything. The plan considered in Exercise 12–6 illustrates a different division.

Regardless of the details of his arrangement with Sturges, it will always be the case that Bridgman can extract up to $2 additional bribe for each additional pound of candy that he agrees not to produce. The forgone opportunity to collect this bribe is a cost of production that acts exactly like a Pigou tax.

Coase Theorem
In the absence of transactions costs, all externalities are internalized, regardless of the assignment of property rights.

We can now state the **Coase Theorem,** in two equivalent forms:

In the absence of transactions costs, private costs equal social costs.

That is, all externalities are automatically internalized, because forgone bribes act exactly like Pigou taxes. Equivalently:

In the absence of transactions costs, the assignment of property rights (or liability rules) has no effect on social welfare.

That is, a socially efficient outcome will be reached regardless of how property rights are assigned. In our example, the property right to noise-free air is at issue. The second and third columns of the table in Exhibit 12–3 correspond to two choices of property rights. A Pigou tax (which assigns the property right to Sturges) leads to an output of Q_0 and a social gain of A. On the other hand, if Bridgman is given the property right, allowing him to make all the noise he pleases, then Sturges will bribe him to produce the quantity Q_0 and the social gain will still be A.

The Coase Theorem is often summarized by saying that the assignment of property rights "does not matter." This means that the choice of property rights does not affect economic efficiency. On the other hand, it certainly does matter to Sturges and Bridgman, as you can see by inspecting the second and third columns of the table in Exhibit 12–3. Sturges prefers to collect the Pigou tax; Bridgman prefers to get bribed.

Alternative Solutions

We have argued that in the absence of transactions costs, private costs rise to equal social costs, regardless of how property rights are allocated. In the case of Bridgman and Sturges, this leads to an output of Q_0 and a social gain of A. Moreover, this output is optimal in the sense that A is the largest social gain possible. But our analysis is still incomplete, because there may be other alternatives, even more desirable than reducing Bridgman's output. Perhaps Bridgman can acquire more modern machinery that can't be heard from Sturges's office. Perhaps Sturges can move his office to the other side of his house. Perhaps Bridgman or Sturges, or both together, can erect a sound barrier between their properties.

Any of these alternatives would eliminate the discrepancy between private and social costs by reducing social costs rather than by raising private costs as a Pigou tax would. In Exhibit 12–3 the MC_S curve would move down to lie on top of the MC_P curve, since the externality would be eliminated. In this case Bridgman would produce Q_E pounds of candy, and the social gain from his operation would increase from A to A + C + D.

However, each of these solutions is costly. The cost of moving Sturges's office cannot be measured by any area in Exhibit 12–3. If that cost is less than C + D, the move is a more efficient solution than any scheme for reducing output to Q_0. If Bridgman can buy a new machine more cheaply than Sturges can move, then that solution is more efficient yet.

The Coase Theorem extends to these other possibilities as well. In the absence of transactions costs, Sturges and Bridgman will find the most efficient of all possible solutions and agree to a system of reimbursements or "bribes" that will make them both better off. This is so regardless of how property rights are initially allocated. The most efficient outcome could be either a cutback in production to Q_0 or some scheme for eliminating or reducing noise damage. There is no way to determine this outcome from the information available in the graph.

To illustrate this point, let us suppose that the possibilities have been narrowed to two: Either Sturges quits practicing medicine or Bridgman stops producing candy.[4] In order to see how the allocation of property rights will affect this decision, we need to make some assumptions about the value of Bridgman's and Sturges's respective businesses. We will present two examples, using different assumptions.

Example 1

Suppose that Bridgman values his confectionery business at $100, reflecting the income that he earns selling candy. Suppose that Sturges earns so much as a doctor that he values his medical practice at $200. These values then also represent the costs to Bridgman and Sturges of leaving their respective industries.

Suppose first that Sturges has the property right, so that he can demand that Bridgman stop making noise. Then Bridgman will be forced out of business and Sturges will be able to practice medicine in peace and quiet.

Now imagine a change in the law. The property right is reassigned to Bridgman, so that he is allowed to make all the noise he wants to. Will he continue to produce candy? In the absence of transactions costs, the answer is no. Sturges is willing to pay up to $200 as a bribe in exchange for Bridgman's closing up shop. For any amount over $100, Bridgman is willing to close. This leaves room for a mutually acceptable payment of, say, $150. Sturges offers this to Bridgman, who accepts it and retires. Each gains $50 more than he would have if Bridgman had exercised his property right. Sturges avoids the loss of a $200 business in exchange for a $150 payment; Bridgman adds $150 to his wallet while sacrificing only $100 worth of income by giving up his business.

Thus, regardless of whether Sturges or Bridgman has the property right, Bridgman will stop producing candy and Sturges will resume his medical practice. The change in the law has no effect on the amounts of medical care and candy that are produced. These outcomes are shown in the first row of the table in Exhibit 12–4.

Example 2

In this example, we reverse the numbers so that Bridgman's business is worth $200, whereas Sturges's is worth $100.

If Bridgman has the property right, he will continue to make candy. Suppose, alternatively, that Sturges has the property right and can order Bridgman to quit. Will he do so? No. Bridgman will offer up to $200 to Sturges in exchange for permission to continue making noise. Sturges will sell this permission for any amount over $100. Thus Bridgman pays Sturges some amount between $100 and $200 (say $150) and stays in business.

---

[4]For purposes of this example, we assume that all other solutions have already been rejected as less desirable. In particular, we are assuming that it is less costly for Bridgman to go out of business altogether than to cut back his production to Q_0. This would be the case if an output of Q_0 does not allow Bridgman to earn enough to cover his fixed costs. Nothing of importance depends on this assumption. Its only purpose is to keep the example manageable.

Exhibit 12–4   Alternative Assignments of Property Rights

	Sturges Has Property Right	Bridgman Has Property Right
Example 1: **Bridgman's Candy Business Worth $100; Sturges's Medical Practice Worth $200**	Sturges forces Bridgman to quit. Society gets medical care, no candy.	Sturges bribes Bridgman $150 to quit. Society gets medical care, no candy.
Example 2: **Bridgman's Candy Business Worth $200; Sturges's Medical Practice Worth $100**	Bridgman bribes Sturges $150. Sturges retires. Society gets candy, no medical care.	Bridgman makes noise, forcing Sturges to retire. Society gets candy, no medical care.

The two rows correspond to two different assumptions about the values of Bridgman's candy business and Sturges's medical practice. In each example, we ask what happens if Sturges is given the property right (enabling him to force Bridgman to stop making noise) and what happens if Bridgman is given the property right (enabling him to make all the noise he wants to). From a social point of view, the allocation of property rights does not matter in either example.

Regardless of who has the property right, Bridgman continues to make candy, and Sturges stops practicing medicine.

Once again, changing the law does not affect the quantities of candy or of medical care. These outcomes are summarized in the second row of the table in Exhibit 12–4.

Comparing the Examples

In Exhibit 12–4 the rows of the table correspond to the two examples, which represent alternative possible economic conditions. The columns correspond to the two possible assignments of property rights, which are alternative possible legal conditions. The social outcome (will society have candy or will it have medical care?) is determined solely by the economic conditions. The choice of column does not affect the outcome.

Of course, this simply illustrates the Coase Theorem: In the absence of transactions costs, the assignment of property rights does not matter from the point of view of economic efficiency. It does, of course, matter to Sturges and to Bridgman.

▷ *Exercise 12.8* Verify that under either set of economic conditions, Sturges is $150 richer with the property right than without it, and the same is true of Bridgman.

Sturges and Bridgman are the names of two real people who were involved in a dispute very similar to the one we have described. The real-world dispute ended up in court, where the judges ruled in the doctor's favor. They did so under the mistaken impression that they were affecting the actual workings of the economic system. They thought that they were voting for medical care over candy. Instead, they were only voting for Sturges over Bridgman. Their decision enriched Sturges at Bridgman's expense, but (assuming no transactions costs) it had no effect on which economic activity was actually pursued.

The Lessons of the Coase Theorem

At this point we can summarize the main points of this section. A classically trained "Pigovian" economist might look at Exhibit 12–1 and say, "The socially optimal outcome is for Bridgman to produce Q_0. We must impose a tax to induce that outcome." Assuming no transactions costs, Coase tells us that the economist is wrong on *both* counts.

First, Q_0 may not be the socially optimal outcome. It might be better to eliminate the noise problem in any of a wide variety of ways. These alternatives include, but are not limited to, one or the other party moving or abandoning his business. (Other possibilities we have already referred to include the construction of sound barriers and the like.)

Second, whatever outcome is socially optimal will be reached with or without a tax, via a bargain between the parties that improves everyone's welfare.[5]

The Coase Theorem with Many Firms

Everything we have said about Bridgman's individual firm applies as well to entire industries. Exhibit 12–5 shows the competitive market for sprockets, which are produced in factories that emit noxious smoke. The industry supply curve is the MC_P curve reflecting producers' costs. The MC_S curve reflects these costs, plus the costs of smoke damage to the neighboring homeowners. Market equilibrium is at quantity Q_E and price P_E. A Pigou tax equal to the amount of the externality imposed on homeowners will move the MC_P curve up to the MC_S curve, leading to the socially optimal output Q_0 being sold at a price P_0. The table displays the gains and losses.

Here again, Coase would raise two objections. First, there may be a solution we haven't thought of. Perhaps the factories could install pollution control equipment that would eliminate the smoke damage. Then optimal output would be Q_E, the sum of producers' and consumers' surpluses would be $A + B + C + D + F + G + H$, and the social gain would be $A + B + C + D + F + G + H$ minus the cost of installing pollution control equipment. This gain might be either more or less than the social gain of $A + B + F$ shown in the second column of the table in Exhibit 12–5.

---

[5]Throughout this section we have assumed no transactions costs. In Section 12.3 we will study Coase's objections to the Pigovian analysis in the case where transactions costs play a significant role.

Exhibit 12–5   A Pigou Tax in a Competitive Industry

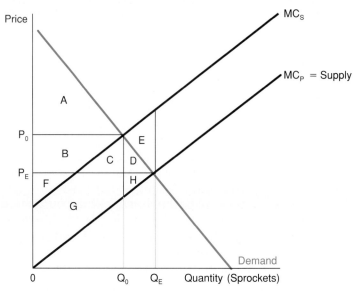

Sprockets are produced competitively in factories that emit noxious smoke. The table below gives the Pigovian analysis of social welfare. However, there are two ways in which the analysis is incomplete. First, it does not consider the possibility of an alternative arrangement under which MC_S is lowered to MC_P, perhaps through the installation of pollution control equipment or the relocation of either the factories or the homes. Second, if there are no transactions costs between factories and homeowners, then forgone bribes will act exactly like a Pigou tax even when there is no tax explicitly imposed.

	With No Tax	With Pigou Tax
Gains:		
Consumers' Surplus	A + B + C + D	A
Producers' Surplus	F + G + H	B + F
Tax Revenue	—	C + G
Losses:		
Smoke Damage	C + D + E + G + H	C + G
Social Gain	A + B + F − E	A + B + F

Second, the optimal outcome, whatever it may be, will be achieved in a world without transactions costs regardless of what taxes are imposed. It should be said, however, that transactions costs probably do play a significant role in an example such as this one, because many different homeowners are affected by the smoke. The logistical problem of getting these homeowners together to jointly bribe the factory owners already constitutes a formidable transactions cost.

The Pigou Tax Reconsidered

If transactions are costless, then the Coase Theorem tells us that the Pigou tax is unnecessary. In fact, we can say more: If only *some* transactions are costless, it is possible for the Pigou tax to be positively harmful.

To see why, suppose in Exhibit 12–5 that sprocket producers and homeowners can transact costlessly. Then by offering side payments, homeowners will bid the MC_P curve up to the level of the MC_S curve. Now suppose that a Pigou tax is imposed, with the revenue collected by some third party. This will move the MC_P curve up higher yet, so that it now lies *above* the MC_S curve! The number of sprockets produced will be *less* than the optimal quantity Q_0.[6]

The problem here is that producers receive a double incentive to reduce their output. When the production of a sprocket causes $2 worth of damage, the producer is both charged $2 tax and made to forgo a $2 bribe, raising his costs by $4. This extra incentive causes him to continue cutting back on output even after the social optimum has been reached.

If *all* parties, including consumers and the recipients of tax revenue, can enter the negotiations, then the social optimum is achieved with or without a Pigou tax. It is always possible to arrange a system of side payments that will benefit everyone when the size of the social pie is maximized. However, the example here shows that when some but not all of the parties can negotiate, the Pigou tax can actually reduce social welfare.[7]

Example: The Nature Conservancy

Environmental pollution is often cited as an example of an externality that cannot be bargained away because of high transactions costs. It is alleged that the large number of people affected suffices to negate any possibility of negotiating side payments. There is undoubtedly much truth in this assertion, but it is far from entirely true.

In Arlington, Virginia, a charitable organization called the Nature Conservancy solicits funds from the public and uses those funds exactly in the way that Coase would predict. It purchases land in ecologically significant areas and maintains that land to preserve threatened species and places of special beauty. Its current holdings comprise 2.8 million acres in 4100 locations. In making its purchases, the Conservancy bids against other potential users of the land, forcing those other potential users to take account of the land's ecological significance.

At the same time, because it pays market prices, the Conservancy must take account of the value of the land in its alternative (nonecological) uses.

---

[6]The problem does not occur if the Pigou tax is paid to the homeowners rather than a third party. If the homeowners are reimbursed for the pollution, they are indifferent to how much pollution occurs and will therefore not offer bribes.

[7]This point seems to have first been clearly exposited by Ralph Turvey in "On Divergences Between Social Cost and Private Cost," *Economica* 30 (1963), 309–313.

When a parcel of land has exceptional value in other uses, the price of the land is high and the Conservancy is less likely to acquire it. Thus from a social point of view, the Conservancy's approach has a distinct advantage over, for example, legally mandating that landowners follow policies that are oriented toward conservation.

Unfortunately, even those who value conservation highly have an incentive to "free ride" on the efforts of groups like the Nature Conservancy, so that the actual level of contributions may inadequately reflect the true demand for conservation. Nevertheless, the organization has been extraordinarily successful. In 1986, it received contributions of $73.4 million. The Nature Conservancy's success is a striking reminder that seemingly insurmountable transactions costs can be at least partially overcome.

External Benefits

Everything we have said about external costs has its analogue regarding external benefits. Suppose that Nabisco can produce a cookie at a (private) marginal cost of 5¢. At the same time, the factory produces a pleasant aroma worth 2¢ to motorists driving by. Then the cookie is produced at a social marginal cost of only 3¢; part of the private costs are returned to society via the external benefit from the aroma. In the presence of external benefits, the social marginal cost curve lies below the private marginal cost curve, and too few cookies are produced.

Just as a Pigou tax internalizes external costs, so a "Pigou subsidy" equal to the benefits conferred on others can internalize external benefits, leading to an efficient level of output. This is illustrated in Exhibit 12–6. However, the Coase Theorem applies in this case as well. In the absence of transactions costs, the recipients of the benefit will offer a bribe in exchange for greater production, and this bribe will operate just like a Pigou subsidy.

Example: The Fable of the Bees

An interesting real-world example is what Professor Steven Cheung of the University of Washington has called "The Fable of the Bees."[8] In the literature of economics, the standard example of a positive externality is the interaction between apple growing and beekeeping. When these two activities are carried on in close physical proximity, one might expect each to confer benefits on the other. More apple trees mean more honey; more bees mean more cross-pollination and eventually more apples. Pigou would have argued (and his disciples did argue) that this situation must result in suboptimal levels of output in both activities. An apple grower stops planting new trees as soon as the marginal cost of planting exceeds

---

[8]Steven Cheung, "The Fable of the Bees: An Economic Investigation," *Journal of Law and Economics* 16 (1973), 11–34.

Exhibit 12–6   **The Market for Cookies**

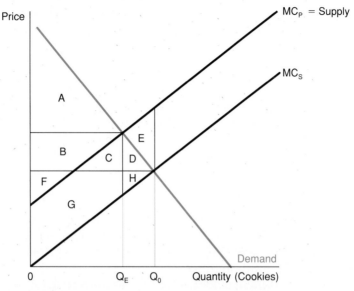

If the production of cookies creates pleasing aromas that benefit passersby, then the social marginal cost curve MC_S lies below the private marginal cost curve MC_P. Only Q_E cookies are produced instead of the optimal quantity Q_0. A Pigou subsidy equal to the amount of the external benefit causes MC_P to move down to the level of MC_S and induces the socially optimal outcome, as displayed in the table.

	With No Subsidy	With Pigou Subsidy
Gains:		
Consumers' Surplus	A	A + B + C + D
Producers' Surplus	B + F	F + G + H
Pleasant Aroma	C + G	C + D + E + G + H
Losses:		
Cost of Subsidy	—	C + D + E + G + H
Social Gain	A + B + C + F + G	A + B + C + D + F + G + H

his private marginal benefit, failing to consider that further trees would benefit his neighbor. The beekeeper performs a similar unfortunate calculation. Both could be made better off by a system of taxes and subsidies that encouraged them to consider their neighbor's welfare as part of their own.

Cheung investigated the accuracy of this fable by interviewing apple growers and beekeepers. He found that, contrary to the expectations of Pigou-style economists and exactly as Coase would have predicted, there is an elaborate system of contracts under which the two groups reimburse each other with "bribes" for increasing output to the socially optimal levels.[9] The evidence that such contracts exist is not hard to find; Cheung pointed out that one need only look in the Yellow Pages under nectar and pollination services. Nevertheless, a generation of economists had somehow managed to deny that such contracts were possible.

▷ **Exercise 12.9** State an appropriate moral for the "Fable of the Bees."

Income Effects and the Coase Theorem

According to the Coase Theorem, assignments of property rights do not matter from the point of view of economic efficiency. In the example of Exhibit 12–4 an even stronger statement can be made. Not only does a change in property rights have no effect on economic efficiency, it also has no effect on the amounts of medical care and candy that are produced. The "resource" consisting of the air around Bridgman's confectionery and Sturges's office is allocated either to the production of candy (via its use as a "dumping ground" for Bridgman's noise) or to the production of medical care (via its use as a quiet, conducive environment in which Sturges can practice), depending on where it is most valuable and regardless of who has the property rights.

We will refer to this outcome as the Strong Coase Theorem:

> *Strong Coase Theorem:* **In the absence of transactions costs, the assignment of property rights has no effect on the allocation of resources.**

The Strong Coase Theorem is not universally true. Suppose that a law were passed requiring all classical music lovers to give half of their wealth to people who like rock and roll. Although this is just a change in property rights, the demand for classical records would fall, the demand for rock records would rise, and resources formerly allocated to producing classical music would be reallocated to the production of rock. However, although the allocation of resources has changed, it is still efficient (that is, Pareto-optimal). Rock fans are happier, classical music lovers are less happy, but social welfare is still being maximized *given* the new wealth distribution. This is an example of what we will call the *Weak Coase Theorem:*

> *Weak Coase Theorem:* **In the absence of transactions costs, the assignment of property rights does not affect the *efficiency* of resource allocation (though it might cause resources to be diverted from one efficient allocation to another).**

The Weak Coase Theorem is always true. The Strong Coase Theorem is true whenever the reallocation of property rights does not change people's wealth enough to have significant effects on market demand curves. (In other words, the redistribution of income that results from the change in property rights should have negligible income effects.)

---

[9]He also discovered that, contrary to a widespread assertion in economic literature, apples produce almost no honey. Therefore he extended his investigation to include many other plants.

Notice that changes in the assets of *firms* do not affect the validity of the Strong Coase Theorem. Only changes in the assets of individuals are relevant, because individuals are the source of demand curves. For the Strong Coase Theorem to fail, there must be large changes in the wealth of enough individuals to make a significant difference in the relevant market.

In Exhibit 12–4 a shift in property rights from Sturges to Bridgman makes Bridgman richer. If Bridgman loves candy, this could raise the demand for candy and cause more candy production; if he loves medical care, it could bring about more medical care. (For that matter, if Bridgman loves carrots, it will raise carrot production.) The fact that Bridgman is a *producer* of candy is irrelevant to how demands will shift. In any event, Bridgman as a consumer is undoubtedly such an insignificant part of either market that no real change will come about.

Example: The Reserve Clause in Baseball

Before 1972 all major league baseball players had contracts containing a "reserve clause." The reserve clause forbade the player from attempting to sell his services to any other team. If the Chicago White Sox wanted to acquire a player from the New York Yankees, the White Sox had to buy that player's contract from the Yankees. They could not simply offer him a higher salary to try to lure him away.

In the 1970s the reserve clause was substantially weakened, and now a number of players are "free agents," who can sell their services to the highest bidder. At the time it was argued that the weakening of the reserve clause would enable the wealthiest teams to buy up all of the best players. Let us subject this assertion to some economic analysis.

The weakening of the reserve clause is a transfer of property rights. Players' services, which used to belong to the teams they played for, now belong to the players themselves. The Coase Theorem suggests that such a transfer of property rights should not affect the allocation of players to teams.

Consider a player, Tinker Evans, who currently plays for the New York Yankees. Having Evans on the team is worth $100,000 to the Yankees. This is because his presence increases the Yankees' revenue by $100,000. He would only be worth $75,000 to the Chicago White Sox.

Under the reserve clause, the Yankees will not sell Evans for any amount less than $100,000, and the White Sox will not offer any amount more than $75,000. No exchange takes place, and Evans continues to play for the Yankees.

On the other hand, suppose that Evans becomes a free agent. Then the Yankees will offer him up to $100,000 to play for them. This is because he can produce an additional $100,000 in revenue for the Yankees and has nothing to do with whether the Yankees are rich or poor. The White Sox will offer Evans up to $75,000. If Evans maximizes his salary, he will play for the Yankees. Thus free agency has no effect on where Evans plays.

We have implicitly made the simplifying assumption that Evans receives no salary under the reserve clause. If he receives $20,000 in salary, then the Yankees will value his contract at $80,000, not $100,000, and the White Sox will value his contract at $55,000. However, the conclusion that he continues to play for the Yankees does not change.

▷ *Exercise 12.10* Assume that Evans is worth $100,000 to the Yankees and $150,000 to the White Sox. For whom does he play under the reserve clause? For whom does he play under free agency?

Now let's throw in a complication. Suppose that Evans hates living in New York, so much so that he would be willing to pay up to $50,000 to move to the White Sox. Under free agency, Evans will move. The White Sox offer him $75,000 and the Yankees offer him $100,000. The additional $25,000 he can earn in New York is not enough to overcome his $50,000 preference for Chicago.

Under the reserve clause, Evans will also move. The White Sox are willing to buy him from the Yankees for $75,000. In addition, Evans himself is willing to "bribe" the Yankees up to $50,000 in exchange for their agreeing to sell him. Thus the Yankees can collect a total of $125,000 for letting Evans go. Since he is only worth $100,000 to the Yankees, Evans ends up in Chicago.

This example illustrates the Strong Coase Theorem. The reallocation of property rights that results from free agency has no effect on where Evans plays.

▷ *Exercise 12.11* Suppose that Evans is only willing to pay $10,000 to live in Chicago. Where does he play under free agency? Where does he play under the reserve clause?

Finally, let's throw in one additional complication. Suppose that Evans's demand for living in Chicago depends upon his income. When he is a poor reserve player, he is willing to pay only $10,000 to live in Chicago, but when he is a rich free agent, he is willing to pay $50,000. Now under the reserve clause, the Yankees can collect a total of only $85,000 for Evans ($75,000 from the White Sox plus a $10,000 bribe from Evans himself) and will not sell. In this case, Evans continues to play for the Yankees. Under free agency, the $25,000 difference in salary offers does not compensate Evans for his $50,000 preference for Chicago, and so he plays for the White Sox.

The preceding paragraph shows how income effects enter the analysis. A change in property rights can affect the allocation of resources (the resource here being Evans) only if it alters incomes in such a way as to change the demand for some resource (in this case Evans's demand to live in Chicago). In such cases, the Strong Coase Theorem fails, but the Weak Coase Theorem is still true. Either allocation of resources is efficient, given Evans's income.

How does free agency affect the allocation of players to teams? If players' preferences about where to live are unaffected by their incomes, then it affects the allocation not at all. Otherwise, it increases the wealth of players and makes it more likely that they will choose the teams that they personally value playing for. This means that with the advent of free agency, it is the teams that are desirable to players, not the wealthy teams, that gain an advantage.

12.3 Transactions Costs

In the presence of transactions costs, it might not be possible to negotiate side payments leading to efficient outcomes. Thus the Coase Theorem need not hold. However, even when there are positive transactions costs, the traditional Pigovian analysis of externalities is incomplete and can lead to wrong conclusions.

Example: Trains, Sparks, and Crops

Railway engines create sparks, and these sparks sometimes set fire to crops planted near the tracks. A large number of farmers are affected, and transactions costs prevent deals from being struck between these farmers and the railroad. If the railroad company is not liable for the ensuing damage, it will not consider the effects of this damage in deciding how many trains to run. A liability rule requiring the railroad to indemnify the farmers (in other words, a Pigou tax with proceeds assigned to the farmers) would provide such an incentive. There would be less rail service but more wheat and corn, which appears to be a social improvement.

The Coase Theorem says that if there were no transactions costs, this argument would be wrong because even without a Pigou tax, farmers would offer side payments to the railroad in exchange for running fewer trains. The railroad would be bribed into cutting back to the optimal level of rail service regardless of liability rules. But Coase made another, equally important point: When there *are* transactions costs, the conclusion that the railroads should be made liable may still be wrong, though for a different reason.

The flaw in the argument is that we do not know the cheapest way to prevent the fires. Suppose that farmers, at very little cost to themselves, can move their crops back a few feet from the railway bed, out of all danger from sparks. This would remove the externality and increase the social gain from the running of the railroad. However, if the railroad reimburses the farmers for all damage done, the farmers have no incentive to move their crops. Crops will be planted and burned, and fewer trains will be run because of the cost of reimbursement. If farmers were made to bear the losses from fires, they would move their crops, to society's benefit.

Exhibit 12–7 shows the picture, which should be familiar: It is identical to panel A of Exhibit 12–1. If the railroad is liable, it runs Q_0 trains and the

Exhibit 12–7   **Sparks from Railroads**

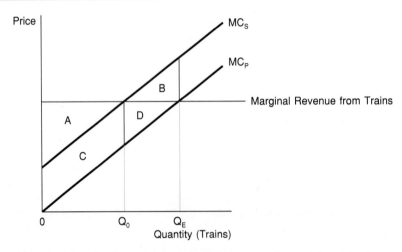

Because railway engines emit sparks that sometimes set fire to crops, the social marginal cost of running trains exceeds the private marginal cost. If the railroad is not liable, it runs Q_E trains and social gain is A − B. If the railroad is made liable, it takes account of all costs and runs Q_0 trains, for a social gain of A. Thus the standard Pigovian analysis suggests that the railroad should be liable.

But this analysis overlooks other possibilities. Suppose that the railroad is not liable and that as a result the farmers decide to move their crops away from the tracks. Then the externality is eliminated. Q_E trains are run (which is now the social optimum) and social gain is A + C + D minus the cost of moving the crops. This gain could be more or less than the gain of A that comes about when the railroad is liable. Thus the graph does not reveal the efficient solution.

social gain is A. If the railroad is not liable and the farmers move their crops, the social marginal cost curve falls to the level of the private marginal cost curve, Q_E trains are run, and the social gain is A + C + D minus the cost of moving the crops. If the cost of moving them is small, the latter is the better solution.

Does this mean that the railroad should not be liable for its actions? Not necessarily. Suppose that the railroad can cheaply install safety equipment that will prevent sparks from being thrown by the engines. If the railroad has no liability for fire damage, it will have no incentive to install this equipment. Once again, it is possible that the low-cost solution has been sacrificed.

Exhibit 12–7 simply does not contain the information necessary to determine how property rights should be allocated. (The property right in question is the right to the unencumbered use of the land adjacent to the tracks—either for agriculture or for spark disposal.) Whoever has the property right has no incentive to seek a solution to the problem. If farmers can move their crops very cheaply, then it is most efficient for the railroad to have the property right so that farmers will have the incentive to move their crops. If the railroad can install safety equipment very cheaply, then it is more efficient for the farmers to have the property right so that the railroad will have the appropriate incentive.

In cases such as this one, courts often concern themselves (or profess to concern themselves) with questions of economic efficiency. If a judge has efficiency foremost in his mind, then he must attempt to determine which party can solve the problem at the lowest possible cost and make that party bear the costs of the damage (that is, the property right should be assigned to the other party). Unfortunately, this can be difficult. If the judge asks the railroad whether it can prevent spark damage at a relatively low cost (planning to make the railroad bear this cost if the answer is yes), the railroad has every incentive to conceal the truth by claiming that controlling the sparks would be prohibitively expensive. The farmers have the same incentive to exaggerate the cost of moving their crops.

When there is a great deal of uncertainty about the costs of various solutions, a judge may be well advised to assign property rights according to some secondary criterion and then to attempt to reduce transactions costs between the parties. If he can do so (say by appointing a spokesman for the farmers and facilitating negotiation between this spokesman and the railroad company), then any mistake in the initial allocation of property rights will tend to be mitigated by the action of the Coase Theorem.

The Reciprocal Nature of the Problem

In Exhibit 12–7, the choice to run Q_E trains when there are crops planted near the railroad tracks is not socially optimal. The market's failure to produce the optimal outcome is due to the divergence between private and social costs. A Pigou tax remedies this divergence by shifting the private marginal cost curve upward. Coase's observation is that the divergence can equally well be remedied by moving the social marginal cost curve downward (for example, by having the farmers move their crops).

Why did economists in the Pigovian tradition fail to recognize the alternative remedy? Coase argues that the error arises from the mistaken notion that the railroad is the "cause" of the fires, and therefore must curtail its activities if the damage is to be reduced. In actuality, the railroad is no more the cause of the fires than the crops are. While it is true that if there were no railroads, there would be no fires, it is equally true that if there were no crops there would be no fires. Ultimately, the problem is caused by the fact that the railroad and the farmers are attempting to use the same land for two different purposes and this is no more one party's fault than it is the other's. Either party might be in possession of the cheapest means of dealing with the problem.

Every case of externalities is similarly reciprocal in nature. The neighborhood residents denounce the owner of a polluting factory; the owner might respond that there would be no externality if it weren't for the existence of the neighbors. The factory owner can mitigate the problem through cutbacks in production or pollution control equipment; the neighbors can equally well contribute to a solution by moving away. Each of these options has a cost.[10] If the factory owner is allowed to pollute without penalty, he has no incentive to reduce pollution. If the neighbors are fully compensated by the factory for damage to their lungs and houses, they have no incentive to move away. Either liability rule might cause the elimination of the low-cost option; the "right" liability rule depends on the actual costs.

It is often argued that the pollution of a lake or river is an economic problem that must be solved, especially if the water would otherwise be available for recreation. If the pollution is curtailed and the lake is reclaimed, it makes equal sense to say that the boaters and fishermen are the source of a problem in that they cause a reduction in the output of a socially valuable product. Which is worth more, the additional product or the boating and fishing? There is no way to tell without examining actual costs and benefits.

Nonsmokers like to view cigarette smoke as a cost imposed on them unfairly by smokers. The problem, however, is a reciprocal one: It is caused by smokers and nonsmokers wanting to use the same air for two different purposes. Conceivably, it could be cheaper (that is, less unpleasant) for the nonsmokers to wear gas masks than for the smokers to curtail their smoking.

Automobiles sometimes hit pedestrians, injuring or killing them. The problem is caused by cars and people being in the same place at the same time; it can be partially alleviated by more care on the part of drivers or by more care on the part of pedestrians. In the 1970s the state of California, seeking to give appropriate incentives to drivers, made them legally responsible for any injury they caused to pedestrians. As a result, pedestrians had a greatly reduced incentive to take precautions, and they do, in fact, take fewer precautions. Whether the net effect has been to reduce accidents is unclear.

Sources of Transactions Costs

An understanding of the nature of transactions costs can be useful to one who is attempting to reduce them. The following series of examples illustrates some of the sources from which transactions costs are likely to arise.

Example: Mining Safety and the Principal–Agent Problem

Coal mining is an inherently dangerous activity. Mining companies are able to reduce the frequency of injury to miners by the purchase of various types of safety equipment. If the companies are liable for injuries sustained on the job, they will have an obvious incentive to invest in such equipment until the marginal cost of one more unit of equipment is equal to the

---

[10]Of course, the cost of moving does not consist only of the fees paid to the moving companies; it includes the value of the dissatisfaction generated by leaving one's friends and gathering places as well.

marginal benefit of that unit in terms of accident prevention. If, on the other hand, the companies bear no liability, you might at first think that they will have no incentive to make any investment in safety. The Coase Theorem suggests that this conclusion is wrong: Miners (who will now have to bear the costs of their own injuries) will be willing to "bribe" the company to buy safety equipment in the optimal amount. The most convenient form of such a bribe is for the miners to accept a lower wage. This is, of course, equivalent to a direct payment from the miners to the mining company.

Now suppose that there is another way to improve mining safety, which involves precautions taken by the miners themselves in the course of their underground activity. If miners bear the costs of their own injuries, they will engage in an appropriate level of precautionary activity. Alternatively, suppose that miners are fully reimbursed for all injuries by the mining company. In this case there appears to be no incentive for miners to take appropriate care. (If they are reimbursed but not fully, then they will take some care but less than the optimal amount.)

In the absence of transactions costs, however, the Coase Theorem suggests that the company itself will offer to pay the miners a bonus in exchange for their agreement to behave cautiously. Both sides benefit, as the miners collect the bonus and there are fewer injuries whose cost the company must bear.

But, unfortunately, there is no way to guarantee that an individual miner will live up to his part of the bargain. There is nothing to stop a miner from collecting the bonus and then behaving recklessly underground, where there is no one to observe him, knowing that he will be compensated by the company for any injury he sustains.

The fact that the miner's behavior is *unobservable* constitutes a transactions cost that can prevent the enforcement of the optimal contract. If all liability is with the company, and if precautionary behavior by miners is totally unobservable, then there will be no precautionary activity, regardless of what the optimal level might be.

In our simplified model of the mining industry, the most efficient liability rule is one that relieves owners of all responsibility to compensate miners for injuries. This in no way affects the incentives of owners to provide safety equipment, because their workers can still bribe them into behaving optimally. It also has the advantage of giving workers appropriate incentives, which they would not otherwise have because of the transactions costs involved in observing their behavior.[11]

Whenever one party contracts to pay another to behave in a certain way, we call the first party a **principal** and the second an **agent**. If the mine owner attempts to pay the workers for behaving cautiously, then the owner is the principal and the workers are the agents. We say that a **prin-**

Principal
Someone who pays someone else to behave in a certain way.

Agent
Someone hired by a principal.

---

[11]An interesting aspect of this choice of liability rule is that in the long run miners themselves will be indifferent to which rule is chosen (unlike Sturges and Bridgman, who cared very much). The reason is that entry and exit from the mining industry will eventually leave mining just as attractive (or just as unattractive) as the alternative occupations.

Principal–Agent
problem
The inability of the
principal to verify the
behavior of the agent.

cipal–agent problem arises when the principal cannot verify that the agent is abiding by the bargain, as in this example.

In general, if A's behavior is observable and B's is not, then, in the absence of other transactions costs, it is efficient for B to bear the costs of damage resulting from interactions between A and B. This gives B the appropriate incentives; A has them already because of the Coase Theorem.

Example: AIDS and Blood Transfusions

The recipients of transfused blood sometimes contract infectious diseases as a result. AIDS is the most significant example. Who should bear the costs of such illnesses, the patient or the doctor?

In the absence of transactions costs, the placement of liability would not matter. If doctors were liable, they would adopt appropriate standards of safety in order to avoid lawsuits; if patients were liable (as, in fact, they are), they would offer higher fees to doctors and elicit the same standard of safety.

Here we face a close analogy with mining accidents. The patient's behavior is perfectly observable: A simple test reveals whether he has contracted AIDS. The doctor's behavior, however, is not. Thus there is a principal–agent problem. If a patient pays extra for blood that is 99% certain to be AIDS-free and is instead given blood that is 95% certain to be AIDS-free, he is likely never to know the difference, whether or not he eventually becomes ill. If he does contract AIDS and suspects the doctor of cheating him, he will have great difficulty proving his suspicion. The inability to monitor doctors' compliance is a transactions cost that suggests that doctors should bear the liability for transfusion-induced illnesses.

We have been assuming that a transfusion patient is unlikely to contract AIDS in any other way. Without this assumption, our analysis must be modified. Suppose that doctors are fully liable when their patients develop AIDS. Then a recent transfusion recipient has reduced incentives to avoid other activities that may lead to the disease. If he contracts AIDS through riotous living, he can blame the doctor and be compensated. As a result, he may engage in such activities to a greater than optimal degree. The unobservability of the patient's behavior constitutes an argument for patient liability.

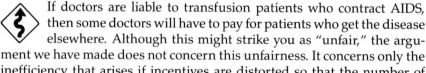 If doctors are liable to transfusion patients who contract AIDS, then some doctors will have to pay for patients who get the disease elsewhere. Although this might strike you as "unfair," the argument we have made does not concern this unfairness. It concerns only the inefficiency that arises if incentives are distorted so that the number of AIDS cases ends up being either more or less than optimal.

Incomplete Property Rights

Transactions costs also arise when property rights are ill-defined or nonexistent. Not knowing who owns something makes it difficult to bargain over its use. If Jack owns a tree that is worth more to Jill than to him, he will sell it to Jill. If Jill owns the tree and values it more than Jack does, she will keep it. If the tree belongs to some third party, he will sell it to whoever values it the most. In any event, the tree ends up in the hands of whoever values it most, regardless of who owns it initially—provided *someone* owns it initially.

Suppose, alternatively, that there are no property rights to trees, and that a tree belongs to the person who takes it. The tree is worth $3 to Jack and $5 to Jill. Nevertheless, if Jack is first to spot the tree, he will claim it for his own. If Jack had a well-defined property right, he could agree to sell the tree to Jill; unfortunately, unless he uses the tree immediately, Jill will claim it for her own. Jack takes the tree for himself.

You might think that Jack could call Jill on the phone, warn her that he is about to claim the tree, and offer to leave it standing for her if she will pay him $4. Unfortunately, Jack has 13 identical cousins, all named Jack, each of whom is prepared to present Jill with the same threat. To save the tree for herself, she would have to pay 13 × $4 = $52, or $47 more than it is worth to her. She passes up this opportunity, and the tree goes to one of the Jacks, who values it less than Jill does.

The lack of property rights in trees can present other problems as well. In the absence of property rights, nobody will plant or nurture trees, even though the benefit from doing so may exceed the cost. Another difficulty arises if Jill values a tree most for its decorative beauty. A tree left standing is a tree left vulnerable to expropriation, so Jill uses the tree for firewood, reducing its value to her and creating a social loss.

Liability Rules as Incomplete Property Rights

In Section 12.2 we treated liability rules and property rights as different ways to describe the same thing. In the examples considered there, this was an accurate depiction. In other instances, however, liability rules can better be viewed as *incomplete* property rights.

Consider again Bridgman the confectioner and Sturges the doctor. Bridgman makes noise damaging to Sturges's practice. If Bridgman is granted the right to make noise, we say either that he has a property right to the air or that there is a liability rule in his favor.

However, we must distinguish between two different legal situations. Is it *Bridgman* personally who is granted a right to the air, or is it *confectioners in general* who have this right? In the first case any other confectioner who wants to make noise in the neighborhood must first purchase the right from Bridgman. And Bridgman will take Sturges's desires into account, because Sturges will offer to pay him *not* to sell the right to a confectioner.

But if all confectioners, just by being confectioners, acquire the right to make noise, and hence the opportunity to be bribed by Sturges, then some people in other industries might become confectioners just in order to collect these bribes. As a result, there will be overproduction of candy, because the bribes from Sturges constitute a subsidy and an artificial incentive to enter the candy industry. Similarly, there will be a suboptimal number of doctors, as each potential doctor recognizes that he will be subject to such extortion and takes this into account in his decision about whether to enter the profession.

The reason for the inefficiency here is that when the air belongs to confectioners generally, it does not really belong to anybody. Like the tree in the forest, it belongs to whoever takes it. If the efficient use of the air is to sell it to Sturges as a quiet zone, this outcome cannot be achieved, because after Sturges pays Bridgman to keep quiet, he will still have to contend with Bridgman's 13 identical cousins, all named Bridgman.

As long as the number of firms in each industry is fixed, a liability rule is the same as a property right. But if the number of practitioners in either industry can change, then the liability rule is likely to convey only a partial property right and hence can lead to inefficiency.[12]

Free Riding

Free riders
People who benefit from the actions of others and therefore have reduced incentives to engage in those actions themselves.

Another important source of transactions costs is the problem of **free riders.** Suppose that a factory causes pollution that adversely affects the lives of 50 families. The families would like to take up a collection to bribe the owner of the factory so that he will reduce the scale of his operation. There are logistical difficulties involved in communicating with so many people at one time, but we shall suppose that these have been overcome. Each family would be willing to pay $100 to reduce pollution and is therefore asked to contribute $100 to the fund. However, each family reasons as follows: "We don't know whether the other families are contributing their share. If they are, the fund-raising drive is bound to be successful even without our contribution. Everyone else will pay and we will share in the benefits; we can 'ride for free' while others pay the fare. Another possibility is that the other families aren't paying, in which case our $100 certainly won't be enough of a bribe to make a significant difference. Either way, let's not contribute."

You might recognize this reasoning; it is precisely that of the prisoners in the Prisoner's Dilemma. It is rational reasoning on the part of each individual family, but it prevents the socially optimal contract from being reached, and as such can be counted as a transactions cost. An alternative view is that this is just another example of ill-defined property rights: If property rights to the newly clean air were well established, those who have bought it could demand payment from other families who make use of it.

---

[12]The importance of this distinction between property rights and liability rules was clarified by H. E. Frech III in "The Extended Coase Theorem and Long Run Equilibrium: The Nonequivalence of Liability Rules and Property Rights," *Economic Inquiry* 17 (1974), 254–268. There has been much confusion among both economists and legal scholars about this issue. Frech points out that in most of the examples that are used to illustrate the Coase Theorem (such as the case of Bridgman and Sturges), there are fixed numbers of participants, so that liability rules and property rights are equivalent.

12.4 **The Law and Economics**

Historically, English and American courts have often expressed a desire to adopt liability rules and systems of property rights that have the effect of fostering economic efficiency. The system of legal precedents that has evolved from centuries of court decisions is known as the **common law.** The common law promotes efficiency both when it directly creates incentives for problems to be solved in the least expensive way and when it acts to reduce transactions costs so that the parties to a dispute can reach low-cost solutions not directly observable by the court.

Common law
The system of legal precedents that has evolved from court decisions.

The Law of Torts

Torts
Acts that injure others.

The law of **torts** provides some interesting examples. A tort is an action that intentionally or unintentionally causes damage to another party. Once this damage has been done, there is generally no way to rectify it. If you hit a pedestrian with your car, causing him injury and six months' lost income, those costs become sunk at the moment of the accident. Regardless of whether the court orders you to pay for these damages, the damages still exist. The court can redistribute income, but it cannot change the size of the social pie. In this sense, it seems that the court's decision is irrelevant to social welfare.

However, this view fails to take account of how the court's decision affects the future behavior of others. While a ruling in favor of the pedestrian will not affect social welfare in the present case, it will send a signal to future drivers in similar situations that they are likely to be held liable as well, and it may affect their behavior in ways that have important social consequences.

Standards of Liability

Negligence
A defendant's failure to take precautions whose cost is less than the damage caused by an accident multiplied by the probability that the accident will occur.

The common law assigns liability according to different standards in different sorts of cases. One standard is the standard of **negligence.** Under this standard a defendant is held liable for the costs of an accident if those costs, multiplied by the probability of the accident occurring, exceed the cost at which he could have prevented the accident. Suppose that your barbecue grill sets fire to your neighbor's garage, causing $1,000 worth of damage, and that the court determines that there was initially a 25% chance of the fire's getting started. Then you are negligent (and hence liable under a negligence standard) if you could have taken safety precautions to prevent the fire at a cost to you of less than $250; you are not negligent if those same precautions would have cost more than $250. This standard encourages low-cost precautions while discouraging precautions whose cost exceeds their value.

There is a problem with the negligence standard, however. Suppose that you can prevent fires at a cost of $200, while your neighbor can fireproof his garage at a cost of $100. In this case a negligence standard will

Contributory negligence
A plaintiff's failure to take precautions whose cost is less than the damage caused by an accident multiplied by the probability that the accident will occur.

hold you liable for fire damage, leaving your neighbor no incentive to implement the true low-cost solution. For this reason the negligence standard is often modified by allowing a defense of **contributory negligence,** under which the plaintiff (that is, the accident victim) cannot collect for damages in cases where he himself could have prevented the accident at a cost less than the cost of the accident multiplied by the probability of occurrence.

The contributory negligence standard can also lead to inefficient outcomes. Continue to assume a $1,000 fire that had a 25% chance of occurring. Suppose that you could prevent the accident at a cost of $100, while your neighbor could fireproof his garage for $200. Under contributory negligence, he cannot collect for damages, so you have no incentive to guard against starting fires, even though it would be efficient for you to do so.

In some cases a negligence standard, with or without the allowance of contributory negligence, can lead to an outcome that is socially undesirable. Suppose that railroads and canals can both be used to transport goods at identical private costs, but that railroads sometimes cause fatal injuries that cannot be prevented at any reasonable cost. In that case railroads would not be liable for these injuries under a negligence standard. On the other hand, such liability would be socially desirable because it would raise the private cost of providing train service, leading to the replacement of railroads by canals, which provide the same service without causing injury. In such a case the efficient standard is one of **strict liability,** under which the railroads are liable for all accidents involving trains, even though there is no negligence.

Strict liability
Liability that exists regardless of whether the defendant has been negligent.

A Positive Theory of Tort Law

Judge Richard Posner, of the Seventh Circuit Court of Appeals, argues that, as a matter of historical fact, the common law has tended to embody standards that encourage economic efficiency.[13] Posner presents this viewpoint as a *positive* (as opposed to normative) theory of tort law. That is, he argues that the positions of the courts can be predicted on the basis of the assumption that they are attempting to promote efficiency. Of course, he makes no attempt to argue that every court decision fits this mold, but he does make the case that the broad outlines of legal doctrine, and the directions in which those doctrines evolve over time, are consistent with this positive theory.

Respondeat superior
The liability of an employer for torts committed by his employees.

We will consider just one of Posner's many examples. According to the legal doctrine of **respondeat superior,** an employer is liable for torts committed by his employees. For example, if you get a job delivering pizza, and you run down a pedestrian in the course of carrying out your duties, the pedestrian can successfully sue your employer. However, respondeat

---

[13]You can read his arguments in "A Theory of Negligence," *Journal of Legal Studies* 1 (1972), 29 in his book *Economic Analysis of Law* (Little, Brown, 1972), and in the recent book *The Economic Structure of Tort Law* by William Landes and Richard Posner (Cambridge, MA: Harvard University Press, 1987). Many of the examples in this section are adapted from these sources.

superior does not usually apply when the victim is a fellow employee. If you run down one of your co-workers in the parking lot, he *cannot* successfully sue the employer. How do these rules help to promote economic efficiency?

The doctrine of respondeat superior creates an incentive for the employer to select employees whom he believes to be cautious, and to oversee their activities. Although it might be more efficient for the burden of care to fall entirely on the employee, thus eliminating the costs of oversight, it is unfortunately the case that liability for accidents cannot deter an employee who has no money. Thus in cases where the employer is much wealthier than the employee, respondeat superior at least ensures that someone will have an incentive to take appropriate safety precautions.

However, if respondeat superior applied to fellow workers as well, then workers would have no incentive to avoid the company of other workers whom they know to be habitually careless. Employees would be less likely to take extra precautions when the reckless drivers were working. They would also have no incentive to report the behavior of such employees to the employer. (Once the habitual carelessness has been reported, the employer does become liable.) The difference between the random pedestrian and the fellow employee is one of transactions costs. Because a pedestrian cannot be expected to know that a particular pizza truck driver is careless, he cannot negotiate with him to drive less recklessly. This high transactions cost makes it necessary to place liability in such a way as to create incentives to solve the problem, and respondeat superior can accomplish this. But fellow employees often have detailed information about each other's behavior, and this information may not be fully available to the employer. By eliminating the employer's liability in cases involving fellow employees, the law encourages workers to use this socially valuable information in an appropriate way.

Normative Theories of Tort Law

A number of authors have proposed changes in the existing system of tort law, often arguing that goals other than economic efficiency should be given greater weight. One of the most eloquent of these is Professor Richard Epstein of the University of Chicago School of Law.[14] Epstein argues that the negligence system should be largely replaced by a system of strict liability. He argues, contrary to Coase, that it is indeed *possible* to develop a consistent set of criteria according to which we can say who is the "cause" of an injury and, contrary to Posner, that it is *desirable* to make this determination and to assign liability accordingly.

Good Samaritan Rule
A bystander has no duty to rescue a stranger in distress.

As an example, Epstein considers the **Good Samaritan Rule.** According to this rule, a bystander has no duty to rescue a stranger in trouble, even when he can do so at low cost to himself. If you are walking along the beach carrying a life preserver and see a man drowning, the law does not

---

[14]Richard Epstein, "A Theory of Strict Liability," *Journal of Legal Studies* 2 (1973), 151 and *A Theory of Strict Liability: Toward a Reformulation of Tort Law* (San Francisco: Cato Institute, 1980).

require you to save him. This rule seems not to conform to the logic of efficiency, since the benefits of the rescue would clearly exceed the costs. Epstein offers this rule as evidence that the common law is not so concerned with efficiency as Posner believes it to be. From a normative point of view, he believes that the rule is a good one, because the bystander is not the cause of the drowning. He argues both that the principles embodied in the Good Samaritan Rule are applied more widely than many scholars believe, and that it would be a good thing if they were applied more widely still.

Optimal Systems of Law

An important role for the legal system is to maintain a system of well-defined property rights. We have seen that uncertainty about property rights can be an important source of inefficiency. For this reason courts are often well advised to adopt standards that are simple and well understood, even when more complicated rules appear to provide more appropriate incentives. The gain from clarity may suffice to justify a more straightforward legal standard.

Consider traffic lights, which constitute a method of allocating the property rights to an intersection. When you are stopped by a red light and there are obviously no cars coming in the opposite direction, property rights have been allocated inefficiently. You have an immediate use for the intersection, but the right has been granted to others who have no use for it. Nevertheless, the law does not allow you to enter the intersection. If it did, there would be ambiguity about when you could and could not take advantage of this exception, and that ambiguity could lead to an increase in the number of accidents. The law accepts inefficient outcomes in some cases in order to have the most efficient possible *system* of outcomes.

Another example is the "reasonable man" standard in tort law, where negligence is judged not by the actual costs of preventing a given accident, but by the typical costs of preventing similar accidents in similar circumstances. In individual cases this may lead to inefficient outcomes, but it has the salutary effect of making it easier to judge whether you or your neighbor is legally responsible for preventing his garage from catching fire. You may not be aware of his individual cost of fireproofing, but you are likely to be aware of the typical costs of fireproofing. The resulting clarification of property rights tends to ensure that at least *someone* will prevent fires, even if not always in the ideal way. Such approximations are often all that could be asked of the legal system by any reasonable man.

Summary

An external cost is a cost imposed on others, such as the damage to neighboring homes from a polluting factory. External costs can lead to a divergence between private costs and social costs, and hence to inefficiency. The reason for the inefficiency is that producers equate marginal benefit to their private marginal cost, whereas the efficient outcome is where marginal benefit equals social marginal cost.

An externality is said to be internalized when the source of the externality counts it as part of his private costs in the course of making decisions. Pigou argued that the way to internalize an externality is to impose a tax (known as a Pigou tax) equal to the amount of the external cost.

Coase found a number of problems with Pigou's analysis. First, in the absence of transactions costs, bargaining will lead to an optimal outcome even when there is no Pigou tax. Second, in the presence of transactions costs, a Pigou tax (or an equivalent property right or liability rule) eliminates the incentives for one party or the other to seek a low-cost solution to the problem. Coase also argued that it makes no sense to identify one party or the other as the "cause" of the externality; externalities arise when two parties want to use the same resource for two different purposes.

Coase's first point is called the Coase Theorem. In its strongest form it says that a reassignment of property rights or a change in liability rules has no effect on the way resources are allocated. However, there are a few important exceptions. First, if there are no transactions costs between a polluting factory and its neighbors, a Pigou tax can actually reduce social welfare by inducing the factory to underproduce. However, this objection vanishes when the proceeds of the Pigou tax are paid to the neighbors, or when the recipients of the tax revenue can costlessly enter the negotiations. Second, a redistribution of property rights affects the distribution of income, possibly changing demand curves and thereby affecting the allocation of resources. Third, many liability rules convey only incomplete property rights and therefore create artificial incentives to enter or leave an industry.

Transactions costs arise when behavior is not observable, when property rights are incomplete, when free ridership problems occur, and in many other situations. In all of these cases Coase's second point applies. That is, the allocation of property rights has important implications for economic efficiency via its effects on the incentive structure.

A court can attempt to promote efficiency by assigning rights so as to create appropriate incentives. Unfortunately, the court may be unaware of the costs of various alternatives, and hence unable to determine what incentives are appropriate. An alternative approach is for the court to attempt to reduce transactions costs. If transactions costs are sufficiently low, the Coase theorem guarantees an efficient outcome regardless of how rights are assigned. In some cases the court's decision itself can affect transactions costs. For example, the unobservability of someone's behavior becomes a transactions cost when he is awarded a right that leads others to attempt to bribe him. (Giving miners the right to be compensated for injuries is an example.)

Posner argues that the law of torts, with its emphasis on the negligence standard, has evolved to promote economic efficiency.

Review Questions

R1. What is a Pigou tax? Explain how it works.

R2. Under what circumstances and in what sense do assignments of property rights "not matter"?

R3. State the Coase Theorem and explain what it means.

R4. Why might it be undesirable to make a railroad liable for the damage its trains cause to neighboring crops? Why might it be desirable? What sorts of information are necessary for determining the optimal liability rule?

R5. What is a principal–agent problem? Give some examples. How does the existence of a principal–agent problem affect the optimal choice of liability rule?

R6. How do incomplete property rights lead to inefficiency? In what way are many liability rules examples of this phenomenon?

R7. What is negligence? What is strict liability? What are some of the ways in which these standards can be conducive or nonconducive to economic efficiency?

Problem Set

1. *True or false:* Monopolies lead to inefficient allocation of resources. Externalities lead to inefficient allocation of resources. Therefore a firm that is both a monopoly *and* a source of negative externalities is an especially serious social problem.

2. A certain brand of soup is widely known to taste delicious and to cause fatal cases of botulism one out of every 10,000 times it is eaten. *True or false:* If the soup company were absolved of all legal liability for these deaths, it would be likely to become more careless, and the number of botulism cases would increase.

   What if a series of contradictory court rulings creates general uncertainty about whether the company is liable?

3. *True or false:* In the absence of transactions costs, every monopolist would act like a competitor.

4.   Stocks are property, yes.
                Bonds are property, yes.
        Machines, land, buildings are property, yes.
                A job is property,
                no, nix, nah nah.
   —Carl Sandburg, *The People, Yes*[15]

   Why might these social arrangements have come about?

5. Discuss the pros and cons of the following statement: "Entry to decreasing-cost industries should be subsidized by the government."

6. Certain brands of over-the-counter medicine have been laced with cyanide, apparently by random psychotics. In some cases the families of the victims have sued the pharmaceutical companies that manufacture the medicines. Assuming that the purpose of the law is to promote efficiency, should they be able to collect? Give some arguments both pro and con.

---

[15]New York: Harcourt Brace Jovanovich, 1936.

7. *True or false:* If universities were made liable to their students for the effects of assaults that occur on campus, the number of such assaults might go up.

8. Farmer Jones keeps rabbits; Farmer Smith grows lettuce on adjoining land. The rabbits like to visit Farmer Smith. *True or false:* Farmer Jones should reimburse Farmer Smith for the damage, since it is caused by the rabbits.

9. *True or false:* In deciding whether it is socially efficient to build a new airport on the edge of town, it is necessary to weigh all of the costs against all of the benefits. One cost that should definitely be counted is the displeasure that nearby residents will suffer as a result of the noise.

10. Suppose that you are the judge in the lawsuit described in the article below. Under various assumptions, discuss the senses in which your decision "matters" and the senses in which it might not. Which of your assumptions seems most reasonable to you?

Bee Trial Brings Up Sticky Insect Mess

If you stay in this business long enough, sooner or later you deal with everything. This column, for example, is about insects depositing waste material—forgive the euphemism—on cars.

The issue comes up because in Macomb, Ill., there is a lawsuit that charges that bees did $25,000 worth of damage to the paint on new cars by dropping their waste on them.

Anyway, the Macomb suit alleges that as much as 1½ million bees were brought to a clover field across the road from a line of new car dealerships. The suit says the beekeeper and the landowner "should have known that said bees would rise up out of their hives and travel the short distance to the Mac Ford [or Kelly Pontiac] lot to deposit the fecal excrement upon said automobiles."

Bee waste, it seems, contains acid that eats through automotive paint, right down to the bare metal, according to Bob Allen, a co-owner of Mac Ford.[16]

Now suppose that the "victim" is not a car dealer but a large collection of motorists whose cars are attacked whenever they drive by the area. How would your answer change? What are some of the important factors that you would take into account in making your decision?

11. The workers at a certain firm are exposed to radiation. This exposure can cause birth defects if the workers have children in future years. (If they don't have children, no health problems arise.) Some ex-workers have had children with birth defects and then sued the firm for large sums of money.
    a. Under what circumstances, and in what sense, does it not matter how the court rules in these lawsuits?

---

[16]*The Chicago Tribune,* 1985.

    b. Suppose that after an employee leaves the firm, all contracts between the employee and the firm become unenforceable. Now does it matter how the court rules?

    c. Suppose that the firm is considering a policy that requires all employees to be sterilized as a condition of employment. How does this possibility affect your analysis?

    d. Suppose that the firm is forbidden by law to adopt the policy described in part c. How does this affect your analysis?

12. Suppose that judges in property disputes universally adopted a policy of holding an auction and awarding property rights to the highest bidder. In what ways would this tend to promote or retard efficiency? (The idea behind this problem is credited to Benjamin Pualwan.)

13. *True or false:* The availability of liability insurance to drivers reduces their incentive to drive carefully, with the result that there are more accidents. Insurance is therefore detrimental to welfare.

14. When a ship carrying cargo encounters peril at sea, it is sometimes necessary for much of the cargo to be thrown overboard quickly. When this occurs, the legal principle of *general average* applies. According to this principle, the owners of the cargo and the owner of the ship share in the loss proportionately to their share in the venture. For example, if the ship and the cargo have equal value, then the shipowner and the cargo owners share equally in the losses. If the ship is worth half as much as the cargo, the shipowner bears one-third of the loss and the cargo owner two-thirds.

    Assume that the captain of the ship acts in the shipowner's interest. When he decides to throw a unit of cargo overboard, how does his private marginal benefit compare to the social marginal benefit? How does his private marginal cost compare to the social marginal cost? Does this law seem to promote economic efficiency?

15. The text suggests an argument for imposing strict liability on doctors whose transfusion patients contract AIDS, and it also suggests a counterargument. Taking account of both arguments, and additional arguments of your own, what do you think would be the efficient liability standard in such cases?

Refer to Answers to Problem Sets for solutions to problems 7, 12, 13, and 14.

Chapter Thirteen

Common Property and Public Goods

In Chapter 12 we learned how incomplete specifications of property rights can lead to inefficient outcomes in the marketplace. Here we will examine some important cases of this phenomenon more deeply. First we will consider the theory of common property, which is property that is not owned by anybody. An example is a lake where anyone can come to fish and nobody has the authority to charge an admission fee. Then we will consider the theory of public goods, which are goods which, once produced, are costlessly available for use by others. An example is a streetlight you install in front of your house, which, once in place, illuminates your neighbors' properties for free.

Each of these theories is a topic in the theory of externalities. The user of a common property resource imposes a negative externality on other users, so that such property tends to be overused from an economic viewpoint. The producer of a public good creates a positive externality, so that such goods tend to be underproduced from an economic viewpoint. We will explore the nature of these problems, and will examine some potential solutions as well.

13.1 **The Tragedy of the Commons**

Incomplete property rights are an important source of economic ineffi-ciency. In this section, we will use an extended example to illustrate several aspects of this phenomenon.

The Giant and the Dwarfs

A race of dwarfs lived near a forest where apple trees grew wild. Any dwarf who wanted to could enter the forest and pick apples for himself and his family to eat. One day a giant came, claimed the forest for his own, and began to charge the dwarfs an entry fee to the forest. We will inquire into how the coming of the giant affected the welfare of the dwarfs.

The Forest as Common Property

Common property
Property without a well-defined owner.

Before the giant's arrival, nobody owned the forest; it was **common prop-erty.** Therefore no dwarf entering the forest took account of the effects his entry had on other dwarfs. Each apple-picking dwarf leaves fewer apples on the trees for other dwarfs to find, making them have to hunt harder and reducing the number of apples they can pick in a day. This is a form of external cost. There may be other external costs as well, as dwarfs clog the forest, congesting the paths and leaving beer cans in their wake.

The fact that the forest is common property raises other potential problems. It means that nobody has an incentive to care for the forest, planting new trees, clearing out those beer cans, and so forth. It also means that dwarfs will not be able to allow apples to ripen before picking them. All dwarfs may prefer ripe apples, but he who waits for the apples to ripen will find all of the apples gone. A related problem is that it might be a good idea to leave some apples in the forest where they will take root and form apple trees for the future, but because there are no property rights to those future trees, there is no one willing to forgo current apple consumption in order to produce them.

The Dissipation of Rents

Let us focus on the important question of how a dwarf's entry affects the number of apples that other dwarfs can pick. Suppose that one dwarf alone in the forest can pick 10 apples per day. He does so by picking the "easiest" apples, those lowest on the trees. When there are two dwarfs in the forest, all of the easiest apples get picked before the day is out, so the dwarfs must go on to slightly more difficult apples; as a result they get only 9 apples apiece per day. For the same reason, each additional dwarf will further reduce the number of apples per dwarf. We might get a table like the one in Exhibit 13–1.

Now suppose that each dwarf must choose to devote his day either to apple picking or to some other activity. The other activity might be coal mining or it might be watching television. We will assume that the value to

Exhibit 13–1   **The Dissipation of Rents**

Number of Dwarfs	Apples per Dwarf	Total Apple Harvest	Marginal Apple Harvest
1	10/day	10/day	10/day
2	9	18	8
3	8	24	6
4	7	28	4
5	6	30	2
6	5	30	0
7	4	28	−2
8	3	24	−4
9	2	18	−6
10	1	10	−8

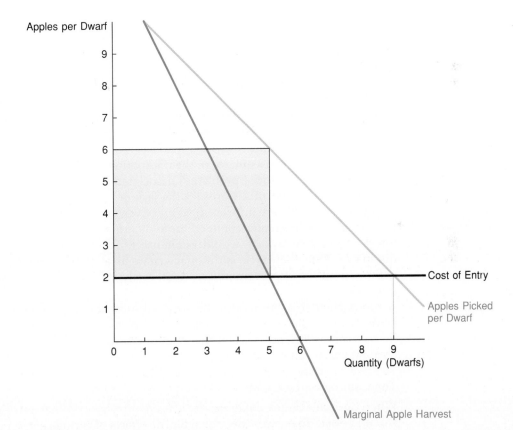

Each time a dwarf enters the forest, he reduces the number of apples picked by all of the other dwarfs. If the cost of entering is 2 apples per day per dwarf, dwarfs will continue to enter until no dwarf can pick more than 2 apples per day. This happens when 9 dwarfs have entered. At this point the rents are completely dissipated and the dwarfs get no benefit at all from the existence of the forest.

If only 5 dwarfs entered, each would gain 4 apples from the existence of the forest, making the total social gain equal to 20 apples, as illustrated by the shaded area.

a dwarf of engaging in this alternate activity is equal to the value of 2 apples. That forgone opportunity is the private cost of apple picking: 2 apples per dwarf per day.

As long as the number of apples that a dwarf can pick in a day exceeds 2, apple picking will be more attractive than the alternative and more dwarfs will enter the forest. This will continue until there are 9 dwarfs in the forest, each picking 2 apples and each indifferent between apple picking and the next best activity. Because each dwarf is indifferent to whether or not he enters the forest, the social gain from the existence of the forest is zero.

The gain to the dwarfs would be greatest if only 5 dwarfs entered the forest. Here the marginal cost of adding a dwarf to the forest just balances his additional contribution to the apple harvest. Each dwarf would pick 6 apples and incur 2 apples worth of cost, for a net gain of 4 apples per dwarf, yielding 20 apples worth of social gain. The optimal gain of 20 apples is the shaded area in Exhibit 13–1. This gain is referred to as *rent* accruing to the dwarfs from their use of the forest.

Because the forest is communally owned, there is no mechanism for restricting entry, so that this optimum cannot be reached. Nine dwarfs will enter and the rent from the forest will be zero. This phenomenon is known, for obvious reasons, as the **dissipation of rents,** or more poetically as the **tragedy of the commons.**

Dissipation of rents or **tragedy of the commons**
The elimination of social gains due to overuse of common property.

An interesting consequence of the dissipation of rents is that many of the other apparent "social problems" associated with communal ownership cease to be problems. Consider the lack of incentive to improve the forest. If the forest were improved, so that dwarfs could pick apples more productively or in greater comfort, more dwarfs would be drawn to the forest. Additional dwarfs would enter until all rents were again fully dissipated. Thus there is no additional welfare to be gained from improvements, and if the improvements are at all costly, it is best that they not be undertaken.

In particular, a mechanism by which dwarfs could claim apples but leave them on the trees to ripen, protected from expropriation by other dwarfs, can be viewed as an improvement to the forest. As such, it would have no social value.

The Coming of the Giant

When the giant claims the forest, he sets an entry price. What entry price should be set? To answer this, consider the effects of various entry prices. First consider an entry price of 8 apples per day. If this is the entry price, then it costs each dwarf a total of 10 apples per day to enter the forest (8 apples entry fee plus 2 apples forgone elsewhere). From the table in Exhibit 13–1, we see that only one dwarf will enter the forest when it costs this much to enter. Thus the giant earns (8 apples per dwarf) × (1 dwarf) = 8 apples.

If the giant sets an entry price of 7 apples per day, it costs each dwarf 9 apples to enter the forest so exactly 2 will enter. The giant earns (7 apples per dwarf) × (2 dwarfs) = 14 apples.

Continuing in this way, we generate a table:

Entry Fee	Number of Dwarfs Entering	Gain to Giant
8 apples per dwarf	1	8 apples
7	2	14
6	3	18
5	4	20
4	5	20
3	6	18
2	7	14
1	8	8
0	9	0

▷ *Exercise 13.1* Check all of the entries in the table.

Inspecting this table, the giant finds that he is best off setting an entry fee of 4 apples per dwarf, attracting 5 dwarfs and earning 20 apples.

Notice that 5 dwarfs is also the social optimum, where the marginal social cost of entry (two apples per dwarf) is equal to the marginal apple harvest from the addition of a dwarf. This is no coincidence. Once the giant arrives, the dwarfs, as before, enter the forest until they themselves gain nothing from its existence. All of the social gains go to the giant. Thus it is not surprising that the giant wants the social gain to be as large as possible.

The giant sets an entry fee that maximizes social gain, and collects all of this gain for himself.

Now that someone (the giant) is earning rents from the forest, it can be both socially and privately desirable to make improvements. Suppose, for example, that the giant decides to fertilize and plant more apple trees. In Exhibit 13–1 the curves representing the apples picked per dwarf and the marginal apple harvest both shift outward. The giant will choose a new, higher entry fee and increase his rents. Whether this is desirable depends on whether the cost of the undertakings exceeds the additional rents to be gained; the important thing is that the giant's incentives and society's coincide, so that the giant's choices will be socially optimal.

The Moral

Because all rents are dissipated, the forest has no value to the dwarfs either before or after the giant's arrival. His takeover of the forest benefits him without hurting the dwarfs. The clarification of property rights improves social welfare, if we count the giant as part of society.

A Variation on the Theme

Our discussion of the commons has assumed that all dwarfs are identical. If this assumption is relaxed, rents are still dissipated, but not completely. Therefore the dwarfs do value the forest as a resource. In such cases the giant's arrival can indeed make a difference to the dwarfs.

The Effect of the Giant When Dwarfs Are Not Identical

Dwarfs may differ either in their ability to pick apples or in their opportunity costs for entering the forest; the two analyses are essentially identical. We will assume differing opportunity costs. In this case the marginal cost curve for adding dwarfs to the forest is upward sloping as in Exhibit 13–2. Dwarfs will enter the forest until the marginal dwarf is indifferent between entering and not entering; a total of Q_C dwarfs will enter. The dwarfs earn a surplus of $F + G + H + I$.

It is important to remember that the marginal cost curve in Exhibit 13–2 does *not* show the marginal cost of picking one more apple. It shows the marginal cost of adding one more dwarf to the forest. The reason that the curve is upward sloping is that the first dwarf to enter is the one with the lowest opportunity cost, and so on. The area $F + G + H + I$ can be broken into successive rectangles, each of which represents one dwarf's gains from entering the forest.

The maximum possible surplus occurs when Q_0 dwarfs enter the forest. In this case the surplus is $C + D + F + G + I$. Dwarfs can be induced to enter in the optimal quantity by an entry fee of $P_2 - P_1$. This is the fee that would be set by a competitive giant. (To see this directly, we would need to consider the market for forests, in which the giant is one of many competitors. However, because we already know that competitive markets maximize social gain, we can guess the competitive price even without working it out.) The giant earns $C + D + F + G$, whereas the dwarfs earn I.

It appears that the dwarfs unambiguously lose $F + G + H$ by the arrival of the giant (even though society as a whole, counting the giant as part of society, gains). This appearance, however, is deceiving. Since dwarfs do earn positive rents in this case, they can benefit from the sorts of improvements that the giant makes to the forest. When he installs benches and beach umbrellas, the dwarfs benefit. We can model this benefit by a rightward shift in the "apples per dwarf" curve. (Even if dwarfs are picking no more apples, they are benefiting in other ways, and the value of those benefits can be measured in apples. Thus we think of a dwarf who gets 8 apples and 7 "apples worth" of suntan as getting the equivalent of 15 apples.)

By undertaking these improvements, the giant can increase all of the areas in the graph and benefit everyone. Without the giant, there is no chance of this occurring.

Exhibit 13–2 **Gains from the Forest When Dwarfs Are Not Identical**

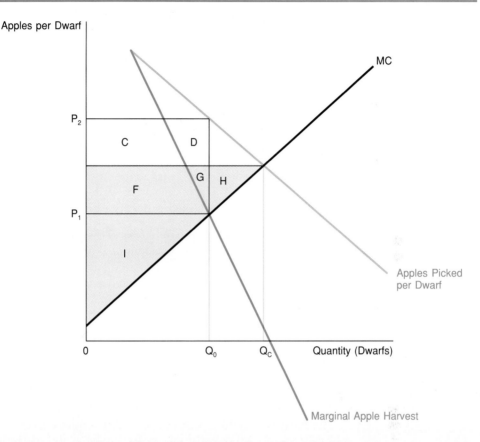

The MC curve shows the cost of adding additional dwarfs to the forest. Dwarfs will continue to enter until the last dwarf has an opportunity cost equal to the number of apples he can pick. This occurs at Q_C, and the dwarfs earn a surplus of $F + G + H + I$. If it were possible to control entry, the optimal number of dwarfs is Q_0, yielding the maximal possible surplus $C + D + F + G + I$.

The Giant as Monopolist

Another possibility to consider is that a giant owning the only forest in the area will act as a monopolist. Such a giant will charge more than the competitive price $P_2 - P_1$ as an entry fee to the forest. At this price fewer than Q_0 dwarfs will enter the forest. Before the giant's arrival there is too much apple picking; afterward there is too little.

▷ *Exercise 13.2*** Here is a challenging exercise for the mathematically talented. Assuming straight-line curves, show that a monopolized forest is more efficient than a communally owned forest if and only if the "marginal number of apples" curve is steeper than the dwarfs' marginal cost curve.

Apples as Common Property

In our examples even the arrival of the giant does not completely alleviate the problem of the forest as common property. Although he charges the dwarfs to enter the forest, we have not allowed the giant to charge them a fee for each individual apple picked. This means that those dwarfs who have already entered the forest and paid their entry fees will continue to view the apples as a common property resource and will overpick from the point of view of efficiency. If you have ever been to Disneyland, you have directly observed the effects of this sort of inefficiency. There is a fee to enter the park, without which congestion would dissipate rents. But there are no fees for the individual rides, as a result of which people queue up for the popular rides without regard to the costs (in waiting time) that they are imposing on others. The result can be waits of several hours, which would be alleviated by well-defined property rights.[1]

This is not a complete analysis of the problem. The next question to ask is: If the pricing system at Disneyland is so inefficient, why don't they change it? The same question occurs for ski lift tickets: Why do resorts sell tickets on a daily basis rather than a per-ride basis, since the latter creates long lines that skiers would be willing to pay to avoid? These questions are difficult, but they have been addressed.[2]

Other Examples of Common Property

The Fishery

Fishery
Common property.

The most commonly cited example of a common-property resource is a lake stocked with fish; the lake is like the forest in the dwarf story, and the fish are like the apples. This example is so common, in fact, that economists often refer to any commonly owned property as a **fishery**. Here the problem of depletion can be especially acute, because a fish eaten today is a fish that does not reproduce tomorrow. As a result, the fish can be overharvested to the point of extinction. The whaling industry presents an important instance (whales are not fish, but whaling is a fishery). The imminent extinction of various species is a direct result of the fact that nobody owns the whales. In the timber industry, by contrast, trees are constantly replenished precisely because they are owned.

---

[1]As always, it doesn't matter who has these rights. If the park claimed them, it could set appropriate prices to discourage inefficient overuse of the rides. If the customers had well-defined, enforceable property rights, the people behind you in line could bribe you to leave, so that only those who valued the rides highly enough to justify the cost would remain.

[2]See R. Barro and P. Romer, "Ski-Lift Pricing, with Applications to Labor and Other Markets," *American Economic Review* 77 (1987), 875–890.

Example: Splitting the Check

Suppose that you are eating dinner at a restaurant as part of a party of 10.[3] It comes time to decide whether to order dessert. You are surprised to discover that the dessert selections are very expensive, all priced at $10, whereas the most you would be willing to pay is $2. Of course, you choose to pass up dessert.

Now the waiter arrives at the table and announces that he forgot to keep separate checks, and as a result will present one bill, which will be split 10 ways. Suddenly the dessert takes on the characteristics of common property: You can have it without paying the full cost. In fact, ordering a $10 dessert will raise everyone's bill, including your own, by only $1. You order dessert. This decision is individually optimal, regardless of what everyone else is doing.

Now, as it happens, everyone else at the table has the same preferences as you do and reasons in exactly the same way. Everyone orders dessert. You end up paying $10 (a $1 share of each of 10 desserts) and getting a dessert that you value at $2.

Perhaps this inefficient outcome should be referred to as the "tragedy of the compotes."

▷ *Exercise 13.3* Find a better pun.

Example: Bumblebees and Property Rights

Often several species of bumblebees compete for nectar from the same flowers.[4] The nectar is a common-property resource, so each species has an incentive to extract more nectar than is optimal from the viewpoint of all of the bees. A system of contracts limiting each species' harvesting would improve each species' welfare.

Evolution has provided an excellent substitute for such a system of contracts. In small locales only a few species of bees tend to be abundant, and these species tend to have tongues of widely varying lengths (typically, there are three species, one very short-tongued, one long-tongued, and one medium-tongued). These differences cause the bees to favor different flowers. Short-tongued bees cannot reach the nectar in flowers with deep corollas; on the other hand, a long tongue can be a clumsy liability on a short-corolla flower.

As a result, each species specializes in taking nectar from particular sorts of flowers. Tongue lengths allocate property rights, and the bees avoid dissipating rents from nectar, without which they could not survive.

---

[3]This example is adapted from David Weimer and Aidan Vining, *Policy Analysis: Concepts and Practice*, Chap. 3 (Englewood Cliffs, NJ: Prentice-Hall, 1989).

[4]This example is taken from the fascinating book *Bumblebee Economics*, by Bernd Heinrich (Cambridge, MA: Harvard University Press, 1979). Copyright © 1979 by The President and Fellows of Harvard College. Reprinted by permission.

13.2 **Public Goods**

Public good
A good where one person's consumption increases the consumption available for others.

A good is said to be a **public good** if one person's consumption of that good increases the amount available to everybody. The most commonly cited example is national defense. An additional missile built to defend your house automatically defends your neighbors' houses as well. Police protection is another example, as are city parks, streetlights, and television programs (a program broadcast to your set is broadcast to other sets as well).

When called upon to make this definition more precise, economists define public goods in different ways. Some define a public good to be one that is **nonexcludable,** meaning that when one person consumes the good, there is no way to prevent others from consuming it as well. Others define a public good to be one that is **nonrivalrous,** meaning that when one person consumes the good, it becomes possible to provide it to others at no additional cost. Yet others define a public good to be one that is both nonrivalrous and nonexcludable simultaneously.

Nonexcludable good
A good that, if consumed by one person, is automatically available to others.

Nonrivalrous good
A good that, if consumed by one person, can be provided to others at no additional cost.

Common property, such as a fishery, is nonexcludable (anyone can use it) but not nonrivalrous (each fisherman reduces the number of fish available to others). Movie showings in uncrowded theaters are nonrivalrous (once the movie is being shown, it costs nothing to allow others to enter the theater) but not nonexcludable (theater owners can refuse admittance to anyone without a ticket). National defense, police protection, and city parks are both nonexcludable and nonrivalrous.

In our examples we will concentrate on goods that are both nonexcludable and nonrivalrous, though much of what we say will be applicable to goods that have only one or the other of these properties.

The Provision of Public Goods

When goods are nonexcludable, their consumption always entails externalities. These externalities are usually external benefits to those who are able to partake of the good for free. Sometimes there are also external costs arising from the fact that others are forced to consume a "good" that they actually view as a bad. If the streetlight that you want installed on your block keeps your neighbor awake at night, or if the missiles that make you feel more secure are viewed by your neighbor as an insane contribution to a dangerous arms race, the externalities are obviously negative.

Because the social benefits of a public good exceed the private benefits, the market tends to supply them in inadequate quantities. Suppose that each of 20 neighbors values a streetlight at $5, and the streetlight would cost $50 to install. The streetlight would provide $100 worth of social value, but no individual will be willing to pay for the streetlight.

Because of this sort of "market failure," public goods are often provided by the government. By installing a streetlight and imposing a tax of $2.50 on each of the 20 neighbors, government can improve social welfare.

There is, however, a crucial difficulty. How can the government determine when it is optimal to purchase a public good? Suppose that some neighbors believe that the streetlight would be a net benefit to the neighborhood and others don't. One possibility is to conduct a vote on the matter. However, a disadvantage of voting is that it does not allow people to register the strengths of their preferences. If 19 people each value the light at $1 apiece and if one person would be willing to pay $40 to prevent its construction, an election will lead to an overwhelming victory for installing the light, even though installing it is socially undesirable.

Another possibility is for the government to ask people not just whether they want the light but how much it is worth to them either to have it or not to have it. This has the disadvantage that people will find it in their interest to exaggerate their preferences. If you want the light at all, you might as well claim that it is worth $1 million to you, just to increase the chance of its being built.

In order to create appropriate incentives, the government might say that your share of the tax burden for installing the streetlight will be proportional to its value to you. This makes it costly to exaggerate the value and discourages overstatements. Unfortunately, it encourages dishonesty of another sort. People will tend to understate their personal valuations so as to shift the tax burden to their neighbors. With everybody understating, there may be a false appearance of insufficient demand to justify installing the lamp.

This is the phenomenon of free riding, and it is another example of the Prisoner's Dilemma. Each individual can rationally argue that if his neighbors are volunteering to be taxed for the installation of a streetlight, then it will be installed without his assistance; if the others are not contributing, then his own contribution will make no difference.

In order for the government to provide public goods in appropriate quantities, it must find ways of gathering information that is initially available only to private individuals with no incentives to reveal it. One possible source of such information is the price of private goods that are similar in nature to the public good being contemplated. For example, suppose that the good under consideration is a dam that will make water available to surrounding farmland. If the farmers are currently purchasing water through a private mechanism, the price of that water is a good indication of its value to farmers.

The more common situation, however, is one in which no such easily observable good exists. The surprising fact is that in such a case it is often possible, by the clever structuring of incentives, to induce people to reveal their true demand for a public good.

Before describing such a mechanism, we present as puzzles two other situations in which there exist surprising mechanisms to elicit the revelation of privately held information. In each case try to figure out the scheme that works before looking at the answer at the end of this section.

Puzzle No. 1 In Joseph Conrad's novel *Typhoon*, each of 200 men on a ship has stored several years' wages in his own personal strongbox. The ship encounters bad weather, the boxes are smashed, and all of the coins are mixed together. The captain gathers up all of the coins and wants to return them to the men, giving each the number of coins to which he is rightfully entitled. Each man knows how many coins were his, but nobody knows how many belong to anybody else. Obviously, each man, if asked, will exaggerate his fair share. How can the coins be returned to their owners?[5]

Puzzle No. 2 Property taxes are levied in proportion to the value of people's homes. Ideally, each individual would be taxed a given fraction of the valuation that he personally places on his house. In practice, this is assumed to be equal to the market value of similar houses. Because no two houses are alike, taxing agencies devote considerable resources to examining individual houses and assessing their values. Homeowners often protest these assessments, leading to costly disputes. How can the tax collector costlessly determine the true value of an individual house (keeping in mind that only the owner himself is initially in possession of this information)?

 In interpreting Puzzle No. 2, keep in mind that the value a homeowner places on his home might be very different from its market value.

A Scheme for Eliciting Information

Now let us return to the optimal provision of public goods. We continue to use the example of a streetlight. To keep the example relatively simple, we will make two assumptions that are not really necessary: (1) that it costs nothing to install the light and (2) that there are only three people living in the neighborhood. The three are named Bob, Cheryl, and Dale. It may be that some or all of these people view the streetlight as a "bad," assigning a negative value to it. Because the streetlight is costless, it should be installed only if the sum of the three values exceeds zero.

Bob, Cheryl, and Dale will each be asked to state the value of the streetlight to him or to her. The streetlight will be installed if the sum of these values is positive, and it will not be installed if the sum is negative. However, we throw in an additional twist. Bob is told that *if* the streetlight is installed, he will receive a payment from the government equal to the sum of the values stated by Cheryl and Dale. (If the sum of those values is negative, he will receive a negative payment; that is, he will have to pay a tax.) Similarly, Cheryl is told that if the light is installed, she will receive the sum of the values stated by Bob and Dale, and Dale is told that if it is installed, she will receive the sum of the values stated by Bob and Cheryl.

[5]The analogy between this problem and the theory of public goods was suggested by Gene Mumy in "A Superior Solution to Captain MacWhirr's Problem," *Journal of Political Economy* 89 (1981). The solution he proposed was substantially more complicated (though identical in spirit) to the one that we will give.

Under this scheme Bob is interested in the following three numbers:

- X = the sum of the values reported by Cheryl and Dale. Bob has no control over X, and it is unknown to him.

- V = the value that Bob personally places on the streetlight. Bob has no control over V, but it is known to him.

- W = the value that Bob reports to the government. Bob gets to choose W. If he were honest, he would set W equal to V.

If the streetlight is installed, Bob will gain X as a payment from Cheryl and Dale, and V in benefits from the streetlight, for a total of X + V. Thus Bob wants the light installed if X + V is positive, and he does not want it installed if X + V is negative.

How does the government decide whether to build the light? It adds the values reported by Cheryl and Dale (totaling X) to the value reported by Bob (W) and builds the light if and only if X + W is positive.

Now what W should Bob choose? By comparing the conclusions of the preceding two paragraphs, you can see that Bob assures himself of the most desirable outcome when he sets W equal to V. In other words, it is to Bob's advantage to tell the truth.

The same is true for Cheryl and Dale. The government, in possession of the truth, will be able to proceed with the optimal policy.

Where Does the Payment Come From?

The scheme we have described is theoretically workable but difficult to put into practice. One problem is that when Bob is paid the amount X, it must not come out of Dale's or Cheryl's pocket: If it did, then Dale and Cheryl would face new incentives to understate their valuations, undercutting the entire plan. (If X is negative, so that Bob is taxed, the tax revenue must not go into Dale's or Cheryl's pocket, for the same reason.) Where then, does the money come from? One solution (at least in theory) would be to use, for example, taxes on the people of California to finance schemes of this sort in New York State and, reciprocally, to use taxes on the people of New York State to finance such schemes in California.

Solutions to Puzzles

Solution to Puzzle No. 1

The captain can ask each man to write down the number of coins he started with. He announces that the numbers will be added up, and that if the sum does not match exactly the total number of actual coins, all of the coins will be tossed overboard.

Solution to Puzzle No. 2

Ask each homeowner what his house is worth to him. The values will be made public, and each owner will be required to sell to anyone who offers him more than the stated value of his house. No truthful owner can be hurt by this scheme; he can only be forced to sell to someone he would be willing to sell to anyway.

Summary

Commonly owned property is an important source of externalities. There is no way to limit use of the property in order to avoid problems of congestion. Also, there is no incentive to improve the property itself. If all users of the property are identical in terms of their opportunity costs, then rents will be dissipated completely. This is because people continue to make use of the property until everyone is indifferent regarding its existence. An owner—any owner—will improve social welfare by setting entry fees that discourage overuse and also by improving the property.

If users of the property vary in their opportunity costs, then rents are partially, but not completely, dissipated in the absence of ownership. An owner who prices competitively increases social welfare. A monopoly owner could increase or decrease social welfare.

Because public goods present incentives for free riding, they represent a type of externality. Since individuals will purchase less than the optimal quantity of public goods, public goods are often provided by the government. This makes it desirable for the government to be able to elicit information about how much people value public goods, which presents a problem in view of individuals' incentives to be untruthful. A number of clever schemes have been devised for eliciting truthful responses in a variety of circumstances.

Review Questions

R1. What is the dissipation of rents? Under what circumstances are rents dissipated completely? Under what circumstances are they dissipated partially? Why?

R2. Describe a mechanism that will induce each party to reveal how much he privately values a certain public good.

Numerical Exercise

Suppose that dwarfs pick apples in a forest that is common property. Since each dwarf who enters the forest imposes externalities on all of the other dwarfs in the forest, the dwarfs have voted to impose a Pigou Tax on all dwarfs who enter.

Let A be the number of apples picked per dwarf and let η be the elasticity of A with respect to the number of dwarfs who enter. Show that the optimal Pigou Tax is $A/|\eta|$ for each dwarf who enters the forest.

Problem Set

1. Two roads go from Hereville to Thereville. One road is very wide and can easily accommodate all of the traffic that would ever want to use it, but it is in poor repair and unpleasant to drive on. The other road is in

excellent repair and goes through the most scenic areas, but it has only one lane in each direction and easily becomes congested.

  a. Explain why, if there are sufficiently many drivers, both roads will be equally pleasant to drive on.

  b. How do the private marginal benefits compare for a driver entering the wide road and a driver entering the narrow road? How do the marginal social benefits compare?

  c. In view of your answer to part b, how could a social planner reallocate one car in order to make a welfare improvement?

  d. How much further reallocation would the planner want to make? How could the same thing be accomplished without a planner?

2. Suppose that dwarfs pick apples in a communally owned forest, and that all dwarfs are identical.

  a. *True or false:* If there are sufficiently few dwarfs, not all rents would be dissipated.

  b. *True or false:* If there are sufficiently few dwarfs, a giant who expropriates the forest and sets entry fees will never improve the welfare of the dwarfs.

3. *True or false:* The monopoly owner of a lake used for fishing might charge exactly the same price as a competitive owner.

4. Suppose that you want to sell your car to one of several people and that you decide to auction it off. You are curious to know the highest price that each of the potential buyers would be willing to pay for the car. You ask each to submit a sealed bid, announcing that the car will go to the high bidder but that he will be charged the amount of the second highest bid. Will the submitted bids be truthful? Why or why not?

5.* A factory that emits noxious smoke is located near a small cluster of homes. It is up to you to decide whether the factory will have to install pollution control equipment. A key variable in your decision is the extent of the cost imposed on the homeowners. How can you discover this cost?

Refer to Answers to Problem Sets for solution to problem 1.

---

*Denotes a problem that is rather difficult.

Chapter Fourteen

The Demand for Factors of Production

In the preceding 13 chapters we have been studying markets for consumption goods. In this and the next two chapters we will study markets for factors of production (also called inputs). Factors of production, such as labor and capital, are supplied by individual households and demanded by firms, which use them to produce output for consumption. In this chapter we will study the firm's demand for inputs.

Firms demand inputs only because they can be used to produce output. Therefore the value of those inputs depends on conditions in the output market. For example, a farmer's demand for fertilizer depends on the price at which he can sell his crops. The need to take account of conditions in the output market means that the derivation of the firm's demand for factors will be more subtle than the derivation of the consumer's demand for consumption goods.

The firm's income is paid out to the various factors of production. Workers receive wages, the owners of capital receive rental payments for the use of their facilities, and so forth. In the last section of this chapter we will use our understanding of the firm's factor demand curves to see what determines how the firm's income is distributed.

14.1 **The Firm's Demand for Factors in the Short Run**

In the short run, only one factor of production is variable, and we will assume that factor to be labor. Thus we will study the demand for labor on the assumption that the firm uses some fixed quantity of capital.

The Marginal Revenue Product of Labor

Marginal revenue product of labor
The additional revenue that a firm earns when it employs one more unit of labor.

Recall from Chapter 6 that the total and marginal product of labor curves are typically shaped like those in the first two panels of Exhibit 14–1. We will also be interested in the **marginal revenue product of labor** (MRP_L), defined to be the additional revenue earned by the firm when one additional unit of labor is employed. The marginal revenue product of labor is measured in dollars per unit of labor, whereas the marginal product of labor is measured in units of output per unit of labor.

For a firm in a competitive industry, the marginal revenue product of labor is equal to the price of output times the marginal product of labor (MP_L). Given the MP_L curve from Exhibit 14–1 and given the price of output (say $7 per unit), we can construct the MRP_L curve simply by changing the units on the vertical axis. We have done so in panel C of the exhibit.

▷ *Exercise 14.1* If the firm in question were a monopolist in the output market, how would the MRP_L curve differ?

Suppose that the firm can hire labor at a going wage rate of $25 per unit of labor. How much labor will it hire? As long as additional units of labor yield marginal revenue products in excess of $25, it will continue hiring. As soon as the MRP_L reaches $25, it will stop. Therefore we see from Exhibit 14–1 that the firm will hire 4½ units of labor. In general, at any given wage rate, the firm will want to hire a quantity of labor read from the downward-sloping portion of the MRP_L curve. We can summarize this by saying:

The firm's short-run demand curve for labor coincides with the downward-sloping portion of the MRP_L curve.

The Role of the Output Market

The three panels of Exhibit 14–2 illustrate the relationship between the labor market and the market for the firm's output. Suppose that the going wage is initially P_L, and the firm's (short-run) marginal cost curve is the curve MC in panel C of the exhibit. As we saw in Chapter 6, the marginal cost curve is determined by the total product curve and the wage rate. Therefore the information in panels A and B dictates the placement of the marginal cost curve in panel C.

Suppose that the price of output is P_X, as shown in panel C. Then from panel A we see that the firm will hire L units of labor, and from panel B we see that when the firm hires L units of labor, it can produce Q units of output. Panel C shows directly that the output of the firm is Q.

Exhibit 14–1   The Total, Marginal, and Marginal Revenue Products of Labor

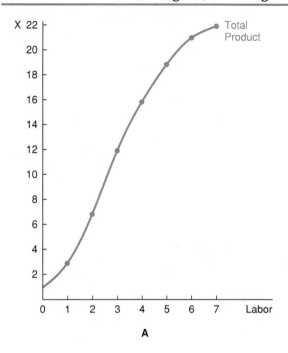

A

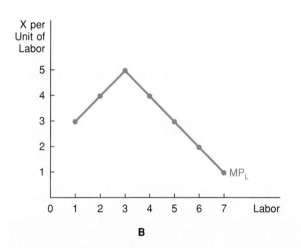

B

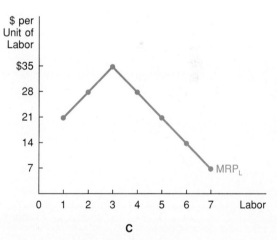

C

The total product and marginal product of labor (MP_L) curves are as in Exhibit 6–5. The marginal product of labor increases until diminishing marginal returns set in at $L = 3$, and it decreases thereafter. If the firm is competitive and sells its output at \$7 per unit, then the marginal revenue product of labor (MRP_L) is given by

$$MRP_L = \$7 \times MP_L.$$

Thus the MRP_L curve can be constructed from the MP_L curve by simply changing the units on the vertical axis, as shown in panel C.

Exhibit 14–2   **The Market for Labor and the Market for Output**

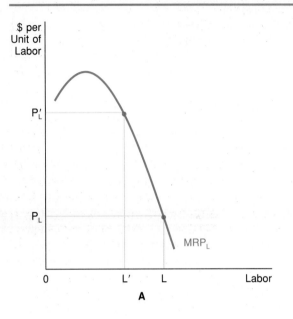

A

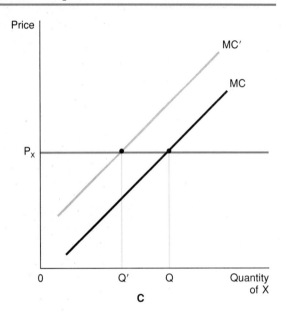

C

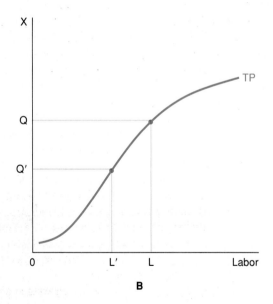

B

The marginal cost curve, MC, in panel C is derived from knowledge of the wage rate of labor, P_L, and the total product of labor curve, TP, in panel B. The derivation was given in Chapter 6. Thus each graph contains some information that is also encoded in the other graphs.

To see the interrelations, notice that when the wage rate is P_L, panel A shows that the firm hires L units of labor, panel B shows that L units of labor will produce Q units of output, and panel C confirms that the firm's output is Q. If the wage rate rises to P'_L, the marginal cost curve rises to MC'. Now panel A shows that the firm hires L' units of labor, panel B shows that the firm produces Q' units of output, and panel C confirms this.

Now suppose that the wage rate rises to P'_L. Then from panels A and B we see that the firm will hire L' units of labor and produce Q' units of output. In panel C the firm's marginal cost curve rises to MC' due to the increase in the wage rate, and the graph confirms that output is Q'.

Changes in the Price of Output

Exhibit 14–3 shows how the market for labor is affected by a change in the price of output. We assume a wage rate of P_L and an output price of P_X. The firm hires L units of labor and produces Q units of output. Now suppose that the price of output rises to P'_X as shown in panel C. Then the marginal revenue product of labor shifts out to MRP'_L in panel A, and the firm hires L' units of labor. Panel B shows that the output with L' units of labor is Q', which is the new quantity supplied as shown in panel C.

The Effect of Plant Size

All of our short-run analysis assumes a fixed plant size (that is, we assume that the firm does not vary its capital usage). It makes a difference what fixed plant size we assume. The marginal product of the fortieth doctor in a major hospital equipped with the latest multimillion-dollar technology is different from the marginal product of the fortieth doctor in a small practice with two offices and one examining room.

Suppose that the firm increases its capital usage. Then any number of workers will certainly be able to produce at least as much as before (they can always just continue what they were doing before, ignoring the new machinery) and will probably be able to produce more. Therefore the total product curve can be expected to rise. This does not necessarily imply that the marginal product of labor will rise. In the two panels of Exhibit 14–4, we show two possibilities. In panel A the total product of labor rises while becoming steeper at each level of output. In this case the marginal product of labor rises, and therefore so does the competitive firm's demand curve for labor. In panel B the total product of labor rises while becoming shallower at each level of output. This leads to a fall in the marginal product of labor, and so to a fall in the competitive firm's labor demand.

Complements in production
Two factors with the property that an increase in the employment of one raises the marginal product of the other.

Substitutes in production
Two factors with the property that an increase in the employment of one lowers the marginal product of the other.

In the first case, which is the typical one, we say that labor and capital are **complements in production.** When labor and capital are complements in production, increases in capital make workers more productive at the margin and lead to increases in the demand for labor. In the second case, we say that labor and capital are **substitutes in production.** When labor and capital are substitutes in production, an increase in capital leads to a fall in labor's marginal productivity and decreases the demand for labor. People who worry about "automation" reducing the demand for workers believe that capital and labor are substitutes in production. As an empirical matter, this case seems to be much rarer than it is often believed to be.

A change in plant size is a long-run phenomenon. Thus when we talk about the marginal product of labor before and after the capital adjustment, we are comparing one initial short-run situation with the new short-run situation that holds following a long-run adjustment.

Exhibit 14–3   A Rise in the Price of Output

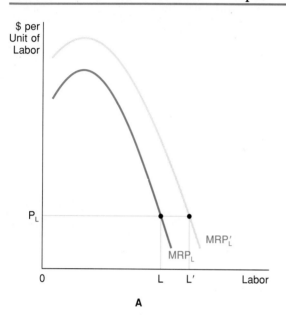

A

C

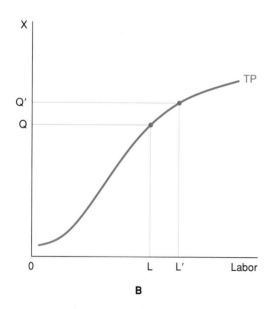

B

Initially, the price of output is P_X and the wage rate of labor is P_L. The firm hires L units of labor and produces Q units of output. When the price of output rises to P'_X, the MRP_L curve shifts out to MRP'_L, employment rises to L', and output increases to Q'.

Exhibit 14–4   **An Increase in Plant Size**

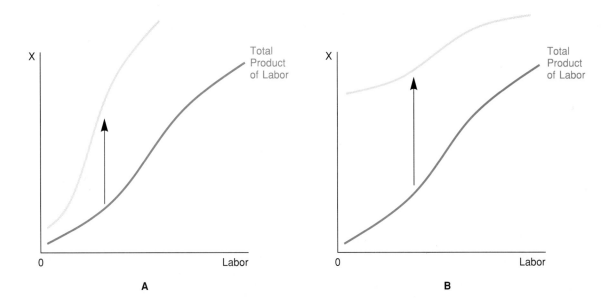

| A | B |

Following an increase in plant size, any quantity of labor can produce more than it did before. Thus the total product curve shifts upward. Typically, it also becomes steeper, as in panel A, so that the marginal product of labor increases as well. In this case we say that capital and labor are *complements* in production. But conceivably the total product could rise but become shallower, as in panel B. In this case the marginal product of labor falls due to the increase in plant size. In this case we say that capital and labor are *substitutes* in production.

14.2   **The Firm's Demand for Factors in the Long Run**

Next we will study the demand for labor in the long run, with both labor and capital treated as variables. (To study the demand for capital, simply interchange the words *capital* and *labor* throughout this section.)

Constructing the Long-Run Labor Demand Curve

Now we will construct the firm's long-run labor demand curve. Throughout the discussion the following are held fixed:

- The technology available to the firm (that is, its isoquant diagram).

- The rental rate on capital, which we denote by P_K.

- The market price of output, which we denote by P_X.

Exhibit 14–5   Constructing a Point on the Labor Demand Curve

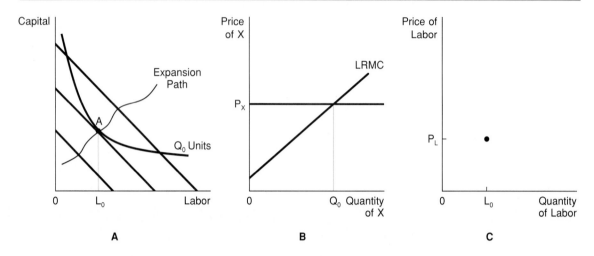

The graphs illustrate the construction of a single point on the firm's demand curve for labor, shown in panel C. The isoquant in panel A and the output price, P_X, shown in panel B are given and are independent of the wage rate. Now we assume a wage rate P_L. This enables us to draw the isocosts in the first panel, which have slope $-P_L/P_K$. These in turn determine the expansion path, also shown in panel A. Using panel A, we can derive the firm's long-run marginal cost (= long-run supply) curve, LRMC, using the methods of Section 6.3. Panel B determines the firm's output, which is Q_0. We now return to panel A to see that when the firm produces the quantity Q_0, it chooses the basket of inputs A, and this basket contains L_0 units of labor. Finally, we conclude that the wage rate P_L corresponds to the quantity of labor L_0, and we record this fact in panel C.

Constructing a Point on the Curve

To find a point on the labor demand curve, we will take a particular wage rate, P_L, as given and see how much labor the firm chooses to employ.

The wage rate P_L determines the slope of the firm's isocosts, which is $-P_L/P_K$. This allows us to draw in the family of isocosts and so to construct the expansion path as in panel A of Exhibit 14–5. In Section 6.3 we saw how the expansion path determines the firm's (long-run) total and marginal cost curves. The long-run marginal cost curve, LRMC, in panel B of Exhibit 14–5 is the one that arises from that process. The firm chooses a level of output, Q_0, so as to maximize its profits. It then looks to the Q_0-unit isoquant and finds the least-cost way of producing Q_0 units. That least-cost way is the basket labeled A in panel A. The firm hires the basket of inputs represented by A. This basket includes L_0 units of labor. Therefore a wage rate of P_L leads to the firm's demanding L_0 units of labor. This entire process allows us to construct a single point on the firm's demand curve for labor, shown in panel C of the exhibit.

Exhibit 14-6   A Rise in the Wage Rate

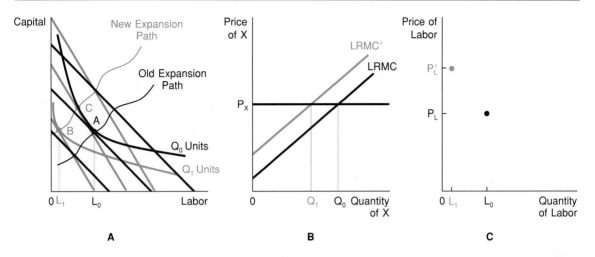

Beginning with the situation in Exhibit 14–5, we assume that the wage rate now rises from P_L to P'_L. The new curves are the colored ones. First we get new isocosts (with slope $-P'_L/P_K$) and a new expansion path in panel A. This yields a new marginal cost curve, LRMC′, and a new quantity of output, Q_1, in panel B. The firm chooses a point on its expansion path where it can produce Q_1 units of output, namely, B in panel A. Thus it hires L_1 units of labor, generating the new point on the demand curve that is shown in panel C.

The Demand for Inputs versus the Demand for Output

The construction of a firm's demand curve for a factor is similar in spirit to that of the consumer's demand curve for an output, but it is also more complicated. The key difference is that a consumer has a budget constraint. Given prices, we can determine that budget constraint and find the basket he consumes. A firm, by contrast, has no budget constraint. Instead, it has an infinite family of isocost lines, and it could choose to operate on any one of them. In order to find out what basket of inputs the firm chooses, we must refer to another market, the market for output (that is, we must use panel B in Exhibit 14–5). The firm's demand curve for a factor of production is called a **derived demand** because it is partly derived from information external to the market for the factor itself.

Derived demand
Demand for an input, which depends on conditions in the output market.

A Change in the Wage Rate

Continuing with the example of Exhibit 14–5, suppose that the price of labor rises, to P'_L. This causes all of the isocosts to become steeper, as in panel A of Exhibit 14–6, yielding a new expansion path shown in blue. The new expansion path leads to new (long-run) total and marginal cost curves. Suppose that the new marginal cost curve is the curve LRMC′ in panel B of Exhibit 14–6. Then the firm reduces output to Q_1 and chooses an input basket where the Q_1-unit isoquant is tangent to an isocost. The new basket is the one labeled B in panel A of Exhibit 14–6. The quantity of labor demanded is L_1. This gives a second point on the firm's demand curve for labor, shown in panel C of the exhibit.

Continuing in this way, we can generate as many points as we want and can connect them to get the firm's labor demand curve.

Substitution and Scale Effects

Substitution effect
When the price of an input changes, that part of the effect on employment that results from the firm's substitution toward other inputs.

Scale effect
When the price of an input changes, that part of the effect on employment that results from changes in the firm's output.

In Exhibit 14–6, when the price of labor rises from P_L to P_L', the firm moves from input basket A to input basket B. In particular, it reduces its employment of labor. This reduction comes about for two quite different reasons.

One reason is that labor is now more expensive relative to capital, so it pays to use less labor and more capital in producing any given quantity of output. In other words, the expansion path in panel A of the exhibit has shifted upward and to the left. (Instead of passing through A, it now passes through B and C.) This is called the **substitution effect** of the wage change.

The other reason is that the firm now faces higher costs and consequently produces less output, so that it wants less of every factor of production, including labor. We see this in panel B of the exhibit, where the higher marginal cost curve causes output to fall. This is called the **scale effect** of the wage change.

The substitution and scale effects of a change in the wage rate are closely analogous to the substitution and income effects that a consumer experiences in response to a change in the price of a consumption good.

An Imaginary Experiment

In order to separate the substitution effect from the scale effect, we can conduct a hypothetical experiment. Suppose that the price of labor were to rise from P_L to P_L' but that the firm kept its output fixed at Q_0. (The experiment is hypothetical because the firm would *not*, in fact, keep its output fixed at Q_0.) In that case where would the firm operate? It would want to be on its new expansion path but to remain on the Q_0-unit isoquant. That is, it would move to point C in panel A of Exhibit 14–6.

The movement from point A to point C is a pure substitution effect. The scale effect, which results from changes in the firm's output level, has been totally eliminated by assuming that the firm holds its output level constant.

Now, in fact, the firm does not hold its output level constant. Instead it moves to point B. The "move" from the hypothetical point C to the firm's actual new basket B is due entirely to the change in output from Q_0 to Q_1. It is the scale effect.

To summarize:

The firm's movement from A to B can be thought of as a movement along the isoquant from A to C (called the *substitution effect*), followed by a movement along the expansion path from C to B (called the *scale effect*).

Exhibit 14–7 **Two Possible Effects of a Rise in the Wage Rate**

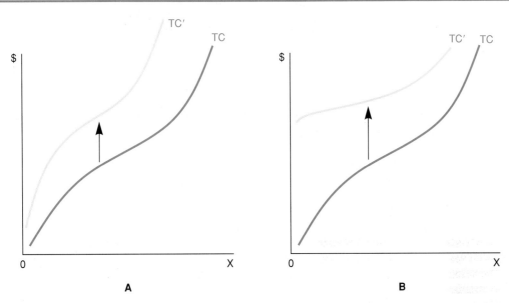

A rise in the wage rate raises the firm's long-run total cost curve, TC, to a new level, TC'. Usually, TC' is steeper than TC, as in panel A. In this case the firm's long-run marginal cost curve moves upward and output decreases, as in panel B of Exhibit 14–6. However, it is possible that TC' could be shallower than TC, as in panel B. In this case long-run marginal cost is reduced and output increases. When the latter case occurs, we say that labor is a regressive factor.

Direction of the Substitution Effect

When the price of labor rises, the substitution effect is a movement along an isoquant to a tangency with a new, steeper isocost. It must be a movement to the left. This is because isoquants become steeper to the left and shallower to the right. In panel A of Exhibit 14–6 this means that point C is to the left of point A and thus represents a basket with less labor.

The substitution effect of a rise in the wage always reduces the firm's employment of labor.

Direction of the Scale Effect

An increase in the wage rate raises the firm's long-run total cost curve. However, this could happen in either of two ways. The long-run total cost curve could both rise and become steeper, in which case long-run marginal cost will rise. Alternatively, the long-run total cost curve could rise and become shallower, in which case long-run marginal cost will fall. The two possibilities are illustrated in Exhibit 14–7.

Panel A of Exhibit 14–7 is by far the more usual case. Here a rise in the wage leads to a rise in marginal cost, as was assumed in Exhibit 14–6. Thus in Exhibit 14–6 output falls, from Q_0 to Q_1. Therefore the scale effect is a movement along the expansion path to a lower isoquant and so must be a movement to the left. Recall that in Exhibit 14–6 the scale effect is the movement from point B to point C. Because B is to the left of C, the scale effect reduces the employment of labor, thereby reinforcing the substitution effect.

However, it is also possible that the rise in the wage rate could lead to an increase in total cost of the sort shown in panel B of Exhibit 14–7 and hence to a fall in the marginal cost curve. If so, we say that labor is a **regressive factor.** For example, the rise in wages might make it profitable for the firm to build a highly automated factory, allowing it to produce at very low marginal cost. This case is shown in Exhibit 14–8, where output rises from Q_0 to Q_2 in panel B. Because of the rise in output, the scale effect is a rightward move, from point C to point B' in panel A. That is, the scale effect causes the firm to employ more labor than it otherwise would.

Regressive factor
A factor with the property that an increase in its wage rate lowers the firm's long-run marginal cost curve.

Combining the Substitution and Scale Effects

Exhibits 14–6 and 14–8 show two possibilities, corresponding to the two panels of Exhibit 14–7. In each case the substitution effect, from point A to point C, is a movement to the left. In Exhibit 14–6, which is the usual case, the scale effect, from C to B, is a further movement to the left. Thus we can conclude that B must lie to the left of A, which is to say that the quantity of labor demanded decreases in response to a rise in the wage rate. That is, in this case the demand curve for labor surely slopes down.

In Exhibit 14–8, where labor is a regressive factor, the substitution and scale effects work in opposite directions. The substitution effect reduces the quantity of labor demanded, whereas the scale effect increases it. That is, C is to the left of A, but B' is to the right of C. Where is B' with respect to A?

From what we can see in the diagram, there is no way to tell for sure whether B' is to the left or to the right of A. However, as a matter of mathematical fact, B' must lie to the left of A. That is, for a regressive factor the substitution effect must be greater than the scale effect. The proof of this is a bit subtle. If you are very talented mathematically, you will learn a lot from trying to discover it.

We can summarize by saying that in any case a rise in the wage rate leads to a fall in the quantity of labor demanded. Put another way:

The competitive firm's demand curve for labor (or any other factor of production) always slopes down.

In fact, the same statement is also true for a monopoly firm's demand curve for labor.

In the case of consumer goods, which we studied in Section 4.3, we had to admit the theoretical possibility of a Giffen good, for which the

Exhibit 14–8   A Rise in the Wage of a Regressive Factor

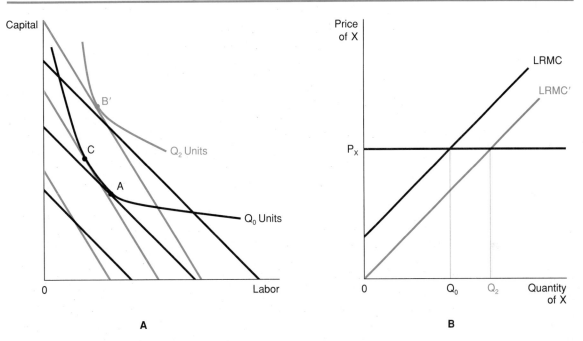

A

B

If labor is a regressive factor, than a rise in the wage rate leads to a fall in marginal cost and an increase in output, from Q_0 to Q_2. Therefore the firm moves from point A on the Q_0-isoquant to point B′ on the higher Q_2-isoquant. The move can be decomposed into a substitution effect (the move from A to C) and a scale effect (the move from C to B′).

consumer's demand curve would slope up. However, there is not even a theoretical possibility of a Giffen *factor*. A firm's derived demand curves for factors of production must slope down.

Relationships between the Short Run and the Long Run

We began this section by studying the case in which labor is the only variable input, and we argued that the firm's demand curve for labor is just the downward-sloping part of the MRP_L curve. We then moved on to the more complicated case in which two factors are variable, and we derived the firm's demand curve for labor via the more complicated process depicted in Exhibit 14–6. What is the relationship between these two approaches to labor demand?

The answer is that in the long run the MRP_L curve shifts due to adjustments in the employment of capital. For example, consider the effect of a rise in the wage when labor and capital are complements in produc-

Exhibit 14–9   Labor Demand in the Short Run and the Long Run

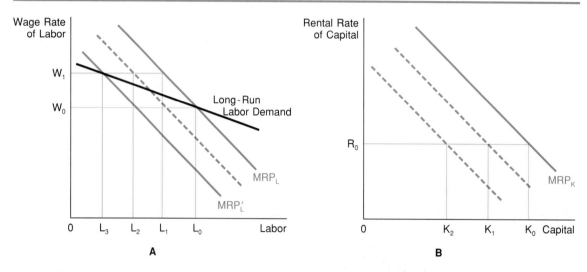

A   B

Initially, the wage rate of labor is W_0 and the rental rate on capital is R_0. The firm hires L_0 units of labor and K_0 units of capital.

Now the wage rate rises to W_1. In the short run the firm reduces its employment of labor to L_1, read off the MRP_L curve. Assuming that capital and labor are complements in production, this causes the MRP_K curve to fall to the level of the middle curve in panel B. The firm reduces its capital employment to K_1.

The reduced capital employment lowers the MRP_L curve to the level of the dashed curve in panel A, causing labor employment to fall to L_2. This lowers the MRP_K still further, causing capital employment to fall to K_2, and the process repeats. Eventually the MRP_L curve settles at the new level MRP_L'. Here the firm hires L_3 units of labor. Thus the long-run labor demand curve (in black) shows that a wage of W_1 corresponds to the quantity L_3 of labor employed.

tion. Exhibit 14–9 shows the adjustment process. Initially, the wage rate of labor is W_0 and the rental rate on capital is R_0. At these prices, the firm hires L_0 units of labor (chosen from the MRP_L curve) and K_0 units of capital (chosen from the MRP_K curve).

When the wage rises to W_1, the firm's short-run response is to move along the MRP_L curve and reduce the employment of labor to L_1. The reduction in labor reduces the marginal product of capital, so that the MRP_K curve moves down to the middle curve in panel B. In the long run the firm reduces its capital employment to K_1, causing the marginal product of labor to fall to the dashed curve in panel A. This causes employment to fall further, to L_2. This in turn leads to a further reduction in the marginal product of capital, which leads to even less capital employed, which reduces the marginal product of labor still further, and so on. After many iterations the marginal product of labor settles down, as indicated in panel A, and the final level of employment is L_3.

In the long run, therefore, the firm hires L_3 units of labor when the wage is W_1. Thus on the long-run labor demand curve, shown in black, the wage W_0 corresponds to L_0 and the wage W_1 corresponds to L_3.

 The adjustment process described here requires, in principle, an infinite number of steps. But since the firm can foresee the outcome of these infinitely many steps, it can simply move directly to the new level of employment without actually stopping at each step along the way.

14.3 The Industry's Demand Curve for Factors of Production

The industry's demand curve for factors of production can be approximated by adding the demand curves of the individual firms. However, this overlooks an important complication. When the wage rate goes up, in the usual case all firms' marginal cost curves move up. As a result, the industry supply curve shifts and the price of output rises. This in turn means that firms will not reduce output by as much as they would if price remained constant. The substitution effect is unchanged, but the scale effect is lessened. Firms reduce their employment of labor by less than Exhibit 14–6 predicts. On similar grounds, a fall in the wage leads to a smaller increase in employment than one would expect from our study of individual firms. The bottom line is that the industry's demand curve for a factor tends to be less elastic than the sum of the demand curves from the individual firms in the industry.

Finally, in any discussion of the demand for labor (or any input), it should be remembered that labor is demanded by many different industries. All of the corresponding industry demand curves must be added together to get "the" demand curve for labor.

Monopsony

Throughout this chapter we have assumed that firms take factor prices as given. This is equivalent to saying that for each factor the firm faces a supply curve that is horizontal at the market wage rate. However, there remains the possibility that a single firm could account for a substantial portion of the market for some factor. In this case the quantity demanded by the firm affects that factor's wage rate. The firm faces an upward-sloping supply curve for that factor.

The most extreme example occurs if there is some factor of production that is demanded by only one firm. In that case the firm in question is a "single buyer," just as a monopolist might be a "single seller." A single buyer is called a **monopsonist.** However, just as we use the word *monopolist* to describe any seller who faces a downward-sloping demand curve, so we shall use the word *monopsonist* to describe any buyer who faces an upward-sloping supply curve.

Monopsonist
A buyer who faces an upward-sloping supply curve.

Exhibit 14–10   **Monopsony**

A monopsony demander of labor faces an upward-sloping labor supply curve (S) and a marginal cost of labor (MC_L) curve that lies everywhere above S. He hires L units of labor (where $MRP_L = MC_L$) and pays the wage W that he reads off the supply curve at that quantity.

In an industry with many firms, the going price for labor would be W_C, and each firm would face a flat supply curve at this price. L_C units of labor would be hired.

To a monopsony demander of labor, the marginal cost of a unit of labor exceeds the wage rate. The reason for this is that when the monopsonist hires an additional worker, there are two ways in which his costs increase: (1) he must pay the new worker's wage and (2) he bids up the wages of all workers.

As a result, the monopsonist faces a marginal cost of labor (MC_L) curve that lies everywhere above the labor supply curve that he faces. He maximizes profits by choosing that quantity where the marginal revenue product of labor and the marginal cost of labor are equal; then he pays a wage read off the supply curve at that quantity. The process is illustrated in Exhibit 14–10.

The monopsonist hires fewer workers and pays a lower wage than would be the case if many firms competed to hire labor. Under competition there would be a going wage rate of W_C in Exhibit 14–10, and employment would be L_C.

How Widespread Is Monopsony?

In order for a firm to have monopsony power, it must constitute a substantial portion of the demand for some factor. Therefore even a firm that is unique in its industry has no monopsony power, provided that there are firms in *other* industries competing with it for the use of factors.

For example, suppose that all of the major auto manufacturers were to merge into one giant firm. At first, this firm could well have monopsony power in the market for auto workers, who would have no other employer competing to hire their valuable skills. However, if the giant auto firm were to exercise this monopsony power to keep wages low, some auto workers would eventually decide to acquire other skills and to sell their services elsewhere—say, as shipbuilders. In the long run the single automaker competes in the labor market with all of the firms in the shipbuilding industry and in countless other industries besides.

The same is true when a single employer dominates a certain geographic area. Although the employer may have some monopsony power in the short run, he may be unable to exercise that power without causing some of the area's residents to move elsewhere. Ultimately, he competes for the local workers with employers all over the world.

14.4 The Distribution of Income

Firms hire factors of production and combine them to create output. This output generates revenue, or income, for the firm. Each factor of production receives a portion of this revenue as its payment for participating in the firm's activity. (Economists persist in speaking of payments to factors of production, even though it would often be more accurate to speak of payments to the *owners* of the factors.) After all of these payments are made, any remaining revenue (positive or negative) accrues to the owners of the firm in the form of profit.

Factor Shares and Rents

We know from the first part of this chapter that the price of any factor is equal to its marginal revenue product. If a firm or an industry hires L units of labor at a wage rate of P_L, labor's income is $P_L \cdot L$. Therefore we can say that labor's income is equal to $MRP_L \cdot L$.

If the supply curve of labor to this firm or industry is upward sloping, the suppliers of labor earn a producers' surplus, or rent, equal to area B in Exhibit 14–11. Labor's income is the sum of areas B and C, so that only a portion of this income can be considered rent.

Do not confuse the word *rent*, meaning producers' surplus, with the rental (that is, wage) paid by the firm to hire a factor of production. The factor earns a producers' surplus equal to the payment it receives from the firm *minus* its opportunity costs. Only when

Exhibit 14–11   **Labor's Share of Income**

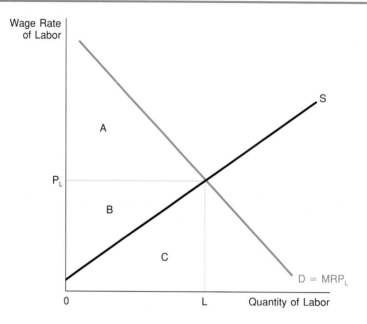

The firm or industry hires L units of labor at the wage P_L and earns a total revenue of A + B + C. Of this revenue, labor receives a share equal to $P_L \cdot L = B + C$. Of this, area C covers workers' opportunity costs and area B is earned as rent.

the factor supply curve is perfectly vertical does the rental payment consist entirely of rent.

The area A + B + C under the MRP_L curve in Exhibit 14–11 is equal to the total revenue of the firm or of the industry. (The area can be broken into rectangles representing the revenue from the first unit of labor employed, the revenue from the second unit, and so on). Because labor receives B + C, the remaining area A must represent the sum of the payments to all other factors, plus any profits that are earned.

What is true of labor is also true of every other factor. Capital earns an income of $MRP_K \cdot K$, of which some portion is rent. There are also intangible factors like "entrepreneurial ability" that are typically supplied by the owners of the firm. Although such factors are not explicitly on the payroll, they should be viewed as implicitly receiving a wage equal to their marginal revenue product. If the owner supplies E units of entrepreneurial ability, with a marginal revenue product of MRP_E, then we think of the firm as paying the owner an income of $MRP_E \cdot E$ in his capacity as a factor of production.

Inputs like entrepreneurial ability are often supplied quite inelastically. The owner of a shoestore has a great deal of knowledge about the specific workings of his own enterprise. Such knowledge is a factor of production that would be much less valuable in any alternative use. As a result, he might supply almost all of this knowledge to his own business regardless of whether he earns a high or a low wage by doing so. Thus the supply curve for the owner's entrepreneurial services is very inelastic, so that a large portion of the income earned by these services tends to be rent.

Profit

The sum of the factor payments may be less than, equal to, or greater than the revenue of the firm. If the factor payments are less than the firm's revenue, then the difference is profit and accrues to the owner of the firm. If the factor payments exceed the firm's revenues, the firm takes a loss, sometimes called a negative profit, equal to the difference. This loss comes from the pocket of the owner of the firm.

Notice that in our analysis the owner of the firm receives two very different kinds of payments. (They are different to the economist, although an accountant or a businessman would see no reason to distinguish them.) First, there is the income that he earns as the supplier of certain factors of production. Much of this income is usually a rent, or a producer's surplus. Second, there is the profit remaining after the firm has made all of its factor payments (including the ones to the owner).

As was discussed briefly in Chapter 7, many economists would prefer not to think of specialized skills, such as knowledge of the workings of a particular shoestore, as factors of production that are hired by the firm. They would prefer to think of the firm as earning positive profits due to the existence of these factors. The two analyses use different words but describe the same outcomes.

Producers' Surplus

In earlier chapters we have talked about the producers' surplus earned by firms. It is often useful to think of producers' surplus in that way. However, in a more careful analysis, we recognize that at least part of the producers' surplus is actually earned by the factors that the firms employ.

In fact, in long-run competitive equilibrium, firms earn zero profits. This means that all of the producers' surplus that we have previously attributed to the firms is actually paid out to factors.

Exhibit 14–12 shows the relationship between the industry-wide markets for output, labor, and capital when each firm earns zero profits. The firms earn total revenue equal to A + B in the output market, of which A is producers' surplus. (The firms' total revenue is also equal to C + D + E in panel B and to F + G + H in panel C.) This revenue is distributed to workers, who earn D + E in panel B, and to the owners of capital, who

Exhibit 14–12   The Distribution of Rent

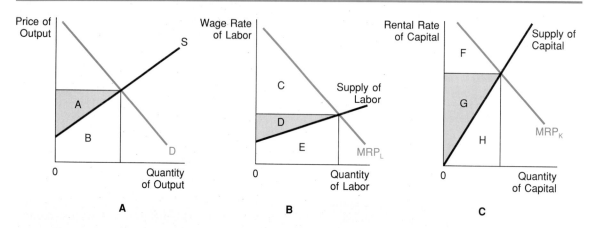

In long-run zero profits equilibrium, the industry's total revenue (given by A + B = C + D + E = F + G + H) is paid out to factors. Since labor's total wages are D + E and the total rental payments to capital are G + H, we have A + B = (D + E) + (G + H). Producers' surplus in the industry is equal to A, of which workers get D and owners of capital get G. Therefore A = D + G.

earn G + H in panel C. Since we assume that firms earn zero profits, these factor payments must exactly account for the firms' total revenue. That is, (D + E) + (G + H) = A + B.

The portion of total revenue that is producers' surplus is exactly A, of which D is earned by workers and G is earned by the owners of capital. Therefore A = D + G. If profits were nonzero, then area A would include those profits in addition to D + G.

 Of course, when there are more than two factors of production, rents are divided among all of them, not just capital and labor.

Who Benefits?

Factors that are supplied relatively inelastically (the most extreme case being a fixed factor) earn more rents than those supplied more elastically. As a result, the more nearly fixed factors have more to gain (or to lose) from changes in the demand for the output of the industry. If the demand for output rises, the derived demand for all inputs rises. This increases producers' surplus by more for those factors with inelastic supply curves than for other factors. By the same reasoning, these factors bear most of the loss when the demand for output falls.

For example, professional football games are produced with many inputs, including professional quarterbacks and footballs. The supply of quarterbacks is quite inelastic, due to the fact that the particular skills of a quarterback have relatively few alternative uses that are anywhere near as valuable. Therefore quarterbacks earn substantial rents. (That is, their wage bills far exceed their opportunity costs.) Footballs are supplied much more elastically, due to the fact that the skills needed to produce footballs are also useful in a variety of other industries. Therefore suppliers of footballs earn comparatively little rent. Any change in the public's demand for football games will have a much greater effect on the fortunes of quarterbacks than it will on the fortunes of football manufacturers.

What matters in this example is not the fact that quarterbacks' wages are high, but that their supply curve is inelastic. Suppose, for example, that all quarterbacks could equally well earn $500,000 a year as movie stars. Then, over a substantial range, the supply curve for quarterbacks would be flat (perfectly elastic) at $500,000 per year. In this case the wage would be high, but there would be no producers' surplus. And, in fact, in this case quarterbacks would not be hurt if the public completely lost interest in football. Changes in the industry's fortunes are felt most by those factors that are inelastically supplied, *not* by those factors whose wage bills are high.

Some factors are fixed in the short run and variable in the long run. An increase in the price of output benefits these factors more in the short run than in the long run. For example, in the short run there are a fixed number of recording studios capable of producing compact disks. A rise in the price of compact disks will raise revenue in the recording industry, and in the short run this increased revenue will largely be paid as rent to the owners of the recording studios. In the long run, however, more recording studios can be built, and the owners of existing recording studios will not continue to reap this windfall benefit.

Quasi-rents
Producers' surplus earned in the short run by factors that are supplied inelastically in the short run.

Short-term rents due to inelastic short-run supply are sometimes called **quasi-rents.**

Finally, we should note that the owners of the factors of production are the same individuals and households that are also the consumers in the economy. In earlier chapters we have maintained a careful distinction between the consumers' surplus earned by individuals and the producers' surplus earned by firms. Now we see that the producers' surplus is actually earned by the same individuals who are earning the consumers' surplus. All gains from trade ultimately accrue to individuals. Who else is there to benefit?

Summary

A factor's marginal revenue product is defined to be the amount of additional revenue the firm can earn by employing one more unit of that factor. The equimarginal principle implies that the firm's demand curve for the factor will be identical with the downward-sloping portion of the factor's marginal revenue product curve.

An increase in employment of one factor will usually raise the marginal productivity of other factors, and hence it will raise the firm's demand curve for other factors. In this case we say that the factors are complements in production. It is also possible that an increase in the employment of one factor will reduce the marginal productivity of other factors, in which case we say that the factors are substitutes in production.

In the long run a change in the wage rate of labor will cause the firm to change its employment of both labor and capital. The firm's marginal cost curve will change, leading to a change in output as well.

In the hypothetical case in which the firm does *not* adjust output, the change in the wage rate leads to a movement along an isoquant, known as the scale effect. The scale effect is always in the expected direction: A rise in the wage rate reduces the quantity of labor demanded, and a fall in the wage rate increases the quantity demanded.

The scale effect of a wage change is that part of the change in employment that is due to the change in output. It is a movement along the new expansion path. The scale effect is usually in the same direction as the substitution effect, but it can go in the opposite direction, in which case we say that labor is a regressive factor. For a regressive factor, however, the substitution effect is always larger than the scale effect. Thus even for a regressive factor the firm's labor demand curve must slope downward.

The firm's revenues are paid out to the factors of production, with each factor earning a wage equal to its marginal revenue product. Among these payments may be payments to the firm's owners for the use of specialized factors such as particular skills. After all of these payments are made, whatever remains is the firm's profit. In long-run competitive equilibrium, profits are zero, so the factor payments exactly exhaust the firm's income.

Payments to factors minus the factors' opportunity costs are the factors' producers' surplus, or rent. The firm's producer's surplus (the area above the firm's supply curve up to the price and out to the quantity supplied) is the sum of all these factor rents plus the firm's profit, if any. Thus the producers' surplus that we have attributed to firms in previous chapters is actually distributed as factor rents.

The more inelastically supplied the factor, the greater the percentage of its income that is rent. Thus inelastically supplied factors benefit the most from the existence of the industry, and they stand to gain or lose the most when the industry's fortunes wax or wane.

Review Questions

R1. What is the relationship between marginal product and marginal revenue product?

R2. Draw total and marginal product diagrams to show how a rise in the price of output affects the employment of labor.

R3. Draw total and marginal product diagrams to show how an increase in plant size affects the employment of labor.

R4. Explain how to construct a point on the firm's long-run demand curve for labor.

R5. Define the substitution and the scale effects of an increase in the wage rate. What can be said about their directions?

R6. Define monopsony. Does a monopsonist employ more or less labor than a firm that hires workers competitively? Why?

R7. In long-run competitive equilibrium, the firm's total revenue is equal to the sum of its factor payments. Why?

R8. What is the relationship between the producer's surplus measured above the firm's supply curve for output and the producers' surpluses measured above the factors' supply curves for their services?

R9. A factor that is supplied perfectly elastically to an industry has nothing to gain or lose from changes in the price of output. Explain why, first using graphs and then giving the verbal interpretation.

R10. A factor that is supplied perfectly inelastically to an industry earns rents equal to its entire wage bill. Thus such a factor participates heavily in the industry's fortunes, be they good or bad. Explain why, first using graphs and then giving the verbal interpretation.

Numerical Exercises

N1. Consider a firm that produces according to the production function

$$Q = \sqrt{KL}$$

where Q is the firm's output and K and L are the quantities of capital and labor that it employs. With this production function, the slope of an isoquant at the point (L,K) is given by $-K/L$.

    a. Suppose that the going wage rate of labor is W, and the going rental rate on capital is R. What is the slope of an isocost? If the firm uses K units of capital and L of labor in long-run equilibrium, derive a formula for K in terms of L, W, and R. Derive a formula for L in terms of K, W, and R. (*Hint:* In long-run equilibrium, the firm operates at a point where the slope of an isocost and the slope of an isoquant are equal.)

    b. Using the production function and the result of part a, write a formula for L in terms of Q, W, and R, and a formula for K in terms of Q, W, and R.

    c. Write a formula for the total cost of producing Q units of output.

    d. Describe the firm's long-run marginal cost curve.

    e. In long-run equilibrium, what must the price of output be? Would you have had enough information to answer this question if your answer to part d had been different than it was?

    f. In terms of Q, how much does the firm pay out to labor and to capital? What is its total revenue? What is its profit?

N2. Consider a perfectly competitive industry with many identical firms, each producing according to the production function

$$Q = \sqrt{KL}.$$

Labor and capital are supplied to the industry according to the supply curves $L = W$ and $K = 4R$.

    a. Suppose that the industry produces Q units of output, using K units of capital and L of labor. Write a formula for L in terms of Q, W, and R and for K in terms of Q, W, and R.

    b. Write down two equations expressing the conditions for equilibrium in the two factor markets. Use these equations to get a numerical value for W/R. (*Hint:* Divide one equation by the other.)

    c. Show that the industry's long-run supply curve is given by

$$Q = P.$$

(*Hint:* Make use of your answers from N1.)

    d. Suppose that the demand curve for the industry's output is given by

$$Q = 1500 - P.$$

What are the price and quantity of output? How much labor is hired, and at what wage? How much capital is rented, and at what rental rate?

    e. Under the conditions of part d, calculate the producers' surplus in the output market. How much producers' surplus is earned by labor and how much by capital? How much profit is earned by firms? Is your answer consistent with your answer to numerical exercise N1f?

Problem Set

1. *True or false:* If the demand curve for a product is vertical, then any rise in the wage rate could be passed on entirely from firms to customers, without any fall in production. Thus a rise in the wage rate would not reduce employment, either in the short run or in the long run.

2. *True or false:* If labor and capital are complements in production, then the long-run labor demand curve is more elastic than the short-run labor demand curve.

3. **a.** Prepare graphs like those in Exhibit 14–9 to illustrate the relationships between short-run and long-run labor demand when capital and labor are substitutes in production.
   b. In this case is the short-run labor demand curve more or less elastic than the long-run labor demand curve?

4. **a.** Use Exhibit 14–9 to show that when labor and capital are the only inputs and when they are complements in production, the long-run labor demand curve must slope downward.
   b. Use the graphs you prepared for Problem 3a to show that when labor and capital are the only inputs and when they are substitutes in production, the long-run labor demand curve must slope downward.

5. *True or false:* The industry demand curve for a regressive factor is likely to be more elastic than the sum of the firms' demand curves.

6. *True or false:* The isocosts of a monopsonist in the labor market are not straight lines.

7. Use a graph to demonstrate the social welfare consequences of monopsony.

8. *True or false:* If there is monopsony in the labor market; a minimum wage law can lead to increased employment.

9. Suppose that labor and capital are both supplied perfectly inelastically to the U.S. economy.
   a. Show the producers' surplus earned by *capital* on a graph of the marginal product of *labor.* Explain where you make use of the fact that the supply of capital is perfectly inelastic.
   b. Suppose that General Motors moves one of its plants to South Korea, increasing the number of workers who can be combined with U.S. capital. Show the gains and losses to (1) American workers, (2) American owners of capital, and (3) South Korean workers.
   c. Does the plant's relocation help or hurt Americans as a whole?

10. *True or false:* If firms earn zero profits and if labor and capital are the only inputs, then a rise in wages must be bad for the owners of capital.

11. *True or false:* If firms earn zero profits and if labor and capital are the only inputs, then labor and capital must be complements in production. (*Hint:* Make use of your answer to Problem 10.)

12. Suppose that there are exactly three factors of production: skilled labor, which is represented by unions; unskilled labor, which is not represented by unions; and capital. Currently, skilled labor earns $15 per hour and unskilled labor earns $5 per hour. Legislation has been proposed to establish a minimum wage of $10 per hour for all workers, and this legislation has been strongly endorsed by the unions.

    Assuming that the unions act in the best interest of their members, can you determine whether skilled and unskilled labor are complements or substitutes in production? What about capital and unskilled labor? Can you predict how the owners of capital will feel about the legislation?

13. In order to promote economic expansion, the town of Hyde Park has declared certain areas of the city to be "no-tax zones." Businesses located in these areas are exempt from all city taxes. As a result, many new firms have started up, each of which rents offices and machinery and hires many workers.

    In the long run, which of the following groups are likely to benefit from the existence of the no-tax zones: the owners of firms, the customers of the firms, landowners in the no-tax zones, the producers of machinery, the workers?

Refer to Answers to Problem Sets for solutions to problems 10, 11, and 12.

Chapter Fifteen

The Market for Labor

There are two types of decision makers in the economy: individuals and firms. The individuals supply factors of production, such as labor, to firms, and demand output in return. The firms demand factors of production, use them to produce output, and supply that output to the same individuals who supply the factors of production.

In a competitive economy all prices and quantities are determined by the intersections of supply and demand curves. The supply of output and the demand for factors are both consequences of technology, and of prices in other markets, as we saw in Chapters 7 and 14. More precisely, output supply depends on both technology and factor prices, and factor demand depends on both technology and output prices. The demand for output depends on individuals' tastes and incomes, and their incomes are determined by factor prices. It remains to study the supply of factors.

In this and the next chapter we will complete our picture of the economy by seeing how individuals' tastes determine the supply of factors. It follows that in a competitive economy all prices and quantities are completely determined by tastes and technology. (Any given price is affected by other prices as well, but these are simultaneously determined by the same tastes and technology.)

We will begin by studying individual labor supply curves. Then we will study the supply of labor to the entire economy and the determination of equilibrium in the labor market. Finally, we will introduce the subject of why wages differ across individuals.

15.1 Individual Labor Supply

Individuals supply labor to the market at a price that we call the wage rate of labor. We will begin by deriving an individual's labor supply curve.

Consumption versus Leisure

Leisure
All activities other than labor.

Each individual is endowed with 24 hours per day that he can allocate between labor and leisure. Labor consists of working in the marketplace for the going wage. **Leisure** consists of all other activities. Thus leisure includes time spent on the beach, but it also includes time spent in productive activities such as managing a firm, going to school, or looking for a better job.

Consumption
All goods other than leisure.

There are two goods relevant to the labor supply decision. One is leisure, and the other is **consumption.** The word *consumption* is used to represent all of the goods that can be purchased in the marketplace. Thus it plays the same role that "all other goods" plays in the derivation of individual demand curves. Consumption stands for all goods other than leisure.

Consumption is often measured in dollars. We will find it more convenient to measure consumption in terms of the output good that the worker is producing. Thus if he is a sausage maker, we will measure all consumption in terms of sausages.

It is often useful to pretend that there is only a single consumption good in the economy, so that all workers receive their wages in the form of this single good.

Indifference Curves

We can draw indifference curves between leisure and consumption, and we will choose to draw them with the leisure axis running *from right to left.* This is pictured in panel A of Exhibit 15–1. Because it is not possible to have more than 24 hours of leisure per day, we have drawn a vertical barrier at the 24-hour mark. The number of hours that the individual devotes to labor is given by 24 minus the number of hours he devotes to leisure. This is indicated in the graph by the second row of labels on the horizontal axis.

In panel B of Exhibit 15–1 we have reproduced panel A without the right-hand vertical axis and with only the labor markings on the horizontal. This panel depicts the individual's indifference curves between labor and consumption. They are upward-sloping, reflecting the fact that labor is considered undesirable. The slope of an indifference curve at any point

Exhibit 15–1   **Consumption versus Leisure**

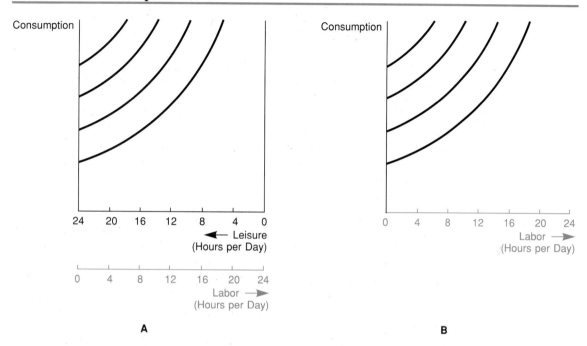

Panel A shows indifference curves between the two goods leisure and consumption, with the leisure axis running from right to left. Because of the reversed axis, the indifference curves appear to slope upward.

The alternate axis in panel A is the labor axis, since the amount of labor supplied per day is always 24 hours minus the amount of leisure taken. Panel B is a duplicate of panel A, with the leisure axis eliminated and only the labor axis shown.

is the amount of consumption needed to just compensate the worker for an additional hour of labor. It is the marginal value of leisure, measured in terms of consumption.

▷ *Exercise 15.1* Use the observation of the preceding sentence to explain why the indifference curves become steeper as you move up and to the right.

Nonlabor income
Income from sources other than wages.

In Exhibit 15–2 we have added the budget constraint. When the individual does not work at all, he earns an income of C_0. This **nonlabor income** is a return to some asset owned by the individual, such as an apple tree, a portfolio of stocks, a small business, or a pension. The slope of the budget line is equal to the wage, which we call W. If consumption is measured in sausages, then W is measured in sausages per hour. Each additional hour of labor yields W additional units of consumption.

Exhibit 15–2   The Worker's Optimum

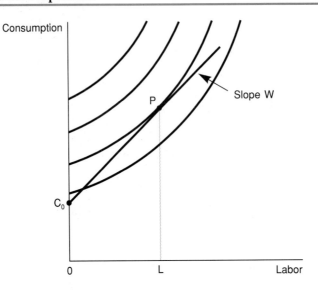

The budget constraint is determined by C_0, which is the worker's income from sources other than labor, and the wage rate W, which gives the slope of the budget line. The optimum is at P, where the worker supplies L units of labor. Here the wage rate (the slope of the budget line) is equal to the marginal value of leisure (the slope of the indifference curve).

The worker chooses his optimum point, which is at a tangency between an indifference curve and the budget line (point P in the exhibit). At the wage W the worker supplies L units of labor. At point P the wage rate (the slope of the budget line) is equal to the marginal value of leisure.

▷ *Exercise 15.2* Justify the worker's choice on economic grounds: If the wage were either more or less than the marginal value of leisure, how could the worker improve his position?

Changes in the Budget Line

The worker's budget line changes if either his nonlabor income C_0 or his wage rate W changes. We will now study how the worker's optimum is affected by each of these possibilities.

Changes in Income

Exhibit 15–3 shows the effect of an increase in the worker's nonlabor income from C_0 to C_1. The new optimum is at P'. If both consumption and leisure are normal (as opposed to inferior) goods, then the worker will choose more of each in response to his higher income; that is, P' will be

Exhibit 15–3 **An Increase in Nonlabor Income**

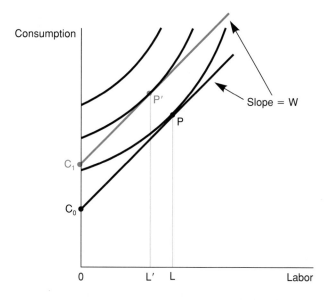

When nonlabor income increases from C_0 to C_1, the worker's budget line shifts upward parallel to itself. The new optimum is at point P'. If consumption and leisure are both normal (as opposed to inferior) goods, then P' lies above and to the left of P. Thus an increase in nonlabor income leads to increased consumption and less labor supplied. The quantity of labor that this worker supplies falls from L to L'.

above and to the left of P. Although it is logically possible for P' to be either below or to the right of P, we will assume that the income effects work in the expected directions, as in the exhibit. With this assumption:

> **An increase in nonlabor income leads to a fall in the quantity of labor supplied.**

An Increase in the Wage Rate

Suppose that the wage rises from W to W' while nonlabor income stays fixed. This has the effect of making the budget line steeper. Since there is no change in nonlabor income, the budget line swings through its intercept with the vertical axis. Exhibit 15–4 shows two possible outcomes. The optimum basket moves from P to Q in panel A of the exhibit or from P to R in panel B.

Income and Substitution Effects

When the wage goes up, there is both a substitution effect and an income effect. The substitution effect is that an additional hour of leisure is now more expensive in terms of forgone consumption. To say the same thing

Exhibit 15–4   A Rise in the Wage Rate

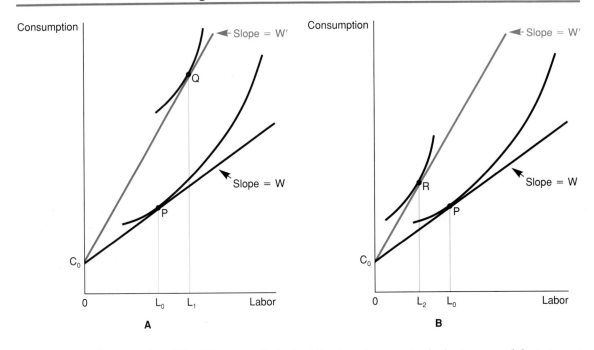

An increase in the wage, from W to W', causes the budget line to swing counterclockwise around the intercept C_0. Depending on the slope of the indifference curves, the new optimum could be at a point like Q, where more labor than before is supplied, or at a point like R, where less labor is supplied.

another way, additional consumption is now less expensive in terms of forgone leisure. In consequence of the substitution effect, the worker chooses more consumption and less leisure. Since he chooses less leisure, he supplies more labor.

The rise in the wage also has an income effect in that it makes suppliers of labor better off. As in Exhibit 15–3, we assume that both consumption and leisure are normal goods, so that the income effect leads the worker to choose more of both. Since the income effect leads the worker to choose more leisure, he supplies less labor.

The income and substitution effects both lead to an increase in consumption (an upward movement in the consumer's optimum). These effects reinforce each other, and we can conclude that the new optimum (Q or R in the two panels of Exhibit 15–4) will be higher than the old optimum (P in either panel).

Regarding leisure, the income and substitution effects are at cross purposes. The higher wage elicits more labor via the substitution effect, but it also makes the worker richer, eliciting more leisure (hence less labor) via the income effect. Either effect can dominate, so that the new optimum can be either to the right of P (as in panel A of Exhibit 15–4) or to the left of P

Exhibit 15–5   **Income and Substitution Effects**

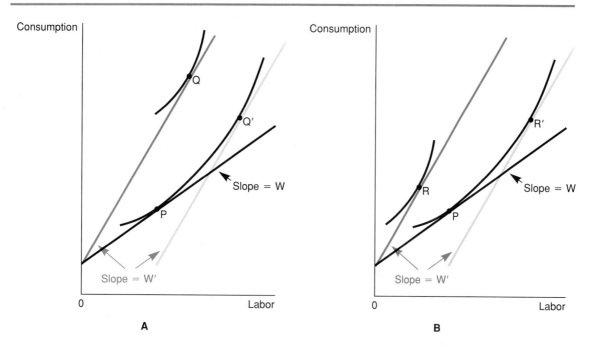

The effect of a wage increase can be decomposed into a substitution effect followed by an income effect.

When the wage goes up, we pretend that the worker loses just enough nonlabor income to keep him on his original indifference curve. In either panel this yields the light-colored budget line. The substitution effect is from P to Q′ in panel A or from P to R′ in panel B; it is a movement along the indifference curve and leads to more labor supplied.

The income effect is from Q′ to Q in panel A or from R′ to R in panel B. It leads to less labor supplied.

In panel A the substitution effect dominates the income effect, so that more labor is supplied after the wage increase. In panel B the opposite is true.

(as in panel B). The worker might supply either more or less labor when the wage rate increases.

The Income and Substitution Effects via Geometry

We can use a graph to sort out the income and substitution effects. After the wage rises from W to W′, we imagine a downward adjustment in the worker's nonlabor income that just compensates for the wage increase, leaving him on the same indifference curve as before. This gives a compensated budget line, shown in light color in each of the panels in Exhibit 15–5. We now imagine the movement to the new optimum as taking place in two steps: from P to Q′ to Q in panel A or from P to R′ to R in panel B. The first movement is the substitution effect and must be upward and to the right (it is a movement along an indifference curve to a steeper point). The second movement is the income effect, as in Exhibit 15–3, which is a movement upward and to the left.

In panel A, the substitution effect is greater than the income effect, while in panel B the reverse is true. Thus in panel A the wage increase leads to more labor supplied and in panel B the wage increase leads to less labor supplied.

Comparing the Two Effects

Which is larger, the income or the substitution effect? First, consider the situation when the wage is very low. In that case the worker supplies very little labor (for example, if the wage is zero, there is no incentive to work at all!). Therefore a change in the wage has little effect on his income, so the income effect is negligible. It follows that at low wages, the substitution effect dominates the income effect as in panel A of Exhibit 15–5. Therefore:

> **When the wage is very low to begin with, an increase in the wage leads to an increase in labor supplied.**

When the wage rate is high, both the income and the substitution effects can be substantial. Therefore at high wage rates there is no way to tell which effect will dominate.

The Worker's Supply of Labor

Deriving the Labor Supply Curve

From graphs like those in Exhibit 15–4, we can derive the labor supply curves of individuals. Exhibit 15–6 depicts the labor supply curves of the two individuals whose indifference curves appear in Exhibit 15–4. Both curves slope upward at low wages, reflecting the dominance of the substitution effect over the income effect. The second curve "bends backward" at higher wages, to reflect the fact that for this individual the income effect eventually comes to dominate the substitution effect. An individual's labor supply curve might or might not be backward-bending.

Using the Labor Supply Curve

Changes in wage rates correspond to movements along the labor supply curve, whereas changes in other things, such as nonlabor income, correspond to shifts of the curve.

Since the early days of the Industrial Revolution, wage rates have increased very substantially and, at the same time, the quantity of labor supplied has decreased. The 60-hour workweeks that were common for unskilled laborers 100 years ago are uncommon today. This evidence is consistent with a backward-bending labor supply curve. However, there is an alternative explanation. Along with the increase in wages has come a substantial increase in nonlabor income. As you can see from Exhibit 15–3, an increase in nonlabor income leads to less labor supplied at any given wage; that is, it causes the labor supply curve to shift leftward. Thus the fall in hours worked might be explained by an upward-sloping labor supply curve that has shifted leftward, as in Exhibit 15–7.

Exhibit 15–6 The Individual's Labor Supply Curve

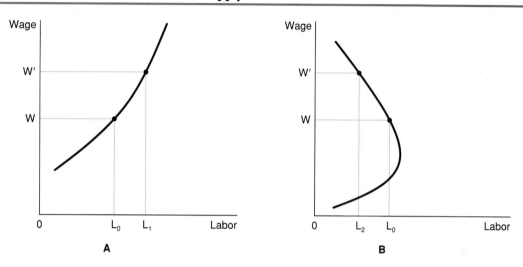

The graphs show the labor supply curves of the two individuals whose indifference curves are depicted in Exhibit 15–4. The enlarged points here are derived from the points P, Q, and R in that exhibit.

Exhibit 15–7 A Rise in the Wage Accompanied by a Rise in Nonlabor Income

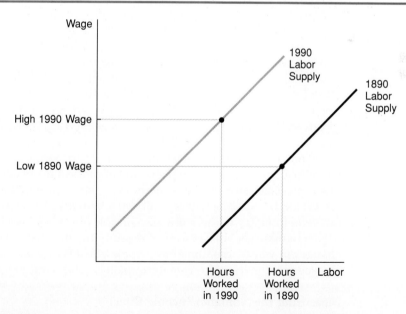

Over the last 100 years both wage rates and nonlabor income have increased. The rise in nonlabor income causes the labor supply curve to shift leftward, as shown. This could explain the observed fall in the quantity of labor supplied.

15.2 Labor Supply to the Entire Economy

In this section we will see how a change in the wage rate affects labor supply in the economy as a whole. Thus instead of asking how any one worker might react to a change in his wage rate, as we did in Section 15.1, we will ask how workers as a group respond to an economy-wide increase in wages.

The Nonlabor Income Effect

Labor income effect
The income effect of a wage change due to the change in the worker's labor income.

We saw in the preceding section that a wage increase has the effect of making workers better off, and we called this the income effect of the wage increase. In this section we will refer to that income effect as the **labor income effect,** so that it can be distinguished from an additional income effect that occurs when wages rise throughout the economy.

The additional income effect comes about because a wage increase reduces the wealth of everyone who hires labor. But this includes everyone in the economy, all of whom are both suppliers and demanders of labor. If a steelworker hires a construction crew to build a house for him, his gains from an economy-wide wage increase are to some degree offset by the rise in the wage bill that he must pay to the house builders. If the same steelworker owns ten shares of General Motors stock, making him an employer of autoworkers, then an increase in wages will reduce the value of his stock, again offsetting at least some of the benefits that he sees in his own paycheck. For many purposes it is important to take account of this **nonlabor income effect** as well as the labor income effect that we introduced in Section 15.1.

Nonlabor income effect
The income effect of a wage change due to the change in the value of the productive assets other than labor that the worker owns.

In fact, we will find that for the average worker the labor income effect and the nonlabor income effect will exactly cancel. This is because every hour of labor supplied by one individual is ultimately being hired by some other individual (perhaps with an intermediary like the General Motors Corporation assisting in the transaction). Therefore the sum of all the (positive) labor income effects from a wage increase is exactly equal to the sum of all the (negative) nonlabor income effects.

When examining the effect of a wage increase for a particular individual or in a particular industry, the nonlabor income effect is insignificant. The typical fast-food worker spends a very small proportion of his income on fast food, and so he will reap all of the benefits of a wage increase in the fast-food industry without any measurable offsetting losses in the form of higher hamburger bills. However, in studying the effects of economy-wide changes in wages, the nonlabor income effect is crucial. Indeed, we have just seen that in the aggregate it completely offsets the labor income effect.

Measuring the Nonlabor Income Effect

To measure the nonlabor income effect, we begin by noting that all nonlabor income derives from the ownership of factors of production other than labor. The steelworker with his General Motors stock owns capital in the form of a small piece of an auto assembly plant. The homeowner who

Exhibit 15–8   **Valuing a Productive Asset**

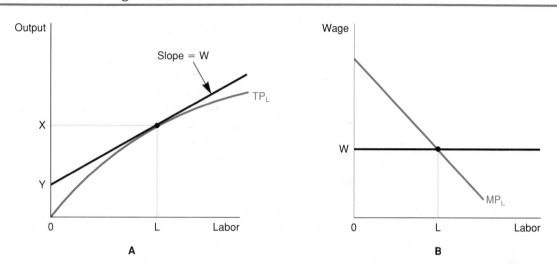

The graphs show how to determine the value of a given farm. Associated with the farm is a total product of labor curve TP_L, which shows how much output (say, wheat) the farm can produce for any given amount of labor. The marginal product of labor curve, MP_L, is derived from the TP_L curve in the usual way.

If the going wage rate is W, then the farmer hires L units of labor (where the wage is equal to the marginal product). This enables him to produce X bushels of wheat (read off the TP_L curve). He must pay his workers $W \times L = X - Y$ bushels, so that he is left with Y bushels for himself. Thus by owning the farm, the farmer earns Y bushels of wheat. The value of the farm in terms of wheat is Y bushels.

hires a handyman to clean his gutters is producing an output—a secure roof over his head—using two inputs: the house (a form of capital) and the handyman (a form of labor). The consumer's surplus that he gets from the transaction is really a rent to the house as a factor of production. When the wage goes up, an individual's losses due to the nonlabor income effect are exactly measured by the fall in value of the other productive inputs that he owns.

Thus we can measure the size of the nonlabor income effect by seeing how a wage increase affects the value of productive inputs other than labor. We will now digress to see how the wage determines the value of such assets, and how a change in the wage causes a change in their value. After we have discussed these points, we will return to the topic of labor supply.

Valuing a Productive Asset

Suppose that you own a farm and that you can hire labor at a going wage of W. (You might provide some of this labor yourself, in which case W measures the opportunity cost of your efforts.) The output of the farm depends on the amount of labor employed, according to the total product of labor curve illustrated in panel A of Exhibit 15–8. The curve becomes shallower to the right, reflecting diminishing marginal returns to labor.

Exhibit 15–9   **A Change in the Wage Rate**

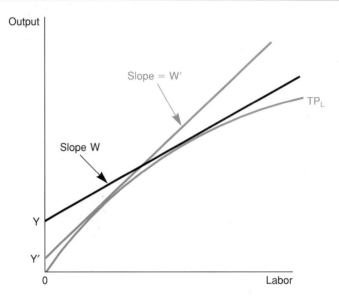

At the starting wage rate of W, the value of the farm is Y, as shown in Exhibit 15–8. When the wage rate rises to W′, the value of the farm falls to Y′.

Panel B of Exhibit 15–8 shows the marginal product of labor. For any given quantity of labor, the marginal product of labor is equal to the slope of the total product curve. Panel B also depicts the going wage of W. You will hire labor until its marginal product is equal to the wage. That is, you will hire L units.[1]

Returning to panel A, we see that L units of labor produce X units of output. The straight line in panel A has a slope equal to the marginal product of L units of labor, which is W. It crosses the vertical axis at a quantity that we denote Y. From our knowledge of the slope, we can calculate that $Y = X - (W \times L)$.

▷ *Exercise 15.3* Perform the calculation.

Suppose that your farm produces X units of output and your total wage bill is $W \times L = X - Y$. The difference, Y, is your nonlabor income as the owner of the farm. Y is a measure of the rent earned by the farm as a factor of production, and this rent accrues as income to you as the owner of the farm.[2] The value of the farm, in terms of the output produced on the farm, is Y.

---

[1]We learned in Section 14.1 that the demand curve for labor is the marginal revenue product curve. When prices and wages are measured in units of the good being produced (as they will be throughout this chapter), the marginal product and the marginal revenue product for a competitive firm are identical.

[2]Thus the vertical distance Y measures the same quantity as the area C in Exhibit 14–12.

Exhibit 15–10   Labor Supply by Three Farmers

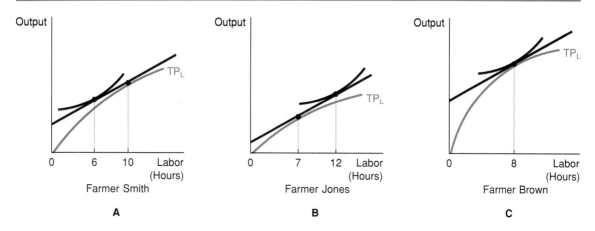

| A | B | C |
| Farmer Smith | Farmer Jones | Farmer Brown |

Each farmer owns a farm with a different production function, and each farmer has different indifference curves. All farmers face the same wage rate W. For each farmer we draw a straight line tangent to his production function, with slope W. This line intersects the vertical axis at a point representing the farmer's nonlabor income, so it is the farmer's budget line. Each farmer then chooses a point where his budget line is tangent to an indifference curve. The horizontal coordinate of this point shows how much labor the farmer supplies.

Each farmer hires labor until its marginal product is equal to the wage W. That is, he hires labor up to the point of tangency between his production function and his budget line. Farmer Smith demands more labor than he supplies, Farmer Jones supplies more labor than he demands, and Farmer Brown supplies and demands exactly the same amounts of labor.

Exhibit 15–9 shows how your nonlabor income is affected by a rise in the wage. At the old wage of W your nonlabor income is Y, whereas at the new, higher wage of W' your nonlabor income falls to Y'.

The Farmer's Budget Line

In panel A of Exhibit 15–8, we drew a straight line tangent to the TP_L curve at the quantity of labor L. The reason we drew this line was to assist in computing the value of the farm, which turned out to be Y. However, the line has another interpretation. It intersects the output axis at Y, which is the nonlabor income of the farmer, and its slope is W, which is the wage rate. These properties characterize the farmer's budget line. Thus the straight line in panel A of Exhibit 15–8 *is* the farmer's budget line.

 In Exhibit 15–2 the vertical axis shows consumption, whereas in Exhibit 15–8 it shows output. But output goods *are* consumption goods, so these are just two different words for the same thing.

The Farmer's Optimum

Exhibit 15–10 depicts the information necessary to determine the labor supply decisions of three different individuals: Farmer Smith, Farmer Jones, and Farmer Brown, each of whom owns a farm. In each case all that we need to start with is the total product curve for the farm (also called the *production function* associated with the farm), the farmer's indifference curves, and the wage. The budget line is determined by drawing a tangent to the production function with slope equal to the wage. Such a line will automatically intersect the vertical axis at the level of the farmer's nonlabor income. The farmer chooses an optimal combination of labor and consumption, at the point where the budget line is tangent to an indifference curve.

Thus Farmer Smith supplies 6 units of labor, Farmer Jones supplies 12, and Farmer Brown supplies 8.

We can also use the graphs to see how much labor each farmer demands. Farmers hire labor until its marginal product (the slope of the production function) is equal to the wage (the slope of the budget line). This occurs at the point of tangency. Thus Farmer Smith hires 10 units of labor, Farmer Jones hires 7, and Farmer Brown hires 8.

Net demander of labor
Someone who demands more labor than he supplies.

Net supplier of labor
Someone who supplies more labor than he demands.

Since Farmer Smith hires 10 units of labor to work on his farm and supplies only 6 units of labor to the marketplace, we say that he is a **net demander of labor.**[3] That is, he demands more labor than he supplies. Farmer Jones supplies more labor than he demands, as he uses only 7 hours of labor on his farm and supplies 12 hours of labor to the marketplace.[4] He is a **net supplier of labor.** Farmer Brown is neither a net supplier nor a net demander, since he supplies exactly the same amount of labor that he demands (8 hours).

The Representative Agent

Representative agent
Someone whose tastes and assets are representative of the entire economy.

To derive the labor supply for the entire economy, it is useful to introduce a fictional character called the **representative agent.** The representative agent holds exactly the average amount of every asset in the economy, and his supply and demand responses are the average responses. If everybody were identical, then everybody would be a representative agent.

When the representative agent changes the amount of labor he supplies, then the labor supply to the entire economy must change in the same direction. Therefore, if we want to understand economy-wide labor supply, we need only study the decisions of the representative agent.

In Exhibit 15–10 Farmer Brown is the representative agent. We know that over the economy as a whole every hour of labor supplied is also an hour of labor demanded. Thus the representative agent must supply the same number of hours that he demands. He can be neither a net supplier nor a net demander of labor.

---

[3]It is quite likely that Farmer Smith works 6 hours on his own farm and hires farmhands for another 4 hours. Labor supplied to one's own farm counts as labor supplied to the marketplace. We view Farmer Smith the landowner as hiring Farmer Smith the farmhand for 6 hours of labor.

[4]Perhaps Farmer Jones works 7 hours for himself and 5 hours for someone else. Or perhaps he works 12 hours for someone else and hires someone to work 7 hours for him.

Sometimes students find it difficult to accept the assertion that Farmer Brown is representative of workers. You might mistakenly believe that the typical worker owns no factors of production other than his own labor services, that he never acts as an employer, or at least that he supplies more labor than he demands. In fact, however, every worker is also an employer. The steelworker who owns stock in General Motors is as much an employer as a farmer who owns a farm. He hires labor (indirectly through the company's managers) and derives rents from his partial ownership of GM's capital. Many a steelworker who might say in casual conversation that he is not a stockholder actually has considerable wealth in the form of a pension fund that in turn owns stocks. And, as we noted earlier, there are other types of capital as well. The couple who combine the physical capital of their house and grounds with labor in the form of painting, gardening, and dishwashing are producing "family life" with two inputs, and they are hiring labor from themselves.

Keep in mind that every hour of labor supplied is an hour of labor demanded, and you will see that the representative agent demands as much as he supplies.

Farmer Brown is the representative agent. At the equilibrium wage his budget line is tangent to both his production function and to an indifference curve at the same point. It follows (as you can see in panel C of Exhibit 15–10) that his optimal basket is on the graph of his production function. This makes good sense. It means that the representative agent consumes exactly as much as he produces.

Deriving the Labor Supply Curve

Now we can return to the subject of labor supply. We can derive an individual's labor supply curve from knowledge of his indifference curves and the production function associated with his assets. Exhibit 15–11 shows the derivation of two such points. When the wage rate is 2 units of output per hour, this worker's nonlabor income is 25 units of output and his budget line is the straight line in panel A of Exhibit 15–11. He elects to supply 1½ hours of labor. When the wage is 6 units of output per hour, his nonlabor income is 8 units of output and he elects to supply 4½ hours of labor. This gives two points on his supply curve, shown in panel C of Exhibit 15–11.

▷ *Exercise 15.4* When the wage rate is 2 units of output per hour of labor, what is the total income of the worker depicted in Exhibit 15–11? Is he a net supplier or a net demander of labor?

▷ *Exercise 15.5* Using the information in Exhibit 15–11, answer the following questions, assuming that the wage rate is 6 units of output per hour of labor: How much labor does the worker employ? Why does he employ that quantity? How much is produced by this labor in conjunction with the productive inputs owned by the worker? How much of

Exhibit 15–11 Deriving the Labor Supply Curve

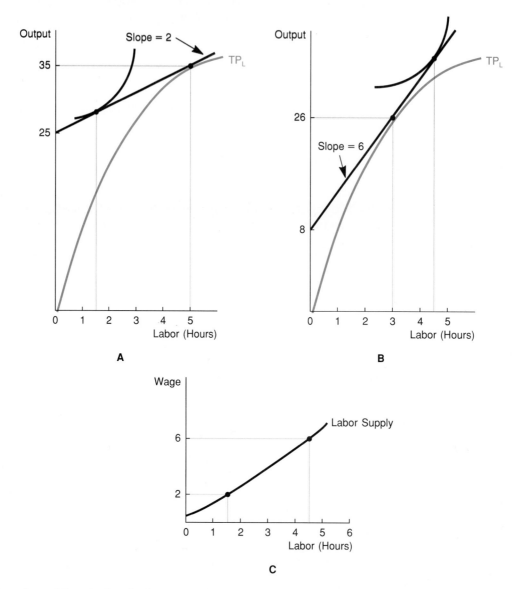

A

B

C

Panel A and panel B each give the derivation of a single point on the labor supply curve in panel C.

We begin by assuming that the wage is 2 units of output per unit of labor. The worker employs labor at his farm (or in association with whatever other productive asset he owns) until its marginal product is equal to the wage. This occurs where the total product curve has a slope of 2, at 5 units of labor. This enables him to produce 35 units of output. His wage bill is $2 \times 5 = 10$ units of output, so that he earns $35 - 10 = 25$ units of output in income from his farm. His budget line is the straight line in panel A. He selects the point of tangency with an indifference curve, where he supplies 1½ units of labor. Thus in panel C a wage of 2 corresponds to 1½ units of labor supplied.

this is paid out in wages? What is the worker's nonlabor income? How much does the worker earn in wages? What is his total consumption? Is he a net supplier or a net demander of labor?

The Shape of the Labor Supply Curve

Let us consider the shape of the representative agent's labor supply curve. When the wage rate changes, the representative agent feels essentially no income effect. As we have mentioned earlier, this is because he demands exactly the same quantity of labor that he supplies, so that a rise in the wage rate lowers his nonlabor income by just the same amount that it raises his labor income. Therefore the representative agent feels only a substitution effect. Since the substitution effect of a wage increase leads to more labor supplied, we can conclude:

The representative agent's labor supply curve must slope upward.

From this it follows that for economy-wide changes in the wage rate:

The market labor supply curve must slope upward.

Comparing the Two Supply Curves

To see the effects of changes in one individual's wages or of wages in a particular industry, we use the (potentially backward-bending) supply curve that was derived in Section 15.1. For economy-wide changes in the wage, affecting not only the wage rate of the worker in question but also the wages of everyone whom he employs, we use the (necessarily upward-sloping) supply curve derived here. The potential for a backward bend is created by income effects: At high wages the worker is richer and may choose to work less. But for economy-wide changes, there is no income effect. Whatever the representative agent gains as a supplier of labor, he loses as a demander of labor.

15.3 Equilibrium in the Labor Market

By plotting the demand and supply curves for labor on the same graph, we can find the equilibrium wage and the equilibrium level of employment. We can then see how the equilibrium moves in response to various changes in the economy.

Effect of an Increase in Wealth

Suppose that one day manna begins to fall from heaven. This does not affect the marginal productivity of labor, which is determined by technological considerations. Therefore it does not affect the demand curve for labor, which is the same thing as the marginal product of labor curve. It does, however, affect the supply of labor. People are richer, and when they are richer, they demand more of everything, including leisure. (We con-

Exhibit 15–12   **Manna from Heaven**

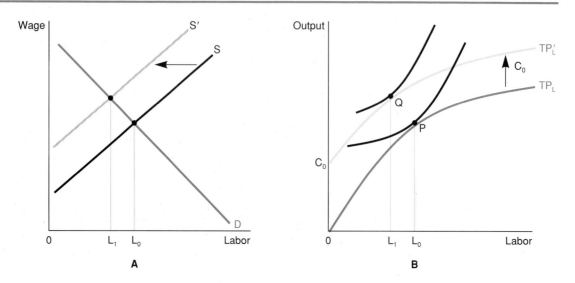

If manna falls from heaven, there is no change in the marginal product of labor, and hence no change in the labor demand curve. However, total product rises by the amount of manna that falls. This is a parallel shift upward in the total product curve, as shown in panel B. People are wealthier and therefore demand more leisure, causing the supply curve of labor to shift to the left in panel A.

    The new equilibrium in panel A corresponds to the point Q in panel B. By looking at either panel, we can see that employment falls. Panel A makes it easy to see that the wage increases, and panel B makes it easy to see that consumption increases.

tinue to assume that neither consumption nor leisure is an inferior good.) This means that they will supply less labor at any given wage. The supply curve of labor moves leftward, as in panel A of Exhibit 15–12. Employment falls, and the wage rate goes up.

    We can check our conclusion by looking at the representative agent's indifference curves, pictured in panel B of Exhibit 15–12. His production function rises as shown (C_0 is the amount of manna that falls from heaven), and he moves from point P to point Q, where he works less and consumes more.

    It is important to recognize that all of the information in panel A is derived from panel B. The demand curve for labor is the marginal product curve, derived from the total product curve; the supply curve for labor is derived by the method of Exhibit 15–11. Therefore, in principle, it is necessary to look at only one panel or the other to see the effect of the manna. However, the increase in the equilibrium wage is most readily visible in panel A, and the increase in consumption is most readily visible in panel B.

Exhibit 15–13   **A Technological Improvement**

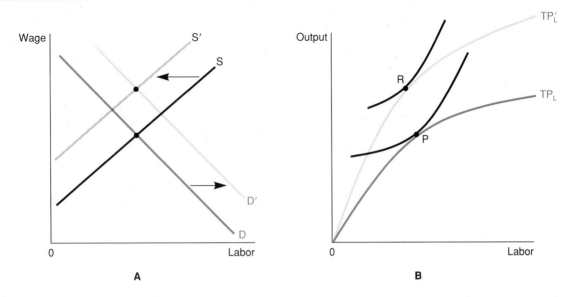

An increase in the marginal product of labor causes the total product curve to become steeper. The demand curve for labor, which is the same as the marginal product curve, moves right, and the supply curve for labor moves left because people are richer. The wage goes up (as seen in panel A) and consumption goes up (as seen in panel B). Employment moves ambiguously.

Effect of a Technological Improvement

Now consider the effect of a technological change that increases the marginal product of labor. Such a change could result from the invention of methods of production or types of capital that were previously unimagined. Alternatively, it could result from something as far beyond human control as a change in the weather (this would be especially important in an agricultural community).

There are two effects. First, the increase in the marginal product of labor translates directly into a shift in the demand curve for labor. Second, the increase in productivity means that people are wealthier, inducing them to provide less labor, just as in the example of Exhibit 15–12. The two effects are shown in panel A of Exhibit 15–13. The wage goes up; employment moves ambiguously.

Again, we can check our conclusion by looking at the effect on the representative agent, whose production function moves upward as in panel B of Exhibit 15–13. The production function becomes steeper at every quantity of labor, reflecting the increase in marginal productivity at every level. Point R is certainly above point P, but it could be either to the left or to the right of it. The substitution effect resulting from the increase in marginal productivity elicits more labor, whereas the income effect elicits less.

Effect of a Change in Working Conditions

Suppose that for some reason working becomes more pleasant than it was before, without becoming more productive. For example, widespread availability of air conditioners might make office work more pleasant in some climates. In this case there is no change in the demand for labor, but the supply curve shifts out. Employment increases and wages fall.

One thing that could increase the attractiveness of working is an increase in interest rates. When you earn a dollar, you can spend part of it and put part of it in the bank to earn interest. At a higher interest rate, earning the dollar is a more attractive proposition, because the part that you save will grow in value more quickly. Thus an increase in interest rates shifts the labor supply curve outward, leading to a fall in the wage and an increase in employment.

Intertemporal Substitution

In all of our supply and demand graphs, the units reflect some standard time period. Thus the quantity of labor is measured in hours *per day*, or hours *per week*, or hours *per year*. For many purposes it doesn't matter how one measures. We can change from hours per week to hours per day simply by dividing all the numbers on the horizontal axis by 7. In the labor market, however, this presents some special problems.

Consider a worker who supplies 8 hours of labor on each weekday, but zero hours on Saturdays and Sundays. Why is there such a sudden shift in the equilibrium? What could cause either the demand curve or the supply curve for his labor to shift so radically every Friday evening and revert to its old position on Monday morning?

The answer is that our supply analysis is incomplete when applied on a daily basis. The worker chooses the number of hours he wants to work in a week (say, 40), but he does not simply divide by 7 to find the number of hours he will work in a day. Instead he works more on some days and less on others, adapting his schedule to the dictates of convenience.

Just as workers vary their labor supply from day to day, so they vary it from week to week, though with less variation from week to week than from day to day. A person may work 40 hours per week for 50 weeks a year, and then suddenly work zero hours for 2 weeks in August before returning to the usual schedule.

A graph like Exhibit 15–1, and the labor supply curves that we derive from such graphs, describe preferences and labor supply decisions over long periods. We can use them to see how many hours per year a person will work, but we cannot necessarily use them to predict how many of those hours will be supplied in one particular day or week as opposed to another.

If we want to draw the labor supply curve for a particular day or week, we must take account of factors not displayed in Exhibit 15–1. For example, suppose that the wage rate fluctuates from day to day. Then people will prefer to supply more labor on the high-wage days and less on the low-wage days. We expect the labor supply curve to shift out to the right when the wage rate is unusually high and in to the left when it is unusually low. This shift is *not* a response to the present wage, since responses to the present wage correspond to movements *along* the supply curve. Rather, it is a response to wages on other days. If the worker expects wages to be high tomorrow, he is likely to cancel tomorrow's vacation and take his vacation today instead. Thus today's labor supply curve moves left.

When workers choose to work more on one day in exchange for working less on another day, they are said to engage in **intertemporal substitution.**

Intertemporal substitution
Adjusting work and vacation times so as to be working when wages are highest.

Effect of a Temporary Technological Improvement

To see the effects of intertemporal substitution, let us return to the example of Exhibit 15–13 (a technological improvement increasing marginal productivity). Let us modify the example by supposing the technological improvement to be a temporary one (perhaps a favorable turn in the weather that cannot be expected to last). When the change was permanent, the labor supply curve moved left because of the income effect. When it is temporary, there are two differences. First, the income effect is much smaller. One week of good weather is worth much less than an eternity of good weather to come. Second, there is an intertemporal substitution effect. Workers can choose to work much harder today, earning the temporary high wages, and compensate by relaxing tomorrow when wages will have returned to normal.

The intertemporal substitution effect moves the labor supply curve to the right, potentially overcoming the greatly diminished income effect that moves it to the left. The result can be a substantial increase in employment, as shown in Exhibit 15–14.

Because of intertemporal substitution, even a small temporary change in productivity can lead to a very large change in employment. Even if wages were only slightly higher on Sundays than on Mondays, many workers might decide to switch their days off from Mondays to Sundays in response. Similarly, in a month when wages are unusually low—even if they are only slightly lower than usual—very many workers might decide to take their vacations, and employment could decrease substantially. This would be more likely if people are largely indifferent about when to schedule their vacations, so that a small wage difference is enough to make them change their plans.

Thus intertemporal substitution may be an important determinant of the severity of recessions. A fall in the wage, if it is perceived as temporary, will induce people to supply less labor. Conceivably, even if the wage decrease is small, the labor supply response could be very large, leading to a dramatic fall in employment.

As an empirical matter, employment falls in recessions by much more than wages do. Intertemporal substitution might play a major role in explaining this fact.

Exhibit 15–14   **A Temporary Technological Improvement**

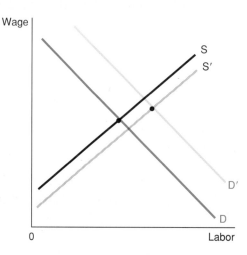

The graph shows the effect of the same technological improvement illustrated by Exhibit 15–13, but with the additional assumption that the improvement is temporary. The demand for labor shifts out exactly as in Exhibit 15–13. The supply of labor, which moved to the left in Exhibit 15–13 because of the income effect, here moves to the right because of intertemporal substitution: Everybody wants to work in the temporary period of high wages. Consequently, there can be a substantial increase in employment.

15.4 Differences in Wages

We have discussed the determination of "the" market wage. Yet it is a common observation that different people earn different wages. In this section we will discuss some of the reasons for these differences.

Human Capital

A firm that hires an employee is often hiring not just raw "labor," but an entire package of productive skills. Some of those skills, like intelligence, may be innate, whereas others, like education and training, are the result of investments by the employee earlier in life. Such skills can productively be viewed as a form of capital, which we will call **human capital.**

Human capital
Productive skills.

We have seen in Section 14.4 that the revenues of the firm are divided among the productive inputs, with each earning its marginal product. A worker who brings both labor and human capital to an enterprise earns both the wage rate for his labor and the market rate of return for his skills. In practice, he usually receives the sum of these returns in a single paycheck, the size of which is described as his "wage." Of course, workers with different amounts of human capital will earn differing returns.

The use of the word *capital* here is more than just a loose metaphor. As we will see in Chapter 16, capital consists of productive resources that have themselves been produced by forgoing consumption at earlier times. This description fits human capital perfectly. When you attend college, you forgo current consumption both by making tuition payments that could be used for other things and by allocating time to your studies that could otherwise be spent earning income. The sum of these costs is an investment in human capital.

In the short run, human capital is a fixed factor (its supply curve is vertical). For this reason, payments to human capital are a form of rent. The difference between the earnings of a college graduate and those of an unskilled laborer constitute the rent on human capital.

In the long run, people can vary their investments in human capital. As more investment takes place, the costs (like college tuition) are driven up and the rents to human capital are driven down. People will continue to invest until the marginal cost and marginal benefit from a unit of human capital are equal.

If all people can make equally productive use of an education, then everyone will be indifferent between becoming educated and not becoming educated. This is because the cost of an education will exactly offset the benefits. (If the benefits of going to college exceed the costs, additional people will enter college until this is no longer the case.) If, on the other hand, people are endowed with varying quantities of other skills (like intelligence or perseverance) that make education more productive, then those who have unusually large endowments of these other skills can benefit from education.

Access to Capital

Wages would also differ if workers had access to capital of differing qualities. A secretary in New York City using the latest word processor might be more productive at the margin than a secretary using a manual typewriter in a locality with no electricity.

In making this argument, it is important not to confuse total productivity with marginal productivity. The lone secretary with the manual typewriter in a developing country can certainly be more productive *at the margin* than the 100,000th word-processing New Yorker. In fact, as long as people can move from country to country, wages will tend to become equal everywhere over time because of people leaving the low-wage countries to enter the high-wage countries. This equalization of wages implies an equalization of marginal products. Therefore the access of different workers to different sorts of capital can explain wage differences in the long run only if there are barriers to the mobility of workers, such as immigration restrictions.

However, even immigration restrictions fail to explain wage differences across countries. If wages are lower in Mexico than in the United

States, we at first expect Mexican workers to cross the border until wages are equalized. Then we are reminded that the immigration laws prevent this. But now we should expect American firms to move their capital across the border into Mexico to take advantage of the low wages there. This will raise wages in Mexico and reduce wages in the United States, and the flow of capital across the border should continue until wages are equalized.

We do see some phenomena like this. In recent years, for example, many firms have relocated from the northern to the southern United States to take advantage of lower wage rates. But there has been nothing like the international movement of capital that one would expect on the basis of standard economic theory. Why not?[5]

An answer to this riddle might be found in the external effects of human capital accumulation.[6] When you invest in training or education, you increase not only your own productivity but that of your fellow workers, through a variety of complicated interactions between you and them. Perhaps some of your new knowledge rubs off in conversations around the water cooler. Perhaps you are more likely to make suggestions or to have ideas that other workers can imitate or that will inspire them to formulate related new ideas of their own. These interactions need not be confined to your own workplace. To paraphrase Adam Smith, people of the same trade seldom meet together, even for merriment and diversion, but the conversation ends in a mutually beneficial exchange of ideas and methods or in some contrivance to increase efficiency.

Through such mechanisms, your accumulation of human capital can raise the productivity not only of your co-workers and of other workers in your industry, but also of the physical capital with which you interact. In that case those owners of physical capital who locate themselves in areas with large concentrations of highly trained people will reap a share of these external benefits. They might be willing to pay higher wages, or higher land rents, in exchange for such an opportunity. Consequently, the difference between land rents in, say, Manhattan and a more remote location might be a tolerably good measure of the value of those external benefits.

If human capital investment yields significant positive externalities, then there will be too little of it. People invest in human capital only up to the point where the marginal cost is equal to the marginal increase in their own productivity, without taking account of how their investment affects the productivity of others. This observation constitutes an efficiency-based argument for subsidizing investments in human capital, such as

---

[5]This riddle was posed by Robert E. Lucas, Jr., in a recent series of lectures titled "On the Mechanics of Economic Development," *Journal of Monetary Economics* 21 (1988). The answer we will propose is also taken from those lectures, although it is offered there as a clue to the solution of a much deeper riddle, namely: Why do different countries have different levels of economic development and different rates of growth?

[6]An alternative possible answer is that after adjusting for human capital differences, Mexican wages really *aren't* any lower than U.S. wages.

education. If, as we have argued, differences in land rents measure the value of human capital externalities, then the size of such rent differentials could be used in a calculation of the size of the optimal subsidy.

Compensating Differentials

Another reason for differences in observed wage rates is that some jobs are more pleasant or less pleasant than others. When there is a large class of equally talented workers available to each of several occupations, these workers must be indifferent as to which occupation they choose.

▷ *Exercise 15.6* Why must the workers be indifferent among occupations? If they were not indifferent, what would happen?

There are many reasons why one occupation might be inherently less pleasant than another. In some occupations the work itself is unpleasant, in others the people employed command less respect, and in still others there are greater degrees of risk. In order for workers to remain indifferent, the less pleasant occupations must pay more. We can view the wage in the less pleasant occupation as the sum of the market wage determined elsewhere plus an additional payment to compensate the worker for the unpleasant aspects of his job. This additional payment is known as a **compensating differential.**

Compensating differential
A wage adjustment that comes about in equilibrium to compensate for a particularly pleasant or unpleasant aspect of a job.

Other occupations are unusually attractive. An employee in such an occupation earns less than one in a more typical job, the compensating differential being negative. For example, many positions offer workers the opportunity to invest in human capital at a cost much lower than the usual market rate. This comes about when an employee, in the course of performing his duties, acquires skills that he will later be able to sell in the marketplace. Such on-the-job training occurs at every level of skill. A postdoctoral instructor in physics at a top university is gaining valuable skills that will increase his marketability in later life, in exchange for which he accepts a wage that might be less than his marginal product. A clerk in a bookstore is observing and learning the business, gaining the skills necessary to be a manager or to open his own shop someday. Again, he pays for this opportunity through a lower wage.

Although on-the-job training is important at every level, it is particularly important at the very bottom of the career ladder, where the skills that are mastered (fundamentals such as knowing the importance of showing up for work on time and how to get along with co-workers) will be useful in any future occupation. In entry-level positions on-the-job training is often a substantial portion of the employee's total compensation.

Signaling

Until now we have assumed that education actually contributes to the acquisition of useful skills. Yet even if education were totally unproductive, and even if this were well understood by everybody, it still might be the case that becoming educated was a road to higher wages.

To see how this could be, let us take the cynical view that nothing whatsoever is learned in college but that only those with at least a certain minimal degree of intelligence and industry are able to successfully graduate. If employers have no other way of distinguishing among high school graduates, they will be willing to pay higher wages to those who have proved themselves in college.

Here is a very simple example. Suppose that there are two kinds of high school graduates: Wise Guys and Dummies. To a Wise Guy the cost of a college education is $10,000 (including all forgone opportunities). A Dummy can also succeed in college, but only at a much higher cost. He has to work much harder, pay extra tuition when he fails courses, and hire both tutors for final exams and ghostwriters for his term papers. All told, it costs a Dummy $20,000 to go through college.

Now suppose that a Wise Guy is worth $30,000 per year to an employer and a Dummy is worth $15,000, and suppose that employers offer one-year contracts to new employees. Then, in equilibrium, all Wise Guys attend college and get paid $30,000 while all Dummies skip college and get paid $15,000.

Signal
An activity that does not directly produce anything socially productive but that conveys information about one's talents, so that it is privately rewarding.

Signaling equilibrium
An equilibrium in which some people engage in signaling and there is no incentive for anyone to change his behavior.

To see that this is an equilibrium, we need to check that no individual has any incentive to deviate from such behavior. A Dummy who deviated by going to college would raise his salary by $15,000 at a cost to him of $20,000—not an attractive proposition, even to a Dummy. A Wise Guy who skipped college would sacrifice $15,000 in salary for a $10,000 saving in educational costs—surely no Wise Guy would make such an error. Employers would find that their expectations were always right: College grads are Wise Guys and non-college grads are Dummies. Thus employers will maintain their behavior as well.[7]

We refer to a college education as a **signal** of certain intrinsic skills, and we call an equilibrium such as the one we have just described a **signaling equilibrium**.[8]

Signaling and Welfare: Should Colleges Be Abolished?

Notice that a signaling equilibrium is not Pareto-optimal. The resources spent on college education constitute pure waste from a social point of view. If all Dummies could be induced to identify themselves voluntarily, employers would still know whom to hire, Dummies would be no worse off than they are now, and Wise Guys would each save $10,000 in educational costs. They could, of course, share part of their $10,000 savings with the Dummies in payment for their honesty.

---

[7]We assume for simplicity that only the first year's income matters to a high school grad deciding whether to attend college. This will be the case if employers can easily distinguish Wise Guys from Dummies after a year on the job, so that future salary is unaffected by college attendance.

[8]Signaling equilibria were introduced by Michael Spence in his quite readable article "Job Market Signaling," *Quarterly Journal of Economics* 87 (1973), 355–374.

For that matter, suppose that college educations were outlawed altogether or that all Wise Guys could be convinced not to attend college, leaving employers with no way to distinguish between Wise Guys and Dummies. Suppose, by way of example, that exactly half of all high school graduates are Dummies. Then employers might figure that a typical job applicant has a 50–50 chance of being either a Wise Guy or a Dummy, and so offer him a wage halfway between $15,000 and $30,000. As a result, Dummies earn $22,500 instead of $15,000—a clear gain. Wise Guys earn $22,500 instead of $30,000, but they save $10,000 in educational costs—a gain to them as well. Employers end up with the same set of employees and the same total wage bill as before—for every Dummy making $7,500 more than he deserves, there is a Wise Guy earning $7,500 less than he deserves. Nobody loses, and both Wise Guys and Dummies are made better off.

Whenever you encounter an equilibrium that is not Pareto-optimal, you should look for an externality lurking in the background. In this case it is not hard to find. Each Wise Guy who goes to college, by confirming employers' beliefs that *all* Wise Guys go to college, reduces the wages of everyone who decides to skip college, without taking this into account in his behavior.

In this example we have assumed that all firms find it equally valuable to hire a Wise Guy instead of a Dummy. But one can easily imagine a situation in which some firms find it more important than others to hire only Wise Guys. Then abolishing college, and with it the signaling, could be very harmful to these firms. Without more information, it is not possible to tell whether the gains would outweigh the losses. It is still the case, however, that everyone could be better off if the Dummies revealed themselves.

Example: Dressing for Success

Signaling behavior is a widespread social phenomenon. "Dressing for success" is an example. Surely the clothes that you wear do not make you a more productive executive, but your ability to choose clothes that are both tasteful and fashionable without being too ordinary is a meaningful signal of your ability to interpret social norms and to be creative within acceptable limits. These are skills that are extremely valuable in business, and it can be rational to invest in displaying them just as it can be rational to invest in an unproductive education to display your intellect.

Two aspects of such a signaling equilibrium bear emphasis. First, it is genuinely rational on the part of the signaler to invest in sending the signal and on the part of the observer to be guided by it. This is just another way of saying that we really have an equilibrium. Second, it can be the case that everyone would be made better off by the elimination of costly signaling mechanisms. We might all be happier with a law that forebade wearing clothes at job interviews.

Example: Signaling in the Animal Kingdom

The male birds of many species—peacocks and birds of paradise are the standard examples—have tails that appear to be too long for their own good. In addition to requiring nutrients that could be put to other productive uses, the tails are cumbersome and can actually hinder locomotion. They might also make the birds more vulnerable to predators.

How could such a characteristic survive the pressures of natural selection? One theory is that we are observing a signaling equilibrium. Suppose that males who are healthier than average are able to bear the burdens of a long tail more cheaply than can males who are less healthy. Suppose also that females have a preference for healthy males (such a preference would be naturally selected for, because healthy males tend to produce healthy offspring, so females with this preference have a greater chance of having grandchildren). Then it might be to the reproductive advantage of each individual male to signal his health with a long tail, even if the tail itself were a burden in everyday life. Females choose males with longer than average tails, and tails get longer over time until the marginal cost of additional growth becomes great enough to outweigh the advantage in terms of attracting females.

Such a signaling equilibrium is nonoptimal from the birds' point of view. Suppose that all males could agree to grow tails half as long as they currently do. Then females would still know who had the longer than average tails and would choose exactly the same mates as at present. No valuable information would be lost, and the costs of growing long tails would be reduced. Unfortunately, such a state is not an equilibrium. It would be to the advantage of any individual male to cheat by not cutting his tail growth.

Education as Consumption

We have repeatedly used education as an example of an investment in higher wages. We have suggested several ways in which this could happen. Perhaps education is a way to acquire human capital; perhaps it is a signal of certain innate skills; perhaps it is some combination of the two.

In fact, highly educated people do earn higher wages than do less highly educated people. However, there is an alternative explanation for this. Rather than education causing high wages, perhaps high wages cause education.

Suppose that people actually enjoy going to college and view it as a consumption good. Then we expect people with greater wealth to consume more of this good. Just as richer people buy more Rolls Royces, so richer people buy more education. No one would suggest that because rich people drive Rolls Royces, buying a Rolls Royce will make you rich.

Undoubtedly, education is partly investment and partly consumption. To some extent, people purchase it to raise their incomes, and to some extent they purchase it because they enjoy it. Here is a question to ponder: What observable data would help you determine what percentage of educational spending is pure consumption?

15.5 Discrimination

The average black person earns less than the average white person, and the average woman earns less than the average man. Parts of these differentials are easy to account for. The average black is about 6½ years younger than the average white, and younger workers generally earn less than older workers do. A larger percentage of blacks live in the South, where wages are lower generally. Women are more likely than men to have studied sociology instead of engineering.

Economists disagree about whether such factors can account for all of the observed wage differentials. The alternative hypothesis is that the differentials are partly due to discrimination. The existence of discrimination is difficult to measure. One must ask not: "Do blacks earn less than whites do?" but: "Do blacks earn less than whites *with comparable market characteristics* (education, experience, age, etc.) do?"[9] The question is an empirical one but a difficult one to settle, because of the difficulty of measuring all of the relevant market characteristics.

The government agencies charged with administering the civil rights and affirmative-action laws have devised various statistical tests for discrimination. When discrimination is found, the firms are required to take remedial action. Many economists have been skeptical of the value of the particular tests that are used, on the grounds that the tests fail to take account of genuine differences in productivity. In the 1970s the Department of Health, Education, and Welfare (HEW)[10] analyzed the employment patterns at universities with the aid of such tests, and it required significant changes in hiring practices on the basis of what it found. Interestingly, an academic turned the tables on HEW. George Borjas reported in 1978 that the very same statistical tests, when applied to data on HEW's own employment practices, appeared to reveal a pattern of discrimination that HEW would have found unacceptable at any university.[11]

---

[9]The real question is: "Do blacks earn less than whites with the same marginal product do?" In view of the difficulty of measuring marginal product directly, we hope to approximate it with a mix of observable market characteristics.

[10]This department has since been renamed the Department of Health and Human Services.

[11]George Borjas, "Discrimination in HEW: Is the Doctor Sick or Are the Patients Healthy?" *Journal of Law and Economics* 21 (1978), 97–110.

Theories of Discrimination

If there is discrimination, employers engage in it at a cost. If blacks earn lower wages than equally productive whites, any employer who hires whites forgoes an opportunity to hire equally productive black labor at a lower wage.

In fact, a relatively small number of nondiscriminating employers could suffice to eliminate all wage differentials, even if the majority of employers discriminate. Suppose that 80% of employers are discriminatory and are unwilling to pay blacks more than half their marginal product. Suppose that the remaining 20% of employers are indifferent between hiring whites and hiring blacks, and that these 20% are enough to employ all of the blacks in the economy. Then as long as blacks are paid less than their marginal product, the nondiscriminating firms will hire more of them. This will continue, bidding up the price of black labor, until blacks are earning their full marginal product, just as whites are.

It is sometimes alleged that employers discriminate not out of any genuine distaste for a particular group, but as a strategy to employ that group at a lower wage. Such a strategy would require the cooperation of thousands of employers and would be subject to exactly the same pressures that cause cartels to break down. Any individual employer could gain by cheating. In fact, such a strategy is far more implausible than a cartel, because a cartel requires cooperation only by the firms in a single industry, whereas the "fake discrimination" ploy requires the cooperation of all firms that hire labor.

One theory of discrimination says that while employers might be indifferent between hiring whites and blacks, they nevertheless discriminate because their white employees have a distaste for associating with blacks. Whenever a black is hired, the employer must increase the white workers' wages or they will leave the firm. Thus because it is especially costly for employers to hire blacks, the demand for blacks is lower and they receive lower wages. If this theory is correct, employers should be able to benefit by hiring all-black work forces, paying the lower black wage without having to worry about the effect on white employees. Employers will adopt this strategy until black wages are bid up to the level of white wages. Thus the theory predicts a heavily segregated work force, with some all-white firms and some all-black firms, but no wage differentials.

Considerable sophistication is needed to find a theory consistent with sustained wage differentials in the face of profit maximization by even some employers. Since most theories predict a tendency toward complete segregation, it is necessary to postulate a force opposing that tendency in order to get realistic results. One possibility is that blacks and whites have different skills, and that those skills are complementary in production. In this case it would pay to combine black and white workers even if it required paying a premium to the whites. Another possibility is to develop a theory of the costs of changing personnel, so that an employer who would ultimately benefit from an all-black work force will find it optimal to stretch the adjustment out over a long period of time.[12]

Wage Differences Due to Worker Preferences

Some apparent discrimination undoubtedly results from the preferences of the workers themselves. Here is an example of how this might come about.

When a worker seeks a job, he or she typically receives several offers at different salaries. Suppose that men and women typically receive the same range of offers, but that men on average are more inclined to accept their highest-paying offer, whereas women apply many other criteria in making their choice. In this case statistics will show that women earn less than men do, even though men and women both receive exactly the same salary offers on average.

Why might men be more inclined than women to accept their highest-paying offers? One reason is that most married men are trained for more lucrative occupations than their wives are. Thus if a married couple must live together in the same city, they usually maximize their total family income by moving to the city where the husband has the brightest prospects.

Imagine, for example, a couple in which the husband is a movie director and the wife a professor. The husband is offered a $100,000 job in California and a $50,000 job in Massachusetts. The wife is offered a $10,000 job in California and a $20,000 job in Massachusetts. In this case the couple maximizes its income by moving to California, where their combined salaries are $110,000 instead of $70,000. The wife will earn $10,000, whereas most male professors (who are not married to movie directors) will live in Massachusetts and earn $20,000.

Statistics will show that female professors generally earn less than their male counterparts do, while perhaps failing to show the reason why. The point of this example is not its empirical significance, which at any rate is unclear.[13] The point is that wage differentials can result from supply decisions (by workers) as well as from demand decisions (by employers) through subtle mechanisms that might not be apparent to the researcher. This is why questions about discrimination are so hard to settle.

---

[12]See K. Arrow, "Some Models of Racial Discrimination in the Labor Market" in A. Pascal (ed.), *Racial Discrimination in Economic Life* (RAND Corporation, 1972), for a survey and detailed discussion of such theories. The first serious attempt by an economist to study questions related to discrimination was in G. Becker, *The Economics of Discrimination* (University of Chicago Press, 1957).

[13]For some evidence, see R. Frank, "Why Women Earn Less: The Theory and Estimation of Differential Overqualification," *American Economic Review* 68 (1978), 360–373.

Human Capital Inheritance

If it is argued that blacks earn less than whites only because of inferior human capital, one must still attempt to account for this interracial difference in human capital. A common explanation is that human capital is largely inherited (we learn much from our parents' skills and attitudes) and that blacks have inherited less because of past discrimination. Of course, this is scant comfort to a black worker who is informed that he earns less than his white colleagues not because he is black, but because his parents were. Yet it surely does make a difference whether blacks and other groups are suffering only from past discrimination or from present discrimination as well. Although two diseases have the same symptoms, the prescribed medications could differ substantially.

Although past discrimination, via human capital inheritance, might play a role in determining the current incomes of blacks, it is at least reasonably certain that this is not true of women. Black people tend to have mostly black ancestors, but women have only the same percentage of female ancestors that their brothers do.

Summary

Individuals supply labor to firms, which produce outputs that individuals demand. Labor supply, like output demand, depends on the tastes of individuals.

Thus we need to study the individual's indifference curves between consumption and labor. We can begin by drawing his indifference curves between consumption and leisure, which are both goods, and then reversing the leisure axis.

The budget line is determined by nonlabor income (which gives the intercept) and the wage rate (which gives the slope). Once we have the indifference curves and the budget line, we can determine how much labor is supplied.

An increase in nonlabor income corresponds to a parallel shift of the budget line. We always assume that consumption and leisure are both normal goods, so that after a rise in nonlabor income, consumption increases and less labor is supplied.

A rise in an individual worker's wage rate has both an income effect and a substitution effect. The substitution effect, which is a movement to a steeper part of the original indifference curve, results in more labor supplied. The income effect, which is a movement to a higher indifference curve, results in less labor supplied. Either effect could dominate. When wages are low, however, income effects are small, so at least at low wages the substitution effect dominates. Thus at low wages the individual's labor supply curve slopes upward, whereas at high wages it could either continue to slope upward or it could bend backward.

To see the economy-wide effect of a rise in wages, we must remember that every worker is also an employer. Thus there is a nonlabor income effect, working in the opposite direction from the labor income effect that we have already considered. Since people on average employ exactly the same amount of labor that they supply, the two income effects wash out and there is only a substitution effect. Thus, for economy-wide changes in the wage, the labor supply curve slopes upward.

To derive a worker's response to an economy-wide wage change, we must see how a wage change affects the value of his productive assets. With any such asset is associated a production function. When the wage is W, the worker hires labor up to the point where its marginal product is W; that is, to the point where the slope of the production function is W. The tangent line at that point is the worker's budget line. He supplies a quantity of labor that is determined by the tangency of an indifference curve with this budget line.

In equilibrium the representative agent supplies and demands equal quantities of labor; thus he is at a point where an indifference curve is tangent to his production function. To see the effects of various changes, we can either manipulate supply and demand diagrams, or we can manipulate the representative agent's production function/indifference curve diagram. The two pictures contain the same information, but some information is easier to see in one picture than in the other. By using both pictures, we can calculate the effects of such things as discoveries of new sources of wealth, increases in productivity, changes in the desirability of working, and so forth.

When wage changes are perceived to be temporary, intertemporal substitution takes place. That is, the labor supply curve shifts to reflect workers' response to their perception that the situation is temporary. If wages are perceived to be temporarily high, workers will reschedule their current vacation plans for later; if wages are perceived to be temporarily low, workers will reschedule their future vacation plans for today. Thus it is possible that even small wage changes, if perceived to be temporary, could yield very large changes in employment. This is consistent with what we know of the history of recessions.

Different workers receive different wages for different reasons. Often, a portion of the worker's paycheck is not really a wage at all, but a return on human capital. Workers can benefit by having access to capital of differing qualities, including their colleagues' human capital, from which they receive external benefits. Some workers receive positive compensating differentials for work that is especially pleasant, or negative ones for work that has special advantages.

There are substantial wage differences between blacks and whites and between men and women. Many factors, including discrimination, might be part of the explanation. Most of these factors, including differences in human capital, are very difficult to measure, making it hard to determine the significance of discrimination. Some wage differences result from the choices of workers themselves, as when married women choose to live in the cities where their husbands can earn the highest wage, rather than in the cities where they themselves can earn the highest wage. Economists do not know how important a role such phenomena play in determining wage differences.

Review Questions

R1. Explain the income and substitution effects of a rise in an individual's wage. Which causes him to work less, and why?

R2. Under what circumstances can we be sure that the substitution effect will outweigh the income effect? What implications does this have for the shape of the individual's labor supply curve?

R3. What are the possible shapes for an individual's labor supply curve? Interpret them in terms of income and substitution effects.

R4. Illustrate how the value of a farm is determined by the total product of labor on that farm and the wage rate. Use your diagram to show how a change in the wage rate affects the value of the farm.

R5. Show how to derive an individual farmer's budget line between consumption and labor, and his labor supply decision. Show how the labor supply decision is affected by an economy-wide increase in the wage.

R6. Explain why the representative agent must always be at a point where an indifference curve is tangent to his production function.

R7. How does the representative agent respond to an economy-wide wage increase? Why?

R8. Draw a supply/demand diagram for labor and draw the representative agent's production function/ indifference curve diagram. How are the following aspects of the first diagram illustrated in the second diagram: The equilibrium wage? The quantity of labor supplied?

R9. Will employment fall more in response to a permanent fall in wages or in response to a temporary fall? Why?

R10. List some reasons why different people earn different wages.

R11. What is a signaling equilibrium? What are its welfare consequences?

R12. List some theories that might explain wage differences between blacks and whites. How might you go about testing some of these theories? What problems might you run into?

Problem Set

1. *True or false:* If an individual suddenly found that he needed less sleep per night than previously, his consumption would go up.

2. Jack can work up to 8 hours a day at a wage rate of W and as much more as he wants at the higher overtime rate of W'. He chooses to work 10 hours. Jill can work as many hours as she wants at a wage of W''. Jack and Jill have the same tastes, the same assets, and are equally happy. What can you conclude about the size of W'' compared to W and W'? What can you conclude about the number of hours Jill works?

3. *True or false:* Workers who like their jobs will be more productive than workers who don't.

4. *True or false:* A man who earns his entire income in wages will respond more sharply to a rise in the wage than will a man whose income is mostly from property.

5. *True or false:* If the capital stock is fixed and if the level of output is fixed, then a rise in the marginal productivity of labor benefits the owners of capital.

6. *True or false:* Someone who hires more labor than he supplies is sure to benefit from a fall in the wage and to be hurt if the wage goes up.

7. How would the wage rate and the level of employment be affected by the invention of a costless pill that made it unnecessary for anyone to sleep?

8. Contrast the effects on employment, output, and wages of (a) a year of bad weather resulting in low agricultural productivity, and (b) nuclear contamination that lowers agricultural productivity permanently.

9. Contrast the effects on employment, output, and wages of (a) an income tax that is expected to be in effect for one year, and (b) an income tax that is expected to be permanent.

10. Suppose that all people have identical tastes and identical talents, but that those who attend college become more productive and hence earn higher wages. On the other hand, college students have to pay tuition.
    a. Explain why college graduates and nongraduates must be equally happy. (*Hint:* What would happen to tuition if they weren't?) Use this observation and an indifference curve diagram to illustrate the equilibrium tuition cost.
    b. *True or false:* Since college graduates earn higher wages, they might choose to work fewer hours than nongraduates.

11. The current federal tax law allows deductions for the depreciation of physical capital. *True or false:* One effect of this deduction is to reduce the average level of education.

12.*a. Prepare a diagram to show how the representative agent is affected by a fall in the wage. Show the substitution effect and show the income effect.
    b. In the text it is argued that the representative agent feels no income effect when the wage changes. Use your diagram to show that this is only an approximation to the truth. In what way is the argument in the text incomplete? (*Hint:* After the wage change, is the representative agent still the representative agent?)
    c. Despite your answer to part b, use your diagram to verify the conclusion that the representative agent's labor supply curve slopes upward.

Refer to Answers to Problem Sets for solutions to problems 1 and 3.

---

*Denotes a problem that is rather difficult.

Chapter Sixteen

Allocating Goods over Time

Markets enable people to trade one kind of good for another. The simplest kind of world in which such trades would occur is a world with two goods. In Chapter 3 we studied the theory of consumer choice in such a world. Although the world we studied was an artificial one, it contained important lessons for the world we live in.

Markets also enable people to allocate their consumption over time, by trading goods delivered at one date for goods delivered at another date. This kind of trade would take place even in a world with only one physical consumption good. In this chapter we will study such a world. The "one-good" assumption is an artifice that enables us to draw appropriate graphs on a two-dimensional piece of paper and to avoid complicating the discussion with peripheral issues. As in our earlier study of consumption, we will see that the model is sufficiently rich to teach us much about reality.

16.1 Interest Rates

Suppose that apples are the only consumption good. Then people face no choices about *what* to eat, but they still have preferences about *when* to eat. An apple today is not the same thing as an apple tomorrow. In this sense, our "one-good" world is really still a "two-good" world after all, with goods distinguished by time of delivery instead of by physical characteristics.

The Consumer's Choice

Exhibit 16–1 displays a typical consumer's indifference curves between "apples today" and "apples tomorrow." Their general shape is the same as the general shape of indifference curves between apples and oranges or between eggs and wine. If you have very few apples today, you will value them highly, and you will be willing to give one up only in exchange for a promise of very many apples tomorrow. In other words, when you have few apples, your marginal rate of substitution (equal to the absolute slope of the indifference curve) is very high. In yet other words, the indifference curves are convex.

The Endowment Point

Endowment
The basket of goods that somebody starts with, prior to any trading.

We suppose that the consumer has an **endowment** consisting of some number of apples today and some number of apples tomorrow. This endowment might consist of apples that grow on the trees in his yard. The endowment can be represented by a point in Exhibit 16–1. A case of particular interest is that in which the consumer's endowment consists of equal numbers of apples on each day. In this case the endowment point is on the 45° line, which has been sketched in the exhibit. At point A, for example, the consumer's endowment consists of 6 apples per day.

The Discount Rate

Ken is a consumer with endowment A. His neighbor, Barb, has offered to trade him an apple today for an apple tomorrow. In general, we expect that Ken would happily accept such an offer. One more apple today is worth more to Ken than one more apple tomorrow, provided that he starts with an equal number of apples on each day.

There are a number of different reasons why Ken might feel this way. One is a natural preference for present over future consumption, which might be called impatience. Another is uncertainty about the future. Since he might be hit by a truck tonight and never have the opportunity to enjoy tomorrow's apples, Ken has an incentive to take his apples while he's sure to get them. Yet a third reason is that apples yield not only immediate pleasure but also a lifetime of pleasant memories. An apple eaten today will yield one more day of these pleasures than an apple eaten tomorrow.

Without committing ourselves fully or exclusively to any of these explanations, we will continue to assume that, to a consumer whose endowment is on the 45° line, one more apple today is worth more than one more apple tomorrow. Another way to say this is that along the 45° line, the marginal rate of substitution, or the absolute slope of the indifference curve, is greater than 1.

Exhibit 16–1 **The Consumer's Preferences**

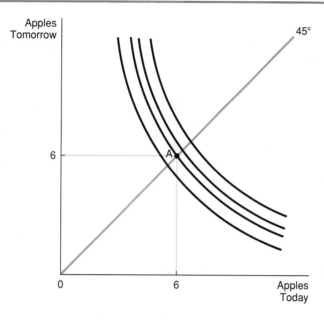

The consumer's preferences are represented by indifference curves. The endowment point A depicts his holdings before he does any trading. In this example the endowment point is on the 45° line, which means that he is endowed with the same number of apples each day.

Since Ken's marginal rate of substitution (MRS) exceeds 1, we can write

$$MRS = 1 + \rho,$$

Discount rate
The MRS between current and future consumption, minus 1.

where ρ is some positive number. For example, if Ken's MRS is 1.2, then $\rho = .2$. The number ρ is called Ken's **discount rate,** and it measures the strength of Ken's preferences for additional current consumption over additional future consumption. When ρ is large, the MRS is large, and it requires many apples tomorrow to compensate Ken for the loss of one apple today.

 Ken's discount rate, like his MRS, depends on what basket he currently owns. If he acquired a different basket, his discount rate would change.

▷ *Exercise 16.1* What would it mean to have a negative discount rate?

The Consumer's Opportunities

Imagine Ken being given the opportunity to trade any number of apples today for apples tomorrow at a price of 1 for 1. We can draw the corresponding budget line. Because the budget line represents the set of baskets that Ken can actually choose, and because point A is certainly one of these (he

Exhibit 16–2   **The Consumer's Choice**

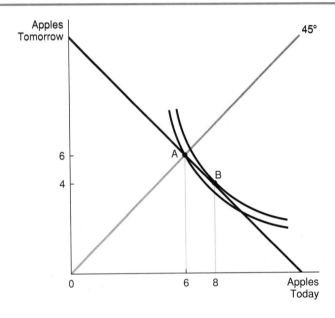

Starting from his endowment at A, Ken is given the opportunity to trade apples today for apples tomorrow (or vice versa) at a relative price of 1 for 1. This enables him to move to any point on the budget line shown, which has slope −1. Since Ken starts with equal numbers of apples today and tomorrow, we expect that he will trade to have more apples today and fewer tomorrow. Thus his optimum, B, is below and to the right of point A.

can achieve point A by simply retaining his endowment and refusing to trade), the budget line must pass through point A. Its slope reflects prices; in this case the slope is −1. The point and the slope suffice to determine the budget line, which is displayed in Exhibit 16–2.

We have assumed that Ken, given his trading opportunities, would prefer to have more apples today and fewer tomorrow. This is reflected in Exhibit 16–2 by the fact that the optimal basket, B, is below and to the right of basket A.

▷ *Exercise 16.2* Explain how the conclusion of the last sentence could have been deduced on purely geometric grounds, given what we already know about the marginal rate of substitution.

The Demand for Current Consumption

When the relative price of an apple today is 1 apple tomorrow, Ken chooses basket B in Exhibit 16–2. That is, he demands a total of 8 apples today (and 4 tomorrow) when the relative price of an apple today is equal to 1 apple tomorrow. This information corresponds to a point B′ on Ken's demand curve for apples today, shown in panel B of Exhibit 16–3.

Exhibit 16–3   **The Demand Curve for Current Consumption**

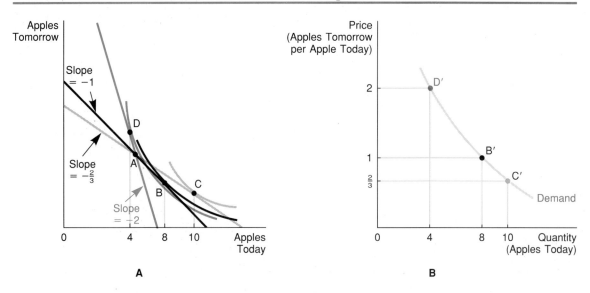

Ken's indifference curves, shown in panel A, can be used to derive his demand curve for apples today, shown in panel B. At a relative price of 1, Ken has the black budget line, chooses point B, and consumes 8 apples today. This is recorded by point B'. At a relative price of ⅔, Ken has the gray budget line, chooses point C, and consumes 10 apples today. This is recorded by point C'. At a relative price of 2, Ken has the blue budget line, chooses point D, and consumes 4 apples today. This is recorded by point D'.

Students are sometimes confused by the statement that Ken demands 8 apples today when the price is 1. They look at Exhibit 16–2 and see that Ken wants to eat 8 apples today, but they remember that he is already endowed with 6. Doesn't this mean that he needs to obtain only 2 additional apples in the marketplace? The answer is yes, he needs to obtain only 2 additional apples. However, we still say that the quantity of apples he demands is 8. "Quantity demanded" refers to the total number of apples that Ken wants to eat. This is the number of apples he demands from the marketplace. The confusion arises from the fact that Ken is both a supplier and a demander in the market for apples. He supplies a total of 6 apples today, and he demands a total of 8 apples, 6 of which he can supply to himself.

We can generate other points on Ken's demand curve by imagining other prices for apples today and examining Ken's optimal basket. If there were a market in which Ken could trade at a rate of ⅔ apple tomorrow for 1 apple today, then he would have the gray budget line in Exhibit 16–3, and he would choose basket C, containing 10 apples today. Thus a price of ⅔ corresponds to a quantity of 10, and we record this fact in panel B by depicting point C′. Similarly, if the price were 2, he would have the blue budget line, choose point D, and consume 4 apples today. This is shown by point D′.

Borrower
Someone who demands more for current consumption than he supplies.

Lender
Someone who supplies more for current consumption than he demands.

A consumer who demands more apples today than he supplies is called a **borrower.** He acquires apples today in exchange for a promise to deliver apples tomorrow. A consumer who supplies more apples today than he demands is called a **lender.** He trades part of his present endowment to somebody else in exchange for a promise of apples delivered tomorrow. At prices of 1 and ⅔, Ken is a borrower. When the price is 2, Ken becomes a lender.

▷ *Exercise 16.3* At each price shown in Exhibit 16–3, how many apples does Ken borrow or lend?

▷ *Exercise 16.4* Draw three points on Ken's demand curve for apples tomorrow (with the price in terms of apples today).

The derivation of the demand curve for apples today is very similar to the derivation of the demand curve for X in Exhibit 4–5 of Section 4.2. When the price of apples today goes down, the budget line swings outward, generating a new optimal basket and a new quantity demanded that can be plotted on the demand curve. The only difference is this: In Chapter 4 we held fixed the consumer's money income and the prices of other goods, which caused the budget line to swing around its Y-intercept. In the present case we hold fixed the consumer's endowment point, which causes the budget line to swing around that endowment point.

After we have generated the consumer's demand curve for apples today, we can do the same for every other consumer in the economy. Then we can add all of the individual demand curves together to get the market demand curve for apples today.

The Supply of Current Consumption

There is also a supply curve for apples today. For the moment we will make two extreme assumptions about the way in which apples today are supplied.

- *Assumption 1:* The number of apples in the world today is determined by people's endowments. These endowments are given and cannot be changed. In other words, we assume that it is not possible to increase your apple endowment by purchasing a stepladder and picking more than the usual number of apples off the trees.

- *Assumption 2:* Apples rot and become useless unless they are eaten immediately.

Assumption 1 limits the number of apples available in the marketplace, and Assumption 2 guarantees that all of the available apples will actually be brought to market for eating (because there is no opportunity to do

Exhibit 16–4   **Equilibrium in the Market for Current Consumption**

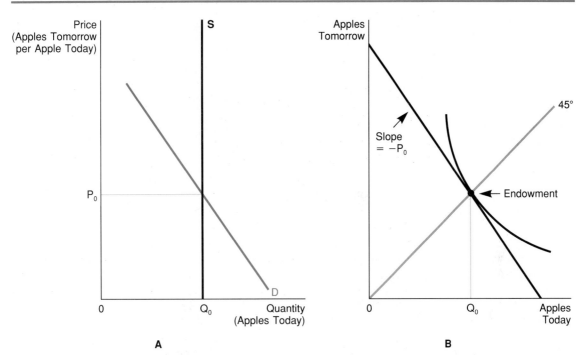

In this example we assume that there is no way to increase the supply of apples and no use for apples other than current consumption. Thus there is a given number of apples today, Q_0, and all of these will be supplied to the marketplace. It follows that the supply curve for apples is vertical.

The equilibrium price for apples today is P_0 apples tomorrow per apple today. Because this is the equilibrium price, the representative agent (that is, the "typical" or "average" consumer) must demand and supply the same quantities. In order for this to be so, the representative agent must choose to consume exactly her endowment, as in panel B.

Representative agent Someone whose tastes and assets are representative of the entire economy.

anything else with them). Taken together, these assumptions imply a vertical supply curve, at a quantity equal to the sum of all of the individual endowments.

Equilibrium

If the market is competitive, the price will be set at the intersection of supply and demand, say at P_0 in panel A of Exhibit 16–4. Each consumer faces a budget line through his endowment with a slope of $-P_0$ and selects an optimal basket.

P_0 is determined by the condition that the total of all quantities demanded is equal to the total of all quantities supplied. This means that at equilibrium the "average" consumer, whom we call the **representative agent,** must demand and supply exactly the same quantity of apples. The representative agent (whose name happens to be Rebecca Representative) chooses to consume exactly her endowment. Rebecca's budget line, with slope $-P_0$, must be tangent to an indifference curve precisely at her endowment point, as shown in panel B of Exhibit 16–4.

▷ **Exercise 16.5** Suppose that Ken, from Exhibit 16–3, were the representative agent. Explain how you know that none of the prices 1, ⅔, or 2 can be the equilibrium price. At each of these prices, is quantity demanded greater or less than quantity supplied? Can you say anything about the value of the equilibrium price?

The Interest Rate

We can reasonably assume that Rebecca's endowment point is on the 45° line. This is tantamount to the assumption that one day is just like another from the point of view of apple harvests. If so, we expect that the absolute slope of her indifference curve through the endowment point (her MRS) is greater than 1. But panel B of Exhibit 16–4 shows that the absolute slope is P_0. From this we conclude that the equilibrium price of apples today in terms of apples tomorrow (that is, P_0) must be greater than 1.

▷ **Exercise 16.6** Suppose that Rebecca expects the great Apple Blight to destroy half of tomorrow's harvest. What does this imply about her endowment point? Suppose, alternatively, that Rebecca expects to win the apple lottery tomorrow. What does this imply? In which of these circumstances is our conclusion that P_0 is greater than 1 still justified?

Because our assumptions imply that P_0 is greater than 1, we can write

$$P_0 = 1 + r,$$

Interest rate
The relative price of current consumption in terms of future consumption, minus 1.

where r is some positive number. This number r is called the **interest rate.** For example, if $r = .10$ (or 10%), it is possible to trade 1 apple today for $1 + .10 = 1.10$ apples tomorrow. One way to think of this transaction is that you forgo eating 1 apple today, in exchange for which you "get back" that apple tomorrow, together with an additional .10 apple in "interest." This way of thinking is often convenient. But it is important to realize that the interest rate is simply a measure of the relative price of one commodity (apples today) measured in terms of another commodity (apples tomorrow).

In equilibrium each individual chooses an optimum where his marginal rate of substitution is equal to the market price. Thus for any individual (not just the representative agent) we have

$$MRS = P_0,$$

which can be rewritten

$$1 + \rho = 1 + r,$$

or

$$\rho = r,$$

where ρ is the individual's discount rate and r is the rate of interest. What is special about the representative agent is that we know that for her this equality occurs at the endowment point, where ρ is positive. From this we can conclude that the interest rate, r, is positive.

▷ **Exercise 16.7** Liz's discount rate exceeds the rate of interest. What transaction will make her better off? Which direction will this move her in an indifference curve diagram? What will become of her discount rate as she moves? How long will this continue? Becky's discount rate is less than the rate of interest. Answer all of the same questions for Becky.

Changes in the Endowment Point

Now that we have found the market equilibrium, we can see how and why that equilibrium might change in response to external forces.

Example: An Increase in the Future Apple Supply

Suppose that a breakthrough in agricultural technology makes it clear that apple trees will become more productive tomorrow. Although each tree was initially expected to produce 6 apples per year each year, we now expect the trees to produce 6 apples this year and 8 apples next year. How will the equilibrium interest rate change?

To answer this question, we can either consult the supply and demand graph or we can consult the indifference curve graph of the representative agent. The two approaches are shown in the two panels of Exhibit 16–5.

Panel A shows the changes in supply and demand. The supply of current apples (6 apples per tree times the number of trees) is unchanged. Demand, however, shifts outward, because people are now effectively wealthier than before. In anticipation of tomorrow's good fortune, they want to begin eating more today. For example, Rebecca, the representative agent, moves from the endowment point A to the endowment point B in panel B, achieving a higher indifference curve. This increase in income raises the demand for both current and future consumption.[1]

In panel A of the exhibit we see that the equilibrium price of apples today increases from P to P'. Since the interest rate is equal to this price minus 1, we can express the same thing by saying that the interest rate increases.

To verify this conclusion, refer to Rebecca Representative's indifference curves in panel B. Initially, her endowment is A, and her budget line is the one shown in black. After the agricultural breakthrough, her endowment is point B. Her new budget line must pass through point B. In equilibrium, its slope is determined by the requirement that Rebecca must be willing to just consume her endowment. Thus her new budget line is

---

[1]We are ignoring the (remote) possibility that current consumption could be an inferior good.

Exhibit 16–5   **An Increase in the Future Apple Supply**

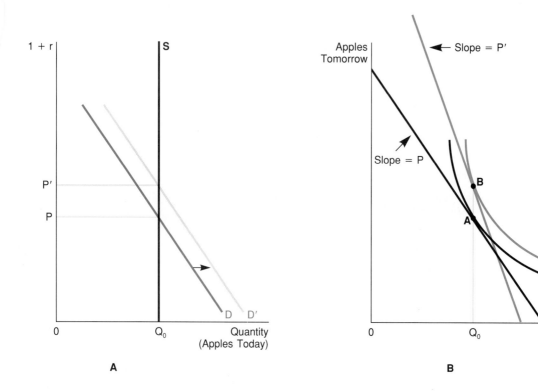

A   B

An increase in the future apple supply moves the representative agent from point A to point B in panel B, increasing wealth and hence increasing the demand for all noninferior goods, including apples today. The demand curve shifts outward in panel A and the equilibrium price rises from P to P′. The interest rate rises from r = P − 1 to r′ = P′ − 1.

The representative agent's budget line shifts from the black line (with slope P) to the blue line (with slope P′). The fact that the blue line is steeper confirms the observation that P′ is greater than P.

the one shown in blue. The slope of this budget line is the new equilibrium price P′. Since the new budget line is steeper than the old budget line, we can be sure that the equilibrium price (and hence the interest rate) has increased.

▷ *Exercise 16.8* Give a careful argument demonstrating that the colored budget line must in fact be steeper than the black one. (*Hint:* Use the assumption that current consumption is not an inferior good.)

Example: An Increase in the Current Apple Supply

Suppose that this year's apple harvest is unusually large (8 apples per tree instead of the expected 6) but that next year's harvest is expected to be back

Exhibit 16–6   An Increase in the Current Apple Supply

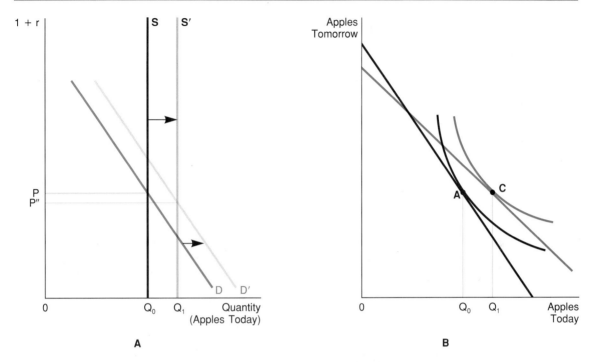

A   B

Because people are wealthier when the current apple supply increases, demand increases as well. The supply and demand graph in panel A does not reveal whether the new equilibrium price, P'', is greater or less than the old price, P. However, we can make this determination on the basis of Rebecca Representative's indifference curves. Her endowment moves from point A to point C, so her budget line changes from the black line to the shallower blue line. As the slope of the budget line is the same as the equilibrium price, we conclude that the equilibrium price (and hence the interest rate) falls.

to normal. In that case the supply of current apples is increased, and so is the demand for current apples, due to the increase in people's wealth. Panel A of Exhibit 16–6 shows the movements of both curves. The equilibrium interest rate moves from $r = P - 1$ to $r'' = P'' - 1$. Is this an increase or a decrease?

From the supply and demand graph alone, we cannot tell. In Exhibit 16–6 P'' appears to be less than P, but by shifting the demand curve a different amount, we could make P'' appear to be greater than P. Thus a rough drawing of the supply and demand picture does not suffice to determine which way the interest rate moves. Fortunately, however, it is easy to tell by looking at Rebecca Representative's indifference curves in panel B.

Rebecca moves from her old endowment at point A to her new endowment at point C. We know that in equilibrium she consumes exactly her endowment, so her budget line changes from the black to the blue line. Since the blue line is evidently less steep than the black line, we conclude that P'' is less than P; hence the interest rate falls.

▷ **Exercise 16.9** Give a careful argument demonstrating that the blue budget line is shallower than the black one. What assumptions must you use?

Investment

Now we will begin relaxing the assumptions that led to our vertical supply curve. The most crucial is Assumption 2. Suppose that, contrary to Assumption 2, there is an alternative use for apples today; namely, suppose that through some technology apples today can be converted into apples tomorrow. One possible such technology is storage. An apple today can be converted into an apple tomorrow if it can be stored without decaying. Alternatively, perhaps one-third of all apples in storage do decay; in that case 3 apples today can be converted to 2 apples tomorrow. A more intriguing possibility is that apples not eaten can be planted in the ground, where they turn into apple trees yielding more than one apple tomorrow for each apple that is planted today.

     Apples that are used in the production of future apples constitute an example of **capital**. Economists use the word *capital* to refer to any good that is used in the production of other goods. When an apple is used as capital—say, by being placed in a refrigerator for future use or by being planted in the ground—that apple is said to be **invested.**

Capital
Goods used to produce future consumption, as opposed to being consumed in the present.

Invested
Used as capital.

The Marginal Product of Capital

Suppose that an apple planted today yields a tree that produces 3 apples tomorrow and then dies.[2] We say that the *gross marginal product* of the planted apple is equal to 3 future apples per apple planted. It is useful to think of this future apple yield in terms of "getting back" the original apple that was planted and obtaining 2 more besides. The *net marginal product* is the number of additional apples earned after "getting back" the first one. In this case the net marginal product of the planted apple is equal to 2 future apples per apple planted, or 200% of what was planted. It is customary to express the gross and net marginal products in percentage terms.

     Because planted apples are a form of capital, their gross and net marginal products are called the **gross marginal product of capital (GMPK)** and the **net marginal product of capital.** The net marginal product of capital is often referred to as the *marginal product of capital* and is

Gross marginal product of capital (GMPK)
The amount of additional future consumption generated by an additional unit of capital.

Net marginal product of capital (MPK)
The GMPK minus 1.

---

[2]We assume that the tree dies after producing its apples so that we avoid having to talk about the apples it produces on the day after tomorrow. In order to talk about these apples, we would need a third dimension in our indifference curve diagrams.

Exhibit 16–7   **The Gross Marginal Product of Capital**

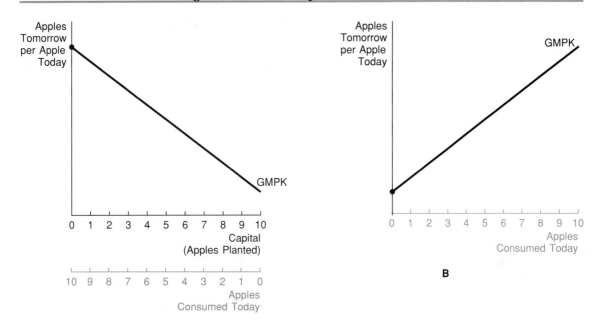

The gross marginal product of capital (GMPK) is the number of apples produced tomorrow by an apple planted today. Due to diminishing marginal returns, the GMPK curve is downward-sloping.

The number of apples planted is determined by the number of apples eaten. If there are 10 apples altogether, then the "apples eaten" axis is as shown in blue below the "apples planted" axis. When the "apples eaten" axis is drawn from left to right, as in panel B, the curve is reversed and appears upward-sloping.

abbreviated *MPK*. The gross and net marginal products of capital are related by the equation

$$1 + \text{MPK} = \text{GMPK}.$$

▷ *Exercise 16.10* Suppose that future apples are produced from present apples via storage, without decay. What is the marginal product of capital? Suppose that one-third of all stored apples are lost to decay. Now what is the marginal product of capital?

We assume that the technology for producing future apples exhibits diminishing marginal returns with respect to the number of present apples invested. The first apple planted is planted in the most fertile soil, the next one in the next most fertile soil, and so on. Alternatively, if all of the soil is uniformly fertile, it is still the case that two planted apples will have to share nutrients and water and will produce less than twice what one planted apple can produce. Panel A of Exhibit 16–7 shows a graph of the gross marginal product of capital as a function of the number of apples planted. Because of the diminishing marginal returns, it is downward-sloping.

The black horizontal axis in Exhibit 16–7 shows the number of apples planted. If we know the total number of apples presently in the world, we can relabel the axis with the number of apples eaten. This is shown in Exhibit 16–7 under the assumption that there are exactly 10 apples in the world. Reading the horizontal axis in panel A *from right to left,* the number of apples eaten increases, the number planted decreases, and the gross marginal product of capital increases. Panel B is a mirror image of panel A. The horizontal axis shows the number of apples currently consumed. Movement to the right means more apples eaten now, fewer planted, and a higher GMPK.

The Marginal Cost of Current Consumption

The marginal cost of eating an apple today is the forgone opportunity to plant that apple and have apples tomorrow. The number of future apples forgone is exactly the gross marginal product of capital. Therefore, when the marginal cost of eating apples today is measured in terms of forgone apples tomorrow, the marginal cost curve is precisely the curve drawn in panel B of Exhibit 16–7. Assuming a competitive market, this marginal cost curve is also the supply curve for apples today.

Equilibrium

The upward-sloping supply curve for apples today can be plotted on the same graph with the downward-sloping demand curve (from panel A of Exhibit 16–4). Exhibit 16–8 shows both curves and the equilibrium in the market for apples today.

Apples today sell at the price P_0 in Exhibit 16–8. This price is equal to the gross marginal product of capital at the equilibrium quantity of apples. Thus we can write

$$P_0 = GMPK.$$

Subtracting 1 from each side, this becomes

$$r = MPK.$$

In equilibrium the interest rate must be equal to the marginal product of capital.

▷ *Exercise 16.11* Suppose that the interest rate were less than the marginal product of capital. How could people exploit this discrepancy to make themselves better off? What would then happen to the marginal product of capital?

Exhibit 16–8   Equilibrium in the Market for Current Consumption

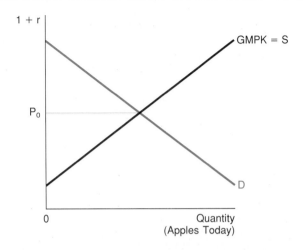

The gross marginal product of capital is equal to the marginal cost of current consumption and hence, in a competitive economy, equal to the supply curve. The graph determines the equilibrium price and quantity of apples consumed today.

We have already seen that each individual chooses his consumption basket in such a way that his discount rate, ρ, is equal to the interest rate, r. Therefore:

In equilibrium the interest rate, each individual's discount rate, and the marginal product of capital must all be equal.

The Rental Rate on Capital

When an individual acquires an apple today for the purpose of eating it, we speak of his "borrowing" the apple, and when he pays the price in future apples we speak of his "repaying the debt with interest." When an individual purchases an apple today for the purpose of planting it, we speak of his "renting" a unit of capital, and when he pays the price in future apples we speak of his "returning the capital plus a rental fee." But an item purchased in a competitive market will sell at the same price regardless of how the buyer intends to use it. Therefore the interest paid on the apple that is eaten must be the same as the rental rate for the apple that is planted. We know from our discussion in this section that the interest rate is the marginal product of capital. We may therefore conclude:

The rental rate for a unit of capital is equal to its marginal product.

This conclusion is not new. We discovered in Section 14.1 that the price of hiring any productive input is equal to its marginal product. The analysis here proceeds from a different viewpoint (focusing on the market for consumption goods instead of on the market for inputs), but it leads to the same conclusion, as of course it must.

Changes in the Equilibrium

Earlier we investigated changes in the equilibrium when the supply curve for current apples is vertical. Now we have seen that the possibility of investment opportunities leads to an upward-sloping supply curve for current apples. Next we will re-examine changes in the equilibrium, taking account of the possibility of investment.

An Increase in Future Productivity

Suppose that people come to expect that apple trees will become more productive in the future, possibly as a result of better weather or improved farming methods.

Exhibit 16–9 shows how this affects the demand for and the supply of current apples. First, the demand is increased, because the improvement in future productivity is an increase in wealth. When people are wealthier, they choose more current consumption at any given price.

The supply curve for current apples is the GMPK curve, which shifts upward, since each planted apple is now expected to be more productive at the margin than it was before. This upward shift represents a fall in the supply of current apples. The intuition is that the owners of current apples now face an increased incentive to plant them and hence a decreased incentive to supply them for current consumption.

When demand increases and supply decreases, price moves up and quantity changes ambiguously. Thus the interest rate rises and the number of apples consumed today could go either up or down.

An Increase in Today's Apple Crop

Suppose that this year apple trees yield an unexpectedly large crop, but that the productivity of apple trees is expected to return to normal next year. In this case the windfall harvest represents an increase in the supply of apples today, and the resulting increase in wealth leads to an increase in the demand for apples today as well. The rightward shifts in the supply and demand curves guarantee that there will be an increase in today's apple consumption, as shown in Exhibit 16–10.

In order to determine the effect on the interest rate, we must ask: Which moves farther—the demand curve or the supply curve? When people unexpectedly receive more apples, do they choose to increase their current consumption by less or more than the amount of the windfall?

The key to answering this question is to notice that the increase in wealth leads people to want more of everything, including *both* current consumption *and* future consumption. If you were given $1,000 for your birthday, you would probably spend part of it now and part of later. Thus

Exhibit 16–9 **An Increase in Future Productivity**

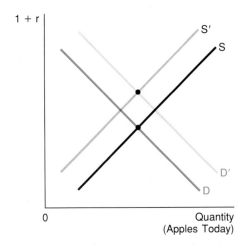

Suppose that agricultural productivity is expected to improve in the future. Then people are wealthier and so demand more apples today at any given price. That is, the demand curve shifts rightward, from D to D'. At the same time, the supply curve for apples today moves leftward, as suppliers prefer to plant more apples and so provide fewer for current consumption. Another way to view the shift in supply is as an upward shift in the GMPK curve. In the new equilibrium, the interest rate moves up and current consumption could move in either direction.

Exhibit 16–10 **An Increase in Today's Apple Crop**

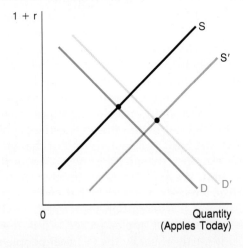

An increase in today's apple crop increases both the demand and the supply for current consumption. But demand increases by less than supply does, so the interest rate must fall.

the demand for *current* consumption increases by less than the windfall gain; in other words, the demand for current consumption increases by less than the supply.

With this observation, we can conclude that the price of current consumption, and consequently the interest rate, must fall.

In Exhibits 16–5 and 16–6 we examined changes in the equilibrium when there was no possibility of investment and hence a vertical supply curve for today's apples. We were able to confirm our analyses by examining the representative agent's indifference curves. When investment is possible, we can do the same thing. However, it is no longer true that Rebecca the representative agent must remain at her endowment point. She can choose to have more apples tomorrow by consuming fewer today. Thus Rebecca chooses an optimum along a budget constraint that passes through her endowment point. The declining marginal product of capital implies that this budget constraint is a curve that bows outward from the origin. Changes in future productivity, current output, and so forth correspond to shifts in this budget constraint and movements to a new optimum.

Relaxing the Assumptions

Our story of the determination of interest rates is highly stylized. We assumed a world in which apples are the only good and in which apples simply fall from trees without regard to any labor input. It turns out that our conclusions remain generally valid when these assumptions are relaxed.

Including the Labor Supply Decision

We began with two assumptions about how apples are produced. Assumption 1 said that people could not increase the current apple supply by working harder; Assumption 2 said that they could not increase the future apple supply by planting, storage, or any other form of investment. Taken together, these implied a vertical supply curve for current consumption.

In the section on investment we dropped Assumption 2 and found that this led to an upward-sloping supply curve. It is also possible to drop Assumption 1. Although this makes the analysis considerably more complicated, the basic conclusions do not change.

For example, consider the effect of a windfall increase in current apple production. We have just seen that this leads to a fall in the interest rate. However, we saw in Chapter 15 that a fall in the interest rate leads to a fall in labor supply. If Assumption 1 is relaxed, a fall in labor supply means that there will be fewer apples picked. Thus the windfall increase in apple supply is partly offset by the fact that people work less hard.

This indicates that including the labor supply decision in the model can sometimes reduce the magnitude of various effects. In most examples, however, it will not change the directions. Thus when we conclude, for example, that a rise in future productivity leads to a rise in the interest rate, our conclusion is not invalidated by our decision to ignore the labor supply decision. If we wanted to estimate the *size* of the interest rate increase, then the effects of labor supply might become important.

The One-Good Assumption

In our simple story we have imagined that a single good—apples—can be used both for consumption and as an input to production. When the demand for apples today goes up, people consume more by eating some of the apples that they would have planted—that is, they consume some of their capital.

In the real world, however, goods are specialized in their uses. Much capital is in the form of industrial machinery. When the demand for food today goes up, it is not possible for people to consume more by eating some of their drill presses. How, then, can we relate our story to the world?

The answer is that there is a sense in which it *is* possible to consume more food by eating drill presses. This is accomplished by manufacturing fewer drill presses and using the freed-up resources to grow food. Economists find it convenient to think of this process as "eating drill presses." Such little fictions are often harmless, and they allow us to reflect the world in much simpler stories than would otherwise be possible.

Real Rates versus Nominal Rates

Suppose that the supply and demand curves for current consumption cross at a price of 1.03. The market interest rate is then .03, or 3%. When you lend to your bank (by making deposits in your account), the bank will agree to pay you 1.03 apples tomorrow for every 1 apple that you deposit today.

Of course, you don't deposit apples. You deposit dollars. However, if dollars can be traded for apples at some constant rate, then the bank will pay you $1.03 tomorrow for every $1 you deposit today, and the dollars can simply be viewed as stand-ins for apples.

There is, however, a possible complication. Dollars might not trade for apples at a constant rate. Suppose that apples cost $1 apiece today but are expected to cost $1.05 apiece tomorrow. Then your deposit of $1 is equivalent to the deposit of 1 apple, and, in order for you to receive the going interest rate of 3%, the bank must pay you tomorrow the equivalent of 1.03 apples. Given tomorrow's price, the bank must pay $1.03 \times \$1.05 \approx \$1.08$.

Real rate of interest The relative price of present consumption goods in terms of future consumption goods, minus 1.

Nominal rate of interest The relative price of current dollars in terms of future dollars, minus 1.

This makes it necessary for us to distinguish the **real rate of interest** (3%) from the **nominal rate of interest** (in this case, 8%). The real rate of interest is the rate of return, in apples, to the lender of an apple (or of a basket of consumption goods). The nominal rate of interest is the rate of return, in dollars, to the lender of a dollar. The two differ when the dollar price of consumption goods is expected to change; that is, when there is expected inflation.

The Relationship between Real and Nominal Interest Rates

Assume, for simplicity, that the current price of apples is $1 apiece and that the real interest rate is some number r per year. Assume that the expected rate of inflation is π per year, by which we mean that market participants expect apples next year to sell at a price of $\$(1 + \pi)$. Then a dollar lent is equal to an apple lent, and the number of dollars returned tomorrow must be:

$$(1 + r) \cdot (1 + \pi) = 1 + r + \pi + r\pi \approx 1 + r + \pi.$$

(The term $r\pi$ will, in general, be small and can be ignored. If you know about the theory of compound interest, you should try to show that with continuous compounding, the approximation becomes an exact formula.)

We see from the preceding formula that the nominal interest rate is $r + \pi$. It is important to realize that the theory of interest rates developed in this chapter is a theory of *real* interest rates. It is the real interest rate, not the nominal rate, that is equal to both the discount rate and the marginal product of capital.

Interest Rates and Welfare

The main lesson of this chapter is that an interest rate is simply a price in a market where goods delivered at one date are traded for goods delivered at another date. (More precisely, the price is 1 plus the interest rate.) The price equates marginal benefits to marginal costs and enables consumers to be better off (as can be seen by the movement from point A to point B in Exhibit 16–2).

Noneconomists sometimes assert that in competitive markets the desire to earn immediate rewards leads to too much present consumption and not enough investment in the future. We can evaluate this statement by examining the social gains created in the market for current consumption. These gains can be calculated exactly as in other markets. In particular, a competitive market allocates apples, like goods generally, across their alternative uses in an efficient manner.

16.2 Present Values

Present value
Relative price in terms of current consumption.

The relative price of an apple delivered today is $1 + r$ apples tomorrow, where r is the interest rate. Therefore the relative price of an apple delivered tomorrow is $1/(1 + r)$ apples today. The value of a future delivery in terms of current consumption is called the **present value** of the future delivery. Thus we can say that the present value of one apple delivered tomorrow is $1/(1 + r)$ apples today, the present value of 2 apples delivered tomorrow is $2 \times 1/(1 + r)$ apples today, and so forth.

Some exchanges involve payments that are more complicated than just a single delivery tomorrow. For example, if you buy a car, you might commit yourself to making payments of a certain size every month for a given period of time. The car that you receive in exchange for these payments is a source of valuable transportation at a series of future dates. Thus in this exchange both your payments and what you receive are spread out over time. In this section we will see how to compute and compare the present values of such streams of income.

Bonds

Suppose that Rosencrantz agrees to trade Guildenstern 10 apples today in exchange for 11 apples tomorrow. In common language, we say that Rosencrantz is lending 10 apples to Guildenstern, and that Guildenstern is borrowing 10 apples from Rosencrantz, at an interest rate of 10% per day.

By definition, it is physically impossible for Guildenstern to deliver his future apples in the present. Instead, he issues a promise to Rosencrantz that he will make such a delivery. This promise may be sealed with a handshake or with a written contract, called a promissory note or an IOU. Another name for a promise is a **bond**. Rosencrantz trades his 10 apples today for Guildenstern's bond, which can be exchanged for 11 apples tomorrow.

Who is the buyer and who is the seller in this transaction? As in any trade, each party is both a buyer and a seller. Rosencrantz is the seller of apples today and the buyer of the bond, while Guildenstern is the buyer of apples today and the seller of the bond.

The buyer of a bond is a lender; the seller of a bond is a borrower.

The **face value** of a bond is equal to the number of future apples that it guarantees. A bond is said to sell at a **discount** equal to the difference between its face value and its price in terms of apples today. When Rosencrantz buys Guildenstern's bond, which has a face value of 11 apples, for a price of 10 apples today, he is buying it at a discount of 1 apple. Of course, the use of the word *discount* should not be interpreted to mean that Rosencrantz is buying the bond at anything other than its going market price.

The bond is said to **mature** at the future date when Guildenstern meets his obligation.

The price of an apple today is $1 + r$ apples tomorrow, where r is the interest rate. Consequently, the price of an apple tomorrow is $1/(1 + r)$ apples today. When r is 10% ($= .10$), this works out to $\approx .91$ apples today. Guildenstern's promise to deliver 11 apples tomorrow is worth $11 \times .91 = 10$ apples today, confirming what we already knew.

Example: Treasury Bills

When the U.S. government borrows, it does so by issuing bonds known as Treasury bills. Treasury bills are issued with a fixed face value and maturity date and then sold at auction to the highest bidder. Thus the size of the discount (and consequently the interest rate) are determined by the auction.

Bond
A promise to pay at some time in the future.

Face value
The amount that a bond promises to pay.

Discount
The face value of a bond minus its current price.

Mature
A bond is said to mature on the date on which it promises payment.

For example, suppose that on January 1, 1990, the Treasury issues a bond that reads "We promise to pay $10,000 on January 1, 1991." The Treasury holds a regular weekly auction at which this bond will be offered for sale. Suppose that after much bidding you are able to purchase this bond for $9,500. In that case, we say that the bond sold at a discount of $500. You have lent $9,500 to the Treasury and will receive $500 in interest, so the interest rate is $500/$9,500 ≈ 5.26%.

After you purchase the bond, you are entitled to sell it to anybody else at whatever price you mutually agree on. Thus the value of the bond could vary quite a bit between the date of purchase and the date of maturity. For example, suppose that immediately after you purchase the bond, the market rate of interest rises to 12%. In that case the value of the bond falls to $10,000 × 1/(1 + .12) ≈ $8,928.57.

Students sometimes want to know the direction of causality: Does a change in the interest rate affect the price of the bond, or does a change in the price of the bond affect the interest rate? The answer is that the interest rate and the price of the bond are two different descriptions of exactly the same thing, and therefore neither can be said to cause the other. The interest rate r is *defined* by the condition that the price of current consumption in terms of future consumption is $1 + r$. It is just a restatement of the definition to say that the price of future consumption in terms of current consumption (that is, the price of a bond) is $1/(1 + r)$.

The More Distant Future

If interest rates do not change over time, we can compute the present value of an apple delivered the day after tomorrow. An apple delivered the day after tomorrow is worth $1/(1 + r)$ apples tomorrow and an apple delivered tomorrow is worth $1/(1 + r)$ apples today. Therefore an apple delivered the day after tomorrow has a present value of

$$\frac{1}{(1 + r)} \times \frac{1}{(1 + r)} = \frac{1}{(1 + r)^2}$$

apples today. By the same reasoning, an apple delivered n days from now has a present value of $1/(1 + r)^n$ apples today.

▷ **Exercise 16.12** Explain why an apple delivered the day after tomorrow is worth $1/(1 + r)$ apples tomorrow. Explain why an apple delivered n days from now has a present value of $1/(1 + r)^n$ apples today.

▷ **Exercise 16.13** What is the present value of an apple delivered yesterday?

Coupon Bonds

We can also discuss the present value of a basket consisting of several apple deliveries on several dates. Suppose on Monday that Guildenstern promises to deliver 2 apples on Tuesday, 3 apples on Wednesday, and 1 apple on Friday. The present value of this multiple promise is the sum of the present

Exhibit 16–11 **A Coupon Bond**

```
┌ ─ ─ ─ ─ ─ ─ ─ ─ ┐   ┌ ─ ─ ─ ─ ─ ─ ─ ─ ─ ┐   ┌ ─ ─ ─ ─ ─ ─ ─ ─ ─ ┐
│                 │   │                   │   │                   │
│  THIS COUPON GOOD │   │  THIS COUPON GOOD   │   │  THIS COUPON GOOD   │
│  FOR 2          │   │  FOR 3            │   │  FOR 1            │
│  APPLES DELIVERED │   │  APPLES DELIVERED   │   │  APPLE DELIVERED    │
│  ON TUESDAY     │   │  ON WEDNESDAY     │   │  ON FRIDAY        │
│                 │   │                   │   │                   │
└ ─ ─ ─ ─ ─ ─ ─ ─ ┘   └ ─ ─ ─ ─ ─ ─ ─ ─ ─ ┘   └ ─ ─ ─ ─ ─ ─ ─ ─ ─ ┘
```

A coupon bond is a promise to make a series of payments at specified dates in the future. To seal his promise, the seller of a coupon bond might issue a set of coupons such as those above.

values of the individual promises it comprises. That is, the present value is:

$$2 \times \frac{1}{(1 + r)} + 3 \times \frac{1}{(1 + r)^2} + 1 \times \frac{1}{(1 + r)^4}$$

apples today (today being Monday). With $r = 10\%$ ($= .10$), this works out to about 4.98 apples today.

Guildenstern's new multiple promise is another example of a bond. A bond of this sort is sometimes called a **coupon bond.** The reason for the terminology is that Guildenstern might seal his promise by providing a set of "coupons" such as those shown in Exhibit 16–11.

Coupon bond
A bond that promises a series of payments on different dates.

Using present values, it is possible to compare different bonds. Suppose that the interest rate is 10% and that you are given a choice between bond A, represented by the three coupons in Exhibit 16–11, and bond B, consisting of 5 apples delivered on Tuesday. We have already calculated bond A's present value to be 4.98 apples today. Bond B's present value is $5 \times 1/(1 + .10) \approx 4.55$ apples today. Bond A is worth more than bond B. If you had bond A, you could trade it in the marketplace for bond B plus an additional .43 apple.

This calculation depends on the interest rate. If r were to rise to 25% per day, the present value of bond A would be 3.93 apples today and the present value of bond B would be exactly 4 apples today. Bond B would now be worth more than bond A.

▷ *Exercise 16.14* Verify the numbers in the preceding two paragraphs.

Durable Goods as Coupon Bonds

Dividends
Streams of benefits.

Many assets are valuable only because of the streams of future benefits that they provide. Another name for these future benefits is **dividends.** Any such asset can be assessed in terms of its present value. Suppose that you are considering buying a sofa that will last for 4 years and then wear out. The alternative is to rent a sofa, which would cost $100 a year, payable at the end of each year. Thus the purchased sofa provides a stream of benefits, or dividends, worth $100 per year for 4 years. At an interest rate of 10% per year, the present value of the stream of dividends is

$$(\$100 \times 1/(1 + .10))$$
$$+ (\$100 \times 1/(1 + .10)^2)$$
$$+ (\$100 \times 1/(1 + .10)^3)$$
$$+ (\$100 \times 1/(1 + .10)^4),$$

which is approximately $317.

If you can buy the sofa for less than $317, you should do so; if the price is over $317, it would be better to rent. For example, suppose that the sofa sells for $325. Instead of spending $325 on the sofa, you could spend $317 to buy a coupon bond that pays $100 at the end of each year. Then you could use the income from the bond to make payments on a rented sofa. This way you would still get 4 years of sofa, and you would have $8 left over.

Again, the present value depends on the interest rate. At an interest rate of 5%, the present value of the benefits from the sofa is approximately $355, and it is better to buy than to rent if the price is anything less than $355.

Perpetuities

Perpetuity
A bond that promises to pay a fixed amount periodically forever.

A **perpetuity** is a promise to pay some fixed amount periodically forever. A perpetuity is like a coupon bond with an infinite number of coupons.

Imagine a perpetuity that pays $1 per year forever, starting one year hence. The present value of such a perpetuity in dollars is:

$$\frac{1}{(1 + r)} + \frac{1}{(1 + r)^2} + \frac{1}{(1 + r)^3} + \frac{1}{(1 + r)^4} + \cdots.$$

Perhaps you know how to sum such an infinite series. If not, don't panic. There is a sneaky but easy way to compute the present value without even thinking about the series.

First, let us imagine a different perpetuity: one that pays $r per year, where r happens to be the interest rate. You can purchase such a perpetuity for $1. If you lend somebody $1 per year forever, he will return $r per year in interest forever. You have essentially traded your dollar (which will never be returned) for a perpetuity.

Since $1 will buy a perpetuity of $r per year forever, it follows that $2 will buy a perpetuity of $(2r) per year forever, and that 50¢ will buy a perpetuity of $(r/2) forever, and so on. How much will $(1/r) buy? The answer is: $1 per year forever. Thus a perpetuity of $1 per year forever must have a present value of $(1/r).

For example, when the interest rate is 10%, the perpetuity has a present value of $1/.10 = \$10$. This means that $10 can be exchanged for an infinite stream of payments of $1 per year. And indeed this is the case. If you put $10 into your bank account at 10% interest and leave it there forever, you have traded your $10 for precisely the perpetuity we have described.

▷ **Exercise 16.15** At an interest rate of 5%, what is the present value of a perpetuity that pays $1 per year forever? Confirm your answer by describing how you could trade this present value for the perpetuity. How could you make the opposite exchange, trading the perpetuity for its present value?

Indestructible Assets as Perpetuities

Indestructible assets yield dividend streams that are perpetuities. If a painting hung on your wall provides you with dividends in the form of viewing pleasure worth $10 per year forever, then its present value is $10 \times (1/r)$. If the interest rate is 5%, this comes to $200.

Bonds Denominated in Dollars

A bond that promises to pay 1 apple next year must sell for $1/(1 + r)$ apples today. However, the face value of a bond is typically measured not in apples, or in any other actual consumption good, but in dollars. We say that such a bond is *denominated* in dollars. In this case the size of the discount must reflect the nominal interest rate rather than the real interest rate. Recall that the nominal interest rate is $r + \pi$, where π is the rate of inflation. Therefore if inflation is nonzero, the present value of a dollar delivered next year is actually $1/(1 + r + \pi)$ dollars, rather than $1/(1 + r)$ dollars.

Default Risk

A bond is a promise to pay, and throughout this section we have assumed that promises are always kept. Those economists (perhaps a minority) who have been in love know better. The buyer of a bond that promises an apple tomorrow is buying not an apple tomorrow, but a *chance* of receiving an apple tomorrow. When he thinks the chance is smaller, he will pay less for the bond. Thus everything we have said about the pricing of bonds applies literally only to cases in which the lender feels quite certain that his bond will be redeemed.

When the borrower is less trustworthy, he will have to sell his bonds at a greater discount in order to attract lenders. This is why different bonds carry different rates of interest.

Default risk
The possibility that the issuer of a bond will not meet his obligations.

The possibility that a borrower will fail to meet his obligations is known as a **default risk.** The higher the default risk, the higher will be the interest rate that the borrower has to pay in order to attract lenders. The additional interest that the borrower receives because of the default risk is called a **risk premium.** We will have more to say on the subject of risk and its effect on asset prices in Chapter 18.

Risk premium
Additional interest, in excess of the market rate, that a bondholder receives to compensate him for default risk.

Treasury Bills: A Risk-Free Asset?

It is widely believed that Treasury bills carry essentially no default risk, and that the U.S. Treasury has never defaulted on its obligations. This is untrue. For example, the Treasury defaulted on Bill #GS7–2–179–46–6606–1 in 1984.

In order to purchase a Treasury bill at auction, the investor (that is, the buyer of the bond) must submit a payment equal to the full face value of the bond. Following the auction the discount is supposed to be returned to the investor immediately. For example, suppose that you want to buy a Treasury bill that promises to pay $20,000 six months from now. To do so, you submit a check for $20,000 before the auction is held. If the bill sells at auction for $19,000, your discount of $1,000 should be returned to you immediately following the auction.

One unfortunate investor followed this procedure on August 14, 1984. His discount, approximately $1,100, was not returned. Following a series of inquiries, the Treasury took the remarkable position that although the default was entirely due to its own clerical errors, there was a strong possibility that the errors were irreparable and that the discount would never be paid. It required nearly 9 months, considerable expense on the investor's part, and the intervention of several senators and congressmen before the Treasury met its obligation. Even then, the Treasury refused to pay interest for the 9 months in which it unlawfully held the funds.

The frequency of such occurrences is not known. In this particular case the investor went on to write a textbook in price theory, yielding a bit more publicity than might ordinarily be expected. If there are many more such cases, and if they become well known, then the risk premium on Treasury bills will grow, so that the price of the bills will fall.

16.3 Government Policy

One of the largest borrowers in the world is the U.S. government. Many people believe that the government's demand for borrowing must bid up interest rates. In this section we will subject that belief to some economic analysis. We will not settle the issue; in fact, there is much disagreement among economists in this area. However, we will be able to present a framework for thinking about the effects of government debt, and we will be able to expose some common arguments as fallacious.

We begin by offering a parable that serves to clarify many of the important issues related to government debt.

A Parable

Suppose that you engage a purchasing agent to do your clothes shopping for you. This agent is empowered to make certain decisions on your behalf. First, he must decide how much to spend on the various components of your wardrobe. Second, he must decide how to finance those purchases.

In order to focus on the second of these decisions, let us suppose that your agent has already resolved to spend $100 on your clothes. There are three methods of financing available to him. First, he can withdraw $100 from your bank account and use it to pay for his purchases up front. Second, he can charge the purchases to your credit card and settle the debt a year from now. In this case, the credit card bill to be paid next year will be $110, assuming a 10% interest rate.

There is also a third option—the agent can charge the $100 to your credit card with no intention of *ever* paying off the principal. In this case you will be billed for $10 interest every year, ad infinitum, and your agent will withdraw $10 per year from your bank to meet these payments.

Now the question is: Which payment scheme do you prefer? Since each of the three schemes requires you to make payments with the same present value ($100 in each case), you will be indifferent between the three options. To verify this, let's consider what your financial status will be one year hence under each of the three options.

We have assumed a prevailing interest rate of 10% and will suppose that your $1,000 bank account earns this prevailing rate. This means that in the absence of any clothes purchases, your balance would rise to $1,100 by this time next year. Any of the three plans that your agent can adopt will partially deplete this $1,000; let's see by how much.

The first plan removes $100 from your bank account today, reducing it from $1,000 to $900. A year from now that $900 will have earned $90 interest, and your balance will be $990. Under the second plan, no payments are made until next year. At that time your bank balance will be $1,100. From this, your agent will withdraw $110 to pay the credit card bill, leaving you with a balance of $990. Finally, there is the third plan, under which the purchases are charged and never paid off. How does your bank balance look after a year on this plan? From a balance (one year from now) of $1,100, your agent will deduct $10 for the first annual interest payment. This leaves $1,090 in your account. Of this $1,090, there is $100 that you dare not touch, because it is needed to generate a yearly income of $10 with which to meet your future obligations. Thus, once again, your usable assets are $990.

In other words, the three plans will all leave you equally wealthy after a year, as we knew they must.

Debt versus Taxation

The government is a purchasing agent. On your behalf it purchases post offices, public radio, and strategic missiles. It can pay for these purchases immediately by taxing you, or it can borrow on your behalf and pay off the debt by taxing you in the future. Yet another alternative is to borrow without ever repaying the debt, but to tax you forever in order to meet interest payments.

The parable of the clothes buyer suggests that it is a matter of indifference which course the government chooses. In fact, the story becomes more realistic when we replace your clothes buyer with the government. We have been assuming that your bank account earns the same rate of interest at which you borrow from the credit card company. This assumption might seem objectionable. But the interest payments on *government* debt are at the Treasury bill rate—which you *can* earn by the simple expedient of buying Treasury bills.

It is important to separate the question of how much to spend from the question of how the spending is financed. The decision to spend $100 on clothes—which is taken as given in the parable— certainly matters to you, although the question of financing does not. If you consider a $100 clothes budget to be either overly profligate or overly frugal, you might be very unhappy with your agent. Similarly, you might be very unhappy with a government that spends either more or less on various programs than you see fit. But once the level of spending has been chosen, the choice between taxation and borrowing is an entirely separate issue.

Government Borrowing and the Rate of Interest

In Section 16.1 we learned how the rate of interest is determined. It is determined by equilibrium in the market for current consumption, as depicted in Exhibit 16–8. Clearly, the equilibrium point can move only if either the demand or the supply curve moves. Thus government borrowing, like anything else, can affect the equilibrium interest rate in only two ways. The first is by causing a shift in the demand curve, and the second is by causing a shift in the supply curve.

Many economists believe that government borrowing does affect interest rates. Most of those economists believe that it does so by causing a shift in the demand for current consumption. Other economists disagree, and still others believe that the answer is not known.

How could government borrowing affect the demand for current consumption? The simplest answer is that borrowing means lower current taxes, making people wealthier and thus increasing demand. However, our parable suggests that this answer is not correct. When the government borrows on your behalf, it must raise future taxes. The present value of those future taxes is equal to the tax that you would pay today if there were no borrowing. Thus it appears that government borrowing does not affect wealth.

Consider Exhibit 16–12, which shows the indifference curves of Terry Taxpayer. Terry lives in a world where the market interest rate is 10%, so that his budget line between current and future apples has a slope of −1.10. He has chosen his optimum point along this budget line, at A.

Now suppose that the government decides to borrow an apple so that it can lower Terry's current tax burden.[3] As a result, Terry has 1 more apple

---

[3]In order to focus on the effects of government borrowing (as opposed to government spending), we assume that government spending is fixed. Therefore increases in government borrowing are used not to increase spending but to decrease taxes.

Exhibit 16–12   **The Effect of Government Borrowing**

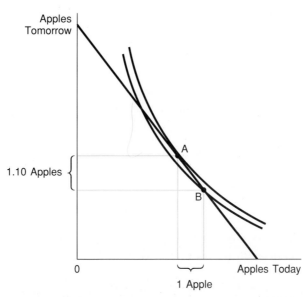

Terry Taxpayer faces an interest rate of 10% and hence a budget line with slope −1.10. He chooses the optimum point A. If the government borrows an apple so as to reduce Terry's taxes by 1 apple, then he has an additional apple today but will have 1.10 fewer apples tomorrow, when he will be taxed to pay the government debt. Thus the government borrowing moves him from point A to point B. But Terry will not stay at B. He will return to his old optimum at A, by lending an apple. Thus the government borrowing has no effect on Terry's demand for current consumption.

today. On the other hand, he knows that next period he will be taxed an additional 1.10 apples so that the government can pay its debt. Thus the new policy causes Terry to move to point B.

Will Terry stay at point B? The answer is no, because his optimum is still at A. He will move from B to A, which he can accomplish by lending 1 apple. There will be no change in Terry's present or future consumption. Thus the government borrowing has no effect on Terry's demand for apples.

Ricardian Equivalence Theorem
The statement that government borrowing has no effect on wealth, consequently no effect on the demand for current consumption, and consequently no effect on the interest rate.

According to this simple story, government borrowing has no effect on wealth, consequently no effect on the demand for current consumption, and consequently no effect on the interest rate. This result is known as the **Ricardian Equivalence Theorem.** The Ricardian Equivalence Theorem is undoubtedly true as a matter of mathematical fact under the simple conditions we have described here. A more interesting question is whether it is true in the world in which we live. Regarding this question there is no consensus among economists. Next we will consider two important differences between our world and the world of Terry Taxpayer.

Do Deficits Matter?

We have seen that government deficits can affect the interest rate only if they affect the demand or supply of current consumption, and that most of those economists who think that deficits matter think that they do so by affecting demand. We have also seen that under simple assumptions it is false that deficits affect demand and therefore false that deficits affect interest rates. Here we shall consider two phenomena that we did not previously consider: default risk and misperceptions. We will see that either of these phenomena can cause deficits to affect the demand for current consumption and consequently the interest rate. The actual importance of these phenomena is a matter of considerable controversy.

Default Risk

Suppose that Terry Taxpayer, because of his poor credit history, is not able to borrow at the market interest rate of 10%, but only at the higher rate of 25%. (He can still *lend* at the market rate, however.) Then Terry's budget constraint has the shape of the black broken line in Exhibit 16–13. If Terry wants to move to the left of his endowment point E, he can do so by lending at a rate of 10%. Thus the budget line has a slope of -1.10 to the left of point E. If Terry wants to move to the right of his endowment (which, in fact, he does), then he must borrow at 25% and so faces a budget line with the steeper slope -1.25. Given this constraint, Terry chooses point X.

Now suppose that the government borrows an apple, reducing Terry's current tax burden but increasing his burden tomorrow by 1.1 apples. This moves his endowment from point E to point F, and the blue broken line becomes part of his new budget constraint. Terry's new optimum is at Y, a point not previously available to him. The government has made additional options available by borrowing for Terry at a rate at which he could not have borrowed for himself.

In this case we see that the effect of government borrowing is to increase Terry's demand for apples today. If there are many people like Terry, the market demand curve for apples will move to the right and the equilibrium price will rise. The deficit will cause an increase in the interest rate.

It is sometimes argued that default risk is especially important in view of the finiteness of life. People who would like to borrow and have their debts paid by their heirs long after they are gone cannot do so, because there is no legal mechanism by which the heirs can be obligated. The certainty of default on such debts makes the interest rate on them essentially infinite. Government borrowing reduces this rate from infinity to something on the order of 10%.

On the other hand, this is an important consideration only if there are a significant number of people who would really like to live well at their children's future expense. The commonly observed phenomenon of parents who work hard in order to leave bequests to their children is evidence to the contrary.

Exhibit 16–13   **Default Risk and Government Borrowing**

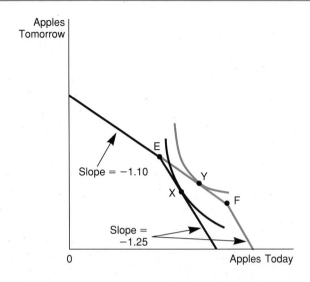

Terry Taxpayer has endowment point E. He can lend at the market rate of 10%, but he can borrow only at 25%. Thus his budget constraint is the black broken line. Along this constraint he chooses point X.

Now suppose that the government borrows an apple at the rate of 10%, cutting Terry's taxes by 1 apple at the same time. Then Terry gains 1 apple today but incurs a future tax burden of 1.10 apples. This moves his endowment to point F, which was not previously available, and makes all of the baskets on the blue broken line available. Given his new opportunities, Terry chooses basket Y. Thus the government borrowing increases Terry's demand for current consumption.

Misperceptions

Suppose that Terry has the black budget line shown in Exhibit 16–14, and the government reduces Terry's taxes by 1 apple. Although Terry will be taxed 1.1 apples tomorrow, suppose that he is unaware of this future tax burden and views the tax reduction as a free gift. Although Terry's endowment has moved to point F, he believes it has moved to point G. In consequence, he believes that his budget line has shifted outward, to the blue line in the exhibit. He chooses point Z on this "false" budget line and consumes 8 apples today. Tomorrow he will discover that he is actually at point W rather than at point Z, but by then it will be too late to change today's consumption.

If Terry had perceived his position correctly, he would have consumed only 7 apples. Thus the deficit fools Terry into consuming more apples than he otherwise would. In this way it causes an outward shift in the demand curve for apples today and consequently an increase in the interest rate.

According to this scenario, deficits matter because people are systematically fooled by them. That hypothesis is very much at odds with the spirit of microeconomics, in which the assumption of rationality plays a major role. As a result, many economists are uncomfortable with the

Exhibit 16–14   **Misperceptions**

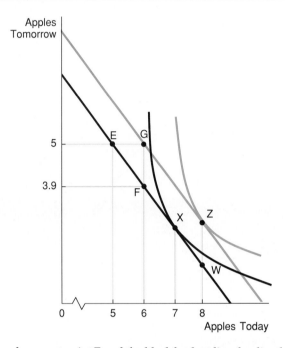

Suppose that Terry has the endowment point E and the black budget line, leading him to choose the optimum point X, where he consumes 7 apples today. The government reduces his tax by 1 apple today, borrows to meet its obligations, and plans to tax Terry 1.1 apples tomorrow to repay the debt. Thus Terry's endowment has moved to point F. His budget line is unchanged and he will still choose point X.

However, suppose that Terry does not realize he will be taxed tomorrow. He views today's tax reduction as a free gift, moving his endowment to point G. This leads him to choose the optimum at Z, where he consumes 8 apples today. Tomorrow he will learn that he is not really at Z but at W; however, by then it will be too late. Terry's demand for current consumption is increased.

notion that misperceptions could be an important factor in determining interest rates. However, there is insufficient empirical evidence to rule out the possibility.

16.4 Some Applications

"Planned Obsolescence"

Larry's Light Bulb Company can produce light bulbs that burn for 1,000 hours or light bulbs that burn for 3,000 hours. The cost of production is the same in either case. Which kind of light bulb should Larry produce?

Many people think that Larry should produce the inferior light bulbs. They argue that if the average bulb is used 1,000 hours per year, the 3,000-hour bulbs will have to be replaced only once every 3 years, whereas the 1,000-hour bulbs will have to be replaced once every year, resulting in 3 times as many sales for Larry.

It is not hard to see that this reasoning cannot be correct if light bulbs are produced competitively. If Larry's competitors have access to the same technology that he does, he will be driven out of business as soon as somebody else decides to produce the better bulb.

However, this argument is actually beside the point. In fact, it is in Larry's interest to make the better bulbs regardless of whether he is a competitor, a monopolist, or anything in between.

To see the reason for this, notice that light bulbs are valuable only because they can be used to produce light. Suppose that customers use each light bulb to produce 1,000 hours of light per year, and that they value an additional year's worth of light at $5. Then the price of a 1,000-hour light bulb will be $5. To compute the price of a 3,000-hour light bulb, think of the bulb as providing $5 worth of service this year, $5 worth next year, and $5 worth the year after that. The present value of this service is

$$\$5 + \frac{\$5}{(1 + r)} + \frac{\$5}{(1 + r)^2},$$

where r is the yearly interest rate. When r = .10, a little arithmetic reveals that this expression is equal to $13.68, which is the price consumers will be willing to pay for a light bulb.

Larry has a choice between manufacturing a light bulb that he can sell for $5 and manufacturing a light bulb that he can sell for $13.68. Each costs him the same to produce. It isn't hard to see what choice he should make.

It is often alleged that firms, and particularly monopolies, engage in the practice of "planned obsolescence" whereby goods are intentionally designed to wear out more quickly than necessary, without any justification in terms of costs of production. We have just seen that as long as customers are aware of differences in quantity, there is never any incentive for any firm to engage in this practice. A profit-maximizing firm will always make a longer-lived product provided that the additional cost of manufacturing such a product is less than the present value of the additional stream of benefits that it provides. (Larry makes the better light bulb as long as its production cost exceeds the production cost of the cheaper bulb by less than $8.68.)

This decision rule by firms is economically efficient from a social point of view. The cost of providing longevity is weighed against its benefits. Because some of the benefits are delayed, they should be assessed at their present values.

Try the following experiment. Ask 25 of your friends what a camshaft is. Now have each of your friends ask his grandfather. You will find that the percentage of correct answers is much higher among the grandfathers.

Most of today's grandfathers learned what a camshaft was about 40 years ago when they had to have theirs repaired, often repeatedly. Most of today's college students will never have that experience. When car manufacturers learned how to make camshafts that lasted, they put their knowledge to work.

Artists' Royalties

When an artist sells a painting, he relinquishes any right to benefit from future increases in its value. Sydney J. Harris, formerly a syndicated columnist, argued repeatedly that artists should share in the benefits when their paintings appreciate. Specifically, whenever a painting is resold, he proposed that the artist should receive a percentage of the increase in value since the last sale. As this textbook went to print, the U.S. Congress was considering enacting a very similar proposal into law. We will evaluate the effect of this proposal from the artist's point of view.

When the artist first sells the painting, its price is equal to the present value of the stream of benefits that it will provide to future owners. At least this is the case if the stream of benefits can be foreseen. More realistically, we should allow for some uncertainty as to how the painting will be valued in the future. The price of the painting will be equal to the present value of the *expected* stream of benefits. We will study expectations and uncertainty more rigorously in Chapter 18.

Suppose that an art lover buying an oil painting expects to derive $10 per year in pleasure from looking at the painting for each of this year and next year, and then he expects to be able to sell the painting for $50. (This $50 is his estimate of how the next buyer will value the future stream of benefits 2 years from now.) In that case he will be willing to pay a price of

$$\$10 + \frac{\$10}{(1 + r)} + \frac{\$50}{(1 + r)^2},$$

where r is the rate of interest.

Now suppose that the "Harris Plan" is enacted into law. The buyer is required to pay the artist 20% of the painting's resale price. In that case the buyer can keep only $40 when he resells the painting, and its present value to him is reduced to

$$\$10 + \frac{\$10}{(1 + r)} + \frac{\$40}{(1 + r)^2}.$$

This is a reduction of $\$10/(1 + r)^2$ from what the painting was worth before the Harris Plan was enacted. The current price of the painting will fall by $\$10/(1 + r)^2$, which is a loss to the artist.

On the other hand, when the painting is resold for $50 in 2 years, the artist will receive a royalty of 20%, or $10. The present value of that royalty is $10/(1 + r)^2$. From the artist's point of view, the benefits of the Harris Plan are equal to its costs. He is indifferent to whether it is enacted.

The foregoing supposes that the buyer is correct in his expectation that he can sell the painting in 2 years for $50. Suppose that he turns out to be wrong. Suppose that the artist's reputation blossoms, and the painting is sold for $100, on which the artist's royalty is $20. The present value of that royalty is $20/(1 + r)^2$. The Harris Plan has benefited this artist. The initial value of his painting fell by $10/(1 + r)^2$, but this is offset by a future royalty with twice that present value.

Another possibility is that the buyer has been too rosy in his expectations. Suppose that in 2 years the artist has been forgotten, and his painting sells for only $15. The royalty is $3, with a present value of $3/(1 + r)^2$. This is insufficient to offset the initial price reduction of $10/(1 + r)^2$. This artist is a loser under the Harris Plan.

Who gains and who loses? The average artist—the one whose career turns out about as expected—just breaks even. The artist whose career goes much better than expected is a winner, and the artist who is less successful than expected is a loser. Thus the Harris Plan is a way to transfer income from unsuccessful artists to successful artists.

Old Taxes Are Fair Taxes

One hundred fifty years ago Coconino County imposed an annual tax of $10 per acre on all landowners. Landowners to this day grumble about the tax. The mayor has decided that the tax represents an unfair burden and has called for its repeal, to correct a historical injustice.

Although the tax might have been a great injustice, repealing the tax is unlikely to correct it. When the tax was imposed, the value of an acre of land plummeted by exactly $10/r$, the value of a perpetuity of $10 per year. Any land sold in the last 150 years has been sold at the new depressed value.

Exhibit 16–15 shows the market for land in Coconino County 150 years ago. After the tax was imposed, the demand curve fell by $10/r$ per acre. The price fell from P to $P - \$10/r$. Producers' surplus fell from $C + D + E$ to just E. Consumers' surplus remained constant at $A + B$. Buyers of land lost nothing as a result of the tax; its burden fell completely on the sellers.

Any parcel of land in Coconino County that has been sold at any time in the last 150 years is now owned by somebody who was fully compensated for the infinite stream of future taxes through a reduced purchase price. If the tax is removed now, the current owners will receive a windfall, as the price of the land rises back to P and its total value increases by $C + D$. The full burden of the tax is still being borne by the heirs of the original owners, now probably scattered and unidentifiable.

Exhibit 16–15   **Old Taxes Are Fair Taxes**

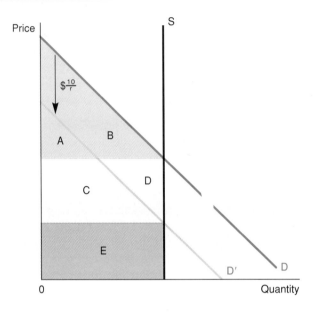

The graph shows the market for land in Coconino County 150 years ago, when an annual $10-per-acre tax on landholdings was first instituted. The demand curve fell by $10/r per acre, and because of the vertical supply curve, the price fell by $10/r. The landowners of Coconino County suffered a loss in producers' surplus of C + D. The buyers of land lost nothing. The price of the land that they bought was reduced by enough to compensate them for the infinite stream of future taxation.

If the tax is repealed, everyone who has bought Coconino County land in the last 150 years will reap a windfall gain. Except in those cases where the land has never changed hands, the winners will be people who were never hurt by the tax in the first place.

The Pricing of Exhaustible Resources

A resource is *exhaustible* if every unit consumed today implies that one less unit will be available in the future. Oil is often said to be an exhaustible resource. The coal available from a given mine is a good example.

When a resource is exhaustible, the forgone opportunity to use it in the future becomes part of the cost of consuming it today. Suppose that coal sells competitively at a going price of P_0 today and is expected to sell at a price of P_1 tomorrow. Suppose also that the cost of digging out any particular nugget of coal is the same on each day. Then any nugget dug out and sold today entails a forgone opportunity to dig out and sell that same nugget tomorrow. The forgone profit on that nugget is $P_1 - MC$, where MC is the marginal cost of physically removing the coal from the ground. The present value of that forgone opportunity is $(P_1 - MC)/(1 + r)$.

The full marginal cost of removing and selling a nugget is equal to the sum of the marginal cost of digging it out and the present value of the forgone opportunity to sell it tomorrow. This comes to

$$MC + \frac{P_1 - MC}{1 + r}.$$

A competitive producer will choose a quantity where the current price is equal to this full marginal cost, or

$$P_0 = MC + \frac{P_1 - MC}{1 + r}.$$

Now a little algebra shows that

$$P_1 = P_0 \cdot (1 + r) - r \cdot MC.$$

This equation predicts the price of an exhaustible resource next year in terms of its price this year and the marginal cost of producing it.

The equation is particularly simple and intuitive when marginal costs are negligible. In this case we get

$$P_1 = P_0 \cdot (1 + r).$$

The price of the exhaustible resource grows at exactly the rate of interest.

There is a great deal of intuitive content to this result. If the price were growing faster than the rate of interest, coal in the ground would be a good investment and mine owners would increase the amount of coal left unmined. This would raise current prices and lower future prices, reducing the rate at which prices grow.

▷ **Exercise 16.16** Explain how the rate of growth of prices would adjust if it were less than the rate of interest.

Summary

To study the allocation of goods over time, we imagine a world with one good, which we can think of as apples. People are endowed with a certain number of apples today and a certain number of apples tomorrow, and they can then trade with each other in the marketplace.

The relative price of current consumption in terms of future consumption is written $1 + r$, and r is defined to be the interest rate. Any individual's marginal rate of substitution (MRS) between current and future consumption is written $1 + \rho$, and ρ is defined to be that individual's discount rate. Individual optimization requires that the relative price and the MRS be equal; in other words, we must have $r = \rho$.

As a first approximation to reality, we assume that people are endowed with a fixed number of apples in each period, and that there is no way to change the total number of apples in existence at any time. In that case the representative agent must be content to consume his endowment. Thus the interest rate is determined by the slope of the representative agent's indifference curve at his endowment point. If that endowment point is on the 45° line, then we assume that the absolute slope of the indifference curve is greater than 1, so that the equilibrium interest rate must be positive.

To study the effects of various phenomena, such as improved harvests in the present or in the future, we can examine supply and demand graphs (in which the supply curve is vertical) or the representative agent's indifference curve graph.

We can make the model richer by incorporating investment, where investment means some technology for converting current apples into future apples. Possible technologies include storage and agriculture. In this case apples that are used to produce future apples are called capital. The gross marginal product of capital (GMPK) is the number of apples produced tomorrow by an additional apple invested today. GMPK is a decreasing function of the number of apples invested, and hence it is an increasing function of the number of apples currently eaten. As a function of the number of apples eaten, it is also the marginal cost of current consumption. Therefore it is also the supply curve for current consumption.

Thus the demand curve for current consumption depends on tastes, and the supply curve depends on technology. Tastes and technology determine the equilibrium interest rate.

A promise to deliver apples in the future is called a bond. The price of the bond is called the present value of the future delivery. Durable assets can be viewed as a sort of bond that promises a stream of future consumption services. The price of such an asset is equal in equilibrium to the present value of the services it provides.

The equilibrium interest rate can be affected only through a change in demand or a change in supply. Some economists believe that government borrowing increases the interest rate by making people feel wealthier (because their taxes are lower) and thus increasing demand. However, the Ricardian Equivalence Theorem demonstrates that under certain conditions government borrowing does not, in fact, make people wealthier. The reason is that when government borrows, the present value of the implied future tax burden is equal to the current tax reduction. Thus if government borrowing increases demand for current consumption, it must do so through a somewhat subtle mechanism. One possible mechanism is an increase in the opportunities of some people who could not previously borrow at market rates due to default risk. Another is the failure of people to accurately perceive the future tax burden. The empirical significance of such phenomena is not known.

Review Questions

R1. What is the meaning of the consumer's discount rate?

R2. Explain how to derive a point on the consumer's demand curve for current consumption.

R3. What assumptions lead to a vertical supply curve for current consumption?

R4. When there are no opportunities for investment, explain how the equilibrium rate of interest can be found by examining the representative agent's indifference curves.

R5. What are the gross and net marginal products of capital?

R6. Explain why the GMPK curve coincides with the supply curve for current consumption.

R7. In equilibrium, what is the relationship between the interest rate, the marginal product of capital, and each individual's discount rate?

R8. What is the relationship between the present value of an apple delivered tomorrow, the price of a bond with tomorrow as its maturity date and one apple as its face value, and the rate of interest?

R9. If you can either buy a house for $10,000 or rent the house forever for $1,000 per year, should you buy or rent? In what way does your answer depend on the interest rate?

R10. Explain why the purchaser of a suit of clothes is indifferent between paying now and paying later, provided that he can borrow at the market rate of interest.

R11. Give a simple argument as to why government borrowing should not affect the equilibrium interest rate. Describe some phenomena that might invalidate this argument.

R12. In general, will the price of an exhaustible resource grow at a rate higher or lower than the rate of interest? Why? Under what circumstances will it grow at exactly the rate of interest?

Problem Set

1. *True or false:* A rise in the interest rate is a bad thing because it makes borrowing more expensive.

2. *True or false:* It is unlikely but possible that current consumption could be a Giffen good.

3. *True or false:* If people are impatient, the equilibrium interest rate must be positive.

4. *True or false:* Because different individuals have different tastes, it is not possible for everyone's discount rate to *simultaneously* equal the marginal product of capital.

5. Explain what you can do to make yourself better off when (a) your discount rate is less than the interest rate, (b) the marginal product of capital is less than the interest rate, and (c) your discount rate is less than the marginal product of capital. In each case, how do your actions cause the variables in question to move?

6. Robinson Crusoe cannot trade with anybody. He divides his time between catching fish and building nets that will help him catch more fish in the future. What interest rate does Robinson face? Is his discount rate equal to the marginal product of his capital?

7. Your local shoemaker can buy a hammer for $10 that will last forever and increase his profits by $1.50 per year. You are thinking of buying the house that you currently rent for $10,000 per year. What is the most you would pay for the house?

8. *True or false:* When the interest rate goes up, investment becomes more desirable.

9. John bought a refrigerator and sold it three years later for exactly what he paid for it. *True or false:* It cost John nothing to use the refrigerator for three years.

10. Contrast the effect on the interest rate of (a) a year of bad weather resulting in low agricultural productivity, and (b) nuclear contamination that lowers agricultural productivity permanently.

11. Explain exactly what is wrong with the following argument: If the government buys me a suit of clothes with borrowed money and never pays off the debt, then my grandchildren will be taxed to make interest payments even though they have never even seen the clothes. Therefore government borrowing allows me to live high on the hog at my grandchildren's expense.

12. **a.** Jeeter owes $1,000 on his student loan. The debt is growing at the market interest rate of 10%. Jeeter would like to pay off the loan now, but the bank will not allow him to do so until 5 years from now. What strategy can Jeeter follow that is equivalent to paying off the loan today?

  b. Jeeter is also concerned about his share of the national debt, which he reckons to be $10,000. He wishes that the government would just tax him today and pay off the debt, so that the accumulation of interest will not cause him to have to pay even more tomorrow. What would you suggest that Jeeter do?

13. You have just been informed that you have two years to live, and you are considering a night of debauchery to take your mind off the news. The consequence of such behavior is eternal damnation, beginning on the date of your death. One year of fire and brimstone is equal in unpleasantness to the loss of $P. The current interest rate is r.

  a. How pleasant would a night of sin have to be in order to be worth the cost?

  b. Which is more likely to deter you from sinning: a doubling of the torments in the underworld or a halving of the interest rate?

14. Write a brief letter in response to the following column:

DEAR ANN LANDERS: This is going to seem like a terrifically trivial problem compared to most you receive, but I've got to get it off my chest.

I'm sure almost every woman in America has gone through this slow burn. You spend two or three bucks for a pair of new pantyhose, and within a week, you have a big ugly runner and have to throw the pair away. Or, they're so stretchy they droop down around your knees and run within the week. Or, they're so NON-stretchy you can't get 'em up above your knees, and they still run within the week!

Why can't the hosiery manufacturers figure out how to make a nylon stocking that fits with a proper degree of stretch and doesn't fall to shreds in six days? Isn't nylon supposed to be one of the toughest substances made by man?

To put this into economic focus: Wanda Worker spends two bucks on nylons every week. That's over a hundred dollars a year, not to mention the aggravation and time spent running to the drugstore on a lunch hour to replace the pair that self-destructed on her way to work.

As I said, Ann, it seems terrifically trivial, but it's maddening. You have contacts all over. Will you please ask somebody who is big in hosiery manufacturing what gives—besides my stockings, that is.

—Ladder Legs in Lima, Ohio

Ann says: You really hit a hot button! I contacted four of the leading hosiery manufacturers, and I have never heard so much double-talk, triple-talk and fancy ways of saying "no comment." All those contacted by my office asked that they not be identified—and would I please not name their companies. I am respecting their wishes.

But, of this you can be sure: The hosiery industry has a mighty sweet thing going and has no intention of letting go. We have been ripped off, if you will pardon the pun, for lo, these many years, ladies. And they will continue to rip us off because the no-run nylons, which they know how to make, would put a serious crimp in their sales. In other words, we are at the mercy of a conspiracy of self-interest.

My advice is this: Shop around. Low-priced, good-fitting nylons are out there. (I wear them myself, and they look as good as the top-dollar variety. Sorry, I can't publish the brand name.) For daily wear, buy nylons with reinforced toe and heel. One final way to get a leg up: If you rip one stocking, cut it off and sew on the good stocking from another pair that similarly failed you.[4]

---

[4]Ann Landers, Los Angeles Times Syndicate. Reprinted with permission.

15. In New York City, every taxicab driver must own a license (called a medallion) to drive a cab. The city has issued a fixed number of medallions, and they are traded on the open market. Because the number of medallions is small, the price of cab rides is higher than it otherwise would be. Suppose that the city decides to abolish the medallion program and allow free entry to the taxicab industry. *True or false:* The owners of medallions will be exactly as well off after the program is abolished as if it had never existed.

16. *True or false:* If a monopolist owned an exhaustible resource, he would control its availability so that the price rose faster than the rate of interest.

Refer to Answers to Problem Sets for solutions to problems 1 and 12.

Chapter Seventeen

Risk and Uncertainty

The future brings surprises. A rainstorm can change the price of wheat. A fire can destroy your house. The invention of the automobile can make you rich if you own rubber plantations, or it can wipe you out if you manufacture buggy whips.

State of the world
A potential set of conditions.

Your wealth tomorrow depends on the **state of the world.** Examples of alternative states of the world are "rain" versus "sunshine," "fire" versus "no fire," and "cars invented" versus "cars not invented."

Markets abound for transferring wealth from one state of the world to another. By placing a bet that it will rain, you increase your wealth in the rainy state of the world while decreasing your wealth in the sunny state. (Of course, you will occupy only one of these states, but at the time you place the bet you don't know which it will be.) Purchasing fire insurance is a mechanism for increasing your wealth in the "fire" state while decreasing your wealth (by the amount of the insurance premium) in the "no fire" state. Organized markets in stocks and commodities afford numerous opportunities for transferring wealth between states of the world.

In this chapter we will begin by studying the individual's choice about how much wealth to transfer from one state of the world to another and the determination of the equilibrium price at which he can do so. We will also examine many of the particular markets in which such transactions take place.

17.1 Attitudes toward Risk

When there are two alternative states of the world, we can use diagrams like those in Exhibit 17–1 to represent your wealth in each of them. The horizontal axis measures your wealth in one state, and the vertical axis measures your wealth in the other. Suppose that your total wealth is $100 but that it will be reduced to $40 if there is a fire. In that case your position is represented by point A in panel A of Exhibit 17–1.

Now suppose that for $20 you purchase an insurance contract that entitles you to collect $60 in the event of a fire. Then if there is no fire, your wealth is reduced to $80, whereas if the fire occurs your wealth is still $80 ($40 plus $60 insurance payment minus $20 to buy the insurance in the first place). Thus your new position is represented by point B.

For another example, suppose that you are a gambler, that you have total assets of $100, and that you have just bet $40 that a certain tossed coin will come up heads. The possible states of the world are "heads" and "tails." In case of heads your wealth will be $140; in case of tails it will be $60. Your position is represented by point D in panel B of Exhibit 17–1. If you had not placed the bet, your wealth would be $100 regardless of whether the coin comes up heads or tails, and your position would be represented by point C.

▷ *Exercise 17.1* What bet would you have to place to move to basket E in Exhibit 17–1?

We can think of each of the points in Exhibit 17–1 as a "basket of outcomes," and we can use indifference curves to represent an individual's preferences among these baskets. However, these baskets of outcomes differ in an important way from the baskets of consumer goods that we studied in Chapter 3. When you own a basket of apples and oranges, you can consume both apples and oranges. But when you own a basket of outcomes, you get only one of the outcomes. Once the state of the world has been determined, we do not need indifference curves to tell us which baskets are preferable to which others. After the coin comes up heads, everyone will agree that point D is better than point C in panel B of Exhibit 17–1. Or after it comes up tails, everyone will agree that C is better than D.

When we talk about preferences between baskets of outcomes, we are referring to the preferences of someone who does not yet know what the state of the world will be. Such preferences are called **ex ante** preferences, as distinguished from the **ex post** preferences of someone who has already learned the state of the world. If we say that Clarence prefers D to C, we mean that he would choose to bet $40 on heads rather than not bet at all, if he were asked *before* the coin was flipped.

Ex ante
Determined before the state of the world is known.

Ex post
Determined after the state of the world is known.

Exhibit 17–1   States of the World

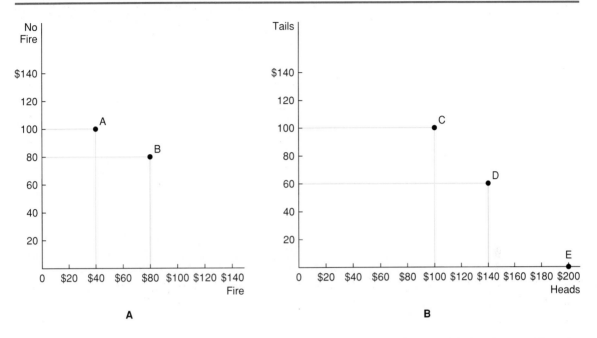

A   **B**

In either panel the two axes represent your wealth in alternative states of the world. Panel A considers the states in which your house is destroyed by fire and in which it is not. Suppose that your wealth is initially $100 but that it will be reduced to $40 in the event of a fire. Then your position is represented by point A. Now suppose that for $20 you purchase an insurance contract that will return $60 in the event of a fire. Then your new position is represented by point B, where your wealth is $80 in either state of the world.

Panel B considers the two possible outcomes of a coin toss. If your initial wealth is $100 and if you do not bet on the outcome of the toss, then your position is represented by point C. If you wager $40 that the coin will come up heads, you move to point D.

Characterizing Baskets

Before drawing budget constraints and indifference curves, we need to introduce two concepts that describe important characteristics of any basket of outcomes. One of these is the expected value of a basket; the other is its riskiness.

Expected value
The average value over all states of the world, with each state weighted by its probability.

Expected Values

The **expected value** of a basket is given by the formula

$$\begin{pmatrix}\text{Probability} \\ \text{of state 1}\end{pmatrix} \times \begin{pmatrix}\text{Wealth in} \\ \text{state 1}\end{pmatrix} + \begin{pmatrix}\text{Probability} \\ \text{of state 2}\end{pmatrix} \times \begin{pmatrix}\text{Wealth in} \\ \text{state 2}\end{pmatrix}.$$

For example, suppose that your basket of outcomes is represented by point A in panel A of Exhibit 17–1, and that the probability of a fire is .25 (so that the probability of "no fire" is .75). Then the expected value of your wealth is

$$.25 \times \$40 + .75 \times \$100 = \$85.$$

In panel B of Exhibit 17–1, if we assume that the coin is unbiased, meaning that it has probability .50 of coming up heads and probability .50 of coming up tails, then the expected value of basket D is

$$.50 \times \$140 + .50 \times \$60 = \$100.$$

▷ *Exercise 17.2* If the coin is unbiased, what is the expected value of basket C? If the coin is weighted so that it comes up heads two-thirds of the time, what are the expected values of baskets C and D? What if the coin is weighted so that it comes up tails two-thirds of the time?

If you repeat the same gamble a large number of times, the average outcome will be approximately equal to the expected value of the gamble. It is possible to formulate this statement more precisely and to prove it mathematically. The careful mathematical formulation is known as the **law of large numbers.**

Law of large numbers
When a gamble is repeated many times, the average outcome is the expected value.

Suppose that state 1 occurs with probability P_1 and state 2 occurs with probability P_2 (so that $P_1 + P_2 = 1$). Then along any line with slope $-P_1/P_2$, all baskets have the same expected value. A family of such "iso-expected value" lines is illustrated in Exhibit 17–2.

▷ *Exercise 17.3* In panel B of Exhibit 17–1, what do the iso-expected value lines look like if the coin is unbiased? If the coin comes up heads two-thirds of the time? If it comes up tails two-thirds of the time? In each case, which point lies on the higher line, C or D? Are your answers consistent with your calculations in Exercise 17.2?

Riskiness

Riskiness
Variation in potential outcomes.

Risk-free
Having the same value in any state of the world.

Baskets differ not only in expected value but also in **riskiness.** Baskets on the 45° line (shown in Exhibit 17–2) are referred to as **risk-free,** because individuals who hold them know with certainty what their wealth will be regardless of the state of the world. Moving away from the 45° line along an iso-expected value line, the baskets become riskier, carrying more uncertainty about what the future will bring. In panel B of Exhibit 17–1 baskets C and E have the same expected value, but a person holding basket C knows for certain what his wealth will be, whereas a person with basket E could come away with either twice as much wealth or with nothing at all.

Opportunities

Suppose that you enter a gambling parlor with $100 in your pocket. Bets are being taken on a coin flip. If you place no bets, your wealth will be $100 in

Exhibit 17–2   Baskets with the Same Expected Value

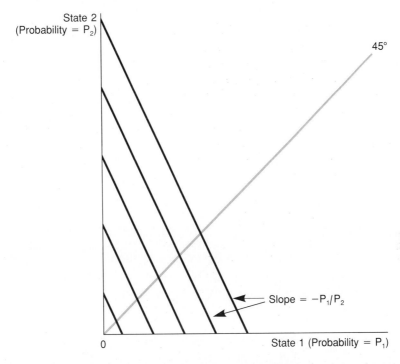

If the probability of state 1 is P_1 and the probability of state 2 is P_2 (so that $P_1 + P_2 = 1$), then all of the baskets along a line of slope $-P_1/P_2$ have the same expected value. The graph shows a family of such lines.

The baskets along the 45° line are risk-free, because a person holding such a basket will have the same wealth in either state of the world. Moving along an iso-expected value line away from the 45° line in either direction, the baskets become successively riskier.

either state of the world. This is your endowment, and it is represented by point C in Exhibit 17–3. Suppose that you are invited to express your opinion about how the coin will turn up, and to bet as much as you would like on the outcome. By betting $50 on tails, you can move yourself to point X, where your wealth will be $150 if you win or $50 if you lose. Other bets can get you to any of the points on the black line shown in Exhibit 17–3. By placing bets, you can trade your endowment for any point along that line. In other words, it is your budget line.

▷ *Exercise 17.4* What would your budget line look like if you were permitted to bet only on heads?

The gambling parlor offers you the opportunity to trade dollars in the heads state of the world for dollars in the tails state at a relative price of 1. This price is reflected in the slope of the budget line, which is 1 in absolute value.

Exhibit 17–3   **Opportunities**

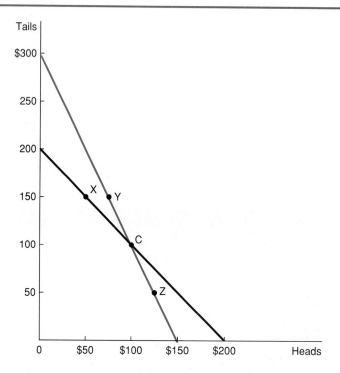

If you enter a gambling parlor with $100 in your pocket and choose not to bet on a coin toss, then your wealth will be $100 in either state of the world. Thus you achieve point C without trading—point C is your endowment. By betting on either heads or tails at even odds, you can achieve any basket along the black budget line, such as X. If the odds are such that tails bettors receive 2 to 1 payoffs, you can achieve any point on the blue budget line. The odds give the relative price of wealth in the tails state in terms of wealth in the heads state, and they therefore determine the slope of the budget line.

Other prices are also possible. Suppose that you are offered the opportunity to bet on tails and given *odds* of 2 to 1. This means that for every $1 you bet, you will win $2 if tails comes up (but you will still lose only $1 if the outcome is heads). Suppose that you are allowed to take either side of this bet: You can bet either on tails at odds of 2 to 1, or on heads, in which case you must grant odds of 2 to 1. You now have an opportunity to trade dollars between the heads state of the world and the tails state of the world. The relative price is 2 "tail-dollars" per "head-dollar." By betting $25 on tails, you can move from point C to point Y in Exhibit 17–3. In so doing, you are selling 25 head-dollars and receiving 50 tail-dollars in return. Alternatively, you could buy head-dollars and sell tail-dollars, moving to a point like Z. Your budget line is the blue line in Exhibit 17–3, with an absolute slope of 2, reflecting the relative price of tail-dollars in terms of head-dollars.

Fair Odds

Fair odds
Odds that reflect the true probabilities of various states of the world.

Odds are said to be **fair odds** if they reflect the actual probabilities of the two states of the world. An unbiased coin is equally likely to come up heads or tails, so the fair odds on the toss of such a coin are 1 to 1. A weighted coin might be twice as likely to come up heads as to come up tails, in which case the fair odds are 2 to 1 for those who bet on tails.

▷ *Exercise 17.5* What are the fair odds on a bet that the roll of a die will turn up 1? What are the fair odds on a bet that it will turn up 4 or less? What are the fair odds on a bet that it will turn up an even number?

What is so fair about fair odds? The answer is that at fair odds the expected value of any bet is the same as the expected value of not betting at all. In other words, if two parties bet with each other repeatedly at fair odds, neither will come out very far ahead or very far behind in the long run. If a coin comes up heads twice as often as it comes up tails, and if the person betting on tails receives twice the payoff for winning that the person betting on heads receives, then each party's wins and losses will just cancel out.

When an individual is offered fair odds, any gamble has the same expected value as any other. Therefore:

> **When an individual is offered fair odds, his budget line coincides with an iso-expected value line.**

Preferences and the Consumer's Optimum

The Frequent Gambler

A gambler who bets frequently with the goal of maximizing his winnings is concerned only with the expected values of his wagers. This is because any wager, when it is repeated sufficiently often, returns its expected value on average. In panel B of Exhibit 17–1, if the coin is unbiased, points C, D, and E all have the same expected value, and hence are equally attractive to the frequent, repetitive gambler. If he holds basket C every day, he will come away with $100 every day. If he holds basket E every day, he will come away with $200 half the time and $0 the other half. Over time, this will average out to the same $100 per day that he can have with basket C.

The frequent gambler is indifferent between two baskets of equal expected value, regardless of the risk associated with each. We say that this

Diversify
To reduce risk.

is because he can **diversify** his risk by playing repeatedly so that he is guaranteed to win the expected value of any gamble in the long run.[1] When someone's preferences among baskets are determined solely on the

---

[1]This assumes that he can always borrow enough to keep playing after he is wiped out by a run of bad luck—or by a single turn of bad luck after a large bet.

Risk-neutral
Caring only about expected value.

basis of their expected values, we describe those preferences as **risk-neutral.** From the definition of risk neutrality, we can see this:

> **The indifference curves of a risk-neutral individual are identical with the iso-expected value lines.**

Risk Neutrality

We have seen that the frequent gambler is risk-neutral. Conceivably, some infrequent gamblers might be risk-neutral as well.

Consider a risk-neutral person who is given the opportunity to play at fair odds. Because he is risk-neutral, his indifference curves are the iso-expected value lines. Because the odds are fair, his budget line is the iso-expected value line through his endowment. The picture is as in panel A of Exhibit 17–4, where the gray iso-expected value lines are the indifference curves, and the black budget line coincides with one of them. This individual is indifferent among all of the points on his budget line. Thus:

> **At fair odds, a risk-neutral individual is indifferent as to how much he bets.**

Suppose that the risk-neutral person has an opportunity to play at other than fair odds. This rotates his budget line through his endowment, either clockwise if the new odds favor betting on tails or counterclockwise if the new odds favor betting on heads. The first possibility is illustrated in panel B of Exhibit 17–4. As you can see, he will now choose a point on the vertical axis, where his wealth becomes zero in the event that the coin turns up heads.

> **A risk-neutral individual faced with unfair odds will bet everything he owns on one or the other outcome.**

 Unlike all of the indifference curves we have encountered previously, the indifference curves of this chapter depend on more than just tastes. They depend also on the probabilities associated with the two states of the world. If a fair coin is replaced by a biased coin, a gambler might change his mind about the desirability of various wagers, even though his underlying tastes have not changed.

Risk Aversion

Now let us consider the preferences of someone who is not a frequent gambler. To such a person the riskiness of his basket can be a significant consideration. He does not expect his gains and losses to cancel out in the long run.

Risk-averse
Always preferring the least risky among baskets with the same expected value.

Many people are **risk-averse.** This means that among baskets with the same expected value, they will choose the one that is least risky. Consequently, when offered fair odds, they will choose the basket that equalizes their incomes in both states of the world. Such baskets are located on the 45° line.

Exhibit 17–4   **Risk Neutrality**

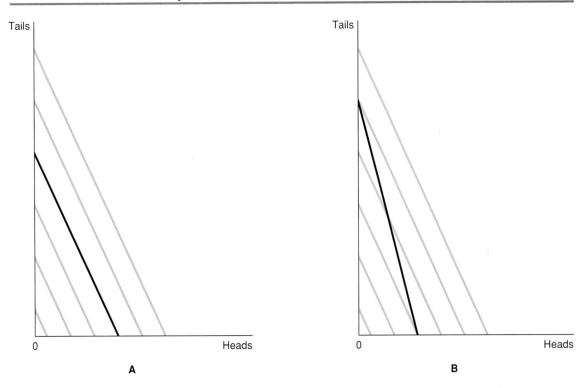

A risk-neutral individual has indifference curves that coincide with the iso-expected value lines, shown in gray in both panels. When he is offered fair odds, his budget line coincides with one of the indifference curves, as in panel A. In that case the individual is indifferent among all of the options available to him. When he is offered any odds other than fair odds, his budget line has a different slope than his indifference curves, like the black budget line in panel B. In that case he will always choose a corner and bet everything he has on one outcome or the other.

The two panels of Exhibit 17–5 show the indifference curves of typical risk-averse individuals facing fair odds. In panel A the individual has an initial wealth of $100 and is offered the opportunity to bet on a coin toss at fair odds. His optimum point occurs right on the 45° line, at his endowment point P. He places no wager.

Panel B shows the situation of a risk-averse person whose wealth is $100, which will be reduced to $40 if there is a fire. His endowment is at point A. We will assume that "fire" occurs with probability .25, so that "no fire" occurs with probability .75.

Suppose that it is possible to buy fire insurance for $1. The insurance pays $4 in the event of fire, and the homeowner can buy as many units of this insurance as he wants to. Buying insurance is exactly like betting that there will be a fire. If there is no fire, he loses his $1. If there is a fire, there is

Exhibit 17–5   **Risk Aversion**

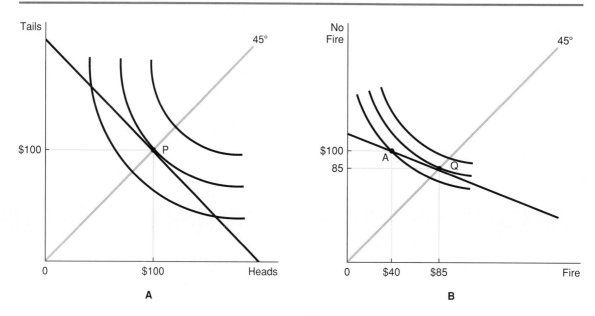

The two panels illustrate the indifference curves of individuals facing fair odds. In panel A the individual has initial wealth of $100 and is offered the opportunity to bet at even odds on the toss of a fair coin. His endowment is at point P, which is already on the 45° line. This is also his optimum, so he places no wager.

In panel B the individual has initial wealth of $100, which will be reduced to $40 in the event of a fire. His endowment is at point A. We assume that the probability of "no fire" is 3 times as great as the probability of "fire." Thus the fair odds for an insurance policy are 3 to 1, and we assume that such a policy is available. This gives the illustrated budget line, which crosses the 45° line at (85, 85). Since he is risk-averse, his optimum is at Q. He achieves this point by purchasing $15 worth of insurance.

a net gain of $3 (a $4 insurance payment minus the $1 cost of the insurance). Therefore this particular insurance policy offers 3 to 1 odds when the homeowner bets that a fire will take place. These happen to be the fair odds, because the probability of "no fire" (.75) is 3 times the probability of "fire" (.25).

The homeowner's budget line has an absolute slope of 1/3, reflecting the odds of 3 to 1. Because the homeowner is assumed to be risk-averse, he will always eliminate risk when he can bet at fair odds. That is, he will choose the point where his budget line crosses the 45° line, at point Q in panel B of Exhibit 17–5. At this point the homeowner is guaranteed that his wealth will be $85 regardless of whether or not the fire occurs. His indifference curves must be like those in the graph, with the optimum at Q.

▷ *Exercise 17.6* Exactly how much insurance does the homeowner buy?

Exhibit 17–6   **Risk Preference**

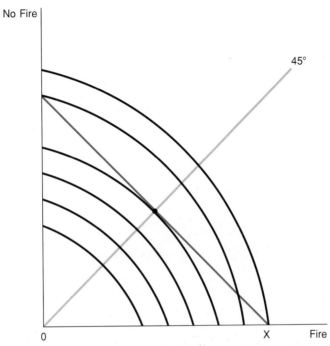

The risk-preferring individual always chooses a corner solution, regardless of the odds he faces. This individual chooses point X, where his wealth becomes zero if there is no fire. He can accomplish this by spending all of his income on fire insurance, hoping for a fire that will make him rich.

Risk-Preference

Risk-preferring
Always preferring the most risky among baskets with the same expected value.

Another type of individual is **risk-preferring.** Given a choice between a "sure thing" and a lottery with the same expected value, he will choose the lottery. Such an individual has indifference curves as shown in Exhibit 17–6. They become tangent to the fair-odds budget lines at points along the 45° line, but this is because the individual considers any such point to be the *worst* he can do when trading at fair odds. You can see from Exhibit 17–6 that a risk-preferring person will always choose a lottery in which he risks sacrificing everything he owns in exchange for a chance at great wealth.

It is also possible for an individual to be risk-preferring in some situations and risk-averse in others. Consider an individual with the indifference curves and budget line shown in Exhibit 17–7. Starting from an endowment at point A, he will indulge his risk preference by gambling to get to either point B or point C. At that point risk aversion will become dominant and he will gamble no further.

Exhibit 17–7   **Risk Preference and Risk Aversion Combined**

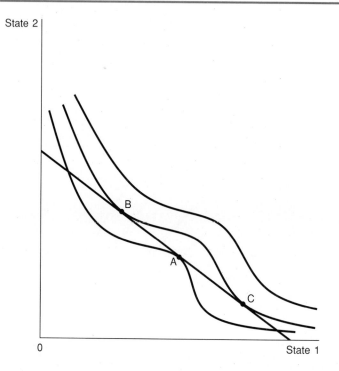

The same individual can exhibit both risk preference and risk aversion at different points on his indifference curve map.

Which Preferences Are Most Likely?

Attitudes toward risk typically vary with income. At very low levels of income, people are probably risk-preferring. To see the reason for this, suppose that $5 per year is the minimum income necessary for survival. In that case an income of $3 per year is no more valuable than an income of zero. Somebody earning $3 per year would be willing to gamble, even at very unfavorable odds, for a chance to earn enough to stay alive.

Even at higher levels of income, we sometimes observe risk preference for similar reasons. If you are determined to purchase a particular sailboat for $20,000 and if your current assets total $19,000, you might be willing to take a very risky bet as long as it offered some chance to win $1,000.

Nevertheless, most individuals exhibit some degree of risk aversion over most ranges of income. A person earning $20,000 per year is unlikely to be willing to trade a year's income for a 50–50 chance at $40,000, or even a 50–50 chance at $50,000. On the other hand, the same person might very well be willing to trade $20 for a 50–50 chance at $50, or $2 for a 50–50 chance at $5. When small amounts are involved, people tend to exhibit risk-neutral behavior. With large amounts at stake, however, risk aversion is the general rule.

Firms, as opposed to individuals, are more likely to exhibit risk neutrality. This is so for several reasons. First, many firms are frequent gamblers that participate in a large number of risky ventures and can expect their good and bad luck to cancel out over time. Second, unlike individuals, firms face no budget constraints. An individual who risks all his assets and loses is wiped out, whereas a firm that risks all its assets and loses can often borrow enough to continue operating. (Of course, the firm must convince lenders that it is showing good business sense in the long run.)

Those firms that are corporations have an additional reason for risk-neutral behavior. Corporate stockholders are able to diversify their risks by holding small amounts of stock in many different companies. Once diversified, they, like the frequent gambler, earn approximately the expected value of the return on their overall portfolios. For this reason the stockholders are interested only in maximizing expected return, and they want the corporation to behave in a risk-neutral way.

Gambling at Favorable Odds

Often we encounter opportunities to gamble at better than fair odds. Suppose that you own a restaurant and have the opportunity to run an advertising campaign that has a 50–50 chance of success. If the campaign succeeds, your profits (net of advertising costs) will increase by $2,000, whereas if it fails, you will lose $1,000. Since success and failure are equally likely, and since the gain from success exceeds the loss from failure, the odds are better than fair. If you run the campaign, you increase the expected value of your wealth. For another example, suppose that you have the opportunity to buy a ticket to a concert that you will enjoy with probability .75. The ticket costs $1, and you receive $2 worth of pleasure if the concert turns out to be good. Thus if the concert is bad, you lose $1, and if it is good, you gain $1 ($2 in enjoyment minus $1 for the ticket). Since the concert is more likely to be good than bad, the odds on this gamble are also favorable.

▷ *Exercise 17.7* For each of the opportunities described in the preceding paragraph, what odds would be fair? What are the actual odds? What is the expected value of your winnings if you gamble?

We have already seen that a risk-neutral person will always accept any wager in which the odds are better than fair, and that he will wager as much as he possibly can at such odds. What will a risk averter do? Will the prospect of a positive expected gain entice him to gamble, or will his risk aversion prevent him from gambling?

Consider an example. Suppose that you are risk-averse, have assets totaling $5, and have the opportunity to gamble at 3 to 1 odds on the toss of

Exhibit 17–8   **Gambling at Favorable Odds**

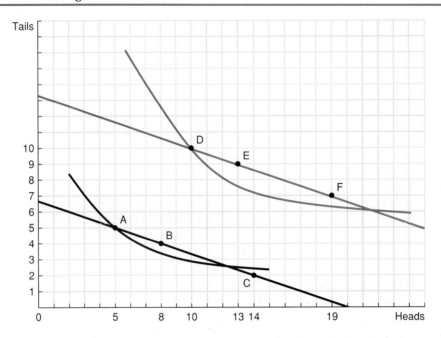

The indifference curves are those of a risk averter facing the opportunity to bet on the toss of an unbiased coin. His initial wealth is $5, so that point A is his endowment. Because he is risk-averse, the absolute slope of the indifference curve at A must reflect the fair odds of 1 to 1; in other words, it has an absolute slope of 1.

This individual is invited to bet on heads at the favorable odds of 3 to 1. By betting $1, he moves to point B, which he prefers to point A. If he bet $3, he would move to point C, which he likes less than point A. Thus if he is allowed to place the small bet of $1, he will do so, but if he must place the large bet of $3, he will decline.

Suppose that this individual has an increase in wealth, to $10. Then his endowment moves to point D. From point D a $1 bet moves him to point E, and a $3 bet moves him to point F. Either of these is an improvement over point D, and if offered either option, he will accept it. With greater initial wealth, he is willing to accept the $3 bet that he previously considered too large. However, he will continue to reject much larger bets.

an unbiased coin. If you bet $1 on heads, then you will either lose $1 (if tails comes up) or win $3 (if heads comes up).

Your budget line is then the black line in Exhibit 17–8. Your endowment is at point A, where you keep your $5 no matter how the coin turns up. We know that if you were offered the fair odds of 1 to 1, you would not bet at all, so the absolute slope of the indifference curve at A must be 1. It follows that the budget line cuts through the indifference curve, as shown in the exhibit.

By betting $1, you move from point A to point B, which is an improvement. Thus if your only options are to bet $1 or to not bet at all, you will choose to bet.

Suppose, alternatively, that the house rules require you to bet either $3 or nothing at all. A $3 bet would move you to point C, which is less desirable than point A. Thus in this case you would prefer not to bet. Therefore the exhibit demonstrates this principle:

A risk-averse person, offered the opportunity to place a sufficiently small bet at favorable odds, will always accept. If only offered the opportunity to place a very large bet at favorable odds, he will always decline.

The largest bet that a risk averter would be willing to make depends on his wealth. Suppose that instead of starting with $5, you started with $10. In that case your endowment would be at point D in Exhibit 17–8. A $1 wager at the favorable odds of 3 to 1 brings you to point E, and a $3 wager brings you to point F. Either of these is preferable to point D. Thus even if the house rules require the relatively large $3 wager, you will still choose to bet.

The indifference curves of Exhibit 17–8 are typical. As a risk averter acquires more wealth, he is willing to enter into larger wagers at favorable odds. However, there is always a limit to the size wager he will accept. Even with the initial wealth of $10, a person with the indifference curves of Exhibit 17–8 will not bet $5 on heads.

Example: Executive Compensation

Attitudes toward risk can be a source of conflict between stockholders and corporate officers. The typical General Motors stockholder, with a diversified portfolio of assets, wants General Motors to choose among risky projects on a risk-neutral basis, taking only expected value into account. The president of GM, if he holds a large percentage of his personal wealth in the form of GM stock, and if he believes that the future of his career is tied to the performance of GM, will want the corporation to exhibit some risk aversion.[2]

As an example, suppose that GM has the opportunity to build electric cars. There is a 50–50 chance that the cars will run. If GM builds the cars and they don't run, each share of its stock will lose $1 in value. If it builds the cars and they do run, each share will gain $3 in value.

The typical GM stockholder, who holds only a small fraction of his wealth in the form of GM stock, views the electric car project as a small wager at favorable odds and wants the project undertaken. The company president, however, views the wager as a much larger one, for two reasons. First, he is likely to hold a substantial percentage of his personal wealth in the form of GM stock. Second, the president's job depends on corporate performance, so that even if he owns very little stock he still has much at stake.

---

[2]Corporate officers are often required or strongly encouraged to hold a substantial amount of corporate stock, so as to ensure their personal stake in the success of the corporation.

Exhibit 17–8 can be reinterpreted to illustrate the conflict. Simply change the axis labels from "Heads" and "Tails" to "Electric Cars Run" and "Electric Cars Don't Run." Suppose that the outside shareholder and the company president each have $5 in assets, but that the shareholder has 1 share of stock while the company president has 3. Then each starts with endowment point A. The electric car project moves the stockholder to point B, which he prefers, but it moves the company president to point C, which he does not prefer.

Exhibit 17–8 also suggests a solution to the conflict. If the company president has $10 in assets instead of $5, then he will favor the project whether he owns 1 share of stock or 3. As long as he is sufficiently wealthy, his potential losses from the project represent only a small fraction of his wealth. When he is sufficiently wealthy, therefore, he will be more likely to undertake risky projects in accord with the shareholders' wishes.

It follows that shareholders have a good incentive to ensure that their corporate executives are relatively wealthy people. This might be one reason why executives' salaries are as high as they are. Stockholders choose to pay high salaries so that executives will be willing to take more risks. When the president of GM must decide whether to introduce a new model line, stockholders do not want him influenced by concern about making next month's mortgage payment.

Alternative Incentive Structures

Can stockholders influence executives' attitudes toward risk in a less expensive way? Let us examine a few options. One way is to monitor the performance of the president, and to fire him if his decisions are not based on risk neutrality. Unfortunately, this monitoring is itself costly—it requires the stockholders to estimate the probabilities of alternative outcomes, which is one of the very things that they hire the president and other officers to do in the first place. If the stockholders could perform these tasks inexpensively, there would be no need for corporate officers.

Another option is to limit stock ownership by corporate officers, so that they would view risky projects as small wagers. Then their personal tendency toward risk aversion would not affect their managerial decisions. Unfortunately, this would reduce the incentive for corporate officers to evaluate projects carefully. It is, in fact, desirable for the officers to have a lot of personal wealth at stake in corporate decisions. If corporate officers must own a lot of stock (so that they have appropriate incentives to evaluate projects) and must also have only a small fraction of their wealth in the form of stock (so that they behave risk-neutrally), then we are led back to the conclusion that corporate officials must be made very wealthy.

One more alternative is to limit the president's downside risk by assuring him that even if things turn out so badly that he is fired, he will still receive a substantial severance payment. These payments are often referred to as "golden parachutes." Many people cannot understand why corporations make payments totaling tens of millions of dollars to officials who have been fired for inadequate performance. The answer is that without the implied assurance of such settlements, the successors of these officials would behave with great caution, contrary to the interests of the stockholders.

The golden parachute policy is similar in flavor, but not the same as, the policy of making the president wealthy by paying him a high salary. Golden parachutes change the odds that the president faces, whereas a high income changes the way he reacts to given odds. Each, however, has the effect of increasing the likelihood that he will consider risky projects in accord with the stockholders' preferences.

Risk and Society

Societies, like corporations, must decide when to undertake risky projects. Just as risk-averse stockholders prefer risk-neutral choices on the part of the corporations that they own, so risk-averse citizens can prefer risk-neutral choices on the part of the societies that they inhabit. However, the individual entrepreneurs who actually make the choices will often have much personal wealth at stake, so that risk aversion enters their decisions. Thus the conflict between stockholders and their corporate officers has its parallel in the conflict between society and its entrepreneurs.

In the 1950s Joseph Wilson (later the head of the Xerox Corporation) had a vision of the copying machine as a tool that would transform American business. At the time few shared his vision. Entrepreneurial visions arise every day, and most do not succeed. Should such visions be pursued?

Suppose that Wilson had a 1 in 100 chance of succeeding in his project. Then from a social point of view, the project should be undertaken if the benefits from a success would be more than 100 times the losses from a failure. The frequency with which such projects arise in society justifies a risk-neutral calculation. But visions are the property of individuals, and individuals are risk-averse. From Wilson's point of view, a mere 100-to-1 payoff would not have sufficed. In order to induce him to risk a substantial fraction of his personal wealth for a 1% chance of success, Wilson might have required the prospect of a 500-fold multiplication of his wealth.

From a social point of view, risk-averse individuals underinvest in risky projects. The existence of corporations helps to solve this problem, since, as we have seen, the shareholders, with diversified portfolios, will encourage appropriate risk-taking. However, intensely personal visions cannot always be effectively pursued by large corporations. In such cases only the prospect of great personal fortune will induce individuals to take great risks. A society that attempted to limit the amassing of great wealth might be a society without copying machines.

17.2 The Market for Insurance

Many markets have developed to facilitate transfers of risk from one party to another. In this and the next two sections we will examine a few of these markets. We have already alluded to the insurance market in Section 17.1. Panel A of Exhibit 17–1 depicts the endowment of a homeowner facing the possibility of a fire. In Exhibit 17–5 we can see how the homeowner, when facing a given price, decides how much insurance to buy. But what determines the market price of insurance?

Insurance companies are highly diversified. If each individual house catches fire with probability .25, you must experience considerable uncertainty about whether yours will be one of those that burn. By contrast, a company that insures 1,000 houses can be sure that almost exactly 250 of them will burn. If there were no other considerations, an insurance company that offered fair odds would just break even. Any insurance company offering less than fair odds would earn profits, causing entry to the insurance industry, and driving the odds down until they were fair. Thus a $1 insurance policy must buy a $4 payoff in case of fire.[3]

There are, however, other considerations. For one thing, there are costs involved with running an insurance company—costs of maintaining an office, a sales force, an actuarial staff to estimate probabilities, assessors to estimate actual damages when they occur, and so forth. A firm offering fair odds could not cover these costs and would not survive. The odds must be tilted in the company's favor by enough so that these basic operating costs can be met.

There are, however, more interesting and more important reasons why insurance is not offered at fair odds. In discussing them, we can safely ignore the relatively minor issue of operating costs. The three reasons we shall examine are known as *moral hazard, adverse selection,* and *uninsurable risks.*

Moral Hazard

Exhibit 17–9 shows the indifference curves of a risk averter with $100 in wealth, which will be reduced to $40 in the event of a fire. Thus his endowment is at point A. The fire occurs with probability .25. If he were allowed to buy insurance at the fair odds of 3 to 1, his budget line would be the black line in the exhibit. As a risk averter, he would choose the risk-free point B on this budget line, where his wealth is $85 regardless of whether a fire occurs. Having made this choice, he would be indifferent as to whether his house caught fire or not. As a result, he would take no precautions against fire if those precautions were at all costly to him. He would stop inspecting electrical wires and start smoking in bed. The probability of a

---

[3]With this policy you lose $1 when there is no fire, and you gain $3 (the $4 payoff minus the $1 premium) if there is a fire. Therefore the policy offers the fair odds of 3 to 1.

Exhibit 17–9   **Moral Hazard**

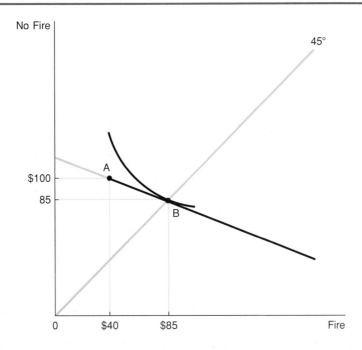

We assume that a fire occurs with probability .25. Then a homeowner with endowment A who can buy fair-odds insurance has the budget line depicted in black. (The gray part of the line is not available if he can only buy, not sell, insurance.) If he is a risk averter, he chooses the risk-free point B by purchasing $15 worth of insurance so that his assets are $85 whether or not a fire occurs. Now, however, because he has no incentive to take precautions, a fire becomes more likely. Thus the 3 to 1 insurance odds are now better than fair, and the insurance company loses money. As a result, the 3 to 1 odds are never offered in the first place.

fire would increase, say from .25 to .50. Thus the 3 to 1 odds would no longer be fair. As a result, no insurance company would offer 3 to 1 odds in the first place.

Moral hazard
The incentive for an individual to take more risks when he is insured.

The problem we have raised is known as the problem of **moral hazard.** A moral hazard arises when an individual, because he is insured, behaves in such a way as to raise the probability of an unfavorable outcome. There is moral hazard when an insured driver is more reckless than an uninsured one, when a homeowner fails to install a security system because he is insured against break-ins, and when a person with health insurance takes more risks on the ski slopes than he otherwise would. All of these things make it impossible for insurance companies to offer premiums that are fair in the sense of expected values. The availability of insurance at fair odds would lead to changes in behavior, the changes in behavior would change the probabilities of the states of the world, and the fair odds would no longer be fair.

Exhibit 17–10   **Insurance with Moral Hazard**

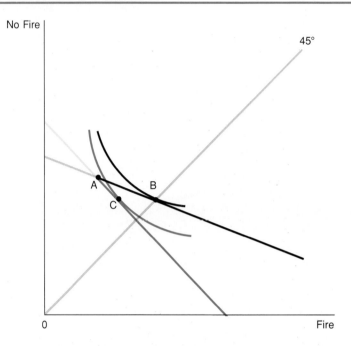

Although the initial probability of fire is .25, the insurance company knows that this will change after the homeowner is insured. Therefore it offers insurance at 1 to 1 odds, rather than 3 to 1. The homeowner's budget line is shown in blue. He chooses point C, where he is partially but not fully insured.

If the insurance company could require the homeowner not to change his behavior after the policy is issued, then it could offer insurance at 3 to 1 odds and the homeowner could achieve the preferred point B.

The insurance company can reduce the extent of moral hazard insofar as it can require certain types of behavior as a condition of being insured. This works only if the behavior is observable, so that the company can be sure that the terms of the contract are fulfilled. Such requirements can benefit both the company and the insured party, who is able to obtain insurance at more favorable rates than before. Some homeowners' policies are offered only to those with burglar alarms, and some health insurance policies are offered only to nonsmokers.

There is another type of moral hazard that arises from the insurance company's inability to ascertain the current state of the world. Suppose that you have insured your diamond ring against theft, and you report it stolen. The insurance company might well wonder whether the ring has really been stolen or not. In order to be compensated for such risks, the company must charge higher premiums than it otherwise would.

In cases where the state of the world is completely unobservable, it might be impossible to have any insurance market. A sudden fire and a sudden urge to go to Hawaii could be equally costly to you, but you can insure against the fire and you cannot insure against the urge.

Although issues of moral hazard prevent insurance from being offered at prices that reflect fair odds, a risk averter will still buy some insurance at less favorable odds if his endowment point is sufficiently far from the 45° line. Suppose that the homeowner in Exhibit 17–9 were offered the opportunity to buy insurance that pays off with odds of 1 to 1. The insurance company offers these odds because it knows that after the homeowner insures himself, his behavior will change so that these odds will be fair. The homeowner's budget line is now the blue line in Exhibit 17–10. He chooses point C, where he is less than fully insured but still better off than if he had no insurance.

Adverse Selection

Adverse selection
The problem that arises when people know more about their own risk characteristics than an insurer does.

Moral hazard arises when the insurance company is unable to monitor people's behavior. **Adverse selection** arises when the insurance company knows less than its customers do about the probabilities of various states of the world. Suppose that most people have a .25 probability of developing a serious illness in the next year. However, a few people (those who have been coughing a lot lately or feeling unusually run down) know that they will become ill in the next year with probability .50. The insurance company cannot distinguish these sickly people from the healthy ones. If the company markets insurance at odds that are fair for "Healthies," the "Sicklies" will buy some. The company will break even on its sales to Healthies and lose money on its sales to Sicklies. Obviously, such a company cannot survive.

Students sometimes confuse the closely related issues of moral hazard and adverse selection. Either one can prevent the normal, healthy people from being able to buy insurance at fair rates. We usually speak of moral hazard when the customers' behavior is involved (a healthy person buys insurance, takes up smoking, and becomes sickly) and of adverse selection when some customers conceal information about risk (like midnight coughing fits) that is not due to their own actions.

How will the insurance company set rates in the presence of an adverse selection problem? For Healthies, with a .25 probability of illness, the fair odds are 3 to 1. For Sicklies, with a .50 probability of illness, the fair odds are 1 to 1. You might guess that the company will market a policy with odds that are some compromise between the two. However, under various sets of assumptions it is possible to prove that there is no equilibrium of this type.[4] We will examine a different strategy available to the company.

---

[4]The argument, which is not difficult, can be found in M. Rothschild and J. Stiglitz, "Equilibrium in Competitive Insurance Markets: An Essay in the Economics of Imperfect Information," *Quarterly Journal of Economics* 90 (1976), 629–650.

Exhibit 17–11 **Adverse Selection**

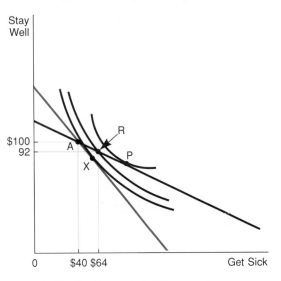

A. Healthy Person's Indifference Curves   B. Sickly Person's Indifference Curves

Healthies and Sicklies both have endowment point A. For Healthies the probability of illness is .25, so that the fair odds for insurance are 3 to 1, which would yield the black budget line. For Sicklies, the probability of illness is .50, so that the fair odds for insurance are 1 to 1, which would yield the blue budget line.

Because the company cannot distinguish Sicklies from Healthies, it cannot forbid Sicklies to buy 3–1 insurance. Thus it adopts a strategy that leads the Sicklies to choose 1–1 insurance voluntarily.

The strategy is to allow anyone to purchase any amount of 1–1 insurance, but to limit each customer to just under $8 worth of 3–1 insurance. Healthies can achieve either point X or point R, and they choose point R. (Actually they achieve a point slightly to the left of R.) Sicklies can achieve point Q or a point slightly to the left of R and choose point Q. Thus the Healthies and Sicklies each voluntarily select the policy that offers them fair odds.

Suppose that each individual has $100 in wealth, which will be reduced to $40 in the event of illness. The two panels of Exhibit 17–11 show the fair-odds budget line for Healthies (in black) and the fair-odds budget line for Sicklies (in blue). Assuming everyone is risk-averse, Healthies have indifference curves tangent to the black budget line where it intersects the 45° line, at point P, as shown in panel A. Similarly, Sicklies have indifference curves tangent to the blue budget line at point Q, as shown in panel B.

Ideally, the company would like to offer 3–1 insurance to Healthies, who would choose point P, and 1–1 insurance to the Sicklies, who would choose point Q. Unfortunately, if such offers were available, the Sicklies would buy the 3–1 insurance and bankrupt the company. Here is an alternative strategy: The company offers two different policies. One is a policy at 1–1 odds, which anyone can purchase in any amount. The other is a policy at 3–1 odds, with a limit of $8 worth per customer.

Let us see how $8 was chosen, and where this leads. A Healthy who buys $8 worth of 3–1 insurance moves from his endowment to point R in Exhibit 17–11. He compares this outcome to the best outcome he can achieve by purchasing 1–1 insurance, namely point X. As we have drawn the indifference curves, he prefers point R to point X. Under reasonable hypotheses about attitudes toward risk, it is possible to prove that he *must* prefer point R to point X. Thus the Healthy chooses to achieve point R by purchasing $8 worth of 3–1 insurance.

A Sickly, with the indifference curve shown in panel B, can achieve point Q by purchasing 1–1 insurance or point R by purchasing $8 worth of 3–1 insurance. Between these options he is indifferent. *The amount $8 was chosen to assure this.* Because the company wants to be certain that the Sickly will choose 1–1 insurance, it might make a slight revision in its offer by limiting each individual to $7.99 worth of 3–1 insurance. Then if the Sickly bought 3–1 insurance, he would achieve a point slightly to the left of R, which would be inferior to point Q. As a result, the Sickly chooses to achieve point Q by purchasing 1–1 insurance.

The bottom line is that all Healthies choose the 3–1 policy and all Sicklies choose the 1–1 policy. Thus each customer voluntarily selects the policy that pays fair odds given his personal probability of becoming ill.[5]

Notice that if the Sicklies revealed their identities, the Healthies would be better off and the Sicklies would be no worse off. This is because the company could then offer the Healthies additional units of 3–1 insurance while continuing to offer the Sicklies the same 1–1 insurance that they purchase under adverse selection. Healthies could reach point P instead of point R, and Sicklies would continue to reach point Q.

Example: The Market for Lemons

Whenever different individuals have access to different information, there can be adverse selection, leading to surprising consequences. George Akerlof has illustrated these consequences with a stylized version of the market for used cars.[6]

Suppose that there are two kinds of used cars, each equally common: "good" used cars and "lemons." The present owners, who are prepared to offer these cars for sale, value the good cars at $100 and the lemons at $50. The potential buyers, who currently have no cars, value the good cars at $120 and the lemons at $60.

If there were separate markets for good cars and for lemons, the buyers would purchase all of the cars at prices that benefit both the buyers and the sellers. Unfortunately, the buyers cannot distinguish a good car from a lemon, although the sellers can. The price that a buyer is willing to pay for a

---

[5]In the paper cited in the previous footnote, Rothschild and Stiglitz prove that this outcome is the only possible equilibrium, although there might be no equilibrium at all.

[6]George Akerlof, "The Market for Lemons: Qualitative Uncertainty and the Market Mechanism," *Quarterly Journal of Economics* 84 (1970), 484–500.

car is equal to its expected value to him. This expected value is equal to the value of the average car being offered for sale.

What will the price of a used car be? First, suppose that the price is greater than $100. At that price, sellers will offer all of their cars for sale. Each car on the market has a 50–50 chance of being either a good car (worth $120 to buyers) or a lemon (worth $60 to buyers). The most a buyer would be willing to pay for such a car is the average of $60 and $120, or $90. Since the going price is over $100, no sales will take place.

Now suppose that the price is between $60 and $100. Then sellers will not be willing to part with their good cars, which they value at $100 apiece. Only lemons will be offered for sale. Buyers, realizing this, will be willing to pay at most $60 for a car. Because the price exceeds $60, no sales will take place.

At a price below $50, no seller would part with a car. Thus the only prices at which sales can occur are between $50 and $60, and at such a price sellers will supply only lemons. It is not possible for the good cars to be sold, even though buyers value them more than sellers do. The market for used cars is a market only for lemons.

Notice that the problem would vanish if the sellers were unable to distinguish good cars from lemons. In that case all of the cars could be sold at any price between $75 and $90.

▷ *Exercise 17.8* If a seller did not know whether he had a good car or a lemon, what is the minimum price at which he would sell? If a buyer did not know whether he was buying a good car or a lemon, what is the maximum amount he would pay? How do your answers justify the sentence preceding this exercise?

Notice also that, as with adverse selection in the insurance market, welfare could be improved if the lemon owners revealed the truth about their cars. They would still be able to sell for the same price that they receive in a lemons market, whereas buyers who wanted good cars would be able to confidently purchase them at a price between $100 and $120. Such truthfulness would benefit some people without hurting anyone. Unfortunately, this social optimum is not an equilibrium, because as long as a market for good cars exists, each individual lemon owner has an incentive to behave dishonestly by claiming that his car is a good one. It is only after the good cars are driven completely out of the marketplace that a (suboptimal) equilibrium can be achieved.

Uninsurable Risks

Uninsurable risk
A risk that cannot be diversified.

Another reason why fair-odds insurance is not always available is that some risks are **uninsurable risks** because they cannot be diversified. This occurs when a large number of people are all adversely affected in the same state of the world.

Suppose that you and your friend must each carry a $10 bill through a bad neighborhood at different times. You can insure against robbery by agreeing that if either one is robbed, the other will ease the burden by paying $5 to the victim. But if you are traveling together, so that if one is robbed the other will also be robbed, then there is no advantage to such a contract and no way you can insure each other.

An insurance company brings together many people, its customers, who effectively insure each other against individual disasters. But a collective disaster cannot be insured against by everybody simultaneously. You cannot buy fair-odds insurance against a nuclear disaster. The insurance company is risk-neutral when it insures 1,000 people against a .25 chance of fire, because it knows that it will have to pay off in only 250 cases. It is no longer risk-neutral, and will not offer fair-odds insurance, when it insures 1,000 people against a .25 chance of a nuclear disaster, because there is a .25 chance that it will have to pay off in 1,000 cases.

17.3 Futures Markets

Suppose that you are a farmer, planting wheat in the spring to be harvested in the fall. You do not know whether the price of wheat will be $3 or $4 a bushel next fall, and you are therefore uncertain both about your future wealth and about the optimal amount of planting to do. If you are risk-averse, you will want to insure against the possibility of a low price.

Futures contract
A contract to deliver a specified good at a specified future date for a specified price.

In practice, this is often accomplished through the medium of a **futures contract.** A futures contract is an agreement to deliver a specified amount of something (in this case wheat) at some future date (in this case next fall) for a price agreed upon today. If the low price of $3 and the high price of $4 are equally likely, then a "fair odds" delivery price is $3.50. By signing a contract to deliver at this price, you can reduce your risk without sacrificing expected value. At the same time the buyer of the contract is able to insure himself against a high price, which is the unfavorable state of the world from his point of view.

Futures market
The market for futures contracts.

Spot market
The market for goods for immediate delivery.

Spot price
Price in the spot market.

The market for futures contracts is called the **futures market** for short. The market for wheat for immediate delivery is called the **spot market.** The **spot price** of wheat is the price of wheat in the spot market; in other words, it is simply what we would ordinarily call "the" price of wheat.

Speculation

Nonfarmers can also sell futures contracts. Suppose that in July wheat for September delivery is selling at $3.50 per bushel. You, however, believe that next September the spot price of wheat is likely to be only $3.25. In that case you can sell a futures contract for $3.50, wait until September, and then buy a bushel of wheat for $3.25 to deliver in fulfillment of your contract. You will earn a profit of 25¢. On the other hand, if you are in error and the spot price next September turns out to be $3.75, then you will have to buy at that price and will end up with a net loss of 25¢.

Somebody who tries to outguess the market and earn profits by buying and selling futures contracts is called a **speculator.** Next we will see that when speculators are successful, they have the effect of improving economic efficiency.

Speculator
One who attempts to earn profits in the futures market by predicting future changes in supply or demand.

Suppose that it is now February. A certain amount of grain is stored in grain elevators, and this is the only source of grain for this month and the next. The sellers (that is, the elevator owners) must decide how much to sell in February and how much to save for sale in March. Panel A of Exhibit 17–12 shows the February demand curve for grain. Panel B shows (in dark blue) the expected March demand curve as foreseen by the sellers. Sellers choose to supply Q_F bushels in February and save Q_M bushels to supply in March. (If they are risk-averse, they sell futures contracts now, promising delivery of Q_M bushels in March.) These quantities are chosen so that the equilibrium prices in the two months are equal. In Exhibit 17–12 the equilibrium price in each month is P_0.

To see why the equilibrium prices must be equal, let us see what would happen if the expected March spot price exceeded the current price. Sellers, sensing a profit, would save more grain for next month, reducing Q_F and increasing Q_M. This would have the effect of raising the current price and reducing the March price and would continue until the two prices are equal.

▷ *Exercise 17.9* Explain what happens if the current price exceeds the expected March spot price.

Actually, sellers equate the current price not to the March price, but to the present value of the March price. We are assuming that the interest rate is small enough so that, for practical purposes, a dollar delivered in March is worth as much as a dollar delivered in February. We are also ignoring storage costs, which, if significant, would make suppliers willing to provide grain at a lower price today than tomorrow. These assumptions simplify the analysis but do not affect the welfare conclusions.

Now suppose that there arrives on the scene a speculator who believes that the market has made a mistake and that the March demand curve will be lower than everyone else expects. He believes that the March demand curve will be the light blue demand curve shown in panel B of Exhibit 17–12. Anticipating a profit, he sells futures contracts, planning to fulfill them by buying cheap wheat on the spot market in March.

The speculator's advertised willingness to provide March wheat at less than the going price of P_0 drives down the expected price of March wheat and along with it the price of a March futures contract.

With the discovery that March wheat is selling for less than P_0, grain suppliers sell more wheat today and save less for March, moving the

Exhibit 17–12   Speculation

Case 1: Speculator Right

Without speculator:
February welfare: A + B + D
March welfare: F + I + M + N
Total: A + B + D + F + I + M + N

With speculator:
February welfare: A + B + C + D + E
March welfare: F + I + M
Total: A + B + C + D + E + F + I + M

Gain due to speculator: C + E − N

Case 2: Speculator Wrong

Without speculator:
February welfare: A + B + D
March welfare: F + G + H + I + J + K + L + M + N
Total: A + B + D + F + G + H + I + J + K + L + M + N

With speculator:
February welfare: A + B + C + D + E
March welfare: F + G + I + J + M
Total: A + B + C + D + E + F + G + I + J + M

Loss due to speculator: H + K + L + N − C − E

A. Supply and Demand for February Grain

B. Supply and Demand for March Grain

The February demand curve for grain is shown in panel A. Suppliers expect the March demand curve to be the dark blue curve in panel B. Thus they supply Q_F bushels in February and Q_M bushels in March, where these quantities are chosen to make the prices equal. The price in either month is P_0.

Now a speculator arrives on the scene, believing that the March demand curve will be the light blue curve in panel B. Thus he offers to sell March futures contracts, driving down the price of March grain and leading suppliers to sell more in February and less in March. The quantities adjust to Q_F' and Q_M'.

The table shows the welfare analysis, first when the speculator proves to be right and then when he proves to be wrong. In each case we must use the appropriate March demand curve—the light blue one if the speculator is right and the dark blue one if he is wrong. If the speculator is right, his arrival increases welfare, and if the speculator is wrong, his arrival decreases welfare.

vertical February supply curve to the right and the vertical March supply curve to the left. This process continues until the speculator no longer perceives any profit to be earned by undercutting the price of March wheat, that is, until the quantities have moved to Q_F' and Q_M' and the price has fallen to P_1.

Speculation and Welfare

The table in Exhibit 17–12 calculates the change in welfare due to the arrival of the speculator, first on the assumption that he is right about the March demand curve and then on the assumption that he is wrong. The marginal cost of providing grain that is already in storage has been taken to be zero, so social welfare is simply the area under the demand curve. To calculate March welfare, we must use the actual March demand curve, which is the light blue curve if the speculator is right and the dark blue curve if he is wrong.

To understand the gains and losses better, keep in mind that the distance from Q_F to Q_F' must equal the distance from Q_M' to Q_M. (Either of these distances is the amount of additional grain sold in February instead of March.) From this it is easy to see that N is less than C + E, so the speculator really increases social welfare when he is right. Similarly, C + E is less than H + K + L + N, so the speculator really decreases social welfare when he is wrong.

Society gains when a speculator correctly alerts it to a coming drop in demand by bidding down the price of futures contracts. This information enables people to increase their current consumption, in recognition of the fact that grain will be less valuable at the margin tomorrow than it is today. Similarly, a speculator who correctly forecasts an increase in tomorrow's demand bids up the price of wheat delivered tomorrow, alerting people today that wheat will be more valuable tomorrow and ought to be conserved.

When the speculator guesses the future correctly, he earns profits and he increases social welfare. When he guesses incorrectly, both he and society lose. By and large, we expect successful speculators to increase the level of their speculative activity over time, and unsuccessful speculators to eventually drop out of the market. Therefore it is a reasonable expectation that the majority of existing speculators serve a welfare-improving function.

17.4 Markets for Risky Assets

Many assets are valued not for their uses in consumption but for their potential to increase their owners' wealth. Corporate stocks are the prime example; real estate is another. The owner of a stock is often entitled to a stream of dividends of uncertain size. In addition, the value of the stock itself might rise or fall. Both the dividends and the changes in the stock

Returns
Gains to the holder of a financial asset, including dividends and increases in the asset's value.

Expected return
The expected value of returns.

Standard deviation
A precise measure of risk.

Investors
Buyers of risky assets.

Portfolios
Combinations of risky assets.

price are referred to as **returns** to the owner of the stock. The expected present value of these returns is called the **expected return** to the stock owner.

A risk-neutral stockholder cares only about expected returns. A risk-averse stockholder cares also about the certainty with which those returns will be realized. Such a stockholder is not indifferent between a stock that returns $5 next year for certain and one that returns either $0 or $10 next year with 50–50 probabilities, even though the expected returns are the same in each case.

The risk associated with a given stock can be described by a number called the **standard deviation** in its returns, abbreviated by σ (the Greek letter *sigma*). If you have taken a statistics course, you know a precise definition of the standard deviation. What you need to know here is that σ is a measure of the "spread" in possible outcomes. A stock that returns $5 with certainty has $\sigma = \$0$. A stock that returns either $0 or $10 with equal probability has $\sigma = \$5$. A stock that returns either $-\$5$ or $15 with equal probability has $\sigma = \$10$.

We shall henceforth measure expected returns and standard deviations as percentages of current asset values. Thus a stock that currently sells for $10 and is expected to return $5 (either by increasing in value or by paying dividends) has an expected return of 50%. If the $5 return is certain, then $\sigma = 0\%$. If the return might be either $-\$5$ or $15, then $\sigma = 100\%$, because $10 is 100% of $10.

People who buy financial assets in the hope of increasing their wealth are often referred to as **investors.** The language is unfortunate, because the purchase of existing stocks, bonds, and real estate does not constitute investment in the sense of Chapter 16. Economists generally reserve the word *investment* to describe the creation of new factors of production. Nevertheless, we will bow to popular usage and refer to the purchaser of stocks as an "investor."

Portfolios

An investor is interested not only in the characteristics of individual stocks; he is also interested in the characteristics of **portfolios,** or combinations of several stocks. In order to compare the characteristics of a portfolio with those of the stocks it comprises, let us consider some examples.

Exhibit 17–13 displays the characteristics of three stocks, each now selling for $10. The stocks are General Air-Conditioning, General Surfboards, and General Snowshoes. The value of each stock tomorrow depends on the state of the world: Either an ice age begins or it doesn't. Exhibit 17–13 shows what will happen to each stock in each state of the world. It also shows the expected return and the standard deviation for each stock, computed on the assumption that the probability of an ice age is .50.

Exhibit 17–13   **Expected Returns and Standard Deviations**

Stock	Current Value	Value If Ice Age Comes	Value If No Ice Age Comes	Expected Return	σ
General Air-Conditioning (GAC)	$ 10	$ 5 (Return = −50%)	$ 25 (Return = 150%)	50%	100%
General Surfboards (GSB)	10	6 (Return = −40%)	22 (Return = 120%)	40	80
General Snowshoes (GSS)	10	25 (Return = 150%)	5 (Return = −50%)	50	100

The table displays the characteristics of three hypothetical stocks. There is a 50% chance of an ice age beginning tomorrow, and each stock's value tomorrow depends on whether the ice age actually arrives. For each stock the expected return is the average of the two possible returns. For each stock the standard deviation is the absolute value of the difference between its return if the ice age arrives and its expected return.

For each stock the expected return is the average of the returns in the two states of the world, and the standard deviation (σ) is equal to the absolute value of the difference between the expected return and either of the possible actual returns. For instance, the possible returns to General Surfboards are −40% and 120%. The average of these is 40%, which is the expected return. The possible returns of −40% and 120% differ from the expected return of 40% by exactly 80% in absolute value, so for General Surfboards $\sigma = 80\%$.

We can now compute the returns and standard deviations on various portfolios. Consider first a portfolio consisting of one share each of General Air-Conditioning and General Surfboards. Such a portfolio has a current value of $20 and could either go down to $11 (the sum of the values of the two stocks if the ice age arrives) or go up to $47 (the sum of the values if the ice age fails to arrive). These outcomes constitute returns of either −45% or +135%. The expected return is 45% and the standard deviation is 90%.

▷ *Exercise 17.10* Verify the numbers in the preceding paragraph.

If you are rash enough to generalize on the basis of this single example, you might be tempted to conclude that the expected return and standard deviation of a portfolio are computed by taking the average expected return and the average standard deviation of the constituent stocks. If you succumbed to such a temptation, you would be right regarding the expected return, but wrong regarding the standard deviation.

Consider a portfolio consisting of one share each of General Air-Conditioning and General Snowshoes. The current value of such a portfolio is $20. In the event of an ice age, its value will be $5 + $25 = $30, and in the event of no ice age, its value will be $25 + $5 = $30. Such a portfolio earns a 50% return with certainty. Its standard deviation is zero.

A portfolio consisting of General Air-Conditioning and General Snowshoes is completely diversified. Whenever one of its constituent stocks goes up, the other goes down. As a result, all of the risk is eliminated and σ is equal to zero. In general, the standard deviation of a portfolio is given by the average of the standard deviations of the individual stocks, *minus* a correction term for any diversification that takes place. Because of this correction term, we can say:

The standard deviation of a portfolio is *at most* equal to the average standard deviation of the individual stocks.

By contrast:

The expected return to a portfolio is *exactly* equal to the average expected return of the individual stocks.

We have seen an example of a completely undiversified portfolio (GAC and GSB) and of a completely diversified portfolio (GAC and GSS). It is also possible to construct a portfolio that is partially, but not completely, diversified. Consider the portfolio that combines one share of General Surfboards with one share of General Snowshoes. This portfolio, initially worth $20, will either go up to $31 or go up to $27. The possible returns are 55% and 35%. The expected return is 45% (the average of the expected returns on the two stocks). The standard deviation is 10%, much less than the average of the standard deviations on the two stocks, but still not zero because the diversification is not complete.

The Geometry of Portfolios

Any individual stock, and any portfolio, can be represented by a point in a diagram as in Exhibit 17–14. The points labeled GSB and GSS represent the stocks General Surfboards and General Snowshoes from Exhibit 17–13.

It is possible for two different stocks to occupy the same position in the diagram. General Air-Conditioning is represented by the same point that represents General Snowshoes.

There is a geometric construction of the portfolio that combines two given stocks. Consider the portfolio consisting of GSB and GSS. We begin by locating the midpoint of the line segment that connects the stocks. That point is labeled X in Exhibit 17–14. It represents a portfolio with the average of the two expected returns and the average of the two standard deviations. Since there is some diversification, the portfolio's standard deviation is less than the average of the two stocks' standard deviations. Thus the portfolio is represented by a point some distance to the left of X. The size of the leftward shift depends on the amount of diversification. In this case we find that the combined portfolio is located at point D.

Exhibit 17–14   **The Geometry of Portfolios**

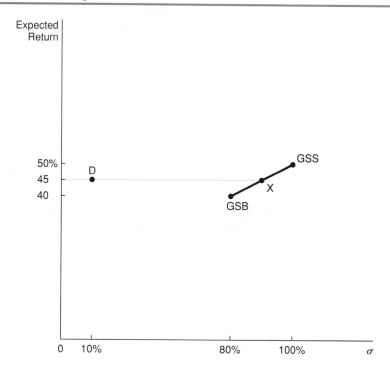

Every stock, and every portfolio, is represented by a point in the diagram. The points GSS and GSB represent General Snowshoes and General Surfboards, which are described in Exhibit 17–13.

The point X, which is midway between the stocks GSS and GSB, represents an asset with the average of their expected returns and the average of their standard deviations. The portfolio containing GSS and GSB has the average expected return but a smaller standard deviation. Thus it is represented by a point directly to the left of X, namely D.

▷ *Exercise 17.11* What point represents the portfolio consisting of GAC and GSS?

Two portfolios can be combined to make a new portfolio, using the same geometric prescription that is used to combine two stocks.

The Efficient Set

In panel A of Exhibit 17–15 there are hypothetical dots representing all of the stocks that might be available at a given time. The shaded area represents all of the available portfolios. Any available stock must be in the shaded region, because one can always hold a portfolio consisting of that stock alone. We have also darkened the northwest boundary of the shaded region.

Exhibit 17–15 **The Efficient Set**

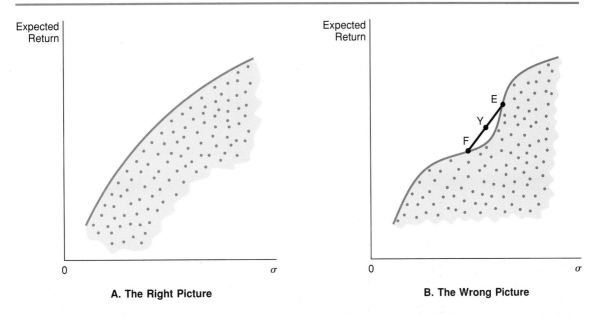

A. The Right Picture

B. The Wrong Picture

The dots represent the stocks available in the marketplace, and the shaded region represents all of the portfolios that can be constructed from those stocks. The picture must look like panel A and cannot look like panel B. In panel B the portfolio that combines portfolios E and F must be located at Y or to the left of Y, where the picture shows no portfolios. Therefore the picture is wrong.

In panel A, which is the correct picture, the northwest boundary of the shaded region is the efficient set. No investor would choose a portfolio that is not in the efficient set.

Efficient set
The northwest boundary of the set of all portfolios.

Efficient portfolio
A portfolio in the efficient set.

It is no accident that the northwest boundary is shaped as it is. Panel B suggests another shape, which we shall argue is impossible. If the boundary were shaped as in panel B, then there would be portfolios represented by points E and F. Combining these portfolios yields a new portfolio, which must be represented either by point Y or by some point to its left. Some such point must therefore be in the shaded region, which is not true. Therefore the shape depicted in panel B is impossible.

The northwest boundary of the shaded region in Exhibit 17–15 is called the **efficient set,** or the set of **efficient portfolios.** These are the only portfolios that a risk-averse individual would ever hold. The reason is that from any other point in the shaded region the investor can always move either upward (increasing expected returns) or to the left (decreasing risk) or both. Because both upward and leftward movements are desirable to the risk-averse investor, he would never remain at a point that was off the efficient set.

Exhibit 17–16   **The Investor's Choice**

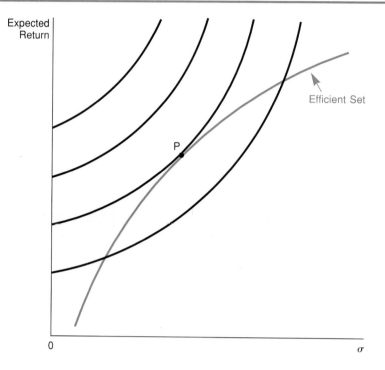

Because the investor views expected return as good and standard deviation as bad, his indifference curves are shaped as shown. Of the portfolios in the efficient set, he selects the one on the "highest" (most northwesterly) indifference curve, which is at the tangency P.

The Investor's Choice

Because the risk-averse investor views expected return as a "good" and standard deviation as a "bad," his preferences among portfolios are represented by indifference curves such as those shown in Exhibit 17–16. He chooses among the portfolios in the efficient set (also shown) so as to be on the highest possible indifference curve (in this case "highest" means "most northwesterly"). That is, he will pick the portfolio where the efficient set is tangent to an indifference curve, as at point P in Exhibit 17–16.

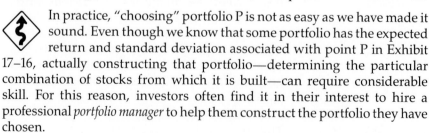

In practice, "choosing" portfolio P is not as easy as we have made it sound. Even though we know that some portfolio has the expected return and standard deviation associated with point P in Exhibit 17–16, actually constructing that portfolio—determining the particular combination of stocks from which it is built—can require considerable skill. For this reason, investors often find it in their interest to hire a professional *portfolio manager* to help them construct the portfolio they have chosen.

In asserting that the investor will choose point P, we have assumed that expected return and standard deviation are the only characteristics of his portfolio that concern him. Conceivably, he could be concerned with other, more subtle, statistical features as well. Suppose that portfolio A could return -6%, -2%, 0, 2%, or 6%, all with equal probability. Portfolio B could return -4% or 4%, each with equal probability. Both portfolios have the same expected return (0%) and the same standard deviation (4%). (If you know the precise definition of standard deviation, you should check this.) Therefore both portfolios occupy the same position in the graph of Exhibit 17–16. Consequently, the theory embodied in that graph must assume that the investor is indifferent between these two portfolios.

The assumption that the investor cares only about expected return and standard deviation is the key assumption of the **capital asset pricing model,** which is often used to study markets for risky assets. A body of empirical evidence indicates that this assumption is not far wrong. We will continue to pursue its implications.

Introduction of a Risk-Free Asset

Suppose now that in addition to all of the stocks shown in Exhibit 17–15, there is a risk-free asset available. It is often asserted that U.S. Treasury bills constitute such an asset (but see the end of Section 16.2 for some contrary evidence). Whatever this risk-free asset might be, it is represented by a point on the vertical axis, like R in Exhibit 17–17.

Let us see what happens when the risk-free asset is combined with a portfolio of stocks. Suppose that an investor holds half of his wealth in the form of stock portfolio A and half in the form of the risk-free asset R. Then his overall portfolio is represented by the point X, midway between A and R. (A risk-free asset cannot contribute to diversification, so the combined portfolio is represented by X rather than some point to the left of X.) Similarly, if the investor holds three-fourths of his wealth in portfolio A and one-fourth in the risk-free asset R, then his overall portfolio is represented by the point Y, three-fourths of the way along the line from R to A.

In general, the investor can achieve any point along the line segment from R to A by combining portfolio A with the risk-free asset. Similarly, he can achieve any point along the line segment from R to B, or from R to any other existing portfolio. The uppermost of these line segments, connecting R with M, contains the most desirable combinations.

Under some circumstances the investor can move past M along the same line. This is possible when he can hold a *negative* amount of the risk-free asset R. For example, if R is a Treasury bill and if the investor is able to borrow at the Treasury bill rate, then such borrowing is equivalent to holding a negative quantity of Treasury bills. (*Borrowing* equals *selling bonds* equals *buying bonds in negative quantities.*) Assuming that this is possible, the investor can achieve any point along the line passing through R and M. This line is called the **market line.**

Capital asset pricing model
A model that assumes that investors care only about expected return and risk, where risk is measured by standard deviation.

Market line
The line through a risk-free asset and tangent to the efficient set.

Exhibit 17–17   **A Risk-Free Asset**

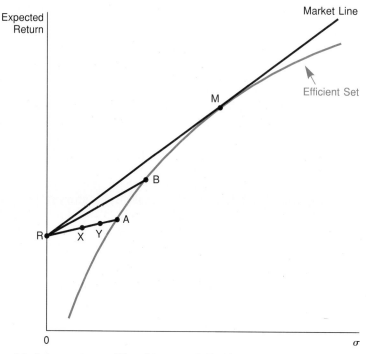

Point R represents a risk-free asset, possibly a Treasury bill. The investor can achieve any point along the illustrated line segments by combining R with portfolios such as A, B, and M. For example, combining R and A in equal amounts yields point X. The line connecting R and M contains the most desirable possibilities; it is called the market line. If R can be held in negative amounts (say by borrowing), then it is possible to move beyond point M along the market line.

No investor would ever want to be off the market line. Therefore every investor wants to hold a portfolio consisting partly of R and partly of a market portfolio M.

Market portfolio
The point of tangency between the market line and the efficient set.

The market line is the line through R that is just tangent to the efficient set. The **market portfolio** is the portfolio represented by the point where the market line touches the efficient set. In Exhibit 17–17 point M represents the market portfolio.

There might be more than one market portfolio, since several portfolios can occupy the same position in the graph.

With the availability of the risk-free asset, an investor is no longer restricted to the old efficient set. He can reach any point on the market line by holding an appropriate combination of risk-free assets and shares of the market portfolio. These options are always preferable to points on the efficient set. For example, an investor holding portfolio A in Exhibit 17–17 could move either directly upward to the market line, increasing his expected return, or directly leftward to the market line, decreasing his risk.

Exhibit 17–18   **The Investor's Choice Revisited**

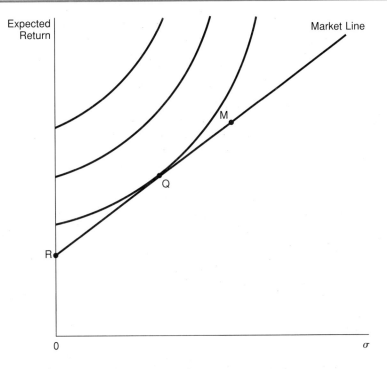

When there is a risk-free asset, the investor is no longer restricted to the old efficient set. He can now reach any point on the market line by combining the risk-free asset with the market portfolio in appropriate proportions. This investor chooses proportions that enable him to reach point Q.

The investor can never do better than to be on the market line. Thus his portfolio of risky assets will always be the market portfolio. There is never any reason to hold any other portfolio of risky assets.

Investors choose only points on the market line. Points on the market line are obtained by combining the risk-free asset R with the market portfolio M. Therefore:

A rational investor always holds a portfolio that combines the risk-free asset with the market portfolio in some proportions.

To see what proportions the investor will choose, we must examine his indifference curves. In Exhibit 17–18 the investor chooses proportions that enable him to reach point Q.

Constructing a Market Portfolio

What happens if we create a giant portfolio consisting of all of the risky assets in the economy? Since every asset is held by somebody, this is the same thing as adding up all of the individual investors' portfolios. Since each investor holds a market portfolio at point M in Exhibit 17–17, we are adding up many portfolios, all at point M. The result must be a portfolio at M, or a portfolio to the left of M if there is further diversification. But we see from Exhibit 17–17 that there are no portfolios to the left of M. It follows that our giant portfolio is itself at point M. In other words:

> **A portfolio that consists of all of the risky assets in the economy, held in proportion to their existing quantities, must be a market portfolio.**

The individual investor wants to hold a combination of two assets: the risk-free asset and a market portfolio. But how is he to construct a market portfolio? The answer is that we have just described one: the portfolio consisting of all of the assets in the economy. An individual investor can hold a miniaturized copy of this portfolio by holding all of the risky assets in proportion to their existing quantities. By choosing an appropriate mix of this particular market portfolio and the risk-free asset, he can reach point Q in Exhibit 17–18, which is his individual optimum.

Unfortunately, practical considerations prevent the investor from really holding all of the risky assets in proportion to their existing quantities. A shopping center in Dubuque, Iowa, might represent a .0001% share of the nation's economy. It is unrealistic to suggest that .0001% of an investor's portfolio should consist of shares in this shopping center. Typically, practical considerations make it necessary for an investor to approximate the market portfolio with a very small number of assets. To some extent he can alleviate this problem by holding shares in mutual funds that in turn hold shares in a large and highly diversified collection of assets. Also, the services of a portfolio manager can be helpful.

17.5 Rational Expectations

In this section we will examine how prices are set in a market where suppliers have to make decisions in the face of uncertain demand. We will discover that equilibrium prices depend very much on the way in which suppliers form their expectations. We will also discover an important reason why economists studying such markets are liable to make predictions that are drastically wrong.

A Market with Uncertain Demand

Suppose that lettuce is sold in a central marketplace. Each day lettuce farmers must decide how much lettuce to load onto their trucks and bring to the market. If they knew what the price was going to be, this decision would be easy. They would simply bring lettuce until the marginal cost of supplying another head was equal to the price. Unfortunately, demand, and therefore price, fluctuates from day to day. The best that farmers can

Exhibit 17–19   **Expectations and Supply**

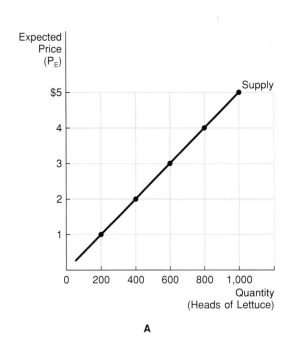

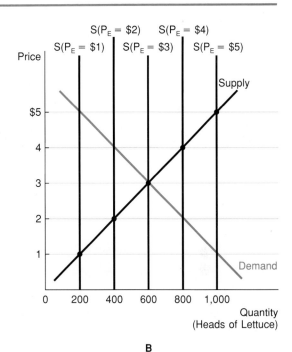

A   B

The curve in panel A shows how much lettuce the farmers bring to market at each expected price. It is like a supply curve, except that it depends on expected price rather than actual price.

When the farmers arrive at the market, the supply curve is vertical. The position of the vertical supply curve depends on the farmers' expectation of the price. Panel B shows the supply curve from panel A superimposed on several possible vertical supply curves. The actual price depends on the expected price (which determines the vertical supply curve) and the actual demand.

do is to form an *expectation* of the price. The amount they bring to market on a given day is given by an upward-sloping "supply curve" as shown in panel A of Exhibit 17–19. The difference between this curve and a true supply curve is that in this case the vertical axis measures not price, but expected price, which we denote by the symbol P_E.

When the farmers actually arrive at the marketplace, the supply curve for lettuce is vertical. The quantity of lettuce is equal to what the farmers have irrevocably decided to bring with them, and all of the lettuce must be sold or it will rot. The location of the vertical supply curve depends on the farmers' expectation of price at the time they start out in the morning. According to Exhibit 17–19, if the farmers expect a price of $1, the supply is 200 heads of lettuce; if they expect a price of $2, the supply is 400 heads, and so forth. Panel B of the exhibit shows the curve from panel A together with

Exhibit 17–20   **Rational Expectations**

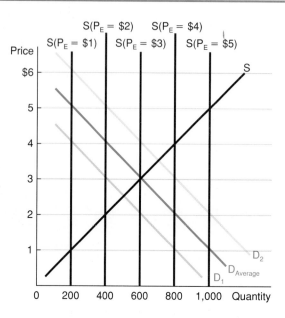

Demand fluctuates between D_1 and D_2; it is $D_{average}$ on the average day. If farmers expect lettuce to sell at $1, they bring 200 heads of lettuce to market and the price on the average day is $5 (where $D_{average}$ crosses the quantity 200). The farmers' expectation is systematically wrong.

    If, on the other hand, the farmers expect lettuce to sell at $3, they bring 600 heads of lettuce to market and the price on the average day is $3. Thus the expectation of a $3 price is correct on average; we say that it is a rational expectation.

the various possible vertical supply curves, each labeled with the corresponding expected price.

    Panel B of Exhibit 17–19 also shows the demand curve for lettuce on a particular day. The market price depends both on the location of this demand curve and on what expectation the farmers have when they start out. If the farmers expect a price of $2, they bring 400 heads of lettuce to market and the actual price is $4. If they expect a price of $4, they bring 800 heads and the actual price is $2. If they expect a price of $3, they bring 600 heads and the actual price is $3. Only in this last case does the farmers' expectation prove to be correct.

▷ *Exercise 17.12* What is the actual price of lettuce if the farmers expect a price of $1? If they expect a price of $5?

    Each day demand is different. Suppose, for example, that the curves D_1 and D_2 in Exhibit 17–20 represent the lower and upper limits of demand. Some days demand is as low as D_1, some days it is as high as D_2, and on the average day it is given by the demand curve $D_{average}$ between them. If farmers consistently expect a price of $1, they will find that the actual price is sometimes as low as $4, sometimes as high as $6, and about $5 on the average day. In other words, they will consistently find that their predictions are drastically wrong.

▷ *Exercise 17.13* Explain how farmers' expectations are confounded if they consistently expect a price of $5.

Now, farmers are not omniscient; nobody expects them to make correct predictions all of the time. But farmers are not foolish either, and when their predictions are consistently off in a systematic way, we expect them to revise those predictions. Farmers who expect a price of $1 will consistently find that they have underestimated, and therefore they will not persist in their belief.

A similar argument can be made about any expected price except for an expected price of $3. If farmers expect a price of $3, then the price will be as low as $2 some days, as high as $4 other days, and $3 on average. Farmers will have no reason to revise their expectations either upward or downward. In this case we say that the farmers have **rational expectations.**

Rational expectations Expectations that, when held by market participants, lead to behavior that fulfills those expectations on average.

An expectation is rational when it does not lead to systematic, correctable errors in prediction. Nevertheless, a rational expectation is not always, nor even usually, a correct expectation. In our example the price might be $2 half of the time and $4 half of the time, in which case the rational expectation of $3 will *never* be correct.

Geometrically, the rational expectation occurs where the average day's demand curve crosses the farmers' upward-sloping supply curve.

Why Economists Make Wrong Predictions

Now let us embellish our model by making an assumption about why demand fluctuates. Suppose that the demand for lettuce is strictly determined by the income of the local lumberjacks. Exhibit 17–21 shows some possible demand curves. When the lumberjacks earn $100, the demand curve is D_{100}; when they earn $150, it is D_{150}; and so on. Let us also assume that on the average day lumberjacks earn $150.

If the farmers have rational expectations, they always expect a price of $3, which is correct on the average day. Thus they always bring 600 heads of lettuce to market. The actual price on any given day is perfectly predictable on the basis of the lumberjacks' income. When the lumberjacks earn $100, the price of lettuce is $2; when the lumberjacks earn $150, the price is $3; and so on.

▷ *Exercise 17.14* What is the price of lettuce when the lumberjacks' income is $200? When it is $250? When it is $300?

▷ *Exercise 17.15* Suppose that the lumberjacks' income averaged $250. What would be the rational expectation of the price of lettuce? How many heads of lettuce would farmers bring to the market? What would be the actual price when the lumberjacks earned $100? When they earned $200? When they earned $300?

Exhibit 17–21   Lumberjacks' Income and the Price of Lettuce

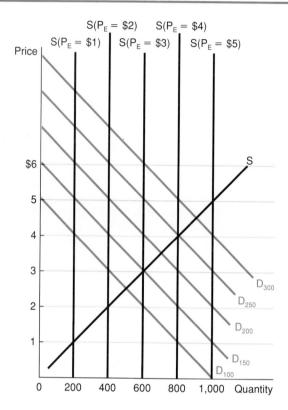

The demand curve for lettuce depends on the lumberjacks' income. When their income is $100, the demand curve is D_{100}; when their income is $150, the demand curve is D_{150}; and so on. Initially, the lumberjacks earn $150 on average. Thus the rational expectation of the price is $3 (where D_{150} crosses the upward-sloping supply curve), so farmers supply 600 heads of lettuce. When the lumberjacks really do earn $150, the rational expectation is fulfilled. On days when the lumberjacks earn $250, the price of lettuce is $5.

Now a paper mill arrives, raising the lumberjacks' income to $250 on average. The new rational expectation for the price is $4. Farmers bring 800 heads of lettuce to market. On the average day the lumberjacks earn $250 and the price of lettuce is $4.

An econometrician extrapolating from past experience would predict that on days when the lumberjacks earn $250, the price of lettuce is $5. Thus he would predict that when the paper mill arrives, the price of lettuce will go up to $5 on average. But he is wrong, because past experience is no longer relevant. When farmers have rational expectations, the additional lettuce that they bring to market invalidates the old relationship between the lumberjacks' income and the price of lettuce.

Suppose now that an econometrician comes to study this market. He is pleased to discover that he can predict the price of lettuce on the basis of the lumberjacks' income, as detailed in the preceding paragraph. He might even be so bold as to summarize his knowledge in an equation:

$$\text{Price of lettuce} = \frac{1}{50} \times \text{Lumberjack's income.}$$

For example, since the lumberjacks earn $150 on average days, the price of lettuce is $1/50 \times \$150 = \$3$ on average days, which is correct.

One day a paper mill is built in the area. The owners of the mill announce that they will be purchasing a lot of lumber. As a result, the lumberjacks' income will now average $250 per day. What does the econometrician predict about the price of lettuce?

Drawing on past experience, the econometrician knows that lumberjack income of $250 implies a lettuce price of $5. Thus he predicts that the price of lettuce will now be $5 on the average day.

But what actually happens? By examining Exhibit 17–21, you can see that the new rational-expectations price of lettuce is $4 (where supply crosses the new average demand curve D_{250}). Farmers now bring 800 heads of lettuce to market each day. When the lumberjacks earn $250, on the average day the price of lettuce is $4, not $5 as the econometrician predicted.

Where did the econometrician go wrong? All past experience supports his equation. It has always been true in the past that on days when the lumberjacks earn $250, the price of lettuce is $5. What happened is that the arrival of the paper mill caused farmers to change their expectations and bring a different amount of lettuce to market. This in turn invalidated the econometrician's equation. The correct new equation is

$$\text{Price of lettuce} = \left(\frac{1}{50} \times \text{Lumberjack's income}\right) - \$1.$$

▷ **Exercise 17.16** Suppose that a tree disease reduces the lumberjacks' average income to $100. What is the new equation for the price of lettuce?

Example: Tweedledum and Tweedledee

Tweedledum and Tweedledee have identical skills and have therefore always had identical incomes. In years when their skills are in demand, their incomes are both high, and at other times their incomes are both low. An econometrician, having carefully collected data, can confidently assert the truth of the equation

Tweedledee's income = Tweedledum's income.

If he can observe Tweedledum's income, the econometrician can use his equation to predict Tweedledee's income, and he will always be right.

One day Tweedledee hired just such an econometrician to advise him on how to increase his income. The econometrician, having discovered the above equation, advised Tweedledee, "It's simple. Your income is always the same as Tweedledum's income, so if you want your income to rise, just give all of your money to Tweedledum." Tweedledee tried it, but it didn't work.

This simple example illustrates that even when equations predict very well, they can be entirely useless as guides to policy. The reason is that changes in policy can invalidate the equations.[7] The equality between Tweedledee's and Tweedledum's incomes existed for a *reason:* the fact that their incomes were derived from selling identical skills in the marketplace. The econometrician's suggestion leads to behavior that eliminates this reason for equality, and as a result the equality itself disappears.

Similarly, we can imagine the econometrician of the preceding subsection advising farmers to try to attract a paper mill to the area, promising that the price of lettuce will rise to $5. When it rises to only $4, the farmers are disappointed, just like Tweedledee. Again the reason is that the policy change eliminates the reason underlying the validity of the very equation that was used to justify the policy change.

The example of Tweedledee and Tweedledum illustrates that this problem with policy evaluation can occur even in exceptionally simple examples. The lumberjacks/lettuce example illustrates that the problem is particularly likely to arise in the presence of rational expectations, since changes in policy lead to changes in those expectations and hence to changes in behavior.

Rational expectations play a central and exciting role in modern macroeconomics, although they are fundamentally a microeconomic concept.[8] Two important areas of research are the attempt to understand the ways in which econometricians can be led astray in their predictions, and the development of new econometric techniques that are appropriate for studying markets in which expectations are rational.

Summary

In many cases an individual's wealth depends on the state of the world. It is possible to transfer income from one state of the world to another in a variety of ways. The gambler who bets that a tossed coin will turn up heads transfers income from the state of the world in which tails comes up to the state of the world in which heads comes up. The homeowner who buys fire insurance transfers income from the state of the world in which his house is undamaged to the state of the world in which his house burns down. The investor who buys a share of stock in a company that makes digital tapes transfers income from the state of the world in which digital tape technology is unsuccessful in the marketplace to the state of the world in which digital tapes completely replace compact disks.

There are thus many ways that an individual can distribute his income across states of the world. We can draw indifference curves to illustrate his preferences among these distributions. The indifference curves depend

---

[7]This point was made forcefully in R. E. Lucas, Jr., "Econometric Policy Evaluation: A Critique," in *The Phillips Curve and Labor Markets,* Vol. 1 of Carnegie-Rochester Conference Series on Public Policy. Editors: Karl Brunner and Allan H. Meltzer. (Amsterdam: North Holland, 1976), 19–46.

[8]Rational expectations were introduced by John Muth to study problems in agricultural economics.

both on the consumer's tastes and on the probabilities of the various states of the world.

A risk-neutral individual is one who always chooses the lottery with the highest expected value, without regard to risk. We expect a frequent gambler to be risk-neutral, since his good and bad luck wash out over time. For someone who is risk-neutral, the indifference curves are straight lines whose absolute slope is the ratio of the probabilities of the states of the world. When he is offered the opportunity to gamble at fair odds, the risk-neutral person is indifferent among all of the opportunities on his budget line. When offered the opportunity to gamble at favorable odds, he will always bet everything he has.

In many situations we expect people to be risk-averse. Among baskets with the same expected value, a risk averter always chooses the one with no risk, that is, the one on the 45° line. Thus at points along the 45° line the risk averter's indifference curves have an absolute slope that reflects the fair betting odds. When offered the opportunity to bet at favorable odds, the risk averter always accepts a small wager, but never a large one. Usually, an increase in income will increase the size of the largest wager that the risk averter will accept at given odds.

Many markets exist to facilitate the transfer of risk across individuals. One is the market for insurance. In a world of perfect information, much insurance would be offered at fair odds (except for a slight tilting in favor of the insurance company to allow it to cover its costs). However, there are important reasons why we do not observe this practice. One is the problem of moral hazard: Insured individuals take fewer precautions. With perfect information moral hazard would not be a problem, since insurance companies could require appropriate behavior as a condition of being insured. Another problem is adverse selection: Different people have different probabilities of becoming ill (or of experiencing a fire, or of being robbed). This makes it impossible for the company to offer unlimited fair-odds insurance to the relatively low-risk group, since members of the relatively high-risk group would purchase it and bankrupt the company. A possible equilibrium involves offering insurance policies that pay off differently, one at the fair odds for the low-risk group and one at the fair odds for the high-risk group, but limiting the amount of the first kind of policy that any individual can buy. If the amount is chosen carefully, then each group chooses to buy the kind of insurance that is appropriate. The resulting equilibrium is suboptimal in the sense that if members of the high-risk group could be costlessly identified, the company would offer policies that benefit the low-risk people without hurting the high-risk people. A final problem is that some risks are undiversifiable, hence uninsurable.

The futures market is another market for transferring risk. It enables farmers to reduce their risks by contracting now for the prices of future deliveries. It also creates the opportunity for speculation, which is welfare-improving when speculators are right and detrimental to welfare when speculators are wrong.

The stock market is yet another market for trading risky assets. In addition to individual stocks, investors can hold portfolios, created by combining various stocks in different proportions. The portfolio consisting of two stocks in equal proportions has the average expected return but may have less than the average standard deviation (riskiness), due to diversification.

By combining the market portfolio (which consists of all of the risky assets in the economy held in proportion to their actual quantities) with a risk-free asset, the investor can create a portfolio that is superior to any other given portfolio in terms of risk and expected return. Thus the only portfolio of risky assets that an investor would ever want to hold is the market portfolio. In practice, however, it is necessary to approximate this portfolio, which can require considerable expertise.

When there is uncertainty about the future, people may form rational expectations, which are expectations that are correct on the average day. If there is a change in circumstances, such as the arrival of a new industry or a change in some government policy, then the rational expectations may change, and consequently so may people's behavior. As a result, equations that have always predicted accurately in the past may prove drastically wrong following a policy change.

Review Questions

R1. Describe the indifference curves (a) of a person who is risk-neutral, (b) of a person who is risk-averse, and (c) of a person who is risk-preferring.

R2. Under what circumstances might a person be expected to be risk-neutral? Why is a firm more likely to be risk-neutral than an individual?

R3. Explain why the stockholders and the executives of a corporation might have different preferences with regard to the corporation's behavior toward risk. Describe some possible remedies and their pros and cons.

R4. What is moral hazard? Give some examples.

R5. What is adverse selection? Give some examples.

R6. Describe a possible equilibrium in an insurance market with adverse selection. In what sense is it suboptimal?

R7. Explain how the market for used cars becomes a market for lemons.

R8. What is an uninsurable risk? Give some examples.

R9. Explain what a futures contract is. How can a farmer or the owner of a grain elevator use futures contracts to eliminate risk?

R10. Explain what happens to the present and future supply of wheat when a speculator expects the price to fall. In what circumstances is this socially beneficial?

R11. What is the efficient set of portfolios? Explain why it is shaped as it is.

R12. Explain why the market portfolio is the only portfolio of risky assets that any investor would want to hold.

R13. What determines the daily equilibrium price in a market where demand fluctuates and suppliers have rational expectations?

R14. Explain how the arrival of a paper mill can cause a change in the relationship between lumberjacks' income and the price of lettuce.

Problem Set

1. *True or false:* If nothing is worth dying for, then going to war is irrational.

2. According to Dr. Johnson, "He is no wise man who will quit a certainty for an uncertainty." Comment.

3. Whenever John is offered the opportunity to take either side of a bet in which the odds are even slightly unfair, he invariably does bet something. *True or false:* John is certainly not risk-averse.

4. Jill likes to bet on heads when the odds are fair, but will bet on tails only if offered very favorable odds. Draw her indifference curves.

5. *True or false:* A risk-preferring person will always bet, no matter how much the odds are against him.

6. Bookmakers organize betting on football games in the following way: First, they determine a "point spread" that one team is expected to beat with 50–50 probability. Then bettors are allowed to bet on whether the team will beat the spread. They may take either side of the bet, and are offered slightly unfavorable odds either way. Show the budget line faced by the bettors. What will a risk-averse bettor do in these circumstances? What will a risk-preferring bettor do? Can you think of any reason why a risk averter might still bet?

7. Many insurance policies have a "deductible" clause that requires the insured to contribute the first $250 toward the cost of an accident, while the insurance company pays the remainder. *True or false:* The deductible provision provides an incentive for the insured to take precautions against accidents.

8. If "sickly" people could insure against illness at the same rates available to healthy people, they would end up preferring illness to good health.

9. *True or false:* Speculators are less harmful to society than they at first appear, because they sometimes err in forecasting the future and their losses due to these errors compensate the rest of us for their gains when they are right.

10. Suppose that the market for grain is initially in equilibrium. A speculator then becomes convinced that next month's demand will be greater than has been expected. What can he do to profit from this expectation? How does this affect prices, and how does it affect the behavior of grain suppliers? Analyze the welfare consequences of the speculator's actions, first on the assumption that he is correct about next month's demand and then on the assumption that he is incorrect.

11. Suppose that houses in California are identical to houses in New York State, and that each state is equally desirable to live in. The only difference is that California houses run the risk of destruction by earthquake, while New York State houses do not. *True or false:* In order for anyone to hold the risky asset consisting of a California house, he must be compensated with a higher rate of return. Therefore California houses will grow in value more quickly than New York State houses will.

12. *True or false:* Nobody would ever hold a stock that was below the efficient set, since there is always an alternative with less risk or greater expected return.

13. Suppose that in reality the number of cars demanded, Q, depends on the real interest rate, r, according to an equation of the form

$$Q = Ar + B,$$

where A and B are constants. An econometrician believes that the number of cars demanded depends on the *nominal* interest rate, i, and uses data to estimate the coefficients C and D in the equation

$$Q = Ci + D.$$

    a.   Express the estimated coefficients C and D in terms of the "true" coefficients A and B and the inflation rate, π.

    b.   Explain why this model will make good predictions as long as the inflation rate is constant.

    c.   Suppose that it is considered desirable to raise the demand for cars and that the government can affect i by adopting policies that lead to a change in π. What will the econometrician advise?

    d.   When the new policy is adopted, what happens to C and D? Explain why the recommended policy won't work.

Refer to Answers to Problem Sets for solutions to problems 1 and 2.

Chapter Eighteen

Transactions and the Role of Money

In a world with only two goods there would be no need for money. People would simply exchange one good directly for another. But in a world with many goods, money serves an important function. Without money, the person who wants to trade a goose for a pig must locate a person who wants to trade a pig for a goose. With money, he can sell his goose in the marketplace for the going money price, and then use the proceeds to buy a pig from any willing seller.

Money facilitates transactions and is therefore desirable. As a result, there is a demand for money. This demand interacts with supply to determine a price. In this chapter we will see how to interpret the notion of "the price of money." We will learn the most important factors determining this price. Also, we will see that holding money conveys a positive externality, and that therefore suboptimal quantities are held. In this connection, we will be able to see why inflation is socially detrimental, and how its opposite, deflation, can improve social welfare.

18.1 The Demand for Money

Students are rarely surprised to learn that money is desirable. Sometimes they think that the demand for money must be unlimited, or infinite. But there is no more reason to think this than to think that the demand for refrigerators, or any other good thing, is infinite. The demand for money is no different in principle than the demand for refrigerators. It depends on income, and it depends on prices.

You hold your wealth in many forms. Some of your wealth is stored in the form of clothing, some in the form of compact disks, some perhaps in the form of stocks or bonds, some in the form of appliances like stereo equipment or refrigerators, and some in the form of money. Presumably, you would choose to have more of any of these than you can own at present, provided that it cost you nothing to do so. Yet we don't say that your demand for sweaters is unlimited just because you would accept an unlimited number if they were free. Your demand for sweaters describes the number of sweaters that you choose to own given the sad fact that each sweater entails a sacrifice of some of the other goods that you enjoy.

The primary reason why students become confused about the demand for money is that they confuse money with wealth. Of course, we would all like to have more wealth than we have. But given our wealth, and given the trade-offs that we face, few of us choose to hold all or even most of our wealth in the form of money.

What is money, and what is its price? In this book the word *money* refers to pieces of green paper bearing pictures of historical figures and the legend "This Note Is Legal Tender for All Debts, Public and Private." In many contexts it is appropriate to include, for example, checking account balances under the definition of money. If you take a course in Money and Banking, you will study the subtleties of what should or should not be included for each of a number of purposes. Those subtleties will not concern us here.

Another thing that you will study in your Money and Banking course (or perhaps in a Macroeconomics course) is a catalog of reasons why people hold money. The only one that will concern us here is that money facilitates transactions. People carry money because they can use it to buy things more easily than they can use their sweaters to buy things. It enables them to deal with unexpected contingencies. If it starts to rain, a person who carries money can hail a cab without having to bargain with the cab driver about trading a sweater for a ride. Someone who habitually carries $100 in his wallet can carry on transactions more easily than someone who habitually carries $50 in his wallet. Of course, he pays a price for this convenience: In order to carry $100 worth of money, he must forgo having $100 worth of something else.

The Price Level and the Cost of Holding Money

Price level
The price of goods in terms of money.

In order to speak about the costs of holding money, we must first have a measure of "the price of goods in terms of money." Such a measure is called the **price level.** When your grandfather tells you that "everything costs ten times as much today as when I was a boy," he means that the price level today is ten times what it was then.

Unfortunately for the definition of the price level, it isn't true that everything costs ten times as much today as when your grandfather was a boy. Computers, for one thing, are a lot cheaper. So are trips to Europe. The price level must refer to the average price of goods, or to the price of some standardized basket of goods. The consumer price index is a measure of the price level. As we saw in Section 3.3, there are a number of difficulties inherent in any specific choice of definition.

We will avoid these difficulties by postulating a world in which apples are the only good. The *price level*, denoted by the letter P, will then unambiguously refer to the price of apples in terms of dollars. This one-good assumption will simplify some of our discussion without seriously affecting any of the arguments.[1]

Notice that when the price level is P, a dollar bill will purchase 1/P apples.

Money Holdings and Real Balances

Real balances
The value of money holdings in terms of goods.

We will use the capital letter M to denote the money holdings of a given individual. A man with $100 in his wallet has set M equal to $100. His **real balances** are defined as the value of his money holdings in terms of apples, or, in other words, the number of apples that he could buy with all of his money. If the price level is $1 per apple, the man's real balances are 100 apples. If the price level is $2 per apple, his real balances are 50 apples. Real balances are denoted by the lower-case letter m. In general, we have

$$m = \frac{M}{P}.$$

Real
Measured in terms of goods.

Notice that actual apples do not count among real balances. Someone with $100 and 600 apples still only has 100 apples worth of real balances if the price level is $1 per apple. Real balances are a measure of the value of money holdings alone, not of total wealth.

Real income
Income measured in terms of goods.

Real versus Nominal Quantities

Money income
or **nominal income**
Income measured in terms of money.

We will always use the prefix **real** to describe things that are measured in terms of apples, as opposed to things that are measured in terms of money. For example, your **real income** is measured in apples per year. Of course, many people are paid in dollars, but we can always measure real income by converting dollars to apples, which simply requires dividing by the price level. Income measured in dollars per year is called either **money income** or **nominal income.** Anything measured in terms of dollars is referred to as **nominal.**

Nominal
Measured in terms of money.

---

[1]The one-good assumption is a bit more disturbing in a discussion of money than it would be elsewhere. The reason for this is that if there were really only one good in the world, then money would be superfluous. Therefore it is important to keep track of the ways in which the one-good assumption is actually used. The alert reader will find that it is never really used at all.

All of the microeconomic theory that we have developed in this book refers to real, rather than nominal, variables. For example, the equilibrium wage rate determined in the market for labor is the equilibrium *real* wage rate. If the labor market is in equilibrium, workers must receive this real wage. This means that if the price level were to double, without any change in the supply of or demand for labor, then the nominal wage rate would automatically double as well in order to maintain equilibrium in the labor market.

The Cost of Holding Money

What is the cost of holding $1? The answer can be measured in forgone apples. In order to add a dollar bill to your wallet, you must forgo the opportunity to exchange that bill for 1/P apples, where P is the price level. To see this another way, suppose that you are in the habit of carrying 5 one-dollar bills in your pocket. One day you decide to reduce your cash holdings down to 4 one-dollar bills. At the time that you reduce your cash holdings, you can acquire 1/P apples that were previously unavailable to you. One dollar bill can be exchanged for 1/P apples.

Thus if we were to graph the supply of and demand for money, the vertical (price) axis would measure the number of apples forgone per dollar held, and it would be labeled 1/P. For some purposes this is an enlightening graph to consider. For our purposes here, however, it will be more convenient to consider the supply of and demand for real balances rather than for dollar bills. First, we must determine the cost of holding real balances.

The Cost of Holding Real Balances

When we measure money holdings, we can use dollar bills as a standard unit. When we measure holdings of real balances, dollar bills will not do, because the quantity of real balances represented by a dollar bill changes when the price level changes. Thus we need a different standard unit for real balances.

We will define a *unit* of real balances to be 1 apple's worth. Thus when the price level is $1 per apple, a unit of real balances is represented by a dollar bill; when the price level is 25¢ per apple, a unit of real balances is represented by a quarter.

What is the cost of holding a unit of real balances? A moment's reflection will convince you that the answer is always 1 apple. Thus the price of real balances never changes; it is always fixed at 1.

The Demand for Real Balances

Although the price of real balances is always equal to 1 apple per unit, we can still ask the hypothetical question: How many units of real balances would be demanded if the price took some other specified value? Asking this question for a variety of hypothetical prices allows us to generate a demand curve for real balances.

Exhibit 18–1   **The Demand for Real Balances**

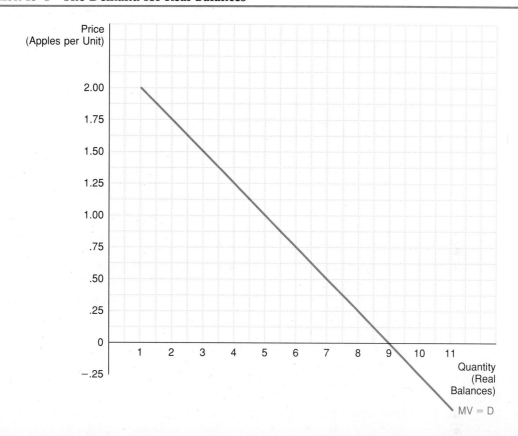

If the price level is $1 per apple, then a unit of real balances is simply a dollar bill, and the graph shows the marginal value of dollar bills. The first bill is so convenient that the consumer would be willing to sacrifice up to 2 apples to acquire it. The second bill is worth 1.75 apples, and so on. The tenth bill has already become a nuisance, and the consumer would be willing to pay up to .25 apple to convert it to some other form of wealth.

If the price level changes, then a unit of real balances will refer to some new quantity of dollar bills. However, the marginal value curve is unaffected by a change in the price level.

Any demand curve can also be viewed as a marginal value curve. Exhibit 18–1 shows a certain consumer's marginal value curve for real balances. It will be easiest to think about this curve if we begin by imagining that the price level is $1 per apple. In that case a "unit of real balances" is simply a dollar bill.

The value of dollar bills lies in the convenience they bring to life. Having a dollar in your pocket means that when you want to purchase a candy bar, you can do so without first running home to get something to trade for it or running to the bank to make a withdrawal. According to Exhibit 18–1, this particular consumer finds that his first dollar bill brings him 2 apples worth of convenience.

Having two one-dollar bills makes life more convenient, but perhaps not twice as convenient as having a single one-dollar bill. The marginal value of the second dollar is still positive (in this case 1.75 apples), but not as high as the marginal value of the first dollar.

Conceivably, there comes a point at which having additional dollar bills becomes a positive nuisance. In addition to stretching out the fabric in the consumer's pants, they make him a target for robbery. Thus the marginal value of dollar bills eventually becomes negative.

It is easy to find Exhibit 18–1 confusing. Why would anybody be willing to sacrifice 2 apples to get his first dollar, which is only enough to buy 1 apple? The answer is that nobody would be willing to sacrifice 2 apples in order to increase his *wealth* by 1 dollar, but that is not the question that the exhibit addresses. The exhibit says that the consumer, with *given* wealth, would be willing to sacrifice up to 2 apples in exchange for the privilege of being able to carry part of his wealth around in the form of a dollar bill.

If the price level were something other than 1 dollar per apple, then a unit of real balances would be something other than 1 dollar bill. However, the marginal value of a unit of real balances is unaffected by a change in the price level. When the price level is 1 dollar per apple, a unit of real balances is a dollar bill and the consumer values his first dollar bill at 2 apples. When the price level is 25¢ per apple, a unit of real balances is a quarter and the consumer values his first quarter at 2 apples. A change in price level does not affect the validity of the graph in Exhibit 18–1.

The Consumer's Choice

We have already observed that the price of real balances is always 1 apple per unit. Thus Exhibit 18–2 shows the consumer's equilibrium. He continues to increase his holdings of real balances as long as the marginal value of a unit exceeds 1 apple, and he stops when the marginal value is equal to one apple. That is, he holds m_0 units of real balances. He earns area A in consumer's surplus. Area A is a measure of how much his life is improved by the convenience of being able to carry money.

Changes in Demand

The demand curve for real balances is affected by anything that makes carrying money either more or less attractive. For example, suppose that all banks installed automatic teller machines on every street corner. In that case people would want to carry less money with them on average. The demand for real balances would fall, so that the equilibrium quantity m would fall. Since m = M/P, and since the quantity M of dollar bills does not change, the fall in m requires a rise in P. Thus the automatic teller machines would lead to a rise in the price level.

For another example, suppose that the rate of interest were to rise. This makes it more desirable to hold interest-bearing assets, such as bonds, and

Exhibit 18–2   **The Consumer's Choice**

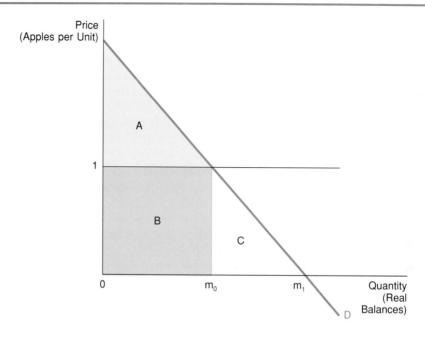

The price of real balances is always 1 apple per unit. Thus the consumer will hold m_0 units of real balances.

consequently less desirable to hold non-interest-bearing assets, such as money. The demand for real balances falls, and, as in the preceding paragraph, the price level rises.

In each of the two examples, we have argued that the price level must rise. How exactly does this happen? When people decide to carry less money, they attempt to convert some of their existing money into other things, such as apples, and thereby bid prices up. The average person is not able to reduce his money holdings, since all of the existing dollar bills must be held by someone. However, as each person *attempts* to spend his money, prices are bid up, thereby automatically reducing everyone's stock of real balances. This process continues until people's real balances are reduced to the new equilibrium level.

Welfare

When you decide to carry money in your pocket, you are deciding to own fewer apples than you could own. This reduces the demand for apples and bids down the price level. This in turn is a boon to anyone else who is holding money: He finds that his real balances automatically increase as the price level is bid down. Therefore the act of holding money conveys a positive externality. We want to measure the size of that externality.

The easiest way to measure the externality is to notice that when you add a unit of real balances to your pocket, you forgo exactly 1 apple, which is now available for someone else to consume. Therefore the price level has to fall by just enough so that others can afford to buy that 1 apple. You bestow 1 apple's worth of benefit on others for each unit of real balances that you carry. When you choose to hold m_0 units of real balances, you bestow m_0 apples' worth of benefit on your neighbors. This can be represented by area B in Exhibit 18–2, which is a rectangle of height 1 and width m_0.

Here is another way to see why the externality is represented by area B. What is the cost of your holding a unit of real balances? The private cost, to you, is exactly 1 apple. But the social cost is zero, because your decision to carry more real balances has no effect on the total number of apples available to society. As a result, the social marginal cost curve lies along the horizontal axis in Exhibit 18–2, and the social gain from your carrying m_0 units of real balances is given by the area under the demand curve, above the social marginal cost curve, and out to the quantity m_0. In other words, the social gain is A + B. Of this, A is consumers' surplus, so B must be the positive externality.

Because of the externality, there is room for improvement. In Exhibit 18–2, if each consumer held m_1 units of real balances, the social gain would be A + B + C, rather than just A + B. The Coase Theorem tells us that when there are social gains available, they will be earned provided there are no transactions costs. The optimal contract is for everybody to agree to carry m_1 units of real balances.[2] Under such a contract we would all have the additional convenience associated with having more money in our pockets, without any sacrifice in apple consumption (the agreement has no effect on the number of apples there are to go around).

Unfortunately, the transactions costs in this situation are enormous. Thus we expect the consumer to hold the suboptimal quantity m_0.

The Optimal Subsidy

Because holding money involves a positive externality, social welfare can be improved by a Pigou subsidy. The optimal subsidy is equal to the amount of the externality, which is 1 apple per unit of real balances held. Suppose that the government contrives to reward you with 1 apple every time you add a unit of real balances to your wallet. This reduces the private cost of real balances from 1 apple per unit to zero, which is equal to the social marginal cost. We can see the result in Exhibit 18–3. You will carry m_1 units of real balances and earn a consumer's surplus of A + B + C. The

---

[2]We assume for convenience that everyone has the demand curve shown in Exhibit 18–2. In general, the optimal contract is for each individual to hold a quantity of real balances determined by the intersection of his marginal value curve with the horizontal axis.

Exhibit 18–3   **A Subsidy to Holding Money**

	Before Subsidy	After Subsidy
Consumer Surplus	A	A + B + C
Gains to Neighbors	B	—
Social Gain	A + B	A + B + C

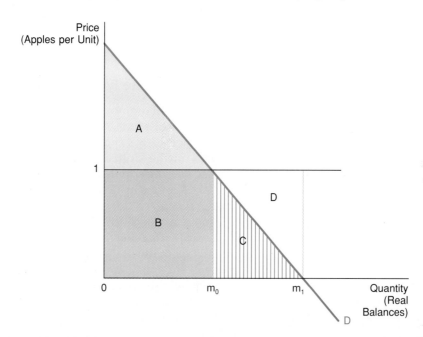

The private cost of holding real balances is 1 apple per unit and the social cost is zero apples per unit. Therefore the consumer holds m_0 units, even though the social optimum is m_1 units. The consumer earns a surplus equal to area A. By forgoing m_0 apples, he makes this many more apples available to his neighbors and thus conveys a positive externality equal to area B.

Now suppose that the government subsidizes money holdings by rewarding each consumer with 1 apple per unit of real balances held. The private marginal cost drops to zero, and the consumer holds m_1 units of real balances. His consumer's surplus increases to A + B + C. The positive externality increases to B + C + D, but this is exactly offset by the fact that the neighbors who benefit from the externality must also pay the subsidy. Thus the increase in social gain is area C, as can be seen in the table.

positive externality conferred on your neighbors is B + C + D. But your neighbors are also the taxpayers who must foot the bill for the subsidy; the bill comes to B + C + D. After subtracting this, your neighbors come out even. The table in the exhibit summarizes the outcome.

The subsidy improves social welfare, and it does so by improving each individual's welfare. Although it appears from the table that your neighbors are losers in this proposition, don't forget that each of them is in the same situation that you are in, and each is gaining additional consumer's surplus that more than offsets the loss in external benefits. Everyone is a winner under this scheme.

How can the government—or anyone—subsidize the maintenance of real balances without randomly spot-checking peoples' wallets in order to see how much they are carrying? Although this might seem an impossible task, we will see in Section 18.3 that there is a practical way to institute the optimal subsidy.

18.2 The Supply of Money and Equilibrium in the Money Market

In the United States the quantity of money in circulation is controlled by the monetary authorities of the Federal Reserve Board, affectionately known as "the Fed." It was not always thus. In the nineteenth century much of the paper currency in the United States was privately issued. Today the Fed exerts control over the supply of money in a variety of ways that you will study if you take a course in Money and Banking. In this book we will adopt a simplified model in which money is supplied in only two ways: It is printed by the monetary authorities, who either give it away or use it to buy apples from private citizens.

Economists sometimes refer to the first of these methods as a *helicopter drop*, because of the image of the monetary authorities flying by in their helicopters, dropping money from the sky. The imagery first appeared in a paper by Milton Friedman[3] that is also the source of many of the ideas in this chapter, especially those in Section 18.3.

Effect of a Helicopter Drop

Imagine that the market for real balances is initially in equilibrium, as shown in Exhibit 18–4. The price of real balances is, of course, 1 apple per unit, and people hold m_0 units. Suppose that the number of dollars in circulation is M_0 and the price level is P_0. Then

$$m_0 = \frac{M_0}{P_0}.$$

Now come the monetary authorities in their helicopters, dropping dollars that are retrieved by a grateful citizenry. After the drop the number of dollars in circulation is M_1, which is larger than M_0. The quantity of real balances held by the public increases to $m_1 = M_1/P_0$, which, according to Exhibit 18–4, is more than people want to hold. The lucky ones who have

---

[3]Milton Friedman, "The Optimum Quantity of Money," in *The Optimum Quantity of Money and Other Essays* (Chicago: Aldine, 1969).

Exhibit 18–4   **Effect of a Helicopter Drop**

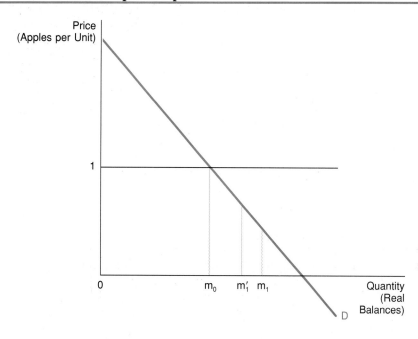

The market is initially in equilibrium, with consumers holding $m_0 = M_0/P_0$ units of real balances. Now helicopters drop additional money, so that the supply of money rises to M_1 and the quantity of real balances rises to $m_1 = M_1/P_0$. As the graph indicates, this is more than people want to hold. They will therefore attempt to convert dollar bills to apples. With all consumers trying to buy apples, the price of apples is bid up, and this increase in the price level reduces the quantity of real balances, say to m_1'. Since this is still more than people are willing to hold, the price level must be bid up still further. The process continues until the quantity of real balances falls to its original equilibrium level m_0. This means that the new price level P_1 must satisfy the equation $M_1/P_1 = m_0 = M_0/P_0$.

acquired the excess dollars attempt to convert them into apples. In so doing, they will bid up the price of apples.

When the price of apples (that is, the price level) rises, the quantity of real balances automatically falls, say to m_1' in Exhibit 18–4. This is still more than people are willing to hold. The excess dollars have changed hands, but they are still held by people who want to dispose of them in exchange for apples. The price of apples is bid up still higher, as the dollars take on the character of "hot potatoes" that nobody wants to be left holding. The process continues until the quantity of real balances is reduced to the equilibrium level m_0. This happens when the price level is bid up to a new level P_1 that must satisfy the equation

$$\frac{M_1}{P_1} = m_0.$$

The equilibrium value for m_0, determined in Exhibit 18–4, cannot change as a result of the authorities' actions. Because the ratios M_0/P_0 and M_1/P_1 are each equal to m_0, they must be equal to each other. Setting M_0/P_0 equal to M_1/P_1 and rearranging terms, we get the important equation

$$\frac{P_1}{P_0} = \frac{M_1}{M_0}.$$

P_1/P_0 is the ratio by which the price level increases; M_1/M_0 is the ratio by which the authorities increased the money supply. The equation tells us:

An increase in the supply of money causes the price level to increase by the same percentage.

After the arrival of the helicopters, how long does it take for the price level to rise to P_1? The answer is that we need not wait for the bidding-up process that we have just described. The appearance of the helicopters means that the price level will soon be bid up to P_1; if people realize this, they will instantly become unwilling to part with apples at any lower price. Therefore the helicopter drop can cause an immediate rise in the price level.

Seigniorage

In the real world the Fed does not use helicopters. However, the Fed does create money and does use it to buy real assets (in practice, it limits itself to the purchase of U.S. Treasury bonds). Let us examine the consequences of such behavior. Suppose that the authorities print up a number of dollar bills, increasing the money supply from M_0 to M_1, and use them to purchase apples. Just as in the story of the helicopter drop, we know that the price level must rise to keep people's real balance holdings unchanged. If the price level failed to rise, nobody would be willing to hold the new money.

The percentage increase in the price level must be the same as the percentage increase in the money supply. The price increase occurs immediately, as soon as the plan to print new money is announced.

Let us determine who gains and who loses as a result of this operation. The authorities are obvious winners; they get apples in exchange for formerly worthless pieces of paper. This gain to the authorities is called **seigniorage.** How many apples do they earn in seigniorage? The number of new dollars printed is $M_1 - M_0$, and these are used to purchase apples at a price of P_1. Therefore the authorities acquire $(M_1 - M_0)/P_1$ new apples. Of course, "the authorities" do not personally pocket this gain any more than the tax collector personally pockets the revenue he collects. As a matter of government policy, the apples purchased by the authorities could be distributed in any way at all to the members of society.

Since there has been no change in the number of apples, the gains to the authorities must be offset by losses to someone else. Who loses? The

Seigniorage
The gain to authorities who can print money and spend it to buy goods.

answer is anyone who was holding money at the time when the new money was created. Such people saw the value of their money holdings fall when the price level went up, and they experienced a real loss. To measure the loss, consider that the total initial money holdings were M_0. The value of these holdings in terms of apples was M_0/P_0, and is now reduced to M_0/P_1. So the holders of money sustain a loss of $M_0/P_0 - M_0/P_1$, and by doing a little arithmetic, you will see that this loss can be rewritten in the form $(M_1 - M_0)/P_1$, which is exactly equal to what the authorities gain.

▷ *Exercise 18.1* Do the arithmetic.

Thus an increase in the money supply can be viewed as a tax on money holders. The revenue from the tax goes to the monetary authorities, who, like any tax collectors, can spend it themselves (which we call seigniorage), distribute it to the citizenry (via a helicopter drop), or use it in any other way.

The single helicopter drop and the single apple purchase in this section are both examples of "one-shot" increases in the money supply. We have not yet analyzed a policy of *repeated* drops or *repeated* purchases. You might think that a policy of weekly helicopter drops would have precisely the same effects as a single helicopter drop, with those effects being repeated week after week. However, we shall see in the next section that this is not true.

18.3 Inflation

Inflation
A continuous rise in the price level.

Inflation is said to occur when the price level rises continuously over a period of time. The one-shot price level increases of Section 18.2 do not constitute inflation. If you wake up one morning to find that prices have doubled overnight, that is not inflation. If you find that prices double overnight on a regular basis, that is inflation.

A one-shot increase in the money supply leads to a one-shot increase in the price level. A continuing sequence of increases in the money supply leads to inflation. Let us see what happens to an economy with initially stable prices when the authorities undertake a policy of increasing the money supply on a continuing basis.

Exhibit 18–5 shows the demand curve for real balances and the equilibrium at m_0. If the money supply is initially stable at M_0, then the price level is initially stable at P_0, where P_0 is determined by the condition that $m_0 = M_0/P_0$. If M_0 were to increase by 10% on a one-shot basis, we know that m_0 would remain unchanged and P_0 would increase by 10%.

Now suppose that the authorities undertake a policy of increasing the money supply on a steady basis, at the rate of 10% per year. Once the policy is underway, the price level will also have to increase steadily at the rate of 10% per year.

Exhibit 18–5   **Inflation**

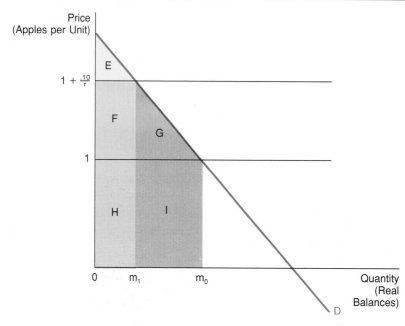

Initially, the money supply is stable at M_0, the price level is P_0, and people hold $m_0 = M_0/P_0$ units of real balances.

Now the authorities institute a policy of increasing the money supply by 10% per year. The price level must eventually also increase by 10% per year. This increases the cost of holding real balances from 1 apple per unit to $1 + .10/r$ apples per unit, where r is the real rate of interest. As a result, people reduce their real balance holdings from m_0 to m_1. This requires an initial period in which the price level grows faster than the money supply so that real balances can fall. The initial period is known as a period of overshooting.

The inflation reduces social welfare from E + F + G + H + I to E + F + H, causing a deadweight loss of G + I.

But this is not the whole story. The advent of inflation adds to the cost of holding money. In an inflationary world, money loses value as it sits in your pocket. In fact, if prices are rising at a rate of 10% per year, then the money in your pocket deteriorates at 10% per year. The deterioration is an additional cost of holding money, or of holding real balances. This increase in the price of real balances leads to a reduction in the quantity that people want to hold.

We can compute exactly the new price of real balances. Suppose that you decide to put 1 unit of real balances in your wallet and to maintain it forever. In order to do so, you place an appropriate number of dollar bills (enough to buy 1 apple) in your wallet today, forgoing the consumption of 1 apple. A year from now you will find to your dismay that your wallet contains only enough to buy .9 apple, because the price of apples has risen 10%. In order just to maintain your unit of real balances, you will have to add another .10 unit to your wallet next year. At that point you will need to forgo the consumption of another .10 apple.

The same thing will happen the following year, and the year after that, and the year after that. The cost of acquiring and maintaining a unit of real balances is 1 apple forgone today, followed by .10 apple forgone every year forever after today. In other words, it is 1 apple plus the present value of a perpetuity of .10 apple per year forever. In Section 16.2 we calculated the value of that perpetuity to be .10/r, where r is the real rate of interest. So the total cost of a unit of real balances is $1 + .10/r$ apples.

In Exhibit 18–5 we see that in view of the new price of real balances, the quantity demanded falls to m_1. In order for the market to clear, the price level must rise by more than the money supply does. If the price level were to rise at the same 10% rate as the money supply, then real balances would be unaffected and people would still be holding m_0 units. But they no longer want to be holding so many units. In their efforts to get rid of the "hot potatoes" in exchange for apples, they must bid the price level up at a rate faster than 10%.

Thus when the new inflation policy is announced, the price level rises more quickly than the money supply, until the quantity of real balances falls to its new equilibrium at m_1. Now that equilibrium is restored in the money market, the price level can rise at exactly the same rate as the money supply, maintaining equilibrium.

The initial period in which the price level rises more quickly than the money supply is called a period of **overshooting.** "Overshooting" is an unfortunate choice of terminology because it often sounds to students like the result of a miscalculation. It is not the result of a miscalculation; it is the result of everyone's simultaneously attempting to reduce his real balances in a thoroughly calculated way.

Overshooting
A percentage increase in the price level that exceeds the percentage increase in the money supply.

Overshooting occurs whenever the rate of growth of the money supply is increased. If money supply growth goes from 10% to 15%, then inflation will go from 10% to something more than 15% and eventually fall back to 15% after real balances have been adjusted to an appropriate new level.

The Inflation Tax

From Exhibit 18–5 we see that a policy of sustained money supply growth creates a social loss equal to the area G + I. (Social gain is reduced from E + F + G + H + I to E + F + H.) Once the policy is underway and prices are rising at 10%, the authorities are, in effect, extracting a 10% per year tax from the holders of real balances, as we saw at the end of Section 18.2. The tax revenue collected (that is, the apples purchased by the authorities with their newly printed money) is exactly equal to the tax revenue paid (that is, the yearly depreciation in the value of existing real balances). But there is an additional loss that is not offset by any gain: the deadweight loss due to the fact that people hold fewer real balances and lose some of the convenience of carrying money.

The inflation tax is just like a tax on any commodity. A one-shot unexpected tax on widget manufacturers would simply transfer income from the widget manufacturers to whomever the authorities wished to bestow it upon. (There is no deadweight loss because there is no way for manufacturers to avoid the tax by altering their behavior.) But a *policy* of taxing widget manufacturers on a regular basis leads to a reduction in the quantity of widgets produced, and a deadweight loss associated with the fall in widget production.

As with widgets, so with any activity, including the holding of real balances. When an activity is taxed, people engage in less of it, and some of the social benefits of that activity are lost.[4]

Historically, inflation rates have sometimes reached spectacular levels. The most famous example is the German hyperinflation of 1921–1923, during which prices multiplied by a factor of 600,000,000 in a single year. At this rate of increase, people holding cash raced to dispose of it. It was of crucial importance to buy now rather than an hour from now. According to Keynes, customers in bars would order several beers at the beginning of the evening, preferring to have to drink them warm and stale than to buy them as they were needed at successively higher prices. The benefits of holding money disappeared almost entirely. The value of these benefits—including, among many other things, the opportunity to drink one's beer cold—is measured by the area under the demand curve for real balances.

Deflation

If inflation is a tax, then deflation is a subsidy. Deflation occurs when prices fall continuously over a period of time. This can be the result of a continuing fall in the money supply. The monetary authorities can bring about such a fall through a policy of selling apples and burning the dollar bills that they collect.

If the money supply falls continuously at the rate of x% per year, then the price level must eventually fall at x% per year in order to maintain the desired stock of real balances. The holder of real balances is now subsidized. Each year his cash holdings increase in value by x%. This enables him to maintain his desired level of real balances while spending the yearly x% increase on apples that he could not have otherwise had.

Every unit of real balances carries with it a subsidy equal to x% of an apple per year. In present value terms, this subsidy is worth (x/r) units, where r is the real rate of interest. In view of the subsidy, the price of holding real balances falls to $1 - (x/r)$ apples per unit. Exhibit 18–6 shows the new equilibrium. The striped area is social gain due to the deflation.

---

[4]For an extraordinarily lucid discussion of the inflation tax, see J. M. Keynes, *A Tract on Monetary Reform,* Chapter 2.

Exhibit 18–6 **Deflation**

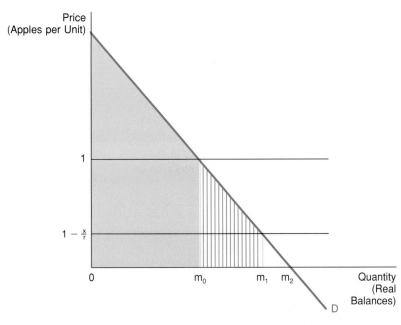

If the price level falls at x% per year, then the holder of a unit of real balances receives a subsidy equal to x% of an apple per unit of real balances held per year. The present value of such a perpetuity is x/r apples. Thus the price of a unit of real balances falls to $1 - (x/r)$ and people increase their holdings to m_1. The striped area is additional social gain due to the deflation.

The Optimal Rate of Deflation

Ideally, people would hold m_2 units of real balances in Exhibit 18–6. To accomplish this, the private marginal cost of holding real balances must be reduced to zero. Thus the optimal subsidy is 1 apple per unit of real balances held. When deflation is x% per year, the actual subsidy is x/r apples per unit held. Putting these two facts together, we find that the optimal rate of deflation—from the point of view of maximizing social gain in the money market—is r% per year, where r is the real rate of interest.

If negative inflation is optimal, why is positive inflation a persistent fact of life? Governments must raise revenue through some form of taxation, and almost any tax leads to some deadweight loss. Given that the government plans to raise a given amount of revenue, it is far from obvious whether it is better to raise that revenue through a tax on money holdings or through a tax on widgets. We are in need of a good theory for predicting how governments decide what to tax and by how much. Until someone finds such a theory, inflation remains neither more nor less mysterious than any other tax.

Summary

Money is desirable because it facilitates transactions. Because of this desirability, there is a demand for money. We must distinguish between the demand for dollar bills and the demand for real balances. The quantity of dollar bills (M) and the quantity of real balances (m) are related by the equation $m = M/P$, where P is the price level. By pretending that apples are the only good in the economy, we can interpret P as the price of an apple in terms of dollar bills.

We define 1 unit of real balances to be the amount sufficient to purchase 1 apple. Then the cost of holding a unit of real balances is exactly 1 apple. The consumer chooses a quantity where the marginal value of holding real balances is equal to this cost.

Although the private cost of holding a unit of real balances is 1 apple, the social cost is zero. This is because the act of holding real balances does not reduce the total number of apples in society. Another way to view this divergence between private and social cost is to call attention to the external effect of holding money: Holding money drives down the price of apples, which benefits all other money holders.

It follows from the existence of this externality that it would be socially desirable to subsidize the act of holding money.

A one-shot increase in the money supply causes the price level to increase by the same percentage as the money supply. This is because the equilibrium level of real balances, m, does not change, so the ratio M/P cannot change. To see the mechanism by which P increases, consider what happens when the new money appears. Whoever holds this money has more money than he wants, so he tries to exchange it for apples. This bids up the price of apples, and the process continues until m returns to its equilibrium value.

If the monetary authorities use new money to buy apples, then the gain to the authorities is exactly equal to the loss to money holders from the increase in P. Thus a one-shot increase in the money supply is a one-shot tax on money holding.

A policy of continuous increases in the money supply yields a continuous rise in the price level, known as inflation. However, at the onset of an inflation there is an additional effect. The fact that money will now "deteriorate" makes it less desirable and reduces the quantity of real balances demanded. Thus P must initially rise faster than M in order for m to reach its new (lower) equilibrium level.

An inflation of x% per year raises the cost of holding real balances to $1 + (x/r)$ apples per unit, where r is the real rate of interest. Similarly, a deflation of x% per year lowers the cost to $1 - (x/r)$ apples per unit. Inflation is a tax on holding money, and deflation is a subsidy. If the authorities choose to set x equal to r, then the optimal subsidy is achieved.

Review Questions

R1. Define the following terms: (a) the price level, (b) real balances, (c) real income, (d) nominal income.

R2. What is the price of money?

R3. What is the private cost of holding real balances? What is the social cost?

R4. In what way does holding real balances create a positive externality?

R5. Use the equation m = M/P to explain why a one-shot rise in the money supply causes the price level to rise by the same percentage.

R6. Suppose that the money supply is M and the price level is P. The authorities announce that they will print an additional M dollars and use them to buy apples. What is the new price level? How many apples can the authorities buy? Where do the apples come from?

R7. What is overshooting? Why does it occur when there is inflation but not in response to a one-shot money supply increase?

R8. Use a diagram to illustrate the deadweight loss due to inflation.

R9. What is the optimal rate of inflation? Why is it optimal?

Problem Set

1. *True or false:* The invention of credit cards would probably cause the price level to rise.

2. *True or false:* If crime in the streets were eliminated, the price level would fall.

3. *True or false:* An increase in the interest rate would cause the price level to rise.

4. *True or false:* The *nominal* quantity of money is determined by what the authorities choose to supply, but the *real* quantity of money is determined by what individuals choose to demand.

5. Suppose that the price level and the money supply have both been steadily growing at the rate of 10% per year when the government announces that henceforth the money supply will increase at only 5% per year. What will happen to the price level? Do you expect "overshooting" or "undershooting"? Why?

6. *True or false:* If all prices, wages, and other payments were indexed so that they automatically adjusted to changes in the price level, then inflation would have no bad effects.

7. Suppose that checking account balances were the only form of money and that all checking accounts paid the market rate of interest. What would be the optimal rate of inflation?

Refer to Answers to Problem Sets for solution to problem 6.

Chapter Nineteen

The Nature and Scope of Economic Analysis

19.1 The Nature of Economic Analysis

Economics is one of several sciences that attempt to explain and predict human behavior. It is distinguished from the other behavioral sciences (psychology, anthropology, sociology, and political science) by its emphasis on rational decision making under conditions of scarcity. Economists generally assume that people have well-defined goals and preferences, and that they allocate their limited resources so as to maximize their own well-being in accordance with those preferences.

Stages of Economic Analysis

Much of economic analysis can be divided into three stages. First, we make explicit assumptions about people's goals and about the constraints on their behavior. This allows us to formulate an economic problem: Within the limits imposed by the constraints, what is the best way to achieve the goals? Second, we determine the solutions to these problems, and we see

591

how the solutions vary in response to changes in the constraints. We assume that the individuals under study can also solve their economic problems and that they behave accordingly. We describe this by saying that the individuals *optimize*. Third, we examine the interactions among individuals: Each person's behavior affects each other person's constraints. In view of these interactions, we are often able to conclude that there is only one possible outcome in which all individuals are simultaneously optimizing. Such an outcome is called an *equilibrium*.

We shall now examine each of these stages in more detail.

Formulating the Individual's Economic Problem

The first step in economic analysis is to make explicit assumptions about individuals' desires and the nature of the constraints that they face. For example, we assume that a consumer has indifference curves that are concave toward the origin and must select a market basket that is within his budget line. Or we assume that a competitive firm wants to maximize profits and must sell its output and purchase its inputs at fixed market prices. Or we assume that a worker views both leisure and consumption as normal goods, but can consume no more than he earns in the marketplace.

Each of the agents in these examples faces an economic problem: a choice among competing alternatives. The consumer can eat more eggs and drink less wine, or he can eat fewer eggs and drink more wine, but once he has allocated his entire income he cannot have more of both. The firm can reduce its costs by cutting back production, but it must accept a reduction in revenues as the consequence if it does. The worker can earn more income, or he can improve his suntan, but he must choose between the two.

The problem of an economic actor is to decide how to allocate scarce resources among competing ends. Such trade-offs can always be expressed in terms of *costs*, which is another word for forgone opportunities. The cost of eating an egg is forgoing some amount of wine; the cost of increasing a firm's revenues is (at least partly) measured by the price of inputs; the cost of a day's wages is a forgone day at the beach. Therefore we can say that the first step in economic analysis is to make explicit assumptions about both the desirability and the cost of various alternatives.

Optimization

The second step in economic analysis is to solve the agent's economic problem. The solution can typically be expressed in terms of the crucial principle of *equimarginality:* If an activity is worth pursuing at all, then it should be pursued until the marginal cost is equal to the marginal benefit. The consumer should buy eggs until the marginal value of an additional egg is equal to the marginal value of the wine that he could trade it for. (This is another way of saying that he should move along his budget line until it is just tangent to an indifference curve.) The firm should produce until its marginal cost is equal to its marginal revenue. It should select an input combination that equates the marginal product of a dollar's worth of labor to the marginal product of a dollar's worth of capital. The worker should relax until the marginal cost in forgone wages is equal to the marginal benefit of relaxation—or, in other words, he should work until the marginal income from working is equal to the marginal cost in forgone leisure.

The economist assumes that people act according to the principle of equimarginality. This is often expressed by saying that the economist assumes that people are *rational*. Indeed, it has been said that a student becomes a true economist on the day when he fully understands and accepts the principle that people equate costs and benefits at the margin. In Section 19.2 we will address the question of whether the economist's assumption is a reasonable one. Here we will pursue its consequences.

In addition to solving the individual's optimization problem, the economist also asks how the solution would change if the constraints changed. For example, in modeling a consumer's behavior, the economist notes first that the consumer's optimum occurs at a point where the budget line is tangent to an indifference curve, but he is also interested in how this tangency moves when there is a shift in the budget line due to a change in prices or a change in income. Although the real-world consumer needs to choose only a single consumption basket, the economist imagines how the consumer would behave in a variety of hypothetical circumstances and predicts the basket that the consumer would choose in each situation. The consumer's demand curve is an example of the economist's solution to a family of optimization problems. The demand curve in Exhibit 4–5 shows that *if* the price of X is $6, the consumer's optimal basket will contain 2 units of X; *if* the price is $3, his optimal basket will contain 3 units; and so forth.

A competitive firm's supply curve constitutes another example of how the economist expresses his solutions to a family of optimization problems. The point corresponding to a price of P shows that quantity at which the firm can equate marginal cost with marginal revenue, given that it is constrained to sell at the market price of P. As the constraint (that is, the price) varies, so does the solution to the problem (that is, the corresponding quantity).

Equilibrium

Solving the optimization problem tells the economist how people respond to various constraints. In order to predict their behavior, he must still determine what constraints are actually in force. The key here is that each individual's actions affect the options available to others. One of the constraints faced by a competitive firm is that it must not offer its wares at a price higher than consumers will pay. That price is determined by the actions of other firms and of the consumers themselves, all of whom are solving their own optimization problems. Those optimization problems in turn involve constraints that are partly the result of the original firm's actions.

In Section 17.3 we saw the same thing in a slightly different context: Farmer Brown attempts to maximize profit under conditions of uncertainty; the constraints that he faces are the probabilities associated with various market prices; these constraints are themselves determined by the amount of wheat that other farmers bring to market, in other words, by the solutions to other farmers' optimization problems. And the entire process comes full circle, because the optimization problems faced by the other farmers include constraints that are partly the result of the actions of Farmer Brown.

In some sense the various optimization problems being solved by economic agents must have solutions that are compatible with each other. This requirement, known as an *equilibrium condition,* enables the economist to "solve" his model and make predictions about actual behavior. Consumers choose an optimal basket given the market prices that they face; firms supply a profit-maximizing mix of goods given those same market prices. In order for the quantity demanded by consumers to equal the quantity supplied by firms, prices cannot be arbitrary. In many circumstances there is only one equilibrium price that equates supply and demand.

Economists use many different equilibrium conditions. A *Nash equilibrium* is one in which each individual optimizes, taking the actions of other individuals as his constraints. The prisoners of Exhibit 11–5 achieve a Nash equilibrium when both confess. A *Walrasian equilibrium* is one in which each individual optimizes, taking market prices as given. The supply and demand diagrams of Chapter 1 illustrate Walrasian equilibria.

The third step in most economic analyses is the choice of an equilibrium condition and a study of the resulting equilibria: Do any exist? How many are there? How can they be computed? How will they change in response to changes in exogenous variables? (An *exogenous variable* is one that is taken to be determined outside the economic model under consideration. For example, the tastes of consumers and the technology available to firms are often treated as exogenous variables.)[1]

Other Aspects of Economic Analysis

The economic study of human behavior consists largely of analyzing problems in the way we have just described: First, specify agents' goals and the nature of their constraints, second, solve the corresponding optimization problems (usually employing the equimarginal principle), and third, impose an equilibrium condition to find out what particular constraints agents must be facing and to describe their behavior.

Not all economic analysis can be fit into this simple mold, however. For example, economists are often concerned with modeling the process by which an equilibrium is achieved. This is known as the study of *economic*

---

[1]The process of studying how equilibria change in response to changes in exogenous variables is known as *comparative statics.* When you solved Problem 5 at the end of Chapter 1, you were performing an exercise in comparative statics.

dynamics. On the other hand, that process is often most productively viewed as the solution to another, more subtle problem of optimization and equilibrium.

Economics also provides tools for analyzing the desirability of outcomes according to various criteria. The efficiency criterion introduced in Chapter 8 is one of the most popular, but economists can and do consider many other criteria as well.

The Value of Economic Analysis

In this book you have seen many examples of economic models. What do such models teach us? Some economic models are intended to reflect certain aspects of the world with sufficient accuracy to allow the economist to make precise numerical predictions. Such models are obviously of interest to anyone who must make decisions today that will be appropriate tomorrow. The shoemaker wants to know what the price of shoes will be next week; the policymaker wants to know how a tax on gasoline will affect the price of cars, or how a "comparable worth" law will affect the average size of firms.

Often, economic models are insufficient to make numerical predictions, but they do allow us to predict directions of change. Using the economic models in this book, you can predict that a tax on shoes will raise the price of shoes, reduce the quantity of shoes traded, and reduce economic efficiency. You can also predict a range for the possible price rise (at least zero and no more than the amount of the tax). A more precise model, incorporating more information about the supply and demand curves, would allow a more precise prediction, but even the rough prediction of the simple model is obviously of interest.

There is also a large class of economic models whose assumptions and conclusions are essentially untestable. Consider the Edgeworth box of Chapter 8. We used this box to describe the outcome of a situation in which exactly two people trade exactly two goods and are constrained to use the artificial medium of a price system in doing so. Outside of an experimental laboratory, no such situation would ever be observed.

Why, then, does the Edgeworth box interest us? The answer is that economists are often interested in understanding the outcomes of real-world situations involving bargaining. Many of these situations are far too difficult to model precisely or to think about in their entirety. But an economist who has studied a wide variety of bargaining models develops a strong "seat of the pants" intuition for what *sorts* of things are likely to affect the outcome. After years of studying abstract models—each one abstract in its own way—the economist develops a sense that certain factors matter in certain ways and others don't matter at all. This intuition is the most powerful tool an economist has for understanding the world, but he can only develop it by first understanding simplifications of the world such as the Edgeworth box.

For example, consider the proposition that the economic incidence of a tax is independent of its legal incidence. In Chapter 1, we proved this proposition under certain conditions—markets are competitive, all taxes are either sales or excise taxes, taxes are flat rate (5 cents per cup) as opposed to something more complicated, and so forth. Economists have examined the impact of taxation in a wide variety of models, each with its own special assumptions, and keep getting the same result: The legal incidence of taxation does not matter. Not only does the economist observe the pattern here, but he begins to develop an intuition into *why* this result obtains in such a wide variety of circumstances. When the economist is asked to comment on the impact of a complicated taxation scheme in the real world, even though it might be the case that none of his models fits the situation exactly, he can predict with confidence that the legal incidence of the tax is irrelevant. He can do so because he understands why it is irrelevant in his models, and he can see that the same intuition is applicable in the case at hand.

Here is another, more general example: The economist's intuition always reminds him of the importance of incentives. Noneconomists are often skeptical that a rise in the price of gasoline will cause people to drive significantly less, that a tax on labor will reduce employment, or that rent controls will reduce the quantity and quality of housing. The economist knows these things to be true. His knowledge derives largely from his study of models of *other* markets, which have revealed the general principle that incentives matter.

In coming to understand the world by first understanding a potpourri of abstract models, the economist is no different from the physicist or any other scientist. Ask a physicist what will happen to your body if you slam on your brakes while going around a curve at 60 miles per hour. He will tell you, with sufficient accuracy to convince you not to do it. He will do so even if he has never written down or studied the physics of the particular situation you are describing. He is able to do so because he has studied the physics of a large number of models, each of which captures some important aspects of the situation, and has observed the common features of what these models predict. In the process he has developed a feel for the sorts of cause-and-effect relationships that are likely to hold. The kind of knowledge embodied in that "feel" is a large part of any successful science.

19.2 The Rationality Assumption

Models start with assumptions. Economic models start with the assumption of rational behavior, usually in the sense that actors accurately solve their optimization problems so as to maximize their well-being within the limits allowed by the constraints (that is, scarcities) with which they must contend. This assumption characterizes economic models. It is perfectly possible to study human behavior productively without assuming rationality, but then one isn't doing economics.

The Role of Assumptions in Science

Students are often uncomfortable with the assumption of universal rationality. Often they point out that the assumption is clearly false, and they are surprised that their economics professors don't seem particularly concerned about this. But the fact of the matter is that all assumptions made in all sciences are clearly false. Physicists, the most successful of scientists, routinely assume that the table is frictionless when called upon to model the motions of billiard balls. They assume that the billiard balls themselves are solid objects. They assume that objects fall in vacuums. They study the behavior of electric charges that are localized at mathematical points and that interact only with a small number of other charges, as if the rest of the universe did not exist.

All scientists make simplifying assumptions about the world, because the world itself is too complicated to study. All such assumptions are equally false, but not all such assumptions are equally valuable. Certain kinds of assumptions lead consistently to results that are interesting, nonobvious, and at some level testable and verifiable. Other kinds of assumptions do not. In any given problem it is important to make simplifying assumptions of the sort that have proved to be successful in the past. It is usually equally important that the model be *robust*; that is, the exact statements of the assumptions should not enter in a crucial way, so that slightly different assumptions would still lead to the same conclusion.

To a large extent, *learning to be an economist consists of learning to make the right simplifying assumptions.* Indeed, we could replace the word *economist* with *physicist* or *anthropologist* or more generally with *scientist,* and this statement would still be true. Unfortunately, no one has ever succeeded in expressing a set of rules for determining the difference between a good and a bad simplification. You undoubtedly discovered this to your frustration when you began working the problems in this book. Often, the problems require assumptions, and often your assumptions probably seemed as good to you as any others, but your teacher did not agree. If you were successful in the course, you gradually developed a sense for what is and what is not the right approach to a problem. If you go on in economics, you will continue to develop this sense, which is what will make you an economist.

Let us take one more example from physics. Physicists are interested in studying the formation of black holes in space. They are also interested in determining the age of the universe. But the very notion of the "age of the universe" cannot be expressed in any model in which black holes can form.[2] When they want to discuss black-hole formation, physicists freely

---

[2]This footnote is just for the physics students. "The age of the universe" presumes a preferred global time coordinate. In some models such a coordinate is given by the world-lines of the galaxies. But in any such model space-time is foliated by three-dimensional leaves corresponding to the universe at different times, and it can be proved that such leaves must be topologically identical. Therefore singularities cannot appear at any time after the Big Bang.

use models that are explicitly inconsistent with the universe having a well-defined age. When they want to talk about that "age," they freely use models that are inconsistent with black-hole formation. Each model is appropriate to its task. The physicist has learned through experience which kinds of inconsistencies (or falsehoods) he can accept with equanimity and which kinds are dangerous.

All We Really Need: No Unexploited Profit Opportunities

The rationality assumption in economics continues to disturb some students at a far more visceral level than the frictionless planes that are assumed in other sciences. It seems plausible that a world without friction could resemble our own world in important ways, but students find it much more difficult to believe that studying the behavior of perfectly rational individuals could have much to do with understanding the behavior of the people they encounter in their everyday life. This difficulty is particularly pronounced among students who live in dormitories.

It is a misconception, however, to believe that a world in which most people are irrational would have to function very differently from a world in which everyone is rational. Imagine a world in which most people are irrational most of the time, but where enough people are rational enough of the time so that there are *no unexploited profit opportunities*. Such a world would function very similarly to one in which everyone is rational. Rather than give a general argument for this proposition, let us examine an illustrative example.

Example: The Law of One Price

Economists believe in the *law of one price*, which says that identical goods will sell for identical prices (here *identical* means identical in all relevant characteristics, including, for example, time of delivery). It is easy to believe that this law would hold in a world of perfectly rational individuals. But it also holds in a world with no unexploited profit opportunities. Why? Because if you value two identical goods at different prices, your neighbor can make money by selling you one and buying from you the other. In the course of doing this, he and others like him will cause the prices of the goods to change and will keep doing this until all of the profit opportunities have been exploited—that is, until the prices of the goods are equal.

Application: The Pricing of Call Options

You may think that the law of one price is a very trivial sort of example. Yet it can be applied to solve very nontrivial problems. One example is the pricing of *call options*.

A call option is a piece of paper entitling you to buy a share of some specified stock at some future date for some prespecified price. These pieces of paper are traded in organized markets called options markets. Exhibit 19–1 shows an example of a call option.

Exhibit 19–1   A Call Option

> This piece of paper entitles the bearer to purchase ten shares of General Motors stock on January 1, 1995, for a price of $1 per share.

Exhibit 19–2   Values of a Call Option

Value of GM Stock on 1/1/95	Value of Call Option on 1/1/95
$1.50	$5
.50	0

We assume that on January 1, 1995, GM stock will surely sell for either $1.50 or $.50. The table shows the value of the call option from Exhibit 19–1. If the GM stock sells for $1.50, the option allows you to buy 10 shares at $1 apiece and to make a $5 profit. If the GM stock sells for $.50, the call option is worthless.

Suppose that it is now January 1, 1994, and General Motors stock is selling at $1.00 per share. Suppose also that on January 1, 1995, it will surely be selling for either $.50 per share or $1.50 per share. Suppose finally that the going rate of interest is 25%. How much should you pay for the call option?

The first thing to ask is what the option will be worth a year from today. If the stock goes up $1.50, then your option will enable you to purchase 10 shares (worth $15) for a price of $10; in other words, it will be worth $5. If the stock goes down to $.50, then you will choose not to exercise your option, so that it is worth zero. In Exhibit 19–2 we record the possibilities.

What is the call option worth today? You might suspect that this depends on the probability that the value of the stock will go up. You might think that if the stock is almost certain to go up, then the option is worth nearly $5, whereas if it is almost certain to go down, then the option is worth nearly zero. However, this is not correct.

To see why, and to price the call correctly, consider your friend Jeeter, who does not deal in options at all, but who adopts a strategy of borrowing $2 to buy 5 shares of stock. What will Jeeter's investment portfolio be worth a year from today? If the stock goes up, his 5 shares are worth $7.50, from which he must subtract $2.50 in order to repay his $2 debt with interest. In other words, his portfolio is worth $5. If the stock goes down, his 5 shares are worth $2.50, from which he must still subtract $2.50, so his portfolio is worth zero. In other words, *Jeeter's portfolio is identical to your call option* in the sense that it will have the same value as your option regardless of what happens to the price of the stock.

Now, by the law of one price, the call option must sell for the same amount of money that it would take to follow Jeeter's strategy. That strategy requires a net outlay of $3 (he takes in $2 in borrowed funds and lays out $5 to buy the 5 shares of stock). Therefore the call option also sells for $3.

We have just seen a highly streamlined example of the *Black-Scholes Option Pricing Model*,[3] which is used to predict real-world option prices with remarkable accuracy. The model not only assumes that all investors are rational; it also assumes that they are extraordinarily clever: Whenever an option is offered, all of the market participants conjure up imaginary friends with portfolios that are identical to the option in order to price it correctly. In fact, even more is assumed. In the full-blown model, prices change continuously and stocks can go up or down by arbitrary amounts (as opposed to our example, where we allowed only two possible future values). In this case, solving the model requires knowledge of a sophisticated area of mathematics called the "Ito calculus." Most professors of mathematics have never heard of the Ito calculus, but Black and Scholes assume that all investors are whizzes at it.

How can such an unrealistic model possibly make accurate predictions? (If your answer is that it can't, be reminded that it does.) The answer is that although the model appears to invoke universal rationality, its conclusions actually follow from the much weaker assumption that there are no unexploited profit opportunities. The few people in the market smart enough to exploit all of the profit opportunities cause prices to behave as if everyone were perfectly rational—and had a Ph.D. in mathematics besides. The same sort of phenomenon occurs in many economic models.

19.3 **What Is an Economic Explanation?**

Economists like to look for puzzling phenomena and see whether they can be explained on the basis of rational behavior. Explanations that have implications beyond the case at hand are especially desirable, since they can be tested in other circumstances. Here are a few examples.

---

[3]This model first appeared in F. Black and M. Scholes, "The Pricing of Options and Corporate Liabilities," *Journal of Political Economy* 81 (1973), 637–654.

Example: Celebrity Endorsements

Why are there celebrity endorsements? Why is a suit advertised by Johnny Carson worth more than the same suit without a famous name attached to it?

One possible explanation is that buyers are either irrational or very foolish: They don't recognize that endorsements carry no information about product quality and are gulled into believing that because Johnny Carson is a famous and accomplished comedian, any suit that he advertises is likely to be of high quality.

To an economist such an explanation is unsatisfactory. Economists insist on seeking explanations that are grounded in rational behavior. There are two reasons for this insistence. First, on the basis of his past experience, the economist is aware of the power and wide applicability of economic analysis, which presumes rationality. Second, by attempting to extend such analysis into realms where it first appears inapplicable, the economist tests the limits and the durability of his theories.

Imagine a physicist sitting in his garden who notices that a baseball lying on the grass has risen of its own accord and begun to hover three feet off the ground. He could "explain" this phenomenon by abandoning his former insistence on the universality of gravitation, or he could attempt to find an explanation that is consistent with all of his previous experience. His gut will lead him to the second course of action. Perhaps it will eventually turn out that the laws of gravitation *are* wrong, but it is most productive to begin with the assumption that there must be some less radical solution to the problem.

If physicists abandoned their theories so easily, physics could never progress. The first physicist to have observed a helium-filled balloon would have admitted that there was no gravity, and the true physics of the situation would not have been discovered. By attempting to fit unfamiliar phenomena into familiar patterns, we arrive at deeper understandings of both the patterns and the phenomena.

So the economist is unwilling to abandon rationality quite so easily. Another easy "solution" presents itself: Perhaps people have a *taste* for wearing celebrity-endorsed clothing. They don't expect higher quality from the endorsed products; they just like wearing products that have been endorsed.

This solution is marginally better than the first one, but only marginally. The objection is that it's just too easy. Any human action can be explained on the basis of someone's having had a taste for that action. If we allow ourselves this easy out, we will never seek for deeper explanations.

The physicist could explain the floating baseball by saying that all of the laws of gravitation are true, but that this one baseball happens to contain a unique antigravity substance that is activated only at 2 p.m. on Tuesdays (or whatever time the physicist happens to be making his observation). We expect our physicists to work harder for their pay. We should expect the same of our economists.

Here is an *economic* explanation of celebrity endorsements: New firms enter the marketplace with different strategies. Some plan to make a quick killing by selling shoddy products and then getting out. Others plan to offer products of high quality, which is expensive for them at first, and to be successful by earning a good reputation that will pay off in future years. Firms of the second type would like to let you know that they are of the second type. One way for them to do so is to hire a celebrity at a very high price. This conveys the information that the firm plans to be around a long time—long enough to earn back its investment in celebrity advertising.

Whether or not this is the correct explanation, it is at least an economic one. It says that firms and individuals face certain constraints, one of which is the inability of firms to issue binding promises that they are not fly-by-nights, and that they optimize within the limits that these constraints impose. They convey the information expensively, which is better than not conveying it at all.

The explanation also has testable implications, which is an extremely desirable feature. It suggests that firms whose reputations are already well established should invest less in celebrity endorsements than firms that are just starting up, and that firms producing products whose quality is easily verified at the time of purchase should invest less in celebrity endorsements than those firms producing products whose quality is revealed only after a long period of use. Real-world observations can now be used to confirm or contest the theory.

Example: The Size of Shopping Carts

Celebrity endorsements are a puzzle, and economists love puzzles. Another puzzle that is very popular among some economists concerns the size of shopping carts. Shopping carts today are larger than they were 20 years ago. Why?

It has sometimes been suggested that the larger shopping carts constitute an attempt on the part of grocery store managers to induce shoppers to make more purchases. The idea is that shoppers are embarrassed to enter the checkout line with a half-full cart.

Not only does this fail as an economic explanation, it fails as any kind of explanation at all! In order to explain a new phenomenon, one must address the issue of why it arose when it did and not earlier. The "embarrassment" theory is a theory of why shopping carts should always be big, not one of why they should grow bigger.

Here is an economic explanation, which might or might not be correct: Over the past 20 years, large numbers of women have entered the marketplace, and relatively few households now have a member who engages in housework (including shopping) on a full-time basis. Therefore people want to allocate less time to shopping and they accomplish this by reducing the number of trips to the store, while buying in larger quantities each time they go. Hence the need for larger shopping carts.

Example: Why Is There Mandatory Retirement?

In 1986 the U.S. Congress severely restricted the practice of mandatory retirement. The fact that it was necessary to pass legislation to curtail this practice is an indication of its popularity. What made mandatory retirement so popular?

Professor Edward Lazear raised this question in a 1979 article,[4] in which he examined the inadequacies of various traditional explanations. Most of those traditional explanations rely on the assertion that workers' productivity declines significantly after a certain age and that employers deal with this through mandatory retirement. However, this cannot be a complete explanation. Among workers of any given age, there is wide variability in productivity. Employers do not refuse to hire the less productive workers; they simply pay them lower wages. Thus "low productivity" cannot be a full explanation of why employers want to eliminate older workers completely.

Lazear offers an alternative explanation of mandatory retirement. Suppose that a worker is employed by a given firm for his entire working life. In competition, the worker will receive a stream of wages whose present value is equal to the present value of his lifetime marginal product. There are many ways in which he can receive this stream of wages. Under Plan A the worker might be paid $20,000 each year, whereas under Plan B he receives less than $20,000 in some years and more than $20,000 in other years. Both the firm and the worker will be indifferent between Plan A and Plan B provided the two streams of wages have the same present value.

Now suppose that the worker agrees to acquire special skills that involve working harder but make him worth $30,000 per year to the company. In exchange for this, the firm pays him a higher wage, and both parties benefit. However, there is a catch: There is no way for the worker to guarantee in advance that he will really perform as promised. If he is paid on Plan A and if his salary is raised from $20,000 per year to $29,000 per year, the firm must be concerned that he will work at the old level of effort for a year, collect the $29,000, and then skip town.

Suppose, alternatively, that the worker is paid under a form of Plan B in which he is paid much less than his marginal product when he is young and much more than his marginal product when he is old. Now the contract to acquire special skills is enforceable: The worker must actually perform before he is compensated. The firm has its guarantee, and both parties benefit since the mutually beneficial contract can now be enforced.

Only one problem remains. The worker agrees to be paid less than he is worth to the firm while he is young in exchange for being paid more than he is worth when he is old. The firm will agree to such an arrangement only if it has a definite ending date. Hence the need for mandatory retirement.

---

[4]Edward Lazear, "Why Is There Mandatory Retirement?" *Journal of Political Economy* 87 (1979), 1261–1284.

You are invited to consider this explanation of the prevalence of mandatory retirement in light of Lazear's criticisms of other explanations. To what extent does Lazear's explanation avoid those problems? To what new criticisms is it susceptible? Is it, on balance, an improvement over other theories? Can you advance a new theory that makes even more sense?

Notice that if Lazear's story, or anything like it, is true, then both employers and employees benefit from mandatory retirement. It is true that any employee approaching his retirement would prefer to be allowed to continue working. But it is also true that the same employee, at the beginning of his working life and taking into account his entire lifetime earnings, is better off when he can commit himself to accepting mandatory retirement than when he cannot. The abolition of mandatory retirement reduces the ability of workers to offer guarantees of performance, reduces the willingness of firms to pay for such guarantees, and thereby reduces both the lifetime productivity and the lifetime compensation of workers.

There is an important moral to be drawn here: In evaluating public policy toward a social institution, it is necessary first to ask why that institution arose. It is impossible to know whether mandatory retirement is a good or a bad thing—by *any* criterion—without knowing why it exists in the first place. Social practices do not arise in vacuums; they arise because somebody finds them useful. It is incumbent upon the critic of these practices to understand who finds them useful and why before discarding them.

Example: "99¢ Pricing"

We close with one more example of an attempt to offer an economic explanation of an apparently "irrational" phenomenon. Consider the following letter to Ann Landers:

Dear Ann Landers: I read your letter to E.A. in Riverside, the man who wanted to know why stores charge odd prices, such as 99 cents, $1.99, $29.99, etc. You answered: "It's a sales gimmick that's been around forever."

I am a 10-year-old boy and I think I have a better answer.

Around 1875, Melville Stone owned a newspaper named the *Chicago Daily News.* The price was a penny. Circulation was good, but after a while it began to drop off. He found that it was because pennies were in short supply.

Mr. Stone persuaded Chicago merchants to sell their merchandise for a penny below the regular price. This put more pennies in circulation and it helped save the paper.

My source is: "Why Didn't I Think of That?" by Webb Garrison.—N.C. Reader

Dear N.C.: When I receive a letter like this from a 10-year-old boy, it gives me fresh hope for the youth of this country. Thanks for writing.[5]

---

[5]Ann Landers, Los Angeles Times Syndicate. Reprinted with permission.

Ann's own explanation ("It's a sales gimmick . . ."), which is also the explanation given by most noneconomists, relies on irrational consumers and therefore doesn't conform to the rules of the economic game. Unfortunately, her correspondent's explanation is far worse, since it makes no sense from any point of view, economic or not. The child psychologist Jean Piaget has determined that most children begin to master the principle of conservation at about age 7. By the age of 8, they understand, for example, that when water is poured from a short thick container into a tall thin container, the quantity of water does not change. One might then expect a 10-year-old to recognize that when a penny changes hands, there are neither more nor fewer pennies in circulation than there were previously.

Here is a suggestion for an economic explanation of how the pricing scheme in question developed. Around the same time that Melville Stone was trying to boost the circulation of the *Chicago Daily News*, the cash register was invented. It was now much easier for store owners to prevent their employees from stealing, because the register kept records of each purchase. However, a sale is recorded only when the register is opened, which would be necessary only if it were required to make change. A clerk can quietly slip a $20 bill into his pocket if the price of the item is $20, but he must ring up the sale and open the register if he has to give a penny in change.

19.4 The Scope of Economic Analysis

We began this chapter by saying that economics is the science that studies human behavior by positing rational action in the face of constraints. Traditionally, such reasoning was applied primarily to the trading of goods and services in the marketplace. However, in the last 30 years it has become clear that the economic way of thinking can be productively applied to a wide range of activities both in and out of the marketplace. Economists study love and marriage, the structure of families, medieval agriculture, religious activity, cannibalism, and evolution. By extending their methods into such areas, many of which are dominated by actors who are traditionally supposed to be engaged in nonrational behavior, economists have demonstrated the power of their approach. In this section we will summarize a few of the most exciting nontraditional applications of economics.

Laboratory Animals as Rational Agents

In a series of remarkable experiments, a group of researchers[6] has demonstrated that laboratory animals respond to economic stimuli in the ways that economic theory would predict.

---

[6]J. H. Kagel, R. Battalio, H. Rachlin, L. Green, R. Basmann, and W. R. Klemm, "Experimental Studies of Consumer Demand Behavior Using Laboratory Animals," *Economic Inquiry* 13 (1975), 22–38. Also R. Battalio, L. Green, and J. H. Kagel, "Income–Leisure Tradeoffs of Animal Workers," *American Economic Review* 71 (1981), 621–632.

Exhibit 19–3   Rats as Rational Consumers

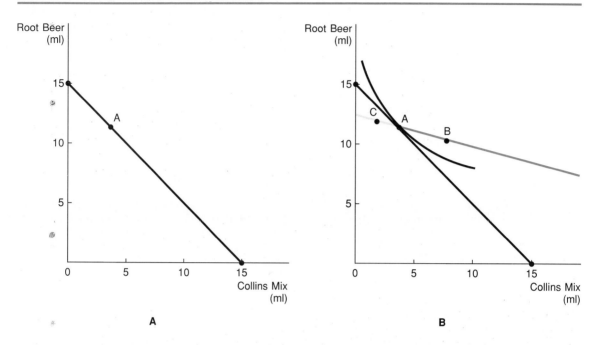

In panel A a rat with the black budget line chose point A. Prices and his income were then adjusted so that he now had the colored budget line in panel B. According to economic theory, the rat must now choose a point like B (on the darker part of the new line) rather than a point like C (on the lighter part). The reason is that if an indifference curve were tangent at C, it would have to cross the original indifference curve. In fact, the rat chose point B, confirming the economic prediction.

Rats as Consumers

In one experiment rats were permitted to "purchase" root beer and collins mix by pressing levers that caused the liquids to be dispensed. The rats were given fixed incomes (for example, 300 lever pushes per day) and prices (for example, one lever push generates .05 ml of root beer or .1 ml of collins mix). Their consumption patterns were noted. Then the rats' incomes and the prices they faced were varied, so that their behavior could be observed under a variety of budget constraints. The rats' behavior demonstrated downward-sloping demand curves and upward-sloping Engel curves, as an economist would expect.

Moreover, the rats' consumption patterns were internally consistent in the sense predicted by economic theory. For example, panel A of Exhibit 19–3 illustrates one rat's consumption point when given an income of 300 lever presses and facing prices of 1 press per .05 ml for both liquids. The rat chose point A. His income and prices were then adjusted to give him the colored budget line shown in panel B. If the rat was a rational maximizer, with an indifference curve tangent to the first budget line at A, then his

Exhibit 19–4 **Pigeons and Labor Supply**

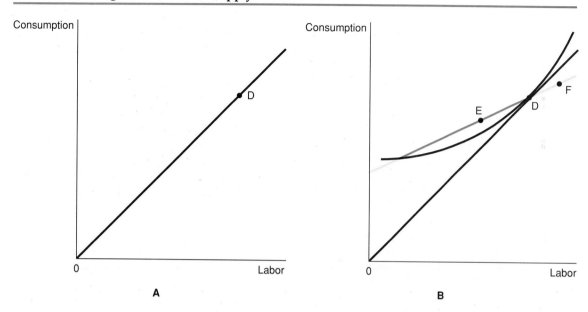

In panel A a pigeon with the black budget line chose point D. His wage and his nonlabor income were then adjusted so that he had the colored budget line. According to economic theory, the pigeon must now choose a point like E (on the darker part of the new line) rather than a point like F (on the lighter part). The reason is that if an indifference curve were tangent at F, it would have to cross the original indifference curve. In fact, the pigeon chose point E, confirming the economic prediction.

new optimum would have to occur at a point below A on the new budget line. In fact, he chose point B, confirming this prediction.

Pigeons as Suppliers of Labor

In a later experiment, pigeons were required to earn their incomes (in this case food) by pecking a response key. Their behavior was observed under variations in both wage rates (amount of food per peck) and nonlabor income (free food delivered at regular intervals). The pigeons demonstrated all of the expected substitution and income effects. In particular, when their nonlabor income was fixed, their labor supply curves were backward bending, as you would expect after having read Section 15.1 of this book.

In one version of the experiment, pigeons were initially presented with no nonlabor income, so that their budget line was as shown in panel A of Exhibit 19–4. They chose point D. Then their wages were lowered, while they were simultaneously given just enough nonlabor income to give them the colored budget line shown in panel B. Assuming that the pigeons are rational maximizers, they must now choose a point on the darker portion of the colored line, such as point E, and, in fact, they do so.

Often noneconomists argue that economists are far too optimistic in their assumption that people have sufficient intelligence to respond appropriately to subtle changes in prices and income. The next time you find yourself in conversation with such a noneconomist, you can ask him whether he thinks that most human beings are as intelligent as rats and pigeons.

Altruism and the Selfish Gene

There is a growing literature on the interface and analogies between economics and biology.[7] One area of mutual interest is the study of *altruism.* Economists have long been aware that people choose to give gifts to others, especially to their children and other close relatives. Perhaps you would not be in college if it weren't for this phenomenon. Such behavior can be explained by saying that people have a "taste" for it, but as we have noted before, economists are distinctly uncomfortable with this kind of glibness. So we must look deeper.

Recently, biologists have begun to explore the notion that altruism is a result of purely selfish (nonaltruistic) behavior on the part of the genetic material that is the true medium for natural selection. If you are carrying a certain gene, then there is a 50% chance that your child is carrying the same gene. The gene's survival probability is enhanced if you behave in a way that improves the survival prospects of your children. Now suppose that some particular gene has the effect of making you feel altruistic toward your children. Then that gene will gain an evolutionary advantage and tend to propagate.[8]

Economists have explored some of the consequences of altruistic behavior in the family. For example, suppose that the household is headed by an altruistic parent who gives bequests to the children in such a way as to equalize the children's "incomes," where these incomes include all of the things that are important to a child. If one child is more satisfied than the others, then the parent will tend to give more attention, presents, and so forth to the other children (and consequently less to the satisfied one) until the situation becomes more equal.

Now suppose that the family contains a "rotten kid" who is thinking of stealing his sister's marbles. Suppose also that the theft of the marbles would be economically inefficient, either because he values them less than she does or because some marbles are likely to be lost in the struggle over their ownership. The Rotten Kid might be deterred from stealing the

---

[7]See, for example, J. Hirshleifer, "Economics from a Biological Viewpoint," *Journal of Law and Economics* 20 (1977),1–52; and G. Tullock, "Biological Externalities," *Journal of Theoretical Biology* 33 (1971), 565–576.

[8]For a fascinating account of this fascinating approach to biology, see R. Dawkins, *The Selfish Gene* (New York: Oxford University Press, 1976). The book's proposed explanations of puzzles in animal behavior are very much in the spirit of economics.

marbles if he feared being found out and punished by the parent. But more remarkably, he will not steal the marbles even if the parent is totally unable to observe or discover the theft. The reason is that the reduction in his sister's level of satisfaction will cause the parent to divert resources to the sister and away from the Rotten Kid, even though the parent has no idea of the reason why the sister has seemed so unhappy lately. The economic inefficiency of the theft means that there will be a smaller social surplus to divide among the children, and an equal share of a smaller pie is not an improvement from the Rotten Kid's own point of view.

This "Rotten Kid theorem" is due to Professor Gary S. Becker, whose book on the economic analysis of family life[9] is a highly recommended (but somewhat technically sophisticated) source of novel and clever economic argument.

The analysis of altruism is by no means a frivolous pursuit. The extent to which parents care about their children's welfare is an important component in understanding savings behavior, responses to taxation, and responses to government debt. (For example, see the discussion of the Ricardian Equivalence Theorem in Chapter 16.) Ultimately, the economic analysis of these important variables (which in turn are critical in the determination of the interest rate and the rate of inflation, among other things) must rest on an understanding of behavior in the household.

The Economics of Scattering

In medieval Europe many small farmers held their land in scattered plots. This means that a typical farmer would own three or four small plots of land at considerable distances from each other. Historians and economists are puzzled by this phenomenon, which seems to entail unnecessary inefficiencies. (Here is an inefficiency you might not have thought of: With so many small plots, there are many more boundaries between neighbors, and consequently many more externalities. Farmers sometimes remove rocks from their own land near the boundary and toss them onto their neighbor's land. With scattering, almost all land is near a boundary, and a lot of energy gets spent tossing rocks back and forth.)

Many explanations have been offered for scattering. Professor Donald McCloskey[10] has examined these explanations and found them wanting from the economist's viewpoint (he is also the source of the parenthetical observation in the preceding paragraph). He has suggested an alternative. Farming communities are subject to localized disasters. Wind, rain, or fire

---

[9]G. S. Becker, *A Treatise on the Family* (Cambridge, MA: Harvard University Press, 1981).

[10]D. McCloskey, "The Open Fields of England: Rent, Risk and the Rate of Interest, 1300–1815," in D. Galenson, ed., *Markets in History: Economic Studies of the Past,* (Cambridge University Press, 1989). This article makes fascinating reading, and applies many of the ideas you have learned in this course both to draw striking conclusions about the past and to refute alternative theories.

can destroy all of the crops in one part of town while leaving those in other parts untouched. If there is no organized market for insurance, a rational farmer will be willing to accept the inefficiencies of scattering in exchange for the corresponding reduction in risk. With scattered plots, he will grow less in the average year, but he is much less likely to face a year in which all of his crops are destroyed.

It is sometimes argued that medieval and modern man differ so radically that the economic models developed in the nineteenth and twentieth centuries for understanding behavior in industrialized societies are not useful tools in the study of the distant past. McCloskey's work indicates the opposite: Peasants in the Middle Ages were willing to pay a price for a reduction in risk just as economic theory would predict (see Chapter 17 of this book), and the price that they were willing to pay was a reasonable one, given the risks involved.

If economic theory applies to rats and pigeons, then surely we should expect it to apply to human beings in situations very different from our own. The scope of economic analysis is being extended every day. This is an exciting time to be studying economics.

Problem Set

1. Reexamine Problem 11 at the end of Chapter 3. What agents are involved in this problem? What are they maximizing and what are their constraints? When you work the problem, at what point are you solving an optimization problem? At what point are you computing an equilibrium?

2. Look back at various other problems in this book. Which are primarily concerned with optimization problems? Which with equilibria? Which with both?

3. *Suppose that General Motors stock is currently selling for $S per share, that one year from today it will either have gone up to $U or down to $D, and that the annual interest rate is r. You are offered a call option that will allow you to buy GM stock next year at a price of $C, where C is between U and D. In terms of S, U, D, r, and C, what is the value of this call option?

4. *True or false:* Television sets will be more expensive in an area with great reception and lots of channels than in an area served by only one channel, which comes in poorly.

5. Why do banks construct elaborate buildings with Greek columns? Does your explanation show why supermarkets don't do the same thing? Does it predict which banks are most likely to construct such buildings?

---

*Denotes a problem that is rather difficult.

6. *Good Housekeeping* tests products and awards its Seal of Approval to those found to be of high quality. Manufacturers who have been judged worthy of the seal must still pay to display it. By being selective about how it awards the seal, the magazine has acquired a reputation for trustworthiness, which makes the seal a valuable commodity. Consider the proposition that Johnny Carson awards the use of his name in the same selective way that *Good Housekeeping* awards its seal, and that his endorsement is valuable for that reason. Contrast this proposition with the explanation offered in the chapter. In what ways does one seem more reasonable than the other? What could you observe in the real world to test the truth of either proposition?

7. Evaluate the explanation of mandatory retirement given in the chapter.

8. Criticize the explanation of "99 cent pricing" given in the chapter. Can you think of an alternative economic explanation? What could you observe in the real world to help establish or refute the validity of the text's explanation?

9. Criticize the Rotten Kid theorem.

10. Suppose that McCloskey's theory of scattering is correct. What exogenous social developments would tend to reduce the preponderance of scattering? How would the amount of scattering be related to the interest rate?

11. Consider the following alternative theory of scattering: Every time a farmer dies, his land is divided among his children, creating several small plots. Whenever there is a marriage, the ownership of several of these plots becomes merged. What flaws are there in this theory? Is it consistent with rational behavior on the part of the peasants? Is it more or less plausible from that point of view than McCloskey's theory?

In the remaining problems, construct theories to explain the phenomena described. Try to base your theories on rational behavior. In each case describe some additional predictions of your theory, and present some ways that you could use real-world observations to test it.

12. Women spend more on medical care than men do.

13. Major rock concerts predictably sell out well in advance of the event, but the promoters don't raise the ticket prices.

14. Blockbuster movies generate long lines at the ticket counter, but theater owners don't raise prices for blockbusters.

15. Firms lay off workers rather than reduce their salaries.

16. When workers go on strike, the firm loses profits and the workers lose wages. If the strike were called off, the two parties would have a bigger pie to divide between them. Nevertheless, there are strikes.

17. People prefer to bet on the sports teams they are rooting for than on the opposing teams.

18. Following an earthquake, sales of earthquake insurance go up.

19. Some items are sold in English auctions (where the item is offered for sale at a low price and buyers bid the price up until only one buyer is left). Others are sold in Dutch auctions (where the item is offered at a high price and the seller calls out successively lower prices until a buyer steps in).

    Can you construct a theory that will predict which sort of auction will be used for which sort of item? Does your theory take into account the incentives that buyers have to attend the auction in the first place?

20. Many societies have strict taboos against baby selling.

21. People voluntarily leave tips in restaurants, even when they know they won't be returning.

22. People give to charitable organizations and to political causes.

23. Over half the electorate turns out to vote for presidential elections, even though the probability of any individual's changing the outcome is negligibly small.

24. Car manufacturers will sometimes offer a $500 rebate on a new car rather than take $500 off the sales price. This is so even though reducing the price would lower the sales tax and thus benefit the consumer by more than $500.

25. *(This problem is due to Marvin Goodfriend.)* Governments are engaged in the business of redistributing income through the tax system. At the same time, private individuals are prohibited by law from redistributing income (via strong arm tactics, breaking and entering, extortion, and the like). Thus the government maintains and enforces a monopoly in the income redistribution market, and there is a general agreement, among both economists and noneconomists, that this is a good thing. But economists generally oppose government monopolies in other areas, such as the postal service. Are they being inconsistent?

Glossary

Absolute price The number of dollars that can be exchanged for a specified quantity of a given good.

Accounting profits Total revenue minus those costs that an accountant would consider; this excludes the opportunity costs of resources owned by the firm.

Adverse selection The problem that arises when people know more about their own risk characteristics than an insurer does.

Agent Someone hired by a principal; alternatively, this term is sometimes used to describe any individual who makes economic decisions.

Average cost Total cost divided by quantity.

Average variable cost Variable cost divided by quantity.

Bertrand model A model of oligopoly in which firms take their rivals' prices as given.

Bond A promise to pay at some time in the future.

Borrower Someone who demands more for current consumption than he supplies.

Budget line The set of all baskets that the consumer can afford, given prices and his income.

Capital Physical assets used as factors of production; goods used to produce future consumption, as opposed to being consumed in the present.

Capital asset pricing model A model that assumes that investors care only about expected return and risk, where risk is measured by standard deviation.

Cartel A group of firms engaged in collusion.

Coase Theorem In the absence of transactions costs, all externalities are internalized, regardless of the assignment of property rights.

Collusion An agreement among firms to set prices and outputs.

Common law The system of legal precedents that has evolved from court decisions.

Common property Property without a well-defined owner.

Comparative advantage The ability to perform a given task at a lower cost.

Compensated demand curve A curve showing how much of a good would be consumed at each possible price if the consumer were income-compensated for all price changes.

Compensating differential A wage adjustment that comes about in equilibrium to compensate for a particularly pleasant or unpleasant aspect of a job.

Competitive equilibrium A point that everyone will choose to trade to, for some appropriate market prices.

Competitive industry An industry in which all firms are competitive and any firm can freely enter or exit.

Complements in production Two factors with the property that an increase in the employment of one raises the marginal product of the other.

Composite-Good Convention The lumping together of all goods but one into a single portmanteau good.

Constant cost industry An industry in which the long-run average cost curve is flat; that is, an industry that produces subject to constant returns to scale.

Constant returns to scale A condition where increasing all input levels by the same proportion leads to a proportionate increase in output.

Consumer price index (CPI) The price index officially reported by the U.S. Department of Labor.

Consumer's surplus The consumer's gain from trade; the amount by which the value of his purchases exceeds what he actually pays for them.

Consumption All goods other than leisure.

Consumption goods Goods that individuals want to consume. *Also called* outputs.

Contestable market A market in which firms can enter and exit costlessly.

Contract curve The set of Pareto-optimal points.

Contributory negligence A plaintiff's failure to take precautions whose cost is less than the damage caused by an accident multiplied by the probability that the accident will occur.

Convex Bowed in toward the origin, like the curves in panel A of Exhibit 3–7.

Corner solution An optimum occurring on one of the axes when there is no tangency between the budget line and an indifference curve.

Cost A forgone opportunity.

Coupon bond A bond that promises a series of payments on different dates.

Cournot model A model of oligopoly in which firms take their rivals' output as given.

Creative response A response to a regulation that conforms to the letter of the law while undermining its spirit.

Deadweight loss A reduction in social gain.

Decreasing cost industry An industry in which the long-run average cost curve is downward sloping; that is, an industry that produces subject to increasing returns to scale.

Decreasing returns to scale A condition where increasing all input levels by the same proportion leads to a less than proportionate increase in output.

Default risk The possibility that the issuer of a bond will not meet his obligations.

Demand A family of numbers that lists the quantity demanded corresponding to each possible price.

Demand curve A graph illustrating demand, with prices on the vertical axis and quantities demanded on the horizontal axis.

Derived demand Demand for an input, which depends on conditions in the output market.

Diminishing marginal returns to labor The circumstance in which each unit of labor has a smaller marginal product than the last.

Discount The face value of a bond minus its current price.

Discount rate The MRS between current and future consumption, minus 1.

Dissipation of rents The elimination of social gains due to overuse of common property. *Also called* tragedy of the commons.

Diversify To reduce risk.

Dividends Streams of benefits.

Economic profits Total revenue minus total cost.

Edgeworth box A certain diagrammatic representation of an economy with two individuals, two goods, and no production.

Effective price ceiling A price ceiling set below the equilibrium price.

Efficiency criterion A normative criterion according to which one policy is better than another if it creates more social gain.

Efficient market A market in which prices fully reflect all available information.

Efficient portfolio A portfolio in the efficient set.

Efficient set The northwest boundary of the set of all portfolios.

Endowment The basket of goods that somebody starts with, prior to any trading.

Endowment point The point representing the initial holdings of an individual in an Edgeworth box.

Engel curve A curve showing, for fixed prices, the quantity of X consumed (on the vertical axis) at each level of income (on the horizontal axis).

Entry price The minimum output price that would cause a firm to enter a given industry.

Envy-free allocation An outcome in which nobody would prefer to trade baskets with anybody else.

Equimarginal principle Principle that an activity should be pursued to the point where marginal cost equals marginal benefit.

Ex ante Determined before the state of the world is known.

Expansion path The set of tangencies between isoquants and isocosts.

Expected return The expected value of returns.

Expected value The average value over all states of the world, with each state weighted by its probability.

Ex post Determined after the state of the world is known.

External costs and benefits Costs and benefits imposed on others. *Also called* externalities.

Face value The amount that a bond promises to pay.

Factor-price effect The effect that an expansion of

industry output has on the price of a factor of production, thereby raising marginal costs in the industry.

Factors of production Goods that are used to produce outputs. *Also called* productive inputs.

Fair odds Odds that reflect the true probabilities of various states of the world.

Fair trade A practice by which the producer of a product sets a retail price and forbids any retailer to sell below that price. *Also called* resale price maintenance.

Fall in demand A decision by demanders to buy a smaller quantity at each given price.

Firm An entity that produces and sells goods, with the goal of maximizing its profits.

First-degree price discrimination Charging each customer the most he would be willing to pay for each item that he buys.

Fishery Common property.

Fixed cost A cost that does not vary with the level of output.

Fixed factor of production One that the firm must employ in a given quantity.

Free riders People who benefit from the actions of others and therefore have reduced incentives to engage in those actions themselves.

Futures contract A contract to deliver a specified good at a specified future date for a specified price.

Futures market The market for futures contracts.

General equilibrium analysis A way of modeling the economy so as to take account of all markets at once, and of all the interactions among them.

Giffen good A good for which the demand curve slopes upward.

Goods Items of which the consumer would prefer to have more rather than less.

Good Samaritan Rule A bystander has no duty to rescue a stranger in distress.

Gross marginal product of capital (GMPK) The amount of additional future consumption generated by an additional unit of capital.

Horizontal integration A merger of firms that produce the same product.

Human capital Productive skills.

Income effect When the price of a good changes, that part of the effect on quantity demanded that results from the change in real income.

Income elasticity of demand The percentage change in consumption that results from a 1 percent increase in income.

Increasing cost industry An industry in which the long-run average cost curve is eventually upward sloping; that is, an industry that produces subject to eventually decreasing returns to scale.

Increasing marginal cost The condition where each additional unit of an activity is more expensive than the last.

Increasing returns to scale A condition where increasing all input levels by the same proportion leads to a more than proportionate increase in output.

Indifference curve A collection of baskets all of which the consumer considers equally desirable.

Inferior good A good that the consumer chooses to consume less of when his income goes up.

Inflation A continuous rise in the price level.

Interest rate The relative price of current consumption in terms of future consumption, minus 1.

Internalize To treat an external cost as a private cost.

Intertemporal substitution Adjusting work and vacation times so as to be working when wages are highest.

Invested Used as capital.

Investors Buyers of risky assets.

Isocost The set of all baskets of inputs that can be employed at a given cost.

Labor income effect The income effect of a wage change due to the change in the worker's labor income.

Labor theory of value The assertion that the value of an object is determined by the amount of labor involved in its production.

Laspeyres price index A price index based on the basket consumed in the earlier period.

Law of demand The observation that when the price of a good goes up, people will buy less of that good.

Law of large numbers When a gamble is repeated many times, the average outcome is the expected value.

Leisure All activities other than labor.

Lender Someone who supplies more for current consumption than he demands.

Liable Legally responsible to compensate another party for damage.

Long run A period of time over which all factors are variable.

Long-run average cost Long-run total cost divided by quantity.

Long-run marginal cost That part of long-run total cost attributable to the last unit produced.

Long-run supply curve A curve that shows what quantity the firm will supply in the long run in response to any given price.

Long-run total cost The cost of producing a given amount of output when the firm is able to operate on its expansion path.

Marginal benefit The additional benefit gained from the last unit of an activity.

Marginal cost The additional cost associated with the last unit of an activity.

Marginal product of labor The additional output due to employing one more unit of labor (with capital employment held fixed).

Marginal rate of substitution (MRS) between X and Y. The value of a consumer's last unit of X, measured by the number of additional units of Y that would just compensate him for its loss.

Marginal rate of technical substitution of labor for capital The amount of capital that can be substituted for one unit of labor, holding output constant.

Marginal revenue product of labor The additional revenue that a firm earns when it employs one more unit of labor.

Marginal value The marginal rate of substitution of X for All Other Goods, often measured in dollars.

Market line The line through a risk-free asset and tangent to the efficient set.

Market portfolio The point of tangency between the market line and the efficient set.

Market power or **monopoly power** The ability of a firm to affect market prices through its actions. A firm has monopoly power if and only if it faces a downward-sloping demand curve.

Mature A bond is said to mature on the date on which it promises payment.

Money income Income measured in terms of money. *Also called* nominal income.

Monopolistic competition The theory of markets in which there are many similar but differentiated products.

Monopsonist A buyer who faces an upward-sloping supply curve.

Moral hazard The incentive for an individual to take more risks when he is insured.

More efficient Having a comparative advantage; preferred according to the efficiency criterion; able to perform a given task at lower cost.

Natural monopoly An industry in which each firm's average cost curve is decreasing at the point where it crosses market demand.

Negative externalities External costs.

Negligence A defendant's failure to take precautions whose cost is less than the damage caused by an accident multiplied by the probability that the accident will occur.

Net demander of labor Someone who demands more labor than he supplies.

Net marginal product of capital (MPK) The GMPK minus 1.

Net supplier of labor Someone who supplies more labor than he demands.

Nominal Measured in terms of money.

Nominal rate of interest The relative price of current dollars in terms of future dollars, minus 1.

Nonexcludable good A good that, if consumed by one person, is automatically available to others.

Nonlabor income Income from sources other than wages.

Nonlabor income effect The income effect of a wage change due to the change in the value of the productive assets other than labor that the worker owns.

Nonrivalrous good A good that, if consumed by one person, can be provided to others at no additional cost.

Normal good A good that the consumer chooses to consume more of when his income goes up.

Oligopoly An industry in which individual firms can influence market conditions.

Optimum The most preferred of the baskets on the budget line.

Outputs Goods that individuals want to consume. *Also called* consumption goods.

Overshooting A percentage increase in the price level that exceeds the percentage increase in the money supply.

Paasche price index A price index based on the basket consumed in the later period.

Pareto criterion A normative criterion according to which one policy is better than another only if every individual agrees that it is preferable.

Pareto-optimal policy A policy to which no other policy is Pareto-preferred.

Pareto-preferred Preferred by every individual.

Perfectly competitive firm One that can sell any quantity it wants to at some going market price.

Perpetuity A bond that promises to pay a fixed amount periodically forever.

Pigou tax A tax equal to the amount of an externality. *Also called* Pigovian tax.

Point of diminishing marginal returns A level of employment beyond which there are diminishing marginal returns.

Portfolios Combinations of risky assets.

Positive externalities External benefits.

Predatory pricing Setting an artificially low price so as to damage rival firms.

Present value Relative price in terms of current consumption.

Price ceiling A maximum price at which a product can be legally sold.

Price discrimination Charging different prices for identical items.

Price elasticity of demand The percentage change in consumption that results from a 1% increase in price.

Price index A measure of the cost of living, based on changes in the cost of some basket of goods.

Price level The price of goods in terms of money.

Principal Someone who pays someone else to behave in a certain way.

Principal-Agent problem The inability of the principal to verify the behavior of the agent.

Private marginal costs Those costs of a decision that are borne by the decision maker.

Producer's surplus The producer's gain from trade; the amount by which his revenue exceeds his variable costs of production.

Product differentiation The production of a product that is unique but has many close substitutes.

Production function The rule for determining how much output can be produced with a given basket of inputs.

Productive inputs Goods that are used to produce outputs. *Also called* factors of production.

Profit The amount by which revenue exceeds costs.

Property right The right to decide how some resource shall be used.

Public good A good where one person's consumption increases the consumption available for others.

Quantity demanded The amount of a good that a given individual or group of individuals will choose to consume at a given price.

Quasi-rents Producers' surplus earned in the short run by factors that are supplied inelastically in the short run.

Rational expectations Expectations that, when held by market participants, lead to behavior that fulfills those expectations on average.

Real Measured in terms of goods.

Real balances The value of money holdings in terms of goods.

Real income Income measured in terms of goods.

Real rate of interest The relative price of present consumption goods in terms of future consumption goods, minus 1.

Region of mutual advantage The set of points that are Pareto-preferred to the initial endowment.

Regressive factor A factor with the property that an increase in its wage rate lowers the firm's long-run marginal cost curve.

Relative price The quantity of some other good that can be exchanged for a specified quantity of a given good.

Rent A payment made by the firm to hire a factor of production. When the firm and the factor are owned by the same person, we imagine the firm paying the factor its opportunity cost and count this as a rent. Also: payments to a factor of production in excess of the minimum payments necessary to call it into existence. In other words, the producer's surplus earned by the factor.

Rental rate The price of hiring capital.

Representative agent Someone whose tastes and assets are representative of the entire economy.

Resale price maintenance A practice by which the producer of a product sets a retail price and forbids any retailer to sell below that price. *Also called* fair trade.

Respondent superior The liability of an employer for torts committed by his employees.

Returns Gains to the holder of a financial asset, including dividends and increases in the asset's value.

Revenue The proceeds collected by a firm when it sells its products.

Ricardian Equivalence Theorem The statement that government borrowing has no effect on wealth, consequently no effect on the demand for current consumption, and consequently no effect on the interest rate.

Rise in demand A decision by demanders to buy a larger quantity at each given price.

Risk-averse Always preferring the least risky among baskets with the same expected value.

Risk-free Having the same value in any state of the world.

Riskiness Variation in potential outcomes.

Risk-neutral Caring only about expected value.

Risk-preferring Always preferring the most risky

among baskets with the same expected value.

Risk premium Additional interest, in excess of the market rate, that a bondholder receives to compensate him for default risk.

Scale effect When the price of an input changes, that part of the effect on employment that results from changes in the firm's output.

Second-degree price discrimination Charging the same customer different prices for identical items.

Seigniorage The gain to authorities who can print money and spend it to buy goods.

Short run A period of time over which some factors are fixed.

Short-run production function The rule for determining how much output can be produced with a given amount of labor input in the short run (with capital employment held fixed).

Short-run supply curve A curve that shows what quantity the firm will supply in the short run in response to any given price.

Shutdown price The output price below which the firm could no longer cover its average variable costs and would therefore shut down.

Signal An activity that does not directly produce anything socially productive but that conveys information about one's talents, so that it is privately rewarding.

Signaling equilibrium An equilibrium in which some people engage in signaling and there is no incentive for anyone to change his behavior.

Social gain The sum of the gains from trade to all participants. *Also called* welfare gain.

Social marginal costs All of the costs of a decision, including the private costs imposed on others.

Speculator One who attempts to earn profits in the futures market by predicting future changes in supply or demand.

Spot market The market for goods for immediate delivery.

Spot price Price in the spot market.

Standard deviation A precise measure of risk.

State of the world A potential set of conditions.

Strict liability Liability that exists regardless of whether the defendant has been negligent.

Substitutes in production Two factors with the property that an increase in the employment of one lowers the marginal product of the other.

Substitution effect When the price of a good changes, that part of the effect on quantity demanded that results from the change in the terms of trade between goods; when the price of an input changes, that part of the effect on employment that results from the firm's substitution toward other inputs.

Sunk cost A cost that can no longer be avoided.

Technologically inefficient A production process that uses more inputs than necessary to produce a given output.

Third-degree price discrimination Charging different prices in different markets.

Torts Acts that injure others.

Total cost The sum of fixed cost and variable cost.

Tragedy of the commons The elimination of social gains due to overuse of common property. *Also called* dissipation of rents.

Transactions cost Any cost of negotiating or enforcing a contract.

Two-part tariff A pricing strategy in which the consumer must pay a fee in exchange for the right to purchase the product.

Uninsurable risk A risk that cannot be diversified.

Unit isoquant The set of all technically efficient ways to produce one unit of output.

Value The maximum amount that a consumer would be willing to pay for an item.

Variable cost The cost of hiring variable factors.

Variable factor of production One that the firm must employ in varying quantities.

Vertical integration A merger between a firm that produces an input and a firm that uses that output.

Wage rate The price of hiring labor.

Welfare gain The sum of the gains from trade to all participants. *Also called* social gain.

Answers to Problem Sets

Chapter 1

5a. An increase in the price of wheat causes an increase in the demand for corn. Consequently, the demand curve for corn shifts out, leading to an increase in price and an increase in quantity.

5c. *A good answer:* The fall in population causes a decrease in the demand for corn. This leads to a fall in price and a fall in quantity. *A more sophisticated answer:* The fall in population means that there are fewer farmers and fewer farm workers. Thus the supply of corn decreases (that is, the supply curve shifts to the left). Together with the decrease in demand, this leads to a fall in quantity. Price can either increase or decrease depending on which curve shifts farther.

Chapter 2

2. False. Suppose that the going wage for child labor on farms is $5 per hour. Then the farmer without children must pay $5 per hour to employ someone else's children; the farmer *with* children must forgo $5 per hour (which he could earn by renting his children out to neighboring farms) to employ his own children. Both farmers face the same cost.

  Students sometimes attempt to argue that the farmer with children incurs costs of clothing, feeding, and education. However, it is *not* correct to count these among the costs of putting the children to work. These are among the costs of having children; once the children exist, these costs must be paid whether the children are working or not.

  Other students attempt to argue that the farmer with children will be wealthier at the end of the year, because he does not actually have to make cash payments to farm workers. Even if this is the case, it is not relevant to the question. The question does not ask which farmer is wealthier; it asks which farmer has higher costs of harvesting. The answer is that both have the same costs. Note that in this case the farmer with children ends up wealthier regardless of whether he employs the children himself or rents them out to another farmer. The increase in his wealth results from his ownership of a valuable resource (the children) and is independent of whether he employs that resource on his own farm or elsewhere.

3. False. The statement of the problem omits the key information that Mary is a highly skilled neurosurgeon, whereas George does not know how to do anything except type. Mary's greater typing speed does not imply that she has a comparative advantage in typing.

  Sometimes students argue that *if* you are an employer who only wants to hire a typist, and *if* George and Mary are available at the same wage rate, then yes, it makes more sense to hire Mary as a typist than to hire George. But even this strained interpretation does not lead to the alleged conclusion. If you can really hire Mary at typist wages, you should set her to doing brain surgery, collect her enormous fees as revenue to your firm, and use a small part of them to hire George to do the typing.

8. It goes wrong exactly where it says that in each case there are the same costs of producing, shipping, and marketing the clothes. If a professional middleman can perform some of these tasks more cheaply than Anderson-Little can, then Brand X might be able to pay the middleman more than enough to cover his costs and still deliver the clothes more cheaply than Anderson-Little.

Chapter 3

4.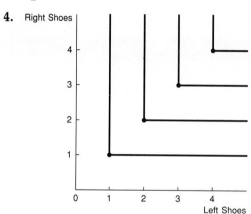

5.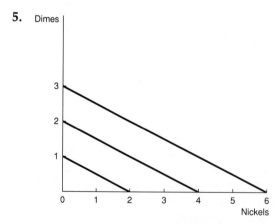

The marginal rate of substitution is ½ dime per nickel.

Chapter 4

2. It means that when your income goes up, your consumption of the luxury good increases by a greater proportion than your income does.

If your income increases by 1%, your consumption of luxury goods increases by more than 1%. But you cannot increase your consumption of *all* goods by more than 1% without violating the budget constraint. Therefore not all goods can be luxuries.

In fact, this can be made more precise. When your income increases by 1%, your expenditures on goods must increase by exactly 1% "on average." Thus the average income elasticity of demand for all goods must be 1. In the averaging process, goods must be weighted according to the share of your income that is spent on them. Suppose that you consume only X and Y. Write k_X for the fraction of your income that you spend on X and write k_Y for the fraction that you spend on Y. Write η_X and η_Y for your income elasticities of demand for X and Y. Then we must have

$$k_X\eta_X + k_Y\eta_Y = 1.$$

If you want to prove this formula, start with the expressions

$$k_X = P_X X/I$$
$$k_Y = P_Y Y/I$$
$$P_X \cdot \Delta X + P_Y \cdot \Delta Y = \Delta I.$$

(First explain what each of these expressions means and why it is true.) Then insert the expressions for k_X, k_Y, η_X, and η_Y into the formula and use algebra to simplify.

3. The illustration below shows the old and new budget lines. The dashed segment is *not* a part of the new budget line, since food stamps cannot be exchanged for goods other than food.

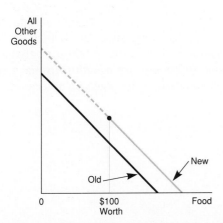

The next two illustrations show two possible configurations for the indifference curves. In the first figure, we know that B is to the right of A (by noninferiority), so that food consumption goes up as you move from A to B. In the second diagram we know that D is to the right of C (by noninferiority) and E is to the right of D (by geometry). In this case you move from C to E, so food consumption goes up in this case as well. Therefore, the statement is true.

622

Chapter 5

2. False, because you've *already* lost a lot of money. The $700-per-ounce loss is a sunk cost and irrelevant to anything in the present.

   Students sometimes argue that the big fall in price means either (a) that further falls in price are likely, so that it would be wise to sell, or (b) that the price is likely to go back up again, so that you would be foolish to sell. In fact, neither theory is correct (as we shall see in Section 9.2), but even if either *were* correct, the price that you paid last year would still be irrelevant to today's decision. If you feel sure that the price will soon rise above $300, then you should not sell (in fact, you should buy more), and if you feel sure that the price will soon fall further, then you should sell. The amount that you paid last year has nothing to do with it.

7. If it must produce a whole number of units, then it produces 2 and sells them at $8 apiece. If it can produce fractional numbers (which is what we usually assume), then it produces some number of units between 2 and 3 (the table does not provide enough information to make this more precise) and the price is somewhere between $6 apiece and $8 apiece.

Chapter 6

1.

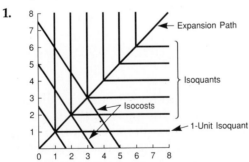

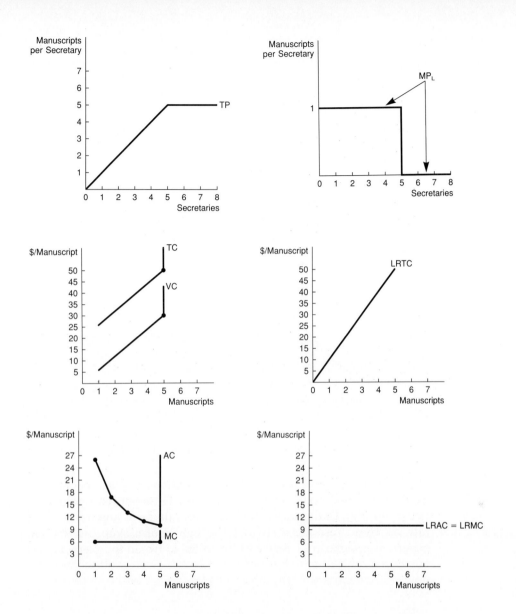

A production function that exhibits L-shaped isoquants and constant returns to scale (like Terry's) is called a *fixed proportions* production function. Such production functions arise when there is only one way to produce a good (such as a manuscript that can be produced only by using exactly one typewriter and one secretary).

3. In the long run, profits are zero, so the question is most interesting in the short run. (But see the additional remarks about the long run at the end of this solution.) At the initial price P, a beer maker's profit per can is given by the distance π in the graph below, since π is the difference between the price per can and the average cost of producing a can. At the new higher price P', the profit per can is π'. Since marginal cost rises more steeply than average cost, π' must be greater than π. Therefore, the statement is true.

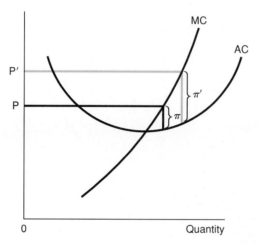

Additional remarks about the long run: An increase in demand will not lead to an increase in price if beer making is a constant-cost industry. The more interesting case is when there is an upward-sloping long-run supply curve due to the fact that some beer makers have access to specialized resources (such as a location near a particular spring). In that case, the increase in demand raises the rental rate on these resources, so that the beer maker who owns them experiences a rise in average cost, from AC to AC' in the graph below. His *profits* remain zero, but nevertheless he is better off, because he now collects more *rent* (from himself) for the use of the resources.

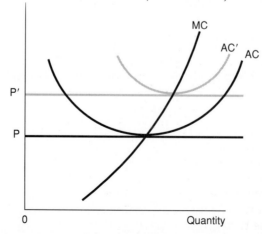

8. Suppose that the wholesale price of gasoline falls by the amount ΔP_W. In the short run (prior to entry), the retail price falls from P to P' in the diagram below. The fall in retail price is less than ΔP_W, so gas station owners are better off. Incidentally, we can see from the second panel that each gas station owner supplies more gasoline after the price falls than he did previously.

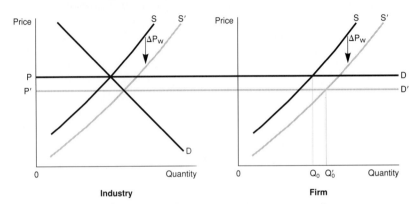

In the long run, suppose first that the industry has constant costs. Then the retail price falls by $P - P' = \Delta P_W$, as shown in the graph below. Since supply and demand both fall by the same amount in the second panel, the quantity supplied by a given gas station remains unchanged at Q_0. Because the retail and wholesale prices have changed by exactly the same amount and the firm continues to sell exactly as much gasoline as before, the owner is neither better nor worse off.

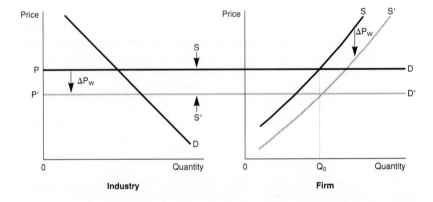

If the industry supply curve is upward-sloping, then the long-run picture looks exactly like the short-run picture in the first part of this solution. Thus the retail price falls by less than the wholesale price, and each existing gas station increases its quantity. However, in the short run we concluded that gas station owners were made better off, whereas in the long run we know that profits must remain zero. How can we reconcile these two statements?

The answer depends on why the long-run supply curve slopes upward. Suppose first that it is because of a factor price effect. In that case, let us ask how the fall in price affects a gas station's average cost curve. First, the fall in the wholesale price by the amount ΔP_W lowers the average cost of providing a gallon of gasoline by ΔP_W. This lowers the average cost curve by the amount ΔP_W. Then the entry of new firms causes the average cost curve to *rise* due to the factor price effect. The final result is that the new average cost curve AC' lies below the old average cost curve AC by an amount that is less than ΔP_W. The picture looks like this:

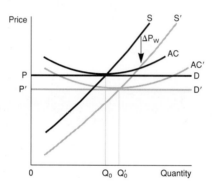

In this case gas station owners continue to earn zero profits: What they gain from the fall in wholesale prices is lost again through the action of the factor price effect (driving up, for example, the wages of mechanics). Gas station owners are made neither better nor worse off.

The final possibility is that the long-run supply curve slopes upward because of differences in ability. In this case, once again the picture for the industry and the firm looks the same as in the short-run picture at the beginning of this solution. Also, the old and new positions of the AC curve are as in the illustration above. Here the story is that the fall in wholesale prices lowers the AC curve by the amount ΔP_W, following which there is entry to the industry. Entry bids up the rental rate on those specialized resources that are available only to some firms, causing the AC curve to rise until it settles at the position of the AC' curve shown in the illustration. Although profits are still zero, the increase in rent is a gain to the owners of the specialized resources. That is, the owners of the more efficient gas stations are made better off. In none of these situations are gas station owners made worse off.

Chapter 8

2a. From buying the widgets.

2b. A gadget.

5. False. It is in fact *more* expensive for society to have people wait in lines. High prices paid from a buyer to a seller are not costs to society; they are transfers of resources from one person's wallet to another's. What the buyer loses, the seller gains. However, time spent in waiting lines is a loss to the buyer that is not offset by a gain to anybody; it is simply lost and therefore represents a real cost to society.

9a. No American will pay more than P_0 for a birdcage, so the price cannot go above P_0. At any price below P_0, quantity demanded exceeds quantity supplied so that price is bid up. The only possible market price is P_0. Q_1 birdcages are produced domestically and $Q_2 - Q_1$ are imported:

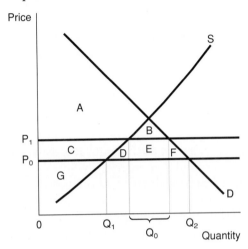

9b. Consumers gain $A + B + C + D + E + F$; producers gain G.

9c. At the price labeled P_1, Americans want to import exactly Q_0 birdcages. At any lower price, they would attempt to import more birdcages, bidding up the price; at any higher price, they would not be willing to import Q_0 birdcages, driving down the price.

9d. Consumers now gain $A + B$ and producers gain $C + G$. Consumers, the losers, lose $C + D + E + F$. Producers, the winners, win C. The losers lose more than the winners win; the difference is $D + E + F$.

9e. The tariff would have to be $P_1 - P_0$ per birdcage. Consumers and producers would be equally well off under the tariff as under the quota. Under the tariff, there would also be tax revenue (measured by area E). Thus, between the tariff and the quota, both consumers and producers are indifferent while recipients of tax revenue prefer the tariff. In principle, these recipients could share their gains with the consumers and producers so as to make *all* Americans better off.

This result makes sense: We saw in the text that the deadweight loss from a tariff is $D + F$, and we saw in part d that the deadweight loss from a quota is $D + E + F$. The tariff creates less deadweight loss, and therefore creates the potential for everyone to benefit relative to the quota situation.

South Moluccans prefer to sell Q_0 birdcages at the price P_1 (under a quota) than to sell Q_0 birdcages at the lower price P_0 (under a tariff). In fact, a switch from tariffs to quotas increases the welfare of South

Moluccans by $Q_0 \times (P_1 - P_0) = E$, which is exactly the amount that the switch causes Americans to lose. Switching from a tariff to a quota is equivalent to taking money from Americans and giving it away to foreigners!

Chapter 9

1. False, or at least not necessarily true. Although the elves want to be as helpful as possible, they have no way of knowing where their services are most valuable. As a result, they might end up spending a lot of time repairing old black and white television sets when they could be repairing the space shuttle. If humans are able to bid against each other for the elves' services, the elves will be able to concentrate their efforts where they do the most good. This makes humans better off; on the other hand, the actual payments to the elves makes people worse off. The net effect on humans could go either way.

2. None of the council members has the expertise to determine the extent of the risk from the chemical plant, and none has the expertise (or information) to determine the extent of the benefits. It is reasonable to expect that the company owners and their insurers (who are experts in assessing risks) have access to more such information than the council has. Under the councilman's proposal, they have the incentive to make use of such information. If the chemical company agrees to bear all of the costs of reimbursement, we may infer that it expects to earn enough from the plant to more than cover these costs. Similarly, if the insurance company is willing to bear the risk in exchange for a price that the chemical company will pay, we may infer that it expects the amount of damage to the townspeople to be less than the gains to the chemical company.

   The councilman's suggestion creates an incentive for those with easiest access to the relevant information to analyze that information and act on it in a socially desirable way.

Chapter 10

1. False, because of the phrase "Unlike a competitor." Anybody can charge any price he wants to for anything. However, there is only one profit-maximizing price to charge, and it is foolish to deviate from this price, whether you are a monopolist, a competitor, or anything in between.

   For a competitor, the profit-maximizing price is the going market price. No one is required to charge this price. You are perfectly welcome to offer wheat at $7,000 a bushel if you want to; the only problem is that you won't sell any, and you won't earn much profit. Similarly, a monopolist can charge either more or less than the price at which marginal cost equals marginal revenue if he wants to. In doing so, he might not be punished as much as the competitor, who loses all of his sales when he charges too much. Nonetheless, he will be punished by earning less profit than he could have earned.

8. False. Natural monopoly requires the average cost curve to be downward-sloping where it crosses demand. Large fixed costs and small marginal costs lead to this condition, but we saw in Chapter 6 that increasing returns to scale also imply a downward-sloping average cost curve. Thus if there are increasing returns to scale over a large range, there is natural monopoly even if there are no fixed costs.

Chapter 11

6. False. Bar owners would all be happier if the price of afternoon drinks were higher. Why don't they all agree to raise prices? Because if they all raised their prices from $1 per beer to $2 per beer, each one of them would have an incentive to "cheat" by selling a whole lot of beer at $1.90. Only with an outside enforcer—the law—can they avoid this problem.

Chapter 12

7. True, since students would have a reduced incentive to take precautions like sticking to well-lighted paths, staying alert to their surroundings, and learning self-defense techniques. If there were no transactions costs between the university and the students, the answer would be false, since the university would offer to pay students enough to induce them to take exactly the same amount of care that students take when the university is *not* liable. However, the key transactions cost here is the unobservability of the students' behavior. Unless the university constantly monitors the students, they will agree to the deal, accept the money, and still behave recklessly. This transactions cost prevents the deal from being struck in the first place.

12. This would ensure that property ultimately ends up in the hands of whoever values it most, which clearly promotes efficiency. On the other hand, it creates uncertainty about property rights between the time when the dispute arises and the time when the judge holds the auction. During this period, nobody knows who will eventually win the property, and hence nobody may have the appropriate incentive to maintain the property. A clear-cut rule (like "Property belongs to whoever plants a flag on it first") has the disadvantage of sometimes allocating rights suboptimally, but it has the advantage of making rights well-defined (so that whoever plants the flag can start immediately to plant a garden, without fear that the property is not really his). Another disadvantage of such a rule is that people waste resources in their attempts to conform to it (the costs incurred by 30 people racing to plant their flags first are all social loss).

Try applying this abstract discussion to concrete examples, as, say, to a dispute between students who want to play their stereos and other students in the same dormitory who want to study. What form do the advantages and disadvantages listed above take in the context of your examples? Can you find some examples in which the advantages clearly outweigh the disadvantages, and vice versa?

13. False. It is true that the availability of liability insurance reduces the incentive to drive carefully and that this can result in more accidents. It is false that this is necessarily detrimental to welfare. The purchase of insurance benefits both the driver and the insurer (otherwise they would not transact). If the insured driver can completely reimburse the victims of any accidents that he causes, then no one is made worse off by the purchase. In the case where accident victims are not fully compensated (for example, because they are killed in the accidents and hence unable to collect), then some people—the victims—are made worse off, while others—the driver and the insurer—are made better off. There could be net social gain or net social loss.

It is a common mistake to think that increasing the number of accidents is always a bad thing. But the optimal number of accidents is not zero. If it were, we would outlaw driving.

14. Suppose, for example, that the value of the ship is one-third the value of the entire venture. The captain must decide whether to toss overboard a block of gold worth $60,000. The social benefit from doing so is that the ship and its cargo have a greater chance of survival. This increased chance of survival has a monetary value of, say, $x. The private benefit to the shipowner is one-third of this, or $/3. The social cost of discarding the gold is $60,000, of which $20,000 is the shipowner's private cost. Thus the socially optimal decision is to discard the gold if and only if $x > 60,000$, whereas the privately optimal decision is to discard the gold if and only if $x/3 > 20,000$. Since the two conditions are equivalent, the captain will always make the efficient decision. Posner offers this as evidence for his view of the common law.

Chapter 13

1a. If the narrow road is more pleasant than the wide road, drivers on the wide road will switch to the narrow road, making the narrow road less pleasant; this continues until the two roads are equally desirable. If the narrow road is less pleasant than the wide road, drivers on the narrow road will switch to the wide road, making the narrow road more pleasant; again, this continues until the two roads are equally pleasant to drive on.

1b. When one driver is added to the narrow road, the private marginal benefit (to the new driver) is the same as when one driver is added to the wide road. This is because we already know that both roads are equally pleasant to drive on. However, the marginal social benefit from adding a driver to the narrow road is equally to his private marginal benefit *minus* the costs he imposes on all other drivers by making the road less pleasant. Thus the marginal social benefit from a driver on the narrow road is less than from a driver on the wide road.

1c. A planner could move one car from the narrow road to the wide road. Since marginal social benefit is greater on the wide road than on the narrow one, total social benefit must increase. Another way to see this is that the driver who is moved was already indifferent about which road to be on, so he neither gains nor loses, but all of the other drivers on the narrow road gain from his departure.

1d. The planner continues until the marginal social benefit from adding a driver is the same on both roads.

    If drivers entering the narrow road had to pay an entry fee equal to the externality that they impose on other drivers, they would completely internalize the externality. Drivers would voluntarily stop entering the narrow road as soon as the marginal social benefit from adding a driver is the same on both roads.

    If the narrow road were owned, the owner would set exactly the optimal entry fee. This is so for the same reason that the giant who owns the forest sets the optimal entry fee. Make sure that you can reproduce the argument in the context of the present question.

Chapter 14

10. True. As the graph shows, a rise in the wage from W to W' causes the revenue earned by capital to fall from A + B to B.

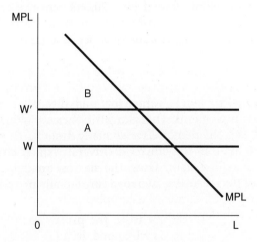

632

11. True. Suppose that labor and capital were substitutes in production. Then an increase in the wage rate would cause an increase in the marginal product of capital from MPK to MPK′ in the graph. The revenue earned by capital would increase from D to D + F + G. But we already saw in Problem 10 that the revenue earned by capital goes down, not up. Thus capital and labor cannot be substitutes in production.

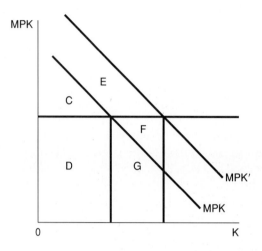

12. The minimum wage law will eliminate much unskilled labor from the market. Apparently the union believes that this will increase the demand for skilled labor; thus skilled and unskilled labor must be substitutes in production.

Temporarily divide inputs into "unskilled labor" and "all other inputs," where "all other inputs" comprises both capital and unskilled labor. Arguing exactly as in Problem 11, we see that unskilled labor and all other inputs must be complements. That is, a fall in the employment of unskilled labor decreases the demand for all other inputs on average. On the other hand, a fall in the employment of unskilled labor increases the demand for skilled labor. Thus a fall in the employment of unskilled labor must decrease the demand for capital. In other words, unskilled labor and capital must be complements.

It follows that the owners of capital will oppose the minimum wage.

Chapter 15

1. True. The budget line shifts out parallel to itself as in the illustration below (which assumes that your need for sleep is reduced from 8 hours per night to 6). Thus there is only an income effect (as opposed to a substitution effect). If consumption is a normal good, people choose to have more of it. (Note that the zero-labor axis moves from the solid position at 16 leisure hours to the dashed position at 18 leisure hours.)

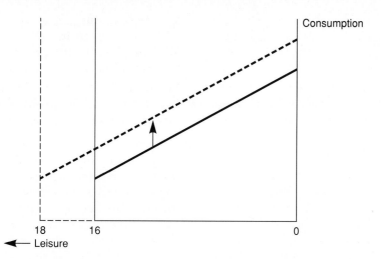

18   16   0

◄— Leisure

3. True or false, depending on how you interpret "productive," but false by the most usual interpretations. People who like their jobs will choose to work more hours and therefore have a lower marginal product. They will also produce less per hour on average. In the diagram, a worker who supplies L_1 hours produces Q_1 units of output, for an average output of Q_1/L_1 per hour, which is the slope of the solid line. A worker who likes his job and therefore supplies L_2 hours has an average output equal to the slope of the dashed line, which is smaller.

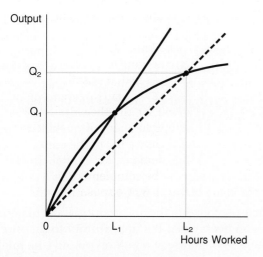

Chapter 16

1. False. It is bad for borrowers, because it makes borrowing more expensive. It is good for lenders, also because it makes borrowing more expensive. The representative agent is neither a borrower nor a lender,

so that "on average" people are made neither better nor worse off when the interest rate changes.

Actually, our assertion that the representative agent neither borrows nor lends is true when there is no investment, but false otherwise. When there is investment, the representative agent is a lender. (He plants seeds today in order to have more trees tomorrow.) In this case, the representative agent benefits from a rise in the interest rate.

The question is not entirely well-posed, since it does not specify what causes the change in the interest rate. Unless there is some change in tastes or technology, the interest rate cannot change. What is true is that an individual lender, with constant tastes, benefits from a rise in the interest rate—but he might either benefit or be hurt by the thing that caused the change in the interest rate. For example, the interest rate in an agricultural society will increase if either the soil becomes more fertile or half of the existing grain is washed away in a flood. (Be sure you understand why!)

12a. Jeeter can spend $1,000 today to buy a bond. He can put the bond in a desk drawer and forget that he owns it. In 5 years, when the loan comes due, he can hand the bond over to the bank. Since the bond grows in value at exactly the same rate that Jeeter's debt to the bank grows, the bond will exactly cover his debt.

This strategy "feels" exactly like paying the loan off for $1,000 today and being done with it.

12b. Jeeter can spend $10,000 to buy Treasury bills. The interest rate on these bills is exactly equal to the rate at which the government debt is growing, since selling Treasury bills is precisely the way in which the government borrows. Whenever the government gets around to taxing Jeeter, he can turn over his Treasury bills, which are guaranteed to be equal in value to his share of the national debt. This strategy "feels" to Jeeter exactly like paying off his share of the debt now and never being charged any interest.

Chapter 17

1. False. Assuming that nothing is worth the certainty of death does not reveal anything about the value of, say, a 50% *chance* of death.

2. It depends on the possible outcomes of the uncertainty, and it depends on the odds. Had Johnson been given the opportunity to sacrifice a certain shilling for a mere 99% chance at a million pounds, he might have reconsidered his position. Indeed, to forgo suicide is to sacrifice the certainty of death for the uncertainties of life, but most of us make this "unwise" choice.

Chapter 18

6. False, since none of these mechanisms addresses the basic issue: People will still hold less money, and they will suffer a loss of convenience as a result.

Index